Handbook of
Forensic Neuropsychology

Arthur MacNeill Horton, Jr., EdD, ABPP, ABPN
Lawrence C. Hartlage, PhD, ABPP, ABPN
Editors

 Springer Publishing Company

Springer Publishing Company, Inc.
536 Broadway
New York, NY 10012-3955

Acquisitions Editor: Sheri W. Sussman
Production Editor: Janice Stangel
Cover design by Joanne Honigman

03 04 05 06 07 / 5 4 3 2 1

Library of Congress Cataloging-in-Publication Data

Handbook of forensic neuropsychology / Arthur MacNeill Horton, Lawrence C. Hartlage, editors.
    p. cm.
    Includes bibliographical references and index.
    ISBN 0-8261-1884-4
    1. Forensic neuropsychology—Handbooks, manuals, etc. 2. Clinical neuropsychology—Handbooks, manuals, etc. I. Horton, Arthur MacNeill, 1947–
II. Hartlage, Lawrence C.
    RA1147.5.H36 2003
    614—dc21   2003042536

Printed in the United States of America by Maple-Vail Book Manufacturing Group.

To my wife, Mary, with all of my love and my parents who were both lawyers.

Arthur MacNeill Horton, Jr.

To Ralph M. Reitan, Ph.D., for inspiration over many years.

Lawrence Hartlage

Contents

Section III: Practice Issues

Section IV: Ethical Issues

Section V: Special Areas

Contributors

Armando de Armas, Ph.D.
Independent Practice
Los Angeles, California

C. Michael Bee, J.D.
Attorney at Law
Morgantown, West Virginia

**Thomas L. Bennett, Ph.D,
ABPN, ABPP.**
Center for Neurorehabilitation
Services
Fort Collins, Colorado

Erin D. Bigler, Ph.D., ABPP
Departments of Psychology and
Neuroscience
Brigham Young University
Provo, Utah

John J. Blasé, Ph.D., ABPN
Independent Practice
Southfield, Michigan

John Montgomery Carson, M.D.
Private Practice
Morgantown, West Virginia

Barry M. Crown, Ph.D., ABPN
Independent Practice
South Miami, Florida and
Department of Psychology
Florida International University

**Raymond S. Dean, Ph. D.,
ABPN, ABPP**
Neuropsychology Laboratory
Ball State University
Muncie, Indiana

Paul S. Ferber, JD
Director of Vermont Law
School's General Practice
Program
White River, Vermont

H. Scott Fingerhut
Attorney at Law
Miami, Florida

Michael D. Franzen, Ph.D.
Department of Psychiatry
Allegheny General Hospital
Pittsburgh, Pennsylvania

Christine L. French, Ph.D.
Department of Educational
Psychology
Texas A & M University
College Station, Texas

**Charles Golden, Ph.D., ABPP,
ABPN**
Department of Psychology
Center for Psychological Studies
Nova Southeastern University
Fort Lauderdale, Florida

Grant L. Iverson, Ph.D.
Department of Psychiatry
University of British Columbia
Vancouver, B.C. Canada

Sheryl J. Lowenthal
Attorney at Law
Miami, Florida

John E. Meyers, Psy.D., ABPN
Mercy Rehabilitation Clinic
Sioux City, Iowa

Peter C. Patch, Ph.D.
Augusta Neuropsychology Center
Evans, Georgia

Dorrie L. Rapp, Ph.D., ABPN, ABPP
Rehabilitation Psychologist
Private Practice
White River, Vermont

Michael J. Raymond, Ph.D., ABPN
Allied Services
John Heinz Institute of
   Rehabilitation Medicine
Fort Collins, Colorado

Cecil R. Reynolds, Ph.D., ABPN, ABPP
Departments of Educational
   Psychology and Neuroscience
Texas A & M University
College Station, Texas

Martha L. Rogers, Ph.D.
Independent Practice
Los Angeles, California

Robert J. Sbordone, Ph.D., ABPP, ABPN
Independent Practice
Laguna Hills, California

Raymond Singer, Ph.D., ABPN
Independent Practice
Santa Fe, New Mexico

Veronica A. Thomas, Ph.D.
Independent Practice
Los Angeles, California

Jeffrey B. Titus, Ph.D.
Neuropsychology Laboratory
Ball State University
Muncie, Indiana

Harold Widdison, J.D.
Attorney at Law
Sioux City, Iowa

Arthur D. Williams, Ph.D., ABPN
Independent Practice
Seattle, Washington

Preface

Great enthusiasm among professional psychologists in independent practice for the specialization of Forensic Neuropsychology can be seen in a number of events. In the last decade, a number of books dealing with Forensic Neuropsychology have been published for the graduate and professional markets, departments of psychology are developing courses and providing training experiences and a new journal entitled the *Journal of Forensic Neuropsychology* has been established. There are also increasing numbers of requests from attorneys and judges for neuropsychologists to interact in the forensic setting by quantifying the nature and extent of cortical damage in cases of automobile or industrial accident or neurotoxin exposure.

Indeed, there is considerable evidence to support the opinion that Forensic Neuropsychology is rapidly expanding, as a professional practice area across the nation. While managed care has reduced reimbursement for psychological services in the last decade, there has still been significant growth in the need for Forensic Neuropsychological services. A salient fact concerning Forensic Neuropsychology is that it is perhaps the prime example of an area of professional specialization that was developed by practitioners. While many Forensic Neuropsychologists engage in full or part-time independent practice, there has been considerable evolution of the traditional independent practitioner role.

In order to address the urgent need for an authoritative reference work for the rapidly growing field, the *Handbook of Forensic Neuropsychology* has been published. The *Handbook of Forensic Neuropsychology* reviews the major areas in which neuropsychologists in independent practice can work effectively within the jurisprudence system. Specific areas covered include the foundations of Forensic Neuropsychology such as the neuropsychological basis of mental abilities, normative and scaling issues, diagnostic decision-making and symptom validity testing. In addition, a number of issues related to brain injury, given the great importance of these issues in personal injury cases, will be addressed. Specific chapters include the epidemiology of traumatic brain injury, Neuro-imaging, behavioral change following traumatic brain injury and disability determination and rehabilitation planning. Also, forensic practice requires an understanding of the unique aspects of a legal case. Specific chapters deal with depositions, the attorney perspective and actual courtroom testimony. Ethical functioning is always a major concern for professional neuropsychologists but the forensic settings holds unique challenges and dilemmas. Specific chapters dealing with ethical concerns and issues include releasing raw data, third-party observers and conflicts of interests for the expert witness. A remaining section includes very specialized areas of practice chapters on forensic neuropsychology with children, forensic neurotoxicology, neuropsychological assessment in criminal law cases, competency/civil commitment decisions. A concluding chapter on the future of Forensic Neuropsychology completes the Handbook.

The *Handbook of Forensic Neuropsychology* is intended for Forensic Neuropsychologists in full or part-time private practice and attorneys and judges who utilized neuropsychological data in their decision-making. Also, other professional who enter the legal arena and rely on neuropsychological opinions such as Forensic Psychiatrists and Forensic Neurologists or clinical psychologists, school psychologists, social workers, counselors and special educators, among other health care and educational professionals, will find the *Handbook of Forensic Neuropsychology* of considerable value. The hope and expectation is that the *Handbook of Forensic Neuropsychology* will make an important contribution in promoting the positive values that Forensic Neuropsychology can bring to the forensic arena and will thereby meet the challenge of alleviating human misery and promoting positive adaptation by brain-injured children and adults in the legal system.

The Editors

Acknowledgments

Many Forensic Neuropsychologists have indirectly contributed to the *Handbook of Forensic Neuropsychology* by their support and advice to the editors. These persons include Ralph M. Reitan, David E. Hartman, Tony Strickland, Arnold Purish, Robert J. McCaffrey, Robert W. Elliott, W. Drew Gouvier, Charles J. Long, Jim Hom, Paul Satz, Pat Pimental, Karen Steingarden, Sue Antell, Eric Zillmer, Joan W. Mayfield, Ralph Tarter, Gerald Goldstein, Deborah Wolfson, Francis J. Fishburne, J. Randall Price, Jeffrey T. Barth, Antonio E. Puente, George W. Hynd. Ira B. Gensemer, Daneen A. Milam, Theodore Blau, Danny Wedding, Randy W. Kamphaus, Robert L. Kane, Katleen Fitzhugh-Bell, Dennis L. Reeves, James A. Moses, Jr., Jeffrey J. Webster, Alan Gessner, Bradley Sewick, Francis J. Pirozzolo, John E. Obrzut, Richard Berg, Mark Goodman, Henry Soper, and Nicole McWhorter, Marvin H. Podd, Greta N. Wilkening, and Cindy K. Westergaard, among others too numerous to mention, have been most helpful. A number of psychiatrists have also been helpful and include Michael K. Spodak, Abdul Malik, Mahmood Jahromi, Daniel Drubach, Scott Spier and Mohammad Haerian, among others too numerous to mention. Also, attorneys such as Tom Talbot, James Sullivan, Mitchell Blatt, Steve Van Grack, Patrick Donahue, Allison Kohler and Jeanie Garner, among others too numerous to mention. Dr. Horton wishes to note that both of his deceased parents were attorneys and they provided him a unique life-long experience of dealing with the highest quality of legal reasoning and ethical decision making. Dr. Hartlage acknowledges the influence of Judges Bork, Borowiec, Quillian, and Williams, who called him to appear as advisor in more than three thousand cases over a thirty year period—and influenced his daughter Mary Beth to pursue a career in the field (Harvard Law 1993).

Foundations

Chapter 1

Overview of Forensic Neuropsychology

Arthur MacNeill Horton, Jr.

The history of psychologists assisting litigating attorneys is brief and recent. Freud (1906) was one of the first clinicians in the medicine–psychology interface to suggest that study of mental processes could be of use in legal arenas. The first psychologists to advocate a role in forensic venues were Munsterberg (1908) and Watson (1913), both of whom were from the field of experimental, not clinical, psychology. Some legal scholars were unsure psychology was ready for the courtroom (Wigmore, 1909). After some decades, however, psychology's efforts in the forensic arena had grown to the point that enough material was available to produce a chapter in the *Annual Review of Psychology* (Tapp, 1976). In the last part of the twentieth century, things moved quickly, and the American Board of Forensic Psychology (Kurke, 1980) was established to board-certify psychologists with legal expertise and interests. Forensic psychologists, of course, are psychologists who have special expertise in legal matters and provide professional services to attorneys and judges, to assist in addressing forensic concerns and legal questions. Examples include expert testimony, education of attorneys in psychological research findings, and jury selection, among other roles.

At the same time, also during the last half-century, interest in human brain–behavioral relationships, or clinical neuropsychology, has increased at a tremendous rate. There are a large number of examples of the cross-cultural validity of neuropsychological research findings, as well as successful applications of neuropsychological assessment intervention methods with adults and children (Hartlage, 1975, 1986; Horton, 1994; Horton & Puente, 1986; Hynd & Willis, 1988; Reitan & Davidson, 1974). These remarkable demonstrations of the power of neuropsychological methods have sparked a great increase in interest in clinical neuropsychology.

NEUROPSYCHOLOGICAL ISSUES AND BRAIN DAMAGE

At this juncture, it might be helpful to provide some basic neuropsychology definitions. *Neuropsychology* was defined by Meier (1974) as "the scientific study of brain–behavior relationships." That definition was particularly apt and is as serviceable today, more than 20 years after it was proposed, as it was at that time. Horton and Puente (1990) note that neuropsychological performance may be influenced by both organic and environmental variables. The organic nature of neuropsychological variables has been clearly demonstrated through the work of famous neuropsychologists such as Ralph M. Reitan, Arthur L. Benton, and A. R. Luria, among others, over a number of decades. Attention to the environmental determinants of neuropsychological performance, however, is of more recent origin. As an example, it should be noted that, in recent years, increased attention has been focused on the practice of behavior therapy with brain-impaired adults and children (Horton & Wedding, 1984; Horton, 1989, 1994).

A brief discussion of the concepts of brain damage and cerebral dysfunction is provided, to clarify the neuropsychological context in which the concepts are applied. Briefly, *brain damage* implies clear and substantial structural injury to the brain (Horton, 1994). Contemporary neurodiagnostic imaging methods, such as positron emission tomography, or magnetic resonance imaging, in many cases, can clearly identify structural brain lesions (Kertesz, 1994). Nonetheless, in some subtle cases, neuroimaging is totally inadequate to reflect changes in the physiological functioning of the brain that may result in behavioral abnormalities. At this point, the behavioral correlates of neuroimaging are still poorly understood. Although brain tumors or strokes often can be easily visualized, other neuropathological conditions, such as sequelae of traumatic brain injury (TBI) and neurotoxic conditions, may produce clear neurocognitive, sensory-perceptual, and motoric deficits, without demonstrating clear structural brain changes under imaging (Horton, 1989). In situations of this sort, in which behavioral changes are clearly documented, but structural lesions in the brain cannot be visualized, the term *cerebral dysfunction* is often used (Horton, 1994). The hope and expectation is that further research in neuroimaging and related procedures and methods will allow more precise detection of abnormalities in cerebral morphology.

ORGANICITY: LOCALIZATION VERSUS GENERALIZED FUNCTION

At this point, attention is turned to the term *organicity*, because this term is also frequently misunderstood. The classic definition, by Davison (1974), is as follows:

> The concept includes the assumption that any and all kinds of brain damage lead to similar behavioral effects and that behavioral differences among the brain damaged are due primarily to severity of damage and premorbid personality characteristics. (p. 14)

The concept of organicity has an interesting history. It originated during the human potentiality–localization debates, which characterized thinking regarding brain–behavior relationships approximately a century ago. Those debates were concerned with how behavioral functions were organized in the human brain (Horton & Wedding, 1984).

A brief review of some of the crucial scientific findings related to these debates may be helpful in understanding them. The debates began, in April of 1861, when a physician named Paul Broca presented the brain of a patient who had been unable to speak, when the patient had been alive, at the Paris Anthropological Society Meeting. Apparently, the patient had been studied, by Broca, while alive, and at that time the patient had been unable to speak. Subsequently, the patient died and his brain became available for inspection. Broca found that the patient had a lesion in the posterior third portion of the inferior frontal convulsion of the left hemisphere. Broca demonstrated that the patient's language difficulty, or aphasia, was not related to either memory difficulties or motoric problems. Rather, Broca postulated that the aphasia was related to the specific brain lesion. The startling hypothesis from this case study was that a specific brain area supported expressive speech, and to this day that particular area is known as *Broca's area* (Horton & Wedding, 1984).

Similarly, in 1874, Carl Wernicke presented a clinical case of a patient, who, when he was alive, had a speech comprehension deficit. After that patient died, his brain became available for inspection and study by Wernicke. The patient's brain was found, by Wernicke, to have a lesion in the posterior third portion of the superior temporal lobe of the left hemisphere. This area today is known as *Wernicke's area* (Horton & Wedding, 1984). These scientific discoveries suggested that specific brain areas could be identified for specific behavioral functions.

Although these advances were exciting instances of the localizationist school of brain–behavioral relationships, there was an opposing school of thought, which proposed that all brain tissue was of equal relevance for subserving behavioral functions. That school described brain tissue of as "equal potentiality" with respect to behavioral functions. This equal potentiality school had its own series of startling scientific discoveries. For example, Marie J. P. Flourens (cited in Luria, 1966) demonstrated, in animal research studies, that the loss of behavioral function were related to the amount of brain tissue impaired, rather than to specific localization of the brain-lesion. Similarly, Kurt Goldstein found similar results in his work with brain-injured veterans of World War I. Goldstein's research suggested that the major difficulty with respect to brain-injured persons was concrete thinking, and that there was, in a rather memorable phrase: "the loss of the abstract attitude" (Horton & Wedding, 1984). It appeared that the French scientists were finding evidence supporting a localization model, whereas the German scientists were finding evidence that endorsed an equal-potentiality paradigm.

One questionable suggestion had been advanced that, since many of these brain lesions were from the Franco-Prussian War or World War I, the different findings could be the result of the fact that the German ammunition in both conflicts, was excellent and tended to remain intact after impact, but the French ammunition, in the same conflicts, was of lessor quality and had a tendency to fragment upon impact. Therefore, it has been suggested that brain lesions caused by German bullets produced relatively prescribed lesions, whereas lesions from French bullets tended to have widespread effects, because bullets were fragments and therefore scattered to various portions of the brain. Whether or not this hypothesis has a basis in fact, it would require a certain amount of historical neuropsychological research to confirm or negate. What does seem clear now, and is generally accepted, is that both the localization and equal potential conceptualizations of brain–behavior relationships fail to fully explain or account for the full range of human neuropsychological abilities.

MULTIPLE BRAIN LEVELS

An integrative solution to the human potentiality–localization debates was proposed by Thomas Hughlings Jackson, an Englishman, who was a contemporary of Broca. Jackson's concepts of brain functioning have been popularized more recently by Luria (1966, 1973). Jackson suggested that human behavioral functions were represented in multiple levels in the brain, which is to say, that there was a vertical organization, with brain functions subsumed at a number of levels. Luria further developed Jackson's theoretical views and described the brain as composed of distinct functional blocks, with each section serving different functions. Basically, Luria saw higher mental processes as involving multiple brain areas interacting in multiple points in time (Horton, 1987). To put this another way, he suggested multicausation of behavioral functions by different brain areas. As was noted by Horton and Wedding (1984),

> Essentially, Luria thought that every complex form of behavior depended on the joint operations of several faculties located in different zones of the brain. Disturbance of any one of the number of faculties located in different areas of the brain will change behavior in a different way. But in another way, this means no single behavior is localized in a specific brain area, and that each behavior is a result of the specific combination of separate brain areas. Also, the damage to a single brain area causes the behavior to be changed but not necessarily lost. (p. 30)

Thus, it can be seen that brain damage is a difficult and complex concept to understand, and complexities go far beyond the simplistic conceptualizations of organicity. Although there are some similarities among brain-injured individuals, there is also a tremendous amount of heterogeneity. Current diagnostic frameworks only poorly capture the degree of complexity inherent in human cerebral functioning.

NEURODEVELOPMENTAL ISSUES

Attention needs to paid to the theoretical ideas of A. R. Luria (1963, 1966, 1973). Luria's cultural and historical model, for example, postulates specific developmental stages, which are related to phases of higher cortical developmental maturation. Luria considered the various stages of mental development, encountered as children mature, as a unique opportunity to study how neurocognitive processes develop (Horton, 1987). As is well known, there are great differences in child neurodevelopmental processes relative to adult neurodevelopmental processes (Rourke, Fisk, & Strang, 1986). Child brains are considerably less studied than adult brains, and there is a greater degree of variability in terms of the expression of neurocognitive abilities in a child's neuropsychological development (Horton & Puente, 1986). Children, for instance, are in a continual process of development, there are various growth spurts and developmental lags to contend with, and there may be specific learning or developmental or behavioral processes that could be related to physical illness or injury (Hynd & Obrzut, 1981; Hynd & Wills, 1988; Reynolds, 1981). These complex neurodevelopmental factors make it particularly difficult to provide a clinical assessment of child neuropsychological abilities and to distinguish subtypes of learning disorders (Broder, 1973; Mattis, French, & Rapin, 1975). Among other critical problems is the difficulty of collecting appropriate normative neuropsychological data (Hartledge, 1986; Klonoff, Crockett, & Clark, 1984). Since neuropsychological abilities may vary in terms of quantity and quality, depending on the various neurocognitive developmental stages, neuropsychological normative data needs to be interpreted in terms of understanding the child's neurocognitive development in the various stages on neuropsychological development (Hynd & Willis, 1988; Reynolds, 1981). The child must have had an opportunity to develop various mental skills before it can be said that the child had lost an ability because of brain injury. For example, if an adult demonstrates an inability to read simple words and phrases, that behavioral deficit might be seen as clear evidence of a brain injury, if the adult had reasonably adequate education experiences as a child. However, it could easily be that the child never had the opportunity to acquire the specific academic skills, and therefore the problem is not one related to brain injury, but rather to inadequate educational opportunities.

Persons who intend to deliver forensic neuropsychological services will need to have a basic understanding of brain–behavior relationships. Since the primary reason that children require neuropsychological services is usually a real or presumed disorder of the brain, an appreciation of the structure and functioning of the cerebral cortex will be invaluable in determining the nature and extent of the presumed brain disorder. Indeed, the central premise upon which all of clinical neuropsychology rests is that there are direct and predictable behavioral correlates of structural lesions in the neocortex (Reitan & Davison, 1974). In child clinical neuropsychology, for example, there is an evolving research literature that has documented specific brain–behavior relationships. The human brain is the prime organ of behavioral functioning. Understanding of the anatomical structure and behavioral functioning of children's brains serves to provide a valuable perspective on methods of clinical neuropsychological assessment and treatment/interventions (Horton, 1994).

DEVELOPMENTAL NEUROANATOMY AND BRAIN LATERALIZATION

This section is intended to be a brief and selective review of brain–behavioral relationships, with particular reference to developmental neuroanatomy and hemispheric lateralization of brain functioning. This discussion is not intended to be a detailed treatment of brain–behavioral relationships. Rather, the reader is referred to other volumes that more adequately address this area of developmental neuroanatomy (Hynd & Willis, 1988; Kolb & Fantie, 1989; Reitan & Wolfson, 1992; Spreen, Risser, & Edgell, 1995). The emphasis is upon the gross structural organization of the human brain, rather than on an examination of the cellular level and neurotransmitter systems. Particular areas addressed are the morphology of the central nervous system (CNS), Luria's neurodevelopmental model of brain functioning, hemispheric lateralization of functioning, specific functioning of the cerebral lobes, and a brief and selective discussion of recovery of function after childhood TBI.

MORPHOLOGY OF THE CNS

The CNS is divided into the brain and the spinal cord. The function of the spinal cord is to transmit sensory impulses to the brain and also to send motor impulses from the brain to the muscles. Various segments (i.e., cervical, thoracic, lumbar, and sacral) make up the spinal cord and refer to various groups of nerves. Injuries to various levels of the spinal cord have serious implications with respect to motoric and sensory functioning. The division of the spinal cord into sensory and motoric areas is also reflected in the gross morphology and organization of the human brain. Understanding the extent of the sensorimotor organization of the human brain is of crucial importance in terms of understanding the structure and functioning of the CNS.

Although the spinal cord is of great importance for the maintainability of life and mobility, its assessment is usually considered to be the domain of the pediatric neurologist; child clinical neuropsychologists more commonly devote their attention to the brain. There are three major divisions to the brain: the hindbrain, the midbrain, and the forebrain. Each of these are briefly reviewed.

Hindbrain

Major areas that make up the hindbrain include the medulla oblongata, the pons, and the cerebellum. Locating the medulla oblongata is best done by first identifying the foramen magnum, which is the opening in the cranial cavity that allows the brain and the spinal cord to be connected. The medulla oblongata lies just above the foramen magnum. Major functions of the medulla oblongata are to control blood pressure, heart rate, and breathing. Just above the medulla oblongata is the pons, which is an enlarged section of the brain stem that has a number of functions. Of the most interest in this context, the pons allows communication to flow from the spinal cord to higher brain areas and includes particular fibers that connect the two cerebral hemispheres to hind areas of the cerebellum. The cerebellum, another hindbrain area, is located behind the pons and has the particular function of monitoring motor control and coordination and, in combination with the pons, coordinates motor impulses in response to movement.

Midbrain

The midbrain sits at the point where the brain stem merges with two other brain areas: the hypothalamus and the thalamus. This area is of particular importance, because brain structures in this area are thought to be in control of attention processes. For instance, the reticular activating system lies in this area and has the function of regulating cortical tone and deciding which, among a large number of incoming stimuli, to focus upon. There has been some speculation that this area is of particular importance in terms of disorders such as attention deficit–

hyperactivity disorder. Often, in cases of severe injury to the reticular activating system, disorders of consciousness, such as a coma, may arise.

Forebrain

This area is often considered to be the primary focus of clinical child and experimental neuropsychology. There are a number of important areas in the forebrain, and these are each briefly described. These include the thalamus, the hypothalamus, the limbic system, the basal ganglia, and the cerebral cortex.

Thalamus

The purpose of the thalamus is to serve as a relay center for sensory information to be transmitted to the brain. Specifically, sensory nerves come to the thalamus and are routed to appropriate cerebral sensory-perceptual areas. There is some speculation that the thalamus is the place in the brain where sensory impulses coming in are "boosted," in terms of power, so that they can be relayed to the higher-level brain areas. The thalamus is also noted for controlling the brain's electrical activity—a crucial matter in terms of information processes. When the thalamus is damaged, in cases of brain injury, the most common problems associated with this site of brain injury involves short-term memory, attention, and concentration. In terms of physical location, the thalamus lies in the center of the brain, above the limbic system. It is composed of two hemispheres, similar to the higher level of the cerebral hemispheres.

Hypothalamus

The hypothalamus is involved in a number of important functions, including the regulation of body temperature, blood pressure, sleeping, eating, drinking, and sexual activities. Clearly, brain injuries to the thalamus and the hypothalamus can have disastrous consequences in terms of life activities. The hypothalamus is generally considered to be located above the roof of the mouth.

Limbic System

The structures commonly associated with the limbic system include the amygdala, cingulate cortex, hippocampus, and septal area. There is a maze of interconnections of the limbic system to other areas of the nervous system. Perhaps the most important of these interconnections are to the frontal lobes. Of the limbic system components, the most studied are the hippocampal area and the amygdala. When the hippocampal area is damaged, the most commonly associated dysfunction is that of memory disorder, particularly with respect to declarative memory for facts that were over-learned. This type of memory for information, compared to skills memory or procedural memory, is often thought to be located in the cerebellum. There also seems to be lateralization in the hippocampus, because when the left hippocampus is damaged, the most common deficit is the inability to acquire new long-term verbal memories (Russell & Espir, 1961), and impairment of the right hippocampal area produces a rather dramatic difficulty with acquisition of new long term nonverbal memories (Milner, 1971). A role in memory production has also been proposed for the amygdala (Mishkin, 1978), as well as an association with the expression of aggressive behavior. Much, however, remains to be learned about these important forebrain structures.

Basal Ganglia

The basal ganglia have been associated with the production of movement and with the unthinking coordination of movement with other components of the extrapyramidal system. The basal ganglia include the putamen, globus pallidus, and caudate nucleuses. The structures of the basal ganglia, along with the cerebral cortex in midbrain, constitute what is often called the extrapyramidal system, which is often associated with the neurological disorder known as Parkinson's disease. Indeed, Parkinson's disease has often been cited as the classic example of an impairment of the extrapyramidal system.

Cerebral Cortex

The area of the forebrain which has been the most studied by clinical child neuropsychologists and other brain researchers has been the cerebral cortex. Many have suggested that the functions of the cerebral cortex are unique in terms of the abilities that allow humans to be human. The most frequently used approach in the United States is to subdivide the cerebral cortex into specific functional areas. The most widely used American system proposes that there are frontal, temporal and parietal, and occipital lobes, and that each lobe has a unique function associated with its structure. In addition, each cerebral hemisphere is considered to have separate frontal, temporal, parietal, and occipital lobes. The frontal and parietal lobes are clearly demarcated by the central sulcus, or the fissure of Rolando, and the temporal lobes are separated from the frontal and parietal lobes by the lateral cerebral fissure, or the fissure of Sylvius. Although, in American neuropsychology, as previously noted (Horton, 1994), four specific lobes are postulated, other brain organization systems are possible. The parietal and occipital lobes are not dramatically separated by a large fissure, but by a relatively small fissure. The parietal-occipital fissure is used to indicate or mark where the parietal lobe ends and the occipital lobe begins. Other non-U.S. models of brain functioning sometimes consider the parietal and occipital lobes to act together as a functional unit.

As is well known, the cerebral cortex is divided into two hemispheres, which, when looked upon from above, appear similar to two footballs placed together (Horton & Wedding, 1984). The cerebral hemisphere that corresponds to the dominant hemisphere, which, in the majority of human beings, is the left cerebral hemisphere, often appears to be a bit larger than the nondominant hemisphere. The two cerebral hemispheres are interconnected by a number of brain structures, perhaps the most important and largest of which is the corpus callosum. The corpus callosum consists of white fibers, which connect areas of the cerebral hemispheres. The corpus callosum allows for direct communication between the two cerebral hemispheres. The cerebral hemispheres are separated by the longitudinal cerebral commissaries, and the surfaces of the cerebral hemispheres have a number of convolutions, which have been described as hills and valleys: The technical terms for these are gyris and sulcis.

The major landmarks of the brain are formed by two very deep valleys, or sulci, in the brain. The most important landmark of the brain is the central valley, also called the central sulcus, or fissure of Rolando, which lies in the middle of each cerebral hemisphere and divides the frontal from the parietal lobes. The unique aspects of the fissure of Rolando are described in greater detail later. The second major landmark of the brain is a lateral valley, also called the lateral cerebral fissure, or the fissure of Sylvius. This particular fissure arises from the bottom of the brain and separates the frontal and temporal lobes. These major landmarks of the brain provide a means of separating the frontal and parietal lobes and the frontal and parietal lobes or temporal lobes from each other.

These functional, structural subdivisions of the brain are important for later understanding of child neuropsychology test-result interpretation and form the underlying basis of the majority of treatment and management recommendations.

The particular areas of the cerebral cortex can, of course, be further classified. Although there are different ways to look at the way the surface of the cerebral cortex has been mapped out by neuroanatomical workers, the most common framework utilized is that of Brodmann (Nauta & Feintag, 1986). In Brodmann's system, particular cortical areas are identified by numbers. For example, in the parietal lobes, just behind the central sulcus, or the fissure of Rolando, lie the primary tactual sensory-perceptual areas, and these have been given numbers 1, 2, and 3, to identify specific functional areas. These particular areas, that is, 1, 2, and 3, must be intact to enable tactile perceptions to be perceived by other portions of the cerebral cortex. In addition, in the temporal lobes lie the primary areas for audition and are identified as area of 41. Also in the occipital lobes are a number of areas supporting primary vision, and they are identified as areas 17, 18, and 19. There are also other specific brain structures associated with various functions. If the particular brain areas mentioned above are severely damaged, then there is difficulty in receiving tactual perceptions hearing sounds or seeing objects.

These primary brain areas interact with other brain areas to produce typically human behaviors, emotions, and cognitions. Although there is a plethora of brain functioning theories, one particularly insightful model for understanding brain functioning is based on the work of A. R. Luria, the famous Russian neurologist and neuropsychologist. The following comments are an oversimplified description of his theoretical paradigm, but are offered for purposes of illustration.

LURIA'S MODEL OF BRAIN FUNCTIONING

Luria (1966, 1973) was a Russian neuroscientist who developed a complex but elegant conceptual model for understanding the organization of higher mental abilities or facilities and proposed human behavioral correlates of brain functioning. In essence, Luria's model of higher cortical functioning involved dividing brain anatomy into three major brain blocks. These were (1) lower brain stem structures, (2) the cerebral cortex posterior to the central sulcus, or the fissure of Rolando, and (3) the cerebral cortex anterior to, or in front of, the central sulcus, or the fissure of Rolando. The blocks of the brain are labeled one, two, and three, corresponding to (1) the brain stem structures, (2) cerebral cortex posterior to central sulcus, and (3) cerebral cortex anterior to the central sulcus. Those major blocks, as conceptualized by Luria, make unique contributions to the human brain functioning. Each is briefly described.

Block One

The lower brain stem structures, or block one in Luria's structure of the brain model, are responsible for maintaining the tone and energy supply of the cerebral cortex. A similar relation might be seen between a personal computer and its electricity supply. For the personal computer to work in a reasonable fashion, it must have a supply of electricity and the level of electricity must be constant. If the electricity supply or current voltage varies, then the arithmetic and logic section and memory banks of the personal computer will have difficulty working in an efficient manner. In a similar fashion, the lower brain stem structures provide for the tone and energy level of the cerebral cortex and must keep this stable and constant, in order for the higher level areas to work in an effective manner.

Block Two

The area posterior to the central sulcus, or the posterior cerebral cortex, which is block two in Luria's structure of the brain model, is the area into which sensory impressions of a visual, auditory, and tactile nature are identified, perceived, and organized for comprehension. The processes of perceiving the incoming sensory stimuli include the function of organizing it in such a way that it can be understood by other areas of the cerebral cortex.

Block Three

This area (block three on Luria's structure of the brain model) is anterior to, or in front of, the central sulcus. This area is involved in the production and monitoring of motor responses. The area of the anterior cerebral cortex is where the information from the posterior sensory impressions comes and where there is a formulation of intention, planning, and production of motor behaviors and evaluation of the effects of motor behaviors. To carry the computer model, mentioned above, a little further, in block two, the input device to the computer, like the keyboard, is a model for the posterior cerebral cortex. Similarly, the anterior cerebral cortex, which makes decisions, is related to the arithmetic and logic unit of the personal computer. The output of information by the printer, or some other output mechanisms, is planned by the anterior cerebral area, but mostly carried out by arms, legs, and the mouth.

Primary, Secondary, and Tertiary Areas of Blocks Two and Three

Luria (1966) further subdivided the second and third blocks of the cerebral cortex into smaller subareas. Luria suggested that the area posterior to the cerebral cortex and the area anterior to the cerebral cortex could be subdivided into primary, secondary, and tertiary areas. Each of these areas is arranged in some organized fashion, in terms of its particular role of dealing with mental stimuli. Perhaps the simplest way to explain this concept is to use the second block, or the posterior cerebral cortex, to illustrate this proposed structure–function neuropsychological arrangement. Grossly oversimplified, the primary areas of the second block perform very simple functions of collecting sensory input of stimuli. More elaborate perceptions of the nature of the stimuli are performed by the secondary areas, and the tertiary areas coordinate the integration of two or more secondary areas to produce higher-level mental activities. For example, using the modalities of touch, the primary area would tell a person whether they had touch, but the secondary area would be necessary to determine some more complex stimuli, or whether the touch was an "X" or an "O" drawn on the skin. The tertiary areas, on the other hand, would subsume more complex activities, such as handwriting, in which the motion of the hand in a complex function and the feedback from touching various materials is important in terms of subserving complex mental activities. Put in another way, information from different areas of the brain combine to subserve higher-level mental functions. Luria (1966) suggested that divergent areas of the brain work together in a functional manner to subsume or support various behavioral functions. That is to say that areas of the brain, in each of the three blocks, were combined in order to support higher-level mental activities. The postulate of this particular notion is that functional systems may use more than one set of brain areas in terms of subsuming the same behavioral functions. In rehabilitation, it may be possible to obtain the same behavioral performance, but reroute or have a different organization in terms of brain areas used.

NEUROPSYCHOLOGICAL DEVELOPMENTAL STAGES

Luria (1966) postulated a number of stages by which neuropsychological functions are developed. These stages apparently interact with environmental stimuli. Luria's work, to a large extent, is based on Lev Vygotsky's cultural and historical theory (Horton, 1987). Vygotsky was a mentor or teacher to A. R. Luria and can be seen as a major influence on Luria's thinking. Vygotsky was an impressive individual, because he initially worked in education, but obtained his PhD based on a dissertation on the works of Shakespeare. This was quite an achievement, considering that he obtained his doctorate in Russia just after the Russian Revolution and Soviet takeover. Vygotsky developed a complex theory related to language and thought processes, and postulated that environmental/cultural influences were important in terms of interacting with neurological structures to develop higher-level mental abilities such as abstraction, memory, and voluntary attention. It was indeed tragic and regrettable that Vygotsky died of tuberculosis at a young age and that he was unable to further develop his interesting neurodevelopmental theories. Nonetheless, Luria apparently used Vygotsky's thinking as his major theoretical framework throughout his life (Horton, 1987). Essentially, Luria, like Vygotsky, believed that the development of higher cortical functions required both the interaction of normal neurological development and specific environmental stimuli of a cultural, historical, and social nature, in order to flourish. The process or the result of the appropriate interaction of neurological development and the appropriate environmental stimuli would be higher cortical functioning, such as language, intention, memory, and abstract thought. Five stages in development were proposed by Luria (1980). It might be expected that the specific stages of neurodevelopment are closely related to Luria's conceptualization of basic blocks of the brain.

As earlier noted, block one was related to the lower brain stem structures, block two was related to the area posterior to the central sulcus, and block three is related to the area anterior to the central sulcus. Essentially, in the first stage, beginning in the first year of life, the brain stem structures are primarily developed. These brain stem structures in block one may be seen as involving the reticular activating system, which was described earlier.

The second stage is related to the activation of the primary sensory areas for vision, hearing, and tactical perception and the primary motor areas for gross motor movement. To put it in terms of neuroanatomy, these would be areas that are immediately adjacent, both posterior and anterior, to the central sulcus. This particular stage relies primarily upon the unfolding of hardwired neurological structures.

The third stage focuses on single modalities in the secondary association areas of the brain. Often, this stage is associated with movement of the child into preschool. The child, at this stage, recognizes and reproduces various symbolic materials and is able to model various physical movements. The different modalities of learning may be separately accessed.

The fourth stage begins about the time of first or second grade. At this time, the tertiary areas of the parietal lobes become activated. The tertiary parietal lobe is the area in which the temporal, parietal, and occipital lobes come together. This enables a coordination of the three major sensory-input channels. In order to help the child make sense of the sensory input, environmental stimulation is particularly important. For instance, the cultural, historical, and social influences are major factors in shaping the crucial academic skills of reading, writing, and arithmetic, which are the primary tasks of the child to learn in the early school years.

The fifth stage becomes activated during adolescence. In this stage, the frontal area, or the area anterior to the central sulcus, comes online in terms of mental functioning. As noted by others (Struss & Benson, 1984), the area anterior to the central sulcus is important for abstract thinking, intentional memory, and the execution, monitoring, and evaluation of complex learning behavior. Luria's model (1980) suggests that there are qualitative differences between children, and different stages in neuropsychological development, and that children could use different functional systems to perform similar tasks. That is to say, combinations of brain areas utilized in mental functioning may vary, although the final behavior performance could be similar. In addition, Luria's thinking suggests that there must be interaction between the child's level of neuropsychological development and sorts of environmental stimulation that are crucial in terms of developing important human adaptive/vocational skills. Luria's model (1980) should be recognized as a unique, elegant, and efficient method with which to understand neuropsychological development and environmental stimuli/stimulation.

HEMISPHERIC LATERALIZATION OF FUNCTIONS

As is well known, the human brain is divided into two cerebral hemispheres (Dean, 1986). These cerebral hemispheres are very similar, but not identical in structure and function. The term *cerebral asymmetry* refers to the differences between the two cerebral hemispheres. As would be expected, given that human beings are dominant on one side of the body versus the other side, one cerebral hemisphere is usually larger than the other. In the vast majority of right-handed individuals, the left cerebral hemisphere is slightly larger than the right cerebral hemisphere, possibly, as is often suggested, because it subserves language functions in the human (Geschwind & Levitsky, 1968). Essentially, the need to support spoken language and various symbolic methods of communication has resulted in areas of the brain that have been further developed as human beings have evolved to an information-intensive society. One might, for sake of humor, coin the phrase "Internet brain," to describe this development. There have been reports, in children with dyslexia, that suggest that their right cerebral hemispheres are slightly larger than their left cerebral hemispheres (Hynd & Willis, 1988). This is clear evidence for a neuroanatomical basis of reading disability.

In addition to cerebral asymmetry, it is also important for the clinical child neuropsychologist to be aware of the concept of *contralateral control.* This refers to the crosswired nervous system organization of the CNS at the level of the cerebral hemispheres. An oversimplified explanation is that the left cerebral hemisphere controls motor and sensory functions on the right side of the body, and the right cerebral hemisphere controls motor and sensory of the left side of the body. All functions of the sensory nature are not 100% lateralized: For example, visual functions do appear to be 100% lateralized; auditory ability is 80% under contralateral control and 20% under ipsolateral, or same-side, control. Similarly, tactile functions are generally thought to be 90% under contralateral control and 10% under ipsolateral control (Horton & Wedding, 1984).

Hemispheric Abilities

As is well known, the cerebral hemispheres are specialized for behavioral functions, which they subserve. Although historical understanding of the functional behavioral correlates of the cerebral hemispheres may be traced as far back as Broca's (Horton & Wedding, 1984) clinical observations of brain-injured subjects and the insightful theoretical formulation of Hughlings Jackson in the 1870s, nonetheless, general acceptance of hemispheric abilities by the neuroscience community only became widespread after the split-brain research of Sperry (1961) was published. Sperry, who had obtained his masters degree in psychology and his doctorate in zoology, conducted an extensive neuropsychological research program with epilepsy patients who had undergone neurosurgical procedures for patients with severe refractory epilepsy. Each patient had been through a neurosurgical procedure that involved cutting the fibers connecting the two cerebral hemispheres.

The theory underlying this surgical procedure was that refractory seizures will move from one cerebral hemisphere to another through these connecting fibers and that cutting the interconnecting fibers would reduce seizure frequency. Usually, the treatment involved the corpus callosum, which is the largest set of interhemispheric connecting fibers. The corpus callosum, however, is not the only group of fibers connecting the cerebral hemispheres. There are also the anterior commissure and the hippocampal commissure, which also connect the cerebral hemispheres, but in smaller collections of fibers. As a general rule, as a result of severing these interhemispheric connecting fibers, the patients were less troubled by their seizures.

Sperry carefully studied a group of these patients, who had operations that had cut the interconnecting hemispheric fibers and, as a result, produced disconnected cerebral hemispheres, or *split brains.* The patient's split-brain operation allows the two cerebral hemispheres to function in an independent fashion (Horton & Wedding, 1984). The split-brain patients were a phenomenal and unique natural laboratory for studying cerebral lateralized brain functioning. They provided a situation in which the two cerebral hemispheres were relatively intact and available for assessment. This allowed comparison within a split-brain patient of the two reasonably well-functioning sides of the brain on a particular experimental manipulation (Nebes, 1974).

In previous research, which usually involved lesion studies in which patients with unilateral brain damage in one cerebral hemisphere were compared to normal subjects, there were multiple cases of confounding influences that could only be poorly controlled. By contrast, the split-brain patients provided a unique situation in which there was relatively exquisite control of past life experiences, demographic variables, substance abuse, and psychiatric history, and many other factors (Nebes, 1974). The research program of Sperry was so successful and produced findings of such great importance that he later received the Nobel Prize in medicine for his contributions.

Essentially, Sperry's research team found that, although split-brain patients had few obvious consequences from the neurosurgical procedure, there were nonetheless subtle neuropsychological changes. For example, information presented in the right visual field would go to the left cerebral hemisphere only and was not be accessible to the right cerebral hemisphere (Gazzaniga, 1977). A fundamental experimental paradigm of Sperry's work was the presentation of stimuli to only one visual field of split-brain patients. An example of how this could work is to present a coin to a split-brain patient's right visual field. As the sensory stimuli are transmitted to the left cerebral hemisphere, the cerebral hemisphere specialized for speech and language, the split-brain patient is able to identify the object by name. On the other hand, or visual field, if the coin is presented to the left visual field, then sensory information is transmitted to the right cerebral hemisphere, which is specialized for visuospatial perception and organization (Nebes, 1974). As a result, the split-brain patient is unable to name the coin, but can match the coin when presented, with alternatives (i.e., a dime is presented, and a nickel, penny, and quarter are other options). Similarly, split-brain patients draw better with the left hand, and right cerebral hemisphere, regardless of their preneurosurgical dominance pattern (Gazzaniga, Steen, & Volpe, 1979).

Since Sperry's major contributions, research has focused on other aspects of hemispheric functioning. Although there is agreement that the two cerebral hemispheres subserve different neurobehavioral functions, there is less agreement regarding at which neurodevelopment stages various behavioral abilities are mediated by particular brain structures (Dean, 1985). It has been postulated, for instance, that hemispheric lateralizarion of functions begins earlier in life and that, by the age of 3 years, more than 90% of children demonstrate left hemisphere language and symbolic processing abilities (Bryden & Saxby, 1985).

Moreover, developmental preferences for hand and foot dominance follow similar age-related patterns. Preference for the right hand in most children appears by age 2 years (Bryden & Saxby, 1985); foot preference develops a little later, in many cases, by age 5 years (Porac & Coren, 1981).

A basic and oversimplified overview of localization of cerebral functioning is presented here. To a great extent, these suggestions for cerebral functioning localization are based on adult chronic lesion study data (Horton & Wedding, 1984). In some cases, the relationships suggested between neurocortex and behavioral function may not generalize to child and adolescent populations. The purpose of this overview, however, is to provide an elementary perspective on brain–behavioral relationships and to demonstrate the specific neurobehavioral functions that may be developing in some children and adolescents. For a more elaborate discussion of lateralization cerebral functioning, the reader may wish to consult the excellent chapter by Dean (1985).

Left Hemispheric Functioning

As is well known, the left cerebral hemisphere, assuming right-handedness, is specialized for language and symbolic processing. Abilities such as speech, writing, arithmetic, and reading are thought to be mediated by the left cerebral hemisphere. In short, the processes of using symbols for communication are generally thought to be subsumed by the left cerebral hemisphere. Generally, the left cerebral hemisphere is also considered to work more in a linear-sequential, or step-by-step fashion, rather than in a synthetic-simultaneous fashion. An example might be that the left hemisphere works more like someone following a cookbook recipe rather than cooking by intuition.

Right Hemispheric Functions

Again, as is well known, thanks to contemporary popular culture, the right hemisphere is specialized for the perception and organization of visuospatial stimuli, certain perceptual-motor skills, and emotional functioning. The various abilities subserved by the right cerebral hemisphere, assuming right-handedness, include orienting oneself in space, reproducing complex geometric and whole–part patterns, recognizing faces, and understanding different emotional tones and patterns of nonverbal behavior (Saxby & Bryden, 1984).

SPECIFIC FUNCTIONS OF THE CEREBRAL LOBES

The knowledge of the specific behavioral correlates of lesions in specific cerebral lobes is based upon a considerable amount of clinical research (Horton & Wedding, 1984). As alluded to earlier, the majority of these research findings were developed from the adult brain-injured population from studies of patients with chronic lesions. Correlation of a behavioral deficit with a chronic lesion in a specific brain area does not always mean that a specific function or behavioral ability can be localized in that particular area of the brain. Rather, the chronic lesion data suggest that some important function that is involved in the production of the behavior may be absent, based on some other particular impaired brain area. As was mentioned earlier, neurobehavioral functions are produced by multiple brain areas working together in a coordinated fashion.

Frontal Lobes

Planning, execution, and evaluation of motor and cognitive behaviors are performed by the frontal lobes, working with other brain areas. The frontal lobes direct behavior toward goals, make judgments with respect to time allocation and passage, and also play a role in making decisions concerning material to be remembered. In addition, there is a relationship between the frontal lobes and emotional responding, because many decisions with respect to emotional expression require input to the frontal lobes.

Left Frontal Lobe

As was earlier mentioned, Broca's area resides in the left frontal lobe and is connected with motor speech or expressive language. With chronic lesions in the left frontal lobe, research has generally shown difficulties of modulating behavior to conform to complex internal speech and difficulties with intentional verbal memory: Luria (1966) described this syndrome as "dynamic aphasia." An example of this problem is an inability to produce words that start with a particular letter (Benton, 1968).

Right Frontal Lobe

The right frontal lobe is particularly involved with visuospatial integration and maze learning (Teuber, 1963; Corkin, 1965). The visuospatial problems, however, may be more related to integration of motor aspects than visual-perceptual components. Also, there may be difficulties in singing or the ability to tell jokes and funny stories.

Temporal Lobes

The perception, analysis, and evaluation of auditory stimuli is the special ability of the temporal lobes (Luria, 1966). In addition, the temporal lobes subserve memory functioning involving both verbal and nonverbal stimuli.

Left Temporal Lobe

As would be expected, verbal stimuli, such as the sounds of letters, words, and numbers, are perceived by the left temporal lobe. Impairment of the left temporal lobe can make it difficult for an individual to appreciate language (Luria, 1966). Problems in phonemic analysis can impair classic academic skills (reading, writing, and spelling skills and the decoding of language), because phonics is a key component in these processes, as well as in verbal short-term memory (Milner, 1958) (a distinction between episodic and declarative memory could be made, but, for ease of understanding, the dated concepts of short- and long-term memory are used in this book).

Right Temporal Lobe

As the left hemisphere is associated with language and verbal short-term memory, the right hemisphere is associated with perception of nonverbal stimuli; therefore, the right temporal lobe is particularly involved with the auditory perception of nonverbal stimuli such as rhythm and pitch (Horton & Wedding, 1984). Impairment of the right temporal lobe can cause a person to be unable to appreciate music; similarly, nonverbal memory is also associated with the right temporal lobe (Meier & French, 1965).

Parietal Lobes

Tactile and kinesthetic perception is based in the parietal lobes. Lesion studies involving the parietal lobes may show deficits in appreciating tactile stimuli, such as an inability to recognize objects perceived through touch and problems integrating tactile and kinesthetic information (Horton & Wedding, 1984). Other deficits include the inability to consider multiple aspects of objects and problems with complex voluntary perceptual-motor skill movements (i.e., apraxia) (Horton & Wedding, 1984).

Left Parietal Lobe

The left parietal lobe is situated in a central location between the temporal and occipital lobes, and, as a result, it plays a special role in terms of verbal information processing. The left parietal lobe, containing numerous connections between the temporal and occipital lobes, is responsible for facilitating communication and integrating information from visual, auditory, and tactile sensory and modalities (Horton & Wedding, 1984). Problems in the perception and comprehension of language can be produced by impairment of this area (i.e., Wernicke's area). Lesion studies, involving the area where the left parietal, occipital, and temporal lobes intersect, demonstrate difficulties with reading, writing, naming, color labeling, and spelling (Horton & Wedding, 1984). Luria (1973) noted that verbal memory deficits associated with the left parietal lobe usually involve difficulties in organizing verbal material, rather than perceiving it.

Right Parietal Lobe

Just as the left parietal lobe is important in verbal information processing, so the right parietal lobe is important is the processing of nonverbal information. The parietal lobe region of the right parietal lobe is particularly important in terms of combining visual, auditory, and tactile stimuli into integrated nonverbal wholes. The perception of faces and the drawing of complex spatial figures is dependent upon intact right parietal lobe functioning. In addition, arithmetic operations in which place values are important, dressing difficulties, and left-sided visual neglect are related to right parietal lobe functioning (Horton & Wedding, 1984).

Occipital Lobes

Just as the temporal lobes subserve the perception of auditory stimuli and the parietal lobes subserve the perception of tactile stimuli, so the occipital lobes mediate visual functions. The occipital lobes in different cerebral hemispheres perceive the contralateral visual field. As earlier noted, the perception of the contralateral visual field is 100%.

Left Occipital Lobe

Visual discrimination and analysis of language-related visual forms, such as symbolic stimuli, are mediated by the left occipital lobe. This includes symbols such as letters, numbers, and words. The inability to integrate visual stimuli, to comprehend multiple aspects of a visual form, can be found in individuals with specific lesions in the left occipital lobe (Luria, 1966). An interesting way of testing for these sorts of deficits is to print a word like *STOP*, then draw diagonal lines through the printed word. The drawing of the lines should make it more difficult for the subject to read a word he or she could read without difficulty before. The reading problem, however, comes from difficulties in visual recognition and scanning, and not from problems in comprehension (Horton & Wedding, 1984).

Right Occipital Lobe

Visual perception of nonverbal forms, compared to verbal forms, is subserved by the right occipital lobe. In chronic lesion studies with patients having impaired right occipital lobes, patients have had difficulty in visual recognition and differentiation of forms and geometric patterns (Horton & Wedding, 1984). In addition, problems in differentiating color hues can be traced to right occipital lobe lesions (Scotti & Spinner, 1970).

RECOVERY OF FUNCTION AFTER BRAIN INJURY

A considerable degree of research on animals has demonstrated that environmental stimulation is important in modifying the CNS. Essentially, it has been suggested that the brain may have some residual capacity to repair itself after injury. The environmental can be crucial in terms of supporting recovery functioning after brain injury. Rosenzweig (1980) performed a number of important studies in this area of research. Essentially, he demonstrated that animals raised in a rich intellectual environment (i.e., for the specific species of animal) would have a larger brain and would have positive neurochemical changes. These physical changes were directly related to prior positive environmental experiences. The suggestion, of course, is that the particular environmental stimulations may be important in allowing the brain to recover, at least to a degree, following some sort of brain injury. It has been suggested that children recover from brain injury in a somewhat different fashion than adults (Reitan, 1974; Horton, 1994), because children are not completely developed as human beings, but are passing through a number of complex developmental phases.

Generally speaking, when adults have a brain injury, assuming that it is not a progressive condition such as a degenerative disease (i.e., Alzheimer's disease, Pick's disease), a degree of recovery might be expected. These are most classically seen in cases of stroke or TBI. Often, adults will recover for a period of 1 or 2 years. With children, a different picture is presented. In a classic study, Teuber and Rudel (1962) studied brain-injured children over a number of years, to assess the residual effects of childhood brain damage. Basically, three possible developmental patterns of recovery of function were postulated. These were fairly straightforward and are briefly described. The first pattern is similar to that seen in adults. There is initial impairment of neuropsychological abilities following brain injury, but the typical progressive pattern of neuropsychological recovery would be seen over time.

The second proposed developmental pattern of neuropsychological functioning after brain injury produces constant and consistent impairment of behavioral abilities over time. This would be similar to individuals with a major stroke in the primary motor area, with significant destruction of brain tissue. In short, no significant recovery of functioning is expected after a brief period of time.

The third pattern was one that was only expected to be seen in children. In that pattern, there would be no clear impairment of behavior abilities initially, but, as the child with a brain injury grows and develops, behavioral impairment would be demonstrated. The behavioral impairment could emerge weeks, months, or years after the initial injury to the brain.

This last pattern relies on the fact that certain neuropsychological brain structures only become active in certain neuropsychological developmental stages. That is to say, the delayed onset of impaired brain functioning is like turning on lights on a Christmas tree. The lights come on only in stages; similarly, a brain injury may impair a brain area that will only become active in a later neurodevelopmental stage. The initial behavioral performance will not be impaired, because the child has not found it necessary to use the particular skill that will only be needed in a later stage of neurobehavioral development. For example, the child may sustain brain injury at age 2 years, and only later, when the child goes to school, could it be apparent that functions, such as reading, writing, and arithmetic, may be impaired to a significant degree. The crux of that matter is that only when the child is called upon to demonstrate specialized neurobehavioral functioning will some neuropsychological deficits emerge.

With respect to Teuber and Rudel's study (1962), the results were unexpected, because brain-injured children displayed all three patterns, depending on the particular tasks assessed. That is to say, in some cases, they had initial impairment followed by significant behavioral over time. In other cases, there was initial impairment of neurobehavioral functioning, which stayed current, and in the third case, there is no clear neurobehavioral impairment initially, but, later, as the child grew up, the neuropsychological deficits emerged. Because of the time lag, if the child had not been followed in a research project, it would not have been clear that he or she was impaired because of childhood brain damage. This research study demonstrates that the effects of brain damage to children are very complex and depends both on the characteristics of tasks under study and the normal developmental sequencing of that task, among other factors (Horton, 1994).

The third pattern is particularly problematic in cases in which someone is attempting to demonstrate the extent of neuropsychological deficits from a childhood TBI, because it essentially undermines any conclusions reached before the child has grown to maturity. The lesion area is either immature or not yet utilized at the time the lesion was sustained, and only later will the degree of neurobehavioral deficit be apparent (Bolter & Long, 1985).

As might be understood after one reflects on the difficulties of longitudinal research, most studies of childhood brain injury have been of limited duration (Teuber & Rudel [1982] followed children for 10 years and is the clear exception to the rule). Most research has concentrated on the first pattern, that is, the recovery of functional ability after TBI in which there is some clear evidence of progressive recovery. Researchers at the University of British Columbia (Klonoff & Low, 1974; Klonoff & Paris, 1977) have done what is perhaps considered to be the most pivotal work in this area. They initiated a number of large longitudinal studies on injuries, involving fairly comprehensive diagnostic assessments. Traumatic head injuries are the most common neurological problem in children and result in 15% of deaths in the 15–24-year age group (Klonoff et al., 1984).

Some of the most important findings from the British Columbia studies were that the most marked improvement after childhood TBI took place in the first 2 years post-head injury, but that children showed evidence of significant improvement for 5 years postinjury. In addition, boys are more likely than girls to have had injury, and factors such as living in a congested residential area, having a lower socioeconomic status, and unstable family lives were related to the likelihood of having a childhood traumatic head injury. Different patterns were seen for younger and older children following traumatic head injury. Younger children demonstrated irritability plus other personality changes; older children were more likely to demonstrate headaches, impaired memory function, and problems in learning (Klonoff et al., 1984).

Test data demonstrated that IQ scores for brain-injured children were lower than those for normal control subjects during the entire 5-year study, and the most marked differences were found at the initial assessment and at the first-year follow-up after postinjury. It was also noted that IQ measures appeared to recover somewhat more rapidly than did neuropsychological measures. The series of studies in British Columbia suggested that full scale IQ scores from the initial testing were the single best predictor of the child's recovery from TBI. This simply underscores the importance of IQ measurements in brain-injured children. The IQ is of a different level of sensitivity with children than it is with adults, in relation to neuropsychological functioning (Benton, 1974). The status of the child after 5 years was best predicted by the initial full-scale IQ, loss of consciousness, and memory problems immediately after injuries (Klonoff et al., 1984).

SUMMARY

The field of clinical neuropsychology is new and rests on an evolving research base. Moreover, the complex nature of clinical neuropsychology makes it a very difficult but rewarding area. The hope and expectation is that this and other chapters of this book will be helpful in facilitating the delivery of forensic neuropsychological services to this needy population of brain-injured adults and children. This chapter presents a basic review of some selected elements of brain–behavior relationships. It addresses, in an oversimplified fashion, the morphology of the CNS, Luria's model of brain functioning, hemispheric lateralization of functions, specific functions of the cerebral lobes, and recovery of functions after TBI.

REFERENCES

Benton, A. L. (1968). Differential effects in the minor hemisphere. *Confinia Neurologica, 6*, 53–60.

Benton, A. L. (1974). Child neuropsychology. In R. M. Reitan & L. A. Davison (Eds.), *Clinical neuropsychology: Current status and application* (pp. 79–82). New York: Wiley.

Bolter, J. F., & Long, C. J. (1985). Methodological issues in research in developmental neuropsychology. In L. C. Hartlage & C. F. Telzrow (Eds.), *Neuropsychology of individual differences* (pp. 41–60). New York: Plenum Press.

Broca, P. (1861). Perte de la parole. *Bulletin of the Society of Anthropology, 2,* 1.

Broder, E. (1973). Developmental dyslexia: A diagnostic approach based on three atypical reading-spelling patterns. *Developmental Medicine and Child Neurology, 15,* 663–687.

Bryden, M. P., & Saxby, L. (1985). Developmental affects of cerebral lateralization. In J. E. Obrzut & G. W. Hynd (Eds.), *Clinical neuropsychology: Vol. I. Theory and Research* (pp. 71–94). Orlando, FL: Academic Press.

Connolly, C. J. (1950). *External morphology of the primate brain.* Springfield, IL: Charles C Thomas.

Corballis, M. C. (1982). The origins and evolution of human laterality. In N. R. Malastesha & L. C. Hartlage (Eds.), *Neuropsychology and cognition, Vol. I* (pp. 1–35). Boston: Martinus Nijhoff.

Corkin, S. (1965). Tactually-guided imaging in man: Effects of unilateral excisions and bilateral hippocampus lesions. *Neuropsychologia, 3,* 339–351.

Craighead, W. E., Kazdin, A. E., & Mahoney, M. J. (1976). *Behavior modification: Principles issues and directions.* Boston: Houghton Mifflin.

Davison, L. A. (1974). Introduction. In R. M. Reitan & L. A. Davison (Eds.), *Clinical neuropsychology: Current status and application* (pp. 1–18). New York: John Wiley.

Dean, R. S. (1985). Foundation and rationale for neuropsychological basis of individual differences. In L. C. Hartlage & C. F. Telzrow (Eds.), *Neuropsychology of individual differences* (pp. 7–40). New York: Plenum Press.

Freud, S. (1906). Psycho-analysis and the certainty of truth in courts of law. *Clinical Papers and Papers on Technique, Collected Papers (1959), 2,* 13–24. New York: Basic Books.

Gazzaniga, M. S. (1977) Consistency and diversity in brain organization. *Annals of the New York Academy of Science, 299,* 415–423.

Gazzaniga, M. S., Steen, D., & Volpe, B. T. (1979). *Functional neuroscience.* New York: Harper & Row.

Geschwind, N., & Levitsky, W. (1948). Human brain left-right asymmetries in temporal speech region. *Science, 161,* 186–187.

Goldstein, K. (1942). *After effect of brain injuries in war.* New York: Grune & Stratton.

Hartlage, L. C. (1975). Neuropsychological approaches to predicting outcome of remedial educational strategies for learning disabled children. *Pediatric Psychology, 3,* 23–28.

Hartlage, L. C. (1986). Pediatric neuropsychology. In D. Wedding, A. M. Horton, Jr., & J. S. Webster (Eds.), *The neuropsychology handbook* (pp. 441–455). New York: Springer.

Horton, A. M., Jr. (1987). Luria's contributions to clinical and behavioral neuropsychology. *Neuropsychology, 1*(2), 39–44.

Horton, A. M., Jr. (1989). Child behavioral neuropsychology with children. In C. R. Reynolds & E. Fletcher-Janzen (Eds.), *Handbook of clinical child neuropsychology* (pp. 521–534). New York: Plenum.

Horton, A. M., Jr. (1994). *Behavioral interventions with brain injured children.* New York: Plenum.

Horton, A. M., Jr., & Puente, A. E. (1986). Behavioral neuropsychology for children. In G. Hynd & J. Obrzut (Eds.), *Child neuropsychology: Clinical practice, Vol. II* (pp. 299–316). Orlando, FL: Academic Press.

Horton, A. M., Jr., & Puente, A. E. (1990). Lifespan neuropsychology: An overview. In A. M. Horton, Jr. (Ed.), *Neuropsychology across the lifespan* (pp. 1–15). New York: Springer.

Horton, A. M., Jr., & Wedding, D. (1984). *Clinical and behavioral neuropsychology.* New York: Praeger.

Hynd, G. W., & Obrzut, J. E. (Eds.). (1981). *Neuropsychological assessment and the school-aged child: Issues and procedures.* New York: Grune & Stratton.

Hynd, G. W., & Willis, W. G. (1988). *Pediatric neuropsychology.* Orlando, FL: Grune & Stratton.

Kertesz, A. (Ed.). (1994). *Localization and neuroimaging in neuropsychology.* New York: Academic Press.

Klonoff, A., Crockett, D. F., & Clark, G. (1984). Head trauma in children. In R. Tarter & G. Goldstein (Eds.), *Advances in clinical neuropsychology* (pp. 139–157). New York: Plenum.

Klonoff, H., & Low, M. (1974). Disordered brain function in young children and early adolescents: Neuropsychological and electroencephalographic correlates. In R. M. Reitan & L. A. Davison (Eds.), *Clinical neuropsychology: Current status and application* (pp. 121–178). New York: Wiley.

Klonoff, H., & Paris, R. (1974). Immediate, short-term and residual effects of acute head injuries in children: Neuropsychological and neurological correlates. In R. M. Reitan & L. A. Davison (Eds.), *Clinical neuropsychology: Current status and application* (pp. 179–210). New York: Wiley.

Kolb, B., & Fantie, B. (1989). Development of the child's brain and behavior. In C. R. Reynolds and E. Fletcher-Janzen (Eds.), *Handbook of clinical child neuropsychology* (pp. 17–40). New York: Plenum.

Kurke, M. I. (1980). Forensic psychology: A threat and a response. *Professional Psychology: Research and Practice, 11,* 72–77.

Luria, A. R. (1963). *Restoration of function after brain injury.* New York: Macmillan.

Luria, A. R. (1966). *Higher cortical functioning in man.* New York: Basic Books.

Luria, A. R. (1973). *The working brain.* New York: Basic Books.

Luria, A. R. (1980). *Higher cortical functions.* New York: Basic Books.

Mattis, S., French, J. H., & Rapin, T. (1975). Dyslexia in children and adults: Three independent neuropsychological syndromes. *Developmental Medicine and Child Neurology, 17,* 150–163.

Meier, M. J. (1974). Some challenges for clinical neuropsychology. In R. M. Reitan & L. A. Davison (Eds.), *Clinical neuropsychology: Current status and application* (pp. 289–324). New York: John Wiley.

Meier, M. J., & French, L. A. (1965). Some personality correlates of unilateral and bilateral EEG abnormalities in psychomotor epileptics. *Journal of Clinical Psychology, 21,* 3–9.

Milner, B. (1958). Psychological deficits produced by temporal lobe excision. *Association for Research in Nervous and Mental Diseases, 36,* 244–257.

Milner, B. (1971). Interhemispheric differences and psychological processes. *British Medical Journal, 27,* 272–277.

Mishkin, M. (1978). Memory in monkeys severely impaired by combined but not separate removal of amygdala and hippocampus. *Nature, 273,* 297–298.

Munsterberg, H. (1908). *On the witness stand.* New York: Doubleday.

Nauta, W. J. H., & Feintag, M. (1986). *Fundamental neuroanatomy.* New York: W. H. Freeman.

Nebes, R. W. (1974). Hemispheric specialization in commissurotomized man. *Psychological Bulletin, 81,* 1–14.

Porac, C., & Coren, S. (1981). *Lateral performances and human behavior.* New York: Springer-Verlag.

Reed, H. B. C., Reitan, R. M., & Klove, H. (1965). The influence of cerebral lesions on the psychological test performance of older children. *Journal of Consulting Psychology, 29,* 247–251.

Reitan, R. M. (1974). Psychological effects of cerebral lesions in children of early school age. In R. M. Reitan & L. A. Davison (Eds.), *Clinical neuropsychology: Current status and applications* (pp. 53–90). New York: John Wiley.

Reitan, R. M., & Davison, L. A. (Eds.). (1974). *Clinical neuropsychology: Current status and applications.* New York: John Wiley.

Reitan, R. M., & Wolfson, D. (1992). *Neuropsychological evaluation of older children.* Tucson, AZ: Neuropsychology Press.

Reynolds, C. R. (1981). The Neuropsychological basis of intelligence. In G. W. Hynd & J. E. Obrzut (Eds.), *Neuropsychological assessment and the school aged child* (pp. 87–124). New York: Grune & Stratton.

Rourke, B. P., Fisk, J. L., & Strang, J. D. (1986). *Neuropsychological assessment of children: A treatment-oriented approach.* New York: Guilford Press.

Rosenzweig, M. R. (1980). Animal models for effects of brain lesions and for rehabilitation. In D. C. Stein, J. J. Rosen, & N. Butters (Eds.), *Plasticity and recovery of function in the central nervous system* (pp. 122–139). New York: Academic Press.

Russell, E. W., & Espir, M. L. E. (1961). *Traumatic aphasia.* London: Oxford University Press.

Saxby, L., & Bryden, M. P. (1984). Left-ear superiority in children processing auditory emotional material. *Developmental Psychology, 20,* 72–80.

Saxby, L., & Bryden, M. P. (1985). Left visual field advantage in children processing visual emotional stimuli. *Developmental Psychology, 20,* 253–261.

Scotti, G., & Spinner, H. (1970). Color imperception in unilateral hemispheric patients. *Journal of Neurology, Neurosurgery and Psychiatry, 33,* 22–41.

Sperry, R. W. (1961). Cerebral organization and behavior. *Science, 133,* 1949.

Spreen, O., Risser, A. T., & Edgell, D. (1995). *Developmental neuropsychology.* New York: Oxford University Press.

Struss, D. T., & Benson, D. F. (1984). Neuropsychological studies of the frontal lobes. *Psychological Bulletin, 95*(1), 23–38.

Tapp, J. L. (1978). Psychology and the law: An overture. *Annual Review of Psychology, 27,* 359–404.

Teuber, H. L. (1963). Space perception and its disturbances after brain injury in man. *Neuropsychologia, 1,* 47–53.

Teuber, H. L., & Rudel, R. G. (1962). Behavior after brain lesions in children and adults. *Developmental medicine and child neurology, 4,* 3–20.

Watson, J. B. (1913). Psychology as the behaviorist views it. *Psychology Review, 20,* 159–177.

Chapter 2

The Neuropsychological Basis of Intelligence Revised: Some False Starts and a Clinical Model

Cecil R. Reynolds and Christine L. French

Intelligence is a neuropsychological phenomenon. By that, we mean that it is steeped in brain function, is closely associated with our biology, but is measured through behavior, as it should be. Intelligence must be manifested through behavior to be seen, to be useful, and to be measured and studied. Behavioral manifestations of intelligence may be overt or covert, although, to assess the latter, we must question, observe, and make inferences from the former. This chapter provides a view of intelligence from a functional, clinical perspective, which we believe will be of utility in clinical practice, but is less of a heuristic for current research. Rather, our intent is to relate a model of the working brain that will aid clinicians in understanding the neuropsychological dynamics of a brain that has been compromised.

We begin by reviewing several false starts that were amazingly, and unduly, influential in educational and related settings. Ultimately, we adopt a current view of Luria's theory of the working brain, integrated with research on lateral cerebral specialization, as a strong, useful paradigm for clinicians.

CEREBRAL DOMINANCE

Cerebral dominance, as a mechanism that will lead to an understanding of the neuropsychological basis and processes underlying human mental

Note: This chapter is based in part on a prior work by the first author: Reynolds, C. R. (1981). The neuropsychological basis of intelligence. In G. Hynd & J. Obrzut (Eds.), *Neuropsychological assessment and the school-aged child*. New York: Grune & Stratton.

abilities, has dominated the thoughts and research of neuropsychologists throughout the history of the field. Cerebral dominance traditionally refers to the hemisphere responsible for controlling language and most language-mediated functions; for the vast majority of individuals, this is the left hemisphere. Indeed, for sometime, the right hemisphere was believed to house few if any important cognitive functions. Cerebral dominance also has been used, in some instances, to refer to the establishment of lateral preference, in relation to handedness, footedness, eyedness, and even earedness. Research over the past three decades has presented serious challenges to this traditional approach to the neuropsychology of intelligence. Past concepts of the relationship between lateral preference and other motoric and sensory indices of cerebral dominance have been revolutionized as more contemporary concepts are introduced.

Lateral Preference and Cerebral Dominance

Lateral preference is distinct from cerebral dominance, in that it is voluntary and involves the peripheral nervous system; individuals have no input regarding their cerebral dominance and central nervous system functioning (Obrzut & Obrzut, 1982). Lateral preference is an important area of interest, given that animals do not demonstrate a preference for a particular hand, foot, eye, or ear (Beaumont, 1997). Based on the human phenomenon of lateral preference, advances in performance can occur more quickly and gain sophistication with relative ease. However, the relationship between handedness or other lateral preference and cerebral dominance can never be directly espied, but only inferred from performance on particular measures or as reported by the individual (Beaumont, 1997).

Handedness and its relationship to cerebral dominance and language functions has been a concern of researchers and theoreticians for some time. Handedness is indeed the most ubiquitously investigated area of lateral preference, with footedness, eyedness, and, more recently, earedness, quickly gaining in popularity. In fact, some researchers are attempting to use facedness as a measure of lateral preference (Borod, Caron, & Koff, 1981) (lateral preference in this instance, and as used throughout this chapter, refers to consistency of hand, eye, foot, and ear dominance). Neurologists, psychologists, and others interested in the field of neuropsychology, with particular emphasis on using lateral preference to predict cerebral dominance, are finding conflicting and often insignificant results based on their investigations (e.g., Beaumont, 1997; Brown & Taylor, 1988; Coren, 1993; Coren & Porac, 1982; DiNuovo & Buono, 1997; Eisenmann, 1993; Grouios, Sakadami, Poderi, & Alevriadou, 1999; Rider, Imwold, & Griffin, 1985; Strauss, 1986). Cerebral dominance, as first described informally by Dax in 1836 (Harris, 1980; Joynt & Benton, 1964; Penfield & Roberts, 1959), and later in formal presentations by Broca (1861, 1863; Harris, 1980), meant the hemisphere of the brain responsible for language functions. Handedness itself has been studied extensively since at least the sixteenth century, and theories of how handedness develops abound. With this in mind, there is a presupposition that supports the notion of lateral preference predicting cerebral dominance. As might be inferred, supporters of this theory assume that cerebral dominance can be determined by observing or measuring motoric and sensory preferences.

In an early review, Harris (1980) discussed five categories of theories of handedness that have been proffered since the 1400s, a number of which stretch the imagination rather vigorously. The categories of theories reviewed by Harris included structural asymmetry (visceral imbalance, blood flow, weight and density of the cerebral hemispheres, arm length, etc.), positional asymmetry (orientation of infant at time of birth or while in the womb), heredity, cultural-conditioning theories (arm used to carry infants, carrying of shield in left hand to protect heart, etc.), and the ambidextral culture (a movement begun in the late 1800s, which proposed humans were "either-handed" and, which, as such movements seem to do, actually started an educational craze toward training pupils to be ambidextrous). Although it now appears that handedness is a preordained, genetic function for most individuals (Saudino & McManus, 1998), deviations from the predetermined state can occur under a variety of conditions (see Hoosain, 1990; Porac, Rees, & Buller, 1990). The issue of precisely how and why handedness develops as it does, and its subsequent effects on the study of brain–behavior relationships, is far from being settled (Annett, 1972; Boklage, 1978; Fuller, 1978; Grouios et al., 1999; Hardyck & Petrinovich, 1977; Harris, 1990; Herron, 1980; Morgan & Corballis, 1978; Robison, Block, Boudreaux, & Flora, 1999; Schwartz, 1990; Yeo, Gangestad, & Daniel, 1993).

A number of motor-based programs intended to affect brain–behavior relationships have been developed over the years. Most of these programs assume that the failure to establish hand (and thus cerebral) dominance or consistent lateral preference is an underlying cause of learning or intellectual deficits. The first such program we have located apparently was a physical exercise therapy program by Buzzard (1882) for the treatment of aphasia, on the theory that the various exercises employed would cause the right hemisphere to develop a "convolution for speech." Probably the most influential programs of this nature in American education have been those of Orton and of Doman and Delacato. Although the Doman and Delacato (D-D) methods have been principally designed from the maxim "Ontogeny recapitulates phylogeny," the notion of cerebral dominance remains central to their theory of brain function and intelligence. Other theories of brain–behavior relationships have affected professional practices in a number of fields (see Harris, 1980; Zarske, 1982).

Samuel T. Orton's Theory

Orton's theory and writings (1925, 1931, 1937) have had marked effect on remedial practices in education, many of which remain today. However, few employing Orton-based techniques can even begin to explain his theory.

Orton's theory of cerebral dominance and reading disability was novel for his time (Obrzut & Obrzut, 1982). He based his theory of cerebral dominance and learning (particularly reading) on the structural symmetry of the brain (although it is now widely known that the human brain does not display perfect morphological or structural symmetry, and it shows sexual dimorphism as well), and he assumed that any event recorded in one hemisphere was recorded in its mirror image in the opposite hemisphere. The dominant, or major, hemisphere was thought to record perceptual events in their correct spatial orientation. Figure 2.1 provides a schematic representation of the recordings of visual-perceptive events, as dictated by Orton's theory. The reversals so often exhibited by dyslexic children were therefore believed to result from competition with the mirror images available in the nondominant, or minor, hemisphere. With incomplete, unestablished, or mixed dominance (as determined by lateral preference), the frequency of reversals occurring would be substantially greater, because of the intrusion of the minor hemisphere into the process, than when a single hemisphere exhibits clear, dominant control over cognitive functions. Orton's (1931) assertions essentially represent a storage or

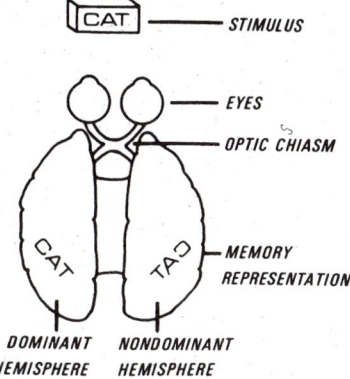

STIMULUS

EYES

OPTIC CHIASM

MEMORY
REPRESENTATION

DOMINANT   NONDOMINANT
HEMISPHERE HEMISPHERE

FIGURE 2.1   Schematic representation of Orton's theory of perception and storge of visual material. (From *The Psychology of Left and Right* by M. C. Corballis and I. L. Beale. Hillsdale, NJ: Lawrence Erlbaum Associates, 1976. Copyright 1976 by Lawrence Erlbaum Associates. With permission).

retrieval problem and not a problem of initial perception, as many believe.

Evidence proliferated, throughout the last century, supporting the view that there is no clear relationship between handedness or other lateral preferences (footedness, eyedness, and earedness) and cerebral dominance (Belmont & Birch, 1963; Benton, 1955, 1959; Brysbaert, 1994; Coren & Porac, 1982; DiNuovo & Buono, 1997; Eisenman, 1993; Hardyck & Petrinovich, 1977; Hardyck, Petrinovich, & Goldman, 1976; Levy & Nagylaki, 1972; Milner, Branch, & Rasmussen, 1964; Naylor, 1980; Penfield & Roberts, 1959; Polemikos & Papaeliou, 2000; Reynolds, Hartlage, & Haak, 1980). The theoretical basis of Orton's position has also been seriously questioned by Corballis and Beale (1976). As part of their convincing argument, Corballis and Beale put forth that Orton is wrong in his basic assumptions:

> It simply does not follow that the two halves of a symmetrical brain would respond to any given stimulus pattern in mirror-opposite ways. This would only happen in general if the pattern were itself symmetrical with respect to the brain's plane of symmetry. . . . It is not at all clear how perceptual input to the nondominant hemisphere could be veridical, yet leave an engram that is reversed. Neither is it clear why the nondominant hemisphere should be the one to suffer this bizarre malfunction. (Corballis & Beale, 1976, pp. 60–61)

Some may assume that, since the majority of individuals are right-handed, those same individuals would therefore demonstrate left hemisphere dominance, which coincides with the contralateral hand preference (Dean & Reynolds, 1997). Notably, reviews of the literature have indicated that, in almost all people, the left hemisphere is the dominant hemisphere for symbolic language and speech, regardless of the handedness of the subject (Bauer & Wepman, 1955; Coren & Porac, 1982; Strauss, 1986; White, 1969). Some exceptions have been noted, however (Lewis & Harris, 1990; McKeever, 1990). Witelson (1980) and others (Coren & Porac, 1982; Hartlage & Gage, 1997) conclude that left-handedness may be associated with a lesser degree of cerebral specialization for speech and language. Dysphasia associated with right-hemisphere lesions in both right- and left-handers has also been reported (e.g., Newcombe & Ratcliff, 1973). Geffen (1978) reports that as many as 6% of normal right-handers have other than left-hemisphere specialization for speech. It is apparent that handedness is not always the best indicator of hemispheric specialization.

It is tempting to hypothesize that the lesser degree of lateralization of cognitive processes found with left-handers is responsible for the Orton effect. However, this is contradicted by evidence related to gender differences in the degree of lateral cerebral specialization of cognitive functioning. With regard to lateralization of verbal functions to the left hemisphere and spatial-oriented functions to the right hemisphere, males show consistently greater lateralization of function than females. Females tend to have a less rigid scheme of specialization than do males. If less lateralization of cognitive function is associated with left-handedness and the lack of established dominance, and these two conditions are subsequently related to intellectual or cognitive dysfunctions, why do males (the more highly lateralized sex) outnumber females four to one in classes for learning-disabled children?

Other problems with using handedness or primarily motoric indices as measures of cerebral dominance stem from disagreements about how these indices should be measured and from research results which, not surprisingly, can differ dramatically, depending on how handedness is measured. Some researchers approach handedness from a dichotomous perspective: Individuals are considered right-handed or nonright-handed. Other researchers define right, left, and either, or no preference, as categories for the study of handedness. More recently, handedness (and hence lateral preference) has come to be considered a continuous variable (Annett, 1972). Subsequently, a variety of efforts have been made to measure lateral preference as a continuous variable. These measures include the use of manual tapping speed instruments (e.g., Peters & Durding, 1978), eye-dominance wands (e.g., Robison et al., 1999), hole-in-the-hand techniques (e.g., Robison et al., 1999), other demonstration techniques (e.g., Brown & Taylor, 1988; Osburn & Klingsporn, 1998), and self-report inventories, such as the Lateral Preference Inventory or other questionnaires, questioning hand, eye, and foot preference for a series of activities (e.g., Coren, 1993; Dean & Kulhavy, 1977; Dean & Reynolds, 1997; Strauss, 1986). Even percentage of time each hand is used for a task has been used as a method for determining lateral preference (Hartlage & Gage, 1997). It appears that measures assessing an individual's hand or eye preference by having them perform tasks (e.g., throwing a ball or looking through a peephole) would result in a more valid and reliable assessment of lateral preference. Presumably, measures of lateral preference based on self-report leave room for error and inaccurate results (see Eisenman, 1993). Truly, how many individuals know which eye they would use to look through the sight of a rifle or which ear they would use to eavesdrop through a closed door?

Measurement of handedness as a continuous variable has not resolved the relationship between dominance and intellectual integrity. Dean (1979), using a self-report measure of lateral preference, recently found that children with higher *Wechsler Intelligence Scale for Children—Revised* (WISC-R) verbal IQs (VIQ) than performance IQs (PIQ) were significantly more bilateral than children with VIQ equal to PIQ and VIQ less than PIQ. The latter children tended to be more right-dominant. Orton's theory states that bilaterality underlies cognitive dysfunction in reading disabilities. However, the right-dominant children in Dean's study display the pattern of VIQ–PIQ discrepancies (PIQ greater than VIQ) that are most frequently found with samples of learning-disabled children (Anderson, Kaufman, & Kaufman, 1976; Kaufman, 1979a; Sattler, 1981; Smith, Coleman, Dokecki, & Davis, 1977; Zingale & Smith, 1978); the bilateral children show the intellectual pattern least often associated with reading deficits.

Reynolds, Hartlage, and Haak (1980) attempted to replicate and extend Dean's (1979) findings, to determine the relationship between lateral preference and IQ–achievement discrepancies. Instead of relying on self-report studies, however, Reynolds et al. determined lateral preference (hand, eye, and foot) by summing each child's score on 26 neuropsychological tests that contrasted the two sides of the body. Correlations were then determined between each child's lateral preference score, VIQ–PIQ difference (with and without the sign retained), and the difference between achievement test scores in reading, spelling, and arithmetic and each of the three WISC-R IQs. Of the 12 correlations generated by this method, none revealed any significant relationship between lateral preference and the variables described above. Neither was lateral preference significantly related to any of the intellectual or achievement variables when taken in isolation. Although the two studies have contradictory results, both are inconsistent with the Orton hypothesis and other traditional theories of dominance and intellectual function.

Eyedness is an even more complex phenomenon than handedness. Rather than each eye being under the principal control of a single cerebral hemisphere, each hemisphere processes visual information from the contralateral visual hemifield of each eye. Because of the complexity of the eyedness phenomenon, it is not surprising to note the disappointing results of numerous studies that have attempted to relate consistency of eye–hand preference in normal controls (Brown & Taylor, 1988; Metalis & Niemiec, 1984; Polemikos & Papaeliou, 2000; Strauss, 1986), school-age children (e.g., Balow, 1963; Balow & Balow, 1964; Coleman & Deutsch, 1964; Hillerich, 1964), and individuals with mental retardation (Robison et al., 1999). These results could have been anticipated, with the knowledge that 40% of the normally functioning 5 to $8^1/2$-year-old population show mixed eye–hand dominance (A. S. Kaufman, personal communication, August, 1978), as determined during standardization of the McCarthy Scales of Children's Abilities.

Although footedness is often related to handedness, earedness is not as simple to measure or equate with other indices of lateral preference. During the past two decades, earedness, like eyedness, has become another sensory index by which investigators are attempting to measure lateral preference and, consequently, cerebral dominance. Unfortunately, the facility with which earedness is measured is troublesome, because it is not something that people are as familiar with, compared to their general knowledge of what hand they prefer. Reiß and Reiß (2000) discuss the various ways in which earedness is measured. Some investigators have relied, not on ear preference, but on relative proficiency of the ears to perform their designed tasks. Proficiency of the right ear does not necessarily mean that the right ear is the preferred ear, therefore contaminating the data and complicating interpretation. Furthermore, if ear preference is measured, it is often measured by means of a self-report inventory (see Coren, 1993; Mandal, Pandey,

Singh, & Asthana, 1992; Polemikos & Papaeliou, 2000; Saudino & McManus, 1998; Strauss, 1986), therefore introducing additional elements of error.

Modifications of Orton's theory have been offered by many researchers, since the 1930s. One modification contends that mixed cerebral dominance creates an antagonistic state of affairs, resulting in the right hemisphere fighting for control of language functions, to the neglect of its normal involvement in perceptual and spatial functions. The antagonism between the two hemispheres, and the subsequent loss of efficiency in perceptual and spatial functions, is believed to play a major role in the development of intellectual dysfunctions during childhood. Noble (1968) has offered another, attractive alternative to Orton's proposal, yet he still relies on mirror-image perceptual transfers between hemispheres. Orton's theory and its derivatives continue to rely on the traditional notion of cerebral dominance. It now seems unlikely that measurements based on hands, eyes, feet, and possibly even ears, can bear more than a peripheral relationship to a dynamic understanding of the cognitive aspects of hemispheric functioning. Based on the theory's presupposition, a major fault of eyedness, handedness, and other indices of cerebral dominance concerns attempts to relate dominance of the motor cortex, for physical activities, to cortical dominance for intellectual functioning and preference for a single mode of cognitive processing. Traditional concepts of dominance must give way to more contemporary notions of hemisphericity and the view of the brain as a dynamic organ, in order to better understand the intellectual workings of the brain (Reynolds, 1978, 1980, 1981).

Doman's and Delacato's Theory

The therapeutic system for children with learning disabilities or problems with motor skills (i.e., children with cerebral palsy), known as the Doman and Delacato (D-D) method, has been described principally in the writings of Delacato (1959, 1963, 1966). The controversial D-D theory relies on vertical and horizontal development and organization of function within the human brain. The roots of Delacato's theoretical work can be traced directly to Orton's (1928) early writings on dominance and structural symmetry. The neuropsychological theory of Doman and Delacato is based on the biogenetic principle, "Ontogeny recapitulates phylogeny" and contends that, if one does not follow this sequential continuum of neurological development, problems of mobility and/or communication will develop. Thus, children with learning disabilities or cerebral palsy are viewed as having inadequate neurological organization, which the D-D method contends to ameliorate. The therapeutic D-D methods are designed to overcome early deficiencies in development, so that the optimal level and pattern of neurological organization may be achieved. In short, the goal of the D-D method is to achieve cerebral dominance, which can only be accomplished by successfully completing all prior levels of development.

Doman and Delacato maintain that there are six major functional attainments of humans: motor skills, speech, writing, reading, understanding, and stereognosis. The attainment of these skills is dependent upon the individual's uninterrupted and successful neuroanatomical progress toward neurological organization. According to Zarske (1982), the D-D method is founded upon an upward developmental trend through primary centers of the central nervous system (i.e., the spinal cord and cerebellum), continuing sequentially through the midbrain and forebrain. Neurological organization is complete when developmental progression extends horizontally through the neocortex.

Each higher level of functioning is dependent on successful progression through the earlier levels. It is proffered by the D-D theory that, if the highest level of functioning (cerebral dominance) is incomplete or unfunctioning, then a lower level of neurological organization dominates the intellectual behavior. The highest level of neurological organization, complete lateral cerebral dominance, is, according to Delacato (1959), what gives humans their great capacity for communication and completely sets them apart from lower animals. Unfortunately for the D-D theory of brain function and intelligence, there is evidence for cerebral dominance in other primates (Dewson, 1977; Gazzaniga, 1971; Johnson & Gazzaniga, 1971a, 1971b; LeMay, 1976; Warren & Nonneman, 1976). In addition, the highest level of neurological organization is deemed to exist only when an individual has achieved consistency of hand, eye, and foot preference. Accordingly, the D-D method utilizes observations of lateral preference (i.e., handedness, footedness, and eyedness) to determine an individual's level of cerebral dominance, and, therefore, complete neurological organization (Zarske, 1982). As noted earlier, mixed eye–hand dominance is a common finding in children at least through age $8^1/2$ years (and likely beyond). Orton and Delacato would have perhaps fared better using a closer review of available literature. Woo and Pearson (1927), after an exhaustive study of 7,000 men, concluded that there was "no evidence whatsoever of even a correlation between ocular and manual lateralities" (p. 181). It is not unreasonable to suspect that the lack of completely consistent hand, eye, and foot preference is the rule rather than the exception, further supported by the earlier discussion of the literature regarding lateral preference.

As mentioned earlier, neurological development is believed to progress upward from the spinal cord through the medulla, the pons, the midbrain (the evolutionarily older portions of the cortex), to the neocortex, resulting in lateral hemispheric dominance. There are any number of cogent theoretical arguments against a theory of neurological organization such as that proposed by D-D (e.g., Bever, 1975; Kinsbourne, 1975), but perhaps the more grave damage to the D-D theory is the lack of positive results from studies of the remedial methods D-D derived from their theoretical formulations.

Although proponents of the D-D method still exist and advocate the brain–behavior relationship tauted by Doman and Delacato, research support for the effectiveness of the D-D methods has been sparse and fraught with methodological difficulties. Glass and Robbins (1967) reviewed 15 studies cited by Delacato as scientific appraisals of his theory of neurological organization. Five of the studies reviewed failed to control for regression effects, and Glass and Robins concluded that it was not possible to determine whether gains reported in these studies were caused by experimental effects or simple regression effects. In 14 of the 15 studies, no random assignment to groups or conditions was made, although no practical reasons for not doing so existed. Further examinations of Doman and Delacato's research support indicated that, in all but one study, control and experimental groups met at different times of day, in different classrooms, and with different teachers. Such confounding severely restricts any interpretations of mean group differences. Glass and Robbins (1967) subsequently offered plausible alternative interpretations of the data presented in the 15 studies, many of which lend themselves to implications directly contrary to the D-D theory. Other studies (e.g., Cornish, 1970; O'Donnell & Eisenson, 1969; Robbins, 1966) continue to find no support for the D-D methods.

The inherent goal of the D-D therapeutic methods is to stimulate and treat the ineffectual areas of the brain (Zarske, 1982). Treatment techniques are designed to pinpoint the level of neurological development and concentrate the remediation toward that area of the brain. Thus, if a child is determined to have deficiencies at a basic level (i.e., spinal cord), treatment would consist of teaching primitive movements. If a child is unable to perform these exercises on their own, the patterning exercises are imposed on the child, some even during sleep. In this procedure, the child's limbs and head are moved by adults while the child lies limp, not actively participating in the movement. A series of studies with both animals and humans (Held, 1965; Held & Bossom, 1961; Held & Freedman, 1963; Held & Hein, 1963) has demonstrated the ineffectual nature of passive participation. As an example, in one particular study (Held, 1965), a group of people were fitted with reversible goggles. Half of the group was then allowed to walk around an enclosure with an homogeneous background. The other half of the group was pushed around the same enclosure on a specially designed cart. Those actively participating in moving about the enclosure adapted to the reversible goggles; the passive participation group showed no adaptation. At least two widely held cognitive theories are also in sharp disagreement with D-D theory (Hunt, 1961).

The practice of passive participation is absent from modern techniques of cognitive rehabilitation. The recent work of Prigatano (2000) enumerates 13 principles of neuropsychological rehabilitation, none of which include anything remotely related to passive participation of the affected individual. In fact, Prigatano and many others (e.g., Ben-Yishay, 2000; Braga & Campos da Paz, 2000; Christensen, 2000; Daniels-Zide & Ben-Yishay, 2000; Trexler, 2000) advocate a comprehensive and dynamic treatment program that consists of cognitive, psychological, and neuropsychological therapeutic interventions.

Traditional dominance-based theories of neurological organization and intelligence find little empirical support. The relationship of dominance to motor functions can only be peripherally related to a preference for intellectual or cognitive processing of information, the forte of intelligent behavior. To cast further doubt upon the functional importance of general dominance by the major hemisphere, as indicated by motor indices of dominance, researchers have reported that hemispheric dominance for many cognitive tasks is quite malleable and responds to training and to the principles of reinforcement (e.g., Bever, 1975; Bever & Chiarello, 1974; Bogen, 1969; Johnson & Gazzaniga, 1971a, 1971b).

Although traditional concepts of dominance will remain an interesting area of theoretical research, reconceptualization of dominance as related to intellectual functioning is clearly necessary. Several influential theorists have developed neuropsychological models of intellectual functioning, with considerably less reliance on traditional notions of cerebral dominance. Luria's theory, in particular, appears to hold great promise for understanding the neuropsychological basis of intelligence and for developing remedial or compensatory techniques for use with cognitively dysfunctional individuals.

HALSTEAD'S THEORY OF BIOLOGICAL INTELLIGENCE

The early work of Halstead and associates, principally described in Halstead (1947) and Shure and Halstead (1959), has greatly affected the development of many of the techniques and methods of clinical neuropsychology. Although the Luria–Nebraska Neuropsychological Test Battery has made tremendous gains since its inception, the Halstead–Reitan Neuropsychological Test Battery (HRNTB) continues to dominate neuropsychological assessment.

Halstead's major thesis regarding the relationship between the brain and intelligence was published in 1947. That volume reported the research of Halstead and his colleagues, which began in 1935 at the Otho S. S. Sprague Memorial Institute and, the Division of Psychiatry of the Department of Medicine at the University of Chicago. Halstead focuses principally on the study of the cortex in relation to intelligence and, more specifically, on the role of the frontal lobes (the frontal lobes also play a major role in Luria's conceptualization of intelligence).

Halstead differentiated between biological intelligence and psychometric intelligence. He considered the latter to be what is measured by intelligence tests, specifically, the measurement of verbal abilities, including vocabulary skills, and the prediction of academic achievement (Broshek & Barth, 2000; Reitan, 1994). Halstead considered the former to be the true, innate ability of the individual. Halstead did not want to weigh down theorists or psychometricians of his time with trying to decipher the dichotomy between the two types of intelligence. In fact, Halstead indicated that the difference between psychometric and biological intelligence could be attributed more to methodology than to true differences between the two measures of intelligence (Pallier, Roberts, & Stankov, 2000). According to Reitan (1994), Halstead considered biological intelligence best viewed as "the adaptive abilities represented by a health brain and nervous system" (p. 55). Halstead did not believe that measures of psychometric intelligence had the capability to denote the true state of the nervous system (Reed, 1985). In fact, Reitan (1994) noted incidences of patients with tremendous loss of brain mass continuing to score relatively high on measures of psychometric intelligence. However, an examination of the biological intelligence of these individuals would result in a greater understanding of their true capabilities. In short, Halstead conjectured that his theory of biological intelligence represented "the normal outcome of the functioning of a healthy nervous system" (p. 56).

Halstead unquestionably realized that psychometric and biological intelligence were not independent of one another. In recognition of this, Halstead, and subsequently Reitan, routinely included a standardized test of intelligence, such as the Henmon–Nelson Tests of Mental Ability or one of the Wechsler series of intelligence scales, in their neuropsychological test battery. Nevertheless, Halstead's research focused on determining the nature and underlying factors of biological intelligence.

From an original battery of 27 behavioral indicators (i.e., psychological tests), Halstead selected 13 measures for his study of biological intelligence. These 13 tests were selected because they yielded objective scores, and because they "seemed likely to reflect some component of biological intelligence" (Halstead, 1947, p. 39). Some of the tests dropped from the larger battery were essentially personality or affective measures (e.g., a modified version of the Rorschach); were one-item, dichotomously scored tests (Halstead Closure Test); or were purely sensory measures (e.g., Halstead–Brill Audiometer).

Based on independent factor analyses of the correlation matrix for this set of tests, determined from the responses of a sample of what Halstead considered normal individuals (50 adults fully recovered from a concussive-type head injury), Halstead extracted four basic factors of biological intelligence, which he labeled *C*, *A*, *P*, and *D*. Halstead hoped that these factors would help others begin to fathom the intricacy of brain–behavior relationships (Reed, 1985). Factor analyses of the data were conducted separately by Karl Holzinger and L. L. Thurstone (Halstead, 1947). Each analysis produced essentially the same results. Halstead defined these four factors as follows.

C, the Integrative Field Factor

Halstead considered this factor to represent an individual's experiences (Reitan, 1994). Central to this factor is the ability to adapt to new situations and to integrate new information and stimuli that were not a part of one's previous experiences, in order to form new symbols and frameworks or orientation, when necessary. The *C* factor creates order from the chaos of new stimuli from the external world constantly bombarding one and gives these stimuli an internal referent. The *C* factor was characterized, in Halstead's initial factor analysis, by large loadings by the Halstead Category Test, the Henmon–Nelson Tests of Mental Ability, the Speech-Sounds Perception Test, the Halstead Finger Oscillation Test, and the Halstead Time-Sense Test.

A, the Abstraction Factor

The *A* factor represents Halstead's conceptualization of a basic factor of intelligence and the aptitude for abstraction. Abstraction is the ability to draw meaning away from a series of events or to hold ideas away from their concrete referents; it is considered difficult. Abstraction includes the ability to grasp essential similarities in the face of apparent differences, and vice versa, without the use or reliance upon past experience. It also includes the ability to abstract, or draw away, a principle or set of rules governing a series of seemingly unconnected stimuli. The *A* factor was characterized, in Halstead's initial factor analysis, by large loadings from the Carlo Hollow-Square Performance Test for Intelligence, the Halstead Category Test, the Halstead Tactual Performance Test (memory component), and Halstead Tactual Performance Test (localization component).

P, the Power Factor

Halstead believed *P* to represent the undistorted power factor of the functioning brain and related it analogously to the reserve power available to an amplifier not already functioning at peak wattage. Halstead's description of the *P* factor relies heavily on flicker-fusion research and indicates that the brain with more available power (*P*) has a higher critical fusion frequency. *P*, to Halstead, was certainly related to the electrical facilitation of cognition (mentation) in the brain and was controlled principally through the frontal lobes. Halstead also proposed some relationships between affect and its effects on intelligence and the *P* factor. According to Reitan (1994), *P* was critical in an individual's expression of their biological intelligence. The *P* factor was character-ized, in Halstead's factor analytic study, by large loadings by the Halstead Flicker-Fusion Test, the Halstead Tactual Performance Test (recall com-ponent), the Halstead Dynamic Visual Field Test (central form), and the Halstead Dynamic Visual Field Test (central color).

D, the Directional Factor

The *D* factor was, in Halstead's interpretation, the most difficult of his biological factors of intelligence to legitimize statistically through factor analysis. Nevertheless, Halstead seemed satisfied with its existence and determined that *D* was the "medium of exteriorization of intelligence, either from within or from without the individual" (Halstead, 1947, p. 84). *D*, then, is a modality factor. Intelligence must be expressed, be it through reading, writing, listening, speaking, composing, or painting, and Halstead believed that *D* represented the modality of expression of intelligence and was also, in one sense, an attentional factor. For, to utilize a modality, one must be able to focus or direct the energy and power of thought toward that modality (some theorists contend that hemispheric specialization for methods of cognitive processing are the result of an attentional bias between the two hemispheres). Results of the factor analysis showed *D* to be characterized by large loadings by the Halstead Tactual Performance Test (speed component) and the Halstead Dynamic Visual Field Test (peripheral component). A poten-tially important secondary loading was apparent by the Halstead Tactual Performance Test (incidental localization component). Halstead be-lieved the various agnosias and apraxias to be strongly related to the *D* factor. However, in the normally functioning human brain, he believed that *D* faded into the background of the other three factors (*C*, *A*, and *P*), except when a new medium of expression was encountered.

As should be clear by now, *C*, *A*, and *P* were considered the process factors of intelligence and *D* the factor through which externalization of these processes occurred. In his subsequent research with brain-injured individuals, Halstead observed these various factors in operation and believed that he had thereby demonstrated the biological validity of these basic factors of intelligence. Unfortunately, no replications of Thurstone and Holzinger's factor analysis have been completed (Bro-shek & Barth, 2000; Reitan, 1994), therefore limiting the validity for the concept of biological intelligence. Once having delineated these factors, Halstead and his associates turned their attention to the localization of intelligence in the brain and to the role of these four factors in various types of psychopathology. It is from this latter work that much current clinical neuropsychology has grown.

The next step in Halstead's validation of his factors of biological intelligence was the development of the now well-known Halstead Impairment Index. Halstead reasoned that, if *C, A, P,* and *D* were indeed biological factors of intelligence, then individuals with known neuropathology should suffer impairment in their ability to perform tasks representing these factors. In developing the Impairment Index, Halstead was also cognizant of its potential pragmatic applications. He found that most of the tests involved in measuring *C, A, P,* and *D* differentiated, at some level, between individuals with a definite history of head injury and a control group with no history of head injury. He then collapsed the 10 best discriminating tests into a battery forming the Impairment Index. Although the various tests were not equivalent in their discriminability, each test was given an equal weighting of .10. An individual scoring within the impaired range on a task was thus assigned a score of .10; scoring in the normal (nonimpaired) range earned a score of 0. Thus, an Impairment Index of 0 represents almost certain neurological integrity. Halstead then set out to investigate the neuroanatomical localization of biological intelligence as indicated by the Impairment Index.

Based on a series of findings with neurosurgical patients for whom the exact site of brain lesion was known, Halstead concluded that the factors of biological intelligence were principally controlled through the frontal lobes. Only a slight difference occurred between left and right frontal lesions; left-sided lesions caused only slightly greater impairment than did right-sided lesions. Frontal lesions (typically in the form of lobotomy) resulted in an impairment index six times that of normal controls and three times that of nonfrontal lesions. The least amount of impairment occurred with occipital lesions, followed by parietal and temporal lesions, although parietal and temporal lesions were very similar in the degree of impairment produced. Although partial replication of these results was proved by Shure and Halstead (1959), the strong relationship between the frontal lobes and Halstead's Impairment Index has not been validated in subsequent research (Reitan, 1975, 1994). However, Halstead retained his interest in the localization of the factors of biological intelligence.

Halstead (1947) has summarized his theory, as follows:

1. Biological intelligence is a basic function of the brain and is essential for many forms of adaptive behavior of the human

organism. While it is represented throughout the cerebral cortex, its representation is not equal throughout. It is distributed in a gradient, with its maximal representation occurring in the cortex of the frontal lobes.

2. The nuclear structure of biological intelligence comprises four basic factors, which, in a unified fashion, enter into all cognitive activities. While these factors make possible the highest reaches of human intellect, their dysfunction, as produced by brain damage, may yield progressively maladaptive forms of behavior, or "biological neurosis."

3. The frontal lobes, long regarded as silent areas, are the portion of the brain most essential to biological intelligence. They are the organs of civilization—the basis of man's despair and of his hope for the future. (p. 259)

Shortly following the publication of Halstead's 1947 monograph, Reitan and others recognized the need for a more diverse array of neuropsychological tests, in order to make more exact and stringent diagnoses of neuropathology. Although Halstead apparently engaged in diagnosing various neurological disorders on the basis of performance on his battery of tests (Reitan, 1975), he was trained as an experimental, physiological psychologist and was principally interested in developing a broad theory of the biology of behavior and concomitant brain–behavior relationships.

Reitan subsequently turned to highly empirical methods, in an almost atheoretical fashion, in expanding Halstead's original battery of tests. Reitan never developed a comprehensive theory of the biological basis of intelligence, although his contributions to the applied field of clinical neuropsychological assessment have been many and of great significance. One of these contributions included laying a foundation for test validation studies. Reitan completed extensive blind studies using test results that were later reviewed and corroborated by others in the field of neuropsychology (Broshek & Barth, 2000; Reitan, 1994). Reitan also modified and updated the test battery and made headway in research based on brain–behavior relationships (Reed, 1985).

In addition, Reitan (1964a) engaged in some evaluation of Halstead's theory. In evaluating the effects of cerebral lesions of various locations within the cortex, Reitan concluded that the consensus of data indicated that nonfrontal lobe lesions are most frequently associated with specific types of disorders, and that frontal lobe lesions result in more general disturbances that are difficult to specify in detail. Reitan apparently felt that these findings disconfirmed Halstead's notion of the frontal lobes as the principal anatomical site of biological intelligence (Reitan, 1975), but this is not necessarily the case. If one conceptualizes intelligence as the coordinating and planning activity of the brain (the "executive" branch), and as directing the processing activities of other areas, then damage to the frontal lobes should produce a more generalized, diverse set of disorders.

Reitan's work (Reitan 1955, 1964a, 1964b, 1966, 1975; Reitan & Davison, 1974; Wheeler & Reitan, 1962) has caused researchers and clinicians to appreciate the complexities of elaborating a theory of brain function and intelligence from deficits in the higher cognitive processes following brain lesions. Considerable research has been done with the HRNTB regarding brain–behavior relationships (Reitan & Wolfson, 1996). In reviewing this research as it applies to clinical assessment and the development of a comprehensive theory of the neuropsychological basis of intelligence, one must keep in mind the methodological difficulties inherent in this line of research. Many of the methodological problems discussed early by Shure and Halstead (1959) remain. Additionally, researchers have not been vigilant in their reporting of subject descriptions in research utilizing the HRNTB (Hevern, 1980; Parsons & Prigatano, 1978).

The following demographic variables are known to affect the outcome of neuropsychological assessment (Golden, Espe-Pfeifer, & Wachsler-Felder, 2000; Hevern, 1980; Parsons & Prigatano, 1978; Reynolds & Gutkin, 1979): age, educational level, sex, socioeconomic status, race, and urban versus rural residence. Hevern's (1980) review indicates that, for most of these variables, less than one half of the studies in the literature since 1975 give adequate information for replication or for accurate comparisons with other studies. Swiercinsky (1979) also has questioned the comprehensiveness of assessment with the HRNTB, indicating that important areas of function, such as receptive speech, concentration, and other information-processing modes, do not receive any independent evaluation through this technique. Nevertheless, the HRNTB continues to be a widely used neuropsychological assessment measure by which multiple interpretive models add power to its clinical use (Nussbaum & Bigler, 1997).

A thorough assessment of Halstead's theory of biological intelligence is not yet available. It appears to have fallen by the wayside, at present, in favor of number-crunching empiricism. A strong theory of the neuropsychological basis of intelligence is requisite to important advances in the field.

THE LURIA MODEL: A KEY TO CLINICAL UNDERSTANDING

Alexander R. Luria was a Russian neuropsychologist who was a major force in the development of the scientific discipline of neuropsychology. His research spans some four decades, but his influence on American neuropsychology was minimal until around the mid-1960s. Luria was a prolific researcher and published extensively throughout his career, which ended with his death in 1977. His later work continued to be published into 1979. In fact, according to Tupper (1999), Luria's works continue to be the most popular books in the field of neuropsychology. Luria's major theoretical contributions to understanding the neuropsychological basis of intelligence are well summarized in his publications of 1961, 1964, 1966, 1969, 1970, and 1973. One of the major contributions Luria made to the field of neuropsychology was the concept of the functional system (Golden et al., 1982). Like Halstead, Luria believed the frontal lobes of man to play a major role in intelligence. Luria's position with respect to frontal lobes is well reflected in the title of his 1969 address to the 19th International Congress of Psychology: "Cerebral Organization of Conscious Acts: A Frontal Lobe Function." Much of the following presentation is taken from the above references to Luria's work and represents a decades-old conceptualization that remains among the most, if not *the* most (in our view), clinically useful conceptualization of brain function.

Luria was greatly influenced in his clinical and experimental research in neuropsychology by the well-known Soviet psychologist L. S. Vygotsky. Throughout Luria's work, one finds that Luria relied extensively on a clinical research methodology not at all unlike the "methodé clinique" of Piaget (Kamphaus, 1993) in addition to his more formalized experimental research. In developing his clinical research methods, Luria designed a rich battery of neuropsychological tests that he used to obtain an essentially qualitative evaluation of an individual's neurological status and integrity. Indeed, it has been the qualitative (often seen as descriptive or subjective; Golden, Purisch, & Hammeke, 1979; Spiers, 1982; Tupper, 1999) nature of Luria's neuropsychological examination that has fostered the reluctance to adopt his techniques in American neuropsychology. However, after Luria's death, a standardized version of the Luria battery was developed and made available for experimental and clinical use in the United States (Golden et al., 1979). A children's version of this battery, the Luria–Nebraska Neuropsychological Test Battery Children's Revision, also has been developed (Golden, 1987).

However, the quantification and standardization of Luria's assessment techniques has been criticized as tending to remove much of the richness that was the essence of Luria's methods. A clear understanding of Luria's theory of the functioning organization of the brain and an appreciation for the brain as a dynamic organ or consciousness should avert the loss of information through the standardization of Luria's methods. Standardization of such methods has a number of advantages that should add to the richness of information about brain function that is available (Golden et al., 1982). However, there still remains, in North American psychology, a general compulsion toward psychometrically sound, data-driven, quantitative research and assessment procedures, whereas the procedures proffered by Luria were driven by theory, flexibility, and were qualitative in nature (Tupper, 1999).

Luria conceptualized the working brain as organized into three major components, which he termed "blocks of the brain." As illustrated in Figure 2.2, the first block of the brain is composed of the brain stem, including the reticular formation, the midbrain, pons, and medulla. The second block of the brain is essentially composed of the parietal, occipital, and temporal lobes—the sections of the brain frequently referred to as the association areas of the cortex. The third block of the brain is essentially composed of the remaining area of the cortex anterior to the central sulcus and the sensorimotor strip—principally the frontal lobes. The three blocks of the brain do not operate independent of each other. In fact, there is a dynamic interaction between the areas, and any weakness in one area of the brain may interact and affect the functioning of the other areas (Languis & Miller, 1992; Reynolds, 1981). Before turning to the localization of function within each of the three blocks of the brain, it is important to fully understand the concept of dynamic localization of function in the human brain.

The sensory and motor functions of the brain have highly specific functional localizations. The locations of these functions have been mapped in precise and meticulous detail by neurologists and psychologists over the past decade. Higher-order, complex mental processes require the coordination of many areas of the brain and are not conducive to such rigid or narrow localization of function. In essence, Luria's

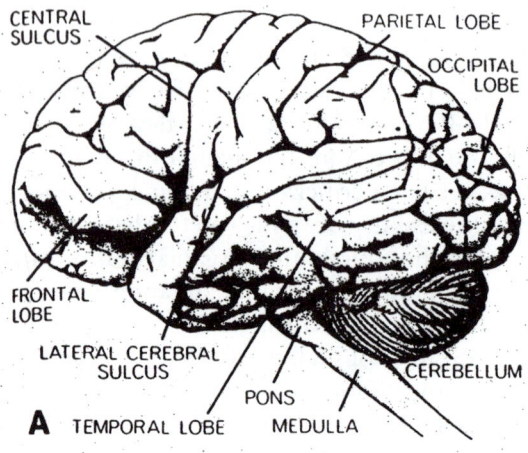

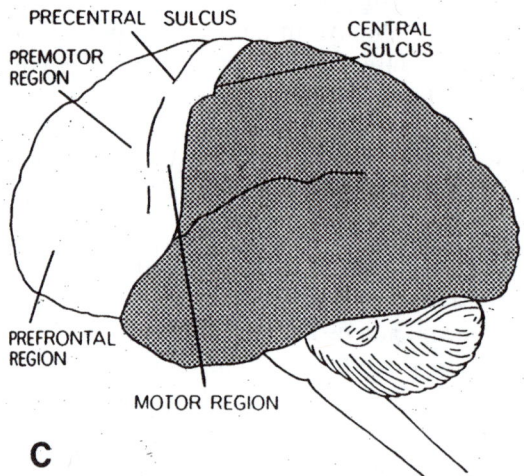

FIGURE 2.2 Lauria's major blocks of the brain. (A) Gross anatomy of the brain, left-hemisphere view. (B) The first block of the brain, the brainstem, and evolutionarilyold cortex. (C) The second block of the brain, the association area, composed of the parietal, occipital, and temporal lobes. (D) Shaded area is the third block of the brain, composed of the frontal areas of the brain, anterior to the central sulcus and including the motor strip of the cortex. (From "The Functional Organization of the brain" by A. R. Luria. *Scientific American*, 1970, 222, 66–78. Copyright 1970 by Scientific American, inc. All right reserved.)

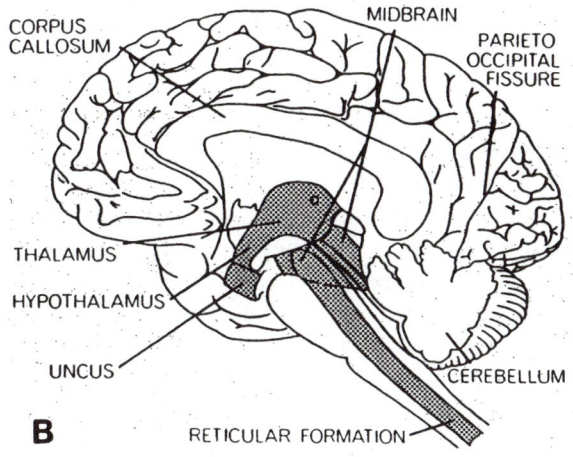

B

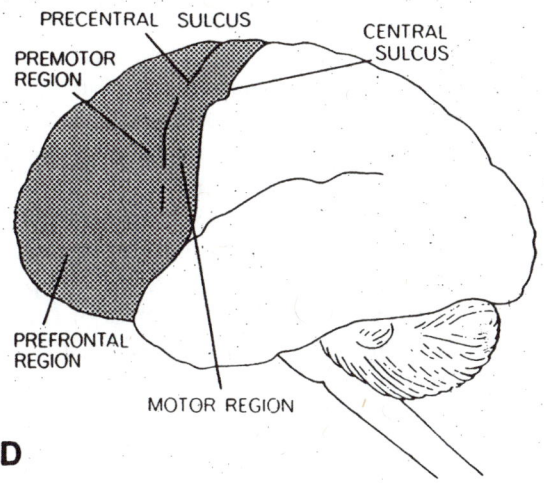

D

FIGURE 2.2 *(continued)*

theory of functional localization could be summed up as structure following function (Languis & Miller, 1992). There is not a direct correspondence between an area of the brain and a specific behavior (Reynolds, 1981). Although it is well known, for example, that impairment and lesions of the right parietal lobe result in extreme difficulty with the Block Design subtest of the Wechsler series, it is incorrect to consider Block Design performance as being localized to the right parietal lobe. Extensive damage to portions of the frontal or occipital lobes may also produce impaired performance on the Block Design task. Yet, if the parietal lobe remained intact, the nature of the difficulty on this task would change, as a function of the localization of any neuropathology. Cortical specialization for cognitive tasks is not task- or stimulus-specific: It is much more process-specific, although processing specialization is gross, and any specific type of information processing itself requires coordination of several anatomical sections of the cortex. Also, functional localization of cognitive processes (compared to purely sensorimotor processes) more closely resembles the integrative, synergistic, and dynamic activities of the brain than a one-to-one correspondence of behaviors to brain areas would achieve (Ashman & Das, 1980).

The notion of the brain as a dynamic functional system is by no means a new idea. Hughlings Jackson presented a similar premise in the nineteenth century, as did Monakow in the early twentieth century. The concept of dynamic localization of higher cognitive processes has perhaps been best explained by Luria (1964). According to Luria, the higher mental processes are formed as a function of people's activity in the process of communication with one another and represent "*complex functional systems* based on jointly working zones of the brain cortex" (pp. 11–12). Once one conceptualizes the brain as an interdependent systemic network, "it becomes completely understandable that a higher (mental) function may suffer as a result of the destruction of *any link which is a part of the structure of a complex functional system* and . . . may be disturbed even when the centres differ greatly in localization" (pp. 12–13). Central to this approach is the contention that each link in the system has a particular function in the processing of the problem at hand. Hence, "when one or another link has been lost, the whole functional system will be disturbed in a particular way, and symptoms of disturbance of one or another higher (mental) function will have a *completely different structure, depending on the location of the damage*" (pp. 11–12).

By thoroughly analyzing the nature of the difficulty experienced in performing a task, such as reading, writing, or counting, one may determine the localizing significance of the observed disturbance. It was for this purpose that Luria developed his qualitative neuropsychological assessment methods. Keeping the concept of dynamic functional localization in mind, it is appropriate to turn to a functional appraisal of Luria's three blocks of the brain.

Block One

The first block of the brain (Figure 2.3), often called the arousal and attention unit, is responsible for regulating the energy level and tone of all other portions of the cortex. In serving this regulatory function, block one provides a stable basis for the conscious organism to organize the various other functions and processes of the brain. The regulatory functions are especially controlled by the reticular formation, the posterior hypothalamic and brain stem portions of which control the waking center of the brain. The reticular formation is responsible for the relative levels of arousal or activation found at any given time in the cortex. Block one of the brain, then, regulates consciousness, and any interruption of impulses from the first block of the brain to the cortex results in complete loss of consciousness. Injuries to block one of the brain can result in coma or a lowering of the level of consciousness in the cortex, giving rise to confused behavior characterized by potentially bizarre associations and great difficulty in stimulus distinction. The subjective experience is not unlike alcohol- or barbiturate-induced intoxication. Although involved in all processes of the brain, the first block seems especially important in the maintenance of Halstead's *P* factor.

Block Two

The second block is undoubtedly the most widely and frequently researched area of the brain. It is essentially the area posterior to the central sulcus and is composed principally of the parietal, occipital, and temporal lobes (Figure 2.2). It is sometimes called the sensory input and integration unit. Most of the (simultaneous or successive) cognitive information processing of the brain, including receiving, processing, and storing of information, occurs in the second block. According to Luria's conceptualization, the various areas of block two that are responsible for the analysis and encoding of specific types of stimuli (e.g., auditory in the temporal region, visual or optic in the occipital region, and kinesthetic or tactile in the parietal lobe) are each organized into three hierarchical zones. The primary zone of each area is responsible for sorting and recording incoming sensory organization. Lesions or dysfunction in this area of block two may result in confabulation and gap filling (Joseph, 1996). The secondary zone organizes and codes information from the primary zone. Damage in the secondary zone may result in agnosias and aphasias (Joseph, 1996). The tertiary zone is where data are merged from multiple sources of input and collated as the basis for organizing complex behavioral responses. Damage to this area of block two may result in apraxia, anomia, impairment to temporal-sequential motor control, and visuospatial neglect (Joseph, 1996).

Damage to the second block of the brain produces the most specific of all behavior changes. For example, damage to the primary zone of the acoustic area of block two may result in a loss of hearing, but is highly unlikely to have any direct effect on the complex, higher mental processes of the brain. As one moves up the hierarchy of processing, however, alterations in behavior become more complex and less predictable. It is within the second block of the brain that the principal information-processing functions of the brain are carried out. The brain essentially uses two methods of processing information, one a sequential, successive method and the other a method of simultaneous synthesis of information. These two modes of cognitive processing are explored further when the work of the Kaufmans (e.g., Kaufman & Kaufman, 1983) and Naglieri and Das (e.g., Naglieri & Das, 1996) are examined.

Block Three

"The third block of the brain, comprising the frontal lobes, is involved in the formation of intentions and programs for behavior" (Luria, 1970, p. 68). It is often called the executive planning and organizing unit and is dependent on the successful operation of the first and second blocks of the brain (Obrzut & Obrzut, 1982). The frontal lobes organize and implement conscious actions on the part of an individual. As Luria points out, the frontal lobes have no responsibility for simple sensory or motor functions. They are, however, intimately involved in every complex, higher-order behavior of humans.

The frontal lobes are also closely tied to the reticular formation and are involved in the activation and regulation of the remainder of the cortex. The frontal lobes serve an important function in regulating and focusing attention in the brain. It is well known that intense anxiety interferes with complex thought and behavior and can produce behavior that appears confused. As a subjective state, anxiety appears to be experienced in the frontal lobes, causing global disruptions of behavior. Violent or highly active victims of psychosis, who experience hallucinations, are, as a rule, intensely anxious. Treatment of such patients through the psychosurgical process of frontal lobotomy (the severing of nerve fibers between the frontal lobes and block one of the brain, particularly the thalamus, resulting in considerable bilateral lesions to the frontal lobes) does not effectively stop hallucinations or many other psychotic symptoms, but does calm the patient, apparently through reducing the intense anxiety promulgated by the psychotic symptomatology. These patients frequently become listless, however, seeming to lose their "will" to behave. The frontal lobotomy causes the loss of ability to plan, organize, and execute complex behavior functions, because of the tremendous loss of communication between the third block and the other blocks of the brain.

The role of the frontal lobes in directing the attentional focus of the association areas is also an important one. The direction of attention is closely related to the method by which information is processed in the brain (simultaneous or successive). Kinsbourne (1978a, 1978b, 1997) believes that an attentional bias between the hemispheres is one potential basis for hemispheric differences and specialization of processing. Attentional biases in the receipt of sensory information are well documented. These attentional biases are probably mediated by the frontal lobes, through interaction with the first block of the brain, although the second block is where the principal processing takes place. The view of the frontal lobes as the executive branch of intelligence in the human brain is neither new nor unique to Luria's model: Halstead (1947) considered the frontal lobes to be the central anatomical locus of intelligence. The frontal lobes play an important role in Pribam's (1971) theory of brain function (though this is not surprising, since Pribam spent 6 months in Luria's laboratory, studying patients with frontal lobe damage). Intelligent behavior, in the Luria model, is the product of the dynamic interplay of the three blocks of the brain, with activation, regulation, and planning of conscious acts falling to the frontal lobes.

Simultaneous and Successive Cognitive Processes

As Naglieri, Kamphaus, and Kaufman (1983) and Gunnison, Kaufman, and Kaufman (1982) noted, the field of psychology is replete with a history of dichotomies, with the simultaneous–successive dichotomy enduring into theoretical formulations and assessment practices today. Luria's theory of cognitive processing arose out of a need to interpret the results of studies that other theories of hierarchical cognitive processing could not explain (Klich, 1987). Luria's model of successive and simultaneous processing, as indicated, is not hierarchical. Rather, the two modes of cognitive processing are complementary, working together in order for the individual to most efficiently and effectively accomplish tasks throughout the day (Hunt, 1980). Simultaneous and successive (or sequential) cognitive processes are the two complementary, principal information-processing strategies of the second block of the brain and therefore are central to any neuropsychological theory of intelligence. These two processes seem to be deployed primarily in the secondary and tertiary zones of block two of Luria's model. Simultaneous and successive processes are neither modality- nor stimulus-specific (Ashman & Das, 1980; McCallum & Merritt, 1983). Verbal or nonverbal information may be processed either simultaneously or successively (Watters & English, 1995). Any type of stimulus information can be processed through simultaneous or successive means; however, certain functions are processed much more efficiently through one process than the other.

Particularly for young children whose preferential means of cognitive processing is not yet solidified, the means of cognitive processing an individual uses for a task may change, depending on the task demands, the individual's level of attention to the task, and the individual's preferred means of completing the task (Hall, Gregory, Billinger, & Fisher, 1988; Watters & English, 1995; Willis, 1985). Watters and English (1995) contend that "individuals adopt strategies in solving problems that use their particular strengths or modes of information processing" (pp. 702–703). McCallum and Merritt (1983) also argue that genetic factors may influence the cognitive processing methods of an individual. In addition, cultural traditions also may influence the cognitive processing method an individual may use. Some populations favor using simultaneous processing for a task; other populations may favor using sequential processes (Cumming & Rodda, 1985). There are always exceptions to any rule, but language is processed at peak efficiency through successive methods, in other words, placing the elements of the composition into a linear sequence, each part of which is dependent upon its preceding component. Figure copying and solving visual analogies are examples of problems most efficiently solved through simultaneous-processing strategies.

Watters and English (1995) discovered a fascinating pattern in their study of 10-year-old children. They found that children who were balanced in their cognitive processing approach (equal levels of simultaneous and successive processing) were viewed by teachers and parents as "well-adjusted, high achieving students, often with a strong interest and ability in mathematics and science" (p. 708). On the other hand, children who employed uneven levels of simultaneous or successive processing (specifically, higher simultaneous processing) were viewed by teachers and parents as underachievers who exhibited acumen and tenacity with regard to difficult tasks. Similarly, Merritt and McCallum (1984) found that individuals with high levels of simultaneous and successive processing capabilities were the most successful in school.

Simultaneous Processing

As described by Das, Kirby, and Jarman, 1979,

> simultaneous integration refers to the synthesis of separate elements into groups, these groups often taking on spatial overtones. The essential nature of this sort of processing is that any portion of the result is at once surveyable without dependence upon its position in the whole. (p. 49)

This type of processing is linked to the occipital and parietal lobes of the brain, usually the right hemisphere (Naglieri et al., 1983; Willis, 1985). Examples include the Backward Digit Span and Similarities subtests of the Wechsler scales. In fact, Naglieri et al. (1983) noted that simultaneous processing closely resembles the Perceptual Organization Index of the Wechsler scales. Simultaneous processing is strongly correlated to inductive reasoning (Watters & English, 1995) and SAT math scores (Wachs & Harris, 1986).

In their research on simultaneous processing, Das et al. (1979) use a form of Raven's Matrices, a figure-copying test, and the Graham–Kendall Memory-for-Designs Test as their principal measures (anchor tests) for assessing simultaneous processing. Although the Raven is known to have a large *g* factor present (the general ability factor believed to underlie the positive intercorrelation occurring between all cognitive measures), it is used because "solution requires the construction of a spatial pattern or scheme. Only after such a scheme has been formed can the option which correctly completes the pattern be chosen" (p. 50). Although Das et al. have not discussed the fact that any of these tasks may be successfully completed through a successive method of processing, it is important to note this possibility for any single individual, even though each of the above tasks is undoubtedly performed most efficiently through simultaneous processing. Most traditional tests of spatial abilities show high correlations with simultaneous processing (Kirby & Das, 1977).

Successive Processing

Das et al. (1979) describe successive (or sequential) information processing as the

> processing of information in a serial order. The important distinction between this type of information processing and simultaneous processing is that in successive processing the system is not totally surveyable at any point in time. Rather, a system of cues consecutively activates the components. (p. 52)

This type of processing is linked to the frontotemporal areas of the brain, usually the left hemisphere (Naglieri et al., 1983; Willis, 1985). Successive information processing, then, is of a linear, sequential fashion, with information being dealt with in an interdependent serial order. The syntactical structure of language makes it a task most efficiently processed through successive methods (although the concept behind the words is of a simultaneous nature). In successive processing, each idea is directly related to the preceding and following ones (Gunnison et al., 1982). The successive processing closely resembles the Freedom from Distractibility Index of the Wechsler scales (Naglieri et al., 1983). In addition, successive processing is significantly correlated with grades in an English composition course (Wachs & Harris, 1986).

Tasks used extensively in research on successive processing by Das et al. are generally tests requiring the maintenance of a temporal order of input of information for the generation of an appropriate response. Examples of the most frequently employed tasks include Digit Span tests (forward only), sequential visual short-term memory tests, and serial recall tests. Obviously, all of these tasks are memory tests, but extensive research (Das et al., 1979) indicates that these tests do not simply define a memory factor. These memory tasks all require the maintenance of a temporal order. Performance on other memory tasks, not requiring the maintenance of any serial or temporal order, correlate no more highly with the successive memory tasks than they correlate with *g*. The various successive memory tasks correlate considerably more highly with one another than with general reasoning ability. Various competing theories of information processing have developed from the past several decades of research on hemispheric specialization, and it is necessary that this research be reconciled with other major neuropsychological models of intelligence, whenever possible.

Although reading is generally noted to be a simultaneous task for fluent readers, there is evidence for sequential processing in early reading and decoding abilities (Gunnison et al., 1982; Kwantes & Mewhort, 1999) and for adults with learning disabilities in reading (Gardiner, 1987). Children learning to read, based on a phonetic approach (not whole language), must identify each letter of the word in succession and pronounce the word, based on the sounds each letter makes. After children have progressed beyond the initial stages of learning to read, they can readily identify words without having to sound them out, based on the order of letters (which then becomes a sequential process). In fact, if an individual expects to be a successful reader in the future, this can only be accomplished by means of successive processing in early reading abilities (Gunnison et al., 1982).

Hemispheric Specialization and Simultaneous and Successive Cognitive Processes

The current literature on lateral cerebral specialization of cognitive functions is immense, and no attempt is made here to review this literature. The hemispheric specialization literature is quite complex as well, and is discussed in this section, in a simplified fashion, dealing with only general conclusions. What was stated at the 1980 meeting of the International Neuropsychological Society is still true today: "To say that the field of hemispheric specialization is in a state of disarray and that the results are difficult to interpret is an understatement. The field can best be characterized as chaotic" (Tomlinson-Keasy & Clarkson-Smith, 1980, p. 1). Nevertheless, research conducted, mostly since 1965 or so, does allow one to draw some conclusions with an adequate degree of confidence.

For the vast majority of individuals, the left cerebral hemisphere appears to be specialized for linguistic, propositional, serial, and analytic tasks and the right hemisphere for more nonverbal, spatial, appositional, synthetic, and holistic tasks (Bever, 1975; Bogen, 1969; Dean & Reynolds, 1997; Gazzaniga, 1970; Harnad, Doty, Goldstein, Jaynes, & Krauthamer, 1977; Kinsbourne, 1978a, 1997; Naglieri et al., 1983; Schwartz, Davidson, & Maer, 1975; Segalowitz & Gruber, 1977; Willis, 1985). One will find in the literature a large number of studies of hemispheric specialization attempting to provide anatomical localizations of performance on motor tasks (i.e., handedness, footedness), sensory tasks (i.e., eyedness, earedness), and higher-order complex tasks utilizing specific means of cognitive processing (i.e., verbal–nonverbal, sequential–simultaneous, analytic–holistic, propositional–appositional, sequential–parallel, rational–metaphoric, fluid–crystallized, convergent–divergent, deductive–inductive). Much of the confusion in the literature stems from the apparently conflicting data of many of these studies. However, the dynamic functional localization principle of Luria, and knowledge that any specific task can be performed through any of the brain's processing modes, should give some insight into the conflicting results that appear in the literature. Some research suggests that differences between hemispheric processes seem to become more notable as tasks become more involved (Posner, Peterson, Fox, & Raichle, 1988).

A review of Table 2.1 suggests that modes of processing are the superior means of reviewing differences in hemispheric processing. Although functions are vital to determining the specific strengths and weaknesses of an individual, processing modes are more important to determining the efficiency of these functions.

Cerebral hemispheric asymmetries of function are process-specific and not stimulus-specific. As mentioned earlier, the mode of processing by which an individual accomplishes a task is widely variable, depending on numerous factors, including task demands, level of attention to the task, individual strengths, genetics, and sociocultural norms and traditions (Cumming & Rodda, 1985; Hall et al., 1988; McCallum & Merritt, 1983; Watters & English, 1995; Willis, 1985). Shure and Halstead (1959) noted early in this line of research that manipulation of stimuli was at the root of hemispheric differences, a notion that is well supported by past and current empirical research (e.g., Dean, 1984; Grimshaw, 1998; Mateer et al., 1984; Obrzut, Obrzut, Bryden, & Bartels, 1985; Ornstein, Johnstone, Herron, & Swencionis, 1980; Piccirilli, D'Alessandro, Mazzi, Sciarma, & Testa, 1991; Tous, Fusté, & Vidal, 1995). Bever (1975) has emphasized this point and elaborated on two

TABLE 2.1 Functions of the Right and Left Hemispheres

Right hemisphere		Left hemisphere	
Processing modes	Representative reference	Processing modes	Representative reference
Simultaneous	Hall, Gregory, Billinger, & Fisher, 1988	Sequential	Bell, 1990; Bloom, 2000
Holistic Visual/nonverbal	Dimond & Beaumont, 1974 Sperry, 1974	Temporal Analytic	Mills, 1977 Morgan, McDonald, & McDonald, 1971
Imagery Spatial reasoning	Seamon & Gazzaniga, 1973 Sperry, 1974		
Nonverbal functions	Representative reference	Verbal functions	Representative reference
Depth perception	Carmon & Bechtoldt, 1969	Speech	Wada, 1949 Reitan, 1955
Melodic perception	Shankweiler, 1966	General language/verbal abilities	Mateer, Rapport, & Kettrick, 1984
Tactile perception (integration)	Boll, 1974	Calculation/ arithmetic	Mitsuda, 1991
Haptic perception	Wittelson, 1974	Abstract verbal thought	Watters & English, 1995
Nonverbal sound recognition	Wright & Ashman, 1991	Writing (composition)	Hecaen & Marcie, 1974
Motor integration	Gorynia & Egenter, 2000	Complex motor functions	Dimond & Beaumont, 1974
Visual constructive performance	Capruso, Hamsher, & Benton, 1995	Body orientation	Gerstmann, 1957
Pattern recognition	Capruso et al., 1995	Vigilance	Dimond & Beaumont, 1974

Note: Adapted from Dean (1984) and Kamphaus & Reynolds (1987).

modes of information processing that are of interest here, because of their similarity to simultaneous and successive cognitive processes.

According to Bever (1975), cerebral asymmetries of function result from two fundamental lateralized processes: holistic and analytic processing. Lateralization of these two processes occurs, according to Bever, because these two methods of information processing are incompatible and cannot coexist in the same physical sense. Analytic processing appears analogous to successive processing and is lateralized, in most individuals, to the left hemisphere. Holistic processing is analogous to simultaneous processing and is typically lateralized to the right hemisphere.

Bever (1975) has put forth four principles of neural organization to account for this localization of function that may be summarized as follows:

1. The mind is self-organizing. "[The mind] differentiates in mental space the location of analytic modes of processing from holistic modes of processing" (p. 252). One will typically have two ways of organizing behavior in response to a given stimulus.

    > We may analyze the stimulus in terms of component parts, or we may respond to the stimulus if it triggers a holistic behavioral "template." . . . A complex stimulus can itself be processed as a primitive whole or be analyzed in terms of its constituent parts and . . . those processes are incompatible. . . . They cannot occur simultaneously in the same place. (p. 252)

2. Analytical processing requires more mental activity than holistic processing. According to Bever, this is "essentially a necessary truth" (p. 252), since the recognition of an object or other stimulus through its component parts will ultimately include recognition of the whole.

3. The dynamic mapping of mental processes onto functional brain structures is maximally simple. Essentially, Bever is asserting here that mental activities that are similar in nature tend to be represented in an anatomically parsimonious fashion and that there is enough flexibility in neural organization to allow for maximal localization of similar processes in the same area of the brain. This view is fundamental to the premise that incompatible processes cannot share the same anatomical location.

4. The left hemisphere is more adaptable at birth. Since analytical processing requires greater mental activity, it will become local-

ized in the more adaptable or flexible hemisphere, the left hemisphere. Since analytical and holistic processing are anatomically and logically incompatible processes, holistic processing must then be lateralized to the right hemisphere. Although Bever (1975) carefully explains that he does not intend to posit here that the right hemisphere is more mature at birth and during the first years of life, this does not seem an attractive hypothesis for explaining the greater plasticity of the left hemisphere early in life. It also has numerous implications for developmental lag hypothesis of the etiology of learning disabilities. The evidence is not totally unequivocal, but there is a considerable body of literature that implicates great maturity of the right hemisphere at birth and in the early years (Carmen & Nachson, 1973; Crowell, Jones, Kapunai, & Nakagawa, 1973; Geschwind, 1978; Giannitrapani, 1967; Reynolds & Kaufman, 1980; Seth, 1973; Woods, 1980). .

Das et al. (1979), Lezak (1995), and others do not agree that simultaneous and successive processing are represented solely in the right and left hemispheres, respectively, but rather believe that are each mode of processing is prominently represented in each hemisphere. This coincides with Bradshaw and Nettleton's (1981) argument that hemispheric specialization is best represented as a continuum, rather than being on opposing sides and acting in complete isolation from the other hemisphere. Furthermore, Beaumont (1997) indicated that the basic biological interconnection between the hemispheres does not support hemispheric specialization hypotheses that divide cognitive processes along the lines of the corpus callosum. According to Bever's (1975) line of reasoning, this is an impossible state of affairs in the normally functioning human brain. Additionally, the hemispheric lateralization literature is highly consistent with the notion of a successive-processing left hemisphere and simultaneous-processing right hemisphere relationship. Das et al. (1979) have developed their theory exclusively on the basis of group data, yet they attempt to discredit hemispheric lateralization of cognitive processing by calling upon anecdotal individual case data. Few would contend that hemispheric specialization for cognitive processing is the same in every single individual. However, this seems to be the requisite state of affairs for Das et al., to accept the hypothesis of lateralization of simultaneous and successive processing. This hardly seems necessary. The sheer weight of evidence at present indicates that, for the vast majority of individuals, the lateralization of simultaneous and successive processes occurs as described above.

The K-ABC and the Luria Model

With the advent of the Kaufman Assessment Battery for Children (K-ABC) (Kaufman & Kaufman, 1983), sequential and simultaneous cognitive processing has earned a notable position in the assessment field. The K-ABC is one of the first measures to be grounded in a convergence of theory and research (Kamphaus, 1993; Kamphaus & Reynolds, 1984, 1987). The K-ABC was developed based on Luria's theoretical framework of cerebral specialization and functional localization (Daleo et al., 1999; Reynolds, Kamphaus, Rosenthal, & Hiemenz, 1997). The structure of the K-ABC mimics the two Lurian methods of cognitive information processing: simultaneous (the integration of elements into simultaneous groups) and successive (the synthesis of sequential elements into a series) cognitive processing. These two modes of information processing represent the functions of block two of Luria's theoretical model of the brain.

Kaufman and Kaufman were the first to present a practical assessment measure that utilized the simultaneous–successive theory proposed by Luria. Reynolds et al. (1997) argued that a child must have the mental ability to synthesize information, regardless of the mode of presentation (spatial or analogic), in order to most efficiently perform the simultaneous processing tasks on the K-ABC. Likewise, a child must have the ability to arrange stimuli in a sequential order, in order to complete tasks in the successive-processing cluster. Although tasks may be completed by any means of information processing, they have been designated into their respective clusters (simultaneous or successive), based on the respective modality by which they can be solved in the most efficient manner.

Shortly after its publication, Majovski (1984) noted that "the K-ABC meets the theoretical, pragmatic, and psychometric standards for assessing certain aspects of a child's thinking processes" (p. 257). Now that nearly two decades have passed since its original publication, the K-ABC is in the process of being revised. As with the original version, the revised version of the K-ABC is sure to bring new understanding to the field of intellectual assessment.

The CAS and the Luria Model

Like the K-ABC, the Cognitive Assessment System (Naglieri & Das, 1996) is based on years of research and theoretical work and incorporates Luria's model of cerebral specialization and functional localization. The Cognitive Assessment System was designed to measure cognitive abilities by ascertaining an individual's abilities in the areas of planning, attention, simultaneous, and successive processes (PASS) (Naglieri, 1997). As can be surmised, the PASS system of assessing cognitive abilities fits nicely with Luria's conceptualization of the three blocks of the brain (Tupper, 1999).

Naglieri and Das (1990) understood that the measures used to assess cognitive functioning greatly influence the interpretation made based on the results of the assessment. Based on this understanding, they have created an assessment tool that is supported by a conglomeration of theory and research. Rather than relying on a single score, *g,* to explain an individual's cognitive functioning, Naglieri and Das (1990) created a battery of tasks, in an attempt to more adequately describe the process of intelligence. Furthermore, the authors of the test were concerned not only with the results of an individual's performance, but the process by which the task is completed (Meikamp, 2001).

HEMISPHERICITY AND COGNITIVE PROCESSING

Hemisphericity, briefly defined, is the tendency of an individual to rely primarily upon the problem-solving or information-processing style of one or the other hemisphere, in the course of normal daily functions. In this theory, there is the presupposition that an individual has a preferred mode of cognitive processing and is possibly able to actively choose the mode of processing (Beaumont, Young, & McManus, 1984). Hemisphericity is conceptualized as a type of dominance for an informa-tion-processing style, is independent of traditional notions of cerebral dominance, and is unrelated to the motorically determined lateral pref-erence of the individual. It is a form of dominance for a style of menta-tion that, if the term had not already acquired an established meaning in psychology, could be described accurately as "a true cognitive style." Hemisphericity, meaning the cognitive style of the two hemispheres, has also been described as modes of consciousness (Deikman, 1971; Galin, 1974). The theory of hemisphericity is utilized in a wide variety of settings beyond the field of neuropsychology (Beaumont et al., 1984).

Conflicting theories of hemisphericity abound today. Allen (1983) noted the theory of unilateral specialization, in which each hemisphere performs its own unique operations, completely independent of, and without integration or interference from, the other hemisphere. This theory of hemispheric specialization was sparked by the research of Dax, Broca, and Hughlings Jackson (Allen, 1983; Finger & Roe, 1999). Some of the functions originally believed to occur in only one hemisphere include language, visuospatial abilities, and motor tasks.

Another theory of hemisphericity is *cooperative interaction*, which was basically what Luria was advocating in his theory of functional lateralization (Allen, 1983). Also known as bilateralization, cooperative interaction occurs when both hemispheres are equally capable of performing a task, although one hemisphere may be slightly better. The hemispheres work cooperatively, therefore integrating functions. The unilateral specialization theory would not lend credit to the maxim "more than the sum of the parts," but cooperative interaction theory does. Other models, including negative interaction (inhibition), parallel, and allocation, also have been touted as plausible explanations for the hemispheric processing of the brain. Indeed, some argue that parallel processing is the most efficient and plausible method of cognitive processing (Beaumont, 1997). However, it seems that Luria's model has once again proven itself and continues to lie at the foundation for current treatment and assessment processes. Recent reviews of cognitive processing and hemispheric specialization continue to support Luria's model (Dean & Reynolds, 1997).

The notion of a dominant or preferential mode of information processing is not new. Bogen et al. (1972) describe the concept of hemisphericity as defined above and measure relative hemispheric dependence as a ratio of performance on appositional and propositional tasks. Das et al. (1979) frequently refer to individuals who display a "habitual mode of information processing." The development of hemisphericity may occur prior to the age of 3 years, but seems well established in most children by $3^1/_2$–4 years of age. A variety of studies have indicated the presence of hemisphericity in adult subjects. Hemispheric specialization has begun to replace cerebral dominance as a major concept in our understanding of brain–behavior relationships. Hemisphericity (the dominant or preferential information-processing modality of an individual) holds great promise for helping to understand both normal and dysfunctional intelligence.

Normally functioning individuals appear to be able to utilize the two modes of information processing separately or in conjunction with one another and possibly shift at will, depending upon the type of information to be processed (Gazzaniga, 1974, 1975), although such decisions are more likely to be made at an unconscious level, in interaction between the stimuli to be processed and the direction of hemisphericity. At the highest level of function, the two modes of processing operate in a complementary manner, achieving maximal interhemispheric integration of processing, or, in Bogen et al.'s (1972) terminology, "cerebral complementarity." For example, right-hemisphere function (simultaneous processing) is important in contributing to letter and word recognition during reading, a function handled primarily through successive processing, because of its linguistic nature, in the formative stages of learning to read (Gardiner, 1987; Gunnison et al., 1982; Kwantes & Mewhort, 1999). Highly skilled readers who have mastered the component skills of reading, making it an automatic function, demonstrate extensive use of both processes in reading (Cummins & Das, 1977).

When first learning to read, successive processing (left-hemisphericity) is most important, and many children with difficulties in learning to read have problems with successive processing (Cummins & Das, 1977; Gardiner, 1987; Gunnison et al., 1982; Kwantes & Mewhort, 1999). This is also consistent with the findings of higher performance than VIQ in most groups of reading-disabled children, discussed earlier. Performance IQ is almost certainly more closely related to the simultaneous processing of information than to successive processing; the converse relationship holds for the VIQ (Bell, 1990; Bloom, 2000).

A variety of direct and indirect methods are available for measuring hemisphericity, including studies on lateral eye movements, self-report questionnaires, electrophysiological measures, dichotic listening tasks, tests of cognitive ability, and others, although there is much controversy regarding their validity. Nevertheless, some interesting relationships have been reported between measures of hemisphericity and cognitive outcome measures. In a blind evaluation of written scenarios of the future (using an objective scoring system developed by Torrance for use in the National Future Problem Solving Program), individuals previously classified as having right-hemisphericity versus left-hemisphericity, on the basis of performance on "Your Style of Learning and Thinking" (Torrance, Reynolds, & Riegel, 1977), were compared on the eight scoring scales of the future scenarios (Torrance & Reynolds, 1978). The right-hemisphericity group significantly outperformed the left-hemisphericity group on seven of the eight scales. This had been anticipated, since future scenario writing is a creative task, and creative functions seem better subserved by simultaneous-processing methods. This is probably related to the nature of simultaneous processing, which makes that entire schema constantly surveyable, making the tryout of new innovations more readily surveyed for outcome and more easily and efficiently modified. Differences in hemisphericity also appear to be partially responsibly for black–white IQ discrepancies observed on traditional left-hemisphere-oriented intelligence tests (Reynolds & Gutkin, 1980; Reynolds, McBride, & Gibson, 1981). Furthermore, differences in reading ability and gender seem to account for at least some of the variance regarding hemisphericity (Newell & Rugel, 1981; Roubinek, Bell, & Cates, 1987).

Much research evidence seems to suggest that traditional concepts of dominance should give way to concepts that pertain more to the dynamics of hemispheric specialization and cerebral complementarity. This is especially true because lateralization of cortical functions may be predisposed genetically (Bradshaw-McAnulty, Hicks, & Kinsbourne, 1984; Gorynia & Egenter, 2000; Kinsbourne, 1975, 1997; Kolb & Fantie, 1997; McCallum & Merritt, 1983; Tous et al., 1995) and, without specific intervention, continues essentially unaltered throughout the normal life span (Borod & Goodglass, 1980; Elias & Kinsbourne, 1974; Woodruff, 1978, Zelinski & Marsh, 1976).

Hemisphericity should take its place in the research literature as a potentially powerful explanatory variable with many pragmatic implications. Although the mode of processing underlying hemisphericity is carried out in block two of the brain, the first block is undoubtedly the decision-making center that directs and coordinates processing and is thus "in charge" of hemisphericity. Hemisphericity can be altered through trauma or training (Bever & Chiarello, 1974; Reynolds & Torrance, 1978; Satz, Strauss, & Whitaker, 1990), or by intense emotional responses, especially anxiety. When experiencing high levels of anxiety, individuals tend to lapse into a single, preferential mode of processing. Notably, with the advent of the "learning styles" movement in the school system, recent research also has focused on identifying students' preferred mode of processing (hemisphericity), in order to remediate problems or facilitate successful academic performance in school (Faust, Kravetz, & Babkoff, 1993; Gunnison et al., 1982; Paquette, Tosoni, Lassonde, & Peretz, 1996; Roubinek et al., 1987; Sonnier, 1992; Sonnier & Goldsmith, 1985).

THE ROLE OF *g* IN NEUROPSYCHOLOGICAL MODELS OF INTELLIGENCE

If one were to apply the theory of parsimony, g would indeed be the most suitable and efficient means of describing the general cognitive abilities of an individual. Rather than attempt to delineate each function as a means of accounting for intelligence, it would be parsimonious to relegate all cognitive functioning to one variable. The idea of using a single variable to describe intellectual functioning is not new, by any means, nor is it completely outdated (Brand, 1996). Aristotle was the first to conceive an individual's intellect based on a single variable, *nous* (Detterman, 1982). However, it has been in vogue during the past few decades, especially as more is learned about the specialized functioning of the two human cerebral hemispheres, to dismiss the notion of *g* as outmoded, archaic, and having little pragmatic or explanatory value. The dismissal of *g* has been especially prominent in processing (Das et al., 1979; Naglieri & Das, 1988) and componential (Sternberg, 1980) models of intelligence. Even one of the foremost authorities and proponents of intelligence testing has seen fit to relegate *g* to the past (Kaufman, 1979b). Similarly, others state that the model of a single variable to explain cognitive functioning is simply not satisfactory (Detterman, 1982).

Unfortunately for supporters of *g*, an individual's cognitive ability (*g*) is impossible to discover without employing numerous tasks to do so (Detterman, 1982). Therefore, *g* is relegated to an average of what might turn out to be tremendous fluctuations in an individual's cognitive abilities as measured by different tasks. In this particular instance, *g* is not the best estimate of an individual's cognitive functioning, and only by further exploration into these fluctuations would the individual's true scope of cognitive abilities be best described (see Kaufman, 1994). Even on the prominent Wechsler scales, which provide a measure of *g* (Full Scale IQ), room is provided for interpreting fluctuations in cognitive abilities, all the way down to the subtest level.

Das et al. (1979) and many others have devoted much time to arguing against even the existence of *g*. Others continue to use g as their means of denoting general intellectual ability (Aluja-Fabregat, Colom, Abad, & Juan-Espinosa, 2000; Kane, 2000). Researchers have made considerable and important progress in documenting the presence of simultaneous and successive cognitive processes across a variety of ages, races, and cultures (Das et al., 1979; Detterman, 1982; Jensen, 1997; Vernon, 1983, 1998). They are able to isolate simultaneous and successive cognitive processes as orthogonal factors in each of the above groups and with separate samples of learning-retarded persons (Das et al., 1979). Das et al. maintain that isolation of these orthogonal factors indicates the nonavailability of g, and they downplay the concept of ability, as well, indicating that processing and not ability is the more correct variable for study.

Regardless, Jensen (1998) continues to insist upon the presence of a general cognitive ability factor. He argues that, "provided the number of tests in the analyzed battery is sufficiently large to yield reliable factors and the tests are sufficiently diverse in item types and information content to reflect more than a single narrow ability, a g factor always emerges" (p. 73). In support of his argument for the presence of g, Jensen (1998) contends that much of the arguments raised by those in favor of ousting the g factor do no take into consideration the need for a large assessment battery, or diverse-item type, as previously mentioned. Furthermore, Jensen proposes that there must be a general cognitive factor, such as g, because it has many biological correlates. Assuredly, the study of g and the study of processing, and even more specific functions of the brain, must be undertaken as complementary, not exclusionary, areas of investigation.

Isolation of simultaneous and successive processes as orthogonal factors does not mean that the performance of these processes is independent of some general ability. Orthogonal isolation only indicates that the two factors can be viewed as distinct, totally separate entities. The mathematics that make this possible do not make performance on the two factors uncorrelated. The VIQ and PIQ factors of the WISC-R are easily isolated as orthogonal factors in many diverse populations (Reynolds, 1981), yet most individuals in the "real world" perform at about the same general level on the two sets of tasks. As Detterman (1982) and Mulaik (1972) have pointed out, factors extracted to be orthogonal in one sample will not be orthogonal in another sample.

However, theories that dismiss g have another, more telling flaw. How can these theories account for individual differences in the level or efficiency of information processing? As Das et al. (1979) and Detterman (1982) have noted, mentally retarded individuals demonstrate just as much evidence for the presence of simultaneous and successive cognitive processes as do normal and even higher-functioning individuals. What differentiates these individuals is not whether they can perform cognitive processing or whether there is a "defect" in one component of their cognitive processing, but rather the level and efficiency with which they perform processing. This is what differentiates the high-average- from low-average- and superior- from very-superior-functioning individuals.

This certainly is not true for all intellectual disorders, however. There is excellent evidence at present that one cause of learning disorders is difficulty with specific types of information processing or an overreliance on a single mode of cognitive processing. Yet the differences between normally functioning individuals with intact brains and cognitive-processing systems cannot be swept under the theoretical rug. Barring trauma or other insult, g controls the level and efficiency of cognitive processing (although almost certainly in interaction with a number of other factors) any individual is able to undertake. A careful review of the literature will find g to have many pragmatic aspects, as well. For example, Travers (1977), Luborsky, Auerbach, Chandler, Cohen, and Bachrach (1971), and Lezak (1995) point out that, in study after study of psychotherapy-outcome research, the general intellectual level (tantamount to g) of the individual turns out to be the best, or one of the best, predictors of success. The premorbid level of general intellectual functioning is also the best predictor of rehabilitative success of patients with acute brain trauma and a number of neurological diseases (Golden, 1978).

What is the nature of g? Undoubtedly, g is determined by the particular anatomy, physiology, and chemistry of the brain of the individual (Brand, 1996; Vernon, 1998). Jensen's (1978) research has given some revitalization to the study of g in psychology. The study of the relationship between cortical-evoked potentials and intelligence gives rise to a physiological determination of g. Likewise, Harmony (1997) asserted that measuring particular physiological variables is useful in determining cognitive activity, that is, g. Harmony (1997) and Languis and Miller (1992) reviewed several studies utilizing electroencephalogram measures, auditory evoked responses, visual evoked responses, and event-related potentials, and lent her support to using physiological measures in order to determine some aspect of cognitive ability (or disability).

Jensen's research on reaction times and stimulus complexity and the study of evoked potentials (e.g., Evans, 1977; Vernon 1983, 1998) leads one to define g in much the same terms as used by Head (1926) to describe psychological vigilance. According to Head, psychological vigilance refers to the general physiological efficiency of the central nervous system. The term *psychological vigilance* has taken on a variety of other meanings and connotations. However, Head's original conceptualization seems to accurately describe what is referred to here as *g*. Ardila (1999) maintained that Head's version of psychological vigilance continues to be a viable definition in current research on reaction time and processing speed, to determine cognitive ability.

Any comprehensive theory of intelligence must not only take into account the method and components of information processing in the brain, but must also account for the ability to use the available information-processing strategies to their fullest potential. Ignoring *g* and its basic properties can easily lead one into such simplistic statements as Bijou's (1966) claim that there is no mental retardation, only retarded behavior. This directly implies that *g* can be "taught" through behavior-modification techniques. We have yet to see any individual, functioning in the mild, moderate, or lower ranges of *g*, become a doctor, lawyer, or other successful professional, even with the most rigorous behavior-modification program. *g* cannot be dismissed with such simplistic statements.

DISCUSSION: BIOLOGICAL AND PSYCHOLOGICAL INTELLIGENCE

Are there separate, independent mechanisms of biological and psychological intelligence? Does *g* represent a biological intelligence based in the physiology of the brain, while psychological intelligence is represented by the executive, coordinating, and planning functions of the frontal lobes in interaction with Luria's first two blocks of the brain? The former type of intelligence would seem necessarily to be much more genetically based, although certainly dependent to some extent on the nurturance of the environment pre- and postnatally, such as is height. Psychological intelligence would be under much greater environmental control, although undoubtedly some genetic template is present, giving guidance to the functional development of the various anatomical structures of the brain.

Biological intelligence, in referring to higher-order thought, represents the general physiological efficiency of the brain. Psychological intelligence is the mechanism, or process, through which intelligence is manifest. Biological intelligence is the principal determinant of an individual's level of function, and psychological intelligence is the principal determinant of an individual's method of performing intelligent functions. The theories of Halstead, Luria, Das and colleagues, and others referred to in this chapter, are all, in reality, theories of psychological intelligence. Their further elaboration will continue to greatly enhance our understanding of how the human brain carries out higher-order thinking. Discovering and elaborating the mechanisms of biological intelligence remains in a primitive state and will likely fall to the neuropsychologist and behavioral neurochemist for resolution.

The notions of biological and psychological intelligence briefly described here are now several decades old and still in need of further elaboration. New approaches to dominance, such as hemisphericity or habitual modes of information processing, are contributing to a rich investigation of early learning in school and of school-related subjects. The reconceptualization of dominance continues to explode into new areas of research in the quest for the aptitude–treatment interaction. Is right- or left-hemisphericity related to performance in particular subject areas? Can accurate measures of hemisphericity be used to predict response to particular curriculum methods? A number of logical connections exist that are amenable to direct experimental investigation. It is not unlikely that an overdependence on right-hemisphere processing will be found to be associated with difficulties in early reading acquisition.

Clearly, level of function, as denoted by g, must be included in any comprehensive theory of human intellect. Psychological intelligence appears to be best described at present by Luria's model of the three blocks of the brain, as elaborated upon by Das et al. (1979), and modified here to account for lateralization of processing in the brain. As new, better, comprehensive measures of psychological intelligence are developed, as they have been in the past two decades (e.g., Kaufman & Kaufman, 1983; Naglieri & Das, 1996), our understanding of brain function will increase and our theories will need modification. However, understanding will come most readily through the use of new techniques of measurement, based on current theories of intelligence. Perhaps, through such methods, the neuropsychologist, the developmentalist, and the psychometrician, all with interests in the origins and development of intelligence, will be able to coalesce their now-divergent views of intelligence. Certainly, each has a unique, significant view to contribute to our ultimate understanding of how the human brain processes information.

REFERENCES

Allen, M. (1983). Models of hemispheric specialization. *Psychological Bulletin, 93,* 73–104.

Aluja-Fabregat, A., Colom, R., Abad, F., & Juan-Espinosa, M. (2000). Sex differences in general intelligence defined as *g* among young adolescents. *Personality and Individual Differences, 28,* 813–820.

Anderson, M., Kaufman, A. S., & Kaufman, N. L. (1976). Use of the WISC-R with a learning disabled population: Some diagnostic implications. *Psychology in the Schools, 13,* 381–386.

Annett, M. (1972). The distribution of manual asymetry. *British Journal of Psychology, 63,* 343–358.

Ardila, A. (1999). A neuropsychological approach to intelligence. *Neuropsychology Review, 9,* 117–136.

Ashman, A. F., & Das, J. P. (1980). Relation between planning and simultaneous-successive processing. *Perceptual and Motor Skills, 51,* 371–382.

Balow, I. H. (1963). Lateral dominance characteristics and reading achievement in the first grade. *Journal of Psychology, 55,* 323–328.

Balow, I. H., & Balow, B. (1964). Lateral dominance and reading achievement in second grade. *American Educational Research Journal, 1,* 139–143.

Bauer, R. W., & Wepman, J. M. (1955). Lateralization of cerebral function. *Journal of Speech and Hearing Disorders, 20,* 171–177.

Beaumont, J. G. (1997). Future research directions in laterality. *Neuropsychology Review, 7,* 107–126.

Beaumont, J. G., Young, A. W., & McManus, I. C. (1984). Hemisphericity: A critical review. *Cognitive Neuropsychology, 1,* 191–212.

Bell, T. K. (1990). Rapid sequential processing in dyslexic and ordinary readers. *Perceptual and Motor Skills, 71,* 1155–1159.

Belmont, C., & Birch, H. (1963). Lateral dominance, lateral awareness, and reading disability. *Child Development, 34,* 257–270.

Benton, A. L. (1955). Right-left discrimination and finger localization in defective children. *Archives of Neurology and Psychiatry, 74,* 583–589.

Benton, A. L. (1959). *Right–left discrimination and finger localization development and pathology.* New York: Hoeber Medical Division, Harper & Row.

Ben-Yishay, Y. (2000). Postacute neuropsychological rehabilitation: A holistic perspective. In A. C. Christensen & B. P. Uzzell (Eds.), *International handbook of neuropsychological rehabilitation* (pp. 127–136). New York: Kluwer Academic/Plenum.

Bever, T. G. (1975). Cerebral asymmetries in humans are due to the differentiation of two incompatible processes: Holistic and analytic. In D. Aaronson & R. Reiber (Eds.), *Developmental psycholinguistics and communication disorders.* New York: New York Academy of Sciences.

Bever, T. G., & Chiarello, R. S. (1974). Cerebral dominance in musicians and nonmusicians. *Science, 186,* 537–539.

Bijou, S. W. (1966). A functional analysis of retarded development. *International review of mental retardation, 1,* 1–19.

Bogen, J. E., DeZure, R., TenHouten, W., & Marsh, J. (1972). The other side of the brain IV: The A/P ratio. *Bulletin of the Los Angeles Neurological Society, 37,* 49–61.

Bloom, A. S. (2000). When academic performance is higher than WISC-III IQs, is the sequential-processing model of intelligence the preferred approach to assessment? *Perceptual and Motor Skills, 90,* 883–884.

Bogen, J. E. (1969). The other side of the brain: Parts I, II, and III. *Bulletin of the Los Angeles Neurological Society, 34,* 73–105, 135–162, 191–203.

Boklage, C. E. (1978). On cellular mechanisms for heritability transmitting structural information. *The Behavioral and Brain Sciences, 2,* 282–286.

Borod, J. C., Caron, H. S., & Koff, E. (1981). Asymmetry of facial expression related to handedness, footedness, and eyedness: A quantitative study. *Cortex, 17,* 381–390.

Borod, J. C., & Goodglass, H. (1980). Lateralization of linguistic and melodic processing with age. *Neuropsychologia, 18,* 79–83.

Bradshaw, J. G., & Nettleton, N. C. (1981). The nature of hemispheric specialization in man. *The Behavioral and Brain Sciences, 4,* 51–91.

Bradshaw-McAnulty, G., Hicks, R. E., & Kinsbourne, M. (1984). Pathological left-handedness and familial sinistrality in relation to degree of mental retardation. *Brain and Cognition, 3,* 349–356.

Braga, L. W., & Campos da Paz, A., Jr. (2000). Neuropsychological pediatric rehabilitation. In A. C. Christensen & B. P. Uzzell (Eds.), *International handbook of neuropsychological rehabilitation* (pp. 283–295). New York: Kluwer Academic/Plenum.

Brand, C. (1996). Doing something about *g. Intelligence, 22,* 311–326.

Broca, P. (1861). Remarques sur le siége de la faculté du language articulé, suivies d'une observation d'aphémie (perte de la parole). *Bulletins do la Societé Anatomique, 6,* 330–357.

Broca, P. (1863). Localisation des functions cérébrales. Siége du language articulé. *Bulletins de la Societé d'Anthropologie de Paris, 4,* 200–203.

Broshek, D. K., & Barth, J. T. (2000). The Halstead-Reitan Neuropsychological Test Battery. In G. Groth-Marnat (Ed.), *Neuropsychological assessment in clinical practice: A guide to test interpretation and integration* (pp. 223–262). New York: John Wiley.

Brown, E. R., & Taylor, P. (1988). Handedness, footedness, and eyedness. *Perceptual and Motor Skills, 66,* 183–186.

Brysbaert, M. (1994). Lateral preferences and visual field asymmetries: Appearances may have been overstated. *Cortex, 30,* 413–429.

Buzzard, T. (1882). *Clinical lectures on diseases of the nervous system.* London: Churchill.

Capruso, D. X., Hamsher, K. D., & Benton, A. L. (1995). Assessment of visuocognitive processes. In R. L. Mapou & J. Spector (Eds.), *Clinical neuropsychological assessment: A cognitive approach* (pp. 137–183). New York: Plenum Press.

Carmen, A., & Nachson, I. (1973). Ear asymmetry in perception of emotional nonverbal stimuli. *Acta Psychologica, 37,* 351–357.

Christensen, A. (2000). Neuropsychological postacute rehabilitation. In A. C. Christensen & B. P. Uzzell (Eds.), *International handbook of neuropsychological rehabilitation* (pp. 151–163). New York: Kluwer Academic/Plenum.

Coleman, R. I., & Deutsch, C. P. (1964). Lateral dominance and right-left discrimination: A comparison of normal and retarded readers. *Perceptual and Motor Skills, 19,* 43–50.

Corballis, M. C., & Beale, I. L. (1976). *The psychology of left and right.* Hillsdale, NJ: Lawrence Erlbaum.

Coren, S. (1993). The lateral preference inventory for measurement of handedness, footedness, eyedness, and earedness: Norms for young adults. *Bulletin of the Psychonomic Society, 31,* 1–3.

Coren, S., & Porac, C. (1982). Lateral preference and cognitive skills: An indirect test. *Perceptual and Motor Skills, 54,* 787–792.

Cornish, R. D. (1970). Effects of neurological training on psychomotor abilities of kindergarten children. *Journal of Experimental Education, 39,* 15–19.

Crowell, D., Jones, J., Kapunai, L., & Nakagawa, J. (1973). Unilateral cortical activity in newborn humans. *Science, 180,* 205–208.

Cumming, C. E., & Rodda, M. (1985). The effects of auditory deprivation on successive processing. *Canadian Journal of Behavioural Science, 17,* 232–245.

Cummins, J., & Das, J. P. (1977). Cognitive processing and reading difficulties: A framework for research. *Alberta Journal of Educational Research, 23,* 245–256.

Daleo, D. V., Lopez, B. R., Cole, J. C., Kaufman, A. S., Kaufman, N. L., Newcomer, B. L., et al. (1999). K-ABC simultaneous processing, Das nonverbal reasoning, and Horn's expanded fluid-crystallized theory. *Psychological Reports, 84,* 563–574.

Daniels-Zide, E., & Ben-Yishay, Y. (2000). Therapeutic milieu day program. In A. C. Christensen & B. P. Uzzell (Eds.), *International handbook of neuropsychological rehabilitation* (pp. 183–194). New York: Kluwer Academic/Plenum.

Das, J. P., Kirby, J. R., & Jarman, R. F. (1979). *Simultaneous and successive cognitive processes.* New York: Academic Press.

Dean, R. S. (1979). Cerebral laterality and verbal-performance discrepancies in intelligence. *Journal of School Psychology, 17,* 145–150.

Dean, R. S. (1984). Functional lateralization of the brain. *Journal of Special Education, 18,* 239–252.

Dean, R. S., & Kulhavy, R. W. (1977). *Dean-Kulhavy lateral preference schedule.* Tempe, AZ: Arizona State University.

Dean, R. S., & Reynolds, C. R. (1997). Cognitive processing and self-report of lateral preference. *Neuropsychology Review, 7,* 127–142.

Deikman, A. J. (1971). Bimodal consciousness. *Archives of General Psychiatry, 25,* 481–489.

Delacato, C. H. (1959). *The treatment and prevention of reading problems: The neuropsychological approach.* Springfield, IL: Charles C Thomas.

Delacato, C. H. (1963). *The diagnosis and treatment of speech and reading problems.* Springfield, IL: Charles C Thomas.

Delacato, C. H. (1966). *Neurological organization and reading.* Springfield, IL: Charles C Thomas.

Detterman, D. K. (1982). Does "g" exist? *Intelligence, 6,* 99–108.

Dewson, J. H. (1977). Preliminary evidence of hemispheric asymmetry of auditory function in monkeys. In S. Harnad, R. Doty, L. Goldstein, J. Jaynes, & G. Krauthamer (Eds.), *Lateralization in the nervous system.* New York: Academic Press.

DiNuovo, S. F., & Buono, S. (1997). Laterality and handedness in mentally retarded subjects. *Perceptual and Motor Skills, 85,* 1229–1230.

Eisenmann, R. (1993). Some problems in the assessment of handedness: Comment on Coren (1993). *Bulletin of the Psychonomic Society, 31,* 285–286.

Elias, M. F., & Kinsbourne, M. (1974). Age and sex differences in the processing of verbal and nonverbal stimuli. *Journal of Gerontology, 29,* 162–171.

Evans, J. R. (1977). Evoked potentials and learning disabilities. In L. Tarnopol & M. Tarnopol (Eds.), *Brain function and reading disabilities.* Baltimore: University Park Press.

Faust, M., Kravetz, S., & Babkoff, H. (1993). Hemisphericity and top-down processing of language. *Brain and Language, 44,* 1–18.

Finger, S., & Roe, D. (1999). Does Gustave Dax deserve to be forgotten? The temporal lobe theory and other contributions of an overlooked figure in the history of language and cerebral dominance. *Brain and Language, 69,* 16–30.

Fuller, J. L. (1978). If genes are not right handed, what is? *The Behavioral and Brain Sciences, 2,* 295.

Galin, D. (1974). Implications for psychiatry of left and right cerebral specialization. *Archives of General Psychiatry, 31,* 78–82.

Gardiner, M. F. (1987). General temporal-sequential processing capability required for reading: New evidence from adults with specific reading difficulties. *Annals of the New York Academy of Sciences, 504,* 283–285.

Gazzaniga, M. S. (1970). *The bisected brain.* New York: Appleton.

Gazzaniga, M. S. (1971). Changing hemisphere dominance by change reward probabilities in split-brain monkeys. *Experimental Neurology, 33,* 412–419.

Gazzaniga, M. S. (1974). Cerebral dominance viewed as a decision system. In S. Dimond & J. Beaumont (Eds.), *Hemisphere functions in the human brain.* London: Halstead Press.

Gazzaniga, M. S. (1975, May). Recent research on hemispheric lateralization of the human brain: Review of the split-brain. *UCLA Educator,* 9–12.

Geffen, G. (1978). Human laterality: Cerebral dominance and handedness. *The Behavioral and Brain Sciences, 2,* 295–296.

Geschwind, N. (1978). Pathological right-handedness. *The Behavioral and Brain Sciences, 2,* 296.

Giannitrapani, D. (1967). Developing concepts of lateralization of cerebral functions. *Cortex, 3,* 353–370.

Glass, G. V., & Robbins, M. P. (1967). A critique of experiments on the role of neurological organization in reading performance. *Reading Research Quarterly, 3,* 5–52.

Golden, C. J. (1978). *Diagnosis and rehabilitation in clinical neuropsychology.* Springfield, IL: Charles C Thomas.

Golden, C. J. (1987). *Luria-Nebraska Neuropsychological Battery Children's Revision.* Los Angeles: Western Psychological Services.

Golden, C. J., Ariel, R. N., McKay, S. E., Wilkening, G. N., Wolf, B. A., & MacInnes, W. D. (1982). The Luria-Nebraska Neuropsychological Battery: Theoretical orientation and comment. *Journal of Consulting and Clinical Psychology, 50,* 291–300.

Golden, C. J., Espe-Pfeifer, P., & Wachsler-Felder, J. (2000). *Neuropsychological interpretations of objective psychological tests.* New York: Kluwer Academic/Plenum.

Golden, C. J., Purisch, A. D., & Hammeke, T. A. (1979). *The Luria-Nebraska neuropsychological test battery: A manual for clinical and experimental uses.* Lincoln: The University of Nebraska Press.

Gorynia, I., & Egenter, D. (2000). Intermanual coordination in relation to handedness, familial sinistrality and lateral preferences. *Cortex, 36,* 1–18.

Grimshaw, G. M. (1998). Integration and interference in the cerebral hemispheres: Relations with hemispheric specialization. *Brain and Cognition, 36,* 108–127.

Grouios, G., Sakadami, N., Poderi, A., & Alevriadou, A. (1999). Excess of non-right handedness among individuals with intellectual disability: Experimental evidence and possible explanations. *Journal of Intellectual Disability Research, 43,* 306–313.

Gunnison, J., Kaufman, N. L., & Kaufman, A. S. (1982). Reading remediation based on sequential and simultaneous processing. *Academic Therapy, 17,* 297–306.

Hall, C. W., Gregory, G., Billinger, E., & Fisher, T. (1988). Field independence and simultaneous processing in preschool children. *Perceptual and Motor Skills, 66,* 891–897.

Halstead, W. C. (1947). *Brain and intelligence.* Chicago: University of Chicago Press.

Hardyck, C., & Petrinovich, L. F. (1977). Left-handedness. *Psychological Bulletin, 84,* 385–404.

Hardyck, C., Petrinovich, L. F., & Goldman, R. D. (1976). Left-handedness and cognitive deficit. *Cortex, 12,* 266–279.

Harmony, T. (1997). Psychophysiological evaluation of neuropsychological disorders in children. In C. R. Reynolds & E. Fletcher-Janzen (Eds.), *Handbook of clinical child neuropsychology* (2nd ed.) (pp. 356–370). New York: Plenum Press.

Harnad, S., Doty, R. W., Goldstein, L., Jaynes, J., & Krauthamer, G. (Eds.). (1977). *Lateralization in the nervous system.* New York: Academic Press.

Harris, L. J. (1980). Left-handedness: Early theories, facts, and fancies. In J. Herron (Ed.), *Neuropsychology of left-handedness.* New York: Academic Press.

Harris, L. J. (1990). Cultural influences on handedness: Historical and contemporary theory and evidence. In S. Coren (Ed.), *Left-handedness: Behavioral implications and anomalies* (pp. 195–258). Amsterdam, The Netherlands: Elsevier Science.

Hartlage, L. C., & Gage, R. (1997). Unimanual performance as a measure of laterality. *Neuropsychology Review, 7,* 143–156.

Head, H. (1926). *Aphasia and kindred disorders of speech: Vol. 1.* New York: MacMillan.

Held, R. (1965). Plasticity in sensory-motor systems. *Scientific American, 213,* 84–94.

Held, R., & Bossom, J. (1961). Neonatal deprivation and adult rearrangement: Complementary techniques for analyzing plastic sensory-motor coordination. *Journal of Comparative and Physiological Psychology, 54,* 33–37.

Held, R., & Freedman, J. (1963). Plasticity in human sensory-motor control. *Science, 142,* 455–462.

Held, R., & Hein, A. (1963). Movement-produced stimulation in the development of visually guided behavior. *Journal of Comparative and Physiological Psychology, 56,* 872–876.

Herron, J. (Ed.). (1980). *Neuropsychology of left-handedness.* New York: Academic Press.

Hevern, V. W. (1980). Recent validity studies of the Halstead-Reitan approach to clinical neuropsychological assessment: A critical review. *Clinical Neuropsychology, 2,* 49–61.

Hillerich, R. L. (1964). Eye-hand dominance and reading achievement. *American Educational Research Journal, 1,* 121–126.

Hoosain, R. (1990). Left handedness and handedness switch amongst the Chinese. *Cortex, 26,* 451–454.

Hunt, D. (1980). Intentional-incidental learning and simultaneous-successive processing. *Canadian Journal of Behavioural Science, 12,* 373–383.

Hunt, J. McV. (1961). *Intelligence and experience.* New York: Ronald Press.

Jensen, A. R. (1978, September). *"g": Outmoded concept or unconquered frontier?* Invited address at the annual meeting of the American Psychological Association, New York.

Jensen, A. R. (1997). Adoption data and two g-related hypotheses. *Intelligence, 25,* 1–6.

Jensen, A. R. (1998). *The g factor: The science of mental ability.* Westport, CT: Praeger.

Johnson, J. D., & Gazzaniga, M. S. (1971a). Some effects of non-reinforcement in split-brain monkeys. *Physiology and Behavior, 6,* 703–706.

Johnson, J. D., & Gazzaniga, M. S. (1971b). Reversal behavior in split-brain monkeys. *Physiology and Behavior, 6,* 706–709.

Joseph, R. (1996). *Neuropsychiatry, neuropsychology, and clinical neuroscience: Emotion, evolution, cognition, language, memory, brain damage, and abnormal behavior* (2nd ed.). Baltimore, MD: Williams & Wilkins.

Joynt, R. J., & Benton, A. L. (1964). The memoir of Marc Dax on aphasia. *Neurology, Minneapolis, 14,* 851–854.

Kamphaus, R. W. (1993). *Clinical assessment of children's intelligence.* Boston: Allyn and Bacon.

Kamphaus, R. W., & Reynolds, C. R. (1984). Development and structure of the Kaufman Assessment Battery for Children. *Journal of Special Education, 18,* 213–228.

Kamphaus, R. W., & Reynolds, C. R. (1987). *Clinical and research applications of the K-ABC.* Circle Pines, MN: American Guidance Service.

Kane, H. D. (2000). A secular decline in Spearman's g: Evidence from the WAIS, WAIS-R and WAIS-III. *Personality and Individual Differences, 29,* 561–566.

Kaufman, A. S. (1979a). *Intelligent testing with the WISC-R.* New York: Wiley-Interscience.

Kaufman, A. S. (1979b). Cerebral specialization and intelligence testing. *Journal of Research and Development in Education, 12,* 96–107.

Kaufman, A. S. (1994). *Intelligent testing with the WISC-III.* New York: John Wiley.

Kaufman, A. S., & Kaufman, N. L. (1983). *Administration and scoring manual for the Kaufman Assessment Battery for Children.* Circle Pines, MN: American Guidance Service.

Kinsbourne, M. (1975). The ontogeny of cerebral dominance. In A. Aaronson & R. Reiber (Eds.), *Developmental psycholinguistics and communication disorders.* New York: New York Academy of Sciences.

Kinsbourne, M. (1978a). Biological determinants of functional bisymmetry an asymmetry. In M. Kinsbourne (Ed.), *Asymmetrical function of the brain* (pp. 163–189). Cambridge: Cambridge University Press.

Kinsbourne, M. (1978b). Evolution of language in relation to lateral action. In M. Kinsbourne (Ed.), *Asymmetrical function of the brain* (pp. 263–289). Cambridge: Cambridge University Press.

Kinsbourne, M. (1997). Mechanisms and development of cerebral lateralization in children. In C. R. Reynolds & E. Fletcher-Janzen (Eds.), *Handbook of clinical child neuropsychology* (2nd ed.) (pp. 102–119). New York: Plenum Press.

Kirby, J. R., & Das, J. P. (1977). Reading achievement, IQ, and simultaneous-successive processing. *Journal of Educational Psychology, 69,* 564–570.

Klich, L. Z. (1987). A focal review of research on the Luria-Das model of cognitive processing. In S. H. Irvine & S. E. Newstead (Eds.), *Intelligence and cognition: Contemporary frames of reference* (pp. 313–347). Dordrecht, The Netherlands: Martinus Nijhoff.

Kolb, B., & Fantie, B. (1997). Development of the child's brain and behavior. In C. R. Reynolds & E. Fletcher-Janzen (Eds.), *Handbook of clinical child neuropsychology* (2nd ed.) (pp. 17–41). New York: Plenum Press.

Kwantes, P. J., & Mewhort, D. J. K. (1999). Evidence for sequential processing in visual word recognition. *Journal of Experimental Psychology: Human Perception and Performance, 25,* 376–381.

Languis, M. L., & Miller, D. C. (1992). Luria's theory of brain functioning: A model for research in cognitive psychophysiology. *Educational Psychologist, 27,* 493–511.

LeMay, M. (1976). Morphological cerebral asymmetries of modern man, fossil man, and nonhuman primate. *Annals of the New York Academy of Sciences, 280,* 349–366.

Levy, J., & Nagylaki, T. (1972). A model for the genetics of handedness. *Genetics, 72,* 117–128.

Lewis, R. S., & Harris, L. J. (1990). Handedness, sex, and spatial ability. In S. Coren (Ed.), *Left-handedness: Behavioral implications and anomalies* (pp. 319–341). Amsterdam, The Netherlands: Elsevier Science.

Lezak, M. D. (1995). *Neuropsychological assessment* (3rd ed.). New York: Oxford University Press.

Luborsky, L., Auerbach, A. H., Chandler, M., Cohen, J., & Bachrach, H. M. (1971). Factors influencing the outcome of psychotherapy: A review of quantitative research. *Psychological Bulletin, 75,* 145–185.

Luria, A. R. (1961). *The role of speech in the regulation of normal and abnormal behavior.* Oxford, England: Pergamon Press.

Luria, A. R. (1964). Neuropsychology in the local diagnosis of brain damage. *Cortex, 1,* 3–18.

Luria, A. R. (1966). *Higher cortical functions in man.* New York: Basic Books.

Luria, A. R. (1969, September). *Cerebral organization of conscious acts: A frontal lobe function.* Speech to the 19th International Congress of Psychology, London, England.

Luria, A. R. (1970). The functional organization of the brain. *Scientific American, 222,* 66–78.

Luria, A. R. (1973). *The working brain.* London: Penguin.

Majovski, L. V. (1984). The K-ABC: Theory and applications for child neuropsychological assessment and research. *Journal of Special Education, 18,* 257–268.

Mandal, M. S., Pandey, G., Singh, S. K., & Asthana, H. S. (1992). Degree of asymmetry in lateral preferences: Eye, foot, ear. *Journal of Psychology, 126,* 155–162.

Mateer, C. A., Rapport, R. L., & Kettrick, C. (1984). Cerebral organization of oral and signed language responses: Case study evidence from amytal and cortical stimulation studies. *Brain and Language, 21,* 123–135.

McCallum, R. S., & Merritt, F. M. (1983). Simultaneous-successive processing among college students. *Journal of Psychoeducational Assessment, 1,* 85–93.

McKeever, W. F. (1990). Familial sinistrality and cerebral organization. In S. Coren (Ed.), *Left-handedness: Behavioral implications and anomalies* (pp. 373–412). Amsterdam, The Netherlands: Elsevier Science.

Meikamp, J. (2001). Das Naglieri Cognitive Assessment System. In J. C. Impara & B. S. Plake (Eds.), *The fourteenth mental measurements yearbook* (pp. 269–271). Lincoln, NE: The Buros Institute of Mental Measurements.

Merritt, F. M., & McCallum, R. S. (1984). The relationship between simultaneous–successive processing and academic achievement. *Alberta Journal of Educational Research, 30,* 126–132.

Metalis, S. A., & Niemiec, A. J. (1984). Assessment of eye dominance through response time. *Perceptual and Motor Skills, 59,* 539–544.

Milner, B., Branch, C., & Rasmussen, T. (1964). Observations on cerebral dominance. In A. V. S. de Rueck & M. O'Conner (Eds.), *Ciba Foundation Symposium on disorders of language.* London: Churchill.

Mitsuda, M. (1991). Successive processing abilities and question aids as determinants of solving arithmetic word problems in mentally handicapped students. *Japanese Psychological Research, 33,* 115–125.

Morgan, M. J., & Corballis, M. C. (1978). On the biological basis of human laterality: II. The mechanisms of inheritance. *The Behavioral and Brain Sciences, 2,* 270–277.

Mulaik, S. A. (1972). *The foundations of factor analysis.* New York: McGraw-Hill.

Naglieri, J. A. (1997). Planning, attention, simultaneous, and successive theory and the Cognitive Assessment System: A new theory-based measure of intelligence. In D. P. Flanagan, J. L. Genshaft, & P. L. Harrison (Eds.), *Contemporary intellectual assessment: Theories, tests, and issues* (pp. 247–267). New York: The Guilford Press.

Naglieri, J. A., & Das, J. P. (1988). Planning-Arousal-Simultaneous-Successive (PASS): A model for assessment. *Journal of School Psychology, 26,* 35–48.

Naglieri, J. A., & Das, J. P. (1990). Planning, attention, simultaneous, and successive (PASS) cognitive processes as a model for intelligence. *Journal of Psychoeducational Assessment, 8,* 303–337.

Naglieri, J. A., & Das, J. P. (1996). *Das Naglieri Cognitive Assessment System.* Chicago: Riverside.

Naglieri, J. A., Kamphaus, R. W., & Kaufman, A. S. (1983). The Luria-Das simultaneous-successive model applied to the WISC-R. *Journal of Psychoeducational Assessment, 1,* 25–34.

Naylor, H. (1980). Reading disability and lateral asymmetry: An information processing analysis. *Psychological Bulletin, 87,* 531–545.

Newcombe, F., & Ratcliff, G. (1973). Handedness, speech lateralization and ability. *Neuropsychologia, 11,* 399–407.

Newell, D., & Rugel, R. P. (1981). Hemispheric specialization in normal and disabled readers. *Journal of Learning Disabilities, 14,* 296–298.

Noble, J. (1968). Paradoxical interocular transfer of mirror-image discrimination in the optic chiasm sectioned monkey. *Brain Research, 10,* 127–151.

Nussbaum, N. L., & Bigler, E. D. (1997). Halstead-Reitan neuropsychological test batteries for children. In C. R. Reynolds & E. Fletcher-Janzen (Eds.), *Handbook of clinical child neuropsychology* (2nd ed.) (pp. 219–236). New York: Plenum Press.

Obrzut, J. E., & Obrzut, A. (1982). Neuropsychological perspectives in pupil services: Practical application of Luria's model. *Journal of Research and Development in Education, 15,* 38–47.

Obrzut, J. E., Obrzut, A., Bryden, M. P., & Bartels, S. G. (1985). Information processing and speech lateralization in learning-disabled children. *Brain and Language, 25,* 87–101.

O'Donnell, D. A., & Eisenson, J. (1969). Delacato training for reading achievement and visual-motor integration. *Journal of Learning Disabilities, 2,* 441–447.

Ornstein, R., Johnstone, J., Herron, J., & Swencionis, C. (1980). Differential right hemisphere engagement in visuospatial tasks. *Neuropsychologia, 18,* 49–64.

Orton, S. T. (1925). "Word-blindedness" in school children. *Archives of Neurology and Psychiatry, 14,* 581.

Orton, S. T. (1928). A physiological theory of reading disability and stuttering in children. *New England Journal of Medicine, 199,* 1046–1052.

Orton, S. T. (1931). Special disability in reading. *Bulletin of the Neurological Institute of New York, 1,* 159–162.

Orton, S. T. (1937). *Reading, writing, and speech problems in children.* New York: Norton.

Osburn, D. M., & Klingsporn, M. J. (1998). Consistency of performance on eyedeness tasks. *British Journal of Psychology, 89,* 27–27.

Pallier, G., Roberts, R. D., & Stankov, L. (2000). Biological versus psychometric intelligence: Halstead's (1947) distinction revisited. *Archives of Clinical Neuropsychology, 15,* 205–226.

Paquette, C., Tosoni, C., Lassonde, M., & Peretz, I. (1996). Atypical hemispheric specialization in intellectual deficiency. *Brain and Language, 52,* 474–483.

Parsons, O. A., & Prigatano, G. P. (1978). Methodological considerations in clinical neuropsychological research. *Journal of Consulting and Clinical Psychology, 46,* 608–619.

Penfield, W., & Roberts, L. (1959). *Speech and brain mechanisms.* Princeton: Princeton University Press.

Peters, M., & Durding, B. M. (1978). Handedness measured by finger tapping: A continuous variable. *Canadian Journal of Psychology, 32,* 257–261.

Piccirilli, M., D'Alessandro, P., Mazzi, P., Sciarma, T., & Testa, A. (1991). Cerebral organization for language in Down's Syndrome patients. *Cortex, 27,* 41–47.

Polemikos, N., & Papaeliou, C. (2000). Sidedness preference as an index of organization of laterality. *Perceptual and Motor Skills, 91,* 1083–1090.

Porac, C., Rees, L., & Buller, T. (1990). Switching hands: A place for left hand use in a right hand world. In S. Coren (Ed.), *Left-handedness: Behavioral implications and anomalies* (pp. 259–290). Amsterdam, The Netherlands: Elsevier Science.

Posner, M. I., Peterson, S. E., Fox, P. T., & Raichle, M. E. (1988). Localization of cognitive operations in the human brain. *Science, 240,* 1627–1231.

Pribam, K. H. (1971). *Languages of the brain.* Englewood Cliffs, NJ: Prentice-Hall.

Prigatano, G. P. (2000). A brief overview of four principles of neuropsychological rehabilitation. In A. C. Christensen & B. P. Uzzell (Eds.), *International handbook of neuropsychological rehabilitation* (pp. 115–125). New York: Kluwer Academic/Plenum.

Reed, J. (1985). The contributions of Ward Halstead, Ralph Reitan and their associates. *International Journal of Neuroscience, 25,* 289–293.

Reiβ, M., & Reiβ, G. (2000). The dominant ear. *Perceptual and Motor Skills, 91,* 53–54.

Reitan, R. M. (1955). Certain differential effects of left and right cerebral lesions in human adults. *Journal of Comparative and Physiological Psychology, 48,* 474–477.

Reitan, R. M. (1964a). Psychological deficits resulting from cerebral lesions in man. In J. M. Warren & K. Akert (Eds.), *The frontal granular cortex and behavior.* New York: McGraw-Hill.

Reitan, R. M. (1964b). Relationships between neurological and psychological variables and their implications for reading instruction. In K. A. Robinson (Ed.), *Meeting individual differences in reading.* Chicago: University of Chicago Press.

Reitan, R. M. (1966). A research program on the psychological effects of brain lesions in human beings. *International review of research in mental retardation, 1,* 153–218.

Reitan, R. M. (1975). Assessment of brain-behavior relationships. In P. McReynolds (Ed.), *Advances in psychological assessment: Vol. III.* San Francisco: Jossey-Bass.

Reitan, R. M. (1994). Ward Halstead's contributions to neuropsychology and the Halstead-Reitan Neuropsychological Test Battery. *Journal of Clinical Psychology, 50,* 47–69.

Reitan, R. M., & Davison, L. A. (1974). *Clinical neuropsychology: Current status and applications.* Washington, DC: V. H. Winston.

Reitan, R. M., & Wolfson, D. (1996). Theoretical, methodological, and validational bases of the Halstead-Reitan Neuropsychological Test Battery. In I. Grant & K. M. Adams (Eds.), *Neuropsychological assessment of neuropsychiatric disorders* (2nd ed.) (pp. 3–42). New York: Oxford University Press.

Reynolds, C. R. (1978, April). *Current conceptualizations of hemisphericity.* Colloquium presented to the Department of Educational Psychology, the University of Texas-Austin, Austin, TX.

Reynolds, C. R. (1980, August). *The neuropsychology of intelligence and a reconceptualization of dominance.* Invited address to the Utah State University conference on Brain Research and Teaching, Logan, UT.

Reynolds, C. R. (1981). The neuropsychological basis of intelligence. In G. Hynd & J. Obrzut (Eds.), *Neuropsychological assessment and the school-aged child.* New York: Grune & Stratton.

Reynolds, C. R., & Gutkin, T. B. (1979). Predicting the premorbid intellectual status of children using demographic data. *Clinical Neuropsychology, 1,* 36–38.

Reynolds, C. R., & Gutkin, T. B. (1980, September). *Intellectual performance of Blacks and Whites matched on four demographic variables: A multivariate analysis.* Paper presented at the annual meeting of the American Psychological Association, Montreal.

Reynolds, C. R., Hartlage, L. C., & Haak, R. (1980, September). *Lateral preference as determined by neuropsychological performance and aptitude/achievement discrepancies.* Paper presented at the annual meeting of the American Psychological Association, Montreal.

Reynolds, C. R., Kamphaus, R. W., Rosenthal, B. L., & Hiemenz, J. R. (1997). Applications of the Kaufman Assessment Battery for Children (K-ABC) in neuropsychological assessment. In C. R. Reynolds & E. Fletcher-Janzen (Eds.), *Handbook of clinical child neuropsychology* (2nd ed.) (pp. 252–269). New York: Plenum Press.

Reynolds, C. R., & Kaufman, A. S. (1980). Lateral eye movement behavior in children. *Perceptual and Motor Skills, 50,* 1023–1037.

Reynolds, C. R., McBride, R. D., & Gibson, L. J. (1981). Black-white IQ discrepancies may be related to differences in hemisphericity. *Contemporary Educational Psychology, 6,* 180–184.

Reynolds, C. R., & Torrance, E. P. (1978). Perceived changes in styles of learning and thinking (hemisphericity) through direct and indirect training. *Journal of Creative Behavior, 12,* 247–252.

Rider, R. A., Imwold, C. H., & Griffin, M. (1985). Comparison of hand preference in trainable mentally handicapped and nonhandicapped children. *Perceptual and Motor Skills, 61,* 1280–1282.

Robbins, M. P. (1966). A study of the validity of Delacato's theory of neurological organization. *Exceptional Children, 32,* 517–523.

Robison, S. E., Block, S. S., Boudreaux, J. D., & Flora, R. J. (1999). Hand–eye dominance in a population with mental handicaps: Prevalence and a comparison of methods. *Journal of the American Optometric Association, 70,* 563–570.

Roubinek, D. L., Bell, M. L., & Cates, L. A. (1987). Brain hemispheric preference of intellectually gifted children. *Roeper Review, 10,* 120–122.

Sattler, J. M. (1981). *Assessment of children's intelligence and special abilities.* Boston: Allyn and Bacon.

Satz, P., Strauss, E., & Whitaker, H. (1990). The ontogeny of hemispheric specialization: Some old hypotheses revisited. *Brain and Language, 38,* 596–614.

Saudino, K., & McManus, I. C. (1998). Handedness, footedness, eyedness and earedness in the Colorado Adoption Project. *British Journal of Developmental Psychology, 16,* 167–174.

Schwartz, M. (1990). Left-handedness and prenatal complications. In S. Coren (Ed.), *Left-handedness: Behavioral implications and anomalies* (pp. 75–97). Amsterdam, The Netherlands: Elsevier Science.

Schwartz, G. E., Davidson, R. J., & Maer, F. (1975). Right hemisphere lateralization for emotion in the human brain: Interactions with cognition. *Science, 190,* 286–288.

Segalowitz, S. J., & Gruber, F. A. (Eds.). (1977). *Language development and neurological theory.* New York: Academic Press.

Seth, G. (1973). Eye-hand coordination and handedness: A developmental study of visuo-motor behaviour in infancy. *British Journal of Educational Psychology, 43,* 35–49.

Shure, G. H., & Halstead, W. C. (1959). Cerebral lateralization of individual processes. *Psychological Monographs: General and Applied, 72*(12).

Smith, M. D., Coleman, J. M., Dokecki, P. R., & Davis, E. E. (1977). Intellectual characteristics of school labeled learning disabled children. *Exceptional Children, 43,* 352–257.

Sonnier, I. L. (1992). Hemisphericity as a key to understanding individual differences. In I. L. Sonnier (Ed.), *Hemisphericity as a key to understanding individual differences* (pp. 6–8). Springfield, IL: Charles C Thomas.

Sonnier, I. L., & Goldsmith, J. (1985). The nature of human brain hemispheres: The basis for some individual differences. In I. L. Sonnier (Ed.), *Methods and techniques of holistic education* (pp. 17–25). Springfield, IL: Charles C Thomas.

Spiers, P. A. (1982). The Luria-Nebraska Neuropsychological Battery revisited: A theory in practice or just practicing? *Journal of Consulting and Clinical Psychology, 50,* 301–306.

Sternberg, R. J. (1980, April). *Factor theories of intelligence are allright almost.* Paper presented at the annual meeting of the American Educational Research Association, Boston.

Strauss, E. (1986). Hand, foot, eye and ear preferences and performance on a dichotic listening test. *Cortex, 22,* 475–482.

Swiercinsky, D. P. (1979). Factorial pattern description and comparison of functional abilities in neuropsychological assessment. *Perceptual and Motor Skills, 48,* 231–241.

Tomlinson-Keasy, C., & Clarkson-Smith, L. (1980, February). *What develops in hemispheric specialization?* Paper presented at the annual meeting of the International Neuropsychological Society, San Francisco, CA.

Torrance, E. P., & Reynolds, C. R. (1978). Images of the future of gifted adolescents: Effects of alienation and specialized cerebral functioning. *Gifted Child Quarterly, 22,* 40–54.

Torrance, E. P., Reynolds, C. R., & Riegel, T. R. (1977). Your style of learning and thinking. Forms A and B: Preliminary norms, abbreviated technical notes, scoring keys, and selected references. *Gifted Child Quarterly, 21,* 563–573.

Tous, J. M., Fusté, A., & Vidal, J. (1995). Hemispheric specialization and individual differences in cognitive processing. *Personality and Individual Differences, 19,* 463–470.

Travers, R. M. W. (1977). *Essentials of learning* (4th ed.). New York: MacMillan.

Trexler, L. E. (2000). Empirical support for neuropsychological rehabilitation. In A. C. Christensen & B. P. Uzzell (Eds.), *International handbook of neuropsychological rehabilitation* (pp. 137–150). New York: Kluwer Academic/Plenum.

Tupper, D. E. (1999). Introduction: Alexander Luria's continuing influence on worldwide neuropsychology. *Neuropsychology Review, 9,* 1–5.

Vernon, P. A. (1983). Recent findings on the nature of g. *Journal of Special Education, 17,* 389–400.

Vernon, P. A. (1998). From the cognitive to the biological: A sketch of Arthur Jensen's contributions to the study of g. *Intelligence, 26,* 267–271.

Wachs, M. C., & Harris, M. (1986). Simultaneous and successive processing in university students: Contribution to academic performance. *Journal of Psychoeducational Assessment, 4,* 103–112.

Warren, J. M., & Nonneman, A. J. (1976). The search for cerebral dominance in monkeys. *Annals of the New York Academy of Sciences, 280,* 732–744.

Watters, J. J., & English, L. D. (1995). Children's application of simultaneous and successive processing in inductive and deductive reasoning problems: Implications for developing scientific reasoning skills. *Journal of Research in Science Teaching, 32,* 699–714.

Wheeler, L., & Reitan, R. M. (1962). The presence and laterality of brain damage predicted from responses to a short aphasia screening test. *Perceptual and Motor Skills, 15,* 783–799.

White, M. J. (1969). Laterality differences in perception: A review. *Psychological Bulletin, 72,* 387–405.

Willis, W. G. (1985). Successive and simultaneous processing: A note on interpretation. *Journal of Psychoeducational Assessment, 4,* 343–346.

Wittelson, S. W. (1980). Neuroanatomical asymmetry in left-handers. In J. Herron (Ed.), *Neuropsychology of left-handedness* (pp. 123–147). New York: Academic Press.

Woo, T. L., & Pearson, K. (1927). Dextrality and sinistrality of hand and eye. *Biometrika, 19,* 165–169.

Woodruff, D. S. (1978). Brain activity and development. In P. B. Bates (Ed.), *Life-span development and behavior: Vol. 1* (pp. 69–82). New York: Academic Press.

Woods, B. T. (1980). The restricted effects of right-hemisphere lesions after age one: Wechsler test data. *Neuropsychologia, 18,* 65–70.

Wright, S. K., & Ashman, A. F. (1991). The relationship between meter recognition, rhythmic notation, and information processing competence. *Australian Journal of Psychology, 43,* 139–146.

Yeo, R. A., Gangestad, S. W., & Daniel, W. F. (1993). Hand preference and developmental instability. *Psychobiology, 21,* 161–168.

Zarske, J. A. (1982). Neuropsychological intervention approaches for handicapped children. *Journal of Research and Development in Education, 15,* 66–74.

Zelinski, E. M., & Marsh, G. R. (1976, September). *Age differences in hemispheric processing of verbal and spatial information.* Paper presented at the annual meeting of the American Psychological Association, Washington DC.

Zingale, S. A., & Smith, M. D. (1978). WISC-R patterns for learning disabled children at three SES levels. *Psychology in the Schools, 15,* 199–204.

Chapter 3

Normative Data and Scaling Issues in Neuropsychology

Charles J. Golden

Neuropsychology has recognized, across all of its theoretical orientations, the need to compare performances across tests, in order to identify relationships between performances on different tests, which allow for the isolation of specific deficits. For example, it is well recognized that a test like Block Design (Wechsler, 1997) can be failed because of a wide variety of deficits, which include motor speed, visual skills, spatial skills, planning, and organization. By comparing performance on Block Design to tests of spatial skills without a motor component, as well as to tests of motor skills without a spatial component, the neuropsychologist can begin to identify which specific factor is impaired.

Although the comparison of neuropsychological tests is recognized as an especially valuable method of inferring the presence and type of brain injury that may be present in a client, there are many pitfalls in such comparisons, which can lead to serious errors. These issues are discussed here, along with those integrative procedures we recognize as being the most useful in interpreting a battery of tests. These concerns should be kept in mind when interpreting any extensive test battery.

NORMATIVE POPULATIONS

Age and Education

One of the most substantial pitfalls in the comparison of tests is the use of tests that were normed on different samples. The underlying samples for the scores on different tests vary considerably in many important variables. The most substantial of these variables are age, education, when the norms were collected, where they were collected, and culture, which can dramatically change how a test score is seen.

For example, if Test A is normed on a 50-year-old group with a 10th-grade education, a score by a 30-year-old with 14 years of education, with a moderate brain injury, may appear to be normal. However, if Test B is given, normed on a group with an average age of 24 years with 18 years of education (graduate students), the score is likely to be abnormal. This may lead to the conclusion that the client is more impaired on Test B, when in fact the difference solely results from the differences in the underlying norm groups. The examiner must be aware of such differences for any tests they adopt.

This is primarily an issue with those tests that do not provide age or education norms or corrections. However, even when those norms are presented, they are often only age-corrected or education-corrected. In such a case, some tests may have age groups that do not have comparable educational levels, or other tests may present norms based on education groups with different ages. None of this represents insurmountable problems, but such deviations must be considered before the results of two tests can be compared.

Comparing a test corrected for age and education to one that is not corrected is potentially very harmful. For example, an elderly man with 6 years of education would often receive significantly better scores on a test with age and education corrections. When that result was compared to the same test based on an uncorrected score, one would conclude that the uncorrected test showed a deficit, which was solely caused by the lack of an age and education correction. Although this would be obvious if one was using the same test twice, it is less obvious when different tests are employed. Thus, if we compare the age-, education-, and gender-corrected norms of the Halstead Category Test to uncorrected norms on the Rey figure, we may again get differences that result solely from the scoring procedures, rather than from real neuropsychological findings. This is a common problem when incorrected tests are compared to the Wechsler Intelligence Tests, which are age-corrected.

This may become a critical issue when properly normed tests are compared to modified procedures or qualitative procedures are used without proper normative data. In such cases, the interpretation of the severity of the score is based upon the clinician's judgment, which is biased by that individual's own background and experience, which will differ considerably among neuropsychologists.

Time Frame

Another related issue is when the norms were generated. In general, research has found that norms collected in the 1950s and 1960s are not comparable to those gathered more recently. This appears to have more impact on the more complex cognitive tests, rather than on tests of simple motor performance or simple recognition. When older norms are used, they may substantially overrepresent how "good" a given performance may actually be. This effect can be seen clearly in the Wechsler Intelligence Tests, in which the normative data of the four versions of the test shows increasing normal performance across nearly all areas, even when the items remain essentially unchanged in any major way.

Geography

Where data is collected may also have a substantial impact. If we pick equivalent populations, which we match on age, education, gender, and race, from one high school in Des Moines, Iowa, and one in Bradenton, Florida, we are likely to get different results on a variety of tests in the normal population. Thus, which population we choose to base a test upon will make a difference in what scores are considered normal and those which are considered abnormal. In neuropsychology, the site of data gathering may vary widely by geography (urban, rural, different states, different countries), setting (academic, medical, community), and inclusion and exclusion criteria. It is, at best, unclear whether norms gathered in the United States are appropriate in Great Britain or Australia, and vice versa, despite the fact that tests are routinely exchanged among the English-speaking countries.

Culture

Cross-cultural and cross-ethnic group problems are also substantial. Data collected on different cultural and ethnic groups cannot be generalized to other groups, whether the tests are verbal or nonverbal. Although differences are often clearer on verbal tests (whether translated into another language or not), there are also differences on nonverbal tests that may reflect differences in style, differences in the meaning of age and education corrections, differences in cultural experiences, and other factors. Some specific problems that arise from focal brain injuries (such as severe construction dyspraxia, dysfluency, loss of receptive skills, paralysis) are indeed cross-cultural, but performances on more complex standardized tests do not hold up as well without renorming and reanalysis.

In general, neuropsychology (and psychology as a whole) has done a poor job of demonstrating the cross-cultural effectiveness of normative, as well as validity and reliability, information. In such cases, applications to these populations must be cautious at best and interfere with an adequate evaluation of the pattern of test results. It cannot be assumed that all tests are equally affected by culture as this is unlikely and certainly unproven. Test data that analyzed clearly for these issues are rare.

It should also not be assumed that all members of a given ethnic group or culture are identical. Golden (1973), for example, studied Japanese university students in Hawaii who were assigned to groups based on whether they were first-, second-, or third-generation Hawaiians. Although all spoke excellent English to avoid any language confound, Golden found that individuals whose families had been in Hawaii the longest performed differently from the other groups on verbal and nonverbal tests and were most similar to a Caucasian control group. It is likely, as well, that minority clients from different socioeconomic levels will also show differences from one another.

Finally, simply including minority groups and different cultures within a standardization group does not make the norms for that test "culture-free." For example, the standardization for the Wechsler Adult and Intelligence Scale—Form III (WAIS-III) made a major effort to include members of different ethnic and cultural groups, based on their percentage in the population. Such an effort probably created norms that are more representative of the normal population in the United States than any other test currently available. Thus, we can compare the performance of anyone (who is cooperative with the test procedure and motivated) with the U.S. population as a whole.

However, this does not tell us the standing of the individual within their own community or cultural or ethnic group. Such information is much more important for neuropsychological analysis. If the individual is unimpaired, compared to their own reference group (rather than to the United States as a whole), there is much less likelihood of neuropsychological dysfunction. Conversely, if they are impaired, compared to their reference group, they may be more likely to have neuropsychological deficits. In any case, comparison to national norms, no matter how well they are constructed, will not tell us this necessary information.

Language

The impact of culture and ethnicity is further complicated by the impact of language issues. A given ethnic group may speak English, but with changes incorporating variations on standard English or words and grammatical structures from another language, such as French, Spanish, or Creole. Such differences may change scores on language-based tests, in ways that will mislead pattern analysis when scores are based on the general population.

Gender corrections are also an issue, although the magnitude of these on most neuropsychological tests are much smaller than those for age, education, when the results were collected, and cultural group. They must be attended to on those tests in which there is a documented influenced and must always be kept in mind when they have not been properly analyzed (many normative samples, for example, come from VA samples, which are entirely male).

Correcting for these issues is not done simply. Some tests have attempted to account for these factors by using large populations chosen to match the U.S. population on many or all of these variables. Thus, a group may include the same percentage of males and females as the general population, drawn in proportion from each region of the country, from urban and rural environments, and include each ethnic/ cultural group in the percentages in which they exist in the general population. Such a procedure may indeed yield norms representative of the United States as a whole, but that does not make the data representative of how any subgroup in the sample may perform. Such biases in the data may again interfere with pattern analysis and lead to inappropriate conclusions.

In all cases, there should be an attempt to use norms that are properly corrected for age, education, and gender, when these factors influence test performance. In the absence of such norms, the possible impact of these variables must be clinically considered before any clinical conclusions are reached.

Unrelated Diagnoses

A related issue is the impact of nonneuropsychological diagnoses. In many cases, normative samples only look at normal people, excluding individuals with psychiatric diagnosis, histories of learning problems, or substantial medical problems, as well as excluding individuals who are hospitalized or involved in litigation. However, many people tested for the impact of a neuropsychological insult will be in hospitals, have pain or other problems relating to accidents or aging, are on major medications, are suing someone, or carry a psychiatric diagnosis such as major depression or schizophrenia. All of these conditions can effect the outcome of neuropsychological testing.

As a result, it would be useful for tests to have at least some of the normative data generated on these groups, which are too often ignored. When they are compared to the "normal" normative samples, they may show deficits that are not neurologically based, but rather are related to these exclusionary conditions. For many tests, such data does not exist, compromising the accuracy of the interpretive strategies employed.

CLASSIFICATION OF SCORES

Once a normative group is finalized, the question arises as to how a test is actually scored: using deviation scores or cutoffs, or a combination of both? There has been the tendency in neuropsychology to focus on cutoff scores, although more recent work has shown increased use of deviation scores (Heaton et al., 1991). Cutoff scores typically dichotomize a score as normal or impaired. This arises from a desire to identify those scores that represent brain injury, rather than just a deviation from the population average. This in turn is often based on underlying assumptions that certain performances are characteristic of brain injury. Cutoffs fail to tell us the severity of a problem and often fail to tell us the likelihood of misclassification rates. Although cutoffs can be useful, they can also be figured in many ways that make comparison of performance across tests difficult.

Defining the Brain-Injured Group

In order to define a cutoff, it is usually necessary to define a brain-injured group to which the normative group can be compared. This process is fraught with potential problems, since all of the issues that apply to the choice of a normal group apply here, along with the additional issues of defining a general brain-injured group. These additional problems include consideration of the cause of the brain injury, the severity, the location, the chronicity, and the degree of treatment. Variations in each of these factors can impact how the brain-injured group performs and, in turn, how the cutoff is determined.

Cause of the Brain Injury

Brain injury may, of course, arise from multiple causes. The common causes include strokes, head injury, tumors, dementia, demyelinating diseases, Parkinson's disease, anoxia, poisoning, and metabolic disorders. Many of these groups can be broken down even further. For example, strokes differ considerably, based on type of stroke (hemorrhagic, occlusive), its size, and its location. Each cause typically produces (when considered with the other factors listed above) a modal pattern of deficits and strengths. Brain-injured groups used in norming will differ considerably, depending on which population the group came from.

Evaluation of different tests will show that the causes of brain injury in the normative group differ widely from test to test, some being all head injury, some being all stroke, some being all dementia, and some reflecting an idiosyncratic combination, usually based on where the study was done (samples of convenience, rather than planned samples, which are very rare). This has a major impact on the pattern of test results and in turn will impact the cutoff points when they are calculated.

Optimization

Depending on the makeup and the severity of the group, the cutoff points established between groups will vary, ranging typically from 1 standard deviation (*SD*) above the normal mean to 2 *SD*s above the normal mean. This will result in widely different error rates for misclassifying normals and brain-injured clients. This method for establishing cutoffs normally is based on a procedure that optimizes correct classification of clients.

The difficulty with such a procedures lies in three major areas. First, the cutoff is dependent on the exact sample used. For example, if one test's cutoff is determined between a matched sample of above-average controls and brain-injured clients, that will not be the same optimal cutoff as if a sample of matched below-average normals and brain-injured had been used. The efficacy of the cutoff when applied to a specific brain-injured client will vary greatly, depending on how appropriate it is for the client being considered. For example, if a study establishes an optimal cutoff for a test when comparing severe head-injured clients to normals, it is likely that a client with mild head injury will be misclassified as normal.

Another major, but related, problem is that cutoffs are often not adequately cross-validated across different populations, again leaving their efficacy in question. Often, a cutoff set up in a single study within a single population is applied across the board with any replication, to see if such a cutoff is stable, even in similar populations. Since population characteristics can potentially impact cutoff points, such replication studies are important to support the generalization of the cutoff across clinical populations.

A second problem is that cutoffs will differ in how many brain-injured are misclassified as normals and how many normals are misclassified as brain-injured. Test A may reach an optimal cutoff by classifying 100% of brain-injured correctly, but only 60% of normals (for a 80% hit rate); Test B may classify 100% of normals correctly, but only 60% of brain-injured (for an 80% hit rate). When used in practice, Test A is much more likely to call someone brain-injured, and Test B is more likely to call someone normal. In such cases, finding a pattern of brain-injured performance on Test A and normal performance on Test B may not reflect differential performance of the client, but rather the ways in which the cutoffs were selected.

Third, cutoffs are usually based on samples of very normal normals, screened for psychiatric problems, any history of neurological problems, any history of learning problems, and so on, and for very clearly brain-injured clients with well-documented injuries. Unfortunately, such samples represent the easiest form of distribution and do not address real-life clinical questions (did the person with severe depression, who was not paying attention while driving, get hurt in the automobile accident?). Such studies meet rigorous, traditional research standards, but such information may not translate into real life. Studies that use controls of individuals with other illnesses (such as orthopedic illnesses or psychiatric disorders) will offer more conservative, but perhaps more relevant, cutoff points.

Discriminant Analysis

This is similar to the hand-optimization level, except that this is decided by a statistical procedure. This procedure is heavily influenced by sample characteristics and can vary widely with changes in the sample and sample size (especially in situations in which sample sizes are uneven). When multiple groups are involved (normal, depressed, and brain-injured, for example), the weightings of each group can heavily influence outcome. Seemingly small changes in options in running discriminant computer programs can also lead to substantial changes in the results. Such programs are unconcerned with the type of error made, leading to cutoffs that may yield very skewed results. Formulas generated to make discriminations based on groups of tests may be overly influenced by chance and not be easily replicable across populations. Again, this can be a useful technique, but use of such cutoffs must be regarded with caution. In general, all of the issues related to optimization also must be considered, when discriminant functions are used.

Cutoffs From Normal Distributions

Increasing numbers of tests use cutoffs based on the normal distribution. Such studies simply may identify the mean and *SD* of normal individuals, then select a point on the normal curve that is said to indicate brain injury. This may be 2 *SDs* from the mean—a very rigorous criteria—but most often is 1 *SD* or slightly more. Such studies may present a single cutoff, or, ideally, may offer cutoffs on scores adjusted for age, education, and gender.

These cutoffs also have disadvantages. First, cutoffs based on normals does not tell us how well the test will identify brain-injured clients (which will also be influenced by the point on the normal curve that defines the cutoff). In some cases, a 1 *SD* cutoff may identify 60% of brain-injured or 80% or 30%. This depends on the distribution of the score in brain-injured clients, which in turn is also influenced by how skewed and how flat both the normal and brain-injured sample curves are, and their relative position to one another. Such issues are important in neuropsychological data, because distributions are often skewed and may indeed not even be truly normal, because of floor and ceiling effects, as well as the basic nature of many of the measures employed.

In such situations, cutoffs that appear to be equal in sensitivity actually vary greatly.

One attempt to deal with the issue of normality is to force the scores into a normal distribution, using statistical techniques. This was done with the various Wechsler scales, in which scores are forced into a normal distribution with a mean of 10 and a *SD* of 3. This was also done by Heaton, Grant, and Matthews (1991), when norming their extended version of the Halstead–Reitan Neuropsychological Test Battery. In general, such procedures force scores into a range from 1 to 19, so that all raw scores are shrunk to fit a distribution up to 3 *SD*s from the mean.

Although this procedure can correct for the distribution problems discussed above, it also introduces several problems, especially with neuropsychological data. In neuropsychological populations, scores can be 10 or even 20 *SD*s from the average of normal individuals. Thus, a wide range of scores are forced together at the bottom of the distribution. As a result, scores that differ in large degree, when compared as raw scores, end up all being represented by a single scale score at the bottom of the distribution. This is not a problem when the possible scores in the distribution fall into a limited range that does not extend outside the 3-*SD* limit, but is an issue with scores, like the time to complete the Trail Making Test, when scores 10 *SD*s from the mean are not unusual.

The question that then arises is whether these raw score differences are meaningful in terms of an understanding of the degree of the client's dysfunction and, by extension, the nature and prognosis of the client's problem. This question has not been answered clearly by research, so we are unsure as to the proper answer. However, in clients whose scores are so low, it is generally useful to look at the raw scores, as well.

Second, such cutoffs may be effected by minor changes in scores that end up being overinterpreted. Thus, the difference between a "normal" *T*-score of 40.01 and an "abnormal" *T*-score of 39.99 may indeed be minuscule and not worthy of the sudden interpretive emphasis given to the lower score. Cutoffs will clearly vary if we choose 1, 2, or some other number of *SD*s to indicate the cutoff point. Even using the same cutoff point (1 *SD*, for example) across tests will result in differing levels of sensitivity and specificity, influencing overall accuracy. This problem, however, exists with all cutoff points that attempt to dichotomize performance as normal and abnormal.

Third, different tests may use cutoffs at 1, 2, 1.5, or some other number of *SD*s, again leading to misleading classifications of test results. As with other cutoffs, sample characteristics may substantially influence results and lead to questionable generalizability.

Age and Education Corrections

The importance of considering age and education issues in adult samples is obvious. However, these lead to several pitfalls, some of which are obvious and others that are more subtle. First, different test norms and cutoffs may address age, education, a combination of both, or neither. Of course, this makes information from the different tests difficult to compare directly, although these scores may be regarded as equivalent by the user. When one test, correcting for age and education, is compared to one that corrects for only age, then apparent differences in scores may again be illusory. In general, tests that correct for all of these factors are seen as more conservative in diagnosing brain injury in populations with higher ages and lower education, but as more liberal in populations with higher educations and lower ages.

A second problem arises from how the corrections are made. Vastly different results may emerge from samples that correct for "over 45" and "under 45" versus those that correct by year, using regression formulas. Bunching of education in groups of "9–11" or "16+" may cause similar problems. In samples that use bunching techniques, sample characteristics among normative groups for each education level may cause variations in norms that are unrelated to brain injury. However, regression formulas that assume linearity of relationships between test performance and demographic variables may err, as well, if the underlying relationship is not linear. In all of these cases, the actual magnitude of the effect of age/education or other demographic factors influences the importance of these issues.

In some cases, however, age and education corrections can lead to serious problems, as when the age or education correction corrects for brain injury itself. In many samples of older normals, we may see decline because of unidentified neurological factors or as a result of systemic disorders (e.g., diabetes, peripheral joint disorders), which act to bias norms toward the impaired side, masking real problems. Similarly, a group of individuals with only a sixth-grade education may have received a sixth-grade education because they were unable to go any farther, because of a neurological disorder, while others dropped out for economic reasons. The effect, however, is to make the test less sensitive to actual (although preexisting) disorders.

Culture and Ethnic Diversity Issues

This is a less-researched (unfortunately), but important, area. The administration of tests to ethnic minorities and to groups whose primary and original language is other than the language the test was normed in is questionable, even in the case of so-called nonverbal tests. Our own work (e.g., Demsky, Mittenberg, Quintar, Katell, & Golden, 1998) suggests that even nonverbal tests yield different results in normal populations, let alone brain-injured samples. Unless a test is appropriately standardized for a group, the use of the norms and cutoffs must be done cautiously and with strong attention to these factors.

The authors believe that simply including a group in a more general normative sample does not make norms culture fair or accurate. We may represent ethnic group X in the normative sample in the 3% ratio in which it exists in the U.S. population, but this does not make the resultant norms fairer or accurate (it does make the norms more representative of the true mean, if we tested everyone in the United States, but this is irrelevant to the question of neuropsychological dysfunction). Only if the norms are appropriately evaluated within that group, with an adequate sample, can we state whether the norms are fair or not.

The issues involved in such norms are complex. For example, when working in Hawaii, the senior author found that norms for second-generation Japanese residents were not equivalent to those for third-generation Japanese residents. Norms for Spanish speakers from Cuba may not be the same as Spanish speakers from Mexico. Norms for a client who is truly bilingual may not be the same for someone who still thinks predominantly in their native language. These issues are unfortunately endless, but must be considered when reaching conclusions.

When analyzing the results of translated tests, differences of up to $2/3$ SD (10 standard score points) may be seen in nonverbal tests; differences twice as large ($4/3$ SD, or up to 20 points) may be caused solely by issues of translation and culture. If a test is translated inappropriately or in an idiosyncratic method, the expected changes in norms, even in normals, may even be larger.

Interpretive Implications

Interpreting a series of tests, with traditional cutoffs for each test, can result in many distortions. As can be seen above, many factors may influence how a cutoff is picked and the degree to which the cutoff generates errors in normals (false positives, when we call a normal person "brain-injured") and in brain-injured clients (false negatives, when we call a brain-injured client "normal"). If Test A generates a high rate of false positives and Test B generates a high rate of false negatives, differences in classification of the tests may not be the result of differences in level of performance, but differences in how the cutoffs are set.

This creates the potential for substantive errors, because tests do differ widely in their overall sensitivity, as well as in the occurrence of false-negative and false-positive outcomes. Users of such cutoffs must be familiar with the psychometric properties of the specific tests that are employed, so as to be able to judge the accuracy of a given classification. Even in such circumstances, however, reliance on cutoff points to classify clients, across a set of tests, is likely to be misleading, because of these factors.

A related interpretive issue is the impact of random chance and premorbid levels, when using cutoffs with multiple tests. Probability rules tell us that, by chance alone, some tests will be performed at levels below the cutoff point, with the likelihood directly related to the degree to which the test is likely to show false-positive results. The more tests that are given, the higher the likelihood of such chance findings. For example, if a battery includes 15 tests or subtests, which each have a cutoff score and an average false-positive rate of 20%, 3 of the tests would be expected, by chance alone, to fall below preset cutoffs (this is made worse by many of the other issues that have already been discussed, such as appropriateness of the normative group initially).

Despite this issue, it is not unusual to see users of such tests interpret the three or four findings as having neuropsychological significance and indicating the presence of brain injury. This represents a substantial overinterpretation of the data and false findings of the presence of brain injury. Similarly, one can argue that chance fluctuations can cause false negatives, as well, so that apparently normal profiles are misinterpreted as indicating the absence of brain dysfunction.

Premorbid levels also clearly influence these outcomes. If a client's premorbid performance on one or more tests is below the cutoff, the impact of a current condition (such as a head injury) will be overinterpreted. In cases in which large numbers of tests are poorly performed premorbidly (e.g., in cases of mental retardation or significant learning disabilities), cutoff scores may be essentially useless. Similarly, high-functioning clients may show decline in function, but still remain above cutoffs, again causing misclassification of the client as uninjured.

It has been argued that the above interpretive problems can be avoided by adjusting cutoffs for such factors as age and education. Although such procedures offer better results, they do not eliminate these problems, because such cutoffs are set for the average person at a given age and education. Thus, if we looked at all individuals who are 40 years old with 12 years of education, then one half of that population would perform better than the mean, and one half would perform worse. We would expect that the overall *SD* for such a group would be smaller than in a more heterogeneous population, but there would still be those who were premorbidly very high and very low, compared to that average. This would induce the same problems, but might reduce false-positive and false-negative rates, so as to minimize the impact of these concerns.

Similar concerns would apply to corrections for gender, ethnic group, race, geographical region, language, and so on. The impact of first language on a person, whose second language was English, would depend on the degree to which the person was fully bilingual and probably on the language the person thinks in (with a poorer performance expected if the individual must continuously translate back and forth between the languages).

PATTERN ANALYSIS

Although cutoffs give us rough ideas of the level of performance of a client, the use of pattern analysis across tests, which ignores cutoffs, and rather focuses on internal variations in the clients own results, in relation to the client's own baseline of current and previous performance, offers a much more powerful tool, especially in more subtle cases or those cases in which we wish to understand the true deficits that underlie a brain injury or whether a brain injury has even occurred. Such a technique ideally translates all scores into a standard score system, with appropriate demographic corrections.

Translation of the scores into a common system is made difficult by the presence of many scoring systems utilizing demographically corrected and uncorrected scores, *T*-scores, standard scores, *z*-scores, raw scores, Wechsler scale scores, and percentiles. These scores must be translated into a common system (most often *T*-scores or standard scores), which are ideally corrected on the same demographic variables. For example, if we evaluate a client with 6 years of education and 45 years of age, we will get widely different results with and without an education correction. If we corrected only for age, an achievement score equivalent to 5 years of education would yield a very low score, but correcting for education, as well, might yield a normal score. If different tests are corrected for different demographic factors, apparent differences in the pattern of scores may only be related to the differences in the scoring corrections.

Client Profile

Once scores have been converted into a common scoring system, client profiles may be plotted or analyzed, looking for score differences that suggest neuropsychological significance. Such analysis must consider the issue of individual variation. When looking at an overall profile, one can calculate the individual's expected scores across all tests administered. In most cases, the full-scale IQ (premorbid) will represent this score. In less severe cases, the current full-scale IQ is often a good estimate, or even the client's average score. In general, research on test batteries seems to suggest that scores for normals will vary about 1 *SD* from this average score (15 points for standard scores on either side of the average, 10 points on either side for *T*-scores). However, this works only when such factors as ceiling or floor limits, demographic equations, or skewed distributions do not influence the profile.

There are several other major exceptions to these rules. First, very-high-functioning clients (90th percentile and above) may show skewed distribution of scores, so that there is a greater variability for scores below their average and less for scores above their average. For example, a client with an full-scale IQ of 145 may have few scores above, but the range for scores below may be as high as 2 *SD*s. Similarly, individuals at the low end of the spectrum may have a tendency to show more high scores than expected (often in motor, sensory, attention, and some memory domains), so the range may be up to 2 *SD*s above the expected score.

Profiles in which scores show less variation than expected are generally considered within the normal range (although that does not prove someone is normal). Profiles with greater variations suggest an unusual degree of variation, which may indicate the presence of cognitive problems or may simply indicate any of the problems with specific tests or scoring procedures, which have already been discussed. Overall, in all clients, a range of scores that reflect only 2 *SDs* are normal; ranges between 2 and 3 *SDs* are probably borderline; and ranges greater than 3 *SDs* suggest that there is a disability (assuming that the differences are not caused by any of the statistical and methodological flaws already discussed).

Variations Between Scores

Below the level of overall profile differences, scores can be compared directly to one another. The degree of difference between scores necessary for neuropsychological significance varies, depending on the underlying relationships of the tests, as well as on variations in the normative samples employed.

The easiest comparisons are between scores representing identical motor or sensory performance on the opposite sides of the body. These scores should be very close to one another and are usually normed on the exact same population, with the same scoring methods, minimizing errors from these sources. Thus, differences of $1/2$ *SD* may be significant.

The second class are tests that are moderately correlated to one another (verbal and performance IQ, performance on two similar drawing tests). If both sets of scores have similar normative populations, then differences of 1 *SD* between scores are usually neuropsychologically significant. If the tests use very different normative populations or different correction methods (e.g., one corrects for education, one does not), a more conservative difference of $1^1/2$ *SDs* should be used.

The third class are tests that are independently normed, but represent areas that theoretically overlap, such as achievement and IQ, executive performance and IQ, or spatial reasoning and construction skills. Such tests normally require differences of $1^1/2$ *SDs*, before neuropsychological differences can be reliably implied. In limited cases, a more liberal difference of 1 *SD* can be applied, but only when there is clear research to back up such an assumption. In most cases, such research is not available, and the more liberal 1 *SD* should not be employed. The final class are tests that are generally unrelated (Block Design and Grammatical skills) and normed on different populations. In such cases, the most conservative criterion of 2 *SDs* should be employed.

However, the presence of a significant deficit between tests does not mean that there is a brain injury or a disability. Since normal people have scores that are typically 1 *SD* above and 1 *SD* below their average or base score, the difference between scores at the extremes are often 2 *SD*s. Only a combination of clear and consistent differences among sets of tests, along with a definite abnormal range of scores, can be clearly interpreted as indicating a disability or brain injury.

OBSERVATIONS

In addition to an analysis of scores, much information can be gained from the qualitative analysis of how a client achieved a score. Although it can be argued that an extensive test battery could be organized so that many, or even most, qualitative variations should be reflected in the quantitative scores, the state of testing at the present time does not have a research base that allows us to demonstrate this argument. Differences between tests, as discussed above, as well as simple error variance, obscure fine differences in client performance. Such problems have less effect on simple classification of performance, such as "impaired," but has many more implications as we attempt to make finer discriminations as to specific problems or specific etiologies.

Under these circumstances, qualitative observations become an important source of collateral information, which should be integrated with the actual data. Neither quantitative nor qualitative data is either better or more perfect, but both offer insights which, when combined, create a more accurate and detailed description of the client. Thus, such observations should be routinely made, along with testing the limits of procedures, when they can further elucidate the reasons behind a client's behavior. All individuals who administer tests, whether doctoral psychologists or technicians, should be trained in making and reporting such observations.

PREMORBID BASELINE

Level-of-performance measures compare a client to population norms, and pattern analysis looks at current intraindividual variations, but there has always been a desire to compare the client to the client's own premorbid level of functioning. This has traditionally been attempted in two ways: using formulas to estimate premorbid levels, and using performance on current "hold" tests to estimate premorbid levels.

The use of formulas has generally focused on the prediction of full-scale IQ as a measure of g, to which all other test scores can be compared. These systems have many problems, because they tend to lump clients into heterogeneous groups, which are not descriptive of the individual. Most of the success of such formulas lies in classifying those in the middle of the normal distribution as being in the middle, but they add little to simply assuming that everyone is normal. When these scores are used, errors of up to 15 standard score points from baseline must be assumed, with scores needing to deviate an additional 15 points before one can reach the conclusion that a score has changed.

The second method involves estimation from hold tests, typically a test of reading recognition (such as the Wide Range Achievement Test—III or Peabody Individual Achievement Test—III) or vocabulary (such as the Peabody Picture Vocabulary Test—Revised or Vocabulary from the WAIS-III). These tests offer decent correlations with g and are easy to give. In the absence of aphasia or severe visual problems, they offer reasonable estimates of the premorbid level, especially when combined with historical information on a person's actual accomplishments. However, even in the best of circumstances, these scores are accurate only within 5–7 standard score points, at the 68% confidence level, and 10–12 points, at the 95% confidence level. This range of error must be considered in any comparisons.

A final caution is the issue of the appropriateness of these baselines. Although they may offer some useful information for premorbid general IQ, they do not predict performance on tests of motor performance, drawing, attention, and other important areas. Thus, care should be taken before generalizing such baselines to such tests, in which the accuracy rate may drop to as low as 20–30 standard score points. There is a paucity of research on the relation of these areas to premorbid scores, and any generalization must be cautious and take into account the other issues discussed in this chapter.

SUMMARY

There are many issues to consider when analyzing a comprehensive test battery, but such an approach remains by far the most accurate and useful method of neuropsychological evaluation. When quantitative and qualitative information are properly integrated with consideration of the issues described above, valid and useful descriptions of client deficits may be identified.

REFERENCES

Demsky, Y., Mittenberg, W., Quintar, B., Katell, A. D., & Golden, C. J. (1998). Bias in the use of standard American norms with Spanish translations of the Wechsler Memory Scale—Revised. *Assessment, 5,* 115–121.

Golden, C. J. (1973). *Cognitive differences among different generations of immigrants to Hawaii.* Unpublished master's thesis, University of Hawaii, Maui.

Heaton, R., Grant, I., & Matthews, C. (1991). *Comprehensive norms for an expanded Halstead-Reitan battery: Demographic corrections, research findings, and clinical applications.* Odessa, FL: Psychological Assessment Resources.

Wechsler, D. (1997). *WAIS-III: Administration and scoring manual.* San Antonio, TX: The Psychological Corporation.

Chapter 4

Diagnostic Decision Making in Neuropsychology

Arthur D. Williams

D iagnostic decision making in neuropsychology must be conducted using the most scientific methods available. This chapter
presents decision rules to assist the neuropsychologist. Decision
rules are presented from the field of logic, from legal cases, and from
the Standards for Educational and Psychological Testing, regarding
assessment of frontal lobe functioning, for evaluating research studies,
and for dissimulation and malingering. A suggested systematic approach
is then presented.

DECISION RULES FROM LOGIC

The task in diagnostic decision making is to distinguish correct reasoning from incorrect reasoning. Copi and Cohen (1998) stated, "*Reason
is the instrument upon which we humans must depend wherever it is
our object to reach judgments upon which we can rely. . . .* Logic is the
study of the methods and principles used to distinguish correct reasoning from incorrect reasoning" (pp. xix, 3). Hughes (2000) said, "Logic is
the science that studies relationships between premises and conclusions
with a view to determining when and to what extent the premises
actually support the conclusion" (p. 25).

To evaluate opinions or arguments, one can use two methods: the
criterial method and the fallacies method. The criterial method begins
by establishing the criteria the argument must satisfy; these criteria are
then used as the basis for assessing arguments (Hughes, 2000). Copi

and Cohen (1998) defined a fallacy as "a type of argument that may seem to be correct, but that proves, on examination, not to be so" (p. 161). Specific types of fallacies are important to identify. Knowledge of these fallacies helps neuropsychologists monitor themselves. It also allows them to identify when they are being inappropriately critiqued by a colleague or when they are being unfairly cross-examined. For a more comprehensive discussion of issues related to logic, the reader is referred to *Introduction to Logic* (Copi & Cohen, 1998) and *Critical Thinking* (Hughes, 2000).

Hughes (2000) said, "An argument is a set of statements that claims that one or more . . . statements, called the premises, support another of them, called the conclusion" (p. 17). A true conclusion cannot be based on a false premise. Ways of assessing whether a premise is false are presented below.

Another important concept is logical strength, wherein the premises, if they are true, actually provide support for the conclusion. Hughes (2000) said, "An argument that has both logical strength and true premises is called a sound argument" (p. 20). It is critical that experts in the forensic arena make sound arguments, since their conclusions can have wide-ranging implications for the patient and the legal system.

A sound argument must be acceptable, relevant, and adequate. To determine if an argument meets these criteria, one must follow seven rules, according to Hughes (2000).

1. Identify the main conclusion. For example, the patient is suffering from persisting neuropsychological deficits from a mild brain injury.
2. Identify the premises. For example, Paced Auditory Serial Addition Task and the Rey Auditory Verbal Learning Test have scores 1 standard deviation (*SD*) from the mean.
3. Identify the structure of the argument. Usually, this is a simple structure, in which the premise (these tests have scores 1 *SD* from the mean) leads to a conclusion (the patient has persisting deficits from a mild brain injury).
4. Check the acceptability of the premises. An empirical truth claim is being presented regarding these tests. This truth claim can be verified, or found to be true, or falsified, and found to be false. The truth claim should be empirically supported by methodologically sound studies. Ways of determining soundness of methodology are discussed. The questions to be verified are: Are these

tests valid and reliable, and do they meet the criteria from the *Standards for Educational and Psychological Testing* (American Psychological Association [APA], 1985)? Are low-average scores on these two tests indicative of deficits? Is it likely these deficits would be related to a mild brain injury?

5. Check the relevance of the premises. Copi and Cohen (1998) stated, "When an argument relies on [premises] that are not relevant to its conclusion, and that therefore cannot possibly establish its truth, the fallacy committed is one of *relevance*" (p. 162).

One type of fallacy of relevance is an appeal to authority. For example, the expert may say that Lezak (1995) stated, "W. R. Russell (1974) pointed out that 'there is no such thing as a "complete recovery" from acceleration concussion of severity sufficient to cause loss of consciousness" (p. 185). Although Lezak has written a frequently cited book, this particular statement is not supported by a methodologically sound study. In fact, Lezak has used a letter to the editor by Russell (1974) as the basis for her statement.

Another common fallacy of relevance, which may be used either in critiques of colleague's work or by cross-examining attorneys, is argument ad hominem, which is "a fallacious attack in which the thrust is directed, not at a conclusion, but at the person who asserts or defends it" (Copi & Cohen, 1998, pp. 166–167). Usually, this is used when the person arguing does not want to address the correctness or incorrectness of the reasoning involved in the argument. Attorneys have been known to say, "If the facts are against you, attack the witness." However, the character of the witness is logically irrelevant to the correctness of his or her reasoning.

Another fallacy is the straw man fallacy, which "is committed when someone attacks a position that appears similar to, but is actually different from an opponent's position, and concludes that the opponent's real position has therefore been refuted" (Hughes, 2000, p. 164).

Another fallacy of relevance is argument ad populum, which is the "fallacious appeal to what is popular. . . . The popular acceptance of a policy or practice does not show it to be wise; the fact that a great many people hold a given opinion does not prove it to be true" (Hughes, 2000, p. 170). For example, Sweet,

Moberg, and Suchy (2000) conducted a 10-year follow-up survey of clinical neuropsychologists and found that a majority use a flexible battery. It is illogical to conclude from this survey that a flexible battery is scientific or accurate. For many reasons completely apart from scientific accuracy, a flexible battery is popular. In the survey by Sweet, Moberg, and Westergaard (1996), the authors commented,

> Given that the involvement of neuropsychologists in forensic activities has apparently been increasing . . . , it would appear that the expectation of comprehensive evaluation in such cases has not increased overall adherence to the standardized approach. However, this does not imply that within specific activities, such as forensic consultation, standardized batteries are not predominant. (p. 215)

Adams (2000) addressed the issue of fixed versus flexible batteries. Although many readers may not agree with his statements, they should be prepared to address the scientific underpinnings (or lack thereof) of a flexible battery approach. His comments were in the context of a review of Mitrushina, Boone, and D'Elia's (1999) book:

> In using the approach espoused here, by some dint of genius one will presumably pick the "right" tests for a job with choices better informed by the normative data here. Rushed onstage to justify this manner of practice is the straw man of "flexible" versus fixed neuropsychological protocols. . . . Naturally, flexible and good, "tailored" to the patient or problem is virtuous. Fixed is stodgy, ignorant of modern developments, and bad. Such practice rationalizations fail to even begin to deal with the dangers of test selection on the basis of face validity, incorrect or incomplete presentation of referral issues, and disregard for the absolute and uncompromising need to base assessment package assembly upon scientific and psychometric collateral that the test assembly will perform as an ensemble. . . . It needs saying: *Ad hoc* creation of test protocols is not flexible, but sloppy science that renders neuropsychologists no more than respondents to whim and fashion. (pp. 300–301)

6. Check the adequacy of the premises. This relates to the strength of the argument, from very tentative to very definite. One way to violate the criterion of adequacy is to jump to conclusions. Another is to use false analogies.

A fallacy of relevance seen in some reports is an argument

ad ignorantium (from ignorance), which is "the mistake that is committed when it is argued that a proposition is true simply on the basis that it has not been proved false, or that it is false because it has not been proved true" (Copi & Cohen, 1998, pp. 162–163). This argument is commonly found in reports regarding mild brain injury and frontal lobe injury. The argument may be that, since the CT scan, the MRI, the neuropsychological testing, and the neurological examination were all negative, this means that the person had a brain injury, because all of these indices are not sensitive to diffuse axonal injury (or frontal lobe injury) and would be expected to be negative. Of course, they would also be negative if the person did not have mild brain injury or frontal lobe injury.

Fallacies of presumption are based on an unjustified assumption. An important type of fallacy of presumption is false cause (non causa pro causa), which involves presuming the reality of a causal connection that does not exist. A common variety of false cause is post hoc ergo propter hoc (after that, therefore because of that). This error in reason is frequent in evaluations of mild traumatic brain injury. Any symptoms or changes in the person's functioning are attributed to the mild brain injury, when there are multiple other more probable explanations: chronic pain, depression, sleep deprivation, medication effects, and so on. All of these alternative explanations need to be systematically explored. *The Specialty Guidelines for Forensic Psychologists* (1991) address this issue in VI. C.:

> As an expert conducting an evaluation, treatment, consultation, or scholarly/empirical investigation, the forensic psychologist maintains professional integrity by examining the issue at hand from all reasonable perspectives, actively seeking information that will differentially test plausible rival hypotheses. (p. 661)

Another fallacy of presumption is called *accident and converse accident*. Copi and Cohen (1998) defined accident as "when we presume the application of a generalization to individual cases that it does not properly govern" (p. 187). Those authors stated that converse accident occurs when we "presume that what is true of a particular case is true of the great run of cases" (p. 187). Converse accident involves the danger of using case reports to generalize about the general population. An example of converse accident would involve arguing that, because a case report in a journal or book chapter described that a patient with orbital frontal damage had average scores on an intelligence test, any given person with average scores on an intelligence test has orbital frontal damage.

7. Look for counterarguments. If there is a sound counterargument (such as deficiencies in the tests or more likely alternative explanations), the given argument (that there are persisting deficits from a brain injury) must be deficient.

DECISION RULES FROM LEGAL CASES

The U.S. Supreme Court decision in *Daubert v. Merrell Dow Pharmaceuticals* (1993) provided four factors to aid the lower courts with their review of scientific evidence. The first factor was whether the theory or technique can be or has been empirically tested using scientific methods to determine possible falsifiability. The Supreme Court used Hempel (1966) and Popper (1989) to define the parameters of scientific inquiry. Hempel (1966) described the nature of the empirical sciences, which

> seek to explore, to describe, to explain, and to predict the occurrences in the world we live in. The statements, therefore, must be checked against the facts of our experience, and they are acceptable only if they are properly supported by empirical evidence. (p. 1)

He is essentially describing an empirical truth claim, which must be verified or falsified. Popper (1989) discussed

> the problem of *drawing a line of demarcation* between those statements . . . which could properly be described as belonging to empirical science, and others which might, perhaps, be described as "pseudoscientific" . . . [Popper] proposed . . . that the *refutability or falsifiability* of a theoretical system should be taken as the criterion of demarcation. (pp. 255–256)

The other factors were: whether the theory or technique has been subjected to peer review and publication, the known or potential rate of error of the technique or method, and whether the theory or technique has obtained general acceptance within the relevant scientific community.

Other relevant cases are: *General Electric v. Joiner* (1997), *United States v. Scheffer* (1998), and *Kumho Tire v. Carmichael* (1999), which reaffirmed the *Daubert* decision. In *Kumho Tire*, the Supreme Court clarified that the Federal Rule reliability analysis applies to all experts. *Chapple v. Ganger* (1994) has suggested that the Court preferred the results of a fixed battery over those of a flexible battery (Reed, 1996).

DECISION RULES FROM THE STANDARDS FOR TESTING

In *Professional Conduct and Discipline in Psychology*, by Bass et al. (1996), published by the APA and the Association of State and Provincial Psychology Boards, DeMers stated,

> One of the hallmarks of a profession is the presence of an organization that standardizes and advances the development of the field. . . . [Organizations such as APA and the Canadian Psychological Association] develop standards and criteria that describe the education, training, competencies, scope of practice, and appropriate conduct or behavior for the members of the profession. Such criteria offer the public a means of recognizing competent practitioners and regulating their conduct. (p. ix)

Therefore, it is necessary to review the standards of the profession.

The *Standards* (APA, 1985) are the standard of care for testing in psychology. The authors stated

> The *Standards* is a technical guide that can be used as a basis for evaluating testing practices. . . . *Primary Standards* are those that should be met by all tests before their operational use and in all test uses, unless a sound professional reason is available to show why it is not necessary, or technically feasible, to do so. Test developers and users . . . are expected to be able to explain why any primary standards have not been met. (pp. 2–3)

Operational use in this context refers to decision making, such as making diagnoses. *Users* are psychologists, who may be cross-examined as to why they did not follow the standards of the profession. All of the standards cited here are Primary Standards.

Standardized Administration

In a discussion of common problem areas, in *Professional Conduct*, Peterson (1996) commented on test misuse: "Psychologists who are poorly trained do not have a systematic approach to diagnosis and assessment and are likely to encounter problems in this area" (p. 74). As an example, she said, "Psychologists may misuse tests by administering under non-standard conditions" (p. 74).

Standard 6.2 states,

> When a test user makes a substantial change in test format, mode of administration, instructions, language, or content, the user should revalidate the use of the test for the changed conditions or have a rationale supporting the claim that additional validation is not necessary or possible. (p. 41)

For example, the manual for the Wechsler Memory Scale—III (WMS-III) states,

> To maintain the validity and reliability of the WMS-III, the uniformity of the administration and scoring procedures, as well as testing conditions, must be adhered to. To obtain results that can be interpreted according to national norms, you should carefully follow all directions in the Stimulus Booklets. Deviations from the standard subtest administration . . . could reduce the validity of the test results. (Wechsler, 1997, p. 28)

Despite this concern stated in the manual, many psychologists administer only subtests, such as the Logical Memory I and II.

Reliability and Validity

Peterson (1996) stated, "Lack of knowledge and skill in application of statistics, especially with regard to test reliability and validity, can result in the misuse of tests" (p. 75). Standard 6.1 states, "Test users should evaluate the available written documentation on the validity and reliability of tests for the specific use intended" (p. 41). For many tests, there is no information about these essential concepts in the manual, if a manual exists.

Peterson (1996) said, "Psychologists can experience difficulty . . . when they use tests on client populations not included in the test validation process" (p. 74). Related to this concern, Standard 6.3 states, "When a test is to be used for a purpose for which it has not been previously validated, or for which there is no supported claim for validity, the user is responsible for providing evidence of validity" (p. 42). Many tests have not been empirically validated.

A test that is used for estimating preinjury intelligence is the North American Reading Test—Revised (NART-R) (Blair & Spreen, 1989). The authors of this test, Blair and Spreen (1989), stated,

> Since the NART-R was standardized and validated on the same sample, additional validation studies in a normal population are needed. Validation studies of the NART-R are also needed for a variety of clinical populations, including demented subjects, other neurologically impaired groups such as head injury and stroke victims, and patients with psychiatric diagnoses. Until such additional studies validate the use of the NART-R, it cannot be employed with confidence for the determination of impairment due to brain disease. (p. 135)

Standard 7.1 states, "Clinicians should not imply that interpretations of test data are based on empirical evidence of validity unless such evidence exists for the interpretations given" (p. 46). It is not unusual for interpretations to be made of test data when there is no empirical evidence for the interpretations.

Use of Norms and the Questionable Normal Distribution

The psychologist must state which norms they used, when there are a multitude of norms that are available. Satz (1999) expressed concern about "norm shopping." He discussed a case in which an expert retained by the other side had used norms from "a very small sample of Australian subjects who were administered a different form of the WMS! Had 'the other side' done 'norm shopping' figuring no one could possibly have access to all the norms and would not discover their possible deception?" (p. ix). For some tests, the same score may be average with one set of norms or "impaired" with another. Psychologists should use the largest sample available that is relevant to the person being tested.

Most psychological tests rely on an assumption that the scores are distributed on a normal curve. Although some issues that are tested are normally distributed, such as intelligence, many are not. Dodrill (1997) stated, "Unlike intelligence, the normal versus abnormal continuum of brain function is not normally distributed. Most people have normal brain functions, and distributions of overall indices of brain functions . . . are highly skewed" (p. 10).

Mitrushina et al. (1999) (p. 16) said,

> The interpretation of individual test scores respective to the normative distribution is based on an assumption of the normality of this distribution. In

order to avoid interpretive errors, the basis for test score interpretation should
be different if distribution is asymmetrical.

They then discussed cases in which the distribution of scores is negatively
skewed. As examples, they cited the Boston Naming Test and the Rey–
Osterrieth Complex Figure Test. These tests are often interpreted as
though the scores were normally distributed, increasing the likelihood
of interpretive error. These authors also noted the Raven's Advanced
Progressive Matrices as an example of a test that is positively skewed.
They concluded, "In both of the above cases resulting in skewed score
distributions, the use of z-score conversions is inappropriate, since such
conversions are based on the assumption of normality (particularly
symmetry) of the distribution" (pp. 16–17).

It is incumbent upon test publishers to provide data regarding the
distribution of scores in the test manuals and for researchers to provide
these data in published studies. Otherwise, the clinician may use inappropriate score conversions and present misleading interpretations.

Despite this concern, many neuropsychologists convert scores, based
on apparently skewed distributions, into derived scores, such as z-scores,
T-scores, and percentiles.

Percentiles are likely to be very misleading. Percentiles are not equally
distributed. Anastasi (1988) stated,

> The chief drawback of percentile scores arises from the marked inequality
> of their units, especially at the extremes of the distribution. If the distribution
> of raw scores approximates the normal curve, . . . then raw score differences
> near the median or center of the distribution are exaggerated in the percentile
> transformation, whereas raw score differences near the ends of the distribu-
> tion are greatly shrunk. (p. 82)

Merely comparing a score on a test to a normative group, usually a
small sample, and using a percentile to describe this score relative to
the normative group, is likely to be misleading.

The manual for the Wide Range Assessment of Memory and Learning, a memory test for children, indicates that one of the scales, Delayed
Recall, is not normally distributed: A scaled score cannot be derived in
a psychometrically sound manner (Sheslow & Adams, 1990). If the
samples are not normally distributed, derived scores (such as percentiles, z-scores, T-scores) may be misleading.

Scores from tests that have been normed on different samples cannot
be compared to one another, since the relationship of the scores to

one another is unknown. This has been pointed out by avid proponents of the flexible battery approach, such as Lezak (1995) and Spreen and Strauss (1998). On a chart, the latter authors have reproduced the following text: "This chart cannot be used to equate scores on one test to scores on another test. . . . [Scores from different tests] do not represent 'equal' standings because the scores were obtained from different groups" (p. 26). This raises questions about the use of pattern analysis with tests that have not been researched together.

The Need for Test Manuals

Standard 6.13 states,

> Test users should not use interpretations of test results, including computer-interpreted test results, unless they have a manual for that test that includes information on the validities of the interpretations for the intended applications and on the samples on which they were based. (p. 44)

For many tests with no manuals, neuropsychologists rely on short descriptions in Lezak (1995) and Spreen and Strauss (1998), who stated, about the Consonant Trigrams Test, "There is no commercial source for this test" (p. 263). For the Buschke Selective Reminding Test, they stated, "There is no commercial source. Users may refer to the following text in order to design their own material" (p. 282).

Differential Diagnosis

Standard 7.3 states,

> When differential diagnosis is needed, the user should choose, if possible, a test for which there is evidence of the test's ability to distinguish between the two or more diagnostic groups of concern rather than merely to distinguish abnormal cases from the general population. (p. 46)

The task in most evaluations is to make a differential diagnosis. Most tests have not been validated with large samples of subjects with a given neurological disorder. If any studies have been done, they have usually been conducted with small samples, raising concerns about generalizability. It is highly preferable to choose a standardized battery that has been developed "to distinguish between the two or more diagnostic groups of concern rather than merely to distinguish abnormal cases from the general population" (APA, 1985, p. 46).

Screening Tests

Standard 6.12 indicates,

> In school, clinical, and counseling applications, tests developed for screening should be used only for identifying test takers who may need further evaluation. The results of such tests should not be used to characterize a person or to make any decision about a person, other than the decision for referral for further evaluation, unless adequate reliability and validity for these other uses can be demonstrated. (p. 43)

Many of the tests used by neuropsychologists are only screening tests. For example, according to the manuals, the Stroop Color and Word Test (Golden, 1978) and the Hooper Visual Organization Test (Hooper, 1993) are screening tests.

Research Editions

Standard 3.20 states, "If a test or part of a test is intended for research use only and is not distributed for operational use, this fact should be displayed prominently in any materials provided for interpreting individual scores" (p. 29). The computer versions of the Category Test and the Wisconsin Card Sorting Test clearly indicate that they are "research editions." These tests are not ready for operational use, meaning for decision-making purposes, such as making diagnoses and making determinations of impairment and disability.

Limits of Data

Section 7.04 (b) of the *Ethical Principles* states, "Whenever necessary to avoid misleading, psychologists acknowledge the limits of their data or conclusions" (p. 46). For example, according to the Technical Manual (Wechsler, 1997), the *Wechsler Adult Intelligence Scale—Third Edition* (WAIS-III) and WMS-III have only been studied on "22 adults who had experienced a moderate to severe single closed head injury," who were administered the WAIS-III and the [WMS-III]" (p. 155). This is too small of a sample to generalize from, and this sample did not include any subjects with mild brain injury. Therefore, it should not be used to diagnose mild brain injury.

Another limitation that would need to be noted would be the use of the WAIS-III in the calculation of the General Neuropsychological Deficit Scale (GNDS) of the Halstead–Reitan Neuropsychological Test Battery. The WAIS was used in the research with the GNDS. Some error may have been introduced into the calculation of the GNDS since the WAIS-III was used.

Comprehensive Assessment

In *Responsible Test Use*, by the Test User Training Work Group of the Joint Committee on Testing Practices (1993), published by the APA, 78 real-life cases are included, which illustrate both proper and improper use of tests. The authors stated that this is not an ethics casebook or the policy of the sponsoring organizations, but it is very valuable in providing guidance for proper test use. One factor is "comprehensive assessment." The authors expressed concern that the referral question was the only area tested, and much important information that is crucial for accurate diagnosis was not gathered.

Base Rates and Biases

Peterson (1996) said, "In addition, psychologists may use faulty decision making during the diagnostic process, such as failure to consider low base rates of certain [phenomena] . . . " (p. 74). Glaros and Klein (1988) have presented a probability formula for assessing the positive and negative predictive value of a test with a consideration of base rates (a discussion of this probability formula goes beyond the scope of this chapter; please refer to Williams [1997]).

Peterson (1996) also said, "Psychologists should also be aware that their own biases may affect the assessment process and should take care in monitoring and ensuring objectivity in the context of the client interview" (p. 74). Neuropsychologists must be aware of the types of bias and debiasing techniques, to help them to reduce the likelihood of bias. This is discussed in more detail in Williams (1997).

DECISION RULES REGARDING
FRONTAL LOBE FUNCTIONS

Decisions in the evaluation of frontal lobe dysfunction may need to be based on behavioral decision rules from the literature. These behavioral decision rules should be explicitly stated in the report. As Dodrill (1997) has pointed out, there are no frontal lobe tests. Regarding assessment of executive functions, he said, "We do not have even one adequately validated test to measure these most important functions" (p. 5). Many of the tests used to diagnose these deficits, such as the Stroop Color and Word Test and the Hooper Visual Organization Test, do not meet the criteria set forth in the *Standards.*

Cummings (1985) described the frontal lobe syndromes in *Clinical Neuropsychiatry,* and, more recently, Cummings and Trimble (1995) have summarized these syndromes. They stated that diseases of the frontal lobe are among the most dramatic in neuropsychiatry.

Dorsolateral Prefrontal Disorders

Cummings and Trimble (1995) stated:

> Dorsolateral prefrontal disorders are marked by executive dysfunction characterized by poor planning when copying constructions and when organizing material to be remembered, impaired set shifting in response to task contingencies, abnormalities of motor programming, compromised attention, and environmental dependency. (p. 58)

Compromised learning strategies are evident on tests of new learning. These patients exhibit the retrieval deficit syndrome, involving poor recall and preserved recognition memory. In the context of frontal lobe dysfunction, amnestic syndromes, with poor recall and poor recognition, occur only with deeply placed lesions affecting the fornix.

Lesions of the dorsolateral area result in inability to integrate disparate sensory elements into a coherent whole, a stereotyped or limited-response repertoire, perseveration and inflexibility, and lack of self-monitoring of errors (Malloy & Richardson, 1994). Working memory may also be affected (Fuster, 1999).

Orbitofrontal Syndrome

Cummings and Trimble (1995) stated, "The orbitofrontal syndrome is the most dramatic of all frontal disorders. Individuals with previously normal behaviors are transformed by the prefrontal lesion" (p. 65). This strong language needs to be emphasized. The patient does not merely suffer increased irritability following a motor vehicle accident: They have been transformed in a dramatic way. The authors said,

> The predominant behavioral change is disinhibition. . . . Patients ignore social conventions and exhibit undue familiarity, talking to strangers and touching or fondling others without permission. They are tactless in conversation and may make uncivil or lewd remarks. They are impulsive, responding immediately and unpredictably to changing environmental circumstances. They lack conscientiousness and fail to complete assigned tasks. They are unconcerned about the consequences of their behavior. . . . They have been labeled "pseudopsychopathic" because of the similarity of some of their behaviors to those of individuals with antisocial personality disorder. (pp. 65–66)

Related to this last point, to do an accurate differential diagnosis, a comprehensive structured interview, such as the *Structured Clinical Interview for DSM-IV for Personality Disorders* (SCID-II) (First, Gibbon, Spitzer, Williams, & Benjamin, 1997), is required, to determine if the patient meets the criteria for antisocial personality disorder. The Hare Psychopathy Checklist—Revised (Hare, 1991) may also be useful for more comprehensive documentation. A thorough history of substance use and abuse with the *Structured Clinical Interview for DSM-IV* (SCID-I) (First, Spitzer, Gibbon, & Williams, 1997) would be essential in determining the contribution of substance use to impulsive behaviors.

Malloy, Bihrle, Duffy, and Cimino (1993) stated that orbitomedial frontal syndrome involves anosmia (loss of smell discrimination); amnesia and confabulation; go-no-go deficits; disinhibited personality change (characterized by sexual and verbal disinhibition, jocularity, lack of concern, and unstable mood; behaviors including facetious humor, inappropriate sexual behavior (sexual overtures to strangers), and labile emotionality; and hypersensitivity to noxious stimuli (such as exaggerated withdrawal of the leg to pinprick of the foot).

Mesial Frontal Syndrome

Cummings and Trimble (1995) stated,

> The medial frontal syndrome is marked by apathy. . . . *Emotionally,* the apathetic individual is unmotivated to initiate new tasks; there is disinterest in establishing or accomplishing goals. . . . *Cognitively,* the apathetic individual fails to formulate or implement plans and activities. . . . Slowing of cognition

may be evident. *Motorically*, apathetic individuals do not engage in activities. They may sit for long periods without participating in functions. (p. 67)

Duffy and Campbell (1994) said that mesial frontal apathetic syndrome is manifested by a client who appears depressed, but lacks the dysphoria, negative cognitions, and neurovegetative signs of a major depression. The patient is sometimes called "pseudodepressed."

DECISION RULES FOR EVALUATING STUDIES

The American Academy of Neurology (1997) presented "Definitions for Classification of Evidence":

Class I:	Evidence provided by one or more well-designed randomized controlled clinical trials.
Class II:	Evidence provided by one or more well-designed clinical studies.
Class III:	Evidence provided by expert opinion, non-randomized historical controls, case series, or case reports.

Definitions of strength of recommendations:

Standards:	Generally accepted principles for patient management that reflect a high degree of certainty that is based on Class I evidence; or, when circumstances preclude randomized clinical trials, overwhelming evidence of Class II studies that directly address the question.
Guidelines:	Recommendations for patient management that may identify a particular strategy or range of management strategies and that reflect moderate clinical certainty based on Class II evidence or consensus of Class III evidence.
Options:	Other strategies for patient management for which there is unclear clinical certainty (i.e., based on inconclusive or conflicting evidence of opinion). (pp. 584–585)

Satz et al. (2000) reviewed the literature regarding persistent postconcussion syndrome from 1960. They concluded that there were only three studies that used an appropriate design, using a noninjury and/ or other injury control group.

Statistical Power Analysis

Aron and Aron (1994) stated: "The statistical power of a psychology experiment is the probability that the study will yield a significant result if the research hypothesis is true" (p. 207). Cohen (1988) stated:

> The power of a statistical test is the probability that it will yield statistically significant results. (p. 1)

> The reliability (or precision) of a sample value is the closeness with which it can be expected to approximate the relevant population value. . . . [Reliability] is *always* dependent on the size of the sample. (p. 6)

> Without intending any necessary implication of causality, it is convenient to use the phrase "effect size" to mean "the *degree* to which the phenomenon is present in the population," or "the degree to which the null hypothesis is false." . . . The larger this value, the greater the *degree* to which the phenomenon under study is manifested. (pp. 9–10)

Aron and Aron (1994) stated: "The extent to which the two populations do not overlap . . . is called the effect size because it describes the degree to which the experimental manipulation has an effect of separating the two populations" (p. 216). Effect sizes are described (Cohen, 1988) as small (.2), medium (.5), and large (.8). For small-effect sizes, the populations of individual cases have an overlap of about 85%; for medium-effect sizes, the overlap is about 67%; and for large-effect sizes, the overlap is about 53%. The smaller the amount of overlap, the higher the power, increasing the probability that the study will yield a significant result, if the research hypothesis is true.

Statistical power is a function of the alpha level, the effect size, and the sample size. In a study, if the effect size is small and the sample size is small, the power would be low. Any conclusions from such a study would be very questionable.

In this context, two studies will be briefly summarized. In an oft-cited study purportedly supporting the concept of the cumulative effect of multiple, mild head injuries, Ewing, McCarthy, Gronwall, and Wrightson (1980) compared two groups of 10 students. This sample size is very small by any standards, and the likelihood that this sample would be representative of the population of interest would be very low. For any meaningful conclusions from a small sample, there would need to be a very large effect size. In this study for the Paced Auditory Serial Addition Task, there was no difference between groups (effect size). There was only a difference on an apparently unpublished "vigilance task" and the Running Digit Span, which was incorporated into the vigilance task. The reliability and validity of these tasks for the purpose intended is unknown. Despite these weak or false premises, the authors provide a strong conclusion:

> These results show that simulated altitude with mild hypoxia will cause a significant decrement in performance of young subjects who have been con-

cussed in the past, when compared to a control group reaction time task. . . .
The most likely explanation of this . . . is that concussion produces some
persisting deficits in intellectual function, although they may be subtle and
only emerge under conditions of stress of further injury. (p. 155)

The authors used no measures of intellectual function. Gronwall (1989)
then used this study as "experimental evidence" for persisting effects of
mild head injury. Lezak (1995) also uncritically stated: "One interesting
study showed that college students who had sustained mild head trauma
and seemed 'recovered' were abnormally prone to mental inefficiency
when physiologically stressed by hypoxic conditions" (p. 185). This
study did not show this. The conclusion does not follow logically from
the premises.

In their review of mild head injury, Binder, Rohling, and Larrabee
(1997) noted an effect size of .2 for attention between those with mild
head injury and controls. This is a negligible effect size, with about an
85% overlap between groups. This should not lead to the conclusion
that there was a deficit in attention found in those with a mild head
injury.

Sample Size

Charter (1999) concluded: "Although the determination of the *N*
needed for reliability studies is somewhat subjective, a minimum of 400
subjects is recommended. Much larger *N*s may be needed for validity
studies" (p. 559). In a "Methodological Commentary" on this article,
Cicchetti (1999) challenged this view. He said that the two fundamental
issues to consider were power and precision. The power decision was
settled by choosing a sample size that would provide power of 80%, with
an alpha level of .05. The precision decision refers to "the *reproducibility of
the power estimate*, or the expected effect size" (p. 567). These two articles
need careful consideration when considering which tests to use and
which studies should be relied upon. Tests and studies should be chosen
based on the sample size and the effect size (the larger the better),
with a power of 80% and an alpha level of .05. Very few tests and studies
would meet these criteria.

There are concerns raised by Fastenau and Adams (1996) about
the commonly used norms by Heaton, Grant, and Matthews (1991).
Fastenau and Adams said there were too many cells and too few subjects,

and the raw data underwent excessive conversions. Regarding sample size, they stated:

> What is the sample size for each subgroup in the *Comprehensive Norms*, from which each table has been derived? . . . Simple mental arithmetic yields a *maximum* of four people per subgroup, with as few as 1 person or even none at all representing at least some cells for at least some measures! . . . It is our responsibility to report the adequacy of our comparison groups. (p. 446)

In addition to these concerns, Heaton et al. assumed the scores were normally distributed, although these scores are unlikely to be normally distributed. If they are not normally distributed, the use of derived scores such as *T*-scores are questionable. In the study by Dikmen, Machover, Winn, and Temkin (1995), the scores on the Halstead–Reitan Battery were not normally distributed. Also, the mean WAIS IQ of the Heaton et al. sample was 113.7, almost 1 *SD* above the mean. This would suggest that the scores from this sample may not be representative of the general population with a mean IQ of 100. This is particularly problematic, since Heaton et al. use 1 *SD* below the mean as evidence of impairment. A score at 1 *SD* below the mean would be considered low average for the best-standardized batteries of tests—the Wechsler Scales and the Woodcock–Johnson Tests. It would be advisable for all psychologists to adopt one way of measuring ranges for scores from very impaired to very superior. The best choice of ranges would be those from the Wechsler Scales and the Woodcock–Johnson Tests.

DECISION RULES FOR DISSIMULATION AND MALINGERING

Rogers (1988) expressed concerns about methodological issues in dissimulation studies. The samples tended to be random, with usually nonpsychiatric subjects. Control groups were usually normal individuals. He suggested psychiatric patients be included. He said that it was rare to have cutting scores for dissimulation measures. There was rarely follow-up for the subjects' compliance. The simulation instructions were often general and vague. There were usually no incentives for simulation subjects to succeed, in marked contrast to true malingerers. The stability of dissimulation was not assessed. He stated: "The majority of psychometric studies put forth little effort to approximate conditions experienced by potential dissimulators in clinical settings" (p. 317). The relationship between the criterion group of simulators and true malingerers is unknown. Therefore, scores from malingering tests should be approached with caution.

Williams (1998) suggested that the neuropsychologist may use three major areas in which discrepancies occur, to construct a malingering index. The first is the relationship of injury severity to cognitive functioning. He said, "In general, injury severity level . . . should allow for general prediction of cognitive outcomes" (p. 122). An appendix in Dikmen et al. (1995) may be used to compare scores from various tests for different levels of severity of traumatic brain injury. It would be unusual for someone with a mild brain injury to have scores similar to the group with very severe injury. The second area involved noting the interrelationship of the tests and subtests. Williams said, "Inconsistencies are expressed as scores that are sufficiently disparate that they violate the known relationships between the tests" (p. 122). The third area involved the relationship between preinjury status and current test results. He said, "The most common situation involves a patient with a mild injury who performs very badly on a test of ability that should maintain premorbid levels" (p. 122). The neuropsychologist can point out inconsistencies, but issues of veracity ultimately should be left for the trier of fact to determine.

SYSTEMATIC ASSESSMENT

Peterson (1996) called for a systematic assessment approach. This is essential to being scientific. A systematic, replicable approach is now presented.

A thorough review of all available records, ideally from birth, will help to differentiate pre- and postinjury factors. It is best to deliberately state preinjury, concurrent, and intervening factors in the report. Discrepancies between the accounts of the patient (and significant others) and the records may raise concerns about informants' reliability.

A replicable test battery may include the Halstead–Reitan Battery, the WAIS-III, the WMS-III, the Western Aphasia Battery, and the Minnesota Multiphasic Personality Inventory-2. For achievement and cognitive abilities, the Woodcock–Johnson Tests may be used. Limitations of each of these tests regarding validity or reliability would be stated in the report.

A history form, such as that developed by Greenberg (1994), is helpful to consistently collect the same data from each patient. The SCID-I covers most Axis I diagnoses in a systematic way, based on criteria from

DSM-IV. SCID-II for Personality Disorders serves the same purpose for Axis II diagnoses. These interviews will provide valuable information about substance use and abuse and the contribution of emotional factors. Decision trees from Appendix A of DSM-IV (American Psychiatric Association, 1994) and the *DSM-IV Handbook of Differential Diagnosis* (First, Frances, & Pincus, 1995) are also useful for a systematic, replicable means of arriving at a diagnosis. For children, the Children's Interview for Psychiatric Syndromes (Rooney, Fristad, Weller, & Weller, 1999), by the American Psychiatric Association, is recommended as a structured interview for the child and the parent.

It is also helpful to ask the patient about activities of daily living from the *Guides for the Evaluation of Permanent Impairment* (1993) of the American Medical Association. Regarding evaluation of sleep disorders, it is helpful to cover areas discussed in *The Principles and Practice of Sleep Medicine* (Kryger, Roth, & Dement, 1994). The Psychosocial Pain Inventory (Getto & Heaton, 1985) is useful for determining the contribution of pain to any problems in functioning.

CONCLUSION

Decision making in forensic neuropsychology is a difficult and demanding task. Using the criterial and fallacies approaches, the neuropsychologist can determine whether the premises support the conclusion. It is best if explicit decision rules are used to evaluate studies, tests, and opinions. Some of these decision rules have been presented in this chapter. *The Standards* (1985) are the standard of care for the profession. For some disorders, such as frontal lobe syndromes, behavioral decision rules must be used. If a comprehensive, scientific, and replicable assessment is conducted, the neuropsychologist's opinion may be helpful to the trier of fact.

ACKNOWLEDGMENTS

To Ernest John and Theresa Marie, thanks for everything. I hope you have found peace. Special thanks to Wilma Ann and Amy Miyako.

REFERENCES

Adams, K. (2000). A normative festival: Now how does the ensemble play together? *Journal of Clinical and Experimental Neuropsychology, 22*(2), 299–302.

American Academy of Neurology Quality Standards Subcommittee. (1997). Practice parameter: The management of concussion in sports [Summary statement]. *Neurology, 48,* 581–585.

American Psychiatric Association (1993). *Guides to the evaluation of permanent impairment* (4th ed.). Washington, DC: American Psychiatric Association.

American Psychiatric Association. (1994). *Diagnostic and statistical manual of mental disorders* (4th ed.). Washington, DC: American Psychiatric Association

American Psychological Association. (1985). *Standards for educational and psychological testing.* Washington, DC: American Psychological Association.

American Psychological Association. (1992). *Ethical Principles of Psychologists and Code of Conduct, 1992.* Washington, DC: American Psychological Association.

Aron, A., & Aron, E. (1994). *Statistics for psychology.* Englewood Cliffs, NJ: Prentice-Hall.

Anastasi, A. (1988). *Psychological testing* (6th ed.). New York: Macmillan.

Bass, L., DeMers, S., Ogloff, J., Peterson, C., Pettifor, J., Reaves, R., et al. (1996). *Professional conduct and discipline in psychology.* Washington, DC: American Psychological Association.

Binder, L., Rohling, M., & Larrabee, G. (1997). A review of mild head trauma. Part I: Meta-analytic review of neuropsychological studies. *Journal of Clinical and Experimental Neuropsychology, 19*(3), 421–431.

Blair, J., & Spreen, O. (1989). Predicting premorbid IQ: A revision of the National Adult Reading Test. *The Clinical Neuropsychologist, 3,* 129–136.

Chapple v. Ganger, 851 F. Supp. 1481 (E.D. Wash. 1994).

Charter, R. (1999). Sample size requirements for precise estimates of reliability, generalizability, and validity coefficients. *Journal of Clinical and Experimental Neuropsychology, 21*(4), 559–566.

Cicchetti, D. (1999). Methodological commentary. *Journal of Clinical and Experimental Neuropsychology, 21*(4), 567–570.

Cohen, J. (1988). *Statistical power analysis for the behavioral sciences* (2nd ed.). Hillsdale, NJ: Lawrence Erlbaum.

Committee on Ethical Guidelines for Forensic Psychologists. (1991). Specialty Guidelines for Forensic Psychologists. *Law and Human Behavior, 15*(6), 655–665.

Copi, I., & Cohen, C. (1998). *Introduction to logic.* Upper Saddle River, NJ: Prentice-Hall.

Cummings, J. (1985). *Clinical neuropsychiatry.* New York: Grune & Stratton.

Cummings, J., & Trimble, M. (1995). *Neuropsychiatry and behavioral neurology.* Washington, DC: American Psychiatric Press.

Daubert v. Merrell Dow Pharmaceuticals, 113 S. Ct. 2786 (1993).

DeMers, S. (1996). Introduction. In L. Bass, S. DeMers, J. Ogloff, C. Peterson, J. Pettifor, R. Reaves, et al. (Eds.), *Professional conduct and discipline in psychology.* Washington, DC: American Psychological Association.

Dikmen, S., Machover, J., Winn, H., & Temkin, N. (1995). Neuropsychological outcome at 1-year post head injury. *Neuropsychology, 8*(1), 80–90.

Dodrill, C. (1997). Myths of neuropsychology. *The Clinical Neuropsychologist, 11*(1), 1–17.

Duffy, J., & Campbell, J. (1994). The regional prefrontal syndromes: A theoretical and clinical overview. *Journal of Neuropsychiatry and Clinical Neurosciences, 6,* 379–387.

Ewing, R., McCarthy, D., Gronwall, D., & Wrightson, P. (1980). Persisting effects of minor head injury observable during hypoxic stress. *Journal of Clinical Neuropsychology, 2*(2), 147–155.

Fastenau, P., & Adams, K. (1996). Heaton, Grant, and Matthews' comprehensive norms: An overzealous attempt. *Journal of Clinical Neuropsychology, 18*(3), 444–448.

First, M., Frances, A., & Pincus, H. (1995). *DSM-IV handbook of differential diagnosis.* Washington, DC: American Psychiatric Press.

First, M., Spitzer, R., Gibbon, M., & Williams, J. (1997). *User's guide for the structured clinical interview for DSM-IV axis I disorders.* Washington, DC: American Psychiatric Press.

First, M., Gibbon, M., Spitzer, R., Williams, J., & Benjamin, L. (1997). *User's guide for the structured clinical interview for DSM-IV axis II personality disorders.* Washington, DC: American Psychiatric Press.

Fuster, J. (1999). Cognitive Functions of the Frontal Lobes. In B. Miller & J. Cummings (Eds.), *The human frontal lobes.* New York: The Guilford Press.

General Electric v. Joiner, 522 U.S. 136 (1997).

Getto, C., & Heaton, R. (1985). *Psychosocial pain inventory manual.* Odessa, FL: Psychological Assessment Resources.

Glaros, A., & Kline, R. (1988). Understanding the accuracy of tests with cutting scores: The sensitivity, specificity, and predictive value model. *Journal of Clinical Psychology, 44,* 1013–1023.

Golden, C. (1978). *Stroop color and word test.* Chicago: Stoelting.

Greenberg, G. (1994). *Neuropsychological history.* Columbus, OH: International Diagnostic Systems.

Gronwall, D. (1989). Persisting effects of concussion on attention and cognition. In H. Levin, H. Eisenberg, & A. Benton (Eds.), *Mild head injury.* New York: Oxford University Press.

Hare, R. (1991). *The Hare Psychopathy Checklist Revised.* North Tonawanda, NY: Multi-Health Systems.

Heaton, R., Grant, I., & Matthews, C. (1991). *Comprehensive norms for an expanded Halstead-Reitan Battery.* Odessa, FL: Psychological Assessment Resources.

Hughes, W. (2000). *Critical thinking.* Orchard Park, NY: Broadview Press.

Hempel, C. (1966). *The philosophy of natural science.* Inglewood Cliffs, NJ: Prentice-Hall.

Hooper, H. (1993). *Hooper Visual Organization Test Manual.* Los Angeles, CA: Western Psychological Services.

Kryger, M., Roth, T., & Dement, W. (1994). *Principles and practice of sleep medicine.* Philadelphia: W. B. Saunders.

Kumho Tire v. Carmichael, 526 U.S. 137 (1999).

Lezak, M. (1995). *Neuropsychological assessment.* New York: Oxford University Press.

Malloy, P., Bihrle, A., Duffy, J., & Cimino, C. (1993). The orbitomedial frontal syndrome. *Archives of Clinical Neuropsychology, 8*(3), 185–201.

Malloy, P., & Richardson, E. (1994). Assessment of frontal lobe functions. *Journal of Neuropsychiatry and Clinical Neurosciences, 6,* 399–410.

Mitrushina, M., Boone, K., & D'Elia, L. (Eds.). *Handbook of normative data for neuropsychological assessment.* New York: Oxford University Press.

Peterson, C. (1996). Common problem areas and their causes relating in disciplinary actions. In L. Bass, S. DeMers, J. Ogloff, C. Peterson, J. Pettifor, R. Reaves, et al., *Professional conduct and discipline in psychology.* Washington, DC: American Psychological Association.

Popper, K. (1989). *Conjectures and refutations.* London: Routledge.

Reed, J. (1996). Fixed vs. flexible neuropsychological test batteries under the Daubert standard for the admissibility of scientific evidence. *Behavioral Sciences and the Law, 14,* 315–322.

Rogers, R. (1988). *Clinical assessment of malingering and deception.* New York: Guilford Press.

Rooney, M., Fristad, M., Weller, E., & Weller, R. (1999). *Administration manual for the ChIPS.* Washington, DC: American Psychiatric Press.

Russell, W. (1974, November 30). Recovery after minor head injury. *The Lancet,* 1314.

Satz, P. (1999). Forward. In M. Mitrushina, K. Boone, & L. D'Elia (Eds.), *Handbook of normative data for neuropsychological assessment.* New York: Oxford University Press.

Satz, P., Alfano, M., Light, R., Morgenstern, H., Zaucha, K., Asarnow, R., et al. (2000). Persistent post-concussive syndrome: A proposed methodology and literature review to determine the effects, if any, of mild head and other bodily injury. *Journal of Clinical and Experimental Neuropsychology, 21*(5), 620–628.

Sheslow, D., & Adams, W. (1990). *Wide range assessment of memory and learning administration manual.* Wilmington, DE: Jastak Associates.

Spreen, O., & Strauss, E. (1991). *A compendium of neuropsychological tests.* New York: Oxford University Press.

Sweet, J., Moberg, P., & Westergaard, C. (1996). Five-year follow-up of practices and beliefs of clinical neuropsychologists. *The Clinical Neuropsychologist, 10*(2), 202–221.

Sweet, J., Moberg, P., & Suchy, Y. (2000). Ten-year follow-up survey of clinical neuropsychologists: Part I. Practices and beliefs. *The Clinical Neuropsychologist, 14*(1), 18–37.

Test User Training Work Group of the Joint Committee on Testing Practices. (1993). *Responsible Test Use.* Washington, DC: American Psychological Association.

United States v. Scheffer, 523 U.S. 303. (1998).

Wechsler, D. (1997). *WMS-III administration and scoring manual.* San Antonio, TX: The Psychological Corporation.

Wechsler, D. (1997). *WAIS-III–WMS-III technical manual.* San Antonio, TX: The Psychological Corporation.

Williams, A. (1997). The forensic evaluation of adult traumatic brain injury. In R. McCaffrey, A. Williams, J. Fisher, & L. Laing (Eds.), *The practice of forensic neuropsychology* (pp. 37–56). New York: Plenum Press.

Williams, J. (1998). The malingering of memory disorder. In C. Reynolds (Ed.), *Detection of malingering during head injury litigation* (pp. 105–132). New York: Plenum Press.

Chapter 5

Detecting Malingering in Civil Forensic Evaluations

Grant L. Iverson

INTRODUCTION

Gradually and systematically, the professional practice of clinical neuropsychology is becoming more sophisticated and psychometrically precise. Clinical judgment is being enhanced with new assessment procedures and more precise methods of interpreting neuropsychological test data. In routine clinical practice, neuropsychologists use the assessment process to document an individual's functioning across numerous ability areas. On the basis of these results, the psychologist draws clinical inferences regarding the putative impact of a brain injury, condition, or disease on these various cognitive and neurobehavioral abilities. Moreover, the clinician attempts to extrapolate real-world implications from the test findings.

Proper interpretation of neuropsychological test results requires careful and systematic consideration of a wide range of factors that can influence performance on any given test. Before assuming that a test score reflects compromised brain functioning secondary to an injury or disease, the clinician must determine that the patient understood the requirements of the test and put forth his or her best effort. The clinician must then try to determine whether a low score represents a premorbid weakness and/or a skill decrement resulting from compro-

Portions of this chapter were presented at the National Academy of Neuropsychology, Orlando, FL, November 16, 2000, and at the American Neuropsychiatric Association Meeting in Fort Myers, FL, in February of 2001.

mised brain functioning. This most basic clinical inference is predicated on a number of assumptions, such as whether (a) the test was administered and scored properly, (b) there was adequate demographically corrected normative data available for comparison, (c) the test has adequate reliability and validity for that specific use with that specific person, and (d) other factors that could adversely affect test performance were systematically ruled out.

Any neuropsychological evaluation that does not include careful consideration of the patient's motivation to give their best effort should be considered incomplete. Moreover, researchers over the past 15 years have provided the clinician with abundant data on strategies for detecting deliberately poor performance. In situations in which there is motivation for exaggerating problems or degree of disability, such as in personal injury litigation, the neuropsychologist should examine for the possibility of negative response bias, just as they examine for possible deficits in concentration, learning, or memory, or the presence of psychological problems such as depression. The clinician should be satisfied that the test results are accurate and that the patient was not attempting to exaggerate or malinger.

To determine if someone is malingering, the psychologist must establish that the patient is deliberately exaggerating or fabricating symptoms and/or deliberately performing poorly on testing. In addition, this must be judged to be goal-directed behavior designed to achieve a readily identifiable external incentive (American Psychiatric Association, 1994; Slick, Sherman, & Iverson, 1999). This determination requires careful consideration of multiple sources of data and the systematic ruling out of several differential diagnoses. This determination should not be made on the basis of a single test result. Fortunately, there are many reviews of this literature in the past few years that can be used to assist the clinician with this process (e.g., Franzen & Iverson, 1997; Iverson & Binder, 2000; Reynolds, 1998; Rogers, 1997; Sweet, 1999; Vickery, Berry, Inman, Harris, & Orey, 2001).

DIAGNOSTIC FORMULATION

Malingering is the intentional production of false or greatly exaggerated symptoms for the purpose of attaining some identifiable external reward (American Psychiatric Association, 1994). Within the context of a neuropsychological evaluation, someone who is malingering may exaggerate subjective symptoms that are difficult to define or to measure precisely. The person may exaggerate pain, stiffness, dizziness, depression, memory disturbance, poor concentration, and/or personality change. Some individuals may fabricate more objective complaints, such as blindness or visual loss, numbness, grossly restricted mobility or range of motion, or severe amnesia. During neuropsychological testing, willful production of poor performance is often associated with malingering. A person may decide to malinger to (a) receive more money in a personal injury lawsuit, (b) receive worker's compensation or disability benefits, (c) obtain prescription medications, (d) avoid prosecution for criminal activities (vis-à-vis a determination of incompetency to stand trial), or (e) avoid criminal responsibility (i.e., not guilty by reason of insanity).

I recommend approaching malingering as a "diagnosis" of exclusion. It is important to be objective and systematic in one's approach to assessing for exaggeration or deliberately poor test performance. Careful examination of personal and professional biases, on a regular basis, may facilitate a fair-minded review of the complete examination.

The presence of exaggeration of symptoms or poor effort on testing should not automatically be equated with malingering. The exaggeration of symptoms in a clinical interview, or intentionally poor performance on psychological or neuropsychological tests, is considered negative response bias. Negative response bias describes the behavior without inferring the motivation. To diagnose malingering, the clinician must determine that the negative response bias was designed to achieve some identifiable external incentive. A number of differential diagnoses and alternative explanations should be considered in this evaluative process.

The diagnostic formulation in cases of known or suspected malingering, although conceptualized as involving an exclusionary approach, does not mean that the presence of a differential precludes the diagnosis of comorbid malingering. Obviously, it is possible to malinger within the course of depression, or malinger in the presence of observed structural brain damage following a traumatic injury. The systematic process of considering multiple differentials is needed to determine if one or more differentials can completely account for the observed exaggeration of symptoms or deliberately poor performance on tests. Important differential diagnoses to consider are factitious disorder, depression, somatization disorder, somatoform disorder not otherwise specified, hypochondriasis, and conversion disorder. The differentials are described in detail in Iverson and Binder (2000).

The psychological constructs of suggestibility and symptom magnification are complex issues that can be difficult to disentangle in neuropsychological evaluations. Babinski (1909/1988) used the term *pithiatism*, which means "caused by suggestion, cured by persuasion," to describe psychologically induced neurological symptoms. Kathol (1996) suggests that pithiatism, or hypersuggestibility, is more likely to be the cause of unexplained neurological complaints than conversion disorder. He reviewed research evidence that patients with hysterical symptoms are more suggestible than other psychiatric patients or normal persons. Kathol also reviewed evidence suggesting that patients with unexplained neurological symptoms (a) are more likely to have friends or relatives who have similar (presumed genuine) problems; (b) frequently do not have extreme stressors, psychological trauma, or early life traumatic experiences that can be casually connected to their complaints; and (c) often respond to reassurance that they do not have a serious neurological problem or disease, especially if they have not had the symptoms for an extended period of time.

The experience of being ill can, in some ways, be rewarding for the patient. For example, the patient may get special privileges and extra attention from their spouse, family, coworkers, and friends. For many years, these issues have been studied in patients with chronic pain syndromes. Researchers have demonstrated that extra attention, changes in household responsibilities and routines, and the avoidance of undesirable activities all can increase patients' reporting of pain and disability. It is reasonable to think that some individuals involved in protracted litigation could derive reinforcement for disability behaviors.

Diagnostic Criteria for Malingering

Slick et al. (1999) proposed diagnostic criteria for definite, probable, and possible malingering (see Table 5.1 for a partial reproduction of the criteria). There are several steps and inferences in the diagnostic process. First, for a diagnosis of definite malingering, there must be clear and compelling evidence of exaggeration or fabrication of cognitive impairment. To be considered malingering, the person's behavior should be conceptualized as volitional and rational. Second, there must not be plausible alternative explanations for this behavior. The clinician should rule out a number of differential diagnoses (e.g., factitious disorder or somatoform disorder). Third, it should be determined that

TABLE 5.1 Criteria for Definite, Probable, and Possible Malingering of Cognitive Dysfunction

Definite Malingering is indicated by the presence of clear and compelling evidence of volitional exaggeration or fabrication of cognitive dysfunction and the absence of plausible alternative explanations. The specific diagnostic criteria necessary for Definite MND are listed below.

1. Presence of a substantial external incentive [Criterion A]
2. Definite negative response bias [Criterion B1]
3. Behaviors meeting necessary criteria from group B are not fully accounted for by psychiatric, neurological, or developmental factors [Criterion D]

Probable Malingering is indicated by the presence of evidence strongly suggesting volitional exaggeration or fabrication of cognitive dysfunction and the absence of plausible alternative explanations. The specific diagnostic criteria necessary for Probable MND are listed below.

1. Presence of a substantial external incentive [Criterion A]
2. Two or more types of evidence from neuropsychological testing, excluding definite negative response bias [two or more of Criteria B2–B6]
   Or
   One type of evidence from neuropsychological testing, excluding definite negative response bias, and one or more types of evidence from self-report [one of Criteria B2–B6 and one or more of Criteria C1–C5]
3. Behaviors meeting necessary criteria from groups B or C are not fully accounted for by psychiatric, neurological, or developmental factors [Criterion D].

Possible Malingering is indicated by the presence of evidence suggesting volitional exaggeration or fabrication of cognitive dysfunction and the absence of plausible alternative explanations. Alternatively, possible MND is indicated by the presence of criteria necessary for Definite or Probable MND, except that other primary etiologies cannot be ruled out. The specific diagnostic criteria for Possible MND are listed below.

1. Presence of a substantial external incentive [Criterion A]
2. Evidence from self-report [one or more of Criteria C1–C5]
3. Behaviors meeting necessary criteria from groups B or C are not fully accounted for by psychiatric, neurological, or developmental factors [Criterion D]
   Or
   Criteria for Definite or Probable MND are met, except for Criterion D (i.e., primary psychiatric, neurological, or developmental etiologies cannot be ruled out). In such cases, the alternate etiologies that cannot be ruled out should be specified.

From Slick et al., 1999. Reprinted with permission.

the exaggeration or fabrication of impairment is not the result of diminished capacity to appreciate laws or mores against malingering or an inability to conform behavior to such standards, as may be the case in persons with certain psychiatric, developmental, or neurological disorders.

The criteria for probable and possible malingering are based on the same principles as the criteria for definite malingering: There is simply less supporting evidence in the former diagnoses. The evidence for suspecting exaggeration or fabrication of impairment is also described by Slick et al. First, there should be evidence of exaggeration of cognitive problems on neuropsychological tests, as demonstrated by one of the following: (a) below-chance performance ($p < .05$) on one or more forced-choice measures of cognitive function; (b) performance consistent with feigning on one or more well-validated tests or indices designed to measure exaggeration or fabrication of cognitive deficits; (c) inconsistency between test results and known patterns of brain functioning; (d) inconsistency between test results and observed behavior; (e) inconsistency between test results and reliable collateral reports; and (f) inconsistency between test results and documented background history. The authors explain these suspicion factors and discuss issues relating to whether these factors are consistent with definite, probable, or possible malingering.

According to Slick et al., evidence from the patient's self-report can be used to support a diagnosis of malingering. The following factors may be considered suspicious, and should be examined carefully: (a) self-reported history that is inconsistent with documented history; (b) self-reported symptoms that are inconsistent with known patterns of brain functioning; (c) self-reported symptoms that are inconsistent with behavioral observations; (d) self-reported symptoms that are inconsistent with information obtained from reliable collateral informants; or (e) evidence of exaggerated or fabricated self-reported problems on psychological tests (e.g., Minnesota Multiphasic Personality Inventory—2 [MMPI-2]). A checklist for using the diagnostic criteria is provided in Table 5.2.

UNDERLYING MOTIVATION FOR DELIBERATE EXAGGERATION

During the twentieth century, malingering has been conceptualized in several different ways. Malingering was once viewed from a pathological

TABLE 5.2   Malingering Criteria Checklist

❏	A. Clear and substantial external incentive
❏	B1. Definite response bias
❏	B2. Probable response bias
❏	B3. Discrepancy between known patterns of brain function/dysfunction and test data
❏	B4. Discrepancy between observed behavior and test data
❏	B5. Discrepancy between reliable collateral reports and test data
❏	B6. Discrepancy between history and test data
❏	C1. Self-reported history is discrepant with documented history
❏	C2. Self-reported symptoms are discrepant with known patterns of brain functioning
❏	C3. Self-reported symptoms are discrepant with behavioral observations
❏	C4. Self-reported symptoms are discrepant with information obtained from collateral informants
❏	C5. Evidence of exaggerated or fabricated psychological dysfunction on standardized measures
❏	D. Behaviors satisfying Criteria B and/or C were volitional and directed at least in part toward acquiring or achieving external incentives as defined in Criteria A
❏	E. The patient adequately understood the purpose of the examination and the possible negative consequences of exaggerating or fabricating cognitive deficits.
❏	F. Test results contributing to Criteria B are sufficiently reliable and valid.

(See Slick et al., 1999.)

perspective; that is, if you malingered, you must be sick. The behavior was considered seriously abnormal, and the "ill" person was in need of treatment. Rogers (1990) discussed the transition from this pathological view to a puritanical view, as represented by the description of malingering in the past several editions of the *Diagnostic and Statistical Manual of Mental Disorders*. Rogers describes this puritanical conceptualization as a "bad person" in a "bad situation," who is a "bad participant," because clinicians are to suspect malingering if the patient (a) has an antisocial personality disorder, (b) is undergoing a forensic evaluation, and/or (c) is uncooperative with the evaluation.

Rogers (1990) proposed an adaptational conceptualization of malingering, in which people assess their situation and deliberately choose a course of action designed to achieve their objectives. From this perspective, it may be less likely that clinicians would ignore evidence of faking because a person did not fulfill the more judgmental criteria.

Moreover, this view is accepting of socially sanctioned malingering, such as when a hostage fakes illness to avoid being mistreated. The DSM-IV expanded the definition from previous editions, by stating that malingering may represent adaptive behavior, such as when a prisoner of war feigns illness.

From a social psychological perspective, malingering occurs on a spectrum of severity; many people have engaged in this behavior from time to time. Some obvious examples include pretending to be sick or exaggerating minor illness to avoid school or work, or pretending to be ill to avoid a social engagement (so as not to hurt your friend's feelings). These examples generally are considered benign. In fact, malingering may not be considered "wrong" unless the issues are much more serious. Examples include people accused of murder who malinger mental illness to be deemed incompetent to stand trial, or the accident victim who fakes whiplash to get an insurance settlement. It is surprising that, when asked directly, many people report that they would consider malingering within the context of personal injury litigation, despite apparent societal mores against this behavior. For example, after participating in an analog malingering study, participants were asked if they would consider malingering if they found themselves in certain situations. Regarding personal injury litigation, 35% of psychiatric inpatients ($N = 20$), 65% of federal inmates ($N = 20$), and 48% of university undergraduates ($N = 40$) reported that they would consider malingering for monetary gain (Iverson, 1996). Clearly, social psychological research into the societal and cultural issues relating to malingering is needed.

Very little is known about a person's underlying motivation to engage in deliberate exaggeration of symptoms or poor test performance. It is presumed that "litigation stress" might be conceptually and causally related to motivation to malinger. However, the effects of litigation stress are poorly understood, and much additional research is needed in this area. Weissman (1990) describes aspects of litigation stress in the following quote:

> Involvement in litigation renders plaintiffs susceptible to stressors and to influences that may lead to increased impairment, biased reportage, and retarded recovery. Underlying personality patterns play a critical role in defining and shaping reactions to trauma, to the stress of litigation, and to treatment interventions. Protracted litigation creates conditions that promote mnemonic and attitudinal distortions, as well as conscious and unconscious motivations for secondary gain. (p. 67)

What is apparent from this quote is Weissman's belief that litigation produces negative effects on the plaintiff's mental state, through multiple pathways, including greater susceptibility to stressors, attitude changes, motivational changes, and biases in self-reported problems.

Plaintiffs with acquired brain injuries or psychological problems find themselves in a very different health care environment than injured or emotionally distressed people not in litigation. For example, individuals other than the injured person have a vested interest in the assessment and rehabilitation of the plaintiff. As well, others have a vested interest in doubting the veracity of the patient's health problems. The effect of these vested interests can be seen in the skepticism frequently attached to diagnoses of postconcussive syndrome, posttraumatic stress disorder (PTSD), or major depression; outside the context of litigation, these diagnoses are accepted with less skepticism.

One result of these vested interests and skepticism is that plaintiffs with alleged postconcussive syndrome or psychological problems will be subjected to more intensive, frequent, and possibly hostile assessment of their health problems. Thus, an individual seeking relief for symptoms while in litigation will experience a very different health care environment than will the person seeking such relief outside the context of litigation. In fact, there might even be pressures to avoid effective treatments and remain off work, in order to illustrate the damages resulting from the cause of action. Undoubtedly, protracted litigation can be very stressful, and a plaintiff who was once significantly injured, but who has mostly recovered, might feel entitled to the compensation anticipated by his lawyer, thus feeling justified in his decision to grossly exaggerate his current disability. Some factors that might be related to a person's underlying motivation to malinger are presented in Figure 5.1.

ASSESSMENT METHODS

There are three general approaches to using tests, within the context of a neuropsychological evaluation, for the purpose of identifying negative response bias. The first approach is to use tests that have response-style indices built in, such as self-report inventories like the MMPI-2 and the Personality Assessment Inventory. The second approach is to use preexisting tests of cognitive ability and to identify unusual cutoff scores or performance patterns on these tests. The third approach is to use specialized tests designed specifically for detecting biased responding.

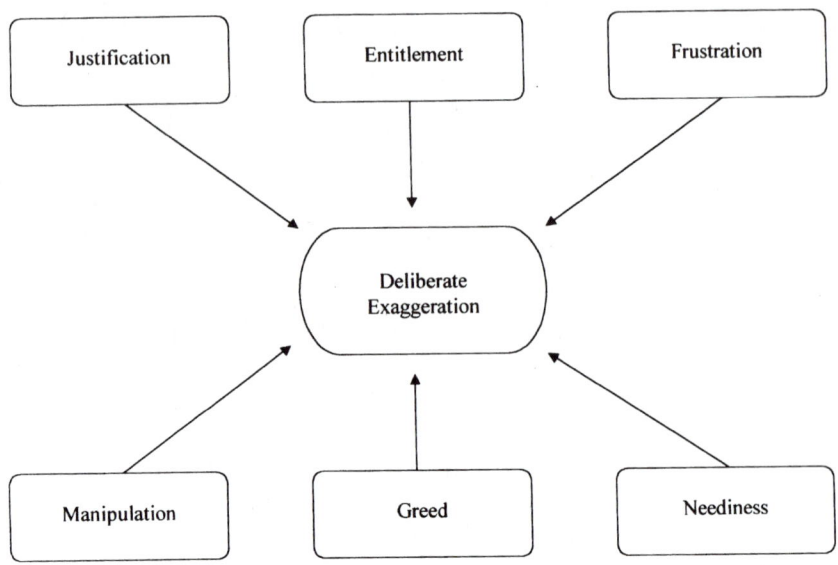

FIGURE 5.1   Factors that might influence exaggeration.

Examples of preexisting (Table 5.3) and specialized tests (Table 5.4), which have been reported in the malingering literature, are provided below. This is not meant to be an exhaustive review of tests and procedures. The interested reader can gather additional information about these and other tests from several books and reviews (e.g., Iverson & Binder, 2000; Reynolds, 1998; Rogers, 1997; Sweet, 1999, Vickery et al., 2001).

The clinician must be careful when applying indices of biased responding from the literature to individual patients. Research results can appear straightforward and ready for use, when they clearly have methodological limitations. For example, Mittenberg, Azrin, Millsops, and Heilbronner (1993) discovered that community volunteers, given instructions to malinger, often suppressed their Attention/Concentration Index (A/C) score, compared to their General Memory Index (GM) score on the Wechsler Memory Scale—Revised (WMS-R). Large GM–A/C difference scores were rare in a sample of nonlitigating patients with head injuries. In follow-up studies, Iverson, Slick, and Franzen (2000) demonstrated that the GM–A/C difference score was positively

TABLE 5.3 Examples of Preexisting Tests that Have Been Used to Identify Biased Responding

Preexisting test	Selected references
Digit Span	Binder & Willis (1991); Greiffenstein, Baker, & Gola (1994), Iverson & Franzen (1994, 1996); Iverson & Tulsky (in press); Meyers & Volbrecht (1998); Suhr, Tranel, Wefel, & Barrash (1997); Trueblood & Schmidt (1993)
Vocabulary—Digit Span Difference Score	Axelrod & Rawlings (1999); Iverson & Tulsky (in press); Mittenberg, Theroux-Fichera, Zielinski & Heilbronner (1995); Millis, Ross, & Ricker (1998)
Wechsler Adult Intelligence Scale—Revised (WAIS-R)	Axelrod & Rawlings (1999); Millis et al. (1998); Mittenberg et al. (1995); Reitan & Wolfson (1996a, 1996b, 1997); Trueblood (1994); Williams & Carlin (1999)
Wechsler Memory Scale—Revised (WMS-R) General Memory–Attention/ Concentration Difference Score	Iverson & Slick (in press); Iverson et al. (2000); Mittenberg et al. (1993)
Wechsler Memory Scale—Third Edition (WMS-III)	Killgore & Dellapietra (2000a, 2000b)
Category Test	Tenhula & Sweet (1996)
Halstead–Reitan Neuropsychological Test Battery	Goebel (1983); Heaton, Smith, Lehman, & Vogt (1978); McKinzey & Russell (1997); Mittenberg, Rotholc, Russell, & Heilbronner (1996)
California Verbal Learning Test	Baker, Donder, & Thompson (2000); Coleman, Rapport, Millis, Ricker, & Farchione (1998); Millis, Putnam, Adams, & Ricker (1995); Trueblood (1994); Trueblood & Schmidt (1993); Slick, Iverson, & Green (in press); Sweet et al. (2000)
Luria–Nebraska Neuropsychological Test Battery	McKinzey et al. (1997); Mensch & Woods (1986)
Recognition Memory Test	Iverson & Binder (2000); Iverson & Franzen (1994, 1998); Millis (1992, 1994); Millis & Dijkers (1993)
Seashore Rhythm Test	Gfeller & Cradock (1998)
Trail Making Test	Iverson, Lange, Green, & Franzen (in press); Ruffolo, Guilmette, & Willis (2000)
Judgment of Line Orientation	Iverson (in press); Meyers, Galinsky, & Volbrecht (1999)

TABLE 5.4 Examples of Specialized Tests that Have Been Used to Identify Biased Responding

Specialized test	Selected citations
Portland Digit Recognition Test	Binder (1993); Binder & Kelly (1996); Binder & Willis (1991); Ju & Varney (2000); Rose, Hall, Szalda-Petree, & Bach (1998)
Computerized Assessment of Response Bias	Allen, Conder, Green, & Cox (1997); Green & Iverson (in press)
Victoria Symptom Validity Test	Doss, Chelune, & Naugle (1999); Grote et al. (2000); Slick, Hopp, Strauss, Hunter, & Pinch (1994); Slick, Hopp, Strauss, & Spellacy (1996); Slick, Hopp, Strauss, & Thompson (1997)
Word Memory Test	Green, Allen, & Astner (1996); Green, Iverson, & Allen (1999); Iverson, Green, & Gervais (1999)
21 Item Test	Arnett & Franzen (1997); Gontkovsky & Souheaver (2000); Iverson (1998); Iverson, Franzen, & McCracken (1991, 1994); Rose et al. (1998)
Validity Indicator Profile	Frederick (1997, 2000); Frederick & Crosby (2000); Frederick, Crosby, & Wynkoop (2000); Frederick & Foster (1991); Frederick, Sarfaty, Johnston, & Powel (1994); Rose et al. (1998)
Test of Memory Malingering	Rees, Tombaugh, Gansler, & Moczynski (1998); Tombaugh (1997)
Rey 15 Item Test	Arnett, Hammeke, & Schwartz (1995); Bernard & Fowler (1990); Goldberg & Miller (1986); Greiffenstein, Baker, & Gola (1996); Guilmette, Hart, Giuliano, & Leininger (1994); Hays, Emmons, & Stallings (2000); Lee, Loring, & Martin (1992); Millis & Kler (1995)

correlated with the GM score. This means that higher scores on the GM are associated with larger-difference scores. This was demonstrated in both inpatient substance abusers (Iverson et al., 2000) and in patients with acute traumatic brain injuries (TBIs) (Iverson & Slick, in press). This is important, because, if a patient scored in the high-average or superior range on the GM, a large-discrepancy score is relatively common, so it would be inappropriate to suggest that this was caused by biased responding. Therefore, the GM–A/C difference score's clinical usefulness was enhanced significantly, based on follow-up research.

Some preexisting tests clearly have more research support, as possible indicators of biased responding, than do others (e.g., the Recognition

Memory Test versus Judgment of Line Orientation or Trail Making Test). A patient's performance on the Judgment of Line Orientation Test or the Trail Making Test might be suspicious (Meyers et al., 1999; Ruffolo et al., 2000) and inconsistent with the known effects of mild traumatic brain injury (MTBI); however, follow-up studies have suggested that these tests should not have special status as "tests for malingering," because they have very low sensitivity to this behavior (Iverson, in press; Iverson et al., in press). Instead, these tests should simply be interpreted carefully, if a patient's score falls in a range that does not appear to make biological or psychometric sense. They may serve as red flags for negative response bias.

The clinician must also be careful when using specialized tests, such as those presented in Table 5.4. For example, there is considerable disagreement in the profession as to whether the Rey 15 Item Test is appropriate as a measure of biased responding. This test has been used in many studies, and administration and scoring procedures have varied considerably. In general, the test is not very sensitive to biased responding; thus, it would be inappropriate to use it as the only specialized test in a battery. Many tests, however, have low sensitivity, so this fact alone should not preclude their use. If simple, brief tests, such as the Rey 15 Item Test or the 21 Item Test are given, it is very important to give them at the beginning of the evaluation, before the patient is exposed to more rigorous testing. Giving them later in the evaluation probably will further reduce their sensitivity.

Forced-choice digit recognition procedures, such as the Hiscock and Hiscock (1989) procedure, Portland Digit Recognition Test (PDRT), Computerized Assessment of Response Bias, and the Victoria Symptom Validity Test (VSVI), have been shown to be relatively insensitive to the effects of brain injury (although the PDRT is presumably the most demanding and likely to be affected by real brain impairment). Most clinicians should now know that there are two ways to interpret these tests: (a) comparison to chance levels via the binomial distribution, and (b) the application of empirically derived basal cutoff scores. Those clinicians who rely on chance performance levels will fail to detect a sizeable percentage of individuals who are not trying their best. This is particularly problematic on the VSVT. Although a well-designed and very useful test, the manual and computer scoring program contain the unfortunate terminology of "valid," "questionable," and "invalid." This is problematic, because the best basal cutoff score for the test falls in the "valid" classification range, meaning that patients who are very likely exaggerating their problems could easily fall into the broad classes of valid or questionable. The VSVT is an excellent test, and recent research is continuing to demonstrate its utility (see Table 5.4), but the clinician should essentially ignore the descriptions of the three classification categories. Instead, the clinician might adopt the classifications "normal," "biased," and "below chance," based on cutoff scores derived from the manual and from the literature.

FUTURE CLINICAL AND RESEARCH DIRECTIONS FOR SPECIALIZED TESTS

The accuracy of a specialized test is influenced by several factors. Sensitivity of a test refers to how often people who are exaggerating are correctly identified (e.g., a sensitivity of .75 means that 75% of people who are exaggerating are correctly identified by the test). Specificity refers to how often people who are not exaggerating are correctly identified (e.g., a specificity of .91 means that 91% of people who are not exaggerating are correctly classified by the test). Base rates refer to the prevalence of exaggeration in the referral base of the lab. For example, in Table 5.5, the base rates of exaggeration in a sample of 10,000 patients referred to a lab are listed in the first row. If the base rate is .10, 1,000 of the patients referred are exaggerating. Thus, a base rate of .50 means that 5,000, or one half of all patients referred, are exaggerating.

Based on data collected to date (Iverson, 1998), the sensitivity of the 21 Item Test to presumed negative response bias is .643 in experimental

TABLE 5.5 Accuracy of the 21 Item Test Forced-Choice Score for Detecting Biased Responding (Sensitivity = .643, Specificity = .988)

Base rate	.10	.20	.30	.40	.50	.60	.70	.80	.90
Correctly identified	.95	.92	.88	.85	.82	.78	.75	.71	.68
True-positive rate	.86	.93	.96	.97	.98	.99	.99	1.00	1.00
True-negative rate	.96	.92	.87	.81	.73	.65	.54	.41	.24
False-positive rate	.01	.01	.01	.01	.01	.01	.01	.01	.01
False-negative rate	.36	.36	.36	.36	.36	.36	.36	.36	.36
Positive predictive power	.86	.93	.96	.97	.98	.99	.99	1.00	1.00
Negative predictive power	.96	.92	.87	.81	.73	.65	.54	.41	.24

malingerers (N = 237), and the specificity in a combined sample of control subjects, heterogeneous neurological and psychiatric patients, and patients with memory deficits, is .988 (N = 406). If 10,000 people are referred for screening, and 30% are exaggerating, then 88% would be correctly identified (see Table 5.5). If the test were positive, it would correctly label the patients as not providing their best performance 96% of the time (positive predictive power [*PPP*] = .96) and if the test were negative, it would correctly classify the patients as providing "full effort" 87% of the time (negative predictive power [*NPP*] = .87). If 10,000 people are referred for screening, and 60% are exaggerating, then 78% would be correctly identified. If the test were positive, it would correctly identify the patients as not providing their best effort 99% of the time (*PPP* = .99), and, if the test were negative, it would correctly classify the patients as providing full effort 65% of the time (*NPP* = .65).

Note that the false-positive rate (i.e., 1%) and the false-negative rate (i.e., 36%) remain constant. However, they only correspond to the predictive power statistics when the base rate is .50, meaning that exactly one half of all patients referred are exaggerating. Otherwise, there is a disproportionate number of patients who are exaggerating (either more or less than 50%), which is then combined with the sensitivity and specificity statistics to create varying levels of predictive power.

Figure 5.2 illustrates the relationship between the predictive power of a test and the prevalence (i.e., base rate) of exaggeration in the referral base of a lab. The graph is based on a sensitivity estimate of .643 and a specificity estimate of .988. Under these conditions, the *PPP* increases rapidly and begins to plateau above 90%, before the prevalence rate hits 20%. In contrast, the *NPP* drops below 80% when the prevalence rate exceeds 40%. This means that, when a person scores below the cutoff, the clinician can be very confident that they are not providing full effort. However, as the base rate of malingering increases in the referral base of the lab, the clinician has less and less confidence in negative results (because the test has a false-negative rate of .36; thus, the *NPP* drops as the base rate increases).

Odds Ratios

The odds ratio can be used to estimate risk for exaggeration, based on screening test cutoff scores. For example, using the data collected to

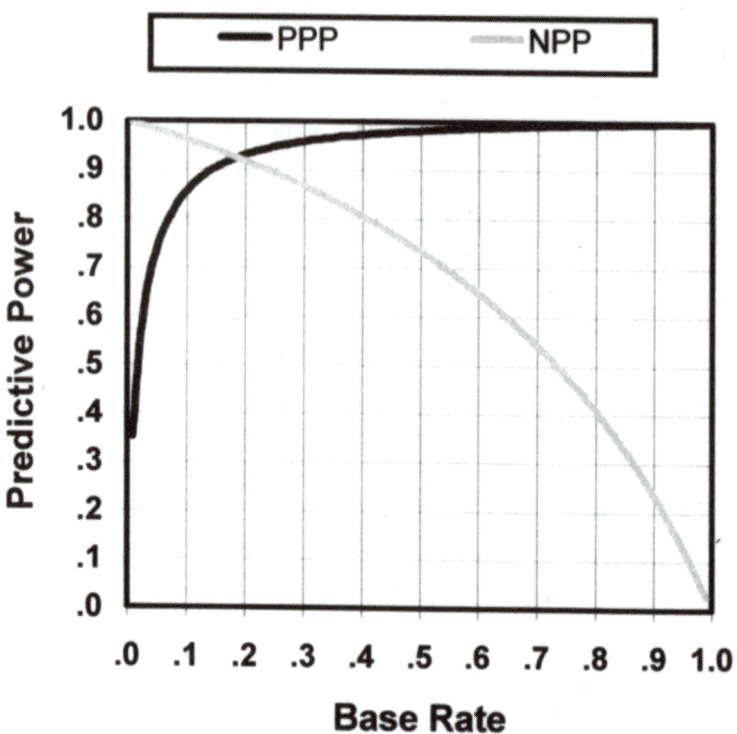

**FIGURE 5.2   Illustration of the relationship between the predictive power
of a test and the prevalence (i.e., base rate) of exaggeration in the referral
base of a lab (sensitivity = .643 and specificity = .988).**

date, it is possible to compute an odds ratio based on a cut-off score
of <12. For these analyses, a combined group of 406 control subjects
and patients were compared to 237 experimental malingerers. A score
of 11 or less on the forced-choice component identified 64.5% of the
malingers and falsely labeled 1.2% of the combined patients and controls (χ^2 (1,643) = 323.8, p < .00001).[1] A patient who scores 11 or less
on the forced-choice component of the 21 Item Test is 146.1 times

---

[1]Odds ratios are relatively easy to calculate by hand; the formula is available in many statistical
texts. Calculating confidence intervals is more cumbersome. Fortunately, this can all be done
in Statistical Program for the Social Sciences under "cross tabs."

more likely to be exaggerating than a patient who scores 12 or more (95% Confidence Interval = 58.1 – 367). The future of negative response bias research and clinical practice should include sophisticated accuracy analyses for all screening tests.

CLINICIANS' RELUCTANCE TO ASSESS FOR BIASED RESPONDING

The term *malingering*, as a description of behavior or as a diagnosis, usually is considered highly pejorative, contentious, and controversial. Clinicians may be very reluctant to address this behavior directly, even if there is strong evidence, because of fear of the consequences (e.g., mislabeling someone, being threatened, or being sued). In contrast, clinicians tend to be much more comfortable diagnosing people with brain damage, schizophrenia, alcohol or drug abuse, or with personality disorders. It could be argued that all of these labels are pejorative and potentially damaging, and thus should be considered very carefully.

Neuropsychologists serving as experts might emphasize the serious consequences of diagnosing malingering, be very cautious in reaching this conclusion, and even suggest that we should err on the side of not finding malingering. Arguably, this approach is systematically biased toward the plaintiff. It is well appreciated that the plaintiff can suffer dire consequences by being falsely labeled a malingerer. The consequences to the defendant, who is the victim of malingering, are frequently overlooked. Certainly, the family of the defendant who is bankrupted by the fraudulent claims of the malingerer will suffer. The emotional costs of protracted litigation, to the defendant, can be hard to quantify. The plaintiff who engages in malingering can also suffer (e.g., through protracted periods of unemployment, changes in role functioning within the family, and reductions in social and recreational activities). Moreover, the plaintiff engaged in malingering for an extended period of time might actually incorporate that disability into his personality (as predicted by social psychological research). Therefore, a scientific approach to the assessment of malingering requires a neutral stance and a willingness to provide the court with the most probable correct answer. Opinions regarding symptom validity should rely heavily on empirical test data that are qualified with information concerning statistical confidence.

There are practical, professional, statistical, and ethical reasons why every civil forensic neuropsychological evaluation should include careful assessment for biased responding. These issues are discussed in detail in the following sections.

Effect Size Considerations

With the recent publication of a malingering meta-analysis, the issue of whether or not it is appropriate to systematically evaluate for negative response bias should be resolved. Vickery et al. (2001) demonstrated clearly that tests designed to measure biased responding are sensitive to that behavior, and they can classify subjects with a reasonable degree of accuracy. The meta-analysis conducted by Vickery et al. can be compared to the meta-analysis by Binder, Rohling, and Larrabee (1997), relating to neuropsychological outcome following MTBI. The overall effect sizes in these meta-analyses were dramatically different. Effect sizes, as proposed by Cohen (1988), are represented as: d = the mean difference between the control group and the depressed group, divided by the pooled standard deviation (SD). Technically, the pooled SD is a weighted SD computed by multiplying the individual group SDs by the proportion of subjects each group contributes to the total sample, then summing these two products. Effect sizes of .2 represent "small effects,".5 "medium effects," and .8 "large effects." A medium effect of .5 means that the groups are separated by one half of a pooled (weighted) SD. Binder et al. reported that the overall effect sized for neuropsychological decrements associated with MTBI was .12 (SD = .18). This is a very small effect, representing approximately one eighth of a pooled SD. In contrast, Vickery et al. reported an overall effect size of 1.13 (95% confidence interval = 1.04 − 1.22; median = 1.4) for decrements in performance associated with biased responding. This is a large effect, representing approximately $1^1/8$ pooled SDs. Frankly, these meta-analyses suggest that neuropsychological tests are minimally sensitive to the effects of MTBI and very sensitive to the effects of negative response bias.

Vickery et al. reported weighted mean effect sizes for specific tests. Some examples are as follows: Digit Memory Test = 1.95, 21 Item Test = 1.46, PDRT = 1.26, and the Rey 15 Item Test = .77. These average weighted effect sizes ranged from $3/4$ to nearly 2 pooled SD decrements in scores. A recent prospective MTBI outcome study can be used for comparison. Ponsford et al. (2000) followed patients with MTBIs from the emergency room to 3 months postinjury. At 1 week postinjury, the patients with MTBIs differed from trauma control subjects on Digit

Symbol, Speed of Comprehension Test, and the Rey Auditory Verbal Learning Test (the MTBI patients actually performed better on the verbal learning test). The effect sizes for Digit Symbol and the Speed of Comprehension Test were .46 and .39, respectively. These are medium effect sizes showing relative decrements in neuropsychological functioning at 1 week postinjury. At 3 months postinjury, there were no statistically significant differences between the patients with MTBIs and the trauma controls.

The data from Vickery et al. can also be compared to effect sizes calculated from the landmark TBI outcome study conducted by Dikmen et al. At 1 year postinjury, patients with MTBIs (i.e., they were able to follow commands in less than 1 hour) did not differ on any neuropsychological test from trauma control subjects. Patients with severe brain injuries, as defined by an ability to follow commands within 14–28 days postinjury, performed significantly worse on all neuropsychological tests than the patients with trauma controls. Effect sizes for some of the neuropsychological tests, calculated using Appendix B (Dikmen, Machamer, Winn, & Temkin, 1995), were as follows: Wechsler Adult Intelligence Scale (WAIS) Verbal IQ = 1.06, WAIS Performance IQ = 1.64, Finger Tapping Test—Dominant Hand = 1.76, Trails A = 1.46, Trails B = 1.29, and Category Test = 1.40. These are all large effect sizes. The important point is that the effect sizes associated with neuropsychological deficits attributable to severe TBIs are comparable to the effect sizes of "neuropsychological deficits" attributable to malingering. This, obviously, illustrates the importance of assessing for malingering in every civil forensic neuropsychological evaluation.

Ethical Considerations

There also are ethical considerations for clinicians who choose to not assess for, or inadequately assess for, biased responding. The ethical issues relate primarily to competence. In civil forensic neuropsychological evaluations of patients with alleged brain injury, many alternative hypotheses should be considered before attributing deficits or unusual test scores to the putative biological effects of a brain injury. Some of these alternative hypotheses are (a) psychiatric conditions, such as depression, PTSD, somatoform, or factitious disorders; (b) medical disorders or conditions, such as Parkinson's disease, hypothyroidism, painful or mobility-limiting bodily injuries, or flu; (c) psychological factors, such as anger or preoccupation; (d) physical states, such as intoxication or fatigue; (e) environmental factors, such as excessive noise; and (f) malingering (Slick & Iverson, in press). Our Ethical Principles of Psychologists and Code of Conduct (American Psychological Association, 1992) requires that "assessments, recommendations, reports, and psychological diagnostic or evaluative statements are based on information and techniques (including personal interviews of the individual when appropriate) sufficient to provide appropriate substantiation for their findings."

> All of the above listed "etiologies" may predate or otherwise be partially or wholly independent of an acquired brain injury, and all may be associated with either reversible or nonreversible cognitive deficits that can mimic those seen in various forms and severity of brain injury. In such cases [point (f) above being an exception], test results may be valid in the sense that they accurately gauge the patient's maximum level of ability or function *at the time of assessment.* However, such results may be of little or no use diagnostically because the presence of these factors can significantly complicate both diagnosis and prognosis. It may be difficult if not impossible to parse out the specific type and severity of any effects of head injury from those associated with other co-occurring conditions. In particular, such data may substantially underestimate the patient's maximum level of function in the absence of a treatable illness or temporary condition, and therefore any conclusions about *permanent* status and *proximal cause* post injury may be highly questionable. (Slick & Iverson, in press)

CASE EXAMPLES

In this section, four cases are presented, which illustrate the diagnostic formulation in cases of possible biased responding. The first case example involved very poor performance on the Word Memory Test (WMT) (Green et al., 1996). The WMT was designed to measure verbal learning and memory. However, it has negative response bias indices built into the original design of the test. The WMT is mostly a computerized test of the ability to learn a list of 20 word pairs, with a noncomputerized administration component. The patient is instructed to watch and remember the list of word pairs, each appearing on the screen for 6 seconds. An immediate recognition subtest is given, in which the patient is instructed to select the original words from a series of target–foil word pairs. After a 30-minute delay interval, the patient is administered a delayed recognition subtest, in which the subject again selects the originally presented words from a new set of target–foil pairs. This is followed by a multiple-choice procedure in which the subject is shown the first words of each pair and asked to select the second word from a list of eight options on the screen. From this point, the examiner begins recording the patient's responses on the computer. For the Paired Associates subtest, the examiner says the first word in the pair aloud and asks the patient to report the second word. The subject is then given a delayed free-recall procedure, in which they are asked to recall all the words from the list, in any order, and not necessarily in pairs. After an additional 20-minute delay, free recall of the word list is tested again (i.e., long-delay free recall). The test takes approximately 7 minutes of the examiner's time and 20 minutes of the patient's time.

The Immediate and Delayed Recognition subtests are designed to detect poor effort. These subtests are passed easily by persons with TBIs and other neurological conditions (Green et al., 1996; Iverson et al., 1999). Moreover, the patient's consistency of responding between immediate and delayed recognition is calculated. Community volunteers and patients with TBIs perform in a consistent manner across these two subtests, but experimental malingerers tend to perform in a highly inconsistent manner (Green et al., 1996; Iverson et al., 1999). Quite simply, a patient who chooses to fail some of the 40 recognition items on initial recognition testing will have considerable difficulty reproducing the errors when given the delayed recognition procedure one-half hour later.

Green et al. (1999) examined the performance of a large sample of head injury litigants on the WMT measures of biased responding. The patients were sorted into two groups on the basis of head injury severity: those with relatively mild head injuries ($n = 234$) and those with moderate to severe brain injuries ($n = 64$). The patients with mild head injuries performed more poorly on the WMT measures of biased responding than the more severely injured patients. A subset of these mild cases fell below the cutoff for biased responding.

Case 1: Probable Malingering/MTBI Litigation

The patient was a 24-year-old man who was seen for a neuropsychological evaluation 2 years after a motor vehicle accident. The patient did not lose consciousness in the accident, nor did he have an appreciable period of posttraumatic amnesia. There was no indication in any medical records that there was suspicion of an MTBI for the first 12 months postinjury. The suspicion of such an injury appears to have emerged in the course of repeated independent medical exams within the context of the personal injury litigation.

Throughout the evaluation, the patient performed extremely poorly on many tests of concentration, learning, memory, and verbal fluency. His performance was far worse than would be expected following MTBI. The psychologist who conducted the evaluation made the following comments in his report regarding the validity of the neuropsychological evaluation.

1. "He was pleasant and cooperative with the assessment process and appeared to exert himself to do the best that he could on the tests."
2. "Nothing was observed in terms of overt behavior that would lead me to question the validity of the results."

The psychologist administered the WMT as part of the evaluation. The following is an excerpt from the computer-generated report that describes the performance of this patient on the WMT.

Very strong evidence of response bias. Three separate measures on the WMT which are sensitive to response bias are below the normal range and provide strong evidence of systematic response bias. This individual has responded in a fashion which is consistent with the pattern obtained by individuals attempting to simulate cognitive deficits. In addition, clinical experience has indicated that many individuals known or suspected to be malingering respond in this fashion. It is quite possible that litigation or other issues of primary or secondary gain are motivating factors for this individual. It is highly unlikely that even an individual who has sustained a severe brain injury would perform this poorly in the absence of symptom exaggeration or malingering issues.

There are three main indices designed to measure biased responding on the WMT. The scores from known groups and from the patient on these indices are presented in Table 5.6. The patient scored well below the cutoff for biased responding on all three indices.

As seen in Table 5.6, patients with TBIs perform well on the three indices of response bias. The maximum score for each is 100. All patients with TBIs reported in the table were involved in litigation at the time of their evaluations. All were administered the Computer-

TABLE 5.6 Performance of Community Volunteers, Patients with TBIs, and Experimental Malingerers on the WMT

Group	Immediate recall (IR)	Delayed recall (DR)	Consistency
Community volunteers ($n = 38$)[1]	97.9% (2.8)	98.6% (2.5)	96.6% (4.0)
Moderate–severe TBI ($n = 15$)[1]	96.5% (3.5)	95.8% (3.4)	93.3% (5.3)
Definite TBI ($n = 62$)[2]	93.4% (8.5)	93.5% (9.5)	90.5% (9.8)
Trivial or mild TBI ($n = 178$)[2]	92.7% (9.7)	92.5% (10.7)	89.3% (11.9)
Suspected exaggerators with trivial–mild injuries ($n = 56$)[2]	73.3% (20.8)	68.6% (20.5)	70.5% (15.5)
Analog malingerers ($n = 15$)[1]	69.0% (14.8)	62.7% (18.9)	62.0% (12.9)
Case 1	62.5%	55.0%	67.5%

The first number represents the percentage correct, out of 100, and the second number is the *SD*. All patients with brain injuries were involved in a litigation-related neuropsychological evaluation. The analog malingerers were well-educated volunteers (psychologists, physicians, etc.) who were given instructions to try to fake memory problems on the test.
[1]Iverson et al. (1999).
[2]Green et al. (1999).

ized Assessment of Response Bias (CARB) and the WMT during the course of this evaluation. The groups with definite TBIs and trivial or mild injuries "passed" the CARB. That is, they scored above the cutoff for suspecting exaggeration. In contrast, the "suspected exaggerators" scored below the cutoff on the CARB; their performances were also much lower on the WMT.

The patient's performance on the WMT was inconsistent with community volunteers or with patients with TBIs who were involved in litigation. His performance was consistent with patients with TBIs who were suspected of exaggerating. Moreover, his performance was most similar to subjects instructed to pretend that they were collecting medical disability payments because of brain injury and to make their best effort to fake memory impairment, without being detected by the test. Application of the diagnostic criteria presented in Tables 5.1 and 5.2 results in a classification of "probable malingering" (A, B2, B6, D).

It would be naïve to assume that malingering cannot occur when a person has genuine brain damage and true impairment. The presence of acquired brain impairment could not possibly preclude deliberate exaggeration of problems. To assume so would be tantamount to assuming that a person with acquired brain damage could not engage in deliberate, goal-directed behavior. Arguably, a person with demonstrable damage to their brain and undisputed deficits in day-to-day functioning may have less underlying motivation to exaggerate, especially in terms of a sense of justification, entitlement, and frustration with the system. Therefore, persons with clearly documented acquired brain damage may be less likely to malinger.

Case 2: Definite Malingering: Comorbidity Issues/Disability Claim

The patient was referred by his neurologist because of complaints of impaired memory functioning. He had a history of a right hemisphere stroke, with excellent recovery, which occurred approximately 2.5 years before the evaluation. Approximately 6 months before the evaluation, he had an "episode" that his family physician believed was a light stroke. However, after reviewing the history, medical records, and MRI results, his neurologist did not think this was a stroke. At the time of the evaluation, the patient was seeking medical retirement and social security disability benefits.

On the Rey 15 Item Test, the patient reproduced six rows, two of which were repeated (Figure 5.3). On the 21 Item Test (Iverson et al., 1991, 1994), the patient recalled seven words on free recall, then only 9/21 words on the forced-choice recognition task. Four of the words he recalled immediately before the forced-choice task, during free recall, he subsequently missed. In addition, he missed

A	B	C
1	2	3
1	2	3
1	1	1
O	O	O
A	B	C

FIGURE 5.3   Rey 15 Item Test performance for case 2.

five words in a row on the two-alternative forced-choice task. Over-all, his recognition score, inconsistency score, and his greatest con-secutive misses score were all in the "highly suspicious" range, according to the research manual (Iverson, 1998). On the Recogni-tion Memory Test, a two-alternative immediate recognition memory test, the patient recalled 19/50 words and 17/50 faces. Both of these scores are below chance, indicating that it is extremely unlikely to obtain a score that low, even if you are responding randomly. In other words, if the patient stood in the hallway while the stimulus faces were being shown, then came in and randomly pointed to his responses, 99% of the time he would obtain a score greater than 17. Thus, he obviously knew the correct answers for some of the items and deliberately chose incorrect responses. Application of the diagnostic criteria presented in Tables 5.1 and 5.2 resulted in a classification of "definite malingering" (A, B1, B2, B6, D).

Case 3: Possible Malingering/MTBI Litigation

The patient was a 37-year-old man who was struck by an automobile while riding a bike. He suffered a dislocated shoulder, rib fractures, and a facial fracture. There was no reported loss of consciousness. There was brief postinjury confusion, but no appreciable posttrau-matic amnesia. He was wearing a helmet, and it showed minor damage. His Glasgow Coma Scale at the scene was 15. His day-of-injury CT scan revealed the facial fracture, but no intracranial abnormality.

He was seen for neuropsychological evaluation 2 years postinjury, in connection with his personal injury litigation. He performed poorly on some of the neuropsychological tests, but for the most part his abilities were within expected limits. However, on the MMPI-2, his performance was consistent with exaggerated psychopathology.

Greene (1997) stated that

> high scores on the F-scale can occur for three reasons: (1) inconsistent patterns of item endorsement, (2) the presence of actual psychopathol-ogy, or (3) malingering. . . . Clinicians are probably safe to conclude that a raw score greater than 26 (T-score > 110) on the F scale does not reflect actual psychopathology, but it could reflect either an inconsistent pattern of item endorsement or malingering. (p. 187)

The patient obtained a raw score of 24 on the *F* scale (*T*-score = 110). This is an extreme elevation, indicating that he endorsed a high number of infrequent items. This score is higher than that obtained by 99.9% of the MMPI-2 normative sample. When compared to the Caldwell dataset, his score was at the 99.7th percentile for the normal subjects and 98th percentile for the clinical subjects. (The Caldwell clinical sample referred to in this review consists of 50,966 patients, and the Caldwell Personnel sample [i.e., "normals"] consists of 6,251 personnel applicants. These samples are presented in Greene [2000]. The MMPI-2 normative sample consists of 2,600 community control subjects.)

On the *Fb* scale, the patient obtained a raw score of 13, which corresponds to a *T*-score of 96. This is an extreme elevation, indicating that he endorsed a high number of infrequent items in the latter part of the test. This means that he endorsed more infrequent symptoms than 99% of the MMPI-2 normative subjects. When compared to the Caldwell dataset, he scored higher than 99.9% of normal subjects and between 84% and 93% of clinical subjects.

The Infrequency-Psychopathology (*F[p]*) scale contains 27 items that are usually not endorsed by psychiatric inpatients. On the *F(p)* scale, the patient obtained a raw score of 5. His score exceeded the 99th percentile for the MMPI-2 normative subjects and the Caldwell normal subjects, and it exceeded the 93rd percentile for Caldwell's clinical subjects. Greene (2000) made the following statement regarding *F(p)* raw, ranging from 4 to 8: "These clients either are experiencing and reporting a significant level of emotional distress or they may be embellishing the severity and extent of their psychopathology" (p. 76).

The variable response inconsistency (VRIN) scale consists of 67 pairs of items with either similar or opposite content. Each time the subject answers a pair of items inconsistently, a point is added to their VRIN total score. Very high scores on VRIN are often associated with random responding on the MMPI-2. The patient obtained a raw score of 2 on the VRIN scale (*T*-score = 38), which means that he answered only 2 of the 67 item pairs inconsistently. This score definitely does not reflect a random or careless approach to taking the test. This score represents a very consistent approach to answering related items.

According to Lees-Haley, English, and Glenn (1991), personal injury malingerers may present with a blended fake-good–fake-bad response set. They portray themselves as premorbidly well-adjusted, high-functioning, honest, conscientious, and hardworking, yet currently psychologically traumatized or disabled. These researchers developed the Fake Bad Scale (FBS) (Lees-Haley et al., 1991) to assess this response set. Using frequency counts of malingerers' MMPI test responses and clinical observations of personal injury malingerers, they selected the 43 questions for the scale on the basis of item content. Greene (1997) reported that the average score on the FBS for men in the MMPI-2 normative sample was 11.67 (SD = 3.81).

Medical outpatients have been instructed to simulate emotional distress under a variety of circumstances, such as in relation to a motor vehicle accident, toxic exposure, and on-the-job stress (Lees-Haley et al., 1991). For these three combined groups of analog malingerers (N = 67), the average score on the FBS was 25 (SD = 8.5). In a sample of 20 mild head injury litigants who obtained below-chance performance on a two-alternative forced-choice test (presumed exaggerators or malingerers), the average FBS score was 29 (SD = 5.1) (Millis et al., 1995). Larrabee (1998) reported that the FBS was sensitive to presumed somatic malingering in litigants who showed evidence of biased responding on cognitive test measures in conjunction with extreme elevations on scales 1 and 3. Eleven of 12 of these patients had elevations on the FBS, compared to only three patients with elevations on the F scale.

The patient obtained a raw score of 24 on the FBS.

In Table 5.7, average scores are reported on three validity scales for multiple groups. The table contains six samples of subjects instructed to fake severe mental problems and six samples of subjects with legitimate mental problems. As seen in this table, the patient's scores on the validity measures are much more similar to those obtained by persons instructed to fake mental illness than to those obtained by patients with mental and emotional problems.

A summary of the MMPI-2 findings is presented below.

1. The patient obtained a low score on the VRIN scale. This means that he did not respond inconsistently to pairs of items that have similar content. It is apparent that his approach to completing the MMPI-2 was not random or careless.
2. The patient obtained a low score on the L scale. This may be an indication of trying to create an "extremely pathological" picture of himself.

TABLE 5.7 Average Scores on Three MMPI-2 Validity Scales for Multiple Groups

Sample	Number of subjects	*F* scale	*Fb* scale	*F* – K
Community volunteers faking PTSD[1]	20	111.3	110.1	27.4
Community volunteers faking paranoid schizophrenia[1]	22	119.4	119.3	36
University students instructed to fake bad[2]	58	114.8	109.3	25.1
Male university students instructed to fake bad[3]	57	117.5	117.2	—
Male inmates instructed to malinger psychopathology[4]	28	112.9	104.8	24.8
Chronic psychiatric patients instructed to fake bad[5]	42	109.6	—	31.6
Patients with PTSD[1]	20	79.8	85.2	4.4
Patients with paranoid schizophrenia[1]	20	80.8	74.3	0
Psychiatric inpatients[2]	95	71.8	73.8	–2.1
Male psychiatric inpatients[3]	30	79.7	83.9	—
Male psychiatric inpatients[4]	51	60.8	69.2	–4.5
Chronic psychiatric patients[5]	42	82.1	—	5.8
Case 3's scores	—	110	96	19

Wetter et al. (1993)[1]; Bagby et al. (1994)[2]; Graham et al. (1991)[3]; Iverson et al. (1995)[4]; Rogers et al. (1995)[5]

3. The patient obtained elevated scores on two of the infrequency scales and an extreme elevation on the third. These scores are uncommon in persons who are being honest and forthright and may reflect exaggerated psychiatric problems.
4. The patient obtained a modest elevation on the FBS, a scale designed to detect a blended fake-good and fake-bad response set believed to be associated with personal injury malingering.

After a careful review of his MMPI-2 profile, it would be reasonable to conclude that there is considerable evidence of distortion and exaggeration of his psychiatric problems, physical problems, and level of disability. Application of the diagnostic criteria results in a classification of "possible malingering" (A, C5, D).

Case 4: Differential Diagnosis

The patient was a 40-year-old woman with occupation-related lead poisoning. Her initial medical workups led to diagnoses of hypotension, postural vertigo, and anemia secondary to lead poisoning. An MRI of her brain was normal. An EEG was considered abnormal, showing paroxysmal, slow-wave left hemisphere activity. After her lead levels returned to normal, she continued to have residual problems. She became seriously depressed and was hospitalized on several occasions. She was seen 2 years after this exposure, in connection with her Worker's Compensation disability claim. Her chief complaints at the time of the evaluation were uncontrollable shaking in her legs, weakness and pain in her legs, progressive loss of vision and hearing, sleep disturbance, migraines, and memory impairment.

During neuropsychological testing (verbal tests), the patient performed unusually poorly on a number of tests in a manner suggestive of suboptimal effort (Digit Span [3 forward; 2 backward; Average Consistent Scale Score = 3]; California Verbal Learning Test: Total = 14; Recognition Memory Test for Words [22/50]; 21 Item Test [Recall = 3, Recognition = 12]).

The patient reported that she was nearly blind. She stated that she could only see lights. She did not know the onset of her blindness. During the evaluation, we were unable to determine what she could or could not see. However, she clearly was able to see more than she reported. This was documented through observation and testing. Examples of observations were as follows: (a) During an extended interview, the patient was describing her history and pointed to a spot on her hand where she had been burned; her eyes were turned downward and the spot was faint; (b) when discussing how she scratches her inner arm, she lifted up her shirt and pointed to additional scratch marks on her stomach; she seemed disconcerted after doing so and quickly pulled her shirt down; (c) she periodically glanced over at one of the examiner's who was sitting off to her left (her eyes would dart over, then back to looking forward;

she was wearing dark glasses but her eye movements could be visualized from the side); and (d) while crying during the interview, she rapidly and effortlessly grabbed tissues that were positioned in a box in front of her.

The patient was told that the brain might be able to process colors without her conscious awareness. Thus, her visual system may be grossly intact, but she simply does not have conscious awareness of the visual input. To test this hypothesis, we simply asked her to guess as to what color folder was being placed in front of her—orange or green (she stated that she had done tasks like this in the past for other doctors). When we placed the folders in front of her, she stated that she could not see the folder or distinguish a color. We then presented multiple trials of alternating folders and instructed her to guess at the color. The folders were slid across the table in front of her as she was instructed to look down at the table. She responded "Orange" nearly every time as a folder passed in front of her. During the last several trials, we varied the rate at which the folders were presented and moved them quietly, above the table, in front of her visual field, so she could not hear them sliding across the table. She responded immediately as the folder entered her visual field, despite no cue that the folder was actually there (no sound, verbal prompt, and the rate of presentation varied). Thus, she had to be able to see something in order to respond. Her total score on the task was within the range of chance level performance (12 correct of 25 trials).

This patient presented a rather confusing diagnostic picture. She had been experiencing cognitive, affective, and vegetative symptoms consistent with major depression. In addition, she had a somatic focus and probably converted psychological stress into physical symptoms. Thus, her psychiatric status clearly was making her physical condition worse. Moreover, the patient appeared to have an exaggerative component to her presentation. She endorsed a litany of symptoms, all of which were extremely severe and disabling. She also appeared to be exaggerating the severity of her visual, cognitive, and motor impairments. The diagnoses listed below were considered.

- Conversion Disorder (300.11; with mixed presentation—motor and sensory). This disorder may be diagnosed in the presence of a neurological or other general medical condition, if the symptoms are not fully explained by the nature and severity of the preexisting condition.

- Psychological Factors Affecting Medical Condition (316) (Major depression delaying recovery from sequelae of lead toxicity)
- Malingering (V65.2) (The exaggeration of existing, or reporting of nonexistent, symptoms for the purpose of avoiding work and obtaining disability compensation)
- Factitious Disorder (300.19) (with combined psychological, i.e., cognitive, and physical signs and symptoms). (The symptoms are intentionally produced or exaggerated for the purpose of assuming the sick role.)
- Major Depressive Disorder, Severe (296.23)

Conclusions

The patient performed substantially below expected levels on many tests of her cognitive abilities. Her intellectual abilities, memory, learning, perceptual-organizational skills, speed of information processing, reasoning, problem solving, and cognitive flexibility were all substantially declined from her estimated optimal level of functioning. At the time of the evaluation, the patient was functioning in the borderline classification range in her intelligence and the impaired classification range in her memory index scores. The etiology of her decline is unknown. It is believed that psychiatric factors played a major role in this decline. However, a general systemic or discrete neurological process also may have been contributing to her presentation (although medical evaluations had not revealed such a process).

Results of psychological evaluation suggested that the patient was experiencing major depression. She also had a somatic focus and probably converted psychological stress into physical symptoms; thus, her psychiatric status was making her physical condition worse. Moreover, the patient appeared to have a volitional, exaggerative component to her presentation. Her symptom magnification pattern may have been the result of her frustration with her illness and her fear that she would not be taken seriously. It also may have reflected some psychological need to maintain a "sick role" a la Factitious Disorder. One also must consider the possibility that she was exaggerating existing symptoms or reporting nonexistent symptoms for the purpose of attaining Worker's Compensation and/ or long-term disability. An attempt to apply the diagnostic criteria from Tables 5.1 and 5.2 yielded an inconclusive result (A, B2, B6, C3; Criterion D not satisfied; possible malingering cannot be ruled out; however, plausible differential diagnoses exist).

CONCLUSIONS AND PRACTICAL SUGGESTIONS FOR CIVIL FORENSIC ASSESSMENTS

There is no standardized, widely accepted approach to assessing for malingering. Some clinicians do not use any tests or specialized procedures designed to detect negative response bias. Other clinicians conduct their assessment in standard fashion, and only include tests designed to detect response bias if they become suspicious during the evaluation. This is a reactive approach to assessment. Many clinicians now include one or more specialized tests in their standard battery. Some clinicians include numerous specialized tests, and examine the standard test results carefully for suspicious performance patterns.

As discussed in this chapter, there are practical, professional, statistical, and ethical reasons why every civil forensic neuropsychological evaluation should include a careful assessment of negative response bias. I recommend that the clinician keep abreast of the literature and follow the four-step procedure listed below.

1. Approach the evaluation proactively, not reactively. Plan for the evaluation of biased responding just as you would plan to evaluate any specific area of functioning. Do not wait for obvious evidence of exaggeration before giving specialized tests. Evaluate for biased responding with the same or greater effort as you evaluate for memory problems or depression.
2. Use a combination of approaches, including specialized tests and examination of performance patterns on standard tests.
3. Give simple specialized tests (e.g., Rey 15 Item Test or 21 Item Test) at the beginning of the evaluation, not the middle or end.
4. Intersperse validity indicators throughout the evaluation. These can be specific tests or general ability tests for which certain "abnormal performance patterns" may be associated with exaggeration.

It is the responsibility of the forensic neuropsychologist to identify and explain test scores that do not make biological or psychometric sense. If the patient demonstrates clear evidence of biased responding on any test within the evaluation, the entire set of test results is questionable. Practitioners should avoid trying to use clinical judgment (i.e., making an educated guess) to determine which test performances are valid, questionable, or biased. Some exaggerating patients might have demonstrable evidence of structural brain damage documented on neuroimaging. Obviously, it would be inappropriate to conclude that they have no neuropsychological decrements or subjective symptoms. Rather, the clinician must conclude that, because the patient did not put forth their best performance, it is not possible to determine relative strengths or weaknesses in the cognitive profile.

Clinicians should also avoid using vague or misleading terminology to describe exaggerated symptoms or deliberately poor test performances. Some psychologists use expressions like "Psychological factors interfered with the test performance." This terminology obfuscates rather than informs. Instead, the clinician should consider phraseology such as the four examples listed below.

1. There is evidence that the patient exaggerated his level of mental and emotional problems.
2. The patient scored below chance on a two-alternative, forced-choice procedure, indicating that she knew the correct answer and deliberately chose the incorrect answer. This performance invalidates the entire set of neuropsychological test results.
3. It is not possible to determine if the plaintiff has significant decrements in her cognitive functioning, because she did not put forth her best effort during testing.
4. The patient's performances on neuropsychological tests, as well as specialized tests designed to detect exaggeration, are very similar to the performances of research participants who are given instructions to malinger. Based on a careful review of the contemporaneous medical record, behavioral observations, and the neuropsychological test results, it is my opinion that the patient is malingering. The presence of malingering during the current evaluation does not preclude the possibility that the patient has some residual problems from the accident in question, but it does preclude a meaningful opinion regarding the nature and severity of these problems.

Some neuropsychologists are very reluctant to infer the underlying motivation for exaggerated symptoms or deliberately poor test performance. Without inferring the underlying motivation (i.e., the antecedents), it is impossible to differentiate malingering from factitious disorder. Those psychologists who refuse to infer "motivation" concerning exaggeration should be equally cautious concerning inferring motives for less contentious behaviors. The neuropsychologist might simply wish to state, "There is considerable evidence that the patient exaggerated his level of disability and deliberately performed poorly during neuropsychological testing. I am not comfortable providing an opinion as to whether this behavior was motivated by general uncooperativeness, a desire for monetary gain (i.e., malingering), or a psychological need to assume the sick or disabled role (i.e., factitious disorder)."

A competent forensic neuropsychological assessment should in most cases be comprised of (a) review of records (e.g., medical and educational); (b) interviews with the plaintiff and other informants, such as spouse or employer, if possible; (c) behavioral observations; (d) neuropsychological measures covering all major domains of cognitive function; (e) measures of psychological adjustment and psychiatric symptoms; and (f) measures for detecting suboptimal or biased performance on cognitive measures (Slick & Iverson, in press). An evaluation that does not include the elements listed above can easily lead to incorrect conclusions about the nature and cause of any observed deficits, and may thus be considered incompetently conducted. A thorough assessment provides the best and, in some cases, only acceptable basis for an expert opinion.

ACKNOWLEDGMENTS

The author thanks Drs. Daniel Slick and Rael Lange for their contributions to this work.

REFERENCES

Allen, L. M., Conder, R. L., Green, P., & Cox, D. R. (1997). *CARB 97 manual for the computerized assessment of response bias.* Durham, NC: CogniSyst.

American Psychological Association (1992). Ethical principles of psychologists and code of conduct. *American Psychologist, 47*(12), 1597–1611.

American Psychiatric Association (1994). *Diagnostic and statistical manual of mental disorders* (4th ed.). Washington, DC: American Psychiatric Press.

Arnett, P. A., & Franzen, M. D. (1997). Performance of substance abusers with memory deficits on measures of malingering. *Archives of Clinical Neuropsychology, 12,* 513–518.

Arnett, P. A., Hammeke, T. A., & Schwartz, L. (1995). Quantitative and qualitative performance on Rey's 15-Item Test in neurological patients and dissimulators. *The Clinical Neuropsychologist, 9,* 17–26.

Axelrod, B. N., & Rawlings, D. B. (1999). Clinical utility of incomplete effort WAIS-R formulas: A longitudinal examination of individuals with traumatic brain injuries. *Journal of Forensic Neuropsychology, 1,* 15–27.

Babinski, J. (1988). Dismembering of traditional hysteria—pithiatism. *Psychiatric Medicine, 6,* 1–16.

Baker, R., Donders, J., & Thompson, E. (2000). Assessment of incomplete effort with the California Verbal Learning Test. *Applied Neuropsychology, 7,* 111–114.

Bernard, L. C., & Fowler, W. (1990). Assessing the validity of memory complaints: Performance of brain-damaged and normal individuals on Rey's task to detect malingering. *Journal of Clinical Psychology, 46,* 432–436.

Binder, L. M. (1993). Assessment of malingering after mild head trauma with the Portland Digit Recognition Test. *Journal of Clinical and Experimental Neuropsychology, 15,* 170–182.

Binder, L. M., & Kelly, M. P. (1996). Portland Digit Recognition Test performance by brain dysfunction patients without financial incentives. *Assessment, 3,* 403–409.

Binder, L. M., Rohling, M. L., & Larrabee, G. J. (1997). A review of mild head trauma. Part I: Meta-analytic review of neuropsychological studies. *Journal of Clinical and Experimental Neuropsychology, 19,* 421–431.

Binder, L. M., & Willis, S. C. (1991). Assessment of motivation after financially compensable minor head trauma. *Psychological Assessment: A Journal of Consulting and Clinical Psychology, 3,* 175–181.

Cohen, J. (1988). *Statistical power analysis for the behavioral sciences* (2nd ed.). Hillsdale, NJ: Erlbaum.

Coleman, R. D., Rapport, L. J., Millis, S. R., Ricker, J. H., & Farchione, T. J. (1998). Effects of coaching on detection of malingering with the California Verbal Learning Test. *Journal of Clinical and Experimental Neuropsychology, 20,* 201–210.

Dikmen, S. S., Machamer, J. E., Winn, H. R., & Temkin, N. R. (1995). Neuropsychological outcome at 1-year post head injury. *Neuropsychology, 9,* 80–90.

Doss, R. C., Chelune, G. J., & Naugle, R. I. (1999). Victoria Symptom Validity Test: Compensation-seeking vs. noncompensation-seeking patients in a general clinical setting. *Journal of Forensic Neuropsychology, 1,* 5–20.

Franzen, M. D., & Iverson, G. L. (1997). The detection of biased responding in neuropsychological assessment. In A. M. Horton, J. Wedding, & J. J. Webster (Eds.), *The neuropsychology handbook: Behavioral and clinical perspectives* (2nd ed.) (pp. 393–421). New York: Springer.

Frederick, R. I. (1997). *Validity Indicator Profile manual.* Minnetonka, MN: NCS Assessments.

Frederick, R. I. (2000). A personal floor effect strategy to evaluate the validity of performance on memory tests. *Journal of Clinical and Experimental Neuropsychology,* 22, 720–730.

Frederick, R. I., & Crosby, R. D. (2000). Development and validation of the Validity Indicator Profile. *Law and Human Behavior, 24,* 59–82.

Frederick, R. I., Crosby, R. D., & Wynkoop, T. F. (2000). Performance curve classification of invalid responding on the Validity Indicator Profile. *Archives of Clinical Neuropsychology, 15,* 281–300.

Frederick, R. I., & Foster, H. G. (1991). Multiple measures of malingering on a forced-choice test of cognitive ability. *Psychological Assessment, 3,* 596–602.

Frederick, R. I., Sarfaty, S. D., Johnston, J. D., & Powel, J. (1994). Validation of a detector of responses bias on a forced-choice test of nonverbal ability. *Neuropsychology, 8,* 118–125.

Gfeller, J. D., & Cradock, M. M. (1998). Detecting feigned neuropsychological impairment with the Seashore Rhythm Test. *Journal of Clinical Psychology, 54,* 431–438.

Goebel, R. A. (1983). Detection of faking on the Halstead-Reitan neuropsychological test battery. *Journal of Clinical Psychology, 39,* 731–742.

Goldberg, J. O., & Miller, H. R. (1986). Performance of psychiatric inpatients and intellectually deficient individuals on a test that assesses the validity of memory complaints. *Journal of Clinical Psychology, 42,* 792–795.

Gontkovsky, S. T., & Souheaver, G. T. (2000). Are brain-damaged patients inappropriately labeled as malingering using the 21-Item Test and the WMS-R Logical Memory forced choice recognition test? *Psychological Reports, 87,* 512–514.

Graham, J. R., Watts, D., & Timbrook, R. E. (1991). Detecting fake-good and fake-bad MMP1-2 profiles. *Journal of Personality Assessment, 57,* 264–277.

Green, P., Allen, L. M., & Astner, K. (1996). *The Word Memory Test: A user's guide to the oral and computer-administered forms, user version 1.1.* Durham, NC.: CogniSyst.

Green, P., & Iverson, G. L. (in press). Validation of the Computerized Assessment of Response Bias in litigating patients with head injuries. *The Clinical Neuropsychologist.*

Green, P., Iverson, G. L., & Allen, L. (1999). Detecting malingering in head injury litigation with the Word Memory Test. *Brain Injury, 13,* 813–819.

Greene, R. L. (1997). Assessment of malingering and defensiveness by multiscale inventories. In R. Rogers (Ed.), *Clinical assessment of malingering and deception* (2nd ed.). New York: Guilford.

Greene, R. L. (2000). *The MMPI-2: An interpretive manual* (2nd ed.). Boston: Allyn and Bacon.

Greiffenstein, M. F., Baker, W. J., & Gola, T. (1994). Validation of malingered amnesia measures with a large clinical sample. *Psychological Assessment, 6,* 218–224.

Greiffenstein, M. F., Baker, W. J., & Gola, T. (1996). Comparison of multiple scoring methods for Rey's malingered amnesia measures. *Archives of Clinical Neuropsychology, 11,* 283–293.

Grote, C. L., Kooker, E. K., Garron, D. C., Nyenhuis, D. L., Smith, C. A., & Mattingly, M. L. (2000). Performance of compensation seeking and non-compensation seeking samples on the Victoria Symptom Validity Test: Cross-validation and extension of a standardization study. *Journal of Clinical and Experimental Neuropsychology, 22,* 709–719.

Guilmette, T. J., Hart, K. J., Giuliano, A. J., & Leininger, B. E. (1994). Detecting simulated memory impairment: Comparison of the Rey Fifteen-Item Test and the Hiscock forced-choice procedure. *The Clinical Neuropsychologist, 8,* 283–294.

Hays, J. R., Emmons, J., & Stallings, G. (2000). Dementia and mental retardation markers on the Rey 15-Item Visual Memory Test. *Psychological Reports, 86,* 179–182.

Heaton, R. K., Smith, H. H., Lehman, R. A. W., & Vogt, A. T. (1978). Prospects for faking believable deficits on neuropsychological testing. *Journal of Consulting and Clinical Psychology, 46,* 892–900.

Hiscock, M., & Hiscock, C. K. (1989). Refining the forced-choice method of detecting malingering. *Journal of Clinical and Experimental Neuropsychology, 11,* 967–974.

Iverson, G. L. (1996, May/June). A comment on the willingness of people to fake problems after motor vehicle accidents or work-related injuries. *Journal of Cognitive Rehabilitation,* 10–13.

Iverson, G. L. (in press). Can malingering be identified with the Judgment of Line Orientation Test? *Applied Neuropsychology.*

Iverson, G. L. (1998). *21 Item Test Research Manual.* Unpublished manuscript.

Iverson, G. L., & Binder, L. M. (2000). Detecting exaggeration and malingering in neuropsychological assessment. *Journal of Head Trauma Rehabilitation, 15,* 829–858.

Iverson, G. L., & Franzen, M. D. (1994). The Recognition Memory Test, Digit Span, and Knox Cube Test as markers of malingered memory impairment. *Assessment, 1,* 323–334.

Iverson, G. L., & Franzen, M. D. (1996). Using multiple objective memory procedures to detect simulated malingering. *Journal of Clinical and Experimental Neuropsychology, 18,* 38–51.

Iverson, G. L., & Franzen, M. D. (1998). Detecting malingered memory deficits with the Recognition Memory Test. *Brain Injury, 12,* 275–282.

Iverson, G. L., Franzen, M. D., & McCracken, L. M. (1991). Evaluation of a standardized instrument for the detection of malingered memory deficits. *Law and Human Behavior, 15,* 667–676.

Iverson, G. L, Franzen, M. D., & McCracken, L. M. (1994). Application of a forced choice procedure designed to detect malingered memory deficits. *Archives of Clinical Neuropsychology, 9,* 437–450.

Iverson, G. L, Franzen, M. D., & McCracken, L. M. (1995). Evaluation of inmates' ability to malinger on the MMP1-2. *Psychological Assessment, 7,* 118–121.

Iverson, G. L., Green, P., Gervais, R. (1999, March/April). Using the Word Memory Test to detect biased responding in head injury litigation. *The Journal of Cognitive Rehabilitation,* 2–6.

Iverson, G. L., Lange, R. T., Green, P., & Franzen, M. D. (in press). Clinical base rates of the Trail Making Test in a TBI sample: Examination of the malingering hypothesis. *Archives of Clinical Neuropsychology.*

Iverson, G. L., & Slick, D. J. (in press). Base rates of the WMS-R Malingering Index following traumatic brain injury. *American Journal of Forensic Psychology.*

Iverson, G. L., Slick, D. J., & Franzen, M. D. (2000). Evaluation of a WMS-R malingering index in a non-litigating clinical sample. *Journal of Clinical and Experimental Neuropsychology, 22,* 191–197.

Iverson, G. L., & Tulsky, D. (in press). Detecting malingering on the WAIS-III: Unusual Digit Span performance patterns in the normal population and in clinical groups. *Archives of Clinical Neuropsychology.*

Ju, D., & Varney, N. R. (2000). Can head injury patients simulate malingering? *Applied Neuropsychology, 7,* 201–207.

Kathol, R. (1996). Unexplained neurological complaints. In M. Rizzo & D. Tranel (Eds.), *Head injury and postconcussive syndrome* (pp. 321–332). New York: Churchill Livingstone.

Killgore, W. D. S., & Dellapietra, L. (2000a). Item response bias on the Logical Memory Delayed Recognition subtest of the Wechsler Memory Scale—III. *Psychological Reports, 86,* 851–857.

Killgore, W. D. S., & Dellapietra, L. (2000b). Using the WMS-III to detect malingering: Empirical validation of the Rarely Missed Index (RMI). *Journal of Clinical and Experimental Neuropsychology, 22,* 761–777.

Larrabee, G. J. (1998). Somatic malingering on the MMPI and MMPI-2 in litigating subjects. *The Clinical Neuropsychologist, 12,* 179–188.

Lee, G. P., Loring, D. W., & Martin, R. C. (1992). Rey's 15-Item visual memory test for the detection of malingering: Normative observations on patients with neurological disorders. *Psychological Assessment, 4,* 43–46.

Lees-Haley, P. R., English, L. T., & Glenn, W. J. (1991). A fake bad scale on the MMPI-2 for personal injury claimants. *Psychological Reports, 68,* 203–210.

McKinzey, R. K., & Russell, E. W. (1997). A partial cross-validation of a Halstead-Reitan Battery malingering formula. *Journal of Clinical and Experimental Neuropsychology, 19,* 484–488.

Mensch, A. J., & Woods, D. J. (1986). Patterns of feigning brain damage in the LNNB. *The International Journal of Clinical Neuropsychology, 8*(2), 59–63.

Meyers, J. E., Galinsky, A. M., & Volbrecht, M. (1999). Malingering and mild brain injury: How low is too low. *Applied Neuropsychology, 6*(4), 208–216.

Meyers, J. E., & Volbrecht, M. (1998). Validation of reliable digits for detection of malingering. *Assessment, 5,* 303–307.

Meyers, J., & Volbrecht, M. (1998). Validation of memory error patterns on the Rey Complex Figure and Recognition trial. *Applied Neuropsychology, 5,* 120–131.

Millis, S. R. (1992). The Recognition Memory Test in the detection of malingered and exaggerated memory deficits. *The Clinical Neuropsychologist, 6,* 406–414.

Millis, S. R. (1994). Assessment of motivation and memory with the Recognition Memory Test after financially compensable mild head injury. *Journal of Clinical Psychology, 50,* 601–604.

Millis, S. R., & Dijkers, M. (1993). Use of the Recognition Memory Test in traumatic brain injury: Preliminary findings. *Brain Injury, 7,* 53–58.

Millis, S. R., & Kler, S. (1995). Limitations of the Rey Fifteen-Item Test in the detection of malingering. *The Clinical Neuropsychologist, 9,* 241–244.

Millis, S. R., Putnam, S. H., Adams, K. H., & Ricker, J. H. (1995). The California Verbal Learning Test in the detection of incomplete effort in neuropsychological testing. *Psychological Assessment, 7,* 463–471.

Millis, S. R., Ross, S. R., & Ricker, J. H. (1998). Detection of incomplete effort on the Wechsler Adult Intelligence Scale—Revised: A cross validation. *Journal of Clinical and Experimental Neuropsychology, 20,* 167–173.

Mittenberg, W., Azrin, R., Millsaps, C., & Heilbronner, R. (1993). Identification of malingered head injury on the Wechsler Memory Scale—Revised. *Psychological Assessment, 5,* 34–40.

Mittenberg, W., Rotholc, A., Russell, E., & Heilbronner, R. (1996). Identification of malingered head injury on the Halstead-Reitan Battery. *Archives of Clinical Neuropsychology, 11,* 271–281.

Mittenberg, W., Theroux-Fichera, S. T., Zielinski, R. E., & Heilbronner, R. L. (1995). Identification of malingered head injury on the Wechsler Adult Intelligence Scale—Revised. *Professional Psychology: Research and Practice, 26,* 491–498.

Ponsford, J., Willmott, C., Rothwell, A., Cameron, P., Kelly, A. M., Nelms, R., et al. (2000). Factors influencing outcome following mild traumatic brain injury in adults. *Journal of the International Neuropsychological Society, 6,* 568–579.

Rees, L. M., Tombaugh, T. N., Gansler, D. A., & Moczynski, N. P. (1998). Five validation experiments of the Test of Memory Malingering (TOMM). *Psychological Assessment, 10,* 10–20.

Reitan, R. M., & Wolfson, D. (1996a). Consistency of responses on retesting among head-injured subjects in litigation versus head-injured subjects not in litigation. *Applied Neuropsychology, 2,* 67–71.

Reitan, R. M., & Wolfson, D. (1996b). The question of validity of neuropsychological test scores among head-injured litigants: Development of a dissimulation index. *Archives of Clinical Neuropsychology, 11,* 573–580.

Reitan, R. M., & Wolfson, D. (1997). Consistency of neuropsychological test scores of head-injured subjects involved in litigation compared with head-injured subjects not involved in litigation: Development of the Retest Consistency Index. *The Clinical Neuropsychologist, 11,* 69–76.

Reynolds, C.R. (Ed.) (1998). *Detection of malingering during head injury litigation.* New York: Plenum Press.

Rogers, R. (1990). Models of feigned mental illness. *Professional Psychology: Research and Practice, 21,* 182–188.

Rogers, R. (1997). *Clinical assessment of malingering and deception* (2nd ed.). New York: The Guilford Press.

Rogers, R., Sewell, K. W., & Ustad, L. L. (1995). Feigning among chronic outpatients on the MMPI-2: A systematic examination of fake-bad indicators. *Assessment, 2,* 81–89.

Rose, F. E., Hall, S., Szalda-Petree, A. D., & Bach, P. J. (1998). A comparison of four tests of malingering and the effects of coaching. *Archives of Clinical Neuropsychology, 13,* 349–363.

Ruffolo, L. F., Guilmette, T. J., & Willis, W. J. (2000). Comparison of time and error rates on the Trail Making Test among patients with head injuries, experimental malingerers, patients with suspected effort on testing, and normal controls. *The Clinical Neuropsychologist, 14,* 223–230.

Slick, D., Hopp, G., Strauss, E., Hunter, M., & Pinch, D. (1994). Detecting dissimulation: Profiles of simulated malingerers, traumatic brain-injury patients, and normal controls on a revised version of Hiscock and Hiscock's Forced-Choice Memory Test. *Journal of Clinical and Experimental Neuropsychology, 16,* 472–481.

Slick, D., Hopp, G., Strauss, E., & Spellacy, F. (1996). Victoria Symptom Validity Test: Efficiency for detecting feigned memory impairment and relationship to neuropsychological tests and MMPI-2 validity scales. *Journal of Clinical and Experimental Neuropsychology, 18,* 911–922.

Slick, D. J., Hopp, G., Strauss, E., & Thompson, G. (1997). *The Victoria Symptom Validity Test.* Odessa: PAR.

Slick, D. J., & Iverson, G. L. (in press). Ethical issues arising in forensic neuropsychological assessment. In I. Z. Schultz & D. O. Brady (Eds.), *Handbook of psychological injuries.* Chicago: American Bar Association.

Slick, D. J., Iverson, G. L., & Green, P. (in press). California Verbal Learning Test indicators of suboptimal performance in a sample of head injury litigants. *Journal of Clinical and Experimental Neuropsychology.*

Slick, D. J., Sherman, E. M. S., & Iverson, G. L. (1999). Diagnostic criteria for malingered neurocognitive dysfunction: Proposed standards for clinical practice and research. *The Clinical Neuropsychologist, 13,* 545–561.

Suhr, J., Tranel, D., Wefel, J., & Barrash, J. (1997). Memory performance after head injury: Contributions of malingering, litigation status, psychological factors, and medication use. *Journal of Clinical and Experimental Neuropsychology, 19,* 500–514.

Sweet, J. J. (1999). Malingering: Differential diagnosis. In J. J. Sweet (Ed.), *Forensic neuropsychology: Fundamentals and practice* (pp. 255–285). Lisse, Netherland: Swets & Zeitlinger.

Sweet, J. J., Wolfe, P., Sattlberger, E., Numan, B., Rosenfeld, J. P., Clingerman, S., et al. (2000). Further investigation of traumatic brain injury versus insufficient effort with the California Verbal Learning Test. *Archives of Clinical Neuropsychology, 15,* 105–113.

Tenhula, W. N., & Sweet, J. J. (1996). Double cross-validation of the booklet category test in detecting malingered traumatic brain injury. *The Clinical Neuropsychologist, 10,* 104–116.

Tombaugh, T. N. (1997). The Test of Memory Malingering (TOMM): Normative data from cognitively intact and cognitively impaired individuals. *Psychological Assessment, 9,* 260–268.

Trueblood, W. (1994). Qualitative and quantitative characteristics of malingered and other invalid WAIS-R and clinical memory data. *Journal of Clinical and Experimental Neuropsychology, 16,* 597–607.

Trueblood, W., & Schmidt, M. (1993). Malingering and other validity considerations in the neuropsychological evaluation of mild head injury. *Journal of Clinical and Experimental Neuropsychology, 15,* 578–590.

Vickery, C. D., Berry, D. T. R., Hanlon Inman, T., Harris, M. J., & Orey, S. A. (2001). Detection of inadequate effort on neuropsychological testing: A meta-analytic review of selected procedures. *Archives of Clinical Neuropsychology, 16,* 45–73.

Weissman, H. N. (1990). Distortions and deceptions in self presentation: Effects of protracted litigation on personal injury cases. *Behavioral Sciences and the Law, 8,* 67–74.

Wetter, M. W., Baer, R. A., Beng, D. T. R., Robison, L. H., & Sumpter, J. (1993). MMP1-2 profiles of motivated fakes given specific information: A comparison with matched patients. *Psychological Assessment, 5,* 317–323.

Williams, R. W., & Carlin, M. (1999). Malingering on the WAIS-R among disability claimants and applicants for vocational assistance. *American Journal of Forensic Psychology, 17,* 35–45.

Issues Unique
to Brain Injury

Chapter 6

Epidemiology of Traumatic Brain Injury

Lawrence C. Hartlage and Peter C. Patch

In recent years, the field of neuropsychology has appropriately recognized the importance of base rate issues in assessing putative sequelae of brain injury attributed to specific events (e.g., Hartlage, 1995; Lees-Haley & Brown, 1993). Just as it is relevant to study the epidemiology of such phenomena as impaired attention, concentration, and memory, so is it relevant and important to attend to the epidemiology of traumatic brain injury (TBI). This is of special relevance and importance in forensic work, especially in cases of mild traumatic brain injury (MTBI), since the integration of symptoms and behavioral changes with the incidence and base rates of these phenomena can provide safeguards against both false-positive and false-negative diagnostic errors (Annegers & Kurland, 1979).

Just as the experienced medical clinician utilizes knowledge of incidence of conditions likely to produce given symptoms in formulating a diagnostic impression (e.g., Richardson, Wilson, Guyett, Cool, & Nishikawa, 1999), the experienced neuropsychologist assesses the likelihood of possible causes of neuropsychological examination findings. Unfortunately, the literature on incidence of MTBI is confusing, inconsistent, and difficult to summarize in ways likely to produce generalized agreement. To some extent reflecting recognition of these factors, the Traumatic Brain Injury Act of 1996 (1996) authorized state surveillance systems to collect information on the number of people affected by TBI and the severity of the TBI. The Centers for Disease Control (CDC) (1999) initiated a TBI surveillance program from 1989 to 1998 and documented approximately 1.5–2 million new TBI cases in the United

States each year, with 5.3 million U.S. citizens living with disability as a result of TBI.

Since requested criterion for TBI included such items as skull fracturing, diagnosed intracranial lesion, listing of head injury on the death certificate, or neurological abnormalities such as aphasia or seizures, it is likely that many cases of MTBI were not reflected in this 1.5–2 million cases per year estimate. A further limiting factor includes classification criteria, including ICD-9 CM codes 800.0–801.9 (fracture to base of skull), 803.0–804.9 (multiple fractures of skull), and 850.0–854.1 (intracranial injury, hemorrhage, etc.). To the extent that MTBI cases may not be formally diagnosed by those or related criterion, they would not be included in the surveillance data (Annegers, Grabow, Kurland, & Laws, 1980; CDC, 1999; Department of Health and Human Services, 1989; Fife, 1986; Fife, Faich, Hollinshead, & Wentworth, 1986; Jagger, Levine, Jane, & Rimel, 1984; Kalsbeek, McLaurin, Harris, & Miller, 1980; Klauber, Barret-Connor, Marhsall, & Bowers, 1981; Krauss & McArthur, 1996; MacKenzie, Edelstein, & Flynn, 1989; Whitman, Coonley-Hoganson, & Desai, 1984). These and other issues related to categorization and classification of TBI contribute to an overall lack of consensus on incidence, as well as other aspects, of the epidemiology of this construct.

Strong evidence indicates that the majority of MTBIs are not detected at all, let alone accurately classified (Zasler, 1993). Estimates, ranging from 500,000 to 1.5 million cases per year, are typically based on hospital primary diagnoses of head injury (Frankowski, 1986). However, careful, detailed, and systematic reviews of injuries in discreet loci have postulated annual incidence in the United States of 7 million to more than 10 million brain injuries (Annegers et al., 1980; Caveness, 1979a, 1979b; Hartlage, 1984, 1990, 1999; Sorenson & Krauss, 1991). Segalowitz and Brown (1991) have indicated a likelihood of dramatic underreporting of mild head injury, which of course clouds the issue when patients, significant others, and treatment providers attempt to identify the etiology of persistent behavioral symptoms sometime after the injury for which head injury was not reported.

Given the apparently inconclusive database concerning incidence of MTBI, and the concurrent importance, in forensic contexts, of relating base rates, with reasonable neuropsychological certainty, to findings from neuropsychological examination, attention is addressed to relevant terminological, methodological, and conceptual issues involved.

BASE RATES OF TBI

There are two approaches to describing the rate of occurrence of a disorder: prevalence and incidence. *Prevalence* refers to the number of cases per given population unit, that is, 10 million individuals with brain injury in a population of 270 million would represent a prevalence of 10 million per 270 million. *Incidence* refers to the number of new cases or admissions during a given time period or some comparable measure of occurrence, which is a major source of distortion of the database (Templer, Spencer, & Hartlage, 1993). In describing TBI, most frequently cited figures refer to incidence (Annegers et al., 1980; Frankowski, 1986; Hartlage, 1990; Hawthorne, 1978; Klonoff & Thompson, 1969; Krauss, 1980).

Although documented history of TBI is substantially more likely in cases of severe brain injury, the large majority of all TBIs are classified as mild (Andresen & McLaurin, 1980; Miller & Jones, 1985; Zasler, 1993), giving rise to the possibility that many cases of brain injury may not be documented. Indeed, statistics documenting brain injury, from the Office of Technology Assessment, compared with estimates of annual incidence of brain injury, raises the possibility that as many as 95% of brain injuries in the United States may not be specifically diagnosed (Hartlage, 1991).

FACTORS LEADING TO UNDERRECOGNITION OF MTBI

Emergency Response Practices

Although a direct blow to the head is not necessary for brain injury from acceleration–deceleration forces to occur, only within recent years has there been neuropsychological documentation of brain injury without head injury, that is, physical trauma to the head (Varney & Varney, 1995). Thus, in cases without obvious or reported blow to the head—such as might occur in restrained drivers, especially with deployed airbags—the need for investigation of sequelae of possible injury to the brain may be unrecognized and, as a result, not pursued.

Similarly, loss of consciousness is not requisite for brain injury and resultant sequelae. As has been recently documented (Iverson, Lovell, & Smith, 2000), there may be no significant differences on attention, learning, memory, language, or executive functions between individuals who did or did not sustain loss of consciousness. In much triage, or even postinjury assessment, however, the absence of loss of consciousness may be regarded as sufficient basis for dismissal of evaluation of possible brain injury resulting from the incident at issue.

Obvious physical injuries, such as fractures or bleeding wounds, typically receive greatest attention by emergency personnel, who may preclude attention to less treatment-critical issues, such as confusion, in favor of the obvious physical signs of acute injury. Even when confusion may be manifest, it may be attributed to shock or to reaction to physical injuries. In general, the more severe and/or obvious the physical injury, the greater is the likelihood that neuropsychological impairment, shy of coma, will be overlooked or not documented.

On-site, emergency treatment personnel are most likely to devote primary attention to obvious physical trauma and potentially life-threatening problems. In some cases, brief loss of consciousness may be resolved by the time EMT personnel arrive on-site. Even when residual confusion is present, it may not be obvious and may be ignored. Absent coma, the assessment of orientation for time, place, and person may be the only assessment of mental status done on-site. If the individual's functioning within this realm is "within normal limits," the tendency is to assume an absence of brain injury, that is, a complete recovery from the loss of consciousness without the possibility or likelihood of lasting effects.

Emergency room assessment is likely to follow a triage-issue model, wherein mild confusion is of low priority, if not attributed to shock from the traumatic event. Since emergency room assessment is normally done sometime following injury, brief lapses of consciousness may have resolved by the time such evaluation is performed. Again, if the patient is oriented to time, place, and person, their mental status may be recorded as normal, in cases in which more concentrated evaluation of mental status would indicate problems.

Patient Self-Report

Even in cases in which emergency room personnel may suspect possible concussive injury, typical diagnostic focus is more likely to assess gross focal neurological abnormalities of computerized tomography (CT) findings to determine the need for active medical (e.g., neurological) intervention. Since the great majority of MTBI cases may not show CT abnormality shortly following injury, there is likelihood that negative CT findings would be interpreted as indicative of neuropsychological impairment.

Interviews of patients sometime after the injury may suggest good recall of the event, in part because of the patient being told by others what occurred (i.e., they confabulate an account of the event based upon information provided by those around them). In this manner, the patient can "fill in the blanks" with what "must have happened," based upon what those around them report, even without direct recall of same, and probably without awareness that they are filling in these blanks with information from others. This can suggest absence of amnesia for the event, when more careful questioning would document either retrograde or anterograde amnestic periods.

Insurance adjusters and defense attorneys may minimize loss of consciousness or periods of postinjury confusion in the interest of minimization of damages and prompt resolution of claims. Even in cases in which symptoms persist and litigation is initiated, absence of hard evidence of brain damage may be invoked as evidence of a lack of brain injury.

Even attorneys representing plaintiffs may view mental complaints following an injury as either irrelevant to the injury or as too difficult to relate to the injury. In cases in which settlement for physical injuries, loss of work, and automobile damages may be delayed if postconcussive injuries are included, it may be considered appropriate to exclude neuropsychological problems from consideration as sequelae of injury.

Diagnosis and Other False-Negative Contributions to Underestimation

It has been recognized for many years that CT is not sensitive to most cases of MTBI (Tsushima & Wedding, 1979; Zasler, 1993). Since CT is the neuroradiologic procedure most likely to be used in emergency room settings to assess possible brain injury in postconcussive cases, the insensitivity of the procedure can obviously lead to considerable potential for false-positive errors in such assessment (Zasler, 1993). Approximately 85% of MTBIs do not show evidence of such injury on the sorts of imaging typically performed, so that behavioral symptoms resultant from the brain injury are likely to be attributed to some etiology other than the brain injury.

Not all neuropsychological examination procedures are sensitive to MTBI. Some test batteries, such as the Halstead–Reitan Neuropsychological Test Battery, have been validated with thousands of patients with known brain injuries, but some approaches use an admixture of tests validated on individuals without brain injury, and attempt to correct via statistical manipulations and weightings, to estimate how individuals with brain injury might perform. In cases in which MTBI is present, but not documented by such procedures, the incidence of TBI is obviously underestimated.

Only a small percentage of individuals who perform neuropsychological examinations have demonstrated competencies through submitting to examination leading to board certification; in most medical specialties, board certification is requisite for claims of expertise in the area of certification. For some reason, much looser criteria are demanded for those producing neuropsychological opinions. There are individuals without board certification in neuropsychology who possess sufficient expertise to make appropriate neuropsychological inferences, and it should be kept in mind that not all individuals with certification make proper diagnoses of all types of neuropsychological disorders. Nonetheless, the uneven skills of those providing neuropsychological diagnostic opinions represents a potential source of failure to recognize some of the subtle features typifying many findings in MTBI.

Psychologists who use computerized interpretations based on actuarial Minnesota Multiphasic Personality Inventory—Second Edition (MMPI-2) profile interpretation (or who use a "cookbook" interpretation based on "normal" or "psychiatric" databases) are at risk for misinterpreting elevations in such scales as *Hs,* implying somatization or somataform disorder, when in fact such elevations reflect accurate reporting of symptoms resultant from brain injury (and perhaps physical injuries sustained in the same incident as the brain injury). A number of researchers have reported appropriate use of differentially weighted scale interpretation with patients with neurologic symptoms (e.g., Derry, Harnadek, McClachlan, & Sontrop, 1997; Gass, 1992) and have identified unique MMPI profile configurations in individuals with head injury (Gass, 1991; Gass & Russell, 1991; Gass, Russell, & Hamilton, 1990; Senior, Lothrop, & Deacon, 1999; Youngjohn, Davis, & Wolf, 1997). Further, patients may be classified as exaggerating symptoms, based on elevations of the *F* or *F(p)* scales, when at least part of such elevations may result from confusion produced by the brain injury (Arbisi & Ben-Porath, 1995, 1997; Gass, 1999).

In a related fashion, posttraumatic stress disorder is not infrequently found following TBI, making it possible that diagnostic conclusions incorrectly attribute behavioral problems to posttraumatic stress disorder, especially when the evaluation is done by a psychiatrist or nonneuropsychological psychologist. Further, this could result in a treatment focus that does not classify, or even consider, behavioral changes to result from MTBI (e.g., Fairbank & Brown, 1987; Kuch, Swinson, & Kirby, 1985; Kuch, 1987). As has been recognized and documented for many years, much of the brain injury sustained from trauma tends, in considerable part because of anatomy and physics, to involve frontal cortical areas (Bigler, 1982). Since damage to frontal areas may produce impairments (e.g., anosomia or microsomia, impaired imitative motor-sequencing movements, and attentional deficits) that will not necessarily be apparent, especially to nonneuropsychological practioners and occasionally neuropsychologists, with admixtures of tests insensitive to such phenomena, such frequent impairments may well be overlooked, adding yet another source of underrecognition of MTBI.

In papers listing myths about TBI, Zasler (1993, 1998) mentions some of the most common reasons for overlooking sequelae of TBI:

1. Loss of consciousness is requisite for TBI to have taken place.
2. The word *mild* as it relates to brain injury means "insignificant."
3. Psychiatric problems following TBI are not serious.
4. A head strike is necessary for TBI.

Obviously, these myths are especially pronounced in cases of MTBI and help illustrate why such a large percentage of MTBI is not registered or documented.

Practical, Physiological, and Psychological Delayed Manifestations Marking TBI

Following an injury that includes fractures or requires surgery, there is likely to be a period of some time before the patient attempts to resume normal activities. During this period, the typical demands on memory, attention, concentration, and executive function, required for effective functioning in work, school, or other settings, are placed in abeyance. The patient is not required to employ such functions at the levels required for work or school settings, so it is unlikely that they will notice difficulty or impairment. When, weeks or even months later, the patient returns to their regular activity setting and notes difficulty in performing activities previously performed with efficiency, it may be attributed to being "rusty" or mentally slack, rather than identified as a decline in neurocognitive function attributable to the injury.

In some cases, the fact that executive-level workers typically make a more prompt return to work status than workers in more routine or lower-level jobs has been attributed to lower motivation to return to work among such workers. Careful study of jobs of "higher" and "lower" level workers reveals that, in many cases, higher-level workers experience postinjury neurocognitive problems that can be overcome or masked by delegation of tasks which prove difficult, but lower-level workers may be required to maintain consistent levels of attention, concentration, and performance. An executive can delegate details and follow-up to others; a fast-food clerk, factory assembly worker, or typist must maintain consistent accuracy and rate of performance. Because those are the types of functions at risk following TBI, their presence may be more pronounced and debilitating, over time, among workers at lower skill levels (Hartlage & Williams, 1992, 1993; Lees-Haley & Brown, 1993).

Lack of Informed Legal Representation

Attorneys representing individuals with MTBI are not always sensitive to the neurobehavioral sequelae of such injuries, or even their possibility. Indeed, in most states, there are only a few attorneys who focus on brain injury cases and have in-depth expertise in recognition of the signs and symptoms of behavioral consequences of MTBI. As a result, it is not uncommon for MTBI to be totally ignored, with no referral for neuropsychological assessment. Such problems are sufficiently common that some law firms have experienced successful growth by litigating cases against attorneys who neglected full potential consequences of brain injury in their settlement of cases (Hartlage, 1991).

SUMMARY AND CONCLUSIONS

As has been shown, the incidence and prevalence of TBI are elusive figures, making the issues surrounding identification, classification, and diagnosis difficult to delineate. What is clear from the research summarized here is that it is a widespread source of neuropsychological impairment, the precise dimensions and parameters of which are unknown. The sources for this confusion abound and start from the moments following injury (EMT response), through emergency treatment (lack of informed and in-depth assessment by emergency room personnel), to shortly after injury (friends and family members attributing behavioral changes to situational factors, rather than to brain injury), to longer periods postinjury (inadequate neuropsychological evaluation procedures), to legal and financial resolution (uninformed legal representation). With as many as 10 million new cases of TBI each year, this lack of information consigns potentially millions of individuals to cognitive and behavioral impairments with no legal or financial redress.

Given the multiplicity of opportunities for failure to recall, recognize, document, or record instances of TBI, combined with reluctance of insurance carriers and their representatives to acknowledge brain injury for which they may be liable, without substantial, unwavering proof of such injury, there is ample basis to expect that a substantial percentage of brain injury (especially mild brain injury) is not recognized and is accordingly undocumented. A reasonable estimate involves the data from early meticulous work by Caveness (1979a), extrapolated to take into account population estimates and automotive mileage records, producing annual incidence, in the United States, of upwards of 10 million occurrences of brain injury per year (Hartlage, 1984). In terms of approximate prevalence, accepting the generally held expectation that the vast majority of TBI is classified as "mild" and that approximately 85% of this MTBI can be expected to resolve without treatment (Lidvall, Linderoth, & Norlin, 1974; Lishman, 1988; Montgomery, Fenton, McClelland, MacFlynn, & Rutherford, 1991; Rimel, Giordani, Barth, Boll, & Jane, 1981), a conservative estimate is that 15% (1.5 million) of the survivors of MTBI present with persistent neurobehavioral symptoms (Alexander, 1995; Dacey, Alves, Rimel, Winn, & Jane, 1986; Gentilini, Nichelli, & Schoenhuber, 1989; Hartlage, 1997; Hatcher, Johnson, & Walker, 1996; Kurtzke, & Kurland, 1993; Levin, Mattis, & Ruff, 1976). With this conservative estimate of 1.5 million individuals each year being added to those left with brain injury residua, prevalence estimates (estimating an average life expectancy for a U.S. population of 270 million) could exceed 100 million individuals. Interest in brain injury and its effect on subsequent adjustment, reflected in attention by the legal profession to such behavioral residua, may translate into emphasis on more precise record keeping. To date, professional interest in TBI has not matched public recognition, which, in a *Wall Street Journal*, page-one feature, as early as 1982, described TBI as a "silent epidemic" (Klein, 1982).

REFERENCES

Alexander, M. P. (1995). Mild traumatic brain injury: Pathophysiology, natural history, and clinical management. *Neurology, 45,* 1253–1260.

Andresen, D. W., & McLaurin, R. L. (1980). The national head and spinal cord injury survey. *Journal of Neurosurgery, 53*, S1–S43.

Annegers, J. F., Grabow, J. D., Kurland, L. T., & Laws, E. R. (1980). The incidence, causes, and secular trends of head trauma in Olmstead County, Minnesota. *Neurology, 30*, 912–919.

Annegers, J. F., & Kurland, L. T. (1979). The epidemiology of central nervous system trauma. In G. L. Odom (Ed.), *Central nervous system trauma research status report, 1979* (pp. 1–8). Durham, NC: Duke University Press.

Arbisi, P. A., & Ben-Porath, Y. S. (1995). An MMPI-2 infrequent response scale for use with psychopathological populations: The Infrequency-Psychopathology Scale, (Fp). *Psychological Assessment, 7*, 424–431.

Arbisi, P. A., & Ben-Porath, Y. S. (1997). Characteristics of the MMPI-2 F(p) scale as a function of diagnosis in and inpatient sample of veterans. *Psychological Assessment, 9*, 102–105.

Bigler, E. D. (1982). Clinical assessment of cognitive deficit in traumatic and degenerative disorders: Brain scan and neuropsychologic findings. In R. N. Malates & L. C. Hartlage (Eds.), *Neuropsychology and cognition, Vol. II, NATO Advanced Study Institute series* (pp. 165–181). The Hague, Netherlands: Martinus Nijhoff.

Caveness, W. F. (1979a). Incidence of cranio-cerebral trauma in the United States. *Transactions of the American Neurological Association, 102*, 136–138.

Caveness, W. F. (1979b). Incidence of cranio-cerebral trauma in the United States 1976, and trend from 1970–1975. In R. Thomson & J. Green (Eds.), *Advances in neurology* (pp. 1–3). New York: Raven.

Centers for Disease Control (1999). *Traumatic brain injury in the United States: A report to congress.* Washington, DC: Centers for Disease Control.

Dacey, R. G., Jr., Alves, W. M., Rimel, R. W., Winn, H. R., & Jane, J. A. (1986). Neurosurgical complication after apparently minor head injury: Assessment of risk in a series of 610 patients. *Journal of Neurosurgery, 65*, 203–210.

Department of Health and Human Services (1989). *Federal interagency head injury task force report.* Washington, DC: Department of Health and Human Services.

Derry, P. A., Harnadek, M. C. S., McLachlan, R. S., & Sontrop, J. (1997). Influence of seizure content on interpreting psychopathology on the MMPI-2 in patients with epilepsy. *Journal of Clinical and Experimental Neuropsychology, 19*(3), 396–404.

Fairbank, J. A., & Brown, T. A. (1987). Current behavioral approaches to the treatment of posttraumatic stress disorder. *The Behavior Therapist, 10*, 57–64.

Fife, D. (1987). Head injury with and without hospital admission: Comparisons of incidence and short-term disability. *American Journal of Public Health, 77*, 810–812.

Fife, D., Faich, G., Hollinshead, W., & Wentworth, B. (1986). Incidence and outcome of hospital-treated head injury in Rhode Island. *American Journal of Public Health, 76*, 773–778.

Frankowski, R. F. (1986). Descriptive epidemiological studies of head injury in the United States 1974–1984. *Advances in Psychosomatic Medicine, 16*, 153–172.

Gass, C. S. (1991). Personality evaluation in neuropsychological assessment. In R. D. Vanderploeg (Ed.), *The clinician's guide to neuropsychological assessment* (pp. 155–194). Mahwah, NJ: Lawrence Erlbaum.

Gass, C. S. (1992). MMPI-2 interpretation of patients with cerebrovascular disease. *Archives of Clinical Neuropsychology, 7,* 17–27.

Gass, C. S. (1999). MMPI interpretation and closed head injury: A correction factor. *Psychological Assessment, 3*(1), 27–31.

Gass, C. S., & Russell, E. W. (1991). MMPI profiles of closed head injury trauma patients: Impact of neurologic complaints. *Journal of Clinical Psychology, 47*(2), 253–260.

Gass, C. S., Russel, E. W., & Hamilton, R. A. (1990). Accuracy of MMPI-based inferences regarding memory and concentration in closed-head trauma patients. *Psychological Assessment, 2*(2), 175–178.

Gentilini, M., Nichelli, P., & Schoenhuber, R. (1989). Assessment of attention in mild head injury. In H. S. Levin, H. M. Eisenberg, & A. L. Benton (Eds.), *Mild head injury* (pp. 163–175). New York: Oxford University Press.

Hartlage, L. C. (1984). Unexpected consequences of apparently insignificant head injuries. *Auto Torts, 7,* 187–191.

Hartlage, L. C. (1990). *Neuropsychological evaluation of head injury.* Sarasota, FL: Professional Resource Exchange.

Hartlage, L. C. (1991). Major legal implications of minor head injuries. *The Journal of Head Injury, 2*(3), 8–11.

Hartlage, L. C. (1995). Neuropsychological complaint base rates in personal injury, revisited. *Archives of Clinical Psychology, 10*(3), 279–280.

Hartlage, L. C. (1997). Is mild brain injury an epidemic, a fad, or a scam? *American Trial Lawyers Association TBI Litigation Group, 4*(2), 5–11.

Hartlage, L. C. (1999). Forensic aspects of mild traumatic brain injury. In M. J. Raymond, T. L. Bennet, L. C. Hartlage, & C. M Cullum (Eds.), *Mild traumatic brain injury* (pp. 135–142). Austin, TX: Pro-Ed.

Hartlage, L. C., & Williams, B. L. (1992). Behavioral screening for exposure to potentially neurotoxic chemicals. *Archives of Clinical Neuropsychology, 7*(4), 333–334.

Hartlage, L. C., & Williams, B. L. (1993). Neuropsychological sequelae of exposure to supposedly safe levels of environmental contaminants. *Archives of Clinical Neuropsychology, 8,* 275.

Hatcher, I., Johnson, C. C., & Walker, J. M. (1996). *More Than Just a Bump on the Head: About concussions: Mild traumatic brain injuries* [Brochure]. Atlanta, GA: Pritchett & Hull.

Hawthorne, V. M. (1978). Epidemiology of head injuries. *Scottish Medicine Journal, 23,* 1–92.

Iverson, G. L., Lovell, M. R., & Smith, S. S. (2000). Does brief loss of consciousness affect cognitive functioning after head injury? *Archives of Clinical Neuropsychology, 15*(7), 643–648.

Jagger, J., Levine, J. I., Jane, J. A., & Rimel, R. W. (1984). Epidemiological features of head injury in a predominantly rural population. *Journal of Trauma, 24,* 40–44.

Kalsbeek, W. D., McLaurin, R. L., Harris, B. S., & Miller, J. D. (1980). The national head and spinal cord injury survey: Major findings. *Journal of Neurosurgery, 53,* S19–S24.

Klauber, M. R., Barret-Connor, E., Marhsall, L. F., & Bowers, S. A. (1981). The epidemiology of head injury: A prospective study of an entire community—San Diego County, California, 1978. *American Journal of Epidemiology, 113,* 500–509.

Klein, F. C. (1982, November 24). Silent epidemic: Head injuries, often difficult to diagnose, get rising attention. *The Wall Street Journal,* p. 1.

Klonoff, H., & Thompson, G. B. (1969). Epidemiology of head injuries in adults. *Canadian Medical Association Journal, 100,* 235–241.

Krauss, J. F. (1980). Injury to the head and spinal cord. The epidemiological relevance of the medical literature 1960–1978. *Journal of Neurosurgery, 53,* 53–59.

Kraus, J. F., & Arthur, D. L. (1996). Epidemiological aspects of brain injury. *Neurologic Clinics, 14*(2), 435–450.

Kuch, K. (1987). Treatment of PTSD following automobile accidents. *The Behavior Therapist, 10,* 241–242.

Kuch, K., Swinson, R. P., & Kirby, M. (1985). Post-traumatic stress disorder after car accidents. *Canadian Journal of Psychiatry, 30,* 426–427.

Kurtzke, J. F., & Kurland, L. T. (1993). The epidemiology of neurologic disease. In R. J. Joynt (Ed.), *Clinical neurology* (pp. 66–89). Philadelphia: J. B. Lippincott.

Lees-Haley, P. R., & Brown, R. S. (1993). Neuropsychological base rates of 170 personal injury claimants. *Archives of Clinical Neuropsychology, 8*(3), 203–209.

Levin, H. S., Mattis, S., & Ruff, R. M. (1976). Neurobehavioral outcome following minor head injury: A three-center study. *Journal of Neurosurgery, 66,* 234–243.

Lidvall, H. F., Linderoth, B., & Norlin, B. (1974). Causes of the post-concussional syndrome. *Acta Neurologica Scandinavica, (Suppl. 56),* 1–144.

Lishman, W. A. (1988). Physiogenesis and psychogenesis in the "post-concussional syndrome." *British Journal of Psychiatry, 353,* 460–469.

MacKenzie, E. J., Edelstein, S. L., & Flynn, J. P. (1989). Hospitalized head-injured patients in Maryland: Incidence and severity of injuries. *Maryland Medical Journal, 38,* 725–732.

Miller, J. D., & Jones, P. A. (1985). The work of a regional head injury service. *Lancet, 1,* 1141.

Montgomery, E. A., Fenton, G. W., McClelland, R. J., MacFlynn, G., & Rutherford, W. H. (1991). The psychobiology of minor head injury. *Psychological Medicine, 21,* 375–384.

Richardson, W. S., Wilson, M. C., Guyett, G. H., Cook, D. J., & Nishikawa, J. (1999). User's guides to the medical literature XV: How to use an article about disease probability for differential diagnosis. *Journal of the American Medical Association, 281*(13), 1214–1219.

Rimel, R. W., Giordani, B., Barth, J. T., Boll, T. J., & Jane, J. A. (1981). Disability caused by minor head injury. *Neurosurgery, 9,* 225–228.

Segalowitz, S. J., & Brown, D. (1991). Mild head injury as a source of developmental disabilities. *Journal of Learning Disabilities, 24,* 551–558.

Senior, G. J., Lothrop, P., & Deacon, S. (1999, November). TBI(f): *An MMPI-2 scale for assessing traumatic brain injury in a forensic setting.* Poster presented at the 19th Annual National Academy of Neuropsychology Conference, San Antonio, TX.

Sorenson, S., & Krauss, J. (1991). Occurrence, severity, and outcomes of brain injury. *The Journal of Head Trauma Rehabilitation, 6,* 1–10.

Templer, D. I., Spencer, D. A., & Hartlage, L. C. (1993). *Biopsychosocial psychopathology: Epidemiological perspectives* (p. vii). New York: Springer.

Traumatic Brain Injury Act of 1996, Pub. L. 104-166, Stat. 1445 (1996).

Tsushima, W. T., & Wedding, D. (1979). Neuropsychology battery and computerized tomography in the identification of brain disorder. *Journal of Nervous and Mental Disease, 167,* 704–707.

Varney, N. R., & Varney, R. N. (1995). Brain injury without head injury. Some physics of automobile collisions with particular reference to brain injuries occurring without physical head trauma. *Applied Neuropsychology, 2,* 47–62.

Whitman, S., Coonley-Hoganson, R., & Desai, B. T. (1984). Comparative head trauma experience in two socioeconomically different Chicago-area communities: A population study. *American Journal of Epidemiology, 4,* 560–580.

Youngjohn, J. R., Davis, D., & Wolf, I. (1997). Head injury and the MMPI-2: Paradoxical severity effects and the influence of litigation. *Psychological Assessment, 9*(3), 177–184.

Zasler, N. D. (1993). Post-concussive disorders: Facts, fallacies, and foibles. *The Journal of Head Injury, 3*(2), 8–13.

Zasler, N. D. (1998). Five myths about traumatic brain injury. *American Trial Lawyers Association TBI Litigation Group, 5*(5), 6–13.

Chapter 7

Neuroimaging in Forensic Neuropsychology

Erin D. Bigler

The origin of contemporary neuroimaging is dated by the introduction of computerized tomography (CT) in the early 1970s
(Hounsfield, 1973), but the more universal use of CT imaging
does not occur until the late 1970s (Eisenberg, 1991). Accordingly, the
first studies examining the interface between CT imaging and neuropsychological assessment do not occur until the late 1970s (Swiercinsky &
Leigh, 1979), and therefore the initial clinical and forensic applications
of neuroimaging in neuropsychology represent a very recent occurrence.

In fact, I believe that the first case of neuroimaging used in conjunction with neuropsychological testimony in the United States occurred
in the case of *Soliz v. Borden Inc*, in 1979 in Austin, Texas (see Bigler,
1980). This was a straightforward case. The patient had the misfortune
of being involved in a car–truck accident in which he was thrown from
the vehicle, striking his head against the curb, which rendered him
unconscious. Because of the level and persistence of coma, an intracranial pressure monitor was placed and the patient was conservatively
treated. He was assessed to have sustained a moderate-to-severe traumatic brain injury (TBI) and spent 2 weeks in the hospital. When this
patient was seen at the Austin Neurological Clinic in 1978, I was in
the midst of collecting CT data that would become one of the early
neuroimaging–neuropsychology studies of brain injury (Bigler et al.,
1984; Bigler, Steinman, & Newton, 1981), and *Neurobehavioral Conse-*

The figures in this chapter appear in color at the end of the chapter *quences of TBI,* by Levin, Benton, and Grossman (1982) had not yet been published.

This new neuroimaging technology, for the first time, permitted an in vivo view of the patient's brain that had been injured. This patient underwent CT imaging several months postinjury, because of significant and persistent cognitive and behavioral deficits. Clearly observable to anyone's view, there was focal frontal atrophy, obviously trauma-related, with some generalized, diffuse atrophy as well. I had seen the patient in my regular duties as a neuropsychologist at the clinic where the patient was being followed. His family reported dramatic changes in personality, with particular deficits in memory, and his employer found him unsuitable to return to his work as a jewelsmith.

Prior to trial, the patient's attorney met with me, and I showed him not only the neuropsychological deficits (i.e., poor copy of the Bender Gestalt and Rey Complex figure, in a gentleman who premorbidly had magnificent fine motor and perceptual motor abilities as a jewelsmith, prior to injury), but odd-looking axial CT images of this man's brain. Once the attorney understood the two-dimensional, flat-surface mental image of this patient's brain, he could see where the brain was damaged. I laid out an atlas (Roberts & Hanaway, 1970) that I had used in my graduate school training in neuroanatomy and showed how a 'normal' image should look. Upon viewing this, the decision was made to show the CT images in the courtroom. I got out my 35mm camera, put the X-ray film on the view box, and took some pictures. A few days later, I walked into the courtroom with pictures in hand and showed the jury how and where this brain was damaged by impact and how these deficits were manifested in the neuropsychological data. With that, to my knowledge, forensic neuropsychology using neuroimaging was inaugurated.

This chapter starts with a recent court case that demonstrates the rich interface between contemporary neuroimaging and neuropsychological practice. The majority of the cases discussed in this chapter are associated with TBI, but damage to the brain from any etiology can be demonstrated by the technologies and techniques described herein.

THE RATIONALE FOR USING NEUROIMAGING FINDINGS AS AN ADJUNCT TO THE NEUROPSYCHOLOGICAL EXAMINATION

No matter how one approaches clinical neuropsychology, the consultation and assessment process is dependent on the cooperation and full effort of the patient for reliable test results. In fact, this has become the focal point of contentiousness in forensic neuropsychology: Is a deficit really a deficit, or is the patient functioning within some realm of either expected (e.g., premorbid baseline) or normal performance? Or, is the patient simply not putting forth appropriate effort, or, worse, is the patient malingering? The tremendous proliferation of so-called "malingering tests" is testament to the importance that some neuropsychologists place on this issue.

In forensic work, so-called "proof" of an injury comes as a by-product of some objective criteria, reproducible deficits, and/or when history and symptom match expected injury sequela. As an example of this point, Figure 7.1 demonstrates a 16-penny nail in a man's head, with the nail passing through the right temporal lobe. This is pretty objective information demonstrating a brain injury. However, documenting brain injury is not always so straightforward. For example, in the American Medical Association guidelines for disability, loss of an arm is easy to quantify. Cocchiarella and Andersson's *Guides to the Evaluation of Permanent Impairment* (2001) indicates that loss of a limb results in 100% upper extremity impairment and 60% whole-person impairment (p. 441). Unlike a physical loss of a limb, outwardly detectable, brain injury may not be so observable. For example, the most distinct outward manifestation of some neurological abnormality is motor impairment, yet extensive areas of the cerebrum can be damaged, resulting in no motor dysfunction whatsoever, as was the case of the patient presented in Figure 7.1. Some have even used the term *silent injury* to denote many of the deficits produced by TBI. Thus, when a patient acquires a significant TBI, yet has no residual motor or speech impairment, how can the deficits be demonstrated accurately and objectively? This is especially true if the case is in litigation and goes to trial. How can all involved "see" the injury, because the patient may outwardly appear normal? I propose that the answer to this is by the interface of neuroimaging with neuropsychology. The case presented below illustrates the point.

THE CASE

A patient is injured, ultimately seen and examined by a neuropsychologist, and the neuropsychologist renders a report. At the time of deposition or trial, the neuropsychologist communicates the findings regarding the patient's cognition, memory, neurobehavioral deficits, executive function, and other brain–behavior relationships. But it is precisely at this level of debate where neuropsychologists may be in diametrically polarized camps. An example of such a case is presented in Figure 7.2. This person sustained a significant TBI in a vehicle–pedestrian collision, wherein the patient sustained a moderate TBI, along with subdural hematoma, which was neurosurgically treated. However, in many respects, by traditional standards, he recovered quite well and was able to return to work. Preinjury, he had completed a college degree and had just established himself early in his career. Despite an excellent recovery, given the severity of injury, he was changed, with different cognitive abilities and temperament, readily recognized by those who knew him before and after the injury. He could walk and talk normally, but had neuropsychological deficits, but a confusing picture was being given because the neuropsychologist retained by the defense indicated that there were no significant deficits in his test performance, because every score was at least within the average range. Who should a juror believe?

It is in exactly such a scenario that contemporary neuroimaging can play a critical role in illuminating the significance of neurobehavioral deficits. Take a close look at the neuroimaging studies presented in Figure 7.2. The magnetic resonance imaging (MRI) findings clearly display regions of encephalomalacia in both temporal lobes and in the inferior frontal region. More detailed inspection of the temporal lobe damage indicates that the left anterior aspect was completely compromised, and there were several areas in the right temporal region that demonstrated distinct changes in brain parenchyma. However, the more revealing findings come with single photon emission computed tomography (SPECT), which demonstrated lack of perfusion in regions that exceeded the boundaries defined by the signal abnormalities in the temporal area. Furthermore, quantitative analysis demonstrated temporal horn dilation and hippocampal atrophy—more so on the left than right side of the brain (see Tate & Bigler, 2000).

What are the neuropsychological correlates of such abnormalities? The left temporal damage spared language centers, so no language deficits would be expected and none were observed. However, memory problems are typically associated with hippocampal atrophy and were present in this patient. Likewise, emotional regulation is another function of the temporal lobes, and this patient had elevated levels of depression, anxiety, and overall psychological distress. As can be seen in Figure 7.2, he has temporal horn dilation, which in TBI is an indicator of loss of white matter integrity in the temporal lobe (Bigler, Anderson, & Blatter, 2001).

Next, the reader should turn attention to the frontal lobes in Figure 7.2. The inferior frontal area (region of the gyrus rectus) has a different MRI signal intensity than observed in tissue located just superior. This is a classic area for inferior frontal contusion in TBI and typically disrupts smell, as the most objective finding. This patient had dysnomia. Such inferior frontal lesions are also important because they occur in regions involved in ascending neuroregulatory pathways for emotional control. Inferior frontal damage is often seen to relate to dysfunctional emotional control. Although structural imaging with MRI in this region did indicate some structural damage, SPECT imaging clearly demonstrated a large left frontal defect (see Figure 7.2). What is important in viewing this defect is that it shows considerable functional impairment in what otherwise looks to be normal-appearing tissue. Such frontal defects are expected to result in changes in executive and personality function. Such problems were reported and also observed in this patient, but were difficult to actually demonstrate with neuropsychological technique, because of very high premorbid functioning. Accordingly, his performance on "executive" tests was not specifically in the impaired range, but on tests in which, before the injury, it would have been expected he would have little difficulty, he now performed in the average to low-average range (although, in the defense neuropsychologist's opinion, this was still interpreted as being "within the average or normal range"). Also, there is no measure in our neuropsychological test armamentarium that truly assesses creativity, which this patient, his employer, and his professional colleagues all felt he had suffered.

Moderate-to-severe TBI is thought to result in significant nonspecific, or what Generalli (1997) and Generalli, Thibault, and Graham (1998) describe as "diffuse brain injury" (see also Smith & Meaney, 2000). Diffuse brain injury is associated with overall loss of white matter integrity and reduced brain volume (Bigler, 2001a; Bigler et al., 2001). Thus, what we expect to see in a patient like the one presented herein is an overall reduction in brain volume, which there was. The reduced brain volume in TBI is a reflection of reduced white matter integrity (Brooks et al., 2000; Friedman, Brooks, et al., 1999; Garnett, Blamire, Corkill, et al., 2000; Garnett, Blamire, Rajagopalan, Styles, & Cadoux-Hudson, 2000), and reduced white matter volume is associated with diminished speed of processing. Accordingly, turning attention to tasks that relate to speed of processing, such as the Trail Making Test and Digit Symbol tasks, these are typically performed less well in TBI subjects (Bigler & Clement, 1997). In this patient, the speed or timed tests were again performed within normal limits, but, in comparison to some nontimed tasks and the estimate of his premorbid ability, were accomplished at the lower end of average.

So, in this actual case, the fallacy of the approach taken by the neuropsychologist retained by the defense was the lack of integrating this information about the actual structural and metabolic damage (readily visible and completely objective) and relying solely on the neuropsychological data. From this defense perspective, test perfor-mance was all within the average or normal range, which was interpreted as being a reflection of normal or recovered neuropsychological func-tion. This approach, by itself, is a difficult one to refute using just the neuropsychological test data. It is difficult for a lay jury to understand the concept that normal performance can still reflect brain damage and diminished ability, compared to preinjury level of function. The integration of neuroimaging with neuropsychological test data offers the best method for presenting the most complete and accurate assess-ment of the patient who has sustained an injury and to address defense polemics when they are unwarranted.

Nonetheless, defense-oriented neuropsychologists still argue this point—that average means normal. In fact, the case presented in Figure 7.3, in which the corpus callosum shows the classic "shear" injury (see Bigler, 2001a, 2001b), the defense neuropsychologist concluded that there was no deficit, because all of the patient's performance was within the average range. This point was even presented to the judge during a bench trial.

This type of posturing, obfuscation, and sophistry by defense neuro-psychologists, in light of definitively objective criteria of damage pre-sented by neuroimaging studies, may provide fodder for legal argument, but does little for the creditability of the neuropsychology profession. We are now at a level of maturity in clinical neuropsychology and assessment when many neuroscience principles can be brought to bear on the evaluation of the brain-injured patient and done objectively, through integration of neuroimaging data with neuropsychological per-formance. In the patient reviewed in Figure 7.2, clearly structural dam-age to the brain has occurred. Temporal lobe damage, in association with hippocampal atrophy, is expected to disrupt memory performance, which was present. Inferior frontal damage is expected to affect olfaction, which it did. Combination of frontal and temporal lobe damage is expected to alter personality, temperament, and emotional control, which were all affected. The diffuse nature of injury, clearly reflected in quantitative analysis of the MRI studies, by the overall reduction in brain volume, is expected to more selectively challenge tasks dependent on speed of processing and responding, which were affected.

Although not a current concern in interpreting the neuropsychological findings, the reduced brain volume has a more ominous implication, which certainly warrants discussion in forensic cases (see Bigler, 2001a). Having sustained a TBI places the individual at increased risk for late-life dementia (Plassman et al., 2000) and specifically for Alzheimer's disease (Guo et al., 2000; Plassman et al., 2000). Since age-related dementias are associated with reduced brain volume, having sustained an injury that results in brain degeneration, reduced brain volume may be one of those precipitating factors that, later in life, contributes to the loss of cognitive ability in those who sustain a brain injury (Bigler, 2001a).

THREE-DIMENSIONAL NEUROIMAGING

As alluded to in the introduction, initially, imaging was strictly two-dimensional (2-D). Accordingly, anyone who was to interpret the images had to be able to generate a mental three-dimensional (3-D) perception, to fully understand the significance of the 2-D image being viewed. Now, damage can be exquisitely shown in 3-D, as exemplified by Figures 7.4 and 7.5. In Figure 7.4, this child sustained a traumatic birth injury that resulted in focal wasting of the left temporal lobe, which is explicitly depicted in the illustration. This focal injury can then be integrated with the neuropsychological findings, to yield a very accurate assessment of the structural and neurobehavioral deficits that occurred with this brain injury. In less-obvious TBI, it is difficult for the inexperienced eye to fully appreciate a shriveled gyrus and widened sulcus (reflections of atrophy) but ventricular expansion can be readily appreciated, and a side-by-side 3-D comparison of a normal versus injured brain makes for a nice comparison, as shown in Figure 7.5. In TBI, when atrophy occurs, there is greater selectivity for white matter damage, which results in prominent ventricular expansion, because so much of the ventricle is surrounded by white matter (Bigler, 2001a). In this case, the dilated ventricular system reflects global atrophy, which, in turn, was related to the generalized cognitive deficits present in this child.

Not only can the damage be shown in 3-D, but the physics of the injury can readily be shown in 3-D and integrated with the clinical imaging. This is shown in Figure 7.6, taken from a patient who was involved in an auto–pedestrian accident, in which the greatest impact occurred when her head struck the ground. CT imaging demonstrated subarachnoid hemorrhaging (see Figure 7.6) and evolution of a subdural hematoma. Biomechanical engineering principles, applied to the known facts of the impact, were able to show that the physical forces of the injury took place in the region of hemorrhage and where functional imaging depicted deficits. This patient had PET imaging that indicated focal parietal changes, also consistent with atrophy (see Figure 7.6), which developed where physical force of mechanical deformation occurred at its peak. Thus, in the images portrayed in Figure 7.6, a complex head injury can be shown in 3-D that is understandable to any lay individual.

NEW IMAGING TECHNIQUES

Technology continually advances in neuroimaging. New techniques, such as diffusion-weighted and tensor imaging, will play an ever-increasing role in evaluating lesions in TBI and other disorders that have a structural–anatomic basis (Klingberg et al., 2000). For example, the case presented in Figure 7.7 shows this principle quite nicely. This patient sustained a mild TBI in a fall. Acute neuroimaging studies demonstrated probable mild nonspecific cerebral edema, but no hemorrhagic lesions. Neuropsychological studies, several months and over 1 year postinjury, did demonstrate deficits consistent with mild TBI (MTBI) (diminished memory performance, variable executive ability, impaired attention/concentration), and follow-up neuroimaging demonstrated presence of multiple areas of hemosiderin staining, distinctly observed in MRI, as shown in Figure 7.7. The neuroimaging findings provided the objective data in support of the neuropsychological findings of mild cognitive impairment secondary to TBI.

FUNCTIONAL NEUROIMAGING FOR IN VIVO NEUROBEHAVIORAL ASSESSMENT

Although having limited spatial resolution, PET imaging studies have demonstrated how certain motor, sensory, language, and cognitive tasks activate different regions of the brain (Orrison, 2000). Recently, Fontaine, Azouri, Remy, Bussel, and Samson (1999) used PET imaging to measure regional cerebral glucose metabolism, to investigate a variety of neurobehavioral tasks in TBI subjects. Their results demonstrated reduced metabolic activity in the cingulate gyrus, to be associated with deficits in memory and executive functioning. Also, Ricker et al. (2000) have shown abnormal frontal activation patterns in TBI patients, using PET imaging techniques. Although PET studies can demonstrate a variety of abnormalities in TBI, there are few PET imaging labs, and therefore PET imaging has not been a practical method for clinical neuroimaging in TBI (see also Balk & Lau, 2001; Bicik et al., 1998). As of this writing, functional MRI (fMRI) and the integration of quantitative MRI procedures with magnetoencephalography (MEG) and quantitative electroencephalography (qEEG) may hold the greatest promise in the forensic assessment, and is discussed below.

fMRI

In an fMRI study, McAllister et al. (1999) reported that, compared to the more discrete bifrontal and biparietal activation in controls during working memory tasks, MTBI subjects showed widespread activation in right parietal and dorsolateral regions of the brain, as shown in Figure 7.8. This indicated greater recruitment offset following MTBI. Chirstodoulou et al. (2001) have also demonstrated working impairment with the fMRI technique, in which TBI patients had more dispersed activation. These studies indicate that central nervous system integration and neural transmission is affected in TBI. The beauty of fMRI is that, simultaneously, the detail and elegance of brain structure, along with MRI resolution, can be combined with functional activation of specific areas known to relate to a neurobehavioral task. Thus, both structure and function can be combined. This technique holds considerable promise in forensic neuropsychology.

MEG

Lewine, Davis, Sloan, Kodituwakku, and Orrison (1999) have shown that MEG abnormalities are often detected in MTBI cases in which MRI is normal. Such a case is presented in Figure 7.9. In this patient,

significant brain injury occurred as a consequence of a motor vehicle
accident, based on acute injury characteristics—positive loss of consciousness, admission Glasgow Coma Scale of 8, CT scan demonstrating
subarachnoid blood, and significant retrograde and anterograde amnesia. Although the initial CT scan demonstrated some subarachnoid
hemorrhaging, follow-up MRI studies, several months postinjury, were
negative (see Figure 7.9). However, the patient continued to have significant cognitive complaints, and neuropsychological studies demonstrated presence of mild cognitive problems. MEG findings, summarized
in Figure 7.9, showed abnormal MEG in multiple areas, despite clinically
normal MRI and SPECT. MEG also holds considerable promise in
forensic neuropsychology, because, combined with 3-D MRI, it can
precisely demonstrate where physiological abnormalities are located.

Quantitative Electroencephalography (qEEG)

qEEG techniques can be integrated with MRI in the demonstration of
cerebral dysfunction from TBI (Arciniegas et al., 2000; Ricker & Zafonte,
2000; Thatcher et al., 2001; Thatcher, Biver, McAlaster, & Salazar, 1998;
Thatcher et al., 1999). qEEG abnormality can be plotted on the 3-D
brain from MRI, similar to what was shown in Figure 7.9 (see also Givens,
1996). These sophisticated technologies provide unique methods for
investigating the physiological abnormalities associated with TBI (see
Thatcher et al., 2001).

Magnetic Resonance Spectroscopy (MRS)

MRS provides a method for assessing intracellular compounds in the
brain. For example, N-acetylaspartate is an amino acid thought to be a
marker of neuronal integrity (Brooks et al., 2000; Friedman et al., 1999;
Garnett, Blamire, Corkill, et al., 2000). A reduction in N-acetylaspartate
has been interpreted as indicating an injury to white matter pathways
(Ross & Ernst, 1998). Choline is also readily assessed by MRS and is
thought to be most involved with membrane metabolism and probably
best reflects integrity of gray matter. Several studies have now examined
human TBI subjects using MRS (Brooks et al., 2000; Friedman, Brooks,
et al., 1999; Garnett, Blamire, Rajagopalan, et al., 2000). For the purposes of this chapter, the study by Garnett et al. (2000) may be the

most important. In that study, MRS was abnormal, even when the MRI was clinically considered to be normal. The abnormalities were distinctly in the white matter and were proportional to the deficit. Friedman, Brooks, et al. (1999) have demonstrated impressive correlations between MRS findings and neuropsychological outcome following TBI.

Although different than MRS, magnetization transfer imaging has been shown, by McGowan et al. (2000) and Sinson et al. (2001), to have the utility of detecting subtle abnormalities in MTBI, when the clinical scan is normal. Obviously, considerable work is necessary, but tremendous potential is present with these technologies. In Figure 7.10, a case of severe anoxic injury in a child is presented, in which the clinical MRI demonstrates significant atrophy, and the MRS findings further specify abnormal *N*-acetylaspartate levels indicative of neuronal loss and a choline/creatine ratio indicative of gliosis.

DAUBERT RULE

Without any debate or discussion, scientific standards must be met, to use any technology in the courtroom. Traditional structural imaging (i.e., CT and MRI) raises no *Daubert* (*Daubert v. Merrell Dow Pharmaceuticals*, 1993) concerns, but the manner in which functional neuroimaging findings are presented does raise some issues. The hallmark of science is the peer review process and reproducibility of results. New technologies will continue to update neuroimaging, and, therefore, the clinician may have an ever-increasing number of neuroimaging techniques to use in evaluating the cognitive and neurobehavioral deficits of an injury. All acceptable methods must first pass the peer review process, in which the best presentation occurs from the rigors of the review process from the best scientific journals within the field. Often, another good index (although not infallible) for the guaranteed use of an imaging procedure in forensic cases is its acceptability within the insurance and medical community. If it is a clinical procedure that is used by other practitioners to make clinical judgments and is reimbursable, that procedure has already passed certain standards that should automatically allow its admissibility.

As implied above, another way *Daubert* issues can be dealt with, using neuroimaging technology, is the reproducibility of the results by independent laboratories. If persisting neurological damage or dysfunction is present, the abnormalities should be there, regardless of how and where they are imaged. A good example of this is present in Figure 7.11. This child was involved in a school bus rollover accident. She was not seat-belted. There was questionable brief loss of consciousness, but also documented vomiting at the scene of the accident. She had ecchymosis over the forehead region, and she sustained a wrist fracture. She was triaged at a local emergency room and found to be neurologically intact. However, within days of the injury, posttraumatic headaches persisted, in association with emotional lability, lethargy, and general malaise. She was seen by her family physician, who reaffirmed that a concussional head injury had occurred and referred her to a neurologist. The neurologist requested MRI, which demonstrated multiple shear lesions, most occurring right at the gray–white junction (see Figure 7.11). When it came time for the independent medical exam, the defense side requested that these imaging studies be duplicated, but in an independent radiology department. The independent medical exam neuroradiological findings were identical. Because, in someone this young, such signal abnormalities are unlikely in an asymptomatic child, other than the history of trauma, the presence of these signal abnormalities was consistent with trauma, and trauma was the most likely explanation. In this case, the neuroimaging and neuropsychological findings met the *Daubert* challenge by their reproducibility and scientific basis.

A BRAIN INJURY IS A BRAIN INJURY

This chapter focuses on neuroimaging methods for displaying structural abnormalities of the brain following some type of acquired injury. However, everything must be kept in perspective. Even with the exciting developments with tensor imaging, in which literal aggregate fiber tracks can be mapped, this technology still does permit anything akin to histological level analysis and certainly does not approach the complexity at the synaptic level. For example, Harding, Halliday, and Kril (1998) recently demonstrated that, in 1 cm within a single layer of cerebral cortex, the number of synapses is estimated to be up to 1.5 billion. Thus, what is observed at the molar level of contemporary neuroimaging may be insensitive to subtler damage/dysfunction below the level of detection.

A good example of this is the current status of research exploring the relationship of head injury to the development of dementia later in life (Guo et al., 2000; Plassman et al., 2000), as previously indicated. The basic premise is that aging is associated with some neuronal loss (apoptosis), simply as a reflection of the normal aging process. There is also a reserve capacity of the brain (Satz, 1993). Normal aging and reserve capacity, along with an individual's genetic endowment and medical history and risk variables, along with environmental effects, probably coalesce to produce an individual's longevity, morbidity, and mortality. Acquired brain injury alters the balance in this equation, just as a history of smoking alters the same balance for lung cancer risk, or a knee injury from high school sports increases the likelihood for orthopedic impairment sometime later in the aging process, even though "full recovery" may have occurred earlier in life.

So, if brain injury is to have a deleterious effect, it should alter this risk balance, and there should be a greater risk for dementia later in life. This is precisely what Plassman et al. (2000) have shown (see Figure 7.12). This means that the cellular environment of the brain has been damaged, regardless of whether imaging findings were positive or negative. This further suggests the importance of the history of head injury, rather than just positive or negative neuroimaging findings. In fact, in our work (unpublished) with mild head injury, even with well-documented loss of consciousness and posttraumatic amnesia, many patients with Glasgow Coma Scale of 13, and higher, have no detectable abnormalities on any neuroimaging or neurophysiological measure. However, Blumbergs et al. (1994) have shown that, in such cases of MTBI, axonal injury can be documented (see also Conti, Raghupathi, Trojanowski, & McIntosh, 1998). Also, in an MTBI case that I recently evaluated, which went to postmortem 7 months postinjury, microhemorrhagic lesions were found that were not detected by standard clinical imaging. This patient, who died 7 months after injury from a heart attack, had classic postconcussional problems when I examined him at 4 months postinjury. His SPECT scan was read as negative, and he had a negative scan on the day of injury. Despite these negative imaging findings, under the microscope, there was obvious perturbation of the white matter that was present (hemosiderin-laden macrophages and scattered lymphocytes). Thus, the absence of a detectable neuroimaging abnormality should not be interpreted as absence of injury or damage. Proof of this comes from the Guo et al. (2000) study, which showed that "mild" TBI, without loss of conscious, increased the risk of Alzheimer's disease by threefold (see also Lye & Shores, 2000). Thus, absence of a neuroimaging abnormality is no guarantee of absence of a neurological abnormality.

On the other hand, presence of an abnormality is going to have some impact on neurobehavioral status. Nonetheless, in the sometimes-strange world of litigation, with its adversarial approach, completely untenable positions are often taken. The last two figures in this chapter illustrate such cases. In Figure 7.13, the patient sustained a severe TBI, but, in the overall scope of likely outcomes, displayed a better recovery than expected, although, as might be anticipated by reviewing the dramatic neuroimaging studies, had significant and permanent motor and language deficits. In an application for Social Security Disability, the psychologist who performed a neuropsychological evaluation felt that the tests represented a good recovery (patient had a performance IQ score of 103) and that the patient could work. Obviously, one look at the MRI studies and clearly this is an untenable conclusion, because damage to this extent will have a profound cognitive influence on the ability to function.

Another non sequitur case is given in Figure 7.14. That patient sustained a significant brain injury in a fall down a flight of ice-covered stairs. On admission to the hospital, initial CT imaging (Figure 7.14) demonstrated numerous small and large hemorrhagic and intraparenchymal contusions. This left the patient with significant frontal lobe disorder, which was contested by the neuropsychologist retained by the defense. The problem with not accepting that these acute imaging findings represent frontal lobe damage, and the cause of the patient's frontal lobe disorder, is that it breaks the principle of Occam's Razor (Weiner, 1999), the basic premise of which is that the most parsimonious and simplest explanation is typically correct. To take the untenable position of the defense neuropsychologist, one would have to conclude that the fall, loss of consciousness, and hemorrhagic contusions of the frontal lobe had no adverse effect on the patient and could not be the basis of the patient's problems.

BUT, A FALLACIOUS CASE IS A FALLACIOUS CASE

There are some situations in which it is impossible that the brain has been injured. It is also true that the mildest forms of injury may represent only transient physiological disruption and no permanent sequelae (Gennarelli, 1997; Gennarelli et al., 1998; Smith & Meaney, 2000). Obviously, minor blows do not necessarily result in injury. In fact, the brain is nicely equipped with the ability to withstand certain impacts.

This is an obvious truism for any parent watching an infant develop ambulatory skills, with all their falls. Likewise, during a lifetime, each of us probably experiences thousands of minor blows and jolts to the head that produce no deficit. One forensic case I had involved a woman who was at a gas pump, having just completed filling her car and gotten back into the driver's seat, when another car pulled behind her. The driver of the second car misjudged the stopping distance, because the driver thought the individual was pulling out, and bumped the lady's rear bumper, with an estimated impact of less than 2 mph (no damage to either car). This was independently observed and documented by eyewitnesses. The lady had no loss of conscious and no posttraumatic amnesia, but ultimately sought legal action, because she claimed to have experienced a serious head injury, for which she sued. A plaintiff-retained neuropsychological evaluation found "abnormalities," yet the physics of such an "injury" (Bandak, Eppinger, & Ommaya, 1996) are completely unsubstantiated by the known and observed facts of impact. Furthermore, her neuroimaging studies showed no abnormalities of any type. Thus, when the history does not support injury, the known physics of the impact do not support injury, and nothing is observed on neuroimaging, the absence of neuroimaging findings can be extremely important in showing that the neuropsychological "impairments" cannot be injury-related.

CONCLUSIONS

Contemporary neuroimaging provides excellent techniques for depicting damage to the brain following some type of acquired injury. Often, neuroimaging will provide the objective, irrefutable "lesions," wherein neuropsychologists can then relate their neurobehavioral data. In the future, neuroimaging and neuropsychological assessment will merge, so that simultaneous evaluation of structure and function will be made with techniques like fMRI, MEG, and/or qEEG. Furthermore, MRS has the potential of tracking chemical composition of the injured brain that relates to neuropsychological outcome, and MR tensor imaging may provide the basis for assessing the integrity of specific tracts in the human brain. If done properly, neuroimaging studies, interfaced with the neuropsychological examination, should yield far more objectivity and less ambiguity to the evaluation of patients who have sustained a brain injury and who have a right to redress within the judicial system.

Also, understanding the clinical utility of neuroimaging should assist in limiting fallacious cases, wherein the brain could not have been injured and any neuropsychological "deficit" could not be related to an injury.

ACKNOWLEDGMENTS

Support for some of the research reported in this chapter was provided from the Ira Fulton Foundation. The technical assistance of Tracy Ablidskov is greatly appreciated, as is the secretarial assistance of Sarah Carter.

REFERENCES

Arciniegas, D., Olincy, A., Topkoff, J., McRae, K., Cawthra, E., Filley, C. M., et al. (2000). Impaired auditory gating and P50 nonsuppression following traumatic brain injury. *Journal of Neuropsychiatry and Clinical Neurosciences, 12*(1), 77–85.

Balk, E., & Lau, J. (2001). PET scans and technology assessment: Deja vu? *Journal of the American Medical Association, 285*, 936–938.

Bandak, F. A., Eppinger, R. H., & Ommaya, A. K. (1996). *Traumatic brain injury: Bioscience and mechanics.* Larchmont, NY: Mary Ann Liebert.

Bicik, I., Radanov, B. P., Schafer, N., Dvorak, J., Blum, B., Weber, B., et al. (1998). PET with fluorodeoxyglucose and hexamethylpropylene amine oxime SPECT in late whiplash syndrome. *Neurology, 51*, 345–350.

Bigler, E. D. (1980). Forensic neuropsychology: A case example. *Texas Psychologist, 32*(1), 7–9.

Bigler, E. D. (2001a). The lesion(s) in traumatic brain injury: Implications for clinical neuropsychology. *Archives of Clinical Neuropsychology, 16*(2), 95–131.

Bigler, E. D. (2001b). Quantitative magnetic resonance imaging in traumatic brain injury. *Journal of Head Trauma Rehabilitation, 16*(2), 1–21.

Bigler, E. D., Anderson, C. V., & Blatter, D. D. (In Press). Temporal lobe morphology in normal aging and traumatic brain injury. *American Journal of Neuroradiology.*

Bigler, E. D., & Clement, P. (1997). *Diagnostic clinical neuropsychology* (3rd ed.). Austin, TX: University of Texas Press.

Bigler, E. D., Paver, S., Cullum, C. M., Turkheimer, E., Hubler, D. W., & Yeo, R. (1984). Ventricular enlargement, cortical atrophy and neuropsychological performance following head injury. *International Journal of Neuroscience, 24*, 295–298.

Bigler, E. D., Steinman, D. R., & Newton, J. S. (1981). Clinical assessment of cognitive deficit in neurologic disorder. *Clinical Neuropsychology, 3*, 5–13.

Blumbergs, P. C., Scott, G., Manavis, J., Wainwright, H., Simpson, D. A., & McLean, A. J. (1994). Staining of amyloid precursor protein to study axonal damage in mild head injury. *Lancet, 344*, 1055–1056.

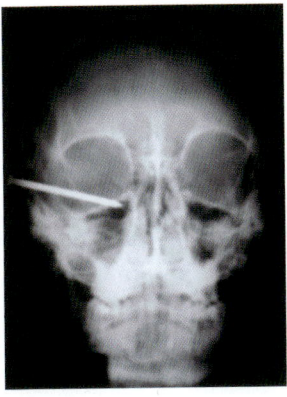

FIGURE 7.1 This is a frontal view of a skull X ray showing a 16-penny nail penetrating through the right temporal bone and lodging in the sphenoid. The nail passed through the temporal lobe and penetrated the hippocampus. The purpose of this illustration is to show an unequivocal indicator of brain damage.

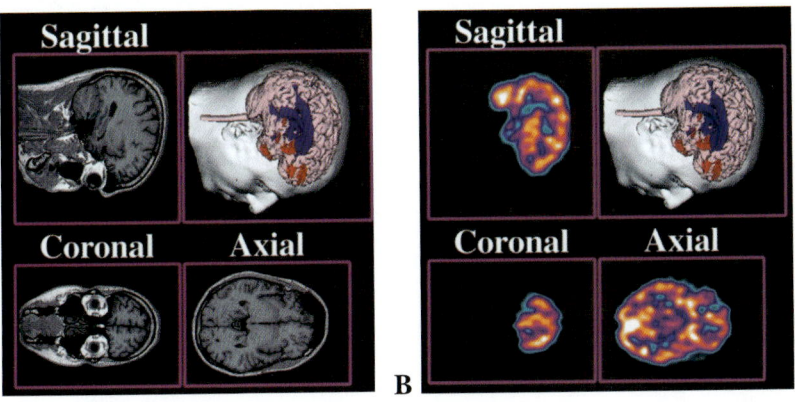

FIGURE 7.2A, B This patient sustained a moderate to severe TBI in an auto–pedestrian accident. He sustained significant frontal and temporal lobe contusion and a right temporal lobe subdural hemotoma. The MRI and SPECT imaging, which is portrayed in this illustration, shows the chronic changes approximately 2 years postinjury. The MRI scan shows frontal and temporal lobe encephalomalacia (MRI in A), but the SPECT imaging (B) shows that the level of disruption as manifested by impaired perfusion is far greater than what is observed in the structural imaging using MRI. For example, the axial MRI shows an indentation in the frontal region, but the axial SPECT scan at the identical level shows even greater disruption in perfusion. This is true for the inferior frontal region in the coronal view and the anterior temporal region in the sagittal.

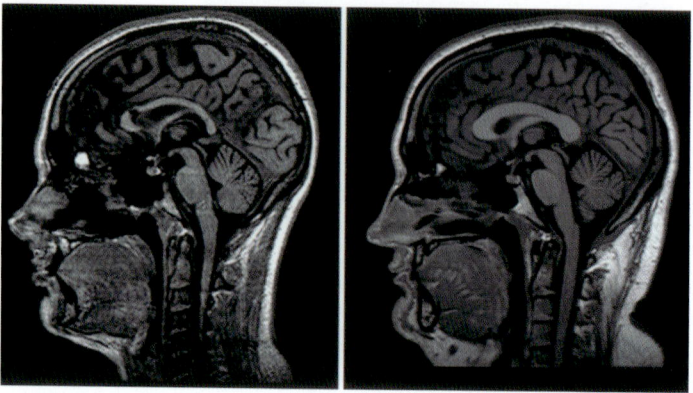

FIGURE 7.3 The illustration on the left is from an older adolescent female who sustained a severe TBI in an auto–pedestrian accident. The image to the right is at approximately the same midsaggital view, but in a normal control subject. Note the global atrophy present in the brain, as well as wasting of the corpus callosum and ventricular enlargement. The corpus callosum shows uniform thinning, but there is a particular lesion noted at the anterior aspect of the corpus callosum, which represents a classic shear-type injury. Literally, the corpus callosum is fractured at this level, and the darkness represents CSF that has filled the void.

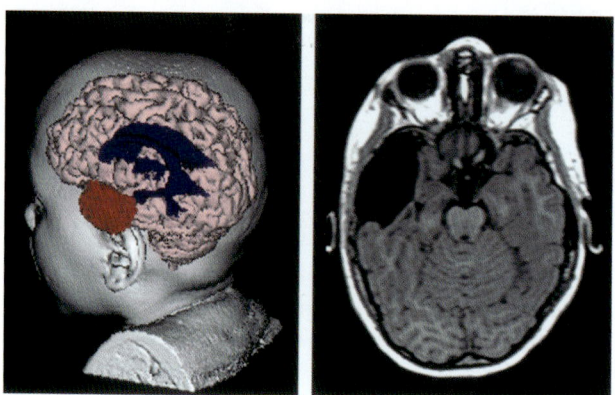

FIGURE 7.4 The upper left figure depicts the ventricular system and cystic formation in the left temporal area, as a consequence of traumatic birth injury. The imaging that was done shortly after this child's birth showed a traumatic injury to the left temporal area, with extensive hemorrhaging. The parenchyma in that area wasted away and left this subarachnoid cystic formation, as seen on the right. The 3-D imaging allows, in a very brief view, the extensiveness of the damage that is present in the brain.

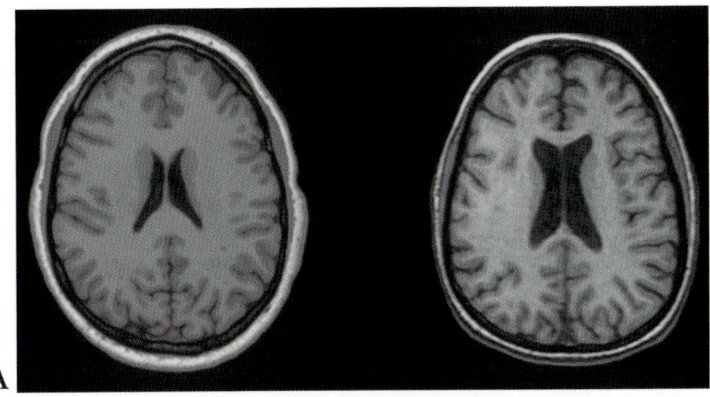

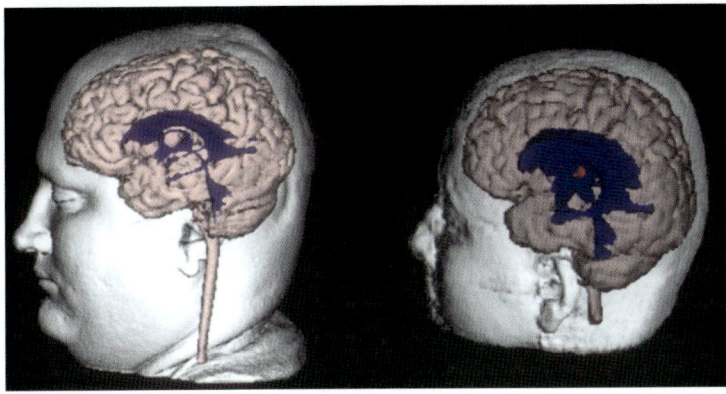

FIGURE 7.5A, B   This patient sustained a severe TBI in an auto–pedestrian accident. The generalized nature of a brain atrophy in severe trauma is characterized by the dilation of the ventricular system (A). (B) 3-D imaging showing the comparison of the patient with the control image on the left shows marked dilation of the entire ventricular system. This is consistent with generalized loss of white matter, with secondary hydrocephalus ex vacuo associated with TBI.

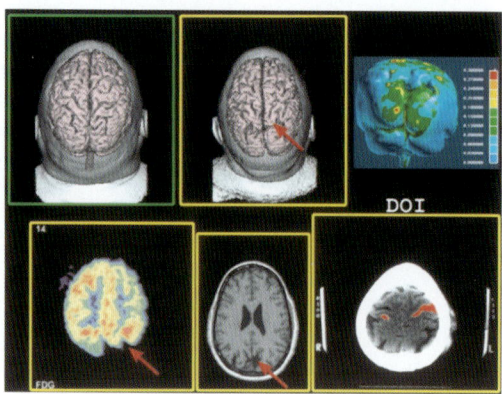

FIGURE 7.6   The image in the upper left is a normal patient of similar age showing normal configuration of the cerebral cortex. The middle-upper panel shows the patient who was injured in an auto–pedestrian accident. The arrow points to prominent sulcal widening and increased CSF space in the parietal area. It is the parietal area that also shows a defect in PET imaging (see arrow, lower-left panel). It is also in this region where she had subarachnoid bleeding, which is depicted in the image in the lower-right. The middle image is the axial MR section, with the arrow pointing to the region of focal atrophy. In the upper right-hand panel is the biomechanical representation of the area of greatest force to injure the brain, which corresponds to the areas of atrophy.

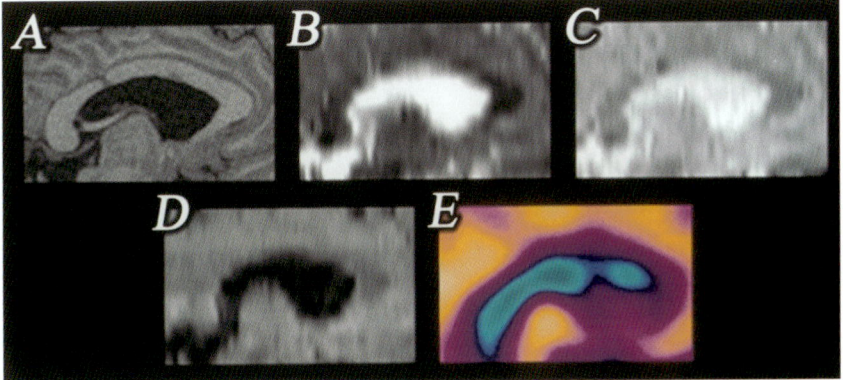

FIGURE 7.7   The image in the upper-left shows a standard T1-weighted midsagittal view (A), compared to other MRI image sequences (B, C, D) and SPECT (E), demonstrating signal intensity differences in the corpus callosum. As already shown in Figure 7.3, the signal in the corpus callosum should be uniform. This is not a classic shear, but the imaging sequence in C demonstrates that it is probably hemosiderin, a blood by-product often indicative of shear injury in TBI. However, using different weightings, it becomes much more apparent where hemosiderin has been deposited in the brain, which is an indication of prior hemorrhaging and, in the context of TBI, a probable index of shearing.

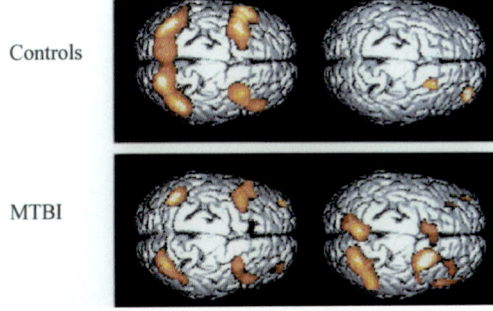

FIGURE 7.8   The location of major cortical activation foci are displayed on a surface-rendered projection showing fMRI patterns of activation performing a task requiring memory and attention. The gyral location of activations (bilateral dorsolateral prefrontal and superior parietal) were similar in both groups, from the 0-back to 1-back condition, which is the easier condition. Major differences, however, were observed in the 1-back to 2-back comparison, a more difficult cognitive task, but, in controls, made easier by the prior experience. Note the more extensive activation of primarily right superior parietal and dorsolateral prefrontal cortex in patients with MTBI. These findings indicate greater recruitment necessary in the brain that has sustained an MTBI.

Brain activation during working memory 1 month after mild traumatic brain injury: A functional MRI study, by McAllister, T. W., Saykin, A. J., Flashman, L. A., Sparling, M. B., Johnson, S. C., Guerin, S. J., Mamourian, A. C., Weaver, J. B., & Yanofsky, N., 1999, *Neurology, 53*, pp. 1300–1308. Reprinted with permission.

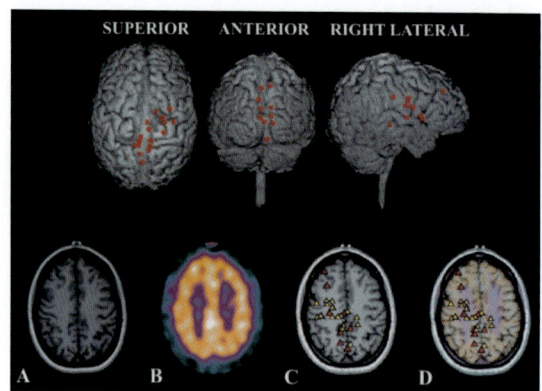

FIGURE 7.9 The imaging at the top demonstrates the position of MEG abnormality depicted on surface morphology from the 3-D MRI. (A) normal MRI scan; (B) normal SPECT scan; (C) MEG abnormalities plotted at the same level; (D) MEG abnormalities plotted at the same MRI level, with the SPECT scan fused with MRI. The 3-D surface morphology shows where the abnormalities are located. Both the MRI and SPECT scans were read as normal. The MEG abnormalities show that physiological abnormalities can exist when brain morphology and perfusion are considered normal.

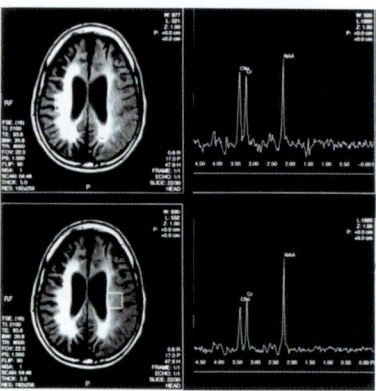

FIGURE 7.10 MRS on a case of severe anoxic brain injury.

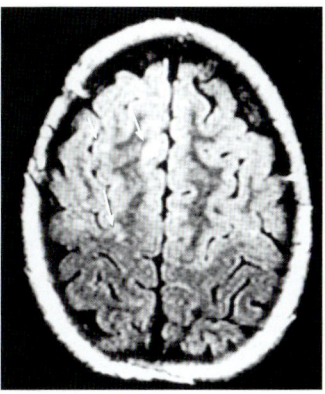

FIGURE 7.11 The arrows point to what are considered to be white matter shear injuries that occurred in MTBI in a child.

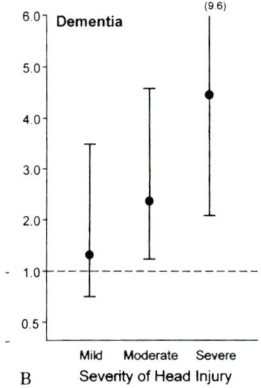

FIGURE 7.12 This illustration demonstrates that the odds ratio of developing dementia increases with the severity of injury.

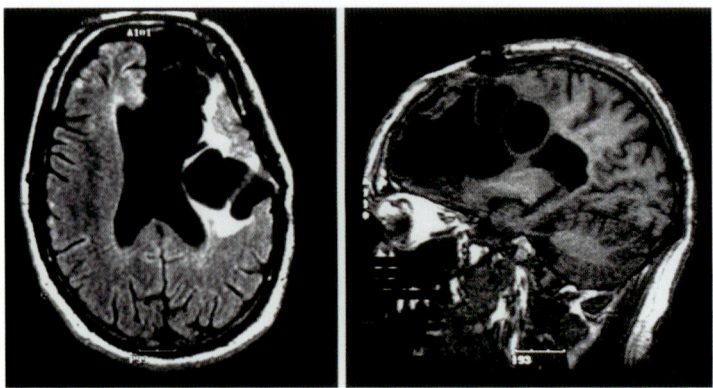

FIGURE 7.13   Top-left axial view showing extensive left hemisphere damage with multicystic formation present. (Right) Sagittal view of the extensive frontal damage with the multicystic formation. As would be expected, the patient was aphasic and had right-side hemiplegia. One of the defense neuropsychologists and a defense neurologist indicated that the patient could work and that the patient had far more potential for functional ability because he had an average performance IQ. Obviously, there is profound brain damage present that will preclude this patient from ever being in the competitive work force.

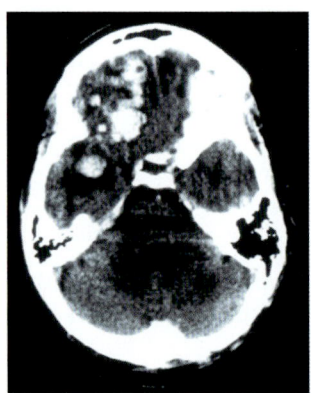

FIGURE 7.14   Axial CT scan showing multiple hemorrhagic contusions in the left frontal and temporal area, as a consequence of a fall down stairs. In this case, the defense neuropsychologist was claiming little-to-no relationship between these injuries and the patient's neuropsychological deficit. Again, objective findings of this type of brain damage typically produce significant neurobehavioral deficits.

Brooks, W. M., Stidley, C. A., Petropoulos, H., Jung, R. E., Weers, D. C., Friedman, S. D., et al. (2000). Metabolic and cognitive response to human traumatic brain injury: A quantitative proton magnetic resonance study. *Journal of Neurotrauma, 17*(8), 629–640.

Christodoulou, C., DeLuca, J., Ricker, J. H., Madigan, N., Bly, B., Lange, G., et al. (2001). Functional magnetic resonance imaging of working memory impairment after traumatic brain injury. *Journal of Neurology, Neurosurgery & Psychiatry.*

Cocchiarella, L., & Andersson, G. B. J. (2001). *Guides to the evaluation of permanent impairment* (5th ed.). Chicago: AMA Press.

Conti, A. C., Raghupathi, R., Trojanowski, J. Q., & McIntosh, T. K. (1998). Experimental brain injury induces regionally distinct apoptosis during the acute and delayed post-traumatic period. *Journal of Neuroscience, 18,* 5663–5672.

Daubert v. Merrell Dow Pharmaceuticals, 113 S. Ct. 2786 (1993).

Eisenberg, R. L. (1991). *Radiology: An illustrated history.* St. Louis, MO: Mosby.

Fontaine, A., Azouvi, P., Remy, P., Bussel, B., & Samson, Y. (1999). Functional anatomy of neuropsychological deficits after severe traumatic brain injury. *Neurology, 53,* 1963–1968.

Friedman, G., Froom, P., Sazbon, L., Grinblatt, I., Shochina, M., Tsenter, J., et al. (1999). Apolipoprotein E-e4 genotype predicts a poor outcome in survivors of traumatic brain injury. *Neurology, 52,* 244–248.

Friedman, S. D., Brooks, W. M., Jung, R. E., Chiulli, S. J., Sloan, J. H., Montoya, B. T., et al. (1999). Quantitative proton MRS predicts outcome after traumatic brain injury. *Neurology, 52,* 1384–1391.

Garnett, M. R., Blamire, A. M., Corkill, R. G., Cadoux-Hudson, T. A. D., Rajagopalan, B., & Styles, P. (2000). Early proton magnetic resonance spectroscopy in normal-appearing brain correlates with outcome in patients following traumatic brain injury. *Brain, 123,* 2046–2054.

Garnett, M. R., Blamire, A. M., Rajagopalan, B., Styles, P., & Cadoux-Hudson, T. A. D. (2000). Evidence for cellular damage in normal-appearing white matter correlates with injury severity in patients following traumatic brain injury: A magnetic resonance spectroscopy study. *Brain, 123,* 1403–1409.

Gennarelli, T. A. (1997). The pathobiology of traumatic brain injury. *The Neuroscientist, 3,* 73–81.

Gennarelli, T. A., Thibault, L. E., & Graham, D. I. (1998). Diffuse axonal injury: An important form of traumatic brain damage. *Neuroscientist, 4,* 202–215.

Givens, A. (1996). Imaging the neurocognitive networks of the human brain. In E. D. Bigler (Ed.), *Neuroimaging I: Basic science* (pp. 133–159). New York: Plenum Press.

Guo, Z., Cupples, L. A., Kurz, A., Auerbach, S. H., Volicer, L., Chui, H., et al. (2000). Head injury and the risk of AD in the MIRAGE study. *Neurology, 54,* 1316–1323.

Harding, A. J., Halliday, G. M., & Kril, J. J. (1998). Variation in hippocampal neuron number with age and brain volume. *Cerebral Cortex, 8*(8), 710–718.

Hounsfield, G. N. (1973). Computerized transverse axial scanning (tomography): Part 1. Description system. *British Journal of Psychiatry, 46,* 1016–1022.

Klingberg, T., Hedehus, M., Temple, E., Salz, T., Gabriella, J. D. E., Moseley, M. E., et al. (2000). Microstructure of temporo-parietal white matter as a basis for reading ability: Evidence from diffusion tensor magnetic resonance imaging. *Neuron, 25*, 493–500.

Levin, H. S., Benton, A. L., & Grossman, R. G. (1982). *Neurobehavioral consequences of closed head injury.* New York: Oxford University Press.

Lewine, J. D., Davis, J. T., Sloan, J. H., Kodituwakku, P. W., & Orrison, W. W. (1999). Neuromagnetic assessment of pathophysiologic brain activity induced by minor head trauma. *American Journal of Neuroradiology, 20*, 857–866.

Lye, T. C., & Shores, E. E. (2000). Traumatic brain injury as a risk factor for Alzheimer's disease: A review. *Neuropsychology Review, 10*(2), 115–129.

McAllister, T. W., Saykin, A. J., Flashman, L. A., Sparling, M. B., Johnson, S. C., Guerin, S. J., et al. (1999). Brain activation during working memory 1 month after mild traumatic brain injury: A functional MRI study. *Neurology, 53*, 1300–1308.

McGowan, J. C., Yang, J. H., Plotkin, R. C., Grossman, R. I., Umile, E. M., Cecil, K. M., et al. (2000). Magnetization transfer imaging in the detection of injury associated with mild head trauma. *American Journal of Neuroradiology, 21*, 875–880.

Orrison, W. W. (2000). *Neuroimaging.* Philadelphia: Saunders.

Plassman, B. L., Havlik, R. J., Steffens, D. C., Helms, M. J., Newman, T. N., Drosdick, D., et al. (2000). Documented head injury in early adulthood and risk of Alzheimer's disease and other dementias. *Neurology, 55*, 1158–1166.

Ricker, J. H., Muller, R.-A., Zafonte, R. D., Black, K., Millis, S. R., & Chugani, H. (2000). Verbal recall and recognition following traumatic brain injury: A [0–15]-water positron emission tomography study. *Journal of Clinical and Experimental Neuropsychology.*

Ricker, J. H., & Zafonte, R. D. (2000). Functional neuroimaging and quantitative electroencephalography in adult traumatic head injury: Clinical applications and interpretive cautions. *J Head Trauma Rehabilitation, 15*(2), 859–868.

Roberts, M. J., & Hanaway, J. (1970). *Atlas of the Human Brain in Section.* Philadelphia: Lea & Febiger.

Ross, B. D., & Ernst, T. (1998). 1H MRS in acute traumatic brain injury. *Journal of Magnetic Resonance Imaging, 8*, 829–840.

Satz, P. (1993). Brain reserve capacity on symptom onset after brain injury: A formulation and review of evidence for threshold theory. *Neuropsychology, 7*, 273–295.

Sinson, G. P., Bagley, L. J., Cecil, K. M., Torchia, M., McGowan, J. C., Lenkinski, R. E., et al. (2001). Magnetization transfer imaging and proton MR spectroscopy in the evaluation of axonal injury: Correlation with clinical outcome after traumatic brain injury. *American Journal of Neuroradiology, 22*, 143–151.

Smith, D. H., & Meaney, D. F. (2000). Axonal damage in traumatic brain injury. *Neuroscientist, 6*(6), 483–495.

Swiercinsky, D. P., & Leigh, G. (1979). Comparison of neuropsychological data in the diagnosis of brain impairment with computerized tomography and other neurological procedures. *Journal of Clinical Psychology, 35*(2), 242–246.

Tate, D. F., & Bigler, E. D. (2000). Fornix and hippocampal atrophy in traumatic brain injury. *Learning and Memory.*

Thatcher, R. W., Biver, C., Gomez, J. F., North, D., Curtin, R., Walker, R. A., et al. (In Press). Estimation of the EEG power spectrum by MRI T2 relaxation time in normals and traumatic brain injury. *Clinical Neuropsychology.*

Thatcher, R. W., Biver, C., McAlaster, R., & Salazar, A. (1998). Biophysical linkage between MRI and EEG coherence in closed head injury. *Neuroimage, 8*, 307–326.

Thatcher, R. W., Moore, N., John, E. R., Duffy, F., Hughes, J. R., & Krieger, M. (1999). QEEG and Traumatic Brain Injury: Rebuttal of the American Academy of Neurology 1997 Report by the EEG and Clinical Neuroscience Society. *Clinical Electroencephalography, 30*(3), 94–98.

Weiner, J. (1999). *Time, love, memory: A great biologist and his quest for the origins of behavior.* New York: Vintage Books.

Chapter 8

Behavioral Change Following Traumatic Brain Injury

Peter C. Patch and Lawrence C. Hartlage

INTRODUCTION

For many years, the overwhelming focus of neuropsychological study and treatment has been a neurocognitive one. The reason for this is both logical and deceptively intuitive. For those cases in which severe cognitive impairment occurs, behavioral changes within the patient are to be expected, because so much of the patient's life has been radically altered and, in many cases, obliterated by what was probably the single most traumatic event in their lives. As with historical views on senility and senile dementia, such changes are to be expected, and there is no question as to what is occurring. Since such individuals are so cognitively impaired, and that cognitive functioning is responsible for their impairment in other areas, that is, social and occupational functioning, there simply was little impetus to pursue the issue of behavior changes within the individual as a concurrent event not necessarily related to or caused by cognitive impairment. Indeed, victims of traumatic brain injury (TBI), who have otherwise recovered from their neurocognitive impairments, can and do suffer behavioral changes as a result of the injury.

PHENOMENOLOGICAL REPORTS

Descriptions of emotional/behavioral changes following TBI are varied, producing the sense that brain insult can result in virtually any sort of behavioral disturbance. The behavioral changes following brain injury are varied indeed. They may encompass neurocognitively based sorts of complaints, including impairment in information-processing capabilities and impairments in concentration and attendance (Binder, 1997; Bohnen, Twijnstra, & Jolles, 1993; Gronwall & Wrightson, 1974; Jennett, 1979; Stuss et al., 1985), epileptic symptoms (Dacey, Vollmer, & Dikmen, 1993; Devinski, 1996; Jennett, 1979), memory (Bigler et al., 1994), emotional lability (i.e., the inability to maintain a steady emotional state appropriate to environmental stimuli), and general nonspecific behavioral disturbances (Blanchard, Hickling, Taylor, & Loos, 1995; Collins et al., 1999; Deb, Lyons, Koutzoukis, Ali, & McCarthy, 1999; Fann, Katon, Uomoto, & Esselman, 1995; Kim, Manes, Kosier, Baruah, & Robinson, 1999; Matser, Kessels, Lezak, Jordan, & Troost, 1999; Oddy, Coughlan, Tyerman, & Jenkins, 1985; Russo et al., 1996; Thomsen, 1984, 1989). Several cited studies have documented such disturbances over time periods ranging from the immediate posttraumatic period to as long as 15 years after the event. In addition, several authors have reported symptoms and behavioral changes, fitting the diagnostic category of posttraumatic stress disorder (PTSD) for time periods ranging from 3 months to 3 years after the initial event (Bryant, 1996; Bryant & Harvey, 1998; Denker, 1944; O'Shanick, 1998; Rimel, Giordani, Barth, Boll, & Jane, 1981; Russell, 1932; Rutherford, Merrett, & McDonald, 1977, 1979). This is not altogether surprising, when one considers the sheer number of possible configurations of head trauma, that is, direct impacts to various areas of the skull, and contracoup injuries, with the skull moving in various directions in response to indirect physical forces, for example, persons being in a car when it is struck. Taken as an amalgam, the research clearly indicates that behavioral changes resulting from head injury can and do occur, and that sequelae can be severe.

Perhaps the most celebrated of case of behavioral disturbance following head injury is that of Phineas Gage (Harlow, 1868), the railroad worker in Vermont, who was participating in the demolition of boulders in order to lay track. While tamping dynamite into a hole in one such boulder, the dynamite exploded, driving the tamping rod through his lower jaw and into his skull. The formerly churchgoing, polite, God-fearing gentleman became a boorish, offensive, loud, profane, womanizing individual whom his family and friend could scarcely recognize. Friends, family, and townspeople alike noted a distinct change in his behavior. He clearly had suffered a severe injury to an area of the brain responsible for behavioral inhibition and other executive functioning, despite the fact that his injury probably would not be scored as "severe," according to contemporary formulations, i.e., he would not have scored highly on the Glasgow Coma Scale, and so on. As a prototype for the phenomenon of behavioral disturbance following TBI, the Phineas Gage case is a classic illustration of the potential contrast between an individual's pre- and postincident functioning.

Severe Head Injury

A traditional explanation has related presence or extent of behavioral abnormalities to severity of brain injury, with behavioral abnormalities typically attributed to deficits in cortical (mainly frontal) processing, combined with reactions to loss of neurocognitive abilities (Binder, Rohling, & Larrabee, 1997; Crooks, 1991; Dikmen, Machamer, Winn, & Temkin, 1995; Gronwall & Wrightson, 1974; Klonoff, Costa, & Snow, 1986; Levin, 1990; Ommaya, 1982).

Three factors account for the focus of research into behavioral sequelae of brain injury on individuals with severe injury. One factor involves the ready availability of such individuals for study. Individuals who have sustained severe brain injury are typically followed for treatment over extended periods, and, indeed, it is from observation of such individuals that many of the traditional notions of the behavioral sequelae of brain injury have been generated. For example, severely disabling dysfunction in all aspects of cognitive functioning, such as serious attentional deficits, behavioral slowing in regard to mental processing and response, long-term memory impairments, interference with ability to use social–emotional and reasoning skills, and impaired linguistic pragmatics, are commonly reported deficits in severe TBI (Prigatano, 1992; Stuss & Buckle, 1992; Wood, 1990). Executive dysfunction involving capacities for self-direction, self-regulation and control, perseveration, inflexibility, and emotional alterations affecting attitudes, responses, and social skills, observed as apathy, disinhibition, impulsivity, lability, or dysphoria, are frequently described symptoms in these patients (Fordyce, Roueche, & Prigatano, 1983; Levin, Goldstein, Williams, & Eisenberg, 1991; Prigatano, 1992).

Mild Traumatic Brain Injury

Figures on the annual incidence of mild traumatic brain injury (MTBI) are extremely elusive, because of the practices, procedures, and priorities inherent in medical examination of physical injuries. Obvious signs of gross injury direct the treating professional's attention to life- and health-threatening conditions, resulting in a de facto de-emphasis on injuries to the head that are not readily apparent. In addition, the symptoms of head injury can easily be overlooked and attributed to emotional reactions to the situation. Diagnostic procedures typically used to assess for brain injury, if used, are not likely to detect the sorts of brain injuries that may result in behavioral impairment, but not overt or long-term cognitive impairment (Varney & Varney, 1995).

Despite these limitations on the recognition and reporting of MTBI, painstaking, systematic analysis of available data place the likely figure for annual MTBI between 7 and 10 million new cases each year (Caveness, 1977, 1979; Hartlage, 1984, 1990; Kraus & Nourjah, 1989; Sorenson & Kraus, 1991), or from 90% to 95% of total new cases of TBI each year (Beers, 1992; Levin, Benton, & Grussman, 1981; Miller, 1996).

There is general, if tentative, agreement that, of the 7 to 10 million annual new cases of TBI each year, 85% can be expected to resolve within 1–3 months, with no apparent after-effects. To what degree such a figure is distorted by the various sources of compensatory behaviors, both those of the head-injured individual and those around him, is unknown at this time. The remaining 15% of individuals whose TBI is considered "mild," a figure which can be extrapolated to approximately 1 million new cases each year, report experiencing persistent symptoms of potentially disabling severity (Alexander, 1995; Barth et al., 1983; Gentilini, Nichelli, & Schoenhuber, 1985; Hartlage, 1997b; Hartlage, Durant-Wilson, & Patch, 2001; Hatcher, Johnson, & Walker, 1996; Kurtzke & Kurland, 1993; Levin et al., 1987; Rimel et al., 1981).

Definition

Research in the field of MTBI has resulted in a variety of formulations of what specifically qualifies an injury as mild, instead of severe (e.g., Annegers, Grabow, Kurland, & Laws, 1980; Eisenberg & Levin, 1989; Gentilini et al., 1989; Jagger, Levine, Jane, & Rimel, 1984; Jennett, 1979; Whitman, Coonley-Hoganson, & Desai, 1984). In an attempt to form some sort of consensus on the issue, the Mild Traumatic Brain Injury Committee of the Head Injury Interdisciplinary Special Interest Group of the American Congress of Rehabilitation Medicine (1993), published the following definition of MTBI:

1. A Glasgow Coma Scale score of 13–15 (after 30 minutes)
2. Less than 30 minutes loss of consciousness
3. 24 hours or less of posttraumatic amnesia (PTA)
4. At least one of the following symptoms: loss of consciousness, altered mental state at time of trauma, retrograde amnesia or PTA, and transient or permanent focal neurological deficits (p. 333)

Frontal Lobe Involvement

The physical forces involved in TBI have been described (Adams, Graham, Gennarelli, 1985; Bigler, 2001; Gean, 1994; Ommaya, 1996; Varney & Roberts, 1999), the frequency of frontal (or frontotemporal) deficits commonly observed in TBI patients is recognized (Bigler, 2001), and the greater incidence of executive and emotional deficits compared with (more posterior) deficits, such as sensory agnosias, has been documented (Bigler & Clement, 1997; Van der Naalt, Hew, van Zomeren, Sluiter, & Minderboud, 1999). Unfortunately, neuropsychological assessment approaches to neurocognitive evaluation do not typically isolate frontal lobe impairments. Such measures as verbal fluency (e.g., FAS and CFL) have been demonstrated sensitive to temporal lobe and caudate nucleus, as well as frontal, lesions (Benton, 1968; Butters, Granholm, Salmon, Grant, & Wolfe, 1987; Micelli, Caltagirone, Masullo, & Silveri, 1981; Milner, 1964; Perret, 1974; Ramier & Hecaen, 1970; Tombough, Kozak, & Rees, 1999), and other research identified verbal fluency most impaired in left-central lesions (Jones-Gotman & Miller, 1977). Indeed, such abilities as planning and integration, as well as features of agitation, although demonstrated to depend on frontal integrity (Tekin et al., 2001; Waltz et al., 1999), are not formally tested by tests normally included in neurocognitive batteries, so that frontal deficits, with their significant implications for behavioral and sociopersonal adjustment, may not be recognized as etiological in adjustment difficulties subsequent to such brain injury.

As Mesulem (1986) observed some years ago, since frontal lobe damage can leave most cognitive and sensorimotor functions relatively intact, the sometimes dramatic alterations of personality and conduct resultant from such damage may not be identified with the frontal lobe damage.

SPECIFIC BEHAVIORAL SEQUELAE OF TBI

Post-Concussive Syndrome

Investigation into the behavioral sequelae of brain injury has produced the diagnostic construct known as *postconcussive syndrome* (Alves, Macciocchi, & Barth, 1993; Cullum & Thompson, 1999; Deb et al., 1999; Straus & Savitsky, 1934). According to this diagnostic formulation, individuals with behavioral sequelae resulting from TBI experience fatigue, irritability, depression, and difficulties with attention and concentration. Other authors describing the syndrome have added several behavioral symptoms to the mix, including confusion, social withdrawal, apathy, dizziness, headaches, nausea, sleep difficulties, heightened sensitivity to noise, and sensory-increased frustration (Boll & Barth, 1983; Ewing, McCarthy, Gronwall, & Wrightson, 1980). This formulation of the postconcussive syndrome has resulted in researchers noting that it is a virtual smorgasbord of symptoms, which support the nonexistence of the syndrome as a coherent diagnostic entity, rather than its existence.

Minnesota Multiphasic Personality Inventory

Perhaps the most common tool used to assess emotional/behavioral function is the Minnesota Multiphasic Personality Inventory (MMPI)/ MMPI-2, one of the most-used psychological assessment instruments. Reliance on this assessment instrument extends to neuropsychological assessments, as well (Alfano, Finlayson, Stearns, & MacLennan, 1991; Alfano, Finlayson, Stearns, & Neilson, 1990; Alfano, Neilson, Paniak, & Finlayson, 1992; Alfano, Paniak, & Finlayson, 1993; Farr & Martin, 1988; Mack, 1979). Use of the MMPI/MMPI-2 has indicated that individuals with varying degrees of head injury experience behavioral changes that can often be quite pronounced, particularly involving scales *Hs, D, Hy,* and *Sc* (Black, 1974; Bornstein, Miller, & van Schoor, 1989; Dikmen & Reitan, 1977; Dikmen, McLean, & Temkin, 1986). Persons experiencing behavioral deterioration marked by these scales can be expected to exhibit symptoms involving preoccupation with somatic functioning, anxiety, depression, and bizarre or unusual sensory experiences. In a series of studies using the MMPI with head-injured individuals, Alfano and his colleagues confirmed these findings (Alfano et al., 1991; Alfano et al., 1990; Alfano et al., 1992; Alfano et al., 1993). They also reported finding elevations in almost every other clinical scale of the MMPI (i.e., *Pd, Pa,* and *Pt*), indicating that the patients in their sample often exhibited high levels of paranoia, antisocial, and obsessive tendencies.

Neurocorrected MMPI Findings

Several authors have reported using the MMPI/MMPI-2 to evaluate behavioral change in individuals with neuropsychological dysfunction unrelated to TBI, including multiple sclerosis (Meyerink, Reitan, & Selz, 1988) and noninjury-induced epilepsy (Bornstein & Kozora, 1990). These authors have suggested that MMPI/MMPI-2 scale scores may be artificially elevated because of the overlapping nature of legitimate neuropsychological symptoms and unusual behavioral functioning of individuals without biological substrates underpinning behavioral abnormalities. In order to address the possibility that such item overlap contributes to the consistent findings of behavioral abnormality in individuals who have experienced traumatic head injury, Alfano and his colleagues undertook to identify and eliminate MMPI items that would artificially elevate clinical scale scores because of overlap with bona fide symptoms of neuropsychological impairment following TBI (Alfano et al., 1991; Alfano et al., 1993). The resulting instrument consisted of 522 items, after elimination of 44 items identified by a panel of experts as likely to contribute to artificial clinical scale score elevation.

The results of these investigations indicated that there is indeed reason to believe that MMPI/MMPI-2 data of victims of TBI must be viewed with caution, using traditional interpretive guidelines. Scale scores for individuals, on the neurocorrected MMPI, ranged from 5 to 8 points lower than scores on the noncorrected version of the MMPI. However, these reductions did not result in mean group profiles free of behavioral disturbance. For instance, although the females in Alfano et al.'s (1993) sample exhibited fewer elevated scale scores (*Pt, Sc,* and *Ma* were no longer elevated), several scales remained elevated, despite the across-the-board reduction in mean scale scores (*Hs* remained above *T*-60; *D* and *Hy* remained above *T*-65). The males in the sample similarly exhibited mean scale scores that were still elevated after the correction (*Hs, Hy, Pd, Pa, Pt,* and *Ma* remained above *T*-60, *D* and *Sc* remained above *T*-65). The results of these investigations would indicate that, for those individuals exhibiting behavioral change post-TBI, even when the potentially confounding effects of symptoms of neuropsychological impairment are removed, behavior disturbance persists at a significant level. Just as an elevated *Hs* score, normally suggestive of overconcern with physical problems, should be viewed with appropriate consideration in cases of individuals completing MMPI questionnaires when in pain and traction following automotive injury, with severe orthopedic and internal damage requiring surgery, so should prudence be exercised in applying interpretive guidelines derived from psychiatrically based samples whose endorsement of behaviors not commonly reported may reflect accurate manifestations of behavioral sequelae of neurologic injury.

One of the most significant obstacles to evaluating behavioral sequelae from traumatic head injury is the traditional source of the data: the patient. As has been cited by many authors (Binder, 1990; Brandt, 1988; Goodyear, 1998; Hartlage, 1997a, 1997b, 1997c; Mendelson, 1987), whether by design, such as in malingering motivated by potential or ongoing litigation (Miller, 1998; Vickery, Berry, Hanlon Inman, Harris, & Orey, 2001) or as a result of preexisting neurotic, personologic, or cognitive variables (Prigitano, 1992), there is ample opportunity for patient self-reports to be slanted or otherwise distorted in one direction or another. Especially in cases of more severe TBI, patients may fail to recognize serious behavioral impairments, or may deny their existence (Prigitano & Schacter, 1991).

Another drawback of behavioral measurement devices, the most often used of which is the MMPI/MMPI-2, as discussed above, is that they are either measures of an individual's current functioning or a more overarching picture of the personality functioning of the individual. Indeed, the MMPI/MMPI-2 is designed to identify and measure personality and behavior tendencies over time, rather than behavioral change. Clearly, when we are discussing the issue of behavior change resulting from traumatic head injury, we are implicating the need for a before-and-after type of assessment instrument. This, combined with the issue of patient self-report reliability, steers us toward a device that will evaluate an individual's behavioral functioning, pre- and postinjury, from multiple points of view, that is, from multiple persons.

Evaluating Behavioral Functioning Before and After TBI

One means of overcoming the issue of (over)reliance on patient self-report is to survey the individual and significant others for information concerning behavior functioning pre- and postinjury (Durant-Wilson, Hartlage, & Patch, 2000; Hartlage, 1989, 1990, 1995, 1997a, 1997b, 1997c; Hartlage, Ball, et al., 1988). The Behavior Change Inventory (BCI) was developed for this purpose. It is a 68-item scale containing behavioral adjectives, which the individual and their significant other(s) endorse as either applying or not applying to the individual. Extensive research has demonstrated this to be a device and procedure sensitive to behavior change following brain injury (Hartlage, 1989, 1990; Hartlage, Williams, & Haney, 1988; Johnson & Hartlage, 1989; Lewis & Hartlage, 1986; Patch & Hartlage, 2001; Roth & Hartlage, 1998; Spencer, 1992).

The BCI can be used as a single inventory of pre- and postinjury behaviors reported by the patient, which helps isolate preexisting phenomena from those with onset noted subsequent to injury. An alternate format, designed to be completed to describe pre- versus postinjury behaviors noted in the patient by others (e.g., spouse, coworker, boss, neighbor, coach, minister, friend), can be used to expand the database. This expanded database is especially helpful in litigated cases in which "unbiased" observations (i.e., those made by individuals not suspected of having any monetary or secondary gain interest in the outcome of the case) are desired. A conservative use of the inventory involves having the patient, and the individual(s) accompanying the patient to examination, complete the BCI completely independent of each of other (i.e., in a separate room, without forewarning or opportunity to collaborate concerning responses), then tabulating as indicators of behavior change only those behaviors so reported by both (or all) respondents.

Although, in cases of severe brain injury, the observations of others may be more sensitive to changes in interpersonal behaviors than the recognition of such by the patient (Prigitano & Schacter, 1991), clinical experience with hundred of cases reveals no significant differences between BCI changes reported by patients and their spouses, in mild brain injury. Indeed, data from only the patient as respondent revealed 94% accuracy in differentiation between brain-injured patients and nonbrain-injured controls, using behavioral changes recorded on the BCI as the criterion measure (Kixmiller, Briggs, Hartlage, & Dean, 1993). An especially attractive feature of the BCI in forensic use involves the ability to target a specific date (e.g., date of putative injury) as baseline, providing some control for preexisting conditions, while allowing sensitivity to exacerbation of preexisting conditions. Accumulated research concerning the procedure has identified 16 homogeneous factors with good accuracy in classification of brain injury.

One recent project used the BCI to assess behavioral changes from preinjury baseline, with 70 consecutive patients referred for neuropsychological examination following MTBI. All patients presented with persistent neurobehavioral problems. Patients were self-assigned to one of two groups, based upon the amount of time that had passed since the brain trauma: within 6 months of injury, or 12 or more months since injury. The reference group used to norm the BCI was used as control (Hartlage, 1989; Kixmiller et al., 1993). The control group had no history of TBI and did not differ substantially from patients on age, education, or gender. Nonparametric analysis was used, in order to evaluate the number of patients (and their significant others) in each experimental group reporting behavior change.

The results of the study indicated that victims of MTBI, at 6 and 12 months postinjury, continued to report, corroborated by independent report by significant others, behavior changes indicative of decreased frustration tolerance, increased anger and irritability, and increased levels of depression, anhedonia, and anxiety-related issues (i.e., fearfulness, rumination, etc.). The differences found between MTBI patients and uninjured control subjects are congruent with those in prior studies, which have indicated vulnerability to behavioral impairment in victims of MTBI (Hartlage, 1989; Kixmiller et al., 1993). Findings from this study expand the database to assess temporal sequence of behavioral changes subsequent to TBI.

Arguments Against Behavioral Changes Caused by TBI

The idea that behavior changes can and do occur as a result of TBI, even supposedly very minor brain injury, is not universally accepted within neuropsychology and related fields. Researchers have examined epidemiological data and research to date and developed alternative hypotheses on the presence or lack of behavior changes resulting from TBI. One of the issues prompting skepticism is the often lengthy interval between injury and reporting of symptoms. There are a myriad of reasons for such delay. As noted previously, behavioral changes within individuals suffering TBI can be, and often are, assumed to be temporary reactions to the trauma itself and the resulting changes in lifestyle. Simply put, the individual and those around them may simply assume that behavioral changes are the normal result of what, by definition, is an abnormal and extraordinary event. Another significant contributor to the failure to recognize behavioral changes resulting from TBI is lower standards and expectations of those around the individual, during what is considered a recuperation period. During such a period, which can be quite lengthy if other injuries require extended recuperation time, performance demands are minimal or nonexistent (i.e., work, school, etc.).

Despite such explanations, some have suggested that bona fide behavior changes within individuals suffering TBI should be expected to emerge immediately after the trauma. They conclude that behavioral effects not emerging immediately after trauma must be the result of purely psychogenic origin (Bryant, 1996; Bohnen et al., 1993; Lishman, 1988; Wrightson & Gronwall, 1981). However, recent research has cast doubt on this contention, by identifying progressive neuronal loss resulting from TBI as a possible etiology for delayed behavioral changes posttrauma (Andersen & Marmarou, 1992; Bergsneider, Hovda, & Shalmon, 1997; Bigler, 1992; Bigler et al., 1994; Crooks, 1991; Hovda, 1998; Levin, Williams, Eisenberg, High, & Guinto, 1992; Oder et al., 1992; Oppenheimer, 1968). Thus, persons who have otherwise recovered from TBI may in fact be continuing to suffer a gradual loss of neuronal functioning related to emotional control and regulation.

Posttraumatic Stress

Although, from a conceptual perspective, PTSD represents a phenomenon completely distinct from brain injury in terms of both etiology and symptomology, there is sufficient overlap in both categories to deserve consideration of personality or behavioral changes following brain injury. Traumatic brain injury is, as might be expected, associated with, and is typically caused by, trauma. Whether resulting from automotive mishap, assault, or other mode of delivery, the brain injury symptoms represent residual sequelae of the trauma. It is not uncommon for stress, resultant either from the precipitating event or the effects of the resultant symptoms, to be present in some form, to varying extent. Estimates of PTSD from serious accident or injury have been estimated at around 17%, with assault-produced incidence over 30% (Zobar, Sasson, Amital, Iancu, & Zinger, 1998). Since TBI can occur from such events, possible overlap is obvious. Further, in brain injury resulting from automotive injury, death or injury to others may be sufficient to produce PTSD.

Posttraumatic stress, which is a frequent corollary of trauma-producing brain injury, can be one of the symptoms of brain injury following trauma; or PTSD may represent a diagnostic entity (DSM code 309.81 [American Psychiatric Association, 1994]) correlated with brain injury only through sharing the same traumatic etiology (Bremner, Randall, et al., 1995; Bremner, Scott, et al., 1993; Bryant, Marrosszeky, Crooks, & Gurks, 2000; Charney et al., 1998; Connor & Davidson, 1998; Harvey & Bryant, 2000; Rauch, Shin, Whalen, & Pitman, 1998; Saigh & Bremner, 1999; Solomon & Bleich, 1998; Ursano et al., 1999; Yeshuda, 1998; Zobar et al., 1998). Issues of comorbidity are certainly relevant (Charney et al., 1998), and attempts to segregate posttraumatic symptoms resulting from brain injury versus PTSD reveal areas of overlap (Zobar et al., 1998).

In forensic practice, there may be an occasional tendency toward focus on what appears to represent the primary disability, using the rationale that, whatever the specific diagnosis, it results from the injury at issue. However, good practice would indicate appropriateness of evaluating against diagnostic criteria for both neurocognitive (e.g., ICD-9-CM Code 294 [Medicode Publications, 1999]) and mental signs of brain injury (e.g., ICD-9-CM Code 310), as well as signs of PTSD, (ICD-9-CM Code 309), since treatment and outcome expectations for brain injury, PTSD, or combined brain injury and PTSD, deserve clarification and documentation.

SUMMARY

There is a growing body of evidence of (oftentimes lasting) behavioral change in survivors of TBI, even so-called "mild" TBI, with damage to the frontal lobe and postinjury progressive neuronal loss being identified as likely sources of such change. Historically, evaluation of the phenomenon has been clouded by the issues of patient self-report and the poor fit of standard behavioral assessment tools vis-a-vis the overlap of bona fide neurological sequelae of head trauma with behavioral ones. The issue of self-report has been addressed effectively with the BCI's before-and-after and self-and-significant-other approach to assessing possible behavior change resultant from head injury, with a growing bibliography supporting its use and effectiveness, as well as the prevalence of the phenomenon (Hartlage, 1989, 1990; Hartlage et al., 1988; Johnson & Hartlage, 1989; Lewis & Hartlage, 1986; Roth, & Hartlage, 1998; Spencer, 1992). The issue of symptom overlap is in the process of being better addressed, by approaches such as Alfano et al.'s (1991, 1993) neurocorrective approach to the use of the MMPI. These advances have particular relevance to forensic settings, and foreknowledge of them should serve both clinical and legal professionals well in serving their clients.

REFERENCES

Adams, J. H., Graham, D. L., & Gennarelli, T. A. (1985). Contemporary neuropathological considerations regarding brain damage in head injury. In D. P. Becker & J. T. Povlishock (Eds.), *Central nervous system trauma. Status report—1985.* Washington, DC: National Institutes of Health.

Alexander, M. P. (1995). Mild traumatic brain injury: Pathophysiology, natural history, and clinical management. *Neurology, 45,* 1253–1260.

Alfano, D. P., Finlayson, M. A., Stearns, G. M., & MacLennan, R. N. (1991). Dimensions of neurobehavioral dysfunction. *Neuropsychology, 5*(1), 35–41.

Alfano, D. P., Finlayson, M. A., Stearns, G. M., & Neilson, P. M. (1990). The MMPI and neurologic dysfunction: Profile configuration and analysis. *The Clinical Neuropsychologist, 4*(1), 69–79.

Alfano, D. P., Neilson, P. M., Paniak, C. E., & Finlayson, M. A. (1992). The MMPI and closed head injury. *The Clinical Neuropsychologist, 6*(2), 134–142.

Alfano, D. P., Paniak, C. E., & Finlayson, M. A. (1993). The MMPI and closed head injury: A neurocorrective approach. *Neuropsychiatry, Neuropsychology, and Behavioral Neurology, 6*(2), 111–116.

Alves, W. M., Macciocchi, S. N., & Barth, J. T. (1993). Postconcussive symptoms after uncomplicated mild head injury. *Journal of Head Trauma Rehabilitation, 8,* 48–59.

American Psychiatric Association (1994). *Diagnostic and statistical manual of mental disorders* (4th ed.). Washington, DC: Author.

Andersen, B. J., & Marmarou, A. (1992). Post-traumatic selective stimulation of glycolysis. *Brain Research, 585,* 184–189.

Annegers, J. F., Grabow, J. D., Kurland, L. T., & Laws, E. R. (1980). The incidence, causes, and secular trends of head trauma in Olmsted County, Minnesota. *Neurology, 30,* 912–919.

Barth, J., Macciocchi, S., Giordani, B., Rimel, R., Jane, J., & Boll, T. (1983). Neuropsychological sequelae of minor head injury. *Neurosurgery, 13,* 529–533.

Beers, S. R. (1992). Effects of mild head injury in children and adolescents. *Neuropsychology Review, 3,* 281–320.

Benton, A. L. (1968). Differential behavioral effects in frontal lobe disease. *Neuropsychologia, 6,* 53–60.

Bergsneider, M., Hovda, D. A., & Shalmon, E. (1997). Cerebral hyperglycolysis following severe human traumatic brain injury: A positron emission tomography study. *Journal of Neurosurgery, 86,* 241–251.

Bigler, E. D. (1992). Three-dimensional image analysis of trauma induced degenerative changes: An aid to neuropsychological assessment. *Archives of Clinical Neuropsychology, 7*, 449–556.

Bigler, E. D. (2001). The lesion(s) in traumatic brain injury: Implications for clinical practice. *Archives of Clinical Neuropsychology, 16*, 95–131.

Bigler, E. D., Burr, R., Gale, S., Norman, M., Kurth, S., Blatter, D., et al. (1994). Day of injury CT scan as an index to pre-injury brain morphology. *Brain Injury, 8*(3), 231–238.

Bigler, E. D., & Clement, P. (1997). *Diagnostic clinical neuropsychology* (3rd ed.). Austin, TX: University of Texas Press.

Binder, L. M. (1990). Malingering following minor head trauma. *Journal of Clinical and Experimental Neuropsychology, 4*, 25–36.

Binder, L. M. (1997). A review of mild head trauma. Part II: Clinical implications. *Journal of Clinical and Experimental Neuropsychology, 19*(3), 432–457.

Binder, L. M., Rohling, M. L., & Larrabee, G. J. (1997). A review of mild head trauma, Part I: Meta-analytic review of neuropsychological studies. *Journal of Clinical and Experimental Neuropsychology, 19*(3), 421–431.

Black, F. N. (1974). WISC Verbal-performance discrepencies as indictions of neurological dysfunction in pediatric patients. *Journal of Clinical Psychology, 30*, 165.

Blanchard, E. B., Hickling, E. J., Taylor, A. E., & Loos, W. (1995). Psychiatric morbidity associated with motor vehicle accidents. *Journal of Nervous and Mental Disease, 183*, 495–504.

Bohnen, N., Twijnstra, A., & Jolles, J. (1993). Persistence of postconcussional symptoms in uncomplicated, mildly head-injured patients: A prospective cohort study. *Neuropsychiatry, Neuropsychology, and Behavioral Neurology, 6*, 193–200.

Boll, T. J., & Barth, J. (1983). Mild head injury. *Psychiatric Developments: Advances and Prospects in Research and Clinical Practice, 1*(3), 263–275.

Bornstein, R. A., & Kozora, E. (1990). Content bias of the MMPI Sc scale in neurological patients. *Neuropsychiatry, Neuropsychology, and Behavioral Neurology, 3*, 200–205.

Bornstein, R. A., Miller, H. B., & van Schoor, J. T. (1989). Neuropsychological deficit and emotional disturbance in head-injured patients. *Journal of Neurosurgery, 70*, 509–513.

Brandt, J. (1988). Malingered amnesia. In R. Rogers (Ed.), *Clinical assessment of malingering and deception* (pp. 65–83). New York: Guilford Press.

Bremner, J. D., Randall, P., Scott, T. M., Bronen, R. A., Seibyl, J. P., Southwick, S. M., et al. (1995). MRI-based measurement of hippocampal volume in patients with combat-related posttraumatic stress disorder. *American Journal of Psychiatry, 152*(7), 973–981.

Bremner, J. D., Scott, T. M., Delaney, R. C., Southwick, S. M., Mason, J. W., Johnson, D. R., et al. (1993). Deficits in short-term memory in posttraumatic stress disorder. *American Journal of Psychiatry, 150*, 1015–1019.

Bryant, R. A. (1996). Posttraumatic stress disorder, flashback, and pseudo memories in closed head injury. *Journal of Traumatic Stress, 9*, 621–629.

Bryant, R. A., & Harvey, A. G. (1998). Relationship between acute stress disorder and posttraumatic stress disorder following mild traumatic brain injury. *American Journal of Psychiatry, 155*(5), 625–629.

Bryant, R. A., Marrosszeky, J. E., Crooks, J., & Gurks, J. A. (2000). Posttraumatic stress disorder after severe traumatic brain injury. *American Journal of Psychiatry, 157*(4), 629–631.

Butters, N., Granholm, E., Salmon, D. P., Grant, I., & Wolfe, J. (1987). Episodic and semantic memory: A comparison of amnesic and demented patients. *Journal of Clinical and Experimental Neuropsychology, 9,* 479–497.

Caveness, W. (1977). Incidence of craniocerebral trauma in the United States, 1970–1975. *Annals of Neurology, 1,* 507.

Caveness, W. F. (1979). Incidence of craniocerebral trauma in the United States 1976, and trend from 1970–1975. In R. Thompson & J. Green (Eds.), *Advances in neurology* (pp. 1–3). New York: Raven.

Charney, D. S., Davidson, J. R. T., Friedman, M., Judge, R., Keane, T., McFarlane, S., et al. (1998, July/August). A consensus meeting on effective research practice in PTSD. *CNS Spectrums,* 6–10.

Collins, M. W., Grindel, S. H., Lovell, M. R., Dede, D. E., Moser, D. J., Phalin, B. R., et al. (1999). Relationship between concussion and neuropsychological performance in college football players. *Journal of the American Medical Association, 282,* 964–970.

Connor, K. M., & Davidson, J. R. T. (1998, July/August). The role of serotonin in posttraumatic stress disorder. *CNS Spectrums,* 42–51.

Crooks, D. A. (1991). The pathological concept of diffuse axonal injury: Its pathogenesis and the assessment of severity. *Journal of Pathology, 165,* 5–10.

Cullum, C. M., & Thompson, L. L. (1997). Neuropsychological diagnosis and outcome in mild traumatic brain injury. *Applied Neuropsychology, 4*(1), 6–15.

Dacey, R. G., Jr., Vollmer, D., & Dikmen, S. S. (1993). Mild head injury. In P. R. Cooper (Ed.), *Head injury* (3rd ed.) (pp. 159–182). Baltimore: Williams & Wilkins.

Deb, S., Lyons, I., Koutzoukis, C., Ali, I., & McCarthy, G. (1999). Rate of psychiatric illness one year after traumatic brain injury. *The American Journal of Psychiatry, 156*(3), 374–378.

Denker, P. G. (1944). The postconcussion syndrome: Prognosis and evaluation of the organic factors. *New York State Journal of Medicine, 44,* 379–384.

Devinski, O. (1996). Epilepsy after minor head trauma. *Journal of Epilepsy, 9,* 104–117.

Dikmen, S. S., Machamer, J., Winn, H., & Temkin, N. (1995). Neuropsychological outcome at 1-year post head injury. *Neuropsychology, 9,* 80–89.

Dikmen, S. S., McLean, A., & Temkin, N. (1986). Neuropsychological and psychosocial consequences of minor head injury. *Journal of Neurology, Neurosurgery and Psychiatry, 49,* 1227–1232.

Dikmen, S., & Reiton, R. M. (1977). Emotional sequelae of head injury. *Annals of Neurology, 2,* 492–494.

Durant-Wilson, D. M., Hartlage, L. C., & Patch, P. C. (2000). Persistent neurobehavioral problems following mild traumatic brain injury. *Archives of Clinical Neuropsychology, 15,* 1–10.

Eisenberg, H. M., & Levin, H. S. (1989). Computed tomography and magnetic resonance imaging in mild to moderate head injury. In H. S. Levin, H. M. Eisenberg, & A. L. Benton (Eds.), *Mild head injury* (pp. 133–141). New York: Oxford University Press.

Ewing, R., McCarthy, C., Gronwall, D., & Wrightson, P. (1980). Persisting effects of minor head injury observable during hypoxic stress. *Journal of Clinical Neuropsychology, 2,* 147–155.

Fann, J. R., Katon, W. J., Uomoto, J. M., & Esselman, P. C. (1995). Psychiatric disorders and functional disability in outpatients with traumatic brain injury. *American Journal of Psychiatry, 152,* 1493–1499.

Farr, S. P., & Martin, P. W. (1988). The MMPI and neurological dysfunction. In R. L. Green (Ed.), *The MMPI: Use with specific populations* (pp. 222–253). Philadelphia: Grune & Stratton.

Fordyce, D. J., Roueche, J. R., & Prigatano, G. P. (1983). Enhanced emotional readiness in clinic head trauma patients. *Journal of Neurology, Neurosurgery, and Psychiatry, 46,* 620–624.

Gean, A. D. (1994). *Imaging of head trauma.* New York: Raven Press.

Gentilini, M., Nichelli, P., & Schoenhuber, R. (1985). Neuropsychological evaluation of mild head injury. *Journal of Neurology, Neurosurgery and Psychiatry, 48,* 137–140.

Gentilini, M., Nichelli, P., & Schoenhuber, R. (1989). Assessment of attention in mild head injury. In H. S. Levin, H. M. Eisenberg, & A. L. Benton (Eds.), *Mild head injury* (pp. 163–175). New York: Oxford University Press.

Goodyear, B. (1998, November/December). Neuropsychological evaluation of mild traumatic brain injury: Detection of malingering and other functional disorders. *The Forensic Examiner,* 32–36.

Gronwall, D., & Wrightson, P. (1974). Cumulative effect of concussion. *The Lancet, ii,* 995–997.

Harlow, J. M. (1868). Recovery from the passage of an iron bar through the head. *Publication of the Massachusetts Medical Society, 2,* 327–346.

Hartlage, L. C. (1984). Unexpected consequences of apparently insignificant head injuries. *Auto Torts, 7,* 187–191.

Hartlage, L. C. (1989). *Behavior change inventory (inventory of pre- versus post-behaviors with brain injury).* Brandon, VT: Clinical Psychology Publishing.

Hartlage, L. C. (1990). *Neuropsychological assessment of head injury.* Sarasota, FL: Professional Resource Exchange.

Hartlage, L. C. (1995). Neuropsychological complaint base rate in personal injury, revisited. *Archives of Clinical Neuropsychology, 10*(3), 279–280.

Hartlage, L. C. (1997a). Clinical detection of malingering. In L. C. Reynolds (Ed.), *Detection of malingering in head injury* (pp. 239–261). New York: Plenum Press.

Hartlage, L. C. (1997b). Forensic aspects of mild brain injury. *Applied Neuropsychology, 4*(1), 69–74.

Hartlage, L. C. (1997c). Is mild brain injury an epidemic, a fad, or a scam? *American Trial Lawyers Association TBI Litigation Group, 4*(2), 5–11.

Hartlage, L. B., Ball, V. C., Gallagher, A. J., Gladden, L. G., Gregory, W. M., Johnson, A. O., et al. (1988, November). *Objective assessment of behavior change following CNS insult: Cross validation.* Paper presented at the annual meeting of the National Academy of Neuropsychology, Orlando, FL.

Hartlage, L. C., Durant-Wilson, D., & Patch, P. C. (2001). Persistent neurobehavioral problems following mild TBI. *Archives of Clinical Neuropsychology, 16*(3), 201–217.

Hartlage, L. C., Williams, B. L., & Haney, K. F. (1988, November). *Differential behavioral sequelae from traumatic vs. chemical insult.* Paper presented at the annual meeting of the National Academy of Neuropsychology, Orlando, FL.

Harvey, A. G., & Bryant, R. A. (2000). Two-year prospective evaluation of the relationship between acute stress disorder and posttraumtic stress disorder following mild traumatic brain injury. *American Journal of Psychiatry, 157,* 626–628.

Hatcher, I., Johnson, C. C., & Walker, J. M. (1996). *More than just a bump on the head: About concussions: Mild traumatic brain injuries* [Brochure]. Atlanta, GA: Pritchett & Hull.

Hovda, D. A. (1998, Spring). The neurobiology of traumatic brain injury: Why is the brain so vulnerable after injury? *Brain Injury Source, 2*(2), 22–25, 42–43.

Jagger, J., Levine, J. I., Jane, J. A., & Rimel, R. W. (1984). Epidemiologic features of head injury in a predominantly rural population. *Journal of Trauma, 24,* 40–44.

Jennett, B. (1979). Severity of brain damage: Altered consciousness and other indicators. In G. L. Odom (Ed.), *Central Nervous System Trauma Research Status Report* (pp. 204–219). Washington, DC: National Institute of Neurological and Communicative Disorders and Stroke.

Johnson, D. J., & Hartlage, L. C. (1989, June). *Specific behavior changes resultant from traumatic head injury.* Paper presented at the annual meeting of the American Psychological Society, Arlington, VA.

Jones-Gotman, M., & Milner, B. (1977). Design fluency: The invention of nonsense drawings after focal cortical lesions. *Neuropsychologia, 15,* 653–664.

Kim, S. H., Manes, F., Kosier, T., Baruah, S., & Robinson, R. G. (1999). Irritability following traumatic brain injury. *Journal of Nervous and Mental Disease, 187,* 327–335.

Kixmiller, J. S., Briggs, J. R., Hartlage, L. C., & Dean, R. S. (1993). Factor structure of emotional and cognitive behaviors for normals and neurologically impaired patients. *Journal of Clinical Psychology, 3*(2), 233–241.

Klonoff, P. S., Costa, L. D., & Snow, W. G. (1986). Predictors and indicators of quality of life in patients with closed-head injury. *Journal of Clinical and Experimental Neuropsychology, 8*(5), 469–485.

Kraus, J., & Nourjah, P. (1989). The epidemiology of mild head injury. In H. S. Levin, H. M. Eisenberg, & A. L. Benton (Eds.), *Mild head injury* (pp. 8–22). New York: Oxford University Press.

Kurtzke, J. F., & Kurland, L. T. (1993). The epidemiology of neurologic disease. In A. J. Joynt (Ed.), *Clinical neurology* (pp. 66–88). Philadelphia: J. B. Lippincott.

Lees-Haley, P., & Brown, R. (1993). Neuropsychological complaint base rates in 170 personal injury claimants. *Archives of Clinical Neuropsychology, 8,* 203–209.

Levin, H. S. (1990). Predicting the neurobehavioral sequelae of closed head injury. In R. L. Wood (Ed.), *Neurobehavioral sequelae of traumatic brain injury* (pp. 89–109). New York: Taylor & Francis.

Levin, H. S., Benton, A. L., & Grossman (1981). *Neuorbehavioral consequences of closed head injury.* New York: Oxford University Press.

Levin, H. S., Goldstein, F. C., Williams, O. H., & Eisenberg, H. M. (1991). The contribution of frontal lobe lesions to the neurobehavioral outcome of closed head injury. In H. S. Levin, H. M. Eisenberg, & A. L. Benton (Eds.), *Frontal lobe function and dysfunction* (pp. 360–374). New York: Oxford University Press.

Levin, H. S., Mattis, S., Ruff, R. M., Eisenberg, H. M., Marshall, L. F., Tabaddor, K., et al. (1987). Neurobehavioral outcome following minor head injury: A three-center study. *Journal of Neurosurgery, 66,* 234–243.

Levin, H. S., Williams, D. H., Eisenberg, H. M., High, W. M., & Guinto, F. C. (1992). Serial MRI and neurobehavioral findings after mild to moderate closed head injury. *Journal of Neurology, Neurosurgery, and Psychiatry, 55,* 255–262.

Lewis, P., & Hartlage, L. C. (1986, August). *Objective assessment of behavioral sequelae of head injury.* Paper presented at the annual meeting of the American Psychological Association, Washington, DC.

Lishman, W. A. (1988). Physiogenesis and psychogenesis in the "post-concussional syndrome." *British Journal of Psychiatry, 353,* 460–469.

Mack, J. L. (1979). The MMPI and neurological dysfunction. In C. S. Newmark (Ed.), *MMPI clinical and research trends* (pp. 53–79). New York: Praeger.

Matser, E. J. T., Kessels, A. G., Lezak, M. D., Jordan, B. D., & Troost, J. (1999). Neurological impairment in amateur soccer players. *Journal of the American Medical Association, 282,* 971–973.

Medicode (1999). International Classification of Disease, 9th Revision, Clinical Modification (ICD-9-CM). Salt Lake City, UT: Author.

Mendelson, G. (1987). The concept of post traumatic stress disorder: A review. *International Journal of Law and Psychiatry, 10,* 45–62.

Mesulem, M. M. (1986). Frontal cortex and behavior. *Annals of Neurology, 19*(4), 320–325.

Meyerink, L. H., Reitan, R. M., & Selz, M. (1988). The validity of the MMPI with multiple sclerosis patients. *Journal of Clinical Psychology, 44,* 764–768.

Micelli, G., Caltagirone, C., Gainotti, G., Masullo, C., & Silveri, M. C. (1981). Neuropsychological correlates of localized cerebral lesions in non-aphasic brain damaged patients. *Journal of Clinical Neuropsychology, 3,* 53–63.

Mild Traumatic Brain Injury Committee of the Head Injury Interdisciplinary Special Interest Group of the American Congress of Rehabilitation Medicine (1993). Definition of mild traumatic brain injury. *Journal of Head Trauma Rehabilitation, 8,* 86–87.

Miller, L. (1996, July/August). Malingering in mild head injury and the postconcussion syndrome: Clinical, neuropsychological, and forensic considerations. *The Journal of Cognitive Rehabilitation,* 6–17.

Miller, L. (1998). Malingering brain injury in toxic court cases. In Wiley Editorial Staff (Eds.), *1998 expert witness update: New developments in personal injury litigation* (pp. 225–289). New York: Wiley.

Milner, B. (1964). Some effects of frontal lobectomy in man. In J. M. Warren & K. Akert (Eds.), *The frontal granular cortex and behavior* (pp. 313–331). New York: McGraw-Hill.

Oddy, M., Coughlan, T., Tyerman, A., & Jenkins, D. (1985). Social adjustment after closed head injury: A further follow-up 7 years after injury. *Journal of Neurology, Neurosurgery, and Psychiatry, 48,* 564–568.

Oder, W., Goldenberg, G., Spatt, J., Podreka, I., Binder, H., & Deecke, L. (1992). Behavioral and psychosocial sequelae of severe closed head injury and regional cerebral blood flow: A SPECT study. *Journal of Neurology, Neurosurgery, and Psychiatry, 55,* 475–480.

Ommaya, A. K. (1982). Mechanism of cerebral concussion, contusion, and other effects of head injury. In J. R. Moumans (Ed.), *Neurological injury.* Philadelphia: W. B. Saunders.

Oppenheimer, D. R. (1968). Microscopic lesions in the brain following head injury. *Journal of Neurology, Neurosurgery, and Psychiatry, 31,* 299–306.

O'Shanick, G. (1998). Personality changes following acquired brain injury. *Brain Injury Source, 2*(4), 20–22, 44, 51.

Patch, P. C., & Hartlage, L. C. (2001). Neurological and emotional sequelae of exposure to ethylene oxide. *International Journal of Neuroscience, 106,* 101–107.

Perret, E. (1974). The left frontal lobe of man and the suppression of habitual responses in verbal categorical behavior. *Neuropsychologia, 12,* 323–330.

Prigatano, G. P. (1992). Personality disturbances associated with traumatic brain injury. *Journal of Consulting and Clinical Psychology, 60,* 360–368.

Prigatano, G. P., & Schacter, D. (1991). *Awareness of deficit after brain injury: Clinical and theoretical issues.* New York: Oxford University Press.

Ramier, A. M., & Hecaen, H. (1970). Role respectif des atteintes frontales et de la lateralisation lesionelle dans les deficits de la "fluence verbale." *Revue Neurologique, 123,* 17–22.

Rauch, S. L., Shin, M., Whalen, P. J., & Pitman, R. K. (1998, July/August). Neuroimaging and the neuroanatomy of posttraumatic stress disorder. *CNS Spectrums,* 30–41.

Rimel, R. W., Giordani, B., Barth, J. T., Boll, T. J., & Jane, J. A. (1981). Disability caused by minor head injury. *Neurosurgery, 9,* 221–228.

Roth, J. S., & Hartlage, L. C. (1998, November). *Reaction time/movement time enhancement of neuropsychological assessment.* Paper presented at the annual meeting of the National Academy of Neuropsychology, Washington, DC.

Russell, W. R. (1932). Cerebral involvement in head injury. *Brain, 55,* 549–603.

Russo, A. A., Barker, L. H., Bigler, E. D., Johnson, S. C., Ryser, D. K., & Blatter, D. D. (1996). Morphological and neuropsychological outcome following traumatic brain injury: Deficits and recovery [Abstracts]. *Archives of Clinical Neuropsychology, 11*(5), 443–444.

Rutherford, W. H., Merrett, J. D., & McDonald, J. R. (1977). Sequelae of concussion caused by minor head injuries. *Lancet, 1,* 1–4.

Rutherford, W. H., Merrett, J. D., & McDonald, J. P. (1979). Symptoms at one year following concussion from minor head injuries. *British Journal of Accident Surgery, 10,* 225–230.

Saigh, P. A., & Bremner, J. D. (1999). *Posttraumatic stress disorder: A comprehensive text.* Des Moines, IA: Allyn & Bacon.

Solomon, Z., & Bleich, A. (1998, July/August). Comorbidity of posttraumatic stress disorder and depression in Israeli veterans. *CNS Spectrums,* 15–21.

Sorenson, S., & Kraus, J. (1991). Occurrence, severity and outcomes of brain injury. *The Journal of Head Trauma Rehabilitation, 6,* 1–10.

Spencer, J. Q. (1992). Behavior change inventory: Review. *Archives of Clinical Neuropsychology, 7,* 451–459.

Straus, I., & Savitsky, N. (1934). Head injury: Neurologic and psychiatric aspects. *Archives of Neurology and Psychiatry, 31,* 893–954.

Stuss, D. T., & Buckle, L. (1992). Traumatic brain injury: Neuropsychological deficits and evaluation at different stages of recovery and in different pathological subtypes. *Journal of Head Trauma Rehabilitation, 7,* 40–49.

Stuss, D. T., Ely, P., Hugenholtz, H., Richard, M. T., LaRochelle, S., Poirier, C. A., et al. (1985). Subtle neuropsychological deficits in patients with good recovery after closed head injury. *Neurosurgery, 17*(1), 41–45.

Tekin, S., Mega, M. S., Masterson, D. M., Chow, T. C., Garakian, J., Vinters, H. V., et al. (2001). Orbitofrontal and anterior cingulate cortex neurofibrillary tangle burden in associated with agitation in Alsheimer Disease. *Annals of Neurology, 49*(3), 355–361.

Thomsen, I. V. (1984). Late outcome of very severe blunt head trauma: A 10–15 year second follow-up. *Journal of Neurology, Neurosurgery, and Psychiatry, 47,* 260–268.

Thomsen, I. V. (1989). Do young patients have worse outcomes after severe blunt head trauma? *Brain Injury, 3*(2), 157–162.

Tombough, T. N., Kozak, J., & Rees, L. (1999). Normative data stratified by age and education for two measures of verbal fluency: FAS and animal naming. *Archives of Clinical Neuropsychology, 14*(2), 167–177.

Ursano, R. J., Fullerton, C. S., Epstein, R. S., Crowley, B., Kao, T. C., Vance, K., et al. (1999). Acute and chronic posttraumatic stress disorder in motor vehicle accident victims. *American Journal of Psychiatry, 156,* 589–595.

Van der Naalt, J., Hew, J. M., van Zomeren, A. H., Sluiter, W. J., & Minderboud, J. M. (1999). Computed tomography and magnetic resonance imaging in mild to moderate head injury: Early and late imaging related outcome. *Annals of Neurology, 46,* 70–78.

Varney, N. R., & Roberts, R. J. (1999). *The evaluation and treatment of mild traumatic brain injury.* Mahwah, NJ: Lawrence Erlbaum.

Varney, N. R., & Varney, R. N. (1995). Brain injury without head injury: Some physics of automobile collisions with particular reference to brain injuries occurring without physical head trauma. *Applied Neuropsychology, 2,* 47–62.

Vickery, C. D., Berry, D. T. R., Hanlon Inman, T., Harris, M. T., & Orey, S. A. (2001). Detection of inadequate effort on neuropsychological testing: A meta-analytic review of selected procedures. *Archives of Clinical Neuropsychology, 16,* 45–73.

Waltz, J. A., Knowlton, B. J., Holyoak, K. J., Boone, K. B., Mishkin, F. S., de Menezes Santos, M., et al. (1999). A system for relational reasoning in human prefrontal cortex. *Psychological Science, 10*(2), 119–125.

Whitman, S., Coonley-Hoganson, R., & Desai, B. T. (1984). Comparative head trauma experiences in two socioeconomically different Chicago-area communities: A population study. *American Journal of Epidemiology, 119,* 570–580.

Wood, R. L. (1990). Neurobehavioral paradigm for brain injury rehabilitation. In R. L. Wood (Ed.), *Neurobehavioral sequelae of traumatic brain injury* (pp. 3–17). New York: Taylor and Francis.

Wrightson, P., & Gronwall, D. (1981). Time off work and symptoms after minor head injury. *Injury, 12,* 445–454.

Yeshuda, R. (1998, July/August). Recent developments in neuroendocrinology of posttraumatic stress disorder. *CNS Spectrums,* 22–29.

Zobar, J., Sasson, Y., Amital, D., Inacu, I., & Zinger, Y. (1998, July/August). Current diagnostic issues and epidemiological insights in PTSD. *CNS Spectrums,* 11–14.

Chapter 9

Utilizing Neuropsychological Assessment in Disability Determination and Rehabilitation Planning

Thomas L. Bennett and Michael J. Raymond

In forensic neuropsychology, not only is the neuropsychologist expected to determine the presence versus absence of brain injury, but also they need to relate the neuropsychological test data to disability. This in turn relates to the ever-present issue about the significance of specific test scores, and patterns of performance of these scores. For example, what does it mean if a person is mildly impaired on a test of attention, moderately impaired on a memory test, or severely impaired on a test of problem solving? Furthermore, what does the pattern of performance on these measures mean? Answering this question in a forensic context requires an understanding of the significance of test performances, not just from a statistical framework, but also from a functional performance perspective. That is, what are the implications of a test score, or pattern of scores, for predicting a person's ability to successfully engage in functional activities of daily living (ADLs)? Two issues that are germane to this question include the nature of disability and the ecological validity of neuropsychological tests.

IMPAIRMENTS, DISABILITIES, AND HANDICAPS

Overview of Concepts

Wilson (1997) has observed that, using the World Health Organization's (1980) conceptual framework, one can classify the sequelae of brain injury (resulting from any neurological condition or injury) into three categories: impairments, disabilities, and handicaps. *Impairments* refer to physical damage (e.g., frontal lobe damage) or deficits on neuropsychological tests, as reflected by test scores (e.g., a mild impairment on a test of attention). Impairments have the potential to produce disability. A person with an impairment, who is able to meet normal life's demands, is then not considered disabled.

Disabilities refer to the functional consequences of the impairment. For example, a mother may forget to pick up her child after school, secondary to a memory deficit associated with temporal lobe damage. Disability is defined, in the American Medical Association's (AMA) *Guides to the Evaluation of Permanent Impairment (4th ed.)*, as "an alteration of an individual's capacity to meet personal, social, or occupational demands, or statutory or regulatory requirements because of an impairment" (p. 173). Scores on neuropsychological tests (impairments) may overestimate or underestimate disabilities.

Handicaps can be conceptualized as problems imposed by the environment on an individual, because of their disability. As Wilson noted, a person is not handicapped in buildings that are wheelchair accessible, but is handicapped in buildings that are not wheelchair accessible. As noted in the AMA *Guides*, "an impaired person is handicapped if there are obstacles to accomplishing life's basic activities that can be overcome only by compensating in some way for the effects of the impairment" (p. 174). However, "if an impaired individual is not able to accomplish a specific task or activity despite accommodations, or if no accommodation exists that will enable completion of the task, then that individual is both handicapped and disabled" (p. 175). Finally, an individual with an impairment who is able to accomplish a specific task is "neither handicapped nor disabled with regard to that task" (p. 176).

In a forensic context, impairments on test scores are important to the extent that they predict disability in the real world (have ecological validity; see Sbordone & Long, 1996). Not all deficits predict disability. A well-known example of this is seen on the Finger Tapping Test. This test was developed for making decisions about lateralization of a brain injury. The fact that a person is mildly slow on finger tapping, or does not show the typical 10% advantage in dominant-hand speed over nondominant-hand speed, does not predict disability in one's functional ADLs. In contrast, if a person has developed a left upper extremity paresis after brain injury, and cannot perform the Finger Tapping Test, that might be considered clinically significant. However, the examiner would know that without even attempting the test.

On the other hand, performance within normal limits does not necessarily indicate lack of disability. The first author of this chapter (Bennett) reevaluated a woman who had a persisting amnestic disorder caused by carbon monoxide overexposure. She successfully completed the Wisconsin Card Sorting Test (WCST). However, throughout the testing, she kept overtly repeating the appropriate sorting principle to stay on task. Overt verbal rehearsal was a compensatory strategy she had learned in occupational therapy to help her successfully stay on task when completing her ADLs. Did her normal performance indicate that her cerebral functions on which this task depends were normal? Certainly, it did not. Is she disabled, despite a lack of impairment on a test score? Probably, but certainly, her disability is reduced by her effective use of a specific compensatory strategy.

If the deficits do indicate that there is a probable disability, or a potential handicap, then the forensic neuropsychologist should be a resource to determine ways to reduce the impact of these deficits. If the forensic neuropsychologist can develop a plan of treatment to reduce a person's disability, or if the environment can be changed to reduce a handicap, then the person will have a better chance of returning to productive activity, and the damages would accordingly be reduced.

Americans with Disabilities Act

Individuals who experience residual neurological and behavioral/cognitive alterations, following acute or chronic injury, illnesses, or diseases, are often forced to make changes to adapt to their environment. Unfortunately, this is often a difficult task and one which has been hindered by societal views and structural or environmental barriers.

With the advent of federal legislation, namely Section 504 of the Rehabilitation Act of 1973 (United States Department of Health, Education, and Welfare, 1977) and the Americans with Disabilities Act (ADA) of 1990 (Pub. L. 101-336), a requirement of nondiscrimination toward individuals with disabilities was enacted. Specifically, Section 504 addressed basic civil rights, indicating that an individual with a disability, who was deemed qualified, could not be excluded from any activity, program, or other benefit that was federally funded. The ADA expanded the rights addressed in Section 504 and included all employers, industries, and private organizations. The ADA also expanded the definition of disability and eligibility requirements. Overall, it protected the civil rights of individuals with disabilities, by mandating equal rights and opportunities in the following areas:

- Employment (Title I)
- State and local government services (Title II)
- Public accommodations (Title III)

Title I: Employment

Title I of the ADA promotes the practice of nondiscrimination against qualified individuals with disabilities. This addresses all phases of employment, including recruitment, completion of the application, hiring, education and training, promotion, compensation, and all other privileges or conditions of employment. For example, if an individual demonstrates the ability to perform essential tasks of a designated position (job), then the employer may not discriminate against the individual. However, the employer is not required to give preference to individuals with disabilities in the aforementioned areas of hiring, promoting, compensating, or retaining, because the ADA is not considered an affirmative action law.

Title II: State and Local Government Services

In Title II of the ADA, state and local governments are prohibited from discriminating against individuals with disabilities by refusing them the opportunities of their services, programs, or activities. Provisions under Title II are regulated by the U.S. Department of Justice, especially regarding accessibility. Specifically, all public agencies, at the time of enactment of this act, were required to submit, in writing, a formal plan to enable program accessibility through structural changes (e.g., barrier removal).

Title III: Public Accommodations

Included in Title III of the ADA is the requirement that all public agencies be accessible to all individuals with disabilities. All businesses that provide public accommodations must not discriminate against those individuals seeking services, procedures, and other associated accommodations. Alterations to public facilities, in order to abide by these requirements, had to be completed in an expedient manner, in addition to minimizing costs. New construction would be free of barriers, and reconstruction would ensure public accessibility. Adherence to these requirements are reviewed and controlled by the U.S. Department of Justice.

In essence, the ADA contends that the problems faced by individuals with disabilities is not disability, but merely a societal misperception and negative response. Dart and West (1995) indicated that "the ADA affirms that disability is a natural fact of the human experience. It rejects the notion that disability is somehow an experience separate and different from the experience of being human" (p. 51).

ECOLOGICAL VALIDITY OF NEUROPSYCHOLOGICAL TESTS

If neuropsychological test scores are to be used in disability determination, they must have ecological validity. This means that the tests are actually reflective of real-life processes. A memory test is useless in a forensic setting, if a person does poorly on it (is impaired) but has no functional memory difficulties at home or at work. Similarly, the test would not have ecological validity if the person did very well on the test, but could not remember to take medicine, turn off stove burners, or remember important phone messages.

One must remember, as Sbordone (1996) has emphasized, that the assessment environment is not the real world. The conditions of testing are set up in such a way as to optimize performance. The assessment environment is typically free from distractions. The environment and the tests are structured, and the examiner is directing the patient concerning what to do and not to do. Feedback is typically clear, immediate, and unambiguous. Time demands are minimized. Instructions are repeated and/or clarified to optimize performance, and prompts are given to facilitate success. The testing environment minimizes the impact of one's emotional state, and, because of the structure of the testing environment, problems with task initiation, organization, and follow-through are minimized. How different this is from the noise and distractions, time demands, lack of structure, and lack of direction and supervision that we typically experience in our homes, schools, workplaces, and communities. Indeed, these observations would suggest that neuropsychological testing data could potentially underestimate cognitive disability.

In evaluating disability, neuropsychologists often place too much emphasis on test scores—an error which the use of demographic norms has reinforced—and they consequently minimize the importance of behavior observations made during testing, which may provide important information about disability.

Goldstein (1942) strongly argued that only qualitative evaluations were valid. He stated that quantitative assessments, with their focus on test scores, would confuse the issues, since a normal and a brain-injured individual might obtain the same score, but arrive at the score quite differently. Goldstein's focus on the importance of behavioral observations is still important today. However, the present authors believe that test scores and behavioral observations are both critically important. Nevertheless, neuropsychologists need to obtain not only test scores, but also observe how the patient approaches and performs each task that contributes to the specific test score. If a person obtains a normal score, but achieves this score in a manner that would never be successful in their ADLs, then the person is still disabled with respect to the cognitive ability being assessed.

It is essential, regarding this latter point, to consider a person's test performance, as well as behavioral observations after completion of rehabilitation. The person may achieve normal scores on the tests in the supportive testing environment, but still report mild difficulties in attention, memory, and organization during everyday activities, especially when in an environment with various external distractions. Is such an individual perfectly normal and not disabled? We do not believe that such a person is without disability, but rather believe the improvements that have occurred during rehabilitation help such an individual compensate to a point at which their disability is significantly reduced. Improvements in test scores, in all likelihood, reflect, to a great extent, compensatory strategies gained during rehabilitation.

IMPROVING THE ECOLOGICAL VALIDITY OF NEUROPSYCHOLOGICAL ASSESSMENT BY INTERFACING WITH ALLIED REHABILITATION PROFESSIONALS

Neuropsychologists can improve the ecological validity of their testing, and thereby improve their ability to evaluate and rehabilitate disability, by combining their assessment procedures with those of allied health professionals. An example of this is found in the multidisciplinary rehabilitation settings of both authors. At these settings, cognitive assessment and the effects of cognitive impairments on functional performance of ADLs are investigated and treated by a team approach, which includes neuropsychology, speech and language therapy, and occupational therapy. The general rehabilitation procedure, which is used across disciplines to reduce disability and handicap, includes the redevelopment of previous skills (remedial training), metacognitive awareness training, and instructing the patient to develop new skills to compensate for their cognitive deficits. Following the learning of new strategies, the patient has the opportunity to incorporate them into simulated or real-life environments (home, work, or community).

For the person with severe deficits, therapy services are initially provided in an inpatient, hospital-based rehabilitation program, followed by home and community-based therapy, to ensure direct generalization as much as possible. For the mild to moderately impaired patient, therapy is initially provided in an outpatient clinic and home settings, and, again, as therapy progresses, the focus therapy is more community-based. For patients with mild brain injuries, who are still able to work, to some extent, services will be provided in the workplace and may include employer/coworker education and job coaching, with the focus often being on removing sources of handicap.

Resulting benefits for the neuropsychologist's assessment process in such a program include the ability to validate hypotheses generated in testing, by evaluating their ecological validity as the patient meets typical challenges in their ADLs. Both the assessment and treatment phases of this program are well integrated, and, therefore, the neuropsychologist can increase the breadth and ecological validity of the neuropsychological assessment process, by including testing results and behavioral observations obtained by allied professionals, such as occupational therapy and speech and language pathology. Evaluations by professionals in these latter two disciplines are different from basic neuropsychological assessments, in that they combine subjective and behavioral assessments of normal ADLs with standardized assessment procedures (tests). They enable the evaluator to more directly assess disability and handicap, by using assessment procedures that more closely reflect normal ADLs than do neuropsychological tests.

Occupational Therapy

Occupational therapy assessment and treatment is "occupational" in nature, because it addresses difficulties in activities that occupy a patient's time and activity. Occupational therapy, by emphasizing task analysis of functional skills, can evaluate the impact of cognitive difficulties (impairments) on ADLs (disabilities). A variety of behavior checklists, interviews, structured and unstructured behavior observations, as well as formal testing procedures to evaluate sensory, motor, sensorimotor integration, balance, and visual-perceptual and visual-motor problems, are utilized to determine the impact of brain injury on a person's ADLs. Major areas that are evaluated, in addition to sensory and motor difficulties, include the following.

Occupational therapy's assessment of one's ability to reengage in normal ADLs utilizes interview and/or observations of such activities as personal care, driving or transportation, community interactive skills, cooking, house cleaning, grocery shopping, organization and decision making in the home, and ability to maintain, and engage in, leisure activities. Assessments are completed at the clinic, in a person's home, and in the community. Return-to-work assessment includes an evaluation of work readiness, a worksite analysis, and a determination of environmental modifications needed to enable a person to return to productive employment and to maintain their productivity. Thus, these procedures directly evaluate disability and handicap.

Functional cognitive assessment will evaluate how a person's cognitive deficits are impacting ADLs and determine the types of compensatory strategies that need to be developed to reduce the impact. Functional cognitive assessment can be completed in the clinic, in the person's home, at work, or in the community. What better way could there be to assess the impact of attention deficits on functional skills than to directly observe how attention/concentration problems are affecting the person when they try to purchase food at a grocery store, find and purchase a shirt at a department store, or stay on task and be productive at work? This information can then be used to validate (or reject) predictions based on the neuropsychological testing.

Neuropsychologists can thereby develop confidence in the predictive validity of their data with respect to meaningful, functional abilities. Information from the occupational therapy evaluation can also aid in determining how such factors as fatigue, balance problems, motor deficits, and visuomotor and visual-perceptual difficulties are interacting with brain-injury-related cognitive impairments to influence our patients' functional abilities.

Speech and Language Pathology

A speech and language pathology assessment is completed to address several areas of functional communication that are typically not directly addressed through a neuropsychological evaluation. In addition, and from a functional evaluation standpoint, specific cognitive difficulties (e.g., speed of processing, attention and concentration, learning and memory, sequencing, and problem solving) may be directly observed through reduced functional communication skills. The communication skills, which we assess through a speech and language assessment, include auditory comprehension, reading comprehension, verbal expression, written language, and math.

As with the occupational therapy evaluation, the speech and language assessment uses standardized testing procedures, along with subjective assessment (e.g., interview and observational data). For example, auditory comprehension translates into how well we can understand what others tell us. Auditory comprehension skills can be evaluated by standardized measures to identify possible problems in the areas of understanding and recalling vocabulary concepts, main ideas, details, and sequential information. A more subjective assessment is conducted via interview, to assess a person's understanding and memory of these parameters during interpersonal communication (e.g., conversation, classroom lectures, understanding information communicated over the phone, and understanding information presented in group conversation).

Other aspects of auditory comprehension are addressed during the assessment, such as the patient's ability to understand and remember language if there is background noise present, if there are distractions present, or if a person can stay on track and listen while doing another activity. Taken together, the results of standardized testing and the subjective interview can be used to describe one's functional auditory comprehension skills.

Similar procedures can be used to evaluate other functional communication skills. Care must be taken, in formulating a rehabilitation program, to determine what a patient's functional communication skills were like before the brain injury and the level of ability that is required for their normal activities. A lawyer, for example, must have a much higher level of verbal expression skills than an over-the-road truck driver.

Deficits observed by the speech and language pathologist thus not only provide information regarding specific communication difficulties, but they also provide greater insight into how these communication deficits are affecting our patients' ADLs, thereby providing additional direct observation of disability and handicap. In addition, they can demonstrate how brain-injury-produced cognitive impairments are affecting one of our most important functional skills: the ability to communicate with others.

Like the occupational therapy evaluation, the speech and language pathology evaluation can be an extension of the neuropsychological assessment. Of greatest benefit is the fact that these evaluations, by allied rehabilitation professionals, can extend the ecological validity of our own investigations, and thereby improve our ability to estimate disability, based on a person's neuropsychological testing performance.

Based on correlations between our own observations of neuropsychological test scores and disability, as well as those made by others, it does appear probable that patterns of cognitive strengths and weaknesses, as reflected by test scores obtained in a neuropsychological evaluation, can help us predict the types of problems (disability and potential sources of handicap) a person might have in their ADLs. The relationship between impairments in neuropsychological test performance and disability in one's ADLs have been discussed by Bennett (1988), Heaton and Pendleton (1981), Prigatano (1986), and others.

IMPLICATIONS OF NEUROPSYCHOLOGICAL TEST IMPAIRMENTS FOR FUNCTIONAL ADLS

In discussing the implications of neuropsychological test impairments for one's ability to function normally and meet typical familial, social, educational, and vocational demands, our observations are based on the expanded Halstead–Reitan Neuropsychological Test Battery (HRNTB), as were Heaton and Pendleton's, and Prigatano's. Examples are provided, but, of course, there are many combinations and permutations when analyzing test score profiles, and it is critical that one integrate test scores across and between cognitive abilities in arriving at conclusions regarding a patient's neuropsychological impairments, strengths, and capabilities. The discussion focuses on acquired cognitive impairments arising from traumatic brain injury. Additional information regarding the neuropsychology of mild brain injury is provided by Raymond, Bennett, Hartlage, and Cullum (1999) and, regarding general traumatic brain injury, by Bennett, Dittmar, and Ho (1997).

Impairments of Sensory and Motor Skills

In general, with the exception of visual-field deficits or significantly reduced visual or auditory acuity, deficits on the Sensory-Perceptual

Exam (unless severe) are not likely to significantly influence one's everyday functioning.

The same can be said for fine motor speed, as measured by the Finger Tapping Test. The Sensory-Perceptual Exam, along with finger-tapping, is more diagnostic of lesion lateralization than functional ability. The exception would be in the case of jobs that require high levels of manual dexterity and sensorimotor integration.

Impairments in sensory abilities that may significantly affect ADLs include balance or vestibular problems and visual tracking, and visual accommodation and visual processing problems secondary to, or associated with, traumatic brain injury (Raymond, Bennett, Malia, & Bewick, 1996). Neuropsychological assessment, at best, only indirectly evaluates these problems. In our programs, these complaints are screened by occupational therapy or physical therapy, with subsequent referrals to specialists for further evaluation, as appropriate (e.g., behavioral or neurooptometrists).

Impairments on Tests of Attention and Concentration

Attention and concentration are critical for higher-level neuropsychological functioning, and impairments in these domains are often the basis for reported disabilities, among brain-injured patients, in learning and memory, communication, reading and writing, and executive functions (Bennett, Raymond, Malia, Bewick & Linton, 1998). Basic attention skills can be evaluated with the Speech Sounds Perception Test and the Seashore Rhythm Test, sustained attention with Digit Vigilance, alternating attention with Trails B, and sustained attention in the face of interference by failures to maintain a correct set on the WCST.

Individuals who perform normally on the Speech Sounds Perception Test, but poorly on the Seashore Rhythm Test, can typically stay on task or track a conversation, if the pace is slow, but they lose track of what is going on if the pace increases. People who make most of their errors on page 2 of Digit Vigilance have trouble processing information for more than a few minutes; they need information presented in small chunks. People whose basic attention skills are intact, but who have trouble maintaining a correct sorting principle on the WCST, are particularly sensitive to outside interference as they go about their ADLs. They need to work in a quiet, nondistracting environment. People who perform normally on Trails A, but are impaired on Trails B, have trouble alternating attention between simultaneous tasks: They need to do one task until it is completed, before moving on to another activity.

Impairments on Tests of Learning and Memory

Disabilities with respect to remembering are the most common symptoms reported among neurological patients with cognitive complaints (Malia, Raymond, Bewick, & Bennett, 1996). Most individuals will report intact memory for premorbid events, but they report difficulties with remembering events that have happened recently. Aside from the Tactual Performance Test and Subtest 7 of the Category Test, the HRNTB does not directly evaluate memory impairments. Fortunately, there are instruments now available to evaluate learning and memory abilities, which also have predictive ecological validity. These include the Memory Assessment Scales, the California Verbal Learning Test (CVLT), and the Rivermead Behavioural Memory Test.

The Rivermead test is especially helpful in making predictions regarding one's functional memory skills, according to data published by Wilson, Cockburn, Baddeley, and Hiorns (1989). This is because the test items and conditions of learning are not highly structured, and because the actual subtests are designed to be analogs of the types of memory challenges we face in our ADLs. Significant impairments on memory batteries that have ecological validity are good predictors as to whether or not a person will have functional memory disabilities.

A strength of the CVLT is its ability to clarify the basis for an individual's memory deficits, and thereby provide helpful information regarding functional memory skills. By assessing memory skills, and by defining the contribution of attention, consolidation, and/or recall deficits to a person's functional memory, one can make recommendations regarding strategies to be used to remediate or compensate for the deficit, make predictions regarding the likely permanence of the memory deficit, and predict how a person will do with respect to functional skills. Some examples follow.

Some individuals have memory disabilities that are solely related to attention problems. If attention is improved and impairments are compensated for, and if distractions can be kept to a minimum, they will be able to consolidate information at a normal rate (and therefore not be disabled). On a long-term basis, such individuals rarely need more than a memory book compensatory system, to demonstrate normal functional memory skills.

Some individuals, after brain injury, will learn information more slowly, but retention is normal following acquisition. Such individuals should be able to engage in regular educational or training programs, with a reduced course load. They will need to study more or have information repeated more often than will their fellow students or coworkers. These patients do not report as many problems in everyday forgetfulness as do individuals with acquired retention deficits.

Some patients demonstrate reasonably normal acquisition, but retention is impaired. Such individuals have significant problems with everyday forgetfulness, as demonstrated by frequently forgetting where things have been placed, what they have been told by others, and what they need to do in the future. In patients with good attention, this disability is most effectively reduced by teaching them compensatory memory strategies that are routine and regimented.

Patients with both significant acquisition and retention deficits, such as those with an hypoxic brain injury, cannot retain new information after their attention has been diverted elsewhere. If attention and executive functions testing results are normal in such individuals, some such patients can be taught, with a great deal of effort and support, memory compensatory strategies that enable them to function independently in a highly structured and routine environment (e.g., Bennett & Moore, 1997). If not compensated for, such deficits render a person unable to work or live independently, or to manage their own affairs.

In essence, these suggestions point to the wealth of information about a neurological patient's capabilities that may accrue following a comprehensive evaluation of learning and memory abilities.

Impairments on Tests of Language and Communication

Some neuropsychologists comprehensively evaluate communication skills, but, for the most part, their evaluation is cursory. The Aphasia Screening Test, from the HRNTB, is just a screening test, and one should not attempt to make significant conclusions based on it. It is designed to elicit pathognomonic signs of left versus right hemisphere damage. The power of this test is in diagnosing the likelihood of brain injury and determining evidence of lateralization of brain injury, not in evaluating a person's communication skills. Adding a test of verbal fluency or a test of naming objects does not add significantly to the Aphasia Screening Test. If a neuropsychologist suspects communication impairments, then a referral should be made to a speech and language pathologist for evaluation of verbal and written expression, verbal and reading comprehension, fluency, articulation, word-finding, and so on.

Impairments on Tests of Executive Functions

Executive cognitive functions include problem solving, sequencing, thinking prospectively, thinking flexibly, making a plan, starting an activity, self-monitoring and self-correcting, and completing a task (Bewick, Raymond, Malia, & Bennett, 1995). Executive functions depend on the integrity of the frontal lobes, but the frontal lobes cannot self-monitor and plan, unless information arriving from the posterior association areas has been properly analyzed and transmitted forward. This is why damage to any quadrant of the brain will disrupt performance on the Category Test.

One can make some general statements regarding impairment on tests of executive functions and one's functional capabilities, but it must always be remembered that it is a long way from the testing room to real life, and some individuals who do very well in the structured testing environment will have significant impairment of executive functions in their ADLs. Indeed, such a disparity is pathognomonic for frontal lobe dysfunction.

Because of the Trails B's dependency on alternating attention, brain-injured individuals who are impaired on Trails B (but do relatively better on Trails A) often have trouble "thinking on their feet." They have difficulty ordering and sequencing information and successfully engaging in activities that require sequential responding.

Performance on the Category Test can reflect, in a general way, a person's ability to cope with the complexities of a normal environment. Patients who are only mildly impaired on the Category Test can usually perform adequately in routine daily activities. These same individuals would, however, have difficulty understanding abstract information they would have understood prior to their brain injury, and thus they would experience difficulty making decisions about matters that were complicated or out of the ordinary. Students who have even mild deficits on the Category Test often report problems with synthesizing and analyzing new information presented in the classroom or in textbooks. Patients who are severely impaired on the Category Test typically should not be making decisions on their own behalf nor live alone. Even routine decisions cannot be made in a reliable fashion by such individuals.

Perseverative responding, as reflected by poor performance on the WCST, can further reduce the adaptive ability of patients with deficits in sequential thinking, logical analysis, and problem-solving ability. Patients with high perseverative response scores on the WCST are, in general, inflexible in their thinking. If they start out with an ineffective approach to a new problem or situation, they will continue with that approach long after most people would try alternative strategies. They have trouble inhibiting an action before it is needed or after it should be stopped. They have trouble learning from mistakes as well as from successes.

As discussed earlier in this chapter, the neuropsychological assessment environment is not the real-world, and in our assessment procedures we typically do not create real-world situations. Neuropsychological assessment has been criticized for being too sensitive, but, in reality, it is often not sensitive enough to detect deficits that follow brain injury. This is particularly true for executive functions, which are assessed with highly structured tests such as Trails B, the Category Test, and the WCST, although the WCST is less structured and probably more sensitive to frontal lobe dysfunction than the other two.

The use of such highly structured tests may render it difficult, if not impossible, for our assessments to adequately evaluate the integrity of the executive control system, because the very process of formally testing executive functions may mask an existing impairment (Sbordone, 1996; Ylvisaker & Szekeres, 1989). This is because the structure provided by the testing environment and the guidance provided by the examiner can serve as a prosthesis for deficits the individual with a brain injury normally has, with respect to task planning, initiation, maintenance, and completion. The examiner typically tells the patient what to do, when to begin, and how to be successful; once the test begins, the examiner keeps the patient on task until it is completed. Formal testing can thus reduce or eliminate deficits in executive functioning that the patient normally experiences.

A test battery with potentially improved ecological validity for predicting executive functions, called the Behavioural Assessment of the Dysexecutive Syndrome, has been published (Wilson, Alderman, Burgess, Emslie, & Evans, 1996). This test should add to our ability to accurately assess executive cognitive functions typically ascribed to the frontal lobes. In addition to using less-structured assessment protocols, executive functions also should be evaluated through observations of patients in their normal activities (Bewick et al., 1995; Kay & Silver, 1989; Sbordone, 1996).

REDUCING DISABILITY BY COGNITIVE REHABILITATION

As indicated earlier in this chapter, if neuropsychological assessment indicates that impairments and consequent disabilities exist, then the forensic neuropsychologist should be a resource for determining ways to rehabilitate the individual. If a plan of treatment can be developed to reduce a person's disability, or if the person's environment can be changed to reduce a handicap, then the person will have a better chance of returning to productive activity. As the AMA *Guides* note, an individual with an impairment, who is able to accomplish a specific task (e.g., their job), is not disabled with respect to that task. Damages would be reduced accordingly.

Cognitive rehabilitation is a methodology that can reduce impairment, and, thereby, reduce disability. Cognitive rehabilitation is the process by which an individual's acquired cognitive deficits, secondary to brain trauma or a neurological condition, are ameliorated. It is widely agreed that treatment must be tailored to each individual case (Raskin & Gordon, 1992). Some general principles regarding cognitive rehabilitation, of which the reader should be familiar, include the following.

Many methods have been developed to address acquired cognitive deficits, including (1) process-specific rehabilitation, such as attention-process training (Sohlberg & Mateer, 1989a); (2) skills-based training, such as prospective memory training (Mayer, Keating, & Rapp, 1986); (3) compensatory strategy training, such as use of a memory book system (Sohlberg & Mateer, 1989b); and (4) metacognitive training, such as providing rehabilitation interventions to improve a person's awareness of deficits and ability to self-monitor (Bewick et al., 1995). These methods and strategies are all incorporated into the comprehensive neurorehabilitation program *Brainwave-R* (Malia, Bewick, Raymond, & Bennett, 1997).

In general, for each patient, combining cognitive rehabilitation methods is the most effective treatment approach. Regardless of what approaches and materials are used in cognitive rehabilitation, the therapist must plan, from the beginning, ways to ensure that generalization of skills acquired during therapy will transfer to real-world activities. Sohlberg and Raskin (1996) describe five principles that they believe will promote generalization: (1) Actively plan for and program generalization from the beginning of the treatment process; (2) identify naturally occurring reinforcers in the person's normal environment that will maintain the newly acquired (or reacquired) cognitive skill or process; (3) utilize training situations that are common to both the training environment and the real world; (4) use sufficient examples when conducting therapy; and (5) select methods for measuring generalization from the clinic to the real world, to evaluate efficacy of the therapy procedures.

Using this framework in our own programs, we generally divide a cognitive rehabilitation session into thirds: The first part of the session is devoted to metacognitive training, the next portion of the session addresses skills-based training and compensatory strategies, and the last part of the session involves process-specific rehabilitation. When conducted appropriately, cognitive rehabilitation does facilitate recovery. As should be apparent to the reader, "conducted appropriately" is far removed from lining people up in front of computers, when the patient's task is to complete repetitive drills. Although the efficacy of cognitive rehabilitation will continue to be debated (as has been the value of rehabilitation in general), a number of published reports have demonstrated the benefits of this therapeutic intervention (e.g., Ben-Yishay & Diller, 1993; Cicerone, 1999; Ho & Bennett, 1997; Malia, Raymond, Bewick, & Bennett, 1998; Sohlberg & Mateer, 1987).

In our clinics, outpatient cognitive rehabilitation is provided by cognitive rehabilitation, speech/language, and/or occupational therapists. The advantage of neuropsychological assessment in planning a formal cognitive rehabilitation program is that test results can be used to specify the nature of the acquired cognitive impairments that are the basis for the patient's disabilities. This can be illustrated by two cases of patients with a presenting complaint of being unable to remember recent events.

For example, a client with mild–moderate overall cognitive impairment, caused by a traumatic brain injury, may complain of problems with everyday forgetfulness. Assessment findings could indicate normal consolidation and retrieval abilities, yet significantly impaired attention and concentration skills. In this situation, the memory problems are not primary, and improvements in everyday memory functions will be realized, if the patient is provided therapy to improve awareness of deficits and situations in which memory problems occur (metacognitive training), strategies to remember what needs to be done each day (prospective memory skills-based training), remediation therapy to improve attention/concentration skills (attention-process training), and a memory-book system (compensatory strategy training).

A different patient, who suffered an hypoxic brain injury, might similarly complain of everyday forgetfulness, but, in this case, the client could demonstrate normal performance on tests of attention and concentration, but severely impaired ability with respect to adding new information to memory. During testing, it could be observed on the CVLT that the person's trial-to-trial performance never improved, and recall after each trial was never greater than one's predicted working memory span. Recall of the list after interference was negligible. Such a person has a primary memory deficit. Focus of therapy, in this latter case, would focus on metacognitive training, skills-based training, and, especially, compensatory strategies.

Skills-based training and compensatory strategy training vary greatly, depending on the typical demands that a client must face in returning to normal ADLs. For example, a receptionist would need to learn skills to filter out distractions in the work environment, stay on task until an activity is completed, double-check the accuracy of messages, and improve organization.

A student, in contrast, would need to learn strategies to improve taking notes during lectures and reading assignments, study skills, and test taking. For students, strategies can be provided to teachers regarding modifications to normal classroom activities, so that the student's ability to meet the demands of the academic environment is enhanced. For the college student, we have had the University Disabled Students Office provide note takers, record textbooks on audio tape, and provide a quiet, nondistracting environment, with a reader, for the student taking an exam. The neuropsychological test data can be used to verify the student's complaints and provide justification for such support. Making such recommendations is dependent on the neuropsychologist being able to predict the ecological significance of the neuropsychological testing results.

When therapy goals are primarily addressed by speech and language therapy, because of acquired communication deficits, the neuropsychologist can recommend metacognitive, process, and skills-based treatments to facilitate speed and efficiency of processing, attention, and self-monitoring. Combined with speech and language therapy, these interventions will promote recovery in areas such as word-finding, tracking conversations, understanding what is read, verbal expression, and one's ability to write in an organized, sequential, and cohesive fashion.

When therapy goals are predominantly being met by occupational therapy, similar neuropsychological assessment-based cognitive interventions will facilitate return to normal ADLs. For example, improvements in attention and concentration can facilitate the use and effectiveness of compensatory strategies acquired in occupational therapy for improving home organization, maintaining one's checkbook, staying with a task until it is completed, cooking, grocery shopping, driving, and employment-related activities. These are a few examples of how forensic neuropsychologists utilize neuropsychological assessment in developing and providing valuable suggestions, to reduce the disability resulting from neurologically based impairments.

REFERENCES

American Medical Association (1993). *Guides to the Evaluation of Permanent Impairment* (4th ed.). Chicago: Author.

Ben-Yishay, Y., & Diller, L. (1993). Cognitive remediation in traumatic brain injury: Update and issues. *Archives of Physical Medicine and Rehabilitation, 74*, 204–213.

Bennett, T. L. (1988). Use of the Halstead-Reitan Neuropsychological Test Battery in the assessment of head injury. *Cognitive Rehabilitation, 6*(3), 18–24.

Bennett, T. L., Dittmar, C., & Ho, M. (1997). The neuropsychology of traumatic brain injury. In A. M. Horton, Jr., D. Wedding, & J. Webster (Eds.), *The neuropsychology handbook: Behavioral and clinical perspectives, Vol. 2* (2nd ed.) (pp. 123–172). New York: Springer.

Bennett, T. L., & Moore, C. (1997). Living with amnesia: The case of Mike S. *Bulletin of the National Academy of Neuropsychology, 13*, 14–17.

Bennett, T. L., Raymond, M. J., Malia, K. B., Bewick, K. C., & Linton, B. S. (1998). Rehabilitation of attention and concentration deficits following brain injury. *Journal of Cognitive Rehabilitation, 16*(2), 8–13.

Bewick, K. C., Raymond, M. J., Malia, K. B., & Bennett, T. L. (1995). Metacognition as the ultimate executive: Techniques and tasks to facilitate executive functions. *NeuroRehabilitation, 5*, 367–375.

Cicerone, K. D. (1999). Efficacy of cognitive rehabilitation in the treatment of mild brain injury. In M. J. Raymond, T. L. Bennett, L. C. Hartlage, & C. M. Cullum (Eds.), *Mild brain injury: A clinician's guide* (pp. 231–253). Austin, TX: Pro-Ed.

Dart, J., & West, J. (1995) Americans with disabilities act. In *Encyclopedia of disability and rehabilitation* (pp. 47–53). New York: MacMillan.

Goldstein, K. (1942). *After effects of brain injury in war.* New York: Grune & Stratton.

Heaton, R. K., & Pendleton, M. G. (1981). Use of neuropsychological tests to predict adult patients' everyday functioning. *Journal of Consulting and Clinical Neuropsychology, 49*, 807–821.

Ho, M., & Bennett, T. L. (1997). Efficacy of neuropsychological rehabilitation for mild-moderate traumatic brain injury. *Archives of Clinical Neuropsychology, 12*, 1–11.

Kay, T., & Silver, S. M. (1989). Closed head trauma: Assessment for rehabilitation. In M. D. Lezak (Ed.), *Assessment of the behavioral consequences of head trauma* (pp. 145–170). New York: Alan R. Liss.

Malia, K. B., Bewick, K. C., Raymond, M. J., & Bennett, T. L. (1997). *Brainwave-R: Cognitive strategies and techniques for brain injury rehabilitation.* Austin, TX: Pro-Ed.

Malia, K. B., Raymond, M. J., Bewick, K. C., & Bennett, T. L. (1996). A comprehensive approach to memory rehabilitation following brain injury. *Journal of Cognitive Rehabilitation, 14*(6), 18–23.

Malia, K. B., Raymond, M. J., Bewick, K. C., & Bennett, T. L. (1998). Information processing deficits and brain injury: Preliminary results. *NeuroRehabilitation, 11*, 239–247.

Mayer, N., Keating, D., & Rapp, D. (1986). Skills, routines, and activity patterns of daily living: A functional approach. In B. P. Uzzell & Y. Gross (Eds.), *Clinical neuropsychology of intervention* (pp. 205–222). Boston: Martinus Nijhoff.

Prigatano, G. P. (1986). *Neuropsychological rehabilitation after brain damage.* Baltimore: Johns Hopkins University Press.

Raskin, S., & Gordon, W. (1992). The impact of different approaches to remediation on generalization. *NeuroRehabilitation, 2*, 38–45.

Raymond, M. J., Bennett, T. L., Hartlage, L. C., & Cullum, C. M. (1999). *Mild traumatic brain injury: A clinician's guide.* Austin, TX: Pro-Ed.

Raymond, M. J., Bennett, T. L., Malia, K. B., & Bewick, K. C. (1996). Rehabilitation of visual processing deficits. *NeuroRehabilitation, 6*, 229–240.

Sbordone, R. J. (1996). Ecological validity: Some critical issues for the neuropsychologist. In R. J. Sbordonne & C. J. Long (Eds.), *Ecological validity of neuropsychological testing* (pp. 15–41). Delray Beach, FL: GR Press/St. Lucie Press.

Sbordone, R. J., & Long, C. J. (Eds.) (1996) *Ecological validity of neuropsychological testing.* Delray Beach, FL: GR Press/St. Lucie Press.

Sohlberg, M. M., & Mateer, C. (1987). Effectiveness of an attention training program. *Journal of Clinical and Experimental Neuropsychology, 9*, 117–130.

Sohlberg, M. M., & Mateer, C. (1989a). *Introduction to cognitive rehabilitation: Theory and practice.* New York: Guilford Press.

Sohlberg, M. M., & Mateer, C. (1989b). Training use of compensatory memory books: A three stage behavioral approach. *Journal of Clinical and Experimental Neuropsychology, 11*, 871–891.

Sohlberg, M. M., & Raskin, S. A. (1996). Principles of generalization applied to attention and memory interventions. *Journal of Head Trauma Rehabilitation, 11*, 65–78.

U.S. Department of Health, Education and Welfare (1997). Nondiscrimination on the basis of handicap. *Federal Register, 42*, 22,679–22,694.

U.S. Office of Education (1994). *Sixteenth Annual Report to Congress on the Implementation of the Individuals with Disabilities Education Act.* Washington, DC: Author.

Wilson, B. A. (1997). Cognitive rehabilitation: How it is and how it might be. *Journal of the International Neuropsychological Society, 3*, 487–496.

Wilson, B. A., Alderman, N., Burgess, P. W., Emslie, H., & Evans, J. J. (1996). *Behavioural assessment of the dysexecutive syndrome.* Bury St. Edmunds, England: Thames Valley Test Company.

Wilson, B. A., Cockburn, J., Baddeley, A., & Hiorns, R. (1989). The development and validation of a test battery for detecting and monitoring everyday memory problems. *Journal of Clinical and Experimental Neuropsychology, 11*, 855–870.

World Health Organization (1980). *International classification of impairments, disabilities, and handicaps: A manual of classification relating to the consequences of disease.* Geneva: Author.

Ylvisaker, M., & Szekeres, S. F. (1989). Metacognition and executive impairments in head injured children and adults. *Topics in Language Disorders, 9,* 34–49.

Practice Issues

Chapter 10

Depositions

John E. Meyers and Harold Widdison

> "The first time I testified, I was so nervous I forgot my age. This gave the judge a really good laugh." (Dr. John E. Meyers)

Another title for this chapter could be "What I wish I had learned about depositions, before I had to do one." In preparation for writing this chapter, it is easy to recall (with near-posttraumatic stress disorder symptoms) the first few depositions one testifies in. Certainly, there are those who feel comfortable in presenting in this arena, but, for the average practitioner, this is a safari onto a strange land. At times, the neuropsychologist may feel like Hansel and Gretel when entering the witch's house, but with full knowledge of whose house it is. The neuropsychological practitioner must first of all not forget that the legal arena is a foreign land, with its own language, customs, and culture. Doubtless, the legal profession could say the same of psychology. However, it is the nature of the daily work of both the legal and neuropsychological profession to interact on a professional level. Thus, we must adapt to the demands of the situation. It is not the purpose of this chapter to review ethics, it is assumed that the reader is familiar with the ethical code of conduct for psychology (American Psychological Association, 1992).

The cooperation of psychological practitioner and attorney in day-to-day professional dealings is essential to the smooth operation of the legal system. It is also in the best interests of our patients and clients. In general, the neuropsychological practitioner should understand that neuropsychological testimony is frequently indispensable to prove or disprove the nature and extent of psychological injuries. Therefore, a neuropsychologist has the responsibility to cooperate in the litigation process. An attorney has the corresponding duty to recognize that a neuropsychologist providing information or testimony, in either a treating or expert capacity, should be accommodated to the extent possible and with a minimum of disruption to the neuropsychologist's practice.

In some situations, a neuropsychologist may be compelled to provide a deposition at a county courthouse at a prescribed time (i.e., under a court order). Needless to say, this might cause some hard feelings between the lawyer and neuropsychologist and strain future working relationships. However, in most cases, a letter will arrive in the mail stating the date and time of the deposition. A phone call or informal contact, to set up the date and time that would work for all parties, usually precedes this letter. Attorneys and neuropsychologists should appreciate that each has continuing and often unpredictable responsibilities to their clients and patients. Further, the courts' dockets cannot be governed by the convenience of the litigants, attorneys, or witnesses, including neuropsychologists. Recognizing these facts, neuropsychologists and attorneys should work to minimize delay and inconvenience in scheduling depositions and trial testimony.

THE DEPOSITION

During a voir dire, some 22 years ago, involving a minor child from Cuba who sought asylum in the United States, the Cuban government hired a Miami attorney to represent their petition that the child belonged in Cuba and must be returned to the island at once.

Attorney:	Were you aware that the (minor child's name) does not have full command of the English language and was raised in Cuba in his formative years and did not come to the U.S. until age 14?
Neuropsychologist:	Yes.
Attorney:	Did you use any tests or neuropsychological measures that were specifically standardized on the Cuban population or culture, or on a Latin American or Hispanic population or culture?
Neuropsychologist:	No.
Attorney:	Have you ever been specifically instructed on testing minorities whose primary language is

	Spanish, or taken any classes in testing Spanish-speaking minorities?
Neuropsychologist:	No.
Attorney:	Have you ever taken any Spanish classes, either before, during, or after your training?
Neuropsychologist:	No.
Attorney:	Well, then, in what language did you interview and test the defendant?
Neuropsychologist:	Spanish.
Attorney:	Well, wait a minute, if you have never been taught how to test Spanish-speaking minorities, never been trained in testing minorities, never been trained in how to interview Spanish-speaking minorities, never took any acculturation classes with respect to the Cuban culture, and never took Spanish language classes, how on earth did you communicate with the defendant?
Neuropsychologist:	In Spanish.
Attorney:	How could that be, if you have never taken any instruction on the Spanish language or been trained to perform psychological examinations in an effective and sensitive manner with Spanish-speaking individuals of Cuban origin and education?
Neuropsychologist:	Because Spanish is my primary language. I speak, read, and write it fluently.
Attorney:	What? How so?
Neuropsychologist:	I was born in Cuba and came to the U.S. in the 5th grade, when I was 10 years old. (laughter in the courtroom—judge admonishes the audience).
Attorney:	I have no further questions, your honor! (more laughter) (Dr. Paul Rosete, personal communication)

As was eluded to earlier, the legal profession has its own language, as does psychology. Therefore, some definitions of terms may be helpful.

A *deposition* is a pretrial discovery device by which one party (through his or her attorney) asks oral questions of the other party or of a witness for the other party. The person who is deposed is called the *deponent.* The deposition is conducted under oath, outside of the courtroom, usually in one of the lawyer's offices. A transcript—word-for-word account—is made of the deposition. Testimony of witness, taken in writing, under oath or affirmation, before some judicial officer in answer to questions or interrogatories (Fed. R. Civil P. 26 et seq.; Fed. R. Crim. P. 15).

An *expert* is one who is knowledgeable in a specialized field, that knowledge being obtained from either education or personal experience. One who, by reason of education or special experience, has knowledge concerning a subject matter about which persons having no particular training are incapable of forming an accurate opinion or making a correct deduction (*Balfour v. State, Ind.*). One who, by habits of life and business, has peculiar skill in forming opinion on subject in dispute (*Brown v. State*). If the scientific, technology, or other specialized knowledge will assist the trier of fact (judge) to understand the evidence or to determine a fact in issue, a witness qualified as an expert may testify in the form of an opinion (FRE 702, 703).

There are five principal uses for testimony given at a deposition:

1. Evidence at the Trial: A deposition may be used as evidence by an opposing party at the trial. Under certain conditions, a lawyer may read a part of the deposition to the jury, and the jury may consider the deposition in the same manner as if the witness gave live testimony.
2. Discovery: A deposition may be used to try to discover leads for evidence, or to develop or discover facts that will help the case. This is often a request for records or other information. Often this comes in the form of a records deposition, in which an attorney may want a copy of the neuropsychologist's records, including raw psychological data. Many states (such as Iowa) have laws specific to the release of raw psychological data. In these states, it is only permissible to release the raw psychological data to another psychologist (with the patient's written authorization). In any event, releasing raw psychological data to attorneys or other unqualified persons should be avoided. All requests for medical records and reports by attorneys, and the furnishing of psychological records, should be in compliance with applicable federal and state statutes, rules of civil procedure, case law, and ethical principles of neuropsychologists. For additional discussion of releasing raw data see Tranel (1994).

There is also a Supreme Court ruling in *Detroit Edison Co. v. NLRB*, 440 1998 U.S. 301 (1998) regarding the release of raw psychological test data. In that case, a labor union sought copies of a statistically validated psychological aptitude test battery and answer sheets from an employer and rejected the employer's offer to release the information to a licensed psychologist selected by the union (*Detroit Edison*). The employer's psychologists, as members of the APA, deemed themselves ethically bound not to disclose test information to unauthorized persons (*Detroit Edison*). The APA, in an amicus curiae brief, argued that, "Unlike the psychologist, the Union [was] under no professional or ethical duty to safeguard against improper dissemination of the test scores and papers" (Brief at 12 n. 15). The Court vacated the judgment of the Sixth Circuit Court of Appeals, on this and other grounds, and stated that disclosure would unnecessarily disserve the empirical validity of the test (*Detroit Edison*). The Court stated that disclosure to the union would not adequately protect the security of the tests and that sanctions against a nonparty for ignoring restrictions on dissemination would likely be unenforceable (*Detroit Edison*).

In workers' compensation cases, in many states, disclosure is automatically authorized by state law, upon proper verification that a claim has been made; when medical records are requested by the patient's attorney or opposing counsel, the request must be in writing and must be accompanied by a written authorization from the patient or the patient's legal representative. Specific consent must be given for mental health records, drug/alcohol treatment records, and HIV/AIDS-related records. If all records in the possession of the neuropsychologist are requested, the signed written authorization must specifically address and authorize disclosure of the mental health records, drug/alcohol treatment records, and HIV/AIDS-related records, in addition to the general request for any other medical records.

All original records of a treating neuropsychologist, made in connection with the treatment and care of the patient, are the property of the neuropsychologist. However, in some cases, the patient is entitled to receive a copy of his/her records upon request. A neuropsychologist may assess a reasonable charge for providing the requested records or reports to either the patient's attorney or opposing counsel. Some jurisdictions have statutes that govern what can be charged for copies of records. In the case of medical records, the reasonable charge should include only copying costs and a charge that reflects the actual time spent by the office staff and the neuropsychologist in reviewing the records and processing the request.

3. Impeachment of a Witness: Deposition testimony may be used to impeach a witness, if the testimony at the trial varies from the deposition testimony. A lawyer is permitted to bring this variation to the jury's attention to reduce the witness's credibility.

4. Review of the Witness: A deposition gives the participating lawyers an opportunity to evaluate a witness for candor, honesty, and responsiveness, and to form opinions as to how the witness might appear to a jury.

5. Preserve Testimony: If a witness is on their deathbed or unavailable for an extended period of time, a deposition may be taken to preserve testimony for a future time.

BEFORE THE DEPOSITION

"I was in a deposition where the attorney had decided to be nastiness personified, not just implying, but stating outright her opinion that I was a shill for the defense. Unfortunately, she had decided to have the deposition at her firm's office conference room, a spacious walnut-paneled room that displayed numerous framed newspaper and legal bulletin articles of major plaintiff 'wins' on their part.

"We had a lunch break and, with nothing else to do, I decided to read the wall. . . . One of those articles lauded a doctor who often worked for them and whose testimony won them multi million dollar awards. The very doctor on the other side of this case.

"After lunch, the attorney continued about how I was defense-evil personified, whereas the doctor that the patient had gone to first was unsullied by the taint of legal context. This, of course, was the same doctor who was detailed in their framed conference room newsletter.

"I said, 'Counselor, I may be wrong, but isn't that neutral doctor you describe the same neutral doctor who has worked for your firm on many similar cases? I was reading the framed articles on your wall and I happened to note his consistently beneficial work for your plaintiffs. Didn't he just win a multimillion dollar damage award for you on a similar case?'

"The attorney looked like a deer in the headlights. She twitched and stood up quickly, knocking down about 500 pages of depositions and questions to the floor. She ended the deposition in the next minute." (Dr. David Hartman, personal communication)

The neuropsychologist has the right to expect reasonable compensation for testimony given as an expert or treating neuropsychologist. It is reasonable that the compensation reflect the time away from the neuropsychologist's practice during both preparation and actual testimony. This is best accomplished by an hourly fee; however, should the neuropsychologist wish to charge a flat fee, that fee must be based on a reasonable calculation of the anticipated overall time the neuropsychologist will spend in preparation and testimony. Ethically, payment of fees for testimony cannot be contingent upon the outcome of the litigation. A written statement of fees for review of records, preparation, and deposition time should be agreed upon before the deposition starts. It is good practice to get (at least) the first hour of deposition fee, or more, before the deposition starts. Some states have laws limiting the fees paid for professional services; therefore, it behooves the neuropsychologist to be aware of any state limits.

Carefully review the chart, re-score the data from any tests that were given. It would be very embarrassing to find your wonderful conclusions were based on a mathematical error. If a diagnosis was given, review the appropriate criteria in DSM-IV (*Diagnostic and Statistical Manual*, 4th ed.) or ICD-9 (*International Classification of Diseases*, 9th ed.). It may be helpful to list the criteria and how specifically the patient does or does not meet the criteria. Of course, the lawyers will want to argue with why you think the patient meets or does not meet specific diagnostic criteria, so prepare for this, and list them on a 3 × 5 card.

It may be helpful to make cue cards: Using separate cards, list the tests, hit rates, reliability and validity data, and so forth. List formulas, cutoff scores, and whatever else may be germane to that specific case. Ensure that there is no extra information or writing on the cards. Once you use a card (to refresh your memory), the attorneys will want the card. Each card should be individual. Stacks of cards pertaining to the testing in one pocket, and specific cards for the case you are being deposed on in the other pocket, will help to reduce search time.

Contact the attorney, case manager, or whomever requested your services, to ask if there has been any additional information on the case. As an example, a video tape of the "demented" wheelchair-bound patient you saw on one day, dancing the next day at a party put on by the patient, could be an important piece of new information that might change or support your assessment conclusions. If additional new information is brought to your attention, if it changes your opinion, this is not a problem. One should not stick to a conclusion just because it was

written in a previous report; if the situation has changed, your opinion
may also change.

Most importantly, "draw a line." This is a phrase used to illustrate
the point past which the neuropsychologist will not go. An examining
lawyer may pursue a line of questioning something like this:

Attorney:	"Now, Doctor, you have testified that he was valid in his responses. Could he have been exaggerating a little bit?"
Neuropsychologist:	"Well, possibly, but not enough to invalidate the testing."
Attorney:	"You have testified that he was exaggerating a little bit. How much would you say was exaggerated, 3% maybe?"
Neuropsychologist:	"Well, possibly."
Attorney:	"Could it have been closer to 5% or 10%?"
Neuropsychologist:	"Well, I could not really say, maybe."
Attorney:	"Could it have been 25%?"
Neuropsychologist:	"I don't think so, possibly."
Attorney:	"It could have been 50% then, and you would not know. So how can you say that the test results are valid, when as much as 50% are exaggerated. . . . "

This is an illustration of the need for "a line." How sure are you of
your data, and what supports your conclusion? It may not be possible
to give a percent, but it is possible to give a line past which you will
not go. Observe the following example:

Attorney:	"Now, Doctor, you have testified that he was valid in his responses. Could he have been exaggerating a little bit?"
Neuropsychologist:	"Well, possibly, but not enough to invalidate the testing."
Attorney:	"You have testified that he was exaggerating a little bit. How much would you say was exaggerated, 3% maybe?"
Neuropsychologist:	"There is no way to give a percent."
Attorney:	"Could it have been closer to 5 or 10%?"
Neuropsychologist:	"There is no way to give a percent. The results were valid, based on . . . "

A skillful attorney may try to swing the unwary neuropsychologist around from a stated opinion to a position more favorable to their case. It is important to establish in the neuropsychologist's mind "where the line is" on a given issue for a case. Not all issues will need a line, but the wise neuropsychologist will (at least mentally) settle on a line, based on clinical judgment and assessment results, that is ethical and within the bounds of neuropsychological sciences.

In preparing for the deposition, remember to keep in mind that a lawyer may not like the conclusions reached by the neuropsychologist. Oftentimes, if the opinion cannot be changed, then the attack moves to the basis of the opinion. The attorney's argument may take this form: "The basis upon which the opinion is based is faulty, and therefore the opinion is faulty." The astute neuropsychologist, therefore, will frame opinions based on defensible methods within the bounds to neuropsychological knowledge, with the foregone conclusion that the methods will be attacked during the deposition.

Plan to have a pre-deposition meeting with the attorney (generally, it is the responsibility of the attorney who hired the neuropsychologist to set up this meeting). Make a list of questions they should ask you, to help the court understand the complicated neuropsychological data. The attorney can discuss the questions they will be asking during the deposition, so the neuropsychologist can be prepared with the answers; and the neuropsychologist can inquire about the need for library research, or if the attorneys would like references or a bibliography. Also, the neuropsychologist can show any charts, graphs, or other visual aids to determine the appropriateness of the visual information. A particular judge may or may not like graphs and charts; usually, the attorney will know something about the hearing judge. It is important that the neuropsychologist not be too informal during these meetings. Whatever is said during these meetings "will come back to haunt" during the deposition.

Probably the most important piece of information to know when preparing for the deposition is what your process was in reaching your conclusions, usually as expressed in your report. Experts must explain why and how they reached their conclusions. Be sure to include enough description in the report to reconstruct how you reached your conclusions. An attorney can disagree with your conclusions, but the conclusions are discredited by attacking how that conclusion was reached. In the court, the "how" of the conclusion being reached may be as important as the conclusion, if not more so. The legal arena is based on procedures. If the procedures are sound, then the conclusion will be sound, and if the basis of reaching the conclusion is flawed, then the conclusion is flawed. It may be years between the evaluation and writing of the report and the deposition: Keep this in mind when writing your report.

Awareness of base rates is also a necessity. Error rates and characteristics of the test battery used in the assessment should be calculated. Simple hit rates, such as "normal versus mild traumatic brain injury," would generally suffice. Normative data and battery characteristics also should be reviewed, including reliability and validity. This information could be recorded on your 3×5 cards, for later reference.

DURING THE DEPOSITION

"I was trying to express the point that we, as a society, are now more aware of mild head trauma. We make kids put on helmets, have side air bags, and restrict our quarterbacks from play after a hit. I summed up with, 'We are past the days when we don't worry that Captain Kirk gets hit multiple times without any effects.' The younger defense attorney looked up, and said, 'Captain who?' In the silence that followed, I replied, 'It's a literary reference.' The judge fell off his chair laughing." (Dr. R. K. McKinzey, personal communication)

Before a deposition can be taken, an expert's opinion must be disclosed, usually in a report (Fed R. Civ. P. 26[a][2][B]). Once an expert has been identified, a subpoena duces tecum may be sent, to get a copy of the chart, and sometimes copies of the expert's tax records for forensic work, and any contracts with independent medical examination companies. The attorney is entitled to documents the expert used to help form their opinion, to refresh their memory or otherwise prepare his/her opinion, or prepare for the deposition (*Hamel v. General Motors, 1989; Trust v. Offenbecher, 1989*). Always review the chart to make sure you know all the information that is in the chart and to ensure that all appropriate information is properly released.

The Expert Witness as Teacher

Sometimes, a deposition will be taken in place of having an expert testify in court. Therefore, the principles that apply to courtroom testimony also apply to the deposition. During the actual trial, someone will be reading your responses to the jury/judge. Remember, regardless of what any particular attorney may wish to present, you probably know more than the attorney about neuropsychology (unless, of course, the attorney is also a neuropsychologist). The role of the expert witness is to provide information to the court (either by deposition testimony or in court). When the expert testifies, this should be a "teaching" presentation. The object is to teach the jury/judge what the expert knows about the subject of the case and to explain the steps and methods used to form the expert's opinion.

The process of teaching or persuading the jury/judge to understand and accept the opinion of the expert has five steps (Hovland, Janis, & Kelly, 1953): attention, comprehension, acceptance, retention, and action.

1. Attention: The expert must find a way to present testimony so that the information is truthful, but is also presented in a way that is understandable to the lay person. The expert should also present how the information is relevant (why the jury/judge should care what the expert's opinion is). Information should not be presented in a "boring" manner, so use charts and graphs to present the neuropsychological profile, use other visuals to help explain the information. Try to avoid distracting clothing: Dress professionally. Distracting mannerisms should be avoided. It is expected that you will be nervous, but do not look like you are nervous. Practice your testimony in front of a video camera before a deposition. Review the practice videotape for any "nervous" behaviors, use some relaxation skills.

2. Comprehension: Establish a basic understanding of neuropsychology with the jury/judge. Define any key words (avoid "psychobabble"). Do not insult the intelligence of the jury/judge by talking down to them, but explain your terms, and use simple words to describe your opinion. Use good teaching techniques: Tell what you will talk about, tell about it, and tell what you have explained. Use plain, easily understood language.

3. Acceptance: What is presented by the expert must make sense to the jury/judge. The use of analogies and real-life examples will make it more easily understood by the average individual on a jury.

4. Retention: Once the information has been presented to the jury/judge, if it is presented appropriately, it will be remembered by the jury/judge. Emphasize the main points of your opinion.

5. Action: This is the culmination of the previous four steps. If the information was presented in a manner that held the jury/judge's attention, was understandable and logical, based on common sense, then it will be accepted by the jury/judge. If appropriate care has been given to explain the complex information, then the opinion of the expert will be retained and the jury/judge will act with the expert's opinion in mind.

Be honest. Your first obligation as a witness at a deposition is to answer questions truthfully and accurately. You are under oath, as if in court. "I do not know" is an acceptable answer.

Concerning when to respond, as a general rule, a witness must answer all questions, unless one of the lawyers present at the deposition directs the witness not to answer. In the event that a lawyer objects to a question during your deposition, you should refrain from answering. If the examining lawyer then directs you to answer the questions, you should do so, unless directed by your lawyer not to do so. Be sure not to talk while the attorney(s) are talking. This helps the court reporter and also gives the attorneys time to object.

Be sure you understand the question. If you do not completely understand a question, do not try to respond based on what you think the question might or should be. Instead, simply say to the examining lawyer that you do not understand the question. You are under no obligation to interpret imprecise or unclear questions. It is the examining lawyer's job to ask questions clearly. The neuropsychologist may legitimately request the examining attorney to rephrase the question.

Look for double meanings. Be especially alert to questions that include terms with more than one meaning. If a question contains a term that is not perfectly clear to you, state that the intended meaning of a term in the question is not clear to you. Also, be careful when long, complex, or double questions are posed to you.

One popular question with a double meaning is, "How much are you being paid for your testimony?" On its surface, one may think that this is asking what one charges for doing a deposition. If the response from the neuropsychologist is simply stating his/her fee, then the implied message to the judge/jury is that your testimony can be bought for that amount of money. In one answer, the lawyer has established that the neuropsychologist is a "prostitute" for the side that hired the neuropsychologist, and will say anything they want for money. A more comfortable response might be, "I am not being paid for my testimony, I am being paid for my time."

Another question is sometimes phrased like this: "I know you are working for (the other attorney), but I want to ask you a few questions. Is that all right with you?" Again, on its face it appears to be a harmless, but wordy, beginning of a conversation. However, by simply stating, "Yes," the neuropsychologist has concluded that he/she is going to give testimony specifically biased for the side that is paying the fee. A more comfortable answer might be, "I am not here to give testimony for either side, I have been asked to come here and present objective testimony as an expert."

Do not begin to respond until the examining lawyer has completed the question and is silent. Even if you feel that you know what information the lawyer is requesting, you run the risk of misinterpretation by breaking into the middle of the question.

Carefully consider your answers. Before responding to a question, consider carefully what you intend to say, and have your answer clearly in mind. Even if you are completely certain of your answer, hesitate for a few moments. This will permit lawyers to object to the question if it is improper and to instruct you not to answer.

Do not be concerned if your deliberations slow the pace of the deposition or involve periods of silence between the questions and the answers. At a deposition, there is no judge or jury to note how long you take to answer, nor is there any record in the deposition transcript that indicates the amount of time it takes you to respond. If the deposition is videotaped, some of the longer pauses can be edited out later by the attorneys. Lawyers have their own procedure for editing videotapes.

Answer the questions asked. When giving your testimony, answer only the question put to you. It is important that you give complete answers to questions. You should give just the response that is sufficient to answer the question, and no more. If you are asked a question that can be answered "Yes" or "No," then do so. It is not your job to educate or to inform the examining lawyer. It is their job to determine carefully and precisely the matters about which to inquire, and to ask questions to elicit that information.

If you are uncertain, be careful to testify only as to those matters within your personal memory or knowledge. If you did not personally witness or observe that about which you are asked, then you are justified in saying you do not know the answer, even though you may have heard secondhand facts or information. Similarly, do not speculate as to what probably happened. There is always a possibility that, at a later time, you may remember what actually did happen, and it may differ from your deposition testimony. Your deposition testimony should rest upon firsthand knowledge and a clear memory, not upon hearsay or speculation.

Be alert to "factual assumptions." You may be asked questions containing factual assumptions that you believe to be inaccurate or about which you have no knowledge. For example, the question, "When Mr. Smith made the decision to fire Ms. Jones, did he consult with you?" contains the assumption that Mr. Smith made the decision to fire Ms. Jones. If he never made that decision, or if you had no knowledge of the decision, then the question is improper. If you find the examining lawyer has asked such a question, you should respond that you are unable to answer. If other lawyers in the deposition object to this kind of question as "assuming facts not in evidence," this should alert you to the defect in the question. Remember that you are under oath and can only testify to what you know. The lawyers are not under oath when they question you, so they do not necessarily have to feed you correct information upon which to answer.

Do not guess details. Be wary of giving exact information (such as measurements, dates, time intervals, and scores). If you are uncertain about the details, examine the chart or your notes or 3 × 5 cards. If the information is not available and you are asked a question of this nature and you are uncertain, respond that you do not remember the exact information. If the information requested is available from certain records, you may add that any answer you give will be your best estimate only, and is subject to verification through applicable records. If your testimony is based on an approximation, you should make this clear to the examining lawyer. Any testimony that is based on estimates should be given only when the record unequivocally reflects that this is the basis for the testimony.

If a lawyer asks you questions that relate to an available document, request to see the document before answering. It is appropriate to consult documents before answering questions. It does not mean your memory is weak. It instead shows you are careful and take the deposition seriously.

No one's memory is completely fool proof or perfect, especially when under the stress of a deposition (assuming you find a deposition stressful). Therefore, when asked for factual information, it is a good idea to also state something like, "That is all I can recall at this time." When the deposition is over, you may remember some other piece of information that had slipped your mind temporarily.

If, at any time during the deposition, you feel a previous answer was incorrect or incomplete, immediately inform your lawyer. Depending on the situation, your lawyer may stop the proceeding to give you an opportunity to correct the inaccuracy or omission. In the event that you recall an omission or inaccuracy after the deposition is completed, you still should bring this matter immediately to the lawyer's attention. A letter from the lawyer to the opposing counsel, which sets forth the error or omission, may spare you considerable embarrassment at the trial.

If you feel fatigued or either physically or mentally uncomfortable at any time during the deposition, immediately inform the lawyer. He or she can request a brief recess.

Be on guard during recesses. There are usually one or more recesses during a deposition, and, from time to time, the lawyers involved will converse off the record. You should always be guarded in your discussion of the case. It is best not to discuss the case at all. Lawyers representing opposing parties have their first loyalty to their clients. When the court reporter is transcribing testimony once again, lawyers can question you about matters that were discussed off the record. In the event that you have a question at any time during the proceedings, you may request an opportunity to consult your lawyer. You have a right to confer with your lawyer at all times, even if it requires a break in the proceedings.

Concerning your personal conduct, you should be courteous, serious, and even-tempered regarding everyone associated with the deposition. An apparent outburst of temper, the use of profanity, or the failure to take the proceedings seriously can be harmful to you as a credible witness. This conduct subsequently can be brought to the attention of the judge or jury.

AFTER THE DEPOSITION

Relax, it's over. You may be asked if you wish to review your deposition. Usually, you should indicate you wish to read and sign your deposition. Review the deposition when it comes to you. The review serves two purposes. The first is to find any misspoken statements or misunderstandings by the court reporter. The accuracy rate of court reporters is quite good, but occasionally the technical words can be misunderstood. Read the deposition over. Any corrections are to be listed (usually on a separate sheet of paper), indicating the page and line of a correction, as well as the correction. Make any corrections now, because, during the court appearance, errors will come back to haunt you. Discuss any errors or corrections with your attorney.

The second, and probably the most important reason to review each deposition, is for training purposes. Look the deposition over, see the types of questions asked and how you answered them. Now that the deposition is over and you have an opportunity to sit back in the cold light of day, how would you have answered differently (if at all)? Would it have been better to use a different word or phrase to explain your results? Do you need to add another card or other information to your "pocket references" (3 × 5 cards) ? Look at the deposition as teaching material for yourself. Once you have completed your review and sent back any corrections, put the deposition away. It is done.

THE EXPERT TRILOGY

> "Increasingly, proof in civil litigation relies on expert testimony. As the world has gotten more complex, so, by necessity, has litigation." (Ollanik, 2000)

There are three cases of particular merit to neuropsychology. These are often referred to as the *Trilogy*. These cases set the stage for expert witnesses. In a 1923 case (*Frye v. United States*), the court ruled that "expert testimony based upon novel scientific evidence is inadmissible unless the technique is 'generally accepted' as reliable in the relevant scientific community" (Ollanik, 2000). New or untested practices or theories were not admissible until such practices became generally accepted. This meant that new or breakthrough scientific progress was not automatically admissible.

New Federal Rules of Evidence (FRE) were adopted in 1975 (FRE 702–706), and, in 1993, the test for admissibility of expert witness testimony set forth in Frye was challenged. The challenge came in *Daubert v. Merrell Dow Pharmaceuticals* (1993). The Supreme Court reexamined the Frye decision in light of the new FRE 702. FRE 702 provides that

> if scientific, technical, or other knowledge will assist the trier of fact [Judge or Jury] to understand the evidence or to determine a fact in issue, a witness

qualified as an expert by knowledge, skill, experience, training, or education may testify thereto in the form of an opinion or otherwise.

In *Daubert*, it was held that no longer would "general acceptance" of a scientific methodology be required in federal trials. However, after *Daubert*, trial courts were required to apply FRE 702 and determine that any proposed expert testimony constituted scientific knowledge and that it will "assist the trier of fact" (Ollanik, 2000). General acceptance was no longer the only standard. The four criteria for expert admissibility were: (1) whether the theory or technique can be, and has been, tested; (2) whether it has been subjected to peer review and publication; (3) the known or potential error rate; and (4) the old criterion of general acceptance. In *Daubert*, the Court emphasized that the four-part test is flexible, and that not all four criteria must be met, but it would make the expert's testimony more acceptable if all criteria are met (Ollanik, 2000). A pretrial hearing may be required for the purpose of qualifying an expert. The *Daubert* decision became the first part of the Trilogy.

The second part of the Trilogy is *General Electric Co. v. Joiner* (1997). One question left unanswered by the Supreme Court in *Daubert* was what the standard was that the appellate courts should use in determining the admissibility of expert testimony (Black, 1999). At the end of 1997, the Supreme Court clarified this issue in Joiner: The Supreme Cout in Joiner held that conclusions and methodology are not entirely distinct from one another and neither *Daubert* nor the Federal Rules of Evidence require a district court to admit opinion evidence just because the expert said so. The expert's opinion cannot be based on "because the expert said so." The Court said experts must explain how and why they reach their conclusions.

The third part of the Trilogy was *Kumho Tire Co. v. Carmichael* (1999). In this decision, the Supreme Court held that a trial court's duty is to scrutinize expert testimony, and this applies to all expert witnesses, not just purely scientific experts.

Validity, Reliability, and Relevance

The Trilogy and Rule 702 established three distinct, but interrelated, tests for the admissibility of expert testimony.

1. Knowledge test: The expert's testimony must be "scientific, technical, or other specialized knowledge" (Kumho et al., 1999). If

an expert's conclusion is not supported by valid reasoning, it fails the knowledge test and must be excluded. The assumption underlying the knowledge test is that invalid reasoning cannot produce a reliable conclusion. It does not follow, however, that valid reasoning necessarily results in conclusions sufficiently reliable or relevant to be helpful for legal purposes. The theory or technique can be, and has been, tested or could be subjected to scientific study to be specialized knowledge.

2. Helpfulness test: This knowledge must assist the judge or jury to understand the evidence or to determine a fact in issue. Even if valid and reliable, an expert's testimony may still be inadmissible on relevancy grounds, for example, testifying outside your area of competency. Additionally, expert testimony that has a wide margin of error, however scientific, may not be acceptable (*State v. Foret*, 1993). The reliability and validity may be enhanced if it has been subjected to peer review and/or publication. The likelihood of admissibility is enhanced if the known or potential error rate is generally accepted in the scientific field of the expert.

3. Qualifications test: The expert must have specialized "knowledge, skill, experience, training, or education" (Kumho et al., 1999). The Rule also allows, but does not require, a qualified expert to testify in the form of an opinion.

Thus, a court's admissibility inquiry should include all three questions: validity, reliability, and relevance. Validity, however, is the most important concept, because the quality of an expert's reasoning is usually the most fundamental issue.

OTHER PROFESSIONAL ISSUES

When a neuropsychologist is testifying under the questioning of the attorney who requested the assessment, this is *direct examination*. This is the time when the neuropsychologist puts on the teaching hat, and educates the jury/judge. When the opposing attorney questions the neuropsychologist, this is *cross-examination*. The purpose of this questioning is to find error with the expert's opinion, and to discredit the neuropsychologist. Weitz (1992) provides a good description of the types of tactics used by lawyers during cross-examination. Assume that the opposing attorney has reviewed your qualifications, professional writings, and previous deposition and trial testimony. Under Fed Rule 26(B), you will have had to provide your opinion, and other cases you have testified in, either by deposition or live at trial, for the past 4 years. You are also required to provide a list of publications within the past 10 years. It would be helpful to maintain a list of this information. Another common question asked is, How many times have you testified at the request of the plaintiff and the defendant? Federal Rule 26(B) only applies when you are testifying as an expert; when testifying as a treating doctor, this rule may not apply, but the attorneys will oftentimes ask for the same information. Additionally, you might be asked to produce tax documents of your income from expert testimony for the past 3 years (*Wrobleski v. Delara,* 1998).

Weitz points out strategies for attacking the expert witness through the use of compound questions (questions with multiple parts), and by questioning in such a way as to put one part of the question factual and another part not factual and asking the expert to agree with the question, thereby, making the expert look like they have changed their testimony or appear as not having done an objective assessment. He points out that jury members expect to see the expert being "attacked."

Countering the Claim of "Junk Science"

Ciresi and Wivell (1991) provide a model for countering the claim of "junk science." First, be knowledgeable in your field of specialty: Have good credentials. Be detail-oriented in your assessment. Actually work in neuropsychology, seeing real patients, not only doing expert testimony. Be recognized by others in your profession (i.e., board certification). Second, show that your findings are consistent with other published studies and know your error rates (i.e., false positive and false negative). Last, show that your methods are similar to other published work. Present literature that uses the same approach and shows that the test approach you used has been previously entered as evidence in court. Spreen and Strauss (1998) and Lezak (1995) can provide information on the interpretation of neuropsychological tests and information on the tests themselves.

Other methods of countering an expert's testimony are through attacking the expert's credentials, showing that the expert is testifying outside his/her area of expertise, or through attacking the examination process and the examination results and interpretation. These are all common strategies. Attempts to fluster or get the expert to contradict their previous testimony are also commonly used. It is also common to save the "zinger" question for last, so that the cross-examining lawyer can end the questioning in "Perry Mason style." Also, at the beginning of the cross-examination, an attorney may also feel that, by "hurting the witnesses early on, you can throw them off balance and firmly establish control." Therefore, some attorneys may attempt to hit the neuropsychologist with a zinger at the beginning and at the end of the testimony.

Based on experience doing depositions, it is best to have a written agreement of payment, for the travel, preparation (including researching) and testifying time, and for the pre-deposition meeting. It is usually best to arrange to be paid in advance. Therefore, the attorney has a clear understanding of the costs involved in the deposition.

Other Helpful References

The MMPI, MMPI-2 & MMPI-A in Court: A Practical Guide for Expert Witnesses and Attorneys, 2nd ed. (Pope, Butcher, & Seelen, 1999), focuses primarily on the use of these tests in forensic psychology and covers many of the questions and responses one might expect during a deposition or court appearance.

Coping with Psychiatric and Psychological Testimony, 5th ed., 3 vols. (Ziskin, 1995), is a book for attorneys, to help neutralize opposing mental health experts by focusing on the limitations of psychiatric and psychological evidence. The suggestions on how to challenge the expertise of psychiatrists and psychologists can be helpful reading.

Effective Expert Witnessing (Matson, 1994). This book discusses many recent court rulings about reliability, relevancy, and admissibility of expert testimony. Discussion of expert witnesses that can survive scrutiny and of federal and state process of keeping unreliable scientific testimony from juries.

CONCLUSIONS

Participation in a deposition can invoke flight-or-fight autonomic responses, but need not. Good preparation is essential both to the neuropsychologist and the attorney. It may be said that lawyers and neuropsychologists are a people separated by a common language. Neuropsychologists are trained to identify and treat cognitive impairment. Neuropsychology is therefore concerned with identifying injury and treating it. One may use several different methods, procedures, and theories to identify and treat the injury. To the neuropsychologist, there are many roads that "lead to Rome." To the attorney, it is not that the neuropsychologist arrived in Rome, but rather that the neuropsychologist followed a verifiable and reliable road map to get to Rome. When testifying, the neuropsychologist needs to be aware of the different agenda of the attorney, and needs to translate neuropsychological methods into a format that is ethical and usable by the court system. It behooves the profession of neuropsychology to present testimony scientifically and appropriately, thus improving the usefulness of the neuropsychological sciences to the court and, most important, to those who are the recipients to neuropsychological services.

APPENDIX A

For convenience, a checklist is included with this chapter. This checklist is presented as a working tool to help the neuropsychologist in preparing for depositions.

Checklist

_____ Received notice of deposition
Date: _____ Time: _____ Place: _____
Attorney name: _____ Phone: _____
_____ Send attorney copy of prepayment policy and request for prepayment.
Received prepayment: _____
_____ Predeposition meeting with attorney
Date: _____ Time: _____ Place: _____
_____ Review chart
Update resume/Vitae. _____
Update publications list/presentations. _____
Re-score and review patient file. _____
Write out 3 × 5 cards. _____
Write out (for yourself) HOW and WHY of opinion. _____
Standard evaluation procedures were used. _____
Valid and reliable tests used _____

Acceptable error of measurement _____

Review relevant studies/publications. _____

Make the "line" of what you can and cannot say under oath. _____

Make drafts of charts and graphs. _____

Make list of questions for attorney. _____

_____ Meet with attorney, discuss file, 3 × 5 cards, HOW and WHY, "the line"; review charts, graphs, and questions for attorney.

_____ Before deposition, re-review patient file and materials, complete any charts, graphs, or visual aids.

_____ Review the suggestions for doing the deposition in this chapter.

_____ Be on time for deposition (leave your cell phone and pager off).

_____ After deposition, review deposition.

Make any notes or changes. _____

Review deposition for learning purposes. _____

REFERENCES

American Psychological Association. (1992). Ethical principles of psychologists and code of conduct. *American Psychologist, 47,* 1597–1611.

Balfour v. State, Ind., 427 N.E.2d 1091, 1094 (____).

Black, B. (1999). *Expert evidence in the wake of the Daubert–Joiner–Kumho tire Trilogy.* Ali-Aba course of study: Products liability. July 22–23, 1999, Boston, MA.

Brown v. State, 140 Ga. App. 160, 230 S.E.2d 128, 131.

Ciresi, M. V., & Wivell, M. K. (1991, November). Protecting your evidence against "junk science" attacks. *Trial,* 35–40.

Daubert v. Merrell Dow Pharmaceuticals, 509 U.S. 509 U.S. 579 (1993).

Denney, R. L., & Wynkoop, T. F. (2000). Clinical neuropsychology in the criminal forensic setting. *Journal of Head Trauma Rehabilitation, 15*(2), 804–828.

Detroit Edison Co. v. NLRB, 440 U.S. 301 (1998).

Frye v. United States, 293 F. 1013 (D.C. Cir, 1923).

General Electric Co v. Joiner, 522 U.S. 136 (1997).

Hamel v. General Motors, 128 F.R.D. 281 (D. Kansas 1989).

Hovland, C. I., Janis, I. L., & Kelly, H. H. (1953). *Communication and persuasion: Psychological studies of opinion change.* New Haven: Yale University Press.

Kumho Tire Co. v. Patrick Carmichael, 119 S. Ct 1167 (1999).

Lezak, M. (1995). *Neuropsychological assessment* (3rd ed.). New York: Oxford University Press.

Matson, J. V. (1994). *Effective expert witnessing* (3rd ed.). Boca Raton, FL: CRC Press.

Ollanik, S. (2000, November). Products cases: An up hill battle for plaintiffs. *Trial,* 20–28.

Pope, K. S., Butcher, J. S., & Seelen, J. (1999). *The MMPI, MMPI-2 & MMPI-A in Court: A practical guide for expert witness and attorneys.* Washington, DC: American Psychological Association.

Spreen, O., & Strauss, E. (1998). *A compendium of neuropsychological tests: Administration, norms, and commentary* (2nd ed.). New York: Oxford University Press.

State v. Foret, 628 So. 2nd 1116 (La. 1993).

Tranel, D. (1994). The release of psychological data to nonexperts: Ethical and legal considerations. *Professional Psychology: Review and Practice, 25,*(1), 33–38.

Trust v. Offenbecher 124 F.R.D. 545 (SDNY 1989).

Weitz, H. (1992, February). Cross-examining the expert at trial. *Trial,* 55–58.

Wrobleski v. Delara, 708 A. 2d 1086 (Md. App. 1998).

Ziskin, J. (1995). *Coping with psychiatric and psychological testimony* (5th ed., Vols. 1–3). Los Angeles, CA: Law and Psychology Press.

Chapter 11

Diagnostic Issues: Attorney Perspective

John Montgomery Carson and C. Michael Bee

The authors, independently, throughout the course of the years of their practices, have noted a direct correlation between persons who suffer whiplash-type neck injuries (also termed *hyperextension/hyperflexion cervical injuries* or *cervical acceleration/deceleration injuries*) with ligamentous injury and/or mild traumatic brain injury (MTBI) in rear-end and frontal motor vehicular collisions, and those who are later diagnosed with either temporomandibular joint (TMJ) dysfunction and/or orofacial pain disorders. This chapter discusses this finding and, further, helps the clinical practitioner, whether medical provider or lawyer, learn how to identify patients and/or clients with TMJ dysfunction and/or orofacial pain disorders, and how then to treat such persons, so that other more serious medical side effects, such as chronic pain disorders and depression, do not occur.

QUESTIONS PRESENTED

1. Is there a correlation between TMJ dysfunction and/or orofacial pain disorders and whiplash-type neck injuries and/or MTBI in frontal and/or rear-end motor vehicle collisions?
2. How do you identify patients and/or clients with TMJ disorders and/or orofacial pain disorders?
3. What, generally, is the course of treatment for persons with TMJ disorders and/or orofacial pain?

DISCUSSION

Is There a Correlation Between TMJ Dysfunction and/or Orofacial Pain Disorders and Whiplash-Type Neck Injuries and/or MTBIs in Frontal and/or Rear-end Motor Vehicle Collisions?

It has been determined that there is a direct correlation between TMJ disorders and/or orofacial pain and whiplash-type neck injuries and/ or MTBI in frontal and/or rear-end motor vehicle collisions. This is particularly true with females, compared to males. Females incur more soft tissue injuries than men, in a ratio of about 2:1. Male fatalities, however, outnumber females 2:1. The disparity in female soft tissue injuries, compared with males, is easy to explain. Females have smaller neck diameters and longer necks, a higher frequency of spinal stenosis, more severe soft tissue injuries, slower recovery, greater disability, and a more guarded prognosis. Females also experience more overall joint injuries, including TMJ disorders, as a result of front-end and rear-end motor vehicle collisions, compared with men. Females exhibit a greater degree of ligament laxity, when compared to male populations, and some current literature suggests that the presence of estrogen receptors may account for a greater degree of pain perception (Dao & LeResche, 2000; Hatch et al., 2001).

A brief review of automobile biomechanics and occupant kinematics, in both rear-end and front-end motor vehicle accidents will facilitate an understanding of the mechanism of injury (Chandler & Christian, 2001; Gurdjian, 1976; Johnson, 1996; Kaneoka et al., 1999). During front-end and/or rear-end motor vehicle impact, essentially three separate collisions occur. The first (Collision I) is vehicle to vehicle. The second (Collision II) is occupant to vehicle interior, and the third (Collision III) involves collision of body parts. The mechanism of injury is the result of energy transfer during these three collisions, which all occur in a time span of 0.1–0.2 seconds. This time frame, for reference, is essentially equivalent to the blink of an eye. Rarely does a vehicle-to-vehicle collision involve identical vehicles, from the standpoint of size and weight, with identical bumper heights. More often, the vehicles differ in size and bumper height, which ultimately results in asymmetric forces being transmitted from the bullet vehicle (striking vehicle) to the target vehicle (vehicle being struck), and subsequently to the occupants.

Collision II will yield significant knowledge and understanding of whiplash-type injuries, brain injury, and injury to the TMJs. There are four phases that occur during Collision II. Reference is directed toward rear-end motor vehicle accidents during this discussion, but the reader should keep in mind that the mechanisms are similar for both rear-end and front-end collision. In a rear-end motor vehicle collision, immediately following impact, both vehicles attain a common velocity. The occupant seat of the target vehicle is displaced toward the point of impact, in this case, to the rear. The legs flex toward the torso, up the hip joint, and the torso undergoes a process referred to as *ramping*, which involves movement of the occupant's torso in a vertical position parallel to the seat back. The head remains stationary, causing both compression and shear forces to be applied to the cervical spine. During Phase 2 of the second collision, the seat back returns to its original position, causing a hyperextension of the cervical spine and posterior rotation of the head. A dramatic increase in shear stresses is present during this phase, and the lower jaw may start to open during Phase 2, as well.

Phase 3 is the time of maximum acceleration for the occupant. The occupant accelerates in a forward direction, causing both flexion and rotation of the head, cervical spine, and pelvis. At this point, the occupant is moving faster than the car, and the head is moving approximately 2.5 times faster than the vehicle. It is obvious that, as forces and force vectors change, injury may occur at any time to the cervical spine, brain, and/or TMJs. During Phase 4, the occupant's head and cervical spine attain maximum hyperflexion. The degree of hyperflexion is dependent on the speed of the collision and the head may not achieve full flexion if the collision velocity is low.

Collision III, as mentioned earlier, involves direct collision of body parts. Most bodily injury occurs during this phase. While the vehicle moves away from the point of impact, the occupants remain stationary relative to the vehicle, but appear to move toward the point of impact. During an offset collision (this kind includes the vast majority of accidents), there will be rotational forces applied to the body, which enhance compression and shear forces. Each vehicle collision is unique. Biomechanical forces applied to occupants are always multidimensional. A force is generated on the impacted side, and a zero force is created on the side away from the impact. This creates a net force on the body, which produces deceleration and injury, thus, a coup–contracoup effect. These forces, as they act on soft tissue, create stretching, tearing, and cellular disruption. The coup–contracoup effect is significant from the standpoint of brain injury, because the initial force generated causes an intracranial compression on the side of the impact, with a secondary impact occurring on the opposite side. This results in disruption of intracranial structures.

Another mechanism of injury is the differential motion of connected adjacent structures. The stability of the TMJs and orofacial musculature is dependent on the integrity of soft tissue elements, such as ligaments and tendons. When forces generated in a motor vehicle collision are sufficient to cause cervical injury and mild-to-moderate TBI, the forces are more than sufficient to cause damage to facial musculature and the TMJs. Soft tissue injury implies injury to connective tissue. Connective tissue is composed of fibers, skeletal muscle, and tendons. Fibers consist of elastin and collagen. Collagen is a major component of cartilage, ligaments, tendons, muscle, and nerve sheaths. It remains flexible unless mineralized. Elastin fibers are far less numerous than collagen fibers. They are poorly organized and, once injured, are nonrepairable. The healing phase of injury to both ligaments and tendons may be quite protracted, as a result of a poor vascular supply, disruption of elastin, and the presence of large amounts of collagen, which heal by scar formation, initially. Replacement of damaged fibers with new collagen may take several years.

During the past several years, the authors have treated and/or represented a number of patients/clients who suffer from TMJ disorders and/or orofacial pain secondary to muscular, tendon, and ligament injuries, when they have been involved in a frontal or rear-end collision. These individuals have each been diagnosed with a documented brain injury and/or whiplash-type neck injury, with permanent ligamentous and/or muscular dysfunction. Below are multiple case reports of patients and/or clients that the authors have either treated or represented. These reports are presented in order to give the reader some perspective on the complexity of issues involved, such as achieving a proper diagnosis and rendering proper effective treatment. A chart is presented, as well, representing significantly more cases. Together, the authors feel that this is a compelling indication that a correlation exists between TMJ disorders, orofacial pain disorders, whiplash-type neck injuries, and/or mild-to-moderate TBIs.

Obviously, for reasons of confidentiality, the names of individuals cannot be provided. Many patient/client records could not be retrieved from archives. The case reports and chart that follows summarize whether the patient was male or female, whether or not the collision was a frontal or rear-end collision, whether or not the party suffered brain injury or whiplash-type neck injuries, and a brief description of the specific types of orofacial pain disorder and/or TMJ dysfunction that followed.

CHART/CASES

A total of 60 recent trauma cases were randomly selected, which involved front-end and rear-end collisions. Of the total, 44 patients were females, ranging in age from 16 to 72 years, and 16 patients were males, ranging in age from 22 to 69 years. Thirty accidents involved front-end collisions and 30 accidents involved rear-end collisions. Of the 30 front-end collisions, 11 cases involved males and 19 cases involved females. Of the rear-end collisions, 4 cases involved males and 26 cases involved females. All 60 cases involved cervical acceleration/deceleration injuries, postaccident orofacial pain, and TMJ disorders. Mild TBI was documented in 42 of the 60 cases. The following chart displays these findings.

Several case studies are presented below, which are representative of these types of injuries. Common salient points are discussed following case presentations.

Case History Report No. 1

A 36-year-old male was involved in a two-vehicle accident. The patient pulled off of a narrow two-lane road to allow an oncoming vehicle to pass and the vehicle overshot a curve in the road on wet pavement and impacted this patient's car head on. The patient was the driver of his vehicle and was restrained with both lap belt and shoulder harness. He experienced what he terms "a questionable loss of consciousness," and is unable to recall the events surrounding impact. Using advanced trauma life support protocol, the patient was transported by way of EMS to a local hospital.

Upon arrival in the emergency department the patient was examined and a CT scan and X rays of the patient's cervical spine obtained. The patient was not admitted and was discharged with an analgesic. Prior to this motor vehicle accident (MVA), the patient was totally free of all symptoms and had no history of previous trauma.

The patient began to experience intensified pain symptoms involving his upper back, neck, head, and face, and also experienced functional jaw joint pain. Seventeen months elapsed from the time of the accident until the patient actively sought medical attention for pain and memory deficit. Neurology and oral and maxillofacial surgery workups were consistent for MTBI secondary to concussion, a bilateral dislocation of the articular disk in the TMJ, and bilateral orofacial pain secondary to facial myospasm, and the patient had symptoms consistent with significant soft tissue injury sustained in a cervical acceleration/deceleration event.

Prior to this MVA, the patient was gainfully employed as a department manager in a retail firm, and subsequently was unable to maintain that job, because of a loss of short-term memory and inability to cope with the day-to-day stress requirements. Following the accident, he also experienced difficulty maintaining interpersonal relationships, which has progressed to the present time.

Long-term prognosis for this individual is guarded, in part, as a result of the time delay from the event of the accident to correct diagnosis and implementation of treatment.

Case History Report No. 2

This case involved a 39-year-old male who was involved in a two car MVA. The patient was at a complete stop in his vehicle. Directly behind him was another vehicle that was at a complete stop. The third vehicle back approached between 30 and 40 mph, rear-ending the second vehicle, which subsequently rear-ended the patient's vehicle. The patient was a driver in the front seat and was restrained using a seat belt and shoulder harness. The patient was dazed at the time following impact, but denies absolute loss of consciousness. The patient experienced extreme pain at the conjunction of his neck and base of the skull after impact.

The patient was not transported to a hospital at the time of the accident. Four days following the accident, the patient was seen at an urgent care center, and an X ray of the C-spine was apparently done at that time. The patient was placed in a cervical collar and prescribed analgesics. The patient was not admitted and was discharged from this center with a diagnosis of "whiplash and a brain bruise." The patient was asymptomatic prior to this MVA and had no history of previous trauma.

Approximately 6 months later, the patient sought treatment at a pain treatment center, because of neck pain, headache, facial pain, and memory impairment. Certain aspects of the patient's pain spectrum were initially approached, and, 21 months after the MVA, the patient was diagnosed with posttraumatic behaviorial changes.

This patient was referred to me 2¹/₂ years following the MVA. Following evaluation, the patient was diagnosed with a displacement of the articular disk and the TMJs bilaterally, orofacial pain secondary to myospasm, cervical pain and concomitant greater occipital neuralgia secondary to cervical acceleration/deceleration injury, and short-term memory loss and concentration deficits secondary to MTBI.

The prognosis for this patient is guarded, because of a delayed diagnosis and implementation of treatment. An early, coordinated, multidisciplinary approach to the diagnosis and treatment of this patient would have been extremely helpful.

Case History Report No. 3

This 51-year-old male patient was involved in an MVA, at which time the patient was slowing to approximately 25 mph in order to make a left turn, and was rear-ended, with the other vehicle traveling at approximately 55 mph.

The patient was the driver of his vehicle and was restrained with both seat belt and shoulder harness. At impact, his seat broke. The patient was dazed at impact and was unable to recall what areas of his head, neck, and upper body he may have hit.

The patient was totally asymptomatic prior to this accident. He had been involved in two previous episodes of trauma, which were minor in nature, and neither resulted in hospital evaluation nor symptomatology.

The patient was transported to a county hospital by private car, after giving a police report. After arriving in the emergency department, he was examined and X rays were taken of his shoulder and cervical spine. He was not admitted and does not recall a discharge diagnosis.

The patient was referred in the same year to a chiropractor, general dentist, and orthopedic surgeon, as well as to a physical therapist. Partial symptomatic relief was obtained, but the patient continued to suffer from headaches and functional jaw pain. The patient experienced short-term memory loss, as well as an inability to concentrate and systematically carry out day-to-day function.

Approximately $2^{1}/_{2}$ years later, the TMJ dysfunction and jaw pain was addressed by means of referral. History, imaging studies, and clinic examination were consistent with TMJ dysfunction, in conjunction with joint capsulitis, orofacial pain secondary to myospasm and temporalis tendonitis, cervicogenic headache with secondary occipital neuralgia secondary to a cervical acceleration/deceleration soft tissue injury, and mental impairment secondary to an MTBI.

The prognosis for this patient is guarded, for a variety of reasons. Initially, the patient's significant complaints were addressed; however, a comprehensive multidisciplinary evaluation of this patient was not accomplished in a timely fashion. The chronic pain aspect of this patient's clinical course contributed to mental deterioration and depression. These matters further complicated the patient's existing stress problems secondary to pain, thus making a favorable prognosis more obscure.

Case History Report No. 4

This 48-year-old male was involved in a two-car MVA, in which the patient experienced a front-end collision. The patient was the driver of his vehicle and was restrained using seat belt and shoulder harness. Subsequent to impact, the patient experienced some loss of consciousness for a short period of time, but he is unsure of the exact length of time.

The patient was totally asymptomatic prior to this event and had no previous history of trauma. The patient was transported to a local city hospital by private automobile. Upon arrival in the emergency department, X rays were taken of his head, arm, back, and left knee. He was given a pain shot and a tetanus shot. He was not admitted, nor was he given a discharge diagnosis prior to release.

Shortly after this accident, the patient was referred for comprehensive pain management, to include a pain management center, neurosurgical consultation, neurology consultation, oral and maxillofacial surgery consultation, neuropsychological evaluation, and consultation by physical rehabilitation medical specialist. Because of the astute timing of consultation, a comprehensive treatment plan was established, using a multidisciplinary approach, and the prognosis for this patient is good.

Case History Report 5

This 29-year-old female was involved in a MVA. She was stopped in traffic and was rear-ended at approximately 30–35 mph. The patient was the driver of her vehicle and was restrained with both lap belt and shoulder harness. The patient denies loss of consciousness at the time of the accident; however, she has very poor recollection of the incidents surrounding impact.

The patient was transported to a local hospital and evaluated in the emergency department. Minimal treatment was rendered and the patient's discharge diagnosis included cervical strain, muscle spasm, and whiplash. The patient was totally asymptomatic prior to this accident and denies any previous accidents or trauma to the face.

The patient was being treated, by her primary care physician, with a nonsteroidal anti-inflammatory medication and a muscle relaxant; however, the patient's pain continued to intensify, and the patient experienced depression and an inability to concentrate and interact with her family in a positive fashion. Her physician then referred her to a psychiatrist, who placed her on Zoloft. Minimal improvement was noted.

Twenty-five months after this accident, the patient was referred to my office for evaluation of headaches and jaw dysfunction. During the initial evaluation of this patient, she was obviously in significant distress and emotionally distraught, and during the course of history-taking became tearful on numerous occasions. Because of the time lapse from accident to presentation in my office, an aggressive, multidisciplinary treatment plan was enacted, which included comprehensive oral and maxillofacial surgery care, neurological consultation and intervention, physical therapy, referral to a pain clinic, and psychotherapy for stress and pain management.

Due to the delay in treating this patient initially, her long-term prognosis is extremely guarded. This case clearly demonstrates the need for early comprehensive multidisciplinary intervention.

Case History Report 6

This 40-year-old female was the driver of her vehicle and was restrained with both shoulder harness and seat belt. She was stopped at a stoplight and was hit from behind. The patient experienced an immediate loss of consciousness and is unable to relate a time frame. She was transported by EMS, using advanced trauma life support protocol, to a local hospital. A CT scan of the head was performed, and the patient was discharged. Following discharge, the patient began to experience extreme dizziness, speech impairment, and confusion. Vision impairment was present for the next few days. The patient was driven back to her home, which was approximately a 6-hour drive.

Fortunately, the patient was employed at a physical rehabilitation hospital and immediately sought consultation with one of the physical medicine rehabilitation physicians at that facility, when she arrived home. A comprehensive, multidisciplinary approach was taken to the diagnosis, treatment, and care of this patient. Neuropsychiatric evaluation revealed that the patient had, indeed, experienced a closed head injury at the time of the accident.

Diagnosis was consistent with TBI, status postcervical acceleration/deceleration injury, orofacial pain, and TMJ dysfunction.

This patient was totally asymptomatic prior to this MVA. She did have a history of what were termed "migraine headaches" in her early twenties, which occurred just prior to the onset of menstruation. Although the prognosis of this patient is guarded at the present time, early diagnosis and treatment certainly improved this patient's chances for a satisfactory recovery.

Case History Report 7

This 50-year-old female was involved in a three-car MVA. The patient was stopped at a stoplight, as was the car behind her. A third vehicle traveling at 40–45 mph rear-ended the car that was directly behind the patient's car, which subsequently impacted the rear-end portion of the patient's vehicle. The patient was the driver of her vehicle and was restrained with both shoulder harness and lap belt. The patient denies loss of consciousness, but was unable to recall the exact events surrounding the accident. Patient refused transportation to the hospital; however, the following day she requested that her husband take her to the emergency department of a local hospital, because of incapacitating head, neck, and back pain. Upon arrival at the emergency department, the patient was examined and cervical spine and back X rays were obtained, with no significant findings. The patient was discharged and told to follow-up with her primary care physician.

The patient chose to follow-up with the physician at her place of employment, since she had not received any medical treatment prior to this accident. The physician subsequently referred this patient for physical therapy. Approximately 10–12 days following the accident, the patient developed vesicles in her left ear and began to experience left facial paralysis. The patient was diagnosed and treated for Bell's palsy, when, in reality, the patient probably had Ramsey–Hunt syndrome. At the same time, the patient started to experience depression, difficulty concentrating, and detachment from her immediate family. The patient received physical therapy, neurological consultation, ear, nose, and throat consultation, and psychiatric consultation, but failed to significantly improve.

The patient was totally asymptomatic prior to this accident and had never been treated by a medical practitioner other than for yearly OB/GYN visits.

The patient was referred for examination approximately $4^1/2$ years following the accident. At the time of initial examination, the patient expressed suicidal contemplation, was severely depressed and tearful, and was experiencing severe back, neck, and head pain. A pronounced facial asymmetry existed. Interdisciplinary consultation was obtained, and the patient began a long road to correction and management of her problems. It is interesting to note that the etiology of this patient's neck and head pain was not well defined until diagnostic trigger point injections were utilized for pain mapping.

Because of the time frame involved from accident to accurate diagnosis and initiation of therapy and treatment, this patient's prognosis is extremely guarded.

Case History Report 8

This case involves a 41-year-old female patient who was referred for evaluation of neck injury and headaches. The patient was involved in a MVA, which occurred approximately 2 years earlier. The patient was involved in a head-on collision at a speed of approximately 40 mph. The patient was the driver of her vehicle and was restrained with both seat belt and shoulder harness. The car was equipped with airbags, which failed to deploy. Although the patient did not lose consciousness, she felt dazed following impact. The patient experienced pain immediately after the accident, but she elected not to seek medical attention at that time. Approximately 2–3 weeks subsequent to the accident, the patient was seen in an immediate care walk-in facility and was placed on muscle relaxants and a nonsteroidal anti-inflammatory agent. A referral was made to an orthopedic surgeon, who recommended physical therapy. The patient was also referred to a neurosurgeon and neurologist, with negative findings. The patient continued with severe headaches, and neck and back pain. The patient progressively became aware of an inability to concentrate, interruption of sleep patterns, and progressive intensity of pain.

Prior to this accident, the patient had been involved in two minor automobile accidents, with no injuries sustained and no medical treatment sought. The patient was totally asymptomatic prior to this accident. This patient was diagnosed with a disk displacement, orofacial pain, cervical headache, and medical manifestation secondary to chronic pain consistent with depression and interruption of sleep patterns.

An interdisciplinary approach to diagnosis treatment and management of this patient has been initiated, with a fair prognosis anticipated.

Observations

Emergency department physicians and staff tend to be oriented toward life-threatening and serious injury. In many instances, the patients represented in these case reports presented to an emergency department with relatively minor injuries, with the exception of pain. Another disturbing fact is that many related a questionable loss of consciousness, or a frank loss of consciousness, and were subsequently discharged from the hospital. Individuals with more serious injuries, who were admitted to the hospital subsequent to evaluation in the emergency department, received more immediate interdisciplinary comprehensive care. Many of the individuals who were discharged following an evaluation became lost in a medical system not trained specifically in diagnostic and treatment of MTBI, cervical acceleration/deceleration soft tissue injuries, orofacial pain, and TMJ dysfunction.

The delay of onset of treatment, in many cases, is responsible for development of chronic pain, which subsequently leads to secondary medical manifestations, which include depression, increased pain, parafunctional, oral habits, and sleep disturbance.

Another problem facing these individuals is the diagnostic acumen of various practitioners treating patients. The fact that many practitioners hold similar degrees and similar training does not, in reality, translate into equal diagnostic and treatment skills. It is essential for both the legal and medical communities to be aware of practitioners who excel in various areas, which are essential to ensuring these patients a long-term favorable prognosis.

As can be seen from the data above, there is a direct correlation between TMJ disorder and/or orofacial pain and whiplash-type neck injuries and/or mild-to-moderate TBI in frontal or rear-end collisions. For this reason, the evaluator, treating health care practitioner, or legal representative should be aware of the symptomotology of TMJ disorders and/or orofacial pain disorders and should assist the individual who suffers these disorders in obtaining competent treatment for these medical problems, so that the individuals involved do not progress to severe and debilitating psychological disorders, such as depression and/or chronic pain disorder.

How Do You Identify Patients and/or Clients with TMJ Disorders and/or Orofacial Pain Disorders?

Temporomandibular joint disorders and/or orofacial pain disorders are frequently overlooked, not detected, or misdiagnosed immediately following injury. Exceptions would include instances in which the presence of facial fractures would direct the clinician to pursue further examination, both clinically and radiographically, of the TMJ areas. Detection of TMJ dysfunction and/or orofacial pain is a simple matter to diagnose and can be tentatively diagnosed by any medical or legal professional. Obviously, a definitive diagnosis must be made by an oral and maxillofacial surgeon, dental practitioner, or other health care professional, specifically trained in diagnosis and treatment of these problems. The untrained medical provider or legal provider should utilize the quick checklist provided below.

The more common symptoms, which are regularly seen with people suffering from TMJ dysfunction and/or orofacial pain disorders, are well documented in the literature and are as follows (Magnusson, Egermark, & Carlsson, 2000; Nassif & Talic, 2001):

1. Sore teeth
2. Teeth that are sensitive to hot and cold
3. Headaches upon awakening in the morning
4. Headaches in the temporal areas
5. Migraine-type headaches
6. Awareness of tooth clenching and grinding
7. Clicking or popping in the jaw joints during movement
8. Inability to fully open one's mouth
9. Jaw pain
10. Pain in the area of the eye sockets
11. Pain when chewing or eating
12. Locking of the lower jaw in either an open or closed position
13. Nonspecific, poorly localized facial pain
14. Earache

This list, obviously, is not exhaustive. If your client/patient is suffering one or more of these symptoms, referral to an appropriate health care provider, well trained in diagnosis and treatment of TMJ disorders, orofacial pain and trauma, is certainly warranted.

A correct and accurate diagnosis is paramount to the success of any proposed treatment (National Institutes of Health, 1996; Ong & Keng, 2001). Evaluation begins by obtaining a well-defined chief complaint, as stated in the patient's own words. A detailed, thoughtful history and comprehensive clinical examination follow this. Adjunctive diagnostic measures are at the clinician's disposal, in order to achieve and confirm the proper diagnosis.

Imaging studies represent an example of such. During initial evaluation, a panoramic X ray should be utilized as a screening tool and should be taken in both open- and closed-mouth positions. The Panorex is a cost-effective study, which, although not diagnostic for more subtle joint pathologies, is an excellent screening device to rule out pain from other etiology, such as dental pathology, cyst or neoplasm involving the upper jaw, lower jaw, and maxillary sinuses.

The use of motion X rays is a new imaging technique that has been employed extensively by the authors. The images are fluoroscopic in nature and provide a dynamic evaluation of both joints, as well as cervical spine, throughout full range of motion. From the standpoint of the TMJs, irregular movements and asymmetric movements are easily observed. Bone abnormalities are visible, as well.

Computerized axial tomography (CAT scanning) and magnetic resonance imaging (MRI) became available for use in the 1980s and are widely used today for examination of both cervical spine and TMJ disorders. CAT scans are the diagnostic tools of choice for examination of bone; MRI studies are traditionally used more for examination of soft tissue structures. Through the use of MRI, the position of the disk in the TMJ, for instance, can be determined in both open- and closed-mouth views and a determination made as to the presence of adhesions and effusions. A variation of the MRI, fast low-angle shot sequencing (FLASH technique), offers a moving image of the disk and condyle structure within the TMJ, providing the clinicians with a dynamic study (Conway & Hayes, 1988).

A new radiographic technique utilizing CAT scan technology is Orthocubic super-high-resolution computed tomography (CT). This technique provides images similar to conventional CT but is less expensive; the instrumentation requires less space and provides the patient with a lower dose of radiation. MRI can also be modified to incorporate individualized oblique/axial scanning planes, which provide a better representation of the relationship of the disks and condyle in both anterior and medial and lateral configurations (Chen et al., 2000).

The source of cervical and facial pain is often difficult to pinpoint. A topically applied surface coolant can be used to identify areas of underlying pain source secondary to muscle spasm. Trigger point injections achieve the same goal, however, with considerably more precision. Diagnostic injections are warranted during an initial evaluation, to determine whether pain originates from myofascial sources, joint sources, or other craniofacial pain syndromes (Jaeger, 1999).

As earlier stated, once TMJ dysfunction and/or an orofacial pain disorder is suspected, prompt referral to an oral and maxillofacial surgeon or other practitioner, well trained in diagnosis and treatment of these entities, is highly recommended. The clinician should then perform an extensive physical evaluation of the patient. Carson has developed an extensive evaluation form, which is attached to this chapter as Exhibit A. This form can obviously be modified to satisfy the particular practitioner's needs and desires. Utilization of this or similar format will assure that a complete and thorough evaluation is performed.

What, Generally, Is the Course of Treatment for Persons with TMJ Disorders and/or Orofacial Pain?

As stated earlier, it is imperative that a person with TMJ disorders and/or orofacial pain disorders receives immediate treatment by a trained professional well versed in these entities. These injuries frequently cause excruciating pain, as well as compromised function. Intricate patterns of referred pain are frequently encountered, which presents the clinician with a diagnostic challenge. Pain originating from TMJ dysfunction and/or orofacial pain is a totally separate entity from pain originating from whiplash-type injuries, however, both are intimately related. Pain originating in one area can cause muscle-guarding, not only in the adjacent areas, but also in distant areas, enhancing the overall perception of pain. As pain increases, protective muscle-guarding increases, and the problem becomes self-perpetuating, if the pain cycle is not broken early on. Because of the intimate relationship of these various elements, it is not at all uncommon for patients suffering from orofacial pain disorders and TMJ dysfunction to experience debilitating headaches, neck pain, shoulder pain, and the like. If this pain goes untreated, a vicious pain cycle is established, which can ultimately devastate the patient's physical and mental health and well-being. It is not uncommon for patients to experience sleep disorders, severe depression, become socially isolated, experience family turmoil and divorce, and either contemplate or commit suicide (Cote, Cassidy, & Carroll, 2000; Ettlin et al., 1992; Riley et al., 2001).

Once a comprehensive evaluation is completed and a firm diagnosis established, confirming TMJ disorders and/or orofacial pain, the problem should be initially managed as conservatively as possible. It cannot be emphasized enough that the potential for successful patient management is dependent upon an accurate clinical diagnosis. For this reason, diagnosis and treatment should only be undertaken by experienced practitioners.

A myriad of alternatives is available for conservative management of these problems. Conservative treatment may consist of one or more of the following (Gessel, 1979; Moore & Hersh, 2001; Rocabado & Iglarsh, 1991).

1. Medications, to include nonsteroidal antiinflammatory medication, hypnotics, antidepressants, analgesics, and/or muscle relaxants
2. Splint therapy, which consists of a removable plastic overlay applied to teeth in either the upper or lower arch, which prevents full contracture of jaw muscles and alleviates direct pressure on the TMJ
3. Physical therapy for both soft tissue injuries and internal derangements of the TMJ
4. Therapeutic trigger point injections, using conventional regimens of local anesthetics and corticosteroids
5. Biofeedback training for stress management
6. Diet modification

A multidisciplinary approach is strongly recommended for patients with mild-to-moderate TBI, cervical spine involvement, and other chronic pain disorders. Consultation and referral to neurologists, pain management specialists, physical rehabilitation medical specialists, behavioral medicine specialists, and orthopedic and/or neurosurgeons may be warranted. A neuropsychologist should be consulted for patients suspected of sustaining closed head injury resulting in mild-to-moderate brain injury (Ong & Keng, 2001).

A multidisciplinary, comprehensive treatment plan should be formulated and coordinated among various clinicians. This is essential in order to prevent redundancy of prescription of medication and/or treatment regimen. Persons with long-standing pain and discomfort should be carefully monitored for symptoms of depression and/or suicidal tendencies, and a prompt referral to a psychologist or psychiatrist made without delay.

Unfortunately, in many instances, conservative treatment fails to resolve the pain associated with soft tissue injury or joint injury. Severe and persistent pain can result from development of occipital neuralgia and/or temporalis tendonitis, resulting in migraine-type headache. Areas of focal hyperirritability can occur in muscle tissue, giving rise to referred pain and tenderness. These areas are referred to as trigger points and are frequently treated by injection and physical therapy. Trigger points may cause radiation of pain into the head, neck, shoulder, and areas of the spine. When this occurs, more aggressive treatment is indicated.

When considering treatment for joint dysfunction, once again, a conservative approach cannot be stressed enough. At this point, we should briefly discuss how joint injury occurs and why various treatment modalities are chosen for certain diagnostic entities. Joint trauma can occur in the form of macrotrauma or microtrauma. In the event of macrotrauma, there is usually a direct blow sustained to the face or lower jaw, or the lower jaw impacts an object in the vehicle, such as the steering wheel, dashboard, or even an airbag. In this instance, the top portion of the lower jaw (condyle) is forced superiorly and posteriorly into the joint space, compressing the disk and ligament structure contained within the capsule surrounding the TMJ. Because of a rich blood supply and nerve supply, hemorrhage into the joint capsule and severe joint pain are not uncommon findings. As the area resolves and heals, scar tissue often forms within the joint, causing adhesions, which may impair the proper movement of the disk and ligaments, leading to disk displacement. At other times, the forces generated may be sufficient to actually tear the ligament or disk inside the joint capsule.

Microtrauma, on the other hand, results from compression of the disk and ligament structure in the joint or compression of the synovial lining of the joint, which results in the release of inflammatory and pain mediators. These can result in pain not only in the joint, but also in the surrounding capsule, resulting in capsulitis (Alstergren et al., 1998; Kopp, 2001).

The initial treatment of choice would be an athrocentesis, whereby a needle is inserted into the joint space and the joint flushed with solution, to decrease the presence of inflammatory agents. Often, this results in significant relief, but, if the etiology remains, one must pursue a greater degree of intervention (Nitzan et al., 1997).

Arthroscopy (Holmlund & Hellsing, 1985; Israel et al., 1999; Montgomery & VanSickels, 1991) is a minimally invasive surgical procedure, whereby a small scope is introduced into the joint space. This gives the clinician an opportunity to directly observe any abnormalities that may be present internally within the joint capsule. Blunt instrumentation can also be used to release any adhesions, thus allowing the disk to return to its normal position. Postoperative physical therapy and splint therapy are mandatory. Should it become evident that internal damage is beyond that which can be repaired using an arthoscopic technique, open joint surgery is then indicated. The joint is entered through an incision usually made in front of the ear. This technique is reserved for instances in which significant ligament or disk perforations are observed, pathologic bone abnormalities or irregularities are observed, and/or additional pathology is present within the joint, necessitating greater access. Once again, following open joint surgery, physical therapy and splint therapy are indicated, often for an indefinite period of time.

There are times when soft tissue injury persists and conservative intervention fails to improve the patient's clinical course. One of the main areas of pain etiology involves the temporalis tendon. The temporalis muscle is positioned along the side of the head; the fibers of that muscle converge in front of the ear and form a tendon, which inserts onto a projection of the lower jaw, called the coronoid process. If a significant amount of orofacial pain can be eliminated, as demonstrated by trigger point injections to the temporalis tendon areas, a procedure called *coronoidectomy* is indicated. In this instance, an incision is made inside the mouth, on both sides, in front of the lower jaw, and the temporalis tendon released from the coronoid process. The coronoid process is then reduced surgically and the incisions closed. Carson has refined and extensively utilized cornoidectomy surgery, often utilized in conjunction with arthocentesis or arthroscopic joint surgery. This allows for relaxation of the temporalis muscle and releases pressure from the tendon. As a result, a significant amount of migraine-type pain and headache is alleviated. In many instances in which patients are reporting subjective pain levels of 9 or 10 on a scale of 0 to 10, with 10 being the greatest, the clinician will observe a postoperative subjective range of pain of 0 to 2. As with other modes of surgical intervention, physical therapy and splint therapy are indicated postoperatively.

Successful surgical outcomes often require prolonged physical therapy, additional trigger point injection therapy, and prolonged splint therapy for an indefinite period of time, each case being unique (Rocabado, 1989).

CONCLUSION

When you evaluate, treat, or represent a person, particularly a female, who has been involved in a rear-end or front-end collision, and who complains of long-term neck, shoulder, and head pain, and a mild-to-moderate TBI, you must consider the strong likelihood that person may be suffering from a TMJ disorder and/or orofacial pain disorder. Unlike permanent neck injury resulting from ligamentous injury, oftentimes the TMJ disorder or orofacial pain disorder can be successfully treated, and one source of direct and/or referred pain can be eliminated. Consequently, we have found that, by utilizing procedures to reduce the orofacial pain and TMJ disorders, the patient suffers significantly less pain, and there is a concurrent reduction in the need for medication, a reduction in depression, and a reduction in chronic pain symptomotology and its sequelae. This, of course, leads to a more fruitful and pain-free life for the patient and/or client.

EXHIBIT A

DR. JOHN M. CARSON   Head & Neck Exam
Oral & Maxillofacial Surgeon
Forensic Consultant

NAME: **DATE:**

SESSION VIDEOTAPED:

PERSONS ACCOMPANYING PATIENT:

SUBJECTIVE:

  CHIEF COMPLAINT:

  MEDICAL HISTORY:

    GENERAL COMMENTS:

    PAST MEDICAL HISTORY:

      SURGERIES:

      ILLNESSES:

      MEDICATIONS:

      ALLERGIES:

      TRANSFUSION:

  DENTAL HISTORY: THE PATIENT GAVE A POSITIVE RESPONSE TO THE FOLLOWING:

  TRAUMA HISTORY:

    GENERAL COMMENTS:

    ACCIDENT INFORMATION:

      DESCRIPTION:

      SPEED OF IMPACT:

PATIENT INFORMATION:

VEHICLES INVOLVED:

ACCIDENT REPORT:

HOSPITAL INFORMATION:

PREVIOUS TRAUMA:

PAIN HISTORY:

BRIEF OVERVIEW:

PREVIOUS TREATMENT: (PRACTITIONER & TREATMENT)

EXACERBATING FACTORS: THE PATIENT GAVE A POSITIVE RESPONSE TO THE FOLLOWING:

MITIGATING FACTORS: THE PATIENT GAVE A POSITIVE RESPONSE TO THE FOLLOWING:

THE FOLLOWING QUESTIONS REQUIRE A NUMERICAL RESPONSE FROM 0 to 10. 0 IS MINIMAL AND 10 MAXIMUM.

NOW: /10

MINIMUM IN THE LAST MONTH: /10

MAXIMUM IN THE LAST MONTH: /10

PAIN-FREE DAYS IN THE LAST MONTH:

HOW MANY DAYS OUT OF 7 W/ A.M. HEADACHES?   /7

HOURS OF SLEEP AT NIGHT:

HOW MANY TIMES DO YOU WAKE UP AT NIGHT?

IF YOU AWAKEN AT NIGHT, HOW MUCH PAIN ARE YOU IN?   /10

HOW MUCH STRESS ARE YOU UNDER AT THIS TIME?   /10

HOW MUCH DO YOU ATTRIBUTE TO THE ACCIDENT?   /10

HOW MUCH DOES THE PAIN INTERFERE WITH YOUR ABILITY TO FUNCTION?   /10

HAS YOUR DIET CHANGED?

IF SO, WHAT ARE YOUR LIMITATIONS?

OBJECTIVE:

IMAGING STUDIES:

  PANOREX:

    MISSING TEETH: R ————————— / ————————— L
                                          /

    CARIOUS TEETH:

    PERIAPICAL LESIONS:

    MAXILLA:

      MALFORMATION:

      RADIOLUCENCIES:

      HORIZONTAL BONE LOSS:

      VERTICAL BONE LOSS:

      IMPLANTS OR BONE PLATES:

    MAXILLARY SINUSES:

      RIGHT:

      LEFT:

    MANDIBLE:

      MALFORMATION:

      RADIOLUCENCIES:

      HORIZONTAL BONE LOSS:

      VERTICAL BONE LOSS:

      IMPLANTS OR BONE PLATES:

    CORONOID PROCESSES:

    CONDYLES:

      CORTICAL PLATE:

      MEDULLARY CYSTS:

      DEGENERATIVE CHANGES:

    ARTICULAR EMINENCE:

      ARCHITECTURE:

      CONDENSING OSTEITIS:

      DEGENERATIVE CHANGES:

    ANTEGONIAL NOTCHING:

RIGHT: /10

LEFT: /10

APPARENT SKELETAL ABNORMALITIES:

VERTICAL ASYMMETRY:

LATERAL ASYMMETRY:

ALVEOLAR DEFICIENCY:

TMJ FILMS:

FOSSAE:

EMINENCE:

CONDYLES:

END OF TRANSLATION:

MOTION VIDEO IMAGING:

MRI IMAGING:

CAT SCAN IMAGING:

JOINTS AND MUSCULATURE:

PRESSURE DURING PALPATION IS MINIMAL UNLESS OTH-ER-

WISE INDICATED.

TMJS:

INTERINCISAL OPENING: MM. MEASURED WITH A BOLEY GAUGE.

OPENING DEVIATION: RIGHT: MM; LEFT: MM

PAIN TO PALPATION: R: /10; L: /10

OPENING CLICKS:

RIGHT: INTENSITY: /10

LEFT: INTENSITY: /10

RIGHT: PAIN: /10

LEFT: PAIN: /10

OPENING CREPITUS:

RIGHT: INTENSITY: /10

LEFT: INTENSITY: /10

RIGHT: PAIN: /10

LEFT: PAIN: /10

LATERAL EXCURSIONS:

TO PATIENT'S RIGHT:

MM:

PAIN: RIGHT: /10; LEFT: 10

JOINT NOISE: RIGHT: /10; LEFT: /10

TO PATIENT'S LEFT:

MM:

PAIN: RIGHT: /10; LEFT: /10

JOINT NOISE: RIGHT: /10; LEFT: /10

PROTRUSIVE:

MM:

DEVIATION: MM

PAIN: /10

JOINT NOISE:
RIGHT:

LEFT:

ROTATION:

RIGHT

LEFT:

TRANSLATION:

RIGHT:

LEFT:

EYES:

PUPILS:

SCLERA:

FUNDOSCOPIC:

EARS:

CANALS:

TEMPOROMANDIBULAR:

MUSCULATURE:

TEMPORALIS:

  ANTERIOR FIBERS: RIGHT: /10; LEFT: /10

  POSTERIOR FIBERS: RIGHT: /10; LEFT: /10

  TEMPORALIS TENDONS: RIGHT: /10; LEFT: /10

MASSETER:

  ORIGIN-FACIAL: RIGHT: /10; LEFT: /10

  INSERTION-FACIAL: RIGHT: /10; LEFT: /10

  ORIGIN-INTRAORAL: RIGHT: /10; LEFT: /10

  INSERTION-INTRAORAL: RIGHT: /10; LEFT: /10

STERNOCLEIDOMASTOID:

  ORIGIN: RIGHT: /10; LEFT: /10

  INSERTION: RIGHT: /10; LEFT: /10

TRAPEZIUS:

  RIGHT: /10

  LEFT: /10

POSTERIOR CERVICAL:

  RIGHT: /10

  LEFT: /10

OCCIPITAL NERVE AREA:

  RIGHT: /10

  LEFT: /10

HEAD RANGE OF MOTION:

  FLEXION:

  EXTENTION:

  RIGHT ROTATION:

  LEFT ROTATION:

NECK:

  ADENOPATHY:

  TRACHEA:

INTRAORAL AND SKELETAL:

  SOFT TISSUE:

TONGUE:

GINGIVA:

BUCCAL MUCOSA:

FLOOR OF THE MOUTH:

HARD AND SOFT PALATE:

PHARYNX:

UVULA:

OCCLUSION:

STABLE: UNSTABLE:

WEAR FACETS:

MX: /10

MD: /10

DENTAL MIDLINES:

MX:

MD:

MOLAR RELATIONSHIP: CLASS

CUSPID RELATIONSHIP: CLASS

CROSS BITES:

RIGHT:

LEFT:

SKELETAL RELATIONSHIP:

CLASS:

CHIN POINT:

CRANIAL NERVES:

TRIGGER POINT INJECTIONS:

MEDICATION USED:

AMOUNT INJECTED PER SITE:

INJECTION SITES:

RIGHT:

1.

2.

    3.

    4.

LEFT:

    1.

    2.

    3.

    4.

FLOURI-METHANE AREAS:

PATIENT DEMEANOR:

ASSESSMENT:

1.

2.

PLAN:

CONSERVATIVE TREATMENT:

    1.

    2.

SURGICAL TREATMENT:

RECOMMENDED REFERRALS:

ADDITIONAL RECORDS REVIEWED:

JOHN M. CARSON, DDS, DAAPM   DATE
ORAL & MAXILLOFACIAL SURGEON
DIPLOMATE, AMERICAN ACADEMY OF PAIN MANAGEMENT

NOTATION: MY CLINICAL FINDINGS AND OPINIONS ARE BASED ON AN EXTENSIVE HISTORY TAKEN FROM THE PATIENT, A CLINICAL EXAMINATION, ACADEMIC BACKGROUND, RESIDENCY TRAINING IN THE SPECIALTY OF ORAL AND MAXILLOFACIAL SURGERY, CERTIFI-CATION IN PAIN MANAGEMENT AND OVER 20 YEARS OF HANDS-ON CLINICAL PRACTICE. THE OPINIONS STATED ABOVE ARE SUBJECT TO CHANGE OR MODIFICATION, SHOULD ADDITIONAL RECORDS, CLINICAL DATA, OR OTHER INFORMATION BECOME AVAILABLE TO WARRANT SUCH A CHANGE.

REFERENCES

Alstergren, P., Emberg, M., et. al. (1998). Interleukin-1beta in synovial fluid from the arthritic temporomandibular joint and its relation to pain, mobility and anterior open bite. *Journal of Oral Maxillofac Surg, 56,* 1059–1065.

Chandler, R. F., & Christian, R. A. (2001). Crash testing of humans in automobile seats. SAE Study No. 700361.

Chen, Y., Gallo, L., Meier, D., et al. (2000). Individualized oblique-axial magnetic resonance imaging for improved visualization of mediolateral TMJ disc displacement. *Journal of Orofacial Pain, 14,* 128–139.

Conway, W., & Hayes, C. (1988). Dynamic magnetic resonance imaging of the temporo-mandibular joint using FLASH sequences. *Journal of Oral Maxillofac Surg, 46,* 930.

Cote, P., Cassidy, J. D., & Carroll, L. (2000). Is a lifetime history of neck injury in a traffic collision associated with prevalent neck pain, headache and depressive symptomatology? *Accid Anal Prev, 32,* 151–159.

Dao, T. T., & LeResche, L. (2000). Gender differences in pain. *Journal of Orofacial Pain, 14,* 169–184.

Ettlin, T. M., Kischka, U., Reichmann, S., et al. (1992). Cerebral symptoms after whiplash Injury of the neck: A prospective clinical and neuropsychological study of whiplash injury. *Journal of Neurol Neurosurg Psychiatry, 55,* 943–948.

Gessel, A. (1979). Electromyographic biofeedback and tricyclic antidepressants in myofacial pain dysfunction (MPD) unresponsive to conventional therapy. *Journal of Dent Res, 58,* 1435.

Gurdjian, E. S. (1976). Cerebral contusions: Re-evaluation of the mechanism of their development. *Journal of Trauma, 16,* 35–51.

Hatch, J. P., Rugh, J. D., Sakai, S., et al. (2001). Is use of exogenous estrogen associated with temporomandibular signs and symptoms? *Journal of American Dental Association, 132,* 319–326.

Holmlund, A., & Hellsing, G. (1985). Arthroscopy of the temporomandibular joint. *Int Journal Oral Surg, 14,* 169.

Israel, H. A., Diamond, B., et al. (1999). The relationship between parafunctional masticatory activity and arthroscopically diagnosed temporomandibular joint pathology. *Journal of Oral Maxillofac Surg, 57,* 1034–1039.

Jaeger, B. (1999). Overview of the head and neck region. In D. Simons, J. Travell, & L. Simons (Eds.), *Myofascial pain and dysfunction: The trigger point manual, Vol I* (2nd ed.). Baltimore: Williams & Wilkins, 239–243.

Johnson, G. (1996). Hyperextension soft tissue injuries of the cervical spine-a review. *Journal of Accid Emerg Med, 13,* 3–8.

Kaneoka, K., Ono, K., Inam, S., et al. (1999). Motion analysis of cervical vertebrae during whiplash loading. *Spine, 24,* 763–770.

Kopp, S. (2001). Neuroendocrine, immune and local responses related to temporomandibular disorders. *Journal of Orofacial Pain, 15,* 9–28.

Magnusson, T., Egermark, I., & Carlsson, G. E. (2000). A longitudinal epidemiological study of signs and symptoms of temporomandibular disorders from 15 to 35 years of age. *Journal of Orofacial Pain, 14,* 310–319.

Montgomery, M., & VanSickels, J. (1991). Success of temporomandibular joint arthroscopy in disk displacement with and without reduction. *Oral Surg Oral Med Oral Path, 71,* 651.

Moore, P. A., & Hersh, E. V. (2001). The role of COX-2 inhibitors in dental practice. *Journal of American Dental Association, 132,* 451–456.

Nassif, N. J., & Talic, Y. F. (2001). Classic symptoms in temporomandibular disorder patients: A comparative study. *Cranio, 19,* 33–41.

National Institutes of Health. (1996). *Management of Temporomandibular Disorders.* Technological Assessment Statement, 1–31. Bethesda, MD: NIH.

Nitzan, D. W., Samson, B., et al. (1997). Long-term outcome of arthrocentesis for sudden-onset, persistent, severe closed lock of the temporomandibular joint. *Journal Oral Maxillofac Surg, 55,* 151–157.

Ong, K. S., & Keng, S. B. (2001). Neuropathic pain of the orofacial region. *American Journal of Pain Management, 11,* 42–52.

Riley, J. R., Benson, M. B., Gremillion, H. A., et al. (2001). Sleep disturbance in orofacial pain patients: Pain-related or emotional distress? *Cranio, 19,* 106–113.

Rocabado, J. (1989). Physical therapy for the post-surgical patient. *Journal of Craniomandib Disord Fac Oral Pain, 3,* 75.

Rocabado, M., & Iglarsh, Z. (1991). *Musculoskeletal approach to maxillofacial pain.* Philadelphia: J. B. Lippincott.

Chapter 12

Neuropsychology in the Courtroom

Lawrence C. Hartlage

It has been estimated that, with the exception of divorce actions, one half of all civil cases in American courts are personal injury cases (Miller, 2001), and a significant proportion of these involve traumatic brain injury (Miller, 1993). Thus, it is likely that most neuropsychologists will see (or have seen) patients involved in litigation and will be (or have been) called to provide court testimony concerning presence/absence, severity, causation, or sequelae of brain injury.

Although the likelihood of a given case going to trial is small (estimated as involving less than 10% of cases filed), it is generally recognized that the best way to prevail without need for a trial is to be fully prepared for trial. This represents the basis for a caveat to keep in mind when agreeing to become involved in a case that may involve litigation: Perform each step as if you plan to defend it in court. Whether reviewing records involving the patient, designing and conducting an assessment procedure for assessing neuropsychological status, interpreting data, or reviewing scientific literature to provide a context for your data, consider how your activities may be presented on direct examination and defended on cross-examination. Any deviation from standard administration or interpretation of a test, for example, needs to be carefully considered, because there must be a clear and cogent reason for such deviation (e.g., sensory or motor impairment), which provides a clear rationale for both choosing to deviate from standard administration and, subsequently, for why the deviation does not affect the validity of findings.

Although, before testifying, you swear to "tell the truth, the whole truth," what you actually testify to in most court settings takes the form of responding to the specific questions posed to you by the attorney.

Since you have little impact on what questions you are asked (on cross-examination) by opposing counsel, the truth you believe is relevant must be presented or otherwise involved in response to questions posed by the attorney who retained or otherwise involved you. And, since you will know more about neuropsychology than the attorney, you can maximize the likelihood that the attorney will give you an opportunity to express relevant facts, by keeping the attorney aware concerning what is relevant from a neuropsychological perspective.

With background in science and the scientific method, and with experience in standardized examination procedures and objective assessment of brain function, neuropsychologists can make special and unique contributions to their patients, the judicial system, and to society, by providing testimony concerning their knowledge and expertise. In the courtroom, the neuropsychologist may find challenges to the scientific method and objective basis of given testimony, since the goal of opposing attorneys is mutually inimical, and what aids one side will be seen as harmful to the other. And, just as neuropsychologists in the role of teacher or mentor will question students or trainees concerning how or why they did certain examinations, or in what sequence, for purposes of ensuring that they consider their practices and learn from understanding their rationale, attorneys in the role of cross-examiners will publicly question neuropsychologists concerning the same matters, not to educate, but to cast doubt on conclusions, adequacy of data to reach conclusions, reasoning process between data and conclusions, or the neuropsychologist himself or herself. Ultimately, such cross-examination will very likely improve the neuropsychologist's awareness of subtle aspects of examination procedures, in terms of how they may be perceived or portrayed by someone intent on discrediting them: Unfortunately, such awareness may be gained at the expense of the patients or defendants involved, while this awareness is being acquired or honed. An example may help illustrate this point.

(Abbreviated from trial format)
Q. Doctor, did you conduct the examination on September 19?
A. Yes.
Q. You did it all in one day, is that correct?
A. Yes.
Q. Why did you do it all in 1 day?
A. The patient lived about 100 miles from my office, and I didn't think it fair to ask the patient to make more than one trip.

Q. How long did your examination take?

A. Just about 8 hours.

Q. And what time did you start?

A. 9:00 a.m.

Q. So, if the trip took 2 hours, in order for the patient to start examination at 9:00 a.m., he would have gotten up about 6:00 a.m., does that sound about right?

A. Yes.

Q. Now, Doctor, do some of the scores and some of your tests depend on speed or alertness?

A. Yes.

Q. Could extreme fatigue or exhaustion affect such tests?

A. Yes.

Q. So, if the patient got out of bed at 6:00 a.m., and drove 2 hours and took $7^1/_2$ hours of testing, can you state with reasonable neuropsychological certainty that he was as alert and would have performed at the same speed during the last half hour as he would have when he was fresh and rested and fully alert?

A. I don't know that I could say this without actually testing for it.

Q. Did you actually test for it?

A. Well, not specifically.

Q. So, your tests done in the last half hour may not be as valid as those in the first half hour?

A. Well, I suppose that's one way of looking at it.

Q. So, Doctor, what I hear you saying is that the validity of the testing you did—and any conclusions or diagnoses you may have based in any part on findings from the testing you did—varies according to the time of day you did your testing?

A. Well, I don't know that I would agree with that.

Q. Let's clarify this for the court. Doctor, can you state with reasonable neuropsychological certainty that the patient's speed or reaction time testing—which you previously stated as being measured in thousandths of a second, would be exactly the same at 5:00 p.m.— after 2 hours of driving and 8 hours of consecutive examination— having gotten up, incidentally, at 6:00 a.m.—would be exactly the same as if you had tested it when the patient was alert, rested, and at his best? Followed by an exhaustive pursuit of possible contamination of validity of fatigue at various intervals (e.g.) after $7^1/_2$ hours; after 7 hours. . . . Doctor, isn't it true that you did not determine at what point your data became invalid due to fatigue?

Now consider how the neuropsychologist's awareness of this potential morass could have been avoided. In response to the question, "Could extreme fatigue or exhaustion affect such tests?" the neuropsychologist who had carefully planned the examination could respond, "Yes, it possibly could and that is why, in examining the patient, I administered such tests (e.g., reaction time) while the patient was fresh, alert, and rested, and deferred tests (e.g., Minnesota Multiphasic Personality Inventory—Second Edition [MMPI-2]) not likely to be sensitive to fatigue or exhaustion until later in the day." Then, if cross-examination attorney pursues this line of inquiry with questions like, "So you deny that fatigue or exhaustion could have influenced your results?" the neuropsychologist could respond that research on the MMPI and MMPI-2 had indicated that fatigue or exhaustion is not likely to influence such factors as introversion/extraversion or masculinity/femininity, and that it is not likely that a person's total personality is going to change over the course of a single day, even if the person gets fatigued.

Thus, by practicing sound testing procedures, the neuropsychologist is prepared to defend such procedures at trial: Preparation for trial testimony needs to begin well before the time it is known whether there may even be trial testimony involved. A good way to anticipate possible challenges is to learn from experiences of other neuropsychologists who have testified: Access to such testimony and its lessons may be available from attorneys who have tried such cases and have transcripts, from books or articles on the topic, or from continuing education or workshops by neuropsychologists, who, in the course of their own court testimony, have made mistakes or otherwise learned some pitfalls to avoid.

NOTHING BEATS GOOD NEUROPSYCHOLOGICAL PRACTICE FOR COURTROOM TESTIMONY

Just like the rural maxim, "You can't make coconut cake out of horse droppings," it is not possible to base good court testimony on poor neuropsychological practice. If the neuropsychological examination was appropriate to the questions at issue; was based on assessment tools with demonstrated validity, reliability, and sensitivity to brain injury; and interpreted findings in a manner congruent with scientific practice, good court testimony can be based on it. The effectiveness of the testimony can be enhanced by the neuropsychologist's level of expertise and skill (or limited by same), but, in any case, must be based on sound and defensible neuropsychological practice.

An examination that is haphazard in conceptualization or context is eminently assailable, and is not acceptable as either a standard of practice or a fair representation to the court or society of what neuropsychology can contribute. Doing an examination with the same tests or approach used by a major professor or favored mentor, without being able to articulate clearly and with some particularity why each test was given, what it means or measures, and how it contributes to the diagnosis, is clearly not an acceptable standard of practice.

Further, technical issues, such as validity, reliability, and sensitivity to brain injury, are increasingly being raised, following *Daubert*. As Reitan (1994) has stated, "Unfortunately, the validity and reliability of many psychological tests are currently being decided by the courts." Specifically, as Reed (1996) has documented in *Chapple v. Ganger* (1994), the *Daubert* standard was applied for the very first time to the use of fixed (standardized) versus flexible (nonstandardized) batteries, with the U.S. Supreme Court giving far greater weight to results from a fixed than a flexible battery. The ruling accepted as scientific evidence the objective results obtained from the fixed Halstead–Reitan Neuropsychological Test Battery (HRNTB), but held that the entire reasoning process, and not simply part of the process upon which the neuropsychologist derives a conclusion, must reflect scientific methodology. What this in effect means is that a flexible battery user must prove the reliability, validity, and sensitivity to brain injury, not only for each test used, but the user must also demonstrate the validity, reliability, and sensitivity to brain injury, for the entire battery. Since, by definition, flexible batteries are not standardized, and thus typically not used and replicated and validated as a battery, this can pose problems in having data from them recognized as meeting scientific criteria: By contrast, a single score (e.g., Impairment Index, Deficit Scale) from the HRNTB has been ruled to be a scientific reasoning process that meets all these criteria.

Similarly, as *Daubert* criteria become more widely accepted by other courts, procedures based on normative corrections for age, education, and so on, extrapolated from the general population (i.e., not brain-injured), may be challenged for failure to meet criteria for sensitivity to brain injury. Since the courts are taking an active role in defining perimeters of neuropsychology practice, which they consider to meet scientific criteria according to guidelines under which they operate, it is important for neuropsychologists planning to testify in a given jurisdiction to be aware of what criteria for admissibility of evidence must be met, in order for their testimony to be admissible.

NEUROPSYCHOLOGIST AS EDUCATOR

Jurors do not represent a professionally trained body of experts maintained by the courts to evaluate evidence. Rather, they are drawn from the ranks of the general population and are assigned the task of producing judgments about complex phenomena, concerning which they typically have little, if any, prior expertise.

An important contribution that the neuropsychologist can make in the courtroom involves the education of the court in such matters as what neuropsychology is and how neuropsychology can provide information of relevance to judgments the jury must make. Just as a good teacher educates students by making complex matters understandable, so can the neuropsychologist help the jury put into perspective the concepts underlying neuropsychological assessment, the tools and procedures used, and the implications of findings for decisions the jury must make. It has been said that the best way to present forensic neuropsychological evidence is by means of testimony that does not sound like testimony, but more like education (Miller, 1997).

Presenting neuropsychological data in a seamless flow takes preparation, but can help jurors feel they are being guided along an intriguing path to knowledge. For this purpose, educational aids can help serve as guidelines along this path to knowledge. Displays of the brain or other visual aids may be helpful in some cases, and sometimes handouts containing illustrations or outlines of the main points may be appropriate. If you plan to use any such aids, they must be approved by the opposing attorney: They will likely be objected to if not preapproved before your testimony. Even though the aids planned for use in educating the jury may be commonly available items, such as a model or picture of the brain, opposing counsel may be counted on to move to suppress it as inadmissible, if it is not reviewed before you are allowed to refer to it.

An advantage of using such aids is that it becomes an exhibit available to jurors, on which they may rely in reaching a conclusion. Tactically, having such an aid available can help highlight a point you consider important or want to emphasize: Breaking the monotony of questions and answers, by leaving the witness box to point out something on a picture or model, can help with enhancing attention. For some jurors, one picture may be worth ten thousand words. Having available some form of visual aid or handout, summarizing the high points of your testimony, may provide a way to help overcome problems, such as having the jury (or some jurors) looking puzzled. Unlike your students or interns, who may be unclear about some part of your presentation, but whom you can help get into the mutually shared knowledge, with a jury, there typically is no preexisting shared knowledge on which you can rely. Accordingly, it is important to carefully build for the jury a relevant fund of information, into the context of which findings from the patient at issue can be placed into focus. Again, unlike with students or interns for whom you can provide illustrations, examples, or possibly sample cases, in the courtroom you can only answer questions. You must make certain the attorney questioning you provides you the opportunity you need to do so in a clear and comprehensive manner.

Although, before testifying, it is important to be thoroughly familiar with such phenomena as base rates, validity, and reliability issues, such matters are typically not likely to be very compelling to jurors. Some experienced neuropsychologists choose not to discuss such areas during direct examination, so that, if cross-examination addresses them, the jury can be bored by the focus of opposing counsel, while remembering the down-to-earth, practical presentation from the direct examination. Jurors, all being human beings living in a real world of relationships, can identify with the patient as a human being and can appreciate how the presence or absence of brain injury will or will not alter such relationships and interactions.

One challenge likely to face a neuropsychologist presenting courtroom testimony, concerning a patient with problems seen as psychiatric or psychological in nature, occurs when such problems represent manifestations of the neuropsychological injury. For more than one-half century, the scientific literature has documented that, following brain injury, patients may have difficulty bearing even small changes in environment or routine, or sustaining close relationships (Goldstein, 1952). Critical review of such behavioral patterns could conclude—or attempt to have the jury conclude—that these behavioral problems, rather than the brain injury at issue, were the patient's real problem:

Q.   Doctor, isn't it true that difficulty bearing even small changes in environment or routine could be characteristic of obsessive–compulsive disorder?

A.   Yes.
Q.   Now then, Doctor (waving current DSM), doesn't it state in the *Diagnostic and Statistical Manual* of the American Psychiatric Association that obsessive compulsive disorder is likely to be a chronic, long-term condition?
A.   Yes, that's true.
Q.   So, Doctor, isn't it true that you are alleging that this condition, which, by your own testimony, is a chronic condition, somehow began about the time this patient decided to seek money damages? Please answer yes or no.

Similarly, cross-examination could focus on difficulty sustaining close relationships as characteristic of a schizoid diagnosis, with the same line of questioning aimed at discrediting psychiatric manifestations of brain injury, and in turn using such psychiatric problems as putative evidence of no brain injury.

One approach toward helping clarify the relationships, if any, between behavioral problems reported following the possible brain injury and the injury itself, involves comparison of preinjury behaviors with postinjury behaviors. By having the patient and, as available, significant others, such as spouse, or parents, or coworkers familiar with the patient before and after the incident allegedly causing brain injury, provide information, it is possible to segregate preincident behavior from postincident behavior, to establish or rule out a temporal relationship (Hartlage, 1989, 1990). A further advantage of such an approach is that it helps identify specific areas of behavior change described as taking place following putative brain injury, to enable determination of whether the behavior changes reported are characteristic of those found resulting from brain injury of given etiology (Hartlage & Williams, 1991; Hartlage, Wilson, & Patch, 2001).

To place these findings concerning reported behavior changes in context, it is helpful to have as much information as possible concerning the patient's functioning in real-life settings. Effectiveness in interpersonal relationships or success in measurable job indices, such as sales volume or work productivity prior to and subsequent to the injury date at issue, can provide job-based indicators of whether, how, and to what extent a concussive episode has produced behavior strange. Global reports of ability to perform a job may be inflated among "higher-level" workers, who can delegate difficult tasks, compared to workers whose work demands for attention, concentration, and consistency are dictated by others (Williams & Hartlage, 1973).

It is not uncommon, following mild traumatic brain injury, for an individual to return to work for a period of weeks or even months, before it is apparent that they cannot meet job requests. Such individuals can often "coast," on the basis of job experience or help by coworkers, giving the impression of greater residual functional abilities than suggested by test data, so it is important, before testimony, to obtain up-to-date information concerning such matters. Since there is typically a considerable duration of time between neuropsychological examination and court testimony, this sort of follow-up, either via brief reexamination or other means, is important for accurate and relevant courtroom testimony.

PLAINTIFF VERSUS DEFENDANT ISSUES

Some writers have elaborated on the issue of possible bias in disproportionate courtroom testimony favoring claimants versus defendants, and many attorneys involved in litigation have labels like "prostitute" for individuals who consistently tend to interpret data in a way favoring one side or the other. Sweet and Moulthrap (1998) suggested self-administered procedures for debasing in adverse situations, and their paper is worth reading as an introduction to the topic. But, as is so frequently the case in forensic issues, exceptions to the Sweet and Moulthrap positions have been registered (Lees-Haley, 1999). The prevailing consensus suggests that a degree of balance between testimony supporting plaintiff or defendant issues is a desideratum. However, neuropsychologists may find referrals made by attorneys representing one or the other side to colleagues, based on the neuropsychologist's prior testimony in a case favoring that side. With attorneys viewing prior testimony helpful to plaintiff (or defense), as indicative that the neuropsychologist will hold views potentially helpful in other plaintiff (or defense) cases. Objectivity, impartiality, and even-handedness, critical and essential to neuropsychologists, may be viewed in less absolute terms by attorneys, with the result that a neuropsychologist can easily develop a reputation as a defense or plaintiff witness, based on prior testimony, and in turn develop a referral network from attorneys pursuing that particular orientation.

Indeed, attempts to be scrupulously fair and evenhanded can produce problems in the adversarial arena of the courtroom. When examining a patient for the defense, use of a highly sensitive approach, such as the HRNTB Neuropsychological Deficit Scale, to make certain the patient got an unequivocally fair opportunity to demonstrate any possible impairment, would be evenhanded, by ensuring that no legitimate impairment was overlooked. Conversely, use of a slightly less sensitive approach (e.g., the more conservative, limited HRNTB Impairment Index) for use with plaintiffs, to ensure that any legal action pursued by the patient would be based on robust data that would not require defense of spurious or questionable cases, could similarly represent an attempt to be fair and evenhanded. Yet the neuropsychologist's use of different assessment approaches, depending on whether retained by plaintiff or defense, could, in courtroom cross-examination, be made to appear biased, even when the choice of different approaches was made in an attempt to be scrupulously fair and evenhanded.

LEGAL ISSUES

Admissibility of scientific testimony in the form of neuropsychological data is typically not at issue. Since 1923, the *Frye* criteria (*Frye v. United States*, 1923) for scientific testimony have involved "the thing from which the deduction is made must be sufficiently established to have gained general acceptance in the particular field in which it belongs." Although some jurisdictions now use the *Daubert* criteria, to which reference has previously been made (i.e., Reed, 1996), *Frye* has been influential and is still operative in some jurisdictions. Thus, there is clearly sufficient general acceptance in the particular field to support neuropsychological testimony as established on scientific principles, that is, meeting *Frye* criteria.

Occasionally, challenges to neuropsychologists' competence to make certain conclusive statements may be challenged. These challenges are usually on very narrow grounds, but can be problematic in given cases. Some years ago, for example, a Georgia appeals court ruled that a neuropsychologist could not diagnosis brain injury: The court's reasoning was based on the fact that, although state medical licensing law permitted physicians to diagnose disease, psychology licensure permitted use of the title without specifying performance of diagnostic or treat activities. Subsequent legislative action amended the situation, but the case provides illustration of the sort of narrowly focused challenges that can be encountered. For the neuropsychologist interested in standards for expert witnesses, reference to Rule 703, "Bases of Opinion Testimony by Experts," will be instructive.

ADMINISTRATIVE HEARINGS

Although not so visible as trials, a venue wherein neuropsychologists are increasingly being involved in providing expert courtroom testimony is as expert witness called by an administrative law judge. Although no overall count is readily available, every applicant for disability benefits, under such programs as Social Security and Railroad Retirement, whose initial and following application for disability benefits had been declined, is entitled to a hearing before an administrative law judge, so there are many thousands of such hearings each year. Neuropsychologists can be certified as medical experts and may be called to specified hearings by the administrative law judge charged with reaching a decision concerning disability. As administrative law judges come to learn how neuropsychological testimony can assist them in reaching appropriate decisions, they will increasingly use neuropsychological testimony. For example, during a 10-year period, 1985–1995, for which I kept a rough count, my testimony had been requested by administrative law judges in more than 2,400 such cases.

Hearings in which neuropsychological expertise and testimony may be sought most frequently involve issues of disability under Social Security. Neuropsychologists are called specifically by the judge as a government expert witness, with fee paid by the government, to review data relevant to whether neuropsychological or related impairments are of severity sufficient to meet criteria for disability; and to provide impartial testimony concerning their opinions. Since the neuropsychologist has been specifically requested to provide testimony by the judge who will issue the decision (i.e., the neuropsychologist has qualifications and background already known to the judge), there is usually no objection to qualifications. Similarly, since all information relevant to the decision will have been made available to the neuropsychologist well before the hearing, there will be little challenge to the sorts of information considered by the neuropsychologist in formulating responses to questions posed by the judge. Further, given the status conferred by the judge in seeking expert testimony of the neuropsychologist, it is uncommon for there to be much in the way of challenges to the neuropsychologist's competency, creditability, or conclusions. Rather, questioning will more likely take the form of initial inquiry by the judge, with hypotheticals, for example, "If I should find that the report of Dr. X is accurate, and should further find that the opinion expressed by Dr. Y is credible, does claimant Z meet criteria for disability?" In order to respond appropriately, the neuropsychologist must know the criterion for disability on which the judge must rely. For example, disability under listing 12.02 (Neurological Disorder) may be established by demonstrating such neuropsychological findings as "Impairment Index . . . in severely impaired range on neuropsychological testing, e.g., LNNB [Luria–Nebraska Neurological Test Battery], Halstead–Reitan [or] Memory Impairment [or] Change in Personality [or] Emotional Liability and Impairment in Impulse Control."

Sciolistic presentations may suffice in the classroom or clinic; they will not survive even moderately knowledgeable cross-examiners' questioning. In the frequently raised issue of possible malingering, for example, an attempt to base credibility solely on "in my professional judgment" may succumb to cross-examination, in the following form:

Q. Doctor, if the patient is malingering, wouldn't that potentially affect validity of your findings?

A. Well, yes, but . . .

Q. Doctor, can you state with reasonable neuropsychological certainty that none of your test data were influenced by malingering?

A. Yes, I believe so.

Q. And on what scientific basis do you base this certainty?

A. Well, I spent several hours examining the patient, observing and interacting with the patient, and, with my 18 years of experience, I believe I'd know if he was malingering.

Q. Doctor, to what scientific tests has your ability to detect malingering been empirically subjected?

A. That's not the way it's usually done.

Q. So, Doctor, you are basing your entire testimony on something which has never been empirically tested for scientific validity, true or false?

A. Well, true, but . . .

Q. Doctor, are you aware of the seminal work of Meehl and his colleagues, proving actuarial prediction is more accurate than clinical judgment?

A. I remember reading something about that.

Q. But you chose to ignore this in favor of relying on your clinical judgment, true?

A. Well, yes . . .

Q. And isn't it true you've never proven your clinical judgment to be more effective than actuarial predictors in any referred study?

A. Well, yes.

Q. Doctor, are you aware of the studies showing approximately 50% ability of clinical judgment to detect malingering (e.g., Heaton, Smith, Lehman, & Vost, 1978)?

A. Yes.

Q. Isn't 50% exactly what you would get by guessing?

A. Yes.

Q. Isn't 50% exactly what you would get by flipping a coin?

A. Yes.

Thank you, Doctor.

An alternative response, going back to the question "On what scientific basis do you base this certainty," could mention profiles of test findings sensitive to malingering, but which did not indicate malingering; describe congruity among findings consistently implicating a given brain area of functional system; mention findings from scales like MMPI validity subscales or *F–K* ratios, VRIN, TRIN, *Fb*, *F(p)*, *S*; then conclude with observations made during testing, which suggested good effort and attempts to cooperate. For example, "On the _____ test, he became frustrated over inability to do it and tried to convince me he really could do it," or "When he was obviously unable to do the _____ required on the _____ test, he got broken up and we had to take a break because he was crying." When citing subtest profiles or configural patterns that suggest no malingering, be prepared to cite studies that support this position. Such information is likely to be more meaningful to the jury than recitation of statistics concerning dissimulation indices based on studies of college students.

CRIMINAL ISSUES

Psychology has been involved for many years in helping courts decide "sanity" issues (e.g., one of the first rulings qualifying psychologists as experts involved Dr. Kenneth E. Clark in *Robinsdale v. Warner Brothers* [1955], and *Jenkins v. United States* [1962] spelled out in counsel-like detail the psychologist as expert witness in matters of mental disease or defect), but, in criminal cases, there has been a growing tendency to involve neuropsychologists in peripheral aspects of this issue. The issues of sanity, ability to understand right from wrong, and participation in one's own defense have addressed the main issue of guilt versus some variant of not guilty by reason of insanity. Psychologists and neuropsychologists continue to provide meaningful assistance in resolving such matters, but the role of neuropsychologists is expanding to address the subordinate issue of possible mitigating circumstances.

In the case of an individual convicted of a crime of passion resulting in murder, neuropsychological testimony may be sought concerning whether an earlier brain injury (or substance abuse, or other phenomenon that could diminish central nervous system function) might have impaired the individual's judgment or impulse control to the extent that sentencing could be ameliorated to take such extenuating circumstances into account. Above-average incidence of central nervous system insult from substance abuse, fights, automobile accidents, resisting arrest, and similar precipitants among a criminal population, has been noted for many years (e.g., Lewis, Pincus, Feldman, Jackson, & Bard, 1986; Mednick & Christianson, 1977; Pontius, 1972; Templer, Spencer, & Hartlage, 1991; Weller, 1986).

Indeed, reports of electroencephalogram (EEG) abnormalities among violent criminals have appeared since the early 1940s (e.g., Hill & Sargant, 1943), and the association between violent crime and EEG abnormalities, with or without epilepsy, has been studied ever since Lewis, Pincus, Shanok, and Glaser (1982) reported a clear relation between degree of violence and EEG abnormality; a review of the work relating EEG abnormalities with crime and violence, up to 1980 (Mednick & Volavka, 1980), provided compelling, if not consistent, documentation of such a relationship. Typical EEG abnormality noted involved slowing within the alpha frequency range (8–13 H2), although there was a wide range of types and loci of abnormality noted.

The rule of neuropsychologists in courtroom testimony has been, and will likely continue to be, sought to a greater extent, for helping the court determine the extent, if any, that possible brain dysfunction ought to be considered in determining severity of punishment. Especially likely to be involved is testimony concerning "the frontal lobe personality" classical constellation (Blumer & Benson, 1975).

Since the courts have great interest in probability, it is important for the neuropsychologist to understand the approximate probability involved in court language. In criminal cases involving matters of guilt or innocence, the standard required to convict "beyond a reasonable doubt" is around 90% or better. However, "reasonable neuropsychological certainty" involves merely the weight of evidence that translates to any probability greater than chance (i.e., 50.01% or better). In matters of terminology, be prepared for cross-examination questions like "Now, Doctor, you previously stated . . . ," followed by a barely describable shift in what you actually stated, to something slightly more favorable to the opposing counsel. In like manner, be prepared for similar misphrasing of statements you made in deposition (i.e., review your deposition to the point you will recognize such alterations of.your deposition testimony, before taking the witness stand).

CONCLUSION

There are many thousands of attorneys representing opposing sides, and each attorney will have a unique style, modus operandi, and store of legal knowledge, and bag of courtroom tricks. You, as a scientifically trained expert in brain behavior relationships, possess a fund of information and knowledge that can help the court better understand some aspects of the question that the court must decide. The extent to which you serve this function depends on both your knowledge and your ability to communicate this knowledge to the court. This chapter mentions a few of the considerations potentially involved in such communications. I would summarize with a brief reprint abbreviating neuropsychology legal testimony from A to Z (Hartlage, 1993).

NEUROPSYCHOLOGY LEGAL TESTIMONY FROM A TO Z

Psychologists' involvement in legal proceedings, either voluntarily or under subpoena, is increasing. Especially in situations involving accidental head injury in which damages are contingent on extent (if any) of loss, neuropsychologists may be requested/required to provide sworn testimony. Since legal requirements involve different concepts than those used by psychologists, the translation of psychological/neuropsychological data into testimony applicable to satisfying legal criteria can be difficult for the psychologist who is not knowledgeable about legal requirements. Forensic work involves specialized skills and knowledge, and, in general, your contributions to a given patient or case will probably be maximized by either seeking consultation or coinvolvement with a colleague sophisticated about and experienced in forensic aspects of neuropsychology. This not only protects the patient's best interest, but may help avoid possible ethical dilemmas (e.g., American Psychological Association Principles 1, 2, 7).

In some cases you may find yourself with no choice, as occurs when you are issued a subpoena for appearance and testimony, either at deposition or trial. The following guides, although covering such situations from A to Z, are not by any means definitive. They are offered as a mnemonic aid for helping keep in mind some caveats that can be helpful.

- **Appearance counts.** Shined shoes, conservatively "dressy" attire can help identify you as a responsible professional.
- **Beware** opposing counsel's summarization of your testimony, to slant it slightly away from your exact testimony.
- **Clarify** your possible areas of testimony with the attorney who issued the subpoena, to be certain you know every topic on which you might be expected to testify.
- **Don't** get angry under questioning, or demonstrate hostility, even when opposing counsel badgers and harasses you.
- **Early** understanding with the attorney, concerning your exact role in diagnosis, treatment, or testimony, can avoid problems.
- **Full** access to all relevant records should be demanded, to help give you a complete picture of the patient's history.
- **Good** preparation of your testimony ahead of time can be a way to help you be relaxed at trial.
- **Happy** is the expert who never testifies to anything that he or she cannot defend against hostile cross-examination.
- **Income** from your practice, or from selected aspects of your practice, can be a question addressed to you at trial.
- **Justice** is not your job. Your job is to answer questions accurately, completely, and truthfully, without elaboration.
- **Killing** time talking to their witnesses is a no-no, and can result in mistrial.
- **Legal** concepts are different from psychological concepts. Be very careful when attempting to translate psychological data into the terminology of attorneys.
- **Money** matters, such as the basis of your charge (flat fee for appearance versus hourly fee; if hourly fee, do you charge for court time, portal-to-portal time, or other basis) should be agreed to before you appear to give testimony.
- **No** aspect of your history is immune; your past work records may be subpoenaed by opposing counsel to search for lack of experience, negative job fitness appraisals, and so on.

- **O**ften, cases are settled on the courthouse steps, and you may have your testimony called off at the last minute.
- **P**rior court testimony by you is discoverable, and you may be asked the names of cases, dates, and so on, on your prior testimony.
- **Q**uarreling with opposing counsel is to be avoided.
- **R**ather, strive to clarify for the court the bases of your apparent differences.
- **S**ay nothing not required to answer the questions; avoid elaboration not related to the question.
- **T**alk to the jury, not the attorney asking the questions.
- **U**nderstand the questions before responding; if you did not understand, get complete clarification.
- **V**erbosity is verboten. An irrelevant elaboration by you can give opposing counsel an avenue to attack.
- **W**ords need to be chosen carefully: Exact meanings are important.
- **X**tra preparation concerning validity, reliability, and standard error of measurement for tests you may mention in testimony can help prevent embarrassing moments.
- **Y**es (or no) responses, even though demanded by counsel, can be explained by you, if you feel the restriction to these responses is misleading.
- **Z**ero deviation from fact. Never try to fill in when you do not have the facts. If you don't know, say so.

The above guidelines, if strictly followed, are not guaranteed to prevent disaster. They may, however, be of some help in ameliorating some of the problems that can arise if they are not followed (American Psychological Association, 1993).

REFERENCES

American Psychological Association. (1992). Ethical Principles of Psychological Code of Conduct. *American Psychologist, 47,* 1597–1611.

American Psychological Association. (1993). *The Independent Practitioner, 13*(5), 229–230.

Blumer, D., & Benson, D. F. (1975). Personality changes with frontal and temporal lobe lesions. In *Psychiatric aspects of neurological disease.* New York: Grune Statton.

Form SSA-2506-BK (12-85). *Disability Examination Under Social Security—A Handbook for Physicians.*

Frye v. United States, 293 F. 1013 (D.C. Civ. 1923).

Goldstein, K. (1952). The effect of brain damage on the personality. *Psychiatry, 15,* 245–260.

Hartlage, L. C. (1989). *Behavior change inventory (inventory of pre- versus post-behaviors with brain injury)*. Brandon, VT: Clinical Psychology.

Hartlage, L. C. (1990). *Neuropsychological evaluation of head injury*. Sarasota, FL: Professional Resource Exchange.

Hartlage, L. C. (1993). Neuropsychology legal testimony from A to Z. *The Independent Practitioner*. Washington, DC: American Psychological Association, *13*, 229–230.

Hartlage, L. C., & Williams, B. L. (1991). Assessment of behavioral sequalae of traumatic and chemical CNS insert. *Archives of Clinical Neuropsychology, 6*, 279–286.

Hartlage, L. C., Wilson, D. D., & Patch, P. C. (2001). Persistent neurobehavioral problems following mild traumatic brain injury. *Archives of Clinical Neuropsychology, 16*, 561–570.

Heaton, R. K., Smith, H. P., Lehman, R. A., & Vost, A. T. (1978). Prospects for faking believable deficits on neuropsychological testing. *Journal of Consulting and Clinical Psychology, 46*, 892–900.

Hill, D., & Sargent, W. (1943). A case of matricide. *Lancet, 244*, 526–527.

Jenkins v. United States. 113 U.S. App. D.C. 300, 367 F. 2d 637 (1962).

Kixmiller, J. S., Briggs, J. R., Hartlage, L. C., & Dean, R. S. (1993). Factor structure of emotional and cognitive behaviors for normal and neurologically impaired patients. *Journal of Clinical Psychology, 49*, 233–241.

Lees Haley, P. R. (1999). Commentary on Sweet and Moulthrop debasing procedure. *Journal of Forensic Neuropsychology, 1*, 43–47.

Lewis, D. O., Pincus, J. H., Shanok, S. S., & Glases, G. H. (1982). Psychomotor epilepsy and violence in a group of incarcerated adolescent boys. *American Journal of Psychiatry, 139*, 882–887.

Lewis, D. O., Pincus, J. H., Feldman, M. A., Jackson, L., & Bard, B. (1986). Psychiatric, neurological and psychoeducational characteristics of 15 death row inmates in the United States. *American Journal of Psychiatry, 143*, 838–845.

Matarazzo, J. D. (1990). Psychological assessment versus psychological testing. *American Psychologist, 45*, 999–1017.

Mednick, S. A., & Christenon, K. O. (1977). *Biosocial bases of criminal behavior*. New York: Gardner Press.

Mednick, S. A., & Volavka, J. (1980). Biology and crime. In N. Morris & M. Tonry (Eds.), *Crime and justice: An annual review of research* (2nd ed., pp. 85–158). Chicago: University of Chicago Press.

Meehl, P. E. (1954). *Clinical vs. statistical prediction*. Minneapolis: University of Minnesota Press.

Miller, L. (1993). *Psychotherapy of the brain-injured patient*. New York: Norton.

Miller, L. (1997, September/October). The neuropsychology expert witness: An attorney's guide to productive case collaboration. *Journal of Cognitive Rehabilitation*, 12–17.

Miller, L. (2001). Not just malingering: Syndrome diagnosis in traumatic brain injury litigation. *Neuro-Rehabilitation, 16*, 1–14.

Pontius, A. A. (1972). Neurological aspects in some types of delinquency, especially among juveniles. *Adolescence, 7*, 289–308.

Reed, J. A. (1996). Fixed vs. flexible neuropsychological test batteries under the Daubert Standard for the admissibility of scientific evidence. *Behavioral Sciences and the Law, 14*, 315–322.

Reitan, R. M. (1994, July). Advanced workshop, Los Angeles, CA.

Robinsdale v. Warner Brothers

Sweet, J. J., & Moulthrop, M. A. (1998). Self-examination questions as a means of identifying bias in adversarial assessments. *Journal of Forensic Neuropsychology, 1,* 73–88.

Templer, D. I., Spencer, D. A., & Hartlage, L. C. (1991). *Psychology: Biosocial epidemiology.* New York: Springer.

Title 28 U.S.C.A.: Article VII Opinions and Expert Testimony, pp. 245–247.

Weller, M. P. (1986). Medical concepts in psychopathy and violence. *Medical Science and Law, 26,* 131–143.

Williams, B. L., & Hartlage, L. C. (1993). Factors influencing return to work following head injury. *Journal of Head Injury, 3,* 48–52.

Ethical Issues

Chapter 13

To Release, Or Not to Release Raw Test Data, That Is the Question[1]

Dorrie L. Rapp and Paul S. Ferber

INTRODUCTION

I, Dr. Rapp, am a solo private practitioner in rural Vermont, who conducts neuropsychological evaluations of individuals with traumatic brain injuries (TBIs) and provides rehabilitation psychology services. I am not an academic, researcher, nor prolific author. I also happen to be married to a law school professor, Paul Ferber, who practiced law for 14 years and was also a member of the Vermont Professional Conduct Board for attorneys. Home at the end of work days, I frequently related exasperating tales about needing to spend clinical time responding to "requests," subpoenas, and court orders to produce raw test data, often fruitlessly trying to explain, to attorneys and judges, the ethical and contractual dilemmas preventing me from doing this. In an effort to solve my problem by improving communication between the professions

---

[1]Disclaimer. This chapter gives the opinions of the authors, and does not provide legal advice nor is it intended to be a substitute for the advice of an attorney in your jurisdiction, because relevant law varies substantially from state to state and context to context. The information does not supersede the American Psychological Association's Ethical Principles of Psychologists and Code of Conduct or the Health Insurance Portability and Accountability Act of 1996 (HIPPA) or any other rules or regulations that may apply.

Editors' Note: The new APA Ethical Principles of Psychologists and Code of Conduct (2002) and the Health Insurance Portability and Accountability Act of 1996 (HIPAA) both impose new requirements relative to release of raw test data and the exact implications are still being decided at this time. Readers will need to be familiar with the New APA Ethics Code (2002) and HIPPA regulations and realize that the material in this chapter may be superceded by new ethics interpretations and legal decisions. In short, ethics and the law are moving targets.

on this issue, we collaborated on an article (Rapp & Ferber, 1994) published in a journal that attorneys would read when not in the heat of any adversarial battle. The article was well received and abstracted in the American Trial Lawyers' Association's *Professional Negligence Reporter.* Subsequently, I have been much more successful in either negotiating reasonable handling of the data, or obtaining a tight protective court order, when a copy of this article, explaining the conflict between the law and ethics, is attached to my letters to attorneys and the courts.

The "release of raw data" controversy has, nonetheless, continued to plague both practitioners and attorneys across the land. Current West Law and Psych Abstracts searches revealed only a few references specifically discussing this issue. It is also likely that many attorneys and neuropsychologists may not be aware of, or read those sources. Happily, the new millennium has produced several new, clear statements on this exact point. This chapter attempts to facilitate effective interprofessional communication, by discussing the release of raw data issue within the contexts of federal and state rules of evidence, case law, and the APA Ethical Principles, but also within the broader scope of scientific and professional integrity, and the future of the practice of neuropsychology. Finally, we provide practical proactive and reactive strategies for coping with the inevitable requests, subpoenas, and court orders that are commonplace in daily practice as a neuropsychologist.

SCENARIO[2]

Between interviewing patients, administering and scoring tests, and writing reports, you receive a telephone call from an attorney who wishes to retain your services as a neuropsychologist, to assess his client, who, he states, was injured in an auto accident and sustained a brain injury. You agree to all terms, such as payment and records to be obtained and reviewed, then you conduct a comprehensive neuropsychological evaluation and produce a report of your opinions. All is going well until you are served with a subpoena duces tecum, which provides:

BY THE AUTHORITY OF THE STATE OF [VERMONT], you are hereby summoned to appear and produce the following documents at the law offices

---

[2]This scenario is fictional and does not represent any real events of any known practitioner. It does, however, represent a compilation of situations and near-miss experiences encountered by many different neuropsychologists.

of the [DEFENDANT]. With respect to your evaluation of the [PLAINTIFF], produce all documents in your possession or control, including, but not limited to: all raw data generated, interview notes, tests and test forms used, normative tables and test manuals, documents, and narratives or drawings made by the [PLAINTIFF]. This you may not omit, or you will answer the default under the pains and penalties of the law in such case made and provided.

You call the attorney and try to explain that you cannot turn over your raw data (defined as the raw test scores, test forms with questions and responses, and the test materials or test manuals) to anyone other than a qualified expert (defined as limited to a licensed psychologist or neuropsychologist, who, by virtue of their training and experience, is in a position to appreciate fully the meaning of the raw data, including considerations of reliability and validity, test construction, and psychological appraisal), who will agree to protect test security by following the same ethical and contractual guidelines as yourself (Tranel, 1994, 1999; Shapiro, 1991). The conversation with the attorney goes something like this:

Neuropsychologist:	I just received a subpoena and have a big problem with reference to some of the material requested.
Attorney:	Problem? I have a copy of the subpoena. The language of the subpoena is standard. The civil rules make them entitled to all documents related to the case. We are making a claim for a brain injury, based on your evaluation. The rules of civil procedure require us to turn over everything you used relating to your evaluation and any other material you used to form your opinions. We call it *discovery.* We have no basis to deny the defense all relevant information. We have to turn those documents over, or the court might not let you testify and might bar us from asserting a claim of brain injury.
Neuropsychologist:	You don't understand. I will be glad to turn over all of those documents directly to the other side's licensed psychologist or neuropsychologist, but I have legal, contractual, and ethical restrictions preventing me from just turning it all over to the opposing attorney. I can't divulge the test materials to anyone other than a properly licensed psychologist or neuropsychologist.

Attorney: That's a distinction without a difference. The psy-
                             chologist on the other side will just turn it all over
                             to the opposing attorney anyway.

Neuropsychologist: She had better not. The same legal, contractual,
                             and ethical restrictions also apply to the psycholo-
                             gist on the other side.

Attorney: Well, I'll talk to the opposing attorney and see
                             what we can do, when I get a chance. (Under her
                             breath, the attorney mumbles something about
                             psychologists being prima donnas, and a mental
                             note about never using you again.)

Result

The attorney eventually calls back saying that the opposing attorney
agrees you should send all the requested materials to her office and
she assures that she will send them on to the psychologist. The opposing
attorney does not want to tell us who that will be, and under the civil
rules, she is not yet required to declare the experts she will use. On
the surface, this seems a reasonable compromise. You have made clear
to the attorney the need to protect raw data and received a commitment
that resolves the conflict between the law relating to discovery and the
law and ethics governing the neuropsychologist's obligations to protect
the raw data. You comply by sending a sealed package of all of the
requested information to the opposing attorney's office, thereby satisfying the subpoena and both attorneys.

Several months later the nightmare unfolds. The other expert turned
out to be a psychologist who is not a member of the APA, and/or
resides in a state that does not require use of either the APA's Ethical
Principles or the Association of States and Provincial Provinces Board
(ASPPB) code of conduct (and/or is actually a psychiatrist without
training and experience in administration or interpretation of the test
results, nor committed to protecting test security [Tranel, 1994, 1999;
Shapiro, 1991; *Watts v. United States*, 1977]). The other expert promptly
made a copy of everything for the opposing attorney. During cross-
examination at trial, you are presented with enlarged exhibits of actual
sections of the copyrighted test protocols, displaying the questions and
your clients' answers, which are entered as exhibits into the public

record. You vigorously object and refuse to answer any questions about the materials. You are held in contempt of court, and all of your testimony is stricken from the record. The jury returns a verdict for the defense. You are later served notice that you are to appear before your state psychology board ethics committee to respond to a complaint that you violated multiple sections of the APA Ethical Principles, which is legally subsumed into the rules and regulations in your state. You have no written documents indicating your efforts to resolve the conflict in an ethical manner, only your cover letter transmitting all of the raw data materials directly to the opposing attorney. You break out in a cold sweat and see your career dissolving before you. End of scenario.

Now that we have your attention, what are the realistic choices for a practicing neuropsychologist? Unscientific sampling of recent E-mail dialogs, among senior practitioners on neuropsychology-related Internet sites, indicated a wide spectrum of opinions and apparent practice. At one end of the spectrum, some simply give all materials when they are requested, reasoning the attorney eventually will get it anyway. Others rely on writing letters of explanation to the retaining attorney, and requesting them to obtain a protective order. At the other end of the spectrum, some believe that the neuropsychologist should retain their own attorney to obtain the necessary protective orders and ensure that those sections of the court record involving test materials are sealed, in every case in which production of raw data is demanded. An extreme resolution is to stop any noninstitutional private practice, and make every effort to avoid becoming involved with any clients having any possibility of litigation (probably an impossible task).

What we have is a major failure of communication between two professions having very different procedures, ethical codes, codes of conduct, and rules of practice. This chapter is about what you need to know, what you can do when faced with these situations, and practical proactive ways of completely avoiding the situation.

THE PROBLEM IDENTIFIED

In the ordinary course of any type of civil litigation, and from time to time in criminal litigation, an attorney will request all data used by the expert in evaluating the plaintiff. In the legal arena, this is a proper request (APA Committee on Legal Issues, in press). Federal courts, and most state courts as well, follow the basic rule that anything relating to the subject matter of the action, or that is likely to lead to admissible evidence, is fair game in preparing for trial. The fundamental principle underlying the rules of discovery is that our legal system will function more fairly if both parties are aware of the strengths and weaknesses of both sides. In theory, trials are likely to yield more appropriate decisions, rather than a result based on one's ability to hide evidence until trial and catch the other side by surprise. In addition, liberal discovery rules should allow both parties to accurately assess their position and thereby encourage settlement at an appropriate level, without even the need for a trial. One can only achieve those goals if there is full disclosure of all aspects the case.

The disclosure of raw test data presents a unique problem: how to balance the discovery rules, which are designed to provide full disclosure of everything a party will rely on at trial, against the scientific, ethical, and contractual obligations of the neuropsychologist and the test publisher's proprietary interests in the testing instruments. Frequently, neither the attorneys nor the courts involved fully understand the unique and highly sensitive aspects of this discovery issue. Indeed, most often, they are unaware of the ethical and contractual conflicts of the neuropsychologist. Therefore, it is important for the neuropsychologist to be able to speak in the attorney's language to explain the problem and proposed resolutions.

WHAT THE NEUROPSYCHOLOGIST NEEDS TO KNOW ABOUT THE LAW AND ATTORNEYS

The Law

The basic philosophy of the procedural rules, in virtually every state and federal court, is that lawsuits should not be about winning by surprising the other side. Therefore, they have adopted a series of rules designed to allow each party to discover the facts and theories underlying the other party's case. This not only encourages trials on the facts, but also encourages settlements before trial.

Federal Rules of Civil Procedure, Rule 26, which has been adopted as the rule in most states, broadly defines the scope of discovery. Litigants are entitled to have access to "any matter, not privileged, which is relevant to the subject matter involved in the pending action" (Federal

Rules of Civil Procedure, Rule 26[b][1]). The Rules further allow discovery of the identity of the other side's expert, the subject matter of their expected testimony, the substance of the expert's substantive facts and opinions, and the bases for the opinion (Rule 26[b][4][A][i]).

The consequence of these rules is that all information dealing with the evaluation of the plaintiff's psychological and cognitive brain–behavior functioning is relevant in a case in which the plaintiff seeks damages for brain injury. The defense is entitled to the plaintiff's expert's written opinion and to take the expert's deposition. The defense is also entitled to obtain all data underlying the expert's opinion, in order to determine the accuracy of testing procedures and scoring, and to evaluate, challenge, or attempt to discredit the expert's opinions.

Attorney's requests for this information can be in the form of an informal telephone call or letter (which can be responded to equally informally in an attempt to negotiate a satisfactory resolutions for all parties). It also may be in the form of a *subpoena* (an order to appear to provide testimony) or *subpoena duces tecum* (an order to appear and bring specific documents), automatically issued by a court officer on request of an attorney; both require a timely response. Finally, a *court order*, signed by the judge, may be issued for your testimony or documents, and it must be responded to in a timely manner, or the neuropsychologist can be held in contempt of court for failing to comply.

Even the APA Ethical Principles (1992) acknowledges that court orders supersede ethics and that test data should be released in response to a court order. In one actual case in our experience, during testimony at trial, the judge stated on the record that he would leave it up to the neuropsychologist to choose to either give all of the raw data to the opposing attorney to review over the lunch break, or all of the neuropsychologist's testimony would be stricken from the record (because of a technical violation by the plaintiff's attorney, who had not given the defense attorney notice that a reevaluation had occurred). Faced with this dilemma, the neuropsychologist asked to speak with the judge off the record, explained the contractual and ethical conflict this decision placed on the neuropsychologist, and asked that the judge issue a court order for the raw data. The judge understood the dilemma of the conflict between the law and ethics, and issued a court order for release and immediate return of the raw test data. This suggests that courts are willing to listen, if the problem is properly presented.

Rule 26 contemplates that there are situations in which circumstances may justify limiting discovery and specifically allows the court to enter an order limiting the use and/or access to sensitive information. The neuropsychologist is entitled to protection under Rule 26(c) as a "person from whom discovery is sought. . . . "

It is incumbent upon the attorney to request, through a motion to the court explaining the reasons requiring that any of the three types of court order be modified or *quashed* (made void or invalid). Rule 26 allows the court to "make any order which justice requires to protect a party or person . . . that a trade secret or other confidential research, development, or commercial information not be disclosed or be disclosed only in a designated way" (Rule 26[c][7]). For additional information on how to respond appropriately to subpoenas or court orders, see Bersoff (1999) for a summary of the APA Committee on Legal Issues *Strategies for Private Practitioners Coping with Subpoenas or Compelled Testimony for Client Records or Data* (1995), or the current 2000 revision in *Professional Psychology: Research and Practice* (in press).

The courts have understood the need to protect confidential research, development, and commercial information, as well as trade secrets. To that end, courts have entered protective orders limiting who has access to such information and how that information can be used. For example, in *Quotron Systems, Inc. v. Automatic Data Processing, Inc.* (1992), the court entered a protective order limiting the category of people who could have access to the information.

When justified, courts have even kept information out of the hands of attorneys. In *Digital Equipment Corp v. Micro Technology, Inc.* (1992), the district court entered a protective order limiting access to the confidential information to only "independent experts, consultants, or translators for a party . . . whose advice and consultation are being or will be used by such party in connection with preparation for trial."

Attorneys often mistakenly believe that the completed test response forms belong to the patient. The test question-and-answer protocols are not released to patients or their guardians. The patient and/or their guardian is entitled to inspect and have the data explained by the neuropsychologist. The neuropsychologist's opinions, and the basis for those opinions are all in the report, which may be released to the patient, if it is appropriately worded and explained by the neuropsychologist, and the report is freely given to parties in litigation, pending appropriate patient release. A federal statute provides that a parent/guardian has a right to inspect test protocols, but not to make copies (20 U.S.C. section 12326 [a][1][A] [FERPA]). This federal statute is consistent with the APA Ethical Principles (1992). This issue is also discussed in the *Statement on Disclosure of Test Data* (1995) by APA's Committee on Psychological Tests, and as summarized in Bersoff (1999).

The Attorneys

This problem varies slightly, depending on whether the neuropsychologist is retained by the plaintiff or the defense attorney. Although generalizations are dangerous, most plaintiffs' attorneys are focused on showing that their client is seriously injured and that it is the defendant's fault. The plaintiff's attorney has no interest in slowing down the case by arguing with the defense attorney over little things like the neuropsychologist's ethics and contractual obligations, or a third-party testing company's commercial interests. Conversely, most defendants' attorneys are focused on showing that the plaintiff is not injured, or at least not severely, and it is not the defendant's fault in any event. The defendant's attorney will immediately be skeptical about any attempts by the plaintiff's neuropsychologist to withhold anything.

The starting point is to recognize that the average attorney is oblivious to the issues of test security and the effects of test disclosure on future public welfare or on the field of neuropsychology itself. Indeed, some continuing legal education programs provide advice to attorneys on how to prepare their clients for independent psychological evaluations, including seeking advanced disclosure of what tests will be administered (Lees-Haley, 1997). Attorneys who have access to raw test data, including the test questions and answers (from release obtained in prior cases, as encouraged by Ziskin & Faust, 1988; Faust, Ziskin, & Hiers, 1991), are encouraged to use this information in advance of testing, to prepare their client to attempt to achieve a specific result.

A survey of 70 practicing attorneys, conducted by Wetter and Corrigan (1995), found that 79–87%, of two groups of attorneys surveyed, felt they should discuss what psychological testing involves with the client before an evaluation, and 48% of the attorneys believed they should always, or at least usually, inform a client about validity measures in psychological tests. The authors noted that the term *discuss* used in the questions, was open to wide interpretation; the attorneys were not directly asked if they coached their clients before testing. However, Youngjohn (1995) reported an attorney who argued that not counseling their client how to answer questions, prior to undergoing a psychological evaluation, may be considered legal malpractice. Rosen (1995) confirmed the existence of coaching by plaintiff's attorneys in personal injury litigation regarding psychological sequelae of traumatic events. As discussed by Lees-Haley (1997), even some other experts, for example, the psychiatrist involved in the mass tort case, *Lailhengue v. Mobil,* 1990, do not see a problem with providing copies of the criteria from the *Diagnostic and Statistical Manual of Mental Disorders* (DSM-IV) (American Psychiatric Association, 1994) directly to plaintiffs to review prior to holding further interviews with the clients.

The results of the Wetter and Corrigan and Youngjohn surveys are surprising, in view of the fact that the improper use of test information, as by coaching a client in advance, could be unethical for attorneys and result in a sanction, which might be as severe as losing the license to practice law. The *Model Rules of Professional Conduct* (American Bar Association, 1998), which are the ethical rules governing lawyers in all but four or five states, have several provisions that would seem to be violated by an attorney's use of confidential testing information to coach a client to achieve a specific result. This situation may stem partly from attorneys not thinking through the full ramifications of their conduct. By understanding the following, the neuropsychologist should be able to put the problem in language that will bring home to attorneys their own liability for improper use of raw data.

Professional Conduct Rule 1.2(d) provides that:

> A lawyer shall not counsel a client to engage, or *assist a client, in conduct that the lawyer knows is* [italics added] criminal or *fraudulent* [italics added], but a lawyer may discuss the legal consequences of any proposed course of conduct with a client and may counsel or assist a client to make a good faith effort to determine the validity, scope, meaning or application of the law.

In addition, Rule 3.3(a)(4) provides that an attorney shall not "offer evidence that the lawyer knows to be false." When an attorney knows that psychological test results have been manipulated by the client's reviewing the test questions and preparing answers in advance, the attorney knows that the results are false. Offering those results at trial, knowing the results are not an accurate reflection of what properly administered testing would produce, would be unethical. It is analogous to altering the test scores, after they were taken, to achieve specific results. Such conduct also violates Rule 3.4(a) and (b), which provide that an attorney shall not:

(a) *unlawfully obstruct another party's access to evidence* or unlawfully alter, destroy or conceal a document or other material having potential evidentiary value. *A lawyer shall not counsel or assist another person to do any such act*;

(b) *falsify evidence,* counsel or assist a witness to testify falsely, or offer an inducement to a witness that is prohibited by law.

THE NEUROPSYCHOLOGIST'S ROLE IN OBTAINING A PROTECTIVE ORDER

The neuropsychologist can aid in an appropriate result by explaining the problem to the attorney, and providing the attorney with the reasons establishing the need for a protective order. The neuropsychologist should provide the retaining attorney with a standard prepared motion and a packet of documents supporting the legal, contractual, and ethical obligations that support the request for a protective order (see Appendix; other examples are also provided in Frumkin, 1995, and Shapiro, 1999). The materials should contain the three categories of information that courts rely on in deciding whether and how to enter a protective order:

1. That significant harm will result from the failure to protect the secrecy of the test materials
2. That the harm from disclosure can be avoided, while still accommodating the opposing side's legitimate need for information to prepare its case
3. The exact restrictions the protective order should contain

Establishing That Harm Will Result Without Protection

The starting point in obtaining a protective order is to establish the need to protect the tests from unrestricted disclosure. There are at least three powerful reasons supporting the need for limiting access to raw data:

1. Protection of the commercial and scientific value of the test instruments themselves
2. Contractual obligations imposed on the neuropsychologist, arising from the purchase of the tests and test forms
3. Ethical obligations imposed on the neuropsychologist

The Need to Protect the Scientific and Commercial Value of the Test Instruments

Several facts demonstrate the need to limit access to the test information. First, unlimited disclosure will destroy the scientific value of the tests. Psychological tests are unlike most tests used by other medical and scientific experts, in which there is no equivalent discovery problem, because the test results are not manipulable. The technology used to create the X ray is not divulged by disclosure of the patient's X ray. A patient's X-ray film cannot be manipulated by explaining to the patient the underlying science of X rays.

Psychological testing, the test documents, and the test results are valid only if the answers are not manipulated. A person with access to the questions and test manual for a psychological test can prepare in advance to answer the questions in a way that produces a desired result. The main control for preventing faking or exaggerating deficits is maintaining test security of the protocol. Failure to enforce secure test standards, keeping the questions and answers and evaluation purposes of each test out of the public domain, would allow widespread coaching and faking of test performances and ultimately destroy the validity of the test. They would lose their usefulness to the medical and psychological communities, as well as their value for forensic, or any other, purposes. Many of the tests involved are the only, or most superior, tests available for important aspects of psychological testing (e.g., Wechsler Intelligence scales, Halstead–Reitan Neuropsychological Test Batteries). In turn, this would have a serious negative impact on the ability of psychologists to assess patients' problems and needs and to develop treatment patterns (Baer, Wetter, & Berry, 1995; Frumkin, 1995; Lees-Haley, 1997; Wetter & Corrigan, 1995; Youngjohn, 1995). If an attorney is having difficulty in grasping this concept, you might ask the attorney to consider what would happen to the validity of the Law School Admission Test or the Multi-State Bar Examination, if the questions used in those examinations were freely available in advance of the examination.

Second, undercutting test validity also destroys the commercial value of the psychological tests, which have been developed at an enormous cost by private parties. Yvette A. Beeman, legal counsel for the Psychological Corporation test manufacturer, summarized the implications as follows:

> For some of our tests, especially the Wechsler Tests, only one highly researched form is currently in use and this one form will continue to be used for ten

to fifteen years. Millions of dollars have been invested by the Psychological Corporation in developing and standardizing these tests over a period of many years. It is crucial that these tests remain strictly secured in order to preserve the commercial value of the tests and in order to preserve the usefulness of these tests to the psychological community and those individuals they serve. (Personal communication, 1994)

See also a similar full letter by Yvette Beeman in Frumkin (1995).

Indeed, the owners of the tests go to great lengths to preserve the security of the tests, by including nondisclosure provisions in every sale and selling the tests only to individuals meeting specific levels of qualifications (e.g., licensed psychologist, member of APA), who must agree to accept the following terms and conditions as part of the purchase of the test equipment (*The Psychological Corporation, 2000* and *Reitan Neuropsychological Laboratory, 2000* catalogs). The attorneys should understand that the end result of all this could be to make the test results inadmissible, because they would no longer have the validity and reliability required under the October 1, 2000, *Daubert* standard. For example, the *Psychological Corporation 2000* test material catalogs specifically state:

> **Maintenance of Test Security. Test Use.** Each person or institution purchasing a test must agree to comply with these basic principles of minimum test security: 1) Test takers must not receive test answers before beginning the test. 2) Test questions are not to be reproduced or paraphrased in any way. 3) Access to test materials must be limited to qualified persons with a responsible, professional interest who agree to safe-guard their use. 4) Test materials and scores may be released only to persons qualified to interpret and use them properly. 5) If a test taker or the parent of a child who has taken a test wishes to examine test responses or results, the parent or test taker may be permitted to review the test and the test answers in the presence of a representative . . . of the institution that administered the test. Such review should not be permitted in those jurisdictions where applicable laws require the institution to provide a photocopy of the test subsequent to review. . . . 6) No reproduction of test materials is allowed in any form or by any means, electronic or mechanical.

See also Frumkin (1995) and APA Committee on Legal Issues (in press), in which pages of test company restrictions are reproduced with permission.

The *Reitan Neuropsychological Laboratory Catalog* of test materials states:

> The tests, manuals (including, without limitation, the standardization and data contained therein), answer sheets, and all related materials sold by

Reitan Neuropsychology Laboratory are protected by the laws of copyright and unfair competition. No purchaser of such materials is authorized to publish, reproduce, translate, or adapt such materials for any purpose by any means, including, without limitation, by photocopying or storing in a database or retrieval system, or by any other means, mechanical or electronic. . . .
4) **Test Security**. By accepting delivery of using the tests, the purchaser acknowledges his/her responsibility for maintaining test security as required by professional standards and applicable state and local polices. Test security involves procedures for receiving, storing, disseminating, and controlling test materials. Maintaining test security is the responsibility of the test purchaser and/or user.

The test owners also protect security by selling them only to purchasers who meet a very narrow definition of a "qualified professional," as exemplified by the following from Reitan Neuropsychological Laboratories:

In accordance with the *Standards for Educational and Psychological Testing* and the *Ethical Principles of Psychologists* published by the American Psychological Association, Reitan Neuropsychological Laboratories, Inc., restricts the sale of tests and books that contain explicit information about the neuropsychological test administration and scoring to the following:
(1) persons who have earned a doctoral degree in psychology or education;
(2) persons who are members of qualified professional organizations in which members routinely use neuropsychological tests; and
(3) persons who are qualified on the basis of professional licensure or certification to use neuropsychological tests.

Ordering Unlimited Disclosure Would Force a Psychologist to Breach Their Contractual Obligations

As the examples of the provisions demonstrate, regarding maintaining the secrecy and integrity of the tests set forth in the previous section, the neuropsychologist takes on important legal obligations by purchasing and using the tests. The failure to abide by those restrictions constitutes breach of the contract under which the tests are purchased.

Thus, the court's forcing unlimited disclosure by a neuropsychologist would constitute a court ordering the neuropsychologist to commit a breach of the contract with the test publishers. The courts have recognized that such a result would be improper. For example, in *Snowden v. Connaught Labs., Inc.* (1991), the court affirmed a magistrates' protective order, which was based on the fact that the "defendants' should not be required to produce documents or records which will require them to violate their contract with [a nonparty]".

The Ethical Obligations of the Neuropsychologist

The APA Ethical Principles applies to all members of APA, and, in many states, this code is a part of the rules and regulations governing the practice of psychology, giving it the force of law for state psychology boards, other public bodies, and the courts. The specific APA enforceable ethical standards applicable to neuropsychological evaluations, forensic neuropsychological evaluations, test security, and release of raw test data, should be familiar to all neuropsychologists, and therefore they will not be explicitly discussed here. Suffice it to say that there are multiple applicable standards in addition to sections 1.02 (Relationship of Ethics and Law), 2.10 (Maintaining Test Security), the 7th section on Forensic Activities, and the 8th section, Resolving Ethical Issues. Applicable sections of the APA Ethical Principles are discussed in detail in, for example, APA Committee on Legal Issues (in press), Tranel (1994), Anderson and Shields (1998), Shapiro (1999), and Binder and Thompson (1995).

The introduction to the Ethical Principles specifically states that

> If the Ethics Code establishes a higher standard of conduct than is required by law, psychologists must meet the higher ethical standard. If the Ethics Code standard appears to conflict with the requirements of law, then psychologists must make known their commitment to the Ethics Code and take steps to resolve the conflict in a responsible manner. If neither law nor the Ethics Code resolves an issue, psychologists should consider other professional materials, and the dictates of their own conscience, as well as seek consultation with others within the field when this is practical. (p. 2)

A footnote in the Ethical Principles indicates that such additional guidelines and standards, whether or not they are adopted by APA or its divisions, are of educative value, but are not enforceable, as the Ethical Principles are. As discussed by Bersoff (1999), Eberlein (1980) presented the case of *Detroit Edison*, in which the Supreme Court agreed with the National Labor Relations Board, that a federal law requiring the disclosure of relevant information (i.e., psychological tests and results), cannot be defeated by the ethical standards and aspirational goals of a private group such as APA. There are circumstances in which psychologists will be faced with overriding obligations imposed by the law.

The Harm from Disclosure Can Be Avoided While Still Accommodating the Opposing Side's Legitimate Need to Prepare Its Case

The next step in demonstrating the appropriateness of a protective order is to establish that legitimate discovery interests will not be compromised by the protective order. Issuing a protective order, limiting access to the raw data to qualified psychologists or neuropsychologists on the side seeking discovery, will protect the security of the tests and still allow adequate discovery.

Even with the protective order covering raw test data, the attorney will obtain the neuropsychological evaluation report and other written notes and other records reviewed, as part of normal discovery. The neuropsychologist's report, analogous to the hospital medical record for a physical injury, should contain all of the information on which the neuropsychologist based their opinions, including sources of the patient's history, the details of any interviews with third parties, identification of all of the records reviewed and tests used, the demographic and other variables that were considered, the interpretation of the raw data results, and the opinions themselves. This contains all the meaningful information the attorney needs to prepare their case.

This raises the debate about whether raw and standard test scores should be included within the neuropsychological reports. Normally, neuropsychological reports do not contain or append all of the quantitative scored test data. However, Freides (1993), as discussed in Anderson and Shields (1998), did advocate routinely appending all qualitative data to neuropsychological reports, citing efficiency, allowing concentration on qualitative observations and inferences from the data, increased integrity by minimizing bias by presenting all data supportive and nonsupportive of the hypotheses, and ease of comparability with other evaluations. The ensuing controversy over this proposal can be reviewed in *The Clinical Neuropsychologist* (Freides, 1995; Matarazzo, 1995; Naugle & McSweeney, 1995).

We agree with Anderson and Shields (1998) that reporting test scores without a thorough explanatory context invites miscommunication and misuse of the results by the nonneuropsychologists who will receive the reports. Anderson and Shields (1998) state that

> Referral sources are unlikely to understand what neuropsychologists mean by "executive functioning." If general terms like "executive functioning" are illustrated by specific examples of the patient's test behaviors, better communi-

cation to referral sources can be achieved. . . . Miscommunication may be avoided by embedding the raw data in an explanatory context and by being careful to include normative comparisons.

They proposed that APA Ethical Principles standard 2.02(b) should be restated, with focus being on adequate communication of test results, rather than on not communicating raw data to unqualified persons. Doing this would ensure that the report provides the attorney with the meaningful information their job requires.

To help the attorneys and the court to fully understand why limiting disclosure of raw test data to only psychological professionals does not impair the attorney's ability to prepare their case, the neuropsychologist needs to explain the testing process and show that the test questions and answers are meaningless, in isolation, to anyone but a qualified professional. The overwhelming number of questions on psychological tests do not call for yes or no answers and do not have clearly right or wrong answers. Rather, the neuropsychologist considers matters such as gender, age, race and ethnicity, national origin, culture and religion, formal education level, socioeconomic status, premorbid functioning, and past evaluation experience, as well as all other test results in their entirety, in order to meaningfully interpret the raw data. The client's test answers, without the psychologist's analysis, are meaningless to, and likely to be misinterpreted by, anyone other than a specifically trained psychologist or neuropsychologist. With rare exceptions, attorneys are not such qualified professionals (Tranel, 1994). Shapiro (1991) discussed the case of *Watts v. the United States* (1977), in which the appellate court denied the claim that a psychiatrist was a qualified person to receive raw psychological data, because there was no evidence that the psychiatrist had the specialized training necessary to interpret that data.

For example, Tranel (1994) presented the following scenario:

An attorney for the defense has obtained all the raw data from a neuropsychologist in a case in which a plaintiff is claiming permanent cognitive disability from a brain injury. In the courtroom, the attorney attempts to convince the jury that the plaintiff cannot possibly be suffering the extent of memory impairment claimed, because the plaintiff was able to complete several difficult nonverbal memory items on a test. The attorney also points out that the items the plaintiff failed are so difficult that it would be unreasonable to expect any normal person to pass them. This line of arguing, perhaps accompanied by exhibits depicting the "difficult" memory items that the patient passed, may be quite compelling to laypersons. . . . Analysis of individual items taken out of context can be quite misleading. Add the likelihood that laypersons have limited understanding of how factors such as age, gender, and educational background may play a role in performance on the test, and one is left with a potentially extremely misleading depiction of the plaintiff's abilities. (p. 34)

In other words, the traditional approach to using evidence does not apply to raw test data.

Only a licensed psychologist or board certified neuropsychologist has the qualifications, training, and competence to evaluate and interpret the test results (Frumkin, 1995; Shapiro, 1991; Tranel, 1994, 1999). They are the appropriate persons to receive all raw test data in discovery. The expert then can review it, along with the neuropsychologist's report and supporting information, then advise the attorney of any scoring errors, omissions, or misinterpretations of the data. To the extent that there is an alleged error in interpreting any particular question, the neuropsychologist being questioned has all of the raw data in her possession at the time of deposition or trial testimony. There is no need for the attorney to have a copy of the raw data, in order to pursue this line of questioning.

In addition, the neuropsychologist is responsible for determining that the requesting party's designated recipient is properly qualified to interpret the raw data, through reviewing evidence, such as the recipient's curriculum vitae (Tranel, 1994). As the result of past negative experiences, we recommend that the neuropsychologist obtain a written agreement from the other expert, indicating that they agree to abide by the APA Ethical Principles, ASPPB code of conduct, and third-party contractual obligations, before releasing the raw test data.

Provisions of a Proposed Protective Order

Rule 26(c) gives the trial judge broad discretion in fashioning a protective order that will guarantee necessary access to important discovery information, while still preserving test security necessary to protect the value of the underlying tools used to gather the information. The specific provisions of the protective order are simple.

First, it should cover "all raw data generated, test materials including manuals, protocols, and scoring sheets related to the neuropsychological evaluation of [patient's name] by [neuropsychologist's name]."

Second, the order should limit the disclosure of such information "to a licensed psychologist or neuropsychologist qualified to administer and interpret such tests, who certifies that s/he will also maintain test security and abide by APA and ASPPB guidelines for doing so." Preferably, the specific name of the expert to whom the raw data will be given should be listed, so that their credentials can be checked to ensure that they are indeed so qualified (by review of the curriculum vitae, checking to see if they are listed in relevant directories of neuropsychological societies, and whether they are indeed a licensed psychologist or board certified neuropsychologist). If the party seeking disclosure of the raw test data has not disclosed the identity of their expert, the protective order should state that the "materials shall be placed in a sealed envelope and delivered to the clerk of the court where the action is proceeding. The clerk shall release the sealed envelope only to the designated licensed psychologist or neuropsychologist, who has been determined to be qualified to receive and interpret the test materials (e.g., by the published standards listed by the publishers of the test materials)."

If the matter reaches the trial stage, the court should also be requested to seal all parts of the record containing any of the test materials, and any exhibits or testimony that make specific reference to any of the raw data materials. The court should also preclude the making of any copies of the materials that are not destroyed or returned to the expert at the conclusion of the trial.

Proactive Strategies for the Neuropsychologist to Use

The adage, "An ounce of prevention is worth a pound of cure," is appropriate here. We suggest that the practicing neuropsychologist create and have available for use the following documents.

1. A standard letter to send to each referring attorney at the outset, before conducting the evaluation of the client, which contains not only the fee agreement and other arrangements, but also a clear statement of how you will handle release of raw data (e.g., only to another qualified expert, through a protective order, motion to seal the portion of the transcript dealing with specifics of test materials, etc.). Some attorneys may object, but you will at least know this and can attempt to resolve the conflict before becoming involved. In our experience, some attorneys have stated that this type of clear statement from the neuropsychologist resulted in their respecting the neuropsychologist as a straightforward expert who would tell them what they really had in their case, rather than what they wanted to hear.

2. Have a standard letter ready to send to the other qualified expert, asking that they acknowledge the agreement to maintain test security, the ethical standards regarding release of raw data to unqualified parties, and the test manufacturer contracts, before sending them the raw data.

3. Have multiple pre-prepared packets, containing a sample protective order and supporting documents, ready to forward to the attorney if/when a request, subpoena, or court order is received in an individual case (see "Provisions of a Protective Order" of this chapter for specific guidance).

4. Consider working with your state's psychological association and legislators to introduce a bill in your state, which will explicitly define how raw test data is to be handled, and define who is qualified to receive the raw test data (see examples of Illinois' and Maryland's laws and Texas's and Quebec's Rules and Regulations for Psychologists, presented in "Current Survey . . . ," later in this chapter).

Importance of Appropriate Attitude and Demeanor

Throughout the process of explaining the issue to the attorneys and the court, it is critical that the neuropsychologist demonstrate an appreciation of the importance of the goals of the discovery process. It is also critical that the neuropsychologist make clear that they are not seeking to withhold rightful discovery, and that the issue has nothing to do with doctor–patient confidentiality (which has been waived when the patient places their mental status at issue in their legal claim). Rather, the neuropsychologist must make clear the ways in which psychological tests and their results differ from other medical and scientific tests, as discussed earlier in this chapter, and that the protective order is necessary for test security. Courts have not recognized other grounds for withholding of test data, as in *Massachusetts v. Trapp* (1985) and *Fitzgibbon v. Fitzgibbon* (1984), as discussed by Shapiro (1991). And, as Tranel (1994 and 1999) stated:

> [T]he attitude or demeanor of the psychologist can influence substantially the degree of cooperation from members of the legal profession (lawyers, judges, etc.). When an attorney senses that the psychologist is trying to conceal something, or to resist cooperation, the attorney is likely to mount an all-out effort to get everything possible out of the psychologist. By contrast, if the

attorney senses that the psychologist is attempting to cooperate fully with the spirit of the proceedings, within the bounds of his or her ethical principles, the attorney is far more likely to go along with the psychologist's recommended course of action. The Ethical Principles do not, in fact, have the force of law; thus, it is very much in the best interest of psychologists to solicit cooperation and collegiality from attorneys.

Conclusion

If the need for protection of test security is properly understood by the attorneys on both sides, this issue should be easily handled by a stipulated protective order. If the attorney seeking discovery refuses to stipulate to an appropriate protective order, the attorney resisting discovery should be prepared, through the neuropsychologist, to provide the court with sufficient acceptable documentation to allow the court to determine that a protective order is appropriate, can provide effective discovery, and at the same time protect the legitimate need for test security. Mutual professionalism, cooperation, and civility will go a long way toward obtaining the objectives of all parties.

ETHICAL STANDARDS AND POLICY STATEMENTS

APA Ethical Principles of Psychologists and Code of Conduct, 1992

The Preamble and Six General Principles are aspirational goals to guide psychologists toward the highest ideals of psychology; the following ethical standards set forth enforceable rules for conduct as psychologists. The APA ethical standards are intentionally written broadly, to apply to all psychologists in varied roles, and they are not exhaustive. They do not provide specific suggestions for what practical actions to take to abide by the standards. Clearly, they were not written specifically for the issues and situations encountered by neuropsychologists acting as forensic experts. Although it is necessary to abide by the specific enforceable ethical standards, following only the enforceable letter of the code is not sufficient, in our opinion. The six aspirational principles are competence, integrity, professional and scientific responsibility, respect for people's rights and dignity, concerns for others' welfare, and social responsibility. The issues of test security and release of test materials into the public domain can clearly impact all of these principles, as well as the validity and, hence, future existence of the practice of neuropsychology.

Also, the APA Ethical Principles, 1992 version, is currently under revision. As recently discussed in the APA Division 40 *Newsletter* (2000), a draft of the revised code proposes substantially changing the standard on release of test data (new 9.04), to: "Psychologists refrain from releasing test data to persons who are not qualified to use such information, except (1) as required by statue or court order or (2) to an attorney or court based on a client release or (3) to the patient or client as appropriate." Professional neuropsychological organizations, such as National Academy of Neuropsychology (NAN) and Div 40, have compiled information and submitted comments about this proposed change (Gordon Chelune, President of APA Division 40, personal communication). This proposed change would substantially relieve the current ethical burden on neuropsychologists needing to obtain protective orders, when raw test data is requested by parties in litigation. However, even if the revised APA Ethical Principles allow release of raw test data to attorneys, based on client release, in our opinion, based on aspirational goals, this should not mean that neuropsychologists should automatically release such data into the public domain, given all of the other crucial remaining issues (i.e., third-party contracts with test publishing companies, harm from invalidating the tests tools, and the scientific validity and practice base of the field of neuropsychology).

Also currently under consideration is a new government rule on *Standards for Privacy of Individually Identifiable Health Information,* as published in 64 Federal Register 59917, November 3, 1999. Some health insurance companies believe that they own the psychologist's record of treatment to the client. The current proposed wording of the rule could be construed to allow the release of responses to psychological test items and/or test data. Regarding release of psychological tests and test data, there is concern that the proposed rule needs to expand protections, under the definition of *psychotherapy notes,* to also include that "test responses, scores, items and forms used in assessment or personal history shall be considered a part of the psychotherapy notes, if the mental health professional determines that such assessment or history contains information directly related to psychological treatment." There is also concern that the proposed rules may be inappropriately interpreted as preempting current state laws that more stringently protect the privacy of mental health records (see Newman [2000]).

Code of Conduct (1991)

Rules of conduct differ in function in critical ways from professional association ethics codes, with which they are sometimes confused. The ASPPB Code of Conduct is a distillation of regulatory codes representing geographic and professional diversity from a wide range of U.S. and Canadian jurisdictions, which were scrutinized and debated by the Model Licensure Committee. Many states, such as Vermont, have incorporated the ASPPB rules of conduct as part of their rules and regulations for psychologist licensure. The ASPPB rules of conduct primarily protect the public interest, and they

> pertain to the process or "mechanics" of the professional relationship, not to the content of the professional judgement itself. . . . They are essentially unambiguous concerning what behavior is acceptable and what is not. . . . They are sufficient unto themselves, without dependence for interpretation on additional explanatory materials, since they will be applied in a judicial/legal context interpreting the regulatory code which they are a part. . . . They are coercive, not advisory or aspirational. They are nontrivial, to the extent that any violation is basis for formal disciplinary action, including loss of licensure.

The ASPPB code is also currently undergoing revision.

The ASPPB Code specifically states that "The psychologist may release confidential information upon court order as defined in section II of this Code, or to conform with state, federal or provincial law, rule, or regulation." The section on assessment procedures is clear and specific.

1. *Confidential information:* The psychologist shall treat an assessment result or interpretation regarding an individual as confidential information.
2. *Communication of results:* The psychologist shall accompany communication of results of assessment procedures to the client, parents, legal guardians or other agents of the client by adequate interpretive aids or explanations.
3. *Reservations concerning results:* The psychologist shall include in his/her report of the results of a formal assessment procedure for which norms are available, any deficiencies of the assessment norms for the individual assessed and any relevant reservations or qualification which affect the validity, reliability, or other interpretation of results.

4. *Protection of integrity of assessment procedures:* The psychologist shall not reproduce or describe in popular publications, lectures, or public presentations psychological tests or other assessment devices in ways that might invalidate them.

Whatever the final status of the newly revised APA Ethical Principles, there may still be other rules and regulations regarding evaluations and test security that will apply to individual neuropsychologists in their states.

Specialty Guidelines for Forensic Psychologists

As discussed in Bersoff (1999), these guidelines are meant to be consistent with the APA Ethical Principles, but are designed to provide more specific guidance to forensic psychologists in monitoring their professional conduct, when acting in assistance to courts and the parties to legal proceedings. These guidelines are a joint statement of the American Law Society and Division 41 of APA (but do not represent an official statement of APA), and are endorsed by the American Academy of Forensic Psychologists. They promote an aspirational model of desirable professional practice by psychologists within any discipline of psychology, when they represent themselves as, and/or are regularly engaged as, providing psychological expertise to the judicial system, and even for individuals who only occasionally provide such services.

Many practicing neuropsychologists would clearly fall into these categories and may find reviewing these guidelines educational. These guidelines provide specific information regarding behavior in all aspects of responsibility, competence, relationships with legal representatives, confidentiality and privilege, specific methods and procedures, and public and professional communications. Of particular interest to the discussion of release of raw data during legal proceedings, the guidelines state the following:

VI. METHODS AND PROCEDURES. . . . B. Forensic psychologists have an obligation to document and be prepared to make available, subject to court order or the rules of evidence, all data that form the basis for their evidence or services. The standard to be applied to such documentation or recording *anticipate* that the detail and quality of such documentation will be subject to reasonable judicial scrutiny; this standard is higher than the normative standard for general clinical practice. 1. Documentation of the data upon which one's evidence is based is subject to the normal rules of discovery, disclosure, confidentiality, and privilege that operate in the jurisdiction in which the data were obtained. Forensic psychologists have an obligation to be aware of those rules and to regulate their conduct in accordance with them.

And, under **"VII. PUBLIC AND PROFESSIONAL COMMUNICATIONS":**

A. . . . a. When disclosing information about a client to third parties who are not qualified to interpret test results and data, the forensic psychologist complies with Principle 16 of the *Standards for Educational and Psychological Testing*. When required to disclose results to a nonpsychologist, every attempt is made to ensure that test security is maintained and access to information is restricted to individuals with a legitimate and professional interest in the data. Other qualified mental health professionals who make a request for information pursuant to a lawful order are, by definition, "individuals with a legitimate and professional interest." **b.** In providing records and raw data, the forensic psychologist takes reasonable steps to ensure that the receiving party is informed that raw data scores must be interpreted by a qualified professional in order to provide reliable and valid information.

CURRENT SURVEY OF THE FIFTY STATES AND PROVINCIAL PROVINCES

We sent a survey to all of the state and provincial psychological association executive directors ($N = 58$, including Washington DC, Virgin Islands, and Guam), asking three questions: (1) Did their state have any written statutes, or (2) rules and regulations, safeguarding release of raw tests data? and (3) Were there any position statements or ethical standards used in their state regarding safeguarding and release of raw test data? Twenty responses were received (34% response rate). Of the respondents ($N = 20$, but a state can be represented in more than one category), 6 stated that they had written statutes that addressed release of raw data, 6 stated they had rules and regulations (3 of these indicated that handling of raw data was subsumed under general confidentiality rules, and 1 indicated raw data was subsumed under release of medical records). Utah has a six-page position statement regarding handling of raw data, complied by members of the Professional Standard's Committee of the Utah Psychology Association. Seven states cited reliance on APA's Ethical Code in their rules and regulations. It is recommended that individual neuropsychologists contact their state's rules and regulations for psychologists, and contact their state psychological association for up-to-date information.

As of July 1, 2000, Vermont has moved from rules and regulations to a statute, incorporating the APA Ethical Principles and the ASPPB Code of Conduct. Texas's State Board of Examiners of Psychologists Rules and Regulations (1999), states, under the Psychological Records, Test Data and Test Protocols section,

> Licensees shall make all reasonable efforts to protect against the misuse of any record or test data. . . . A licensee shall release information about a patient or client only upon written authorization by the patient, client or appropriate legal guardian pursuant to a proper court order or as required by applicable state or federal law. . . . Test data are not part of a patient's or client's record. Test data are not subject to subpoena. Test data shall be made available only to another qualified mental health professional and only upon receipt of a written release from the patient or client for purposes of continuity of care or pursuant to a court order.

Also, Quebec's Code of Ethics of Psychologists (1998) states, under Standards for Psychological Tests Use, "A Psychologist shall not entrust the raw, uninterpreted data from a Psychological consultation to anyone but another Psychologist."

Two states provided copies of their laws, which directly address the issue of test security and release of raw data. Illinois' *Mental Health and Developmental Disabilities Confidentiality Act*, paragraph 803 (c) states that:

> Psychological test material whose disclosure would compromise the objectivity or fairness of the testing process may not be disclosed to anyone including the subject of the test and is not subject to disclosure in any administrative, judicial or legislative proceeding. However, any recipient who has been the subject of the psychological test shall have the right to have all records relating to that test disclosed to any psychologist designated by the recipient. Requests for such disclosure shall be in writing.

As of July 1, 2000, Maryland's *Medical Records—Confidentiality Act* includes section III(E)(1) stating:

> Except as otherwise provided in paragraphs (3), (4), and (5) of this subsection, if the disclosure of a portion of a medical record relating to a psychological test would compromise the objectivity or fairness of the test or the testing process, a mental health care provider may not disclose that portion of the medical record to any person including the subject of the test. (2) The raw test data relating to a psychological test is only discoverable or admissible as

evidence in a criminal, civil, or administrative action on the determination by the court or administrative hearing officer that the expert witness for the party seeking the raw test data is qualified by the appropriate training, education, or experience to interpret the results of that portion of the raw test data relating to the psychological test. (3) (I) A recipient who has been the subject of a psychological test may designate a psychologist licensed under Title 18 of the Health Occupations article or a psychiatrist licensed under Title 14 of the Health Occupations Article to whom a health care provider may disclose the medical record.

Individual neuropsychologists may want to consider working with their state psychological association and their legislators, to introduce a specific bill in an attempt to authoritatively resolve the issue of how and when to release raw data within their state.

DIFFICULTIES INVOLVED IN BEING ETHICAL IN THE LEGAL ARENA

Although this chapter concentrates primarily on release of raw test data and test security, in our view, these issues cannot be considered in isolation from the broader perspectives of the judicial system, ethics and morals, and the integrity of the profession of neuropsychology. Bersoff (1999) provides a collection of many thoughtful commentaries on these complex interactions. These closing comments may provide insightful reflections for neuropsychologists who find themselves immersed in contentious situations.

Sales and Simon (1993) remind us that "Standards of practice, including ethical principles and standards, do not guarantee excellence. They only institutionalized the minimum level of acceptable performance-competence." And, as Adams and Putnam (1994) stated,

> Psychologists called to court are best advised to act as psychologists first and best, allowing the legal arena to evolve as it must and will. Psychologists and lawyers are professionals with different goals, cultures, and rules who operate in epistemologically diverse ways. (p. 6)

Bersoff (1999a) stated that it is imperative that social scientists remain true to the primary role they serve in society:

> [W]hile unbridled advocacy may be a moral imperative for attorneys, it may be directly antagonistic to the ethical principles that control the behavior of

psychologists. Social scientists must continually be conscious of the fact that their data, interpretations, and opinions will be tested in the crucible of court-room cross-examination whose very purpose it is to destroy credibility and evoke evidence of bias. . . . [Psychologists] must offer more situation-specific, ecologically valid, objective data that serve science, not a particular adversary. (p. 493)

Anderten, Staulcup, and Grisso's (1980) comments remain equally true now, when they

urge psychologists to be assertive concerning the establishment of a truly collaborative relationship with the attorney and client. . . . Careful joint prepa-ration will reduce the number of 'surprises' encountered by psychologists in the courtroom and allow the psychologists to avoid various ethical pitfalls. It is also through active involvement with the attorney that the psychologist can best educate the attorney regarding ethical problems as they arise. . . . As more psychologists take the witness stand, the courtroom may become a major source of information with which the public forms its impressions of psychology as a science and a profession. There is a commensurate responsibil-ity for psychologists to adequately prepare themselves to meet the special ethical demands of the expert witness role, not only because they represent the profession in the public's eye but also for the welfare of the clients who are served.

We agree with Bersoff's (1999b) commentary and with the quotation of Butcher and Pope (1993), that

The psychologist who conducts forensic assessments holds a sometimes over-whelming power over the lives of others. . . . The explicit ethical and profes-sional standards reviewed . . . are the profession's attempt to ensure that this power is used competently, carefully, appropriately, and responsibly. Our responsibility as forensic practitioners includes not only upholding these standards in our own work of conducting assessments but also constantly rethinking the nature of these standards, their presence in our education and training, the degree to which the profession ensures accountability or, alternatively, passively tolerates and tacitly accepts or encourages violations, and the care with which we spell out responsibilities that fit the current and constantly evolving demands of forensic assessment. (p. 285)

APPENDIX: SOURCES OF SUPPORTING INFORMATION FOR THE NEUROPSYCHOLOGIST

Independent Supporting Documentation

Several new, short, clear statements are available to assist the neuropsy-chologist's understanding and practice, which can be used as attached documents to submit to attorneys and courts in support of the neuropsychologist's position. These include the "Test Security, Protecting the Integrity of Tests" editorial published in the December 1999 *American Psychologist; Standards for Educational and Psychological Testing* (1999); the APA Committee on Psychological Tests and Assessment's "Statement on the Disclosure of Test Data" (1996); and the APA Committee on Legal Issues's statement of "Strategies for Coping With Subpoenas or Compelled Testimony for Test Data" (1996, and 2000 in press).

Practical Step-by-Step Guides

The following provide short, clear guides for the process of responding to requests, subpoenas, and court orders for release of raw test data: Frumkin (1995); Committee on Legal Issues, APA, "Strategies for Private Practitioners Coping with Subpoenas or Compelled Testimony for Client Records or Test Data" (the in-press version includes a handy flowchart; see also the 1996 version); and as summarized in Bersoff (1999), pp. 321–326.

Sources for Example Letters and Protective Orders

Example response letters, which can be adapted for the individual neuropsychologist's use, are provided in Shapiro (1991, 1999), Rapp and Ferber (1994), and Frumkin (1995).

NAN Test Security Position Statement (1999)

This position statement is available directly from NAN, and it was published in the NAN *Bulletin* (2000) and in the *Archives of Clinical Neuropsychology* (2000). This position statement provides a succinct discussion of the issues, and a useful appendix containing a question and answer outline the neuropsychologist can use when they receive a request for raw data, guiding them through the suggested process for handling each request, depending on its exact nature.

REFERENCES

Adams, K. M., & Putnam, S. H. (1994). Coping with professional skeptics: Reply to Faust. *Psychological Assessment, 6,* 5–7.

American Bar Association. (1998). *Model Rules of Professional Conduct.* Chicago: Author.

American Educational Research Association, American Psychological Association, & National Council on Measurement in Education. (1999). *Standards for educational and psychological testing.* Washington, DC: American Educational Research Association.

American Psychiatric Association. (1994). *Diagnostic and Statistical Manual of Mental Disorders.* Washington DC: Author.

American Psychological Association. (1985). *Standards for educational and psychological testing.* Washington DC: Author.

APA. (1992). Ethical principles of psychologists and code of conduct. *American Psychologist, 47,* 1597–1611.

APA. (1996). Statement on the disclosure of test data. *American Psychologist, 51,* 644–648.

APA. (1999). *Standards for educational and psychological testing.* Washington DC: Author.

APA. (1999). Test security. Protecting the integrity of tests. *American Psychologist, 54,* 1078.

APA. (2002). Ethical principles of psychologists and codes of conduct. *American Psychologist, 52,* 1060–1073.

American Psychological Association (APA) Committee on Ethical Guidelines for Forensic Psychologists. (1991). Specialty guidelines for forensic psychologists. *Law and Human Behavior, 15,* 655–665.

APA Committee on Legal Issues. (1995). *Strategies for coping with subpoenas or compelled testimony for test data.* Washington DC: American Psychological Association.

APA Committee on Legal Issues. (2000). Strategies for coping with subpoenas or compelled testimony for test data. *Professional Psychology.* (In press).

APA, Division 40. (2000). Ethics Code Task Force. *Newsletter Division 40, 18,* 8.

Anderson, R. M., Jr., & Shields, H. (1998). Ethical issues in neuropsychological assessment. In R. M. Anderson, T. L. Needles, & H. V. Hall (Eds.), *Avoiding ethical misconduct in psychology specialty areas* (pp. 131–141). Springfield, IL: Charles C Thomas.

Anderten, P., Staulcup, V., & Grisso, T. (1980). On being ethical in legal places. *Professional Psychology, 11,* 764–773.

Association of State and Provincial Psychology Boards Code of Conduct. (1991). Montgomery, AL: Author.

Baer, R., Wetter, M., & Berry, D. (1995). Effects of information about validity scales on underreporting of symptoms on the MMPI-2: An analogue investigation. *Assessment, 2,* 189–200.

Bersoff, D. N. (1999). *Ethical conflicts in psychology* (2nd ed.). Washington, DC: American Psychological Association.

Bersoff, D. N. (1999a). Psychologists and the judicial system: Broader perspectives. In D. N. Bersoff, *Ethical conflicts in psychology* (2nd ed., pp. 492–494). Washington, DC: American Psychological Association.

Bersoff, D. N. (1999b). On being ethical in legal places. In P. Anderten, V. Staulcup, & T. Grisso (Eds.), *Ethical conflicts in psychology* (2nd ed., pp. 541–542). Washington, DC: American Psychological Association.

Binder, L. M., & Thompson, L. L. (1995). The ethics code and neuropsychological assessment practices. *Archives of Clinical Neuropsychology, 10,* 27–46.

Butcher, J. N., & Pope, K. S. (1993). Seven issues in conducting forensic assessments: Ethical responsibility in light of new standards and new tests. *Ethics and Behavior, 3,* 267–288.

Confidentiality of Medical Records Act. Section 4-307 of the Health General Article, Annotated Code of Maryland. 1994 replacement, vol. 2000 supplement.

Detroit v. National Labor Relations Board. 440 U.S. 301. (1979).

Digital Equipment Corp v. Micro Technology, Inc. 142 F.R.D. 488, 1992.

Eberlein, L. (1980). Confidentiality of industrial psychological tests. *Professional Psychology, 11,* 749–754.

Editor officiel du Quebec. (1998). *Quebec Code of Ethics of Psychologists.*

Faust, D., Ziskin, J., & Hiers, J. B. (1991). *Brain damage claims: Coping with neuropsychological evidence.* Los Angeles: Law and Psychology Press.

Federal Statute. 20 U.S.C. section 12326 (a)(1)(A) (FERPA).

Fitzgibbon v. Fitzgibbon, 484 A.2d 46 (N.J. Sup. Ct., 1984).

Freides, D. (1993). Proposed standard of professional practice: Neuropsychological reports display all quantitative data. *The Clinical Neuropsychologist, 7,* 234–235.

Freides, D. (1995). Interpretations are more benign than data? *The Clinical Neuropsychologist, 9,* 248.

Frumkin, I. B. (1995). How to handle attorney requests for psychological test data. *Innovations in Clinical Practice: A Source Book, 14,* 275–292.

Halstead-Reitan Neuropsychological Tests and Other Products. (2000). *Reitan Neuropsychological Laboratory.* Tucson, AZ: Author.

Law School Admission Test. Princeton: Law School Admission Services.

Illinois Statute (740 ILCS 110/3(c), formerly Ill. Rev. Statutes. 1991 ch. 91 1/2, 803.

Laihengue v. Mobil. Civil Action No. 90-4425, U.S. Dist. Ct. for E. Dist. of LA. (1990).

Lees-Haley, P. R. (1997). Attorneys influence expert evidence in forensic psychological and neuropsychological cases. *Assessment, 4,* 321–324.

Massachusetts v. Trapp, 485 N.E. 2d 162 (Mass. Sup. Jud. Ct., 1985).

Matarazzo, R. G. (1995). Psychological report standards in neuropsychology. *The Clinical Neuropsychologist, 9,* 248.

National Academy of Neuropsychology. (2000). Test Security. Official Position Statement of the National Academy of Neuropsychology. *Archives of Clinical Neuropsychology, 15*(5), 383–386.

National Conference of Bar Examiners. *Multi-State Bar Examination.* Iowa City: Author.

Naugle, R. I., & McSweeney, J. (1995). On the practice of routinely appending neuropsychological data to reports. *The Clinical Neuropsychologist, 9,* 245–247.

Newman, R. (2000). *Comments on proposed rule on standards for privacy of individually identifiable health information.* Government Relations Practice Directorate. Washington, DC: American Psychological Association (www.APA.org).

Proposed Rule on Standards for Privacy of Individually Identifiable Health Information. (1999). 64 Federal Register 59917, November 3, 1999.

Psychological Assessment, Tests and Other Products. (2000). *The Psychological Corporation.* San Antonio, TX: Harcourt Brace.

Quotron Systems, Inc. v. Automatic Data Processing, Inc. 141 F.R.D. 37 (S.D.N.Y., 1992).

Rapp, D. L., & Ferber, P. S. (1994, December). Discovery and protective orders relating to raw data in psychological or neuro-psychological testing. *The Vermont Bar Journal & Law Digest*, 22–34.

Rosen, G. M. (1995). The Aleutian Enterprise sinking and posttraumatic stress disorder: Misdiagnosis in clinical and forensic settings. *Professional Psychology, 26*, 82–87.

Rule 26. *Federal Rules of Civil Procedure.*

Sales, B. D., & Simon, L. (1993). Institutional constraints on the ethics of expert testimony. *Ethics and Behavior, 3*, 231–249.

Shapiro, D. L. (1991). *Forensic psychological assessment: An integrative approach.* Needham Heights, MA: Allyn and Bacon.

Shapiro, D. L. (1999). *Criminal responsibility evaluations. A manual for practice.* Sarasota, FL: Professional Resource Press.

Snowden v. Connaught Labs., Inc. 137 F.R.D. 325, 332 (D. Kan., 1991).

Texas State Board of Examiners of Psychologists. (1999). *Rules and Regulations.* Austin, TX: Author.

Tranel, D. (1994). The release of psychological data to nonexperts: Ethical and legal considerations. *Professional Psychology, 25*, 33–38.

Tranel, D. (1999). The release of psychological data to nonexperts: Ethical and legal considerations. In D. N. Bersoff (Ed.), *Ethical conflicts in psychology* (2nd ed., pp. 303–307). Washington, DC: American Psychological Association.

Watts v. the United States, 77-1428, U.S. Ct. of App., DC., 1977.

Wechsler Intelligence Scales. New York: Psychological Corporation.

Wetter, M. W., & Corrigan, S. K. (1995). Providing information to clients about psychological tests: A survey of attorneys' and law students' attitudes. *Professional Psychology, 26*, 474–477.

Youngjohn, J. R. (1995). Confirmed attorney coaching prior to neuropsychological evaluation. *Assessment, 2*, 279–283.

Ziskin, J., & Faust, D. (1988). *Coping with psychiatric and psychological testimony* (4th ed.). Marina del Rey, CA: Law and Psychology Press.

Chapter 14

Trained Third-Party Presence During Forensic Neuropsychological Evaluations

John J. Blase

The presence of an observer during forensic neuropsychological evaluations is an issue that has created controversy and discussion in the field of neuropsychology. The interest has been spearheaded by the decision, in many jurisdictions in various states, that an outside observer is permissible as part of the discovery process in litigated matters. Some courts have ruled that attorneys may be present at the evaluation of their clients, and others have advised that the examinee has a right to have a doctor of their choice present during such an evaluation. However, lawmakers in California and Iowa have passed legislation banning the presence of a third-party observer. The opinions of neuropsychologists as to the appropriateness of this type of observation are mixed.

McCaffrey, Fisher, Gold, and Lynch (1996) present several reasons to oppose the presence of observers during neuropsychological examinations. The main position McCaffrey et al. espouse is based on the theory of social facilitation, and an extensive bibliography on the subject is offered. Other objections cited include (a) the compromise of test security and misuse of tests; (b) potential ethical violations, because tests were not standardized with a third-party present; and (c) the impact of ethical and professional standards on a request to a neuropsychologist to be a third-party observer. Many of McCaffrey et al.'s cautions appear to be relevant for third-party observers, but may not apply to trained third-party observers. Since the appearance of McCaffrey et al.'s article in 1996, there has been a published opinion by McSweeney et al. (1998)

and a policy statement made by the National Academy of Neuropsychology (NAN) (1999). Both appear to rely on an independent review of the literature, but seem to rely on McCaffrey et al.'s analysis concerning social facilitation and a reiteration of the Ethical Principles of Psychologists and Code of Conduct (1992).

An unpublished policy statement for the American Academy of Clinical Neuropsychology, authored by Hamsher, Baron, and Lee (1999), makes the important distinction between an involved third party, such as an attorney, parent, or relative, and an uninvolved third party, such as a health care professional, student professional, or technical personnel. Of note is Hamsher et al.'s opinion that the purpose for the presence of uninvolved parties is to learn about test procedure and to focus on observation of the examiner, not the examinee. He also makes reference to the absence of involved third parties in the standardization of test instruments, but does not include this same caution concerning uninvolved third parties in making reference to test standardization. It would appear that Hamsher et al.'s reference to the presence of an uninvolved third-party observer during a forensic neuropsychological assessment is similar to, if not indistinguishable from, the presence of a supervisor during the training of neuropsychologists, either by videotape or actual presence.

This chapter proposes to examine and clarify the issues being addressed concerning the presence of a trained third party observer during a forensic neuropsychological evaluation. The focus of this chapter is purposely narrowed to consider only trained third-party observers who are defined as neuropsychologists or technicians trained in the use and administration of neuropsychological tests. This definition is akin to Hamsher et al.'s uninvolved third party. This restriction of using only trained third-party observers should obviate the concern about test security or the misuse of tests. The current author would not suggest or condone as appropriate the presence of any untrained observer, such as a parent, spouse, or attorney, during a neuropsychological assessment. He also would have concerns about audio or videotaping that could allow future viewing by untrained individuals, unless assurances, in the form of a protective order, could be obtained from the court that such a recording would not be released into the public domain. Use of trained observers would help to ensure that the observer adheres to the American Psychological Association's Ethical Principles (1992), to act professionally and not engage in distraction or any other behavior that would interfere with the test administration.

This chapter reviews the literature on social facilitation that has been proposed as relevant to the issue of third-party observers and comments on its applicability to trained third-party observers. Known research findings are presented, as well as suggestions concerning trained third-party observers and future research topics. Finally, there is discussion of the relevance of observing the examiner, rather than the examinee, during forensic assessments. To date, the focus has been on the observation of the individual being evaluated and how such observation will effect the validity of neuropsychological testing. It would seem that this should not be the sole focus of attention in forensic evaluations, since it is the examiner's methods that are to be observed and not necessarily the examinee's behavior. McCaffrey et al. (1996) point out that "attorneys, especially those who fear that the examiner would elicit incriminating information concerning how the injury occurred, or who felt that the exam would otherwise be conducted in a biased manner, were usually permitted to attend" (p. 435). Clearly, the emphasis in this statement is on the observation of the examiner, not the examinee. The request for a trained third-party at an evaluation should be to address concerns about what questions will be asked, how these questions will be phrased, and what questions are omitted. Questions are appropriate about what tests are employed, whether the tests are administered in a standardized fashion, if appropriate time is allowed for examinee response, and similar methodological inquiries. These are examination details that cannot be observed by merely reviewing the raw test data. The focus needs to be on how the examinee is evaluated by the examiner, not how the examinee performs. The importance of this focus becomes evident in the discussion that follows.

FORENSIC VERSUS CLINICAL EVALUATIONS

The request for a trained third-party observer is almost always confined to the forensic examination. Forensic neuropsychological assessments are substantially different from clinical assessments. The American Psychological Association (1992) has recognized this difference and the need to define special codes of conduct specific to forensic activities. For instance, in a forensic assessment, there is no doctor–patient relationship established. The person being evaluated is not a *patient* in the clinical sense and is usually referred to as an *examinee* or a *plaintiff*. There is limited confidentiality for the information gathered and no promise or attempt to provide treatment. The Ethical Principles (1992), in section 1.21, requires the psychologist to inform the examinee of the differences between a forensic and a clinical evaluation. The evaluating forensic neuropsychologist has a relationship with a third party—usually an insurance company, municipality, or an attorney—and no therapeutic relationship with the examinee. The examinee is not evaluated voluntarily, and, in some instances, there is an adversarial aspect to the evaluation. There are no individual tests or battery of tests that have been validated and/or normed specifically for use in a forensic evaluation.

The forensic examinee or plaintiff is different from clinical patients, in that they have made their injury complaints public and are aware of the fact that their behavior is open to scrutiny. This scrutiny can take the form of interrogatories, depositions, and/or sworn testimony in a court of law before a jury of peers. Examinees or plaintiffs in forensic evaluations are generally aware that their actions may be observed, recorded, and/or videotaped for public scrutiny. Insurance companies routinely assign case managers who accompany examinees into medical exams—a practice rarely, if ever, tolerated in a clinical examination. In other words, plaintiff examinees are accustomed to and expect a different set of rules to apply during examinations in anticipation of litigation.

The ethical codes for psychologists are liberally invoked as a reason to prevent a third-party observer at a neuropsychological examination. There is some question as to whether or not this same line of reasoning should be applied to trained third-party observers during a forensic assessment. The current author would agree that a third party observer is not appropriate during a clinical assessment, except when a foreign language interpreter is needed. In the clinical supervision setting, the supervisor is a trained third-party observer, and the person being assessed is the examiner, not the patient. Tests administered in a supervised setting are considered to be both reliable and valid. Trained third-party observers, during both clinical supervision and observation of a forensic examination, are asked to answer the same question: Is the test administration being conducted properly and according to established practices? If distraction of the examinee or patient occurs, the distraction exists equally in both a supervisory session and a forensic examination that includes a trained third-party observer. If controlled properly, there is no reason to believe that distractions would be significant factors influencing the outcome of either type of assessment.

Sanders and Baron (1975) studied the effects of distraction on task performance; they conclude: "To the question 'Does distraction *necessar-*

ily impair task performance?' the present research provides a firm 'No.' Even though distraction does take time and/or attention away from the task at hand, additional factors are apparently involved" (p. 962). Both simple and complex tasks were studied, and the authors concluded that a compensatory process, most likely in the form of an increase in general drive level of the performer, accompanies the process of distraction. Trained third-party observers would be aware of appropriate testing procedures and will also understand the importance of being unobtrusive and refraining from distraction. Reports of inappropriate interference by a trained observer are rare if they exist at all. However, inappropriate behavior by a relative or attorney, which interrupts the testing process, is a too commonly reported phenomenon.

SOCIAL FACILITATION

Social facilitation is a much-studied concept in the field of social psychology. Zajonc (1965, 1980) championed an instinct theory of social facilitation, by proposing that the mere presence of others was the sufficient condition to bring about a change in a person's behavior. He proposed, further, that the presence of others produced an increased drive state, resulting in social facilitation on simple tasks and socially mediated impairment on complex tasks. Thus, Zajonc suggests that an audience will impair the acquisition of new responses and facilitate the emission of responses that are well learned or instinctive. Key to Zajonc's theory is that the mere presence of a second party is sufficient to produce these changes in behavior.

Cottrell (1972) proposed a revision to Zajonc's theory, by suggesting that the presence of others is a learned source of drive, rather than a source of drive that is innate or "wired into" the organism. He designed experiments that allowed for the presence of another during an experiment, but had the second party blindfolded. Since the mere presence of the blindfolded second party did not have the predicted influence proposed by Zajonc, Cottrell concluded that the presence of others will enhance the emission of dominant responses only when the spectators can evaluate the individual's performance.

Various researchers (Henchy & Glass, 1968; Paulus & Murdock, 1971) conducted experiments that demonstrated that the mere presence of others is not a sufficient condition to enhance emission of dominant responses, but that these effects do occur when there is the anticipation of later praise or criticism. Guerin and Innes (1982) reviewed the social facilitation research literature prior to 1982. Approximately 50% of that research appeared to lend support to the drive theory proposed by Zajonc, and 50% supported the learning theory of Cottrell.

Schmitt, Gilovich, Goore, and Joseph (1986) conducted a study that strongly supported Zajonc's contention that mere presence of another person is sufficient to increase people's generalized arousal and to produce the standard social facilitation effects. However, they go on to state: "No advocate of the mere presence hypothesis, for example, would deny that evaluation apprehension is an important variable that can indeed increase people's general arousal level and thus further facilitate their dominant response tendencies" (p. 246).

Whether one accepts the instinct theory or the learning theory as explanatory to social facilitation, there is no dispute that the presence of another does influence the behavior of a person being examined. This finding would seem to lend support to the conclusions of McCaffrey et al. (1996), that the phenomenon called social facilitation may pose an important threat to the validity of a neuropsychological evaluation in the presence of a third-party observer. McCaffrey et al. (1996) state further that

> the literature on social facilitation provides empirical evidence to suggest that the presence of an observer(s) alters cognitive/motor performance. . . . The social facilitation literature provides a theoretical framework to support arguments that the presence of a third party observer during neuropsychological evaluation may alter the results of the evaluation. (p. 441)

The question that needs to be addressed is just how the presence of a third party during neuropsychological evaluation alters the result of the evaluation, and by how much?

SECOND- VERSUS THIRD-PARTY OBSERVATION

A review of the extensive bibliography provided by McCaffrey et al. (1996) will reveal that most of the social facilitation research refers to studies in which the experimental design provided for a comparison of an individual working alone with an individual working with an examiner/experimenter. The process of social facilitation, in both the drive theory proposed by Zajonc and the learning theory proposed by Cottrell, refers to the influence on the examinee by the mere presence of the examiner (Zajonc) and/or the evaluative characteristic of the examiner (Cottrell). Manstaed and Semin (1980) note:

> While it might be argued that an experimenter does not constitute an audience, it is difficult to see how, from the perspective of a mere presence theorist, our experimenter did not satisfy the conditions of being "merely present," since to suggest that there is some phenomenological difference between the mere presence of an experimenter and that of a third party is to invoke the very cognitive processes which mere presence must by definition not involve. (p. 131)

In some studies (Guerin, 1983; Knowles, 1983; Rittle & Bernard, 1977), the examiner was blindfolded, sometimes placed behind the examinee, sometimes in front of the examinee, and sometimes at a distance, simulating indifference or nonattention. In each instance, the comparison was between the "alone condition" and one in which an examiner was present. In other words, social facilitation occurred by virtue of the presence of an examiner, not the presence of a third party. Therefore, the relevant question in neuropsychological examinations is: Since social facilitation already exists by virtue of the fact that neuropsychological examinations involve the presence of both an examinee and an examiner, what is the possible effect on the examinee by introducing another person into the testing situation? This question has relevance for the presence of a trained third-party observer during a forensic assessment or a supervisory session, or as an interpreter for non-English-speaking examinees.

Knowles (1983) measured the effects of audience size and distance on social judgments and behavior. The audience size varied from 2 to 4 to 8 members, and distances varied from 3 to 10 to 24 feet. The distance of the audience had no reliable effects on the drive-related measures, even though subjects accurately recalled the distance of the audience and were influenced by it in judging their crowdedness. There was a tendency for the alone condition to take somewhat less time per trial than the audience conditions, but, within audience conditions, the size and distance of the audience did not significantly effect times.

Laughlin and Wong-McCarthy (1975) designed an experiment requiring the solving of three concept-attainment problems in an orthogonal design. The variables to be manipulated were the number of observers, comparing the examiner alone with an additional observer. Videotaping, audiotaping, and task complexity did not appear to diminish performance, when compared to the control condition of no observer. The presence of an additional observer had no effect on performance. Those authors point out that previous findings, in which the presence of an observer degrades performance, may be the result of the observer as recorder of information about performance, rather than to his physical presence per se.

Laughlin and Jaccard (1975) compared individuals and cooperative pairs, varying the size of the audience between no, one, or two persons, as they solved three successive concept attainment problems. Their findings indicated that an audience of either one or two persons hindered the performance of individuals, compared to unobserved controls, but had no effect upon the performance of cooperative pairs.

Cohen and Davis (1973) emphasize that the presence of others is a vague psychological dimension. Although the most parsimonious conclusion from research is that presence of others generally implies evaluation, the saliency of evaluation can clearly be increased by instruction. Evaluation of performance may or may not imply a relationship to the needs and purposes of the person being evaluated.

Tolman (1965) commented on animal behavior and noted that the running of chicks in a 4-foot runway for food was facilitated by the mere presence of conspicuous companions. This effect was a disinhibitory one. A similar interpretation was given to data obtained on rhesus monkeys by Stamm (1961) and by Ross and Ross (1949), in discussing their results on feeding behavior in dogs. Cottrell (1972) opined that humans are trained by their past experience, in that other persons who watch them as spectators often praise or criticize them. He cites several authors who produce research findings akin to his, demonstrating that, when anticipations of praise or criticism are eliminated, the presence of others does *not* (italics added) increase the individual's drive level.

When a nonrivalrous coaction arrangement is encountered, the presence of coactors does not serve to increase the individual's drive level. Sasfy and Okun (1974) concluded that audience characteristics and the form of evaluation could be considered interactive determinants of evaluation potential. Their findings supported Cottrell's notion that the potential for evaluation characterized a social situation that is the chief source of audience and coaction effects in humans.

Green (1983) conducted an experiment comparing subjects evaluated with the promise of future help with those evaluated with no such promise. His conclusion was that evaluation apprehension was reduced when subjects were told that an otherwise evaluative observer would be a source of future help. He concluded, further, that such a finding suggests that evaluation apprehension during observation is a function of the anticipation of negative outcomes. Evaluation resulting from being observed facilitates performance on an easy task, even though it inhibits performance on a more difficult one. Green (1985) noted that fear of failure, engendered by test anxiety and experimenter evaluation, caused subjects to become overly cautious and withhold responding. Shaver and Liebling (1976) state:

> There is probably no such thing as the "mere presence" of an observer *in a task situation*; a task observer will always be perceived as somewhat evaluative or will at least arouse some uncertainty concerning evaluation and hence will tend to increase task-relevant drive. (p. 270)

Evaluative audiences are frequently noted in social facilitation research, with the conclusions emphasizing the importance of audience expectation on the test performance (Bond, 1982; Criddle, 1971; Ganzer, 1968; Green, 1979; Guerin, 1983, 1986; Haas & Roberts, 1975; Innes & Gordon, 1985; Innes & Young, 1975; Lombardo & Catalano, 1975, 1978; Seta, Donaldson, & Wang, 1988; Zajonc, 1980). Sanna and Shotland (1990) concluded that whether the presence of an evaluative audience improves or impairs performance depends upon whether a positive or a negative evaluation is anticipated.

Robinson-Staveley and Cooper (1990) studied the effects of mere presence, expectations for success, gender, and level of computer experience, on reactions to computers. They concluded:

> It is not inconsistent with models of social facilitation that performance could be impaired because of low expectations for success. . . . Low expectations could result in the energization of irrelevant response tendencies, in embarrassment, or in withdrawal, all of which would be expected to impair performance. When expectations for success are high, however, the result could be increases in task-relevant drive, self-presentational strategies, and matching to standards that would lead to facilitation of performance. (p. 181)

Lombardo and Catalano (1975) noted that their findings indicate that anticipation of performance evaluation is the mediating mechanism for drive arousal. Zajonc (1980) reported the effects of stress on performance. He concluded that stress often elicits fixed response patterns and that different stress conditions elicit different responses in different species. Furthermore, to the extent that stress responses conflict with the behavior under observation, the presence of others interacts with the performance of this observed behavior, accordingly. The level of stress in companions promoting efficient behavior is unimportant; and implied evaluative threats may increase stress. Additionally, the possibility exists that others may prevent the occurrence of avoidance responses and thus reduce emotional reactions to stress. Green and Gange (1977) noted that the presence of others leads to increased arousal only when the others are stimuli for anticipation of negative outcomes. Reassuring subjects viewing a stressful film, in the presence of a familiar and trusted figure, inhibited the anxiety normally elicited by the film.

SURVEY OF NEUROPSYCHOLOGISTS

Social facilitation research provides some useful information concerning the presence of others during evaluation, but, as of 1998, there was no comprehensive survey among professionals regarding trained third-party observation. Sewick, Blase, and Besecker (1998) sent a questionnaire to 3,167 members of the NAN, asking whether or not a neuropsychologist or a trained technician acting as a third-party observer was appropriate in certain forensic settings. Respondents were asked about the appropriateness of actual presence of a trained third party, as well as the use of videotape to record the session for future observation. There was a response rate of 26%, or a return of 817 questionnaires. Fifty questionnaires were discarded when it became evident that one individual copied the original questionnaire and submitted 49 invalid documents. All invalid documents advocated no trained third-party observation. After elimination of these invalid responses, the number of respondents advocating the inclusion of a trained third party totaled 572, or 70%, in agreement. When asked about videotaping the procedure, 515, or 63%, were in agreement. Thus, a majority of respondents to this questionnaire believe that inclusion of a trained third-party observer during a forensic evaluation is an appropriate procedure.

CONCLUSIONS

Current review of the literature suggests that the use of social facilitation research to support the objections to third-party observation is questionable. Social facilitation research does not provide empirical evidence to suggest that the presence of an observer, in addition to the examiner, alters examinee performance. Social facilitation research suggests that there is no appreciable effect on the examinee by the introduction of a trained observer, in addition to the examiner, when the examiner is the individual being observed. The use of social facilitation research to support the conclusions in the August 1999 published opinion of the Executive Board of the NAN, concerning third-party observers in forensic evaluations, raises questions about the scientific basis for this opinion. The NAN position advocates a third-party observer during supervision, but not in a forensic assessment. This position places a distinction on the setting for the evaluation, rather than on the use of a trained versus an untrained observer. Social facilitation research appears to lend support to the conclusion that the presence of a trained third-party observer, during both forensic evaluations and training sessions requiring supervision of the examiner, does not produce a clinically significant change in examinee responses.

Social facilitation research does posit some interesting questions concerning the instructions given to an examinee regarding the presence of a trained third-party observer and how this perception could actually enhance test performance. Advising examinees that an trained observer, either a person or a recording device, will be present to observe the examiner, may have a beneficial effect on those examinees anticipating a negative outcome. It is reasonable to conclude that the presence of a trained third-party observer, who is perceived as a monitor of the examination process, could raise the examinee's drive level and thereby improve test performance.

The presence of a perceived neutral party observing the process in a forensic independent medical examination (IME) evaluation could help to reduce the anticipated negative evaluation in this potentially adversarial situation. Although it is not reasonable to conclude that all IME evaluations are biased or will generate negative expectations from examinees, this is a common enough perception that it may warrant the recommendation for a trained third-party observer in many situations. Social facilitation research suggests that other IME evaluations, in addition to neuropsychological assessments, are likely candidates for some type of observation. What forensic neuropsychologist has not heard of the 10-minute complete and comprehensive neurology or orthopedic examination?

Because we have little or no scientific research that supports an objection to trained third-party observation during forensic evaluations, it is recommended that examining forensic neuropsychologists utilize trained third-party observers, in order to adhere to the principles of freedom of information and full disclosure. Defining the appropriate conditions for observation allows our profession the opportunity to exercise reasonable precautions and avoids the imposition of a court order by a judge who may not have the knowledge base or the understanding to exercise an informed decision. At the same time, neuropsychologists would be helping to prevent distribution of the tests and knowledge about test administration into the public domain, which would jeopardize the validity of our instruments. Future research pertaining to the effects of trained third-party observers on the evaluation process could investigate (1) the advising that the focus of attention is on the examiner versus the examinee and (2) the effect of advising the examinee that the examiner is a biased versus an impartial IME examiner.

REFERENCES

American Psychological Association. (1992). Ethical principles of psychologists and code of conduct. *American Psychologist, 47,* 1597–1611.

Bond, C. F. (1982). Social facilitation: A self-presentational view. *Journal of Personality and Social Psychology, 42,* 1042–1050.

Cohen, J. L., & Davis, J. H. (1973). Effects of audience status, evaluation, and time of action on performance with hidden-word problems. *Journal of Personality and Social Psychology, 27,* 74–85.

Cottrell, N. B. (1972). Social facilitation. In C. G. McClintock (Ed.), *Experimental social psychology* (pp. 185–236). New York: Holt.

Criddle, W. D. (1971). The physical presence of other individuals as a factor in social facilitation. *Psychonomic Science, 22,* 229–230.

Ganzer, D. (1968). Effects of audience presence and test anxiety on learning and retention in a serial learning situation. *Journal of Personality and Social Psychology, 8,* 194–199.

Green, R. G. (1979). Effects of being observed on learning following success and failure experiences. *Motivation and Emotion, 3,* 355–371.

Green, R. G. (1983). Evaluation apprehension and the social facilitation/inhibition of learning. *Motivation and Emotion, 7,* 203–211.

Green, R. G. (1985). Evaluation apprehension and response withholding in solution of anagrams. *Personality and Individual Differences, 6,* 293–298.

Green, R. G., & Gange, J. J. (1977). Drive theory of social facilitation: Twelve years of theory and research. *Psychological Bulletin, 84,* 1267–1288.

Guerin, B. (1983). Social facilitation and social monitoring: A test of three models. *British Journal of Social Psychology, 22,* 203–214.

Guerin, B. (1986). The effects of mere presence on a motor task. *The Journal of Social Psychology, 126,* 99–401.

Guerin, B., & Innes, J. M. (1982). Social facilitation and social monitoring: A new look at Zajonc's mere presence hypothesis. *British Journal of Social Psychology, 21,* 7–18.

Haas, J., & Roberts, G. C. (1975). Effect of evaluative others upon learning and performance of a Complex motor task. *Journal of Motor Behavior, 7,* 81–90.

Hamsher, K., Baron, I. S., & Lee, G. P. (1999). Third party observers. *Policy Statement for the American Academy of Clinical Neuropsychology.* Unpublished manuscript.

Henchy, T., & Glass, D. C. (1968). Evaluation apprehension and the social facilitation of dominant and subordinate responses. *Journal of Personality and Social Psychology, 4,* 446–454.

Innes, J. M., & Gordon, M. I. (1985). The effects of mere presence and a mirror on performance. *The Journal of Social Psychology, 125,* 479–484.

Innes, J. M., & Young, R. F. (1975). The effect of an audience, evaluation apprehension, and objective self awareness on learning. *Journal of Experimental Social Psychology, 11,* 35–42.

Knowles, E. S. (1983). Social physics and the effects of others: Tests of audience size and distance on social judgement and behavior. *Journal of Personality and Social Psychology, 45,* 1263–1279.

Laughlin, P. R., & Jaccard, J. J. (1975). Social facilitation and observational learning of individuals and cooperative pairs. *Journal of Personality and Social Psychology, 32,* 873–879.

Laughlin, P. R., & Wong-McCarthy, W. J. (1975). Social inhibition as a function of observation and recording of performance. *Journal of Experimental Social Psychology, 11,* 560–571.

Lombardo, J. P., & Catalano, J. F. (1975). The effect of failure and the nature of the audience on performance of a complex motor task. *Journal of Motor Behavior, 7,* 29–35.

Manstead, A. S. R., & Semin, G. R. (1980). Social facilitation effects: Mere enhancement of dominant responses? *British Journal of Social and Clinical Psychology, 19,* 119–136.

McCaffrey, R. J., Fisher, J. M., Gold, B. A., & Lynch, J. K. (1996). The presence of third parties during neuropsychological evaluations: Who is evaluating whom? *The Clinical Neuropsychologist, 10*(4), 435–449.

McSweeny, A. J., Becker, B. C., Naugle, R. I., Snow, W. G., Binder, L. M., & Thompson, L. L. (1998). Ethical issues related to third party observers in clinical neuropsychological evaluations. *The Clinical Neuropsychologist, 12*(4), 552–559.

National Academy of Neuropsychology. (1999, Summer). Presence of third party observers during neuropsychological testing. *National Academy of Neuropsychology Bulletin, 10*(3), 15–16.

Paulus, J. F., & Murdock, S. A. (1971). Anticipated evaluation and audience presence in the enhancement of dominant responses. *Journal of Experimental Social Psychology, 7,* 280–291.

Rittle, R. H., & Bernard, N. (1977). Enhancement of response rate by the mere physical presence of the experimenter. *Personality and Social Psychology Bulletin, 3,* 127–130.

Robinson-Staveley, K., & Cooper, J. (1990). Mere presence, gender, and reactions to computers: Studying human-computer interaction in the social context. *Journal of Experimental Social Psychology, 26,* 168–183.

Ross, A. C., & Ross, R. J. (1949). Social facilitation of feeding behavior in dogs: I. Group and solitary feeding. *Journal of Genetic Psychology, 74,* 97–108.

Sanders, G. S., & Baron, R. S. (1975). The motivating effects of distraction on task performance. *Journal of Personality and Social Psychology, 32,* 956–963.

Sanna, L. J., & Shotland, R. L. (1990). Valence of anticipated evaluation and social facilitation. *Journal of Experimental Social Psychology, 26,* 82–92.

Sasfy, J., & Okun, M. (1974). Form of evaluation and audience expertness as joint determinants of audience effects. *Journal of Experimental Social Psychology, 10,* 461–467.

Schmitt, B. H., Gilovich, T., Goore, N., & Joseph, L. (1986). Mere presence and social facilitation: One more time. *Journal of Experimental Social Psychology, 22,* 242–248.

Seta, J. J., Donaldson, S., & Wang, M. A. (1988). The effects of evaluation on organizational processing. *Personality and Social Psychology Bulletin, 14,* 604–609.

Sewick, B. G., Blase, J. J., & Besecker, T. (1999, November) *Third-party observers in neuropsychological testing: A 1999 survey of NAN members.* Paper presented at the 19th Annual Meeting of the National Academy of Neuropsychology, San Antonio, TX.

Shaver, P., & Liebling, B. A. (1976). Explorations in the drive theory of social facilitation. *The Journal of Social Psychology, 99,* 259–271.

Stamm, J. P. (1961). Social facilitation in monkeys. *Psychological Reports, 8,* 470–484.

Tolman, C. W. (1968). The role of the companion in social facilitation of animal behavior. In E. Simmel, R. Hoppe, & G. Milton (Eds.), *Social facilitation and initiative behavior* (pp. 33–54). Boston, MA: Allyn & Bacon.

Zajonc, R. B. (1965). Social facilitation. *Science, 149,* 269–274.

Zajonc, R. B. (1980). Compresence. In P. Paulus (Ed.), *Psychology of group influence* (pp. 35–60). Hillsdale, NJ: Lawrence Erlbaum.

Chapter 15

Conflicts of Interest and Other Pitfalls for the Expert Witness

Barry M. Crown, H. Scott Fingerhut, and Sheryl J. Lowenthal

> I will teach you wisdom's ways and lead you in straight paths. If you live a life guided by wisdom, you won't limp or stumble as you run.
>
> Proverbs 4:11–12

INTRODUCTION

Expert testimony is big business, and its growing importance in modern litigation cannot be understated. Indeed, many cases, particularly those involving complex issues of mental states, ability, or causation, often boil down to a battle between the experts (Richmond, 1997). It has been said, perhaps unfairly, that "the business of being an expert has become a cottage industry" (*Cordy v. Sherwin-Williams Co.*, 1994, p. 582). In a far less sinister light, however, it has been stated with equal force that expert witnesses "play as great a role in the organization and shaping and evaluation of their client's case as do the lawyers" (*Murphy v. A. A. Mathews*, 1992, p. 682; Richmond, 1997, p. 485). The balance between counsel, their experts, and the just resolution of causes is a delicate one. For, although there is certainly nothing necessarily inappropriate about the proliferation of their testimony, the perception exists, nonetheless, that "trial lawyers are drawn to expert witnesses like moths to light" (Richmond, 2000, p. 909).

The reason for the attraction is manifest. By its very nature, modern litigation calls out to a vast array of properly qualified professionals to testify as expert witnesses—to "peer into the past," as well as to "predict the future" (Lubet, 1999, p. 465). It is expert testimony that often provides that ever-critical aura of reliability enabling a party to prevail (Richmond, 2000). As a consequence, underlying these concerns is the more fundamental tenet of access to courts. Our notions of justice, both civil and criminal, take care to foster the ability of rich and poor alike to litigate justiciable claims. Thus, "one of the paramount goals of the American legal system is to ensure that injured persons have realistic access to the courts" (Parker, 1991, p. 1368).

"Courts have not stood still in the face of what appears to be an expert witness explosion" (Richmond, 1997, p. 490). To date, however, the judiciary's focus on the problems presented by expert witness testimony has been, for the most part, on evidentiary matters of admissibility, reliability, and relevance, especially to prevent dubious scientific evidence from infecting trials (see, generally, *Daubert v. Merrell Dow Pharmaceuticals, Inc.*, 1993; *Kumho Tire Co. v. Carmichael, Weisgram v. Marley Co.*, 1999; Richmond, 1997, 2000). With trial courts as gatekeepers, admissibility has been scrutinized not only of scientific information, but expert testimony based on technical and other specialized knowledge, to discern problems posed by unreliable, speculative, misleading, or unfairly prejudicial testimony, which may rightfully be excluded from the factfinders' view (*Kumho*; Richmond, 2000).

In federal courts, six closely intertwined rules of evidence govern expert witness testimony:

1. Rule 104(a): the trial court's preliminary resolution of questions of admissibility, such as witness competency, privilege, scientific knowledge, and whether the testimony will assist, rather than obfuscate, the trier of fact's effort to understand or determine a fact in issue
2. Rule 702: mandating that expert witnesses be qualified to render opinions that clarify issues
3. Rule 703: the types of facts and data upon which an expert may base their opinion or inference
4. Rule 705: permitting the expert to testify in the form of an opinion or inference without necessarily testifying first as to its foundational basis, that is, in the form of a "naked opinion"
5. Rule 403: recognizing the trial court's broad discretion to balance probative value against undue prejudice arising from the admission of evidence

6. Rule 704: permitting an expert to render their opinion as to the ultimate issue in the litigation (Richmond, 1997)

Ultimately, it is not the court's function to decide whether an expert's opinions are correct, but "merely whether the bases supporting the conclusions are reliable" (*Joiner v. General Electric Co.,* 1997, p. 533; Richmond, 1997, p. 499).

In the name of zealous advocacy, and buffered by the availability of ardent cross-examination, attorneys have responded in kind, to insist that a party is free to solicit the expert of its choice and elicit any opinion that suits its theory of the case. A threefold curative rationale has thus developed to keep the playing field even, while recognizing the importance of role experts serve in facilitating justice. "First, expert testimony which borders on the fantastic, or which is wholly incredible, undermines the integrity of the adversary system" (Richmond, 1997, p. 486). Second, an expert witness should neither be "a party's advocate" or "the litigation equivalent of hired guns" (Richmond, 1997, p. 486). Rather, "an expert witness should be an advocate of the truth with testimony to help the court and the jury reach the ultimate truth in a case, which should be the basis of any verdict" (*Selvidge v. United States,* 1995, p. 156).

And, concededly,

third, expert witnesses merit special attention because their testimony can be powerful and simultaneously very "misleading because of the difficulty in evaluating it." Absent judicial guidance, jurors may "abdicate their fact-finding obligations" and, instead, simply adopt the opinions of the expert witnesses whose testimony they find persuasive. (Richmond, 1997, p. 487)

Each of these concerns, which have caused, and continue to cause, increased scrutiny of "professional experts," are ominously summarized thusly:

Expert testimony often becomes a point of contention in cases in which an expert witness is alleged to be a "professional expert." Professional experts usually are compelling witnesses whose primary function is persuading the jury; the expert's demeanor, personality and communications skills are far more important than the subject of the expert's testimony. Professional expert witnesses freely change their theories and qualifications to suit their immediate employers. . . . Novel scientific testimony sprouts like weeks. Some scientific testimony borders on the absurd. (Richmond, 1997, pp. 487–488)

Some noted examples have included experts specializing in footprint-to-person matching, later debunked as "complete hogwash," forensic dentistry matching bite marks via ultraviolet light, detectable solely by that single "expert" and, more recently, psychological syndrome evidence, such as child sexual abuse accommodation, rape trauma, battered woman, posttraumatic stress, parental alienation, and false memory syndromes, which, unlike diseases, "follow no specified temporal course, nor is their pathology clear" (Richmond, 1997, p. 488).

Curiously, the field of expert witness professional ethics and professionalism, and the ramifications of conduct resulting in disqualification, is rather undeveloped (Lubet, 1999). *Professional ethics* typically refers to the "distinct, mandatory responsibilities undertaken by individuals in the course of practicing a trade or calling" (Lubet, 1999, p. 465). Because of their obligatory nature, breaches here are those that may result in professional discipline, fee forfeiture, or other adverse consequences (Lubet, 1999). By contrast, the more forgiving term *professionalism* is generally used to "identify admirable, model or ideal conduct that is generally expected within a given profession—but not absolutely required" (Lubet, 1999, pp. 465–466).

To be sure, all expert witnesses are governed by a society-driven code of personal ethics, and all must obey rules of courts, evidence and procedure in the jurisdictions in which they appear (Lubet, 1999).

> Still, there is no single source that we can look to for a definitive statement of expert witnesses' professional ethics. A few organizations have attempted to draft codes of conduct for expert witnesses, but none have achieved broad acceptance (Lubet, 1999, p. 467). Despite the absence of an enacted code or other distinct, formal guidance for expert witnesses, this is certainly not to imply an "absence of content-related professional standards." (Lubet, 1999, p. 467)

Regrettably, however, most seminal authority addressing misconduct has not arisen in the psychiatrist–patient context (Lubet, 1999). A prime example, the Model Code of Professional Responsibility, is set forth in three parts: First, *canons* are statements that express the standards of professional conduct to be expected of the professional, and embody the general concepts that comprise the latter two components of the Code; second, *ethical considerations* are aspirational, representing the several objectives to which experts are to aspire; third, *disciplinary rules* are mandatory and relate the minimum level of conduct below which no professional can fall, lest they be subject to discipline (Parker, 1991).

These concerns and issues are what this chapter endeavors to survey, particularly, the often overlooked area broadly defined as *conflicts of interest.* In the more formal usage of the term, a conflict of interest arises in connection with public officials, fiduciaries, and their relationship to matters of private interest or gain, that is, a "clash between public interest and the private pecuniary interest of the individual concerned" (*Black's Law Dictionary*, 1979, p. 271). Stated another way, a conflict of interest is "the circumstance of a public officeholder, corporate officer, etc., whose personal interests might benefit from his or her official actions or influence" (Random House Webster's College Dictionary, 1991, p. 285).

For our purposes, a conflict of interest broaches not only the breach of a fiduciary relationship between parties, but may also incorporate any of a number of nettlesome conflicts and pitfalls of which the expert witness must be aware, from the incipience of the engagement of their professional services, lest they soon find themselves, and perhaps retaining counsel as well, unemployed.

"As modern litigation continues its march toward increasing technical complexity, it will become more important to define and understand issues of ethics and professionalism as they relate to expert witnesses" (Lubet, 1999, p. 488). Under this large umbrella, this chapter attempts a broad examination for the expert witness, as a primer, and highlights several areas of concern, not only conflicts of interest in the traditional sense, but the related quagmires of compensation, in its various forms, permissible and impermissible alike, as well as the expert's conduct during discovery and trial.

The upshot of this sweeping analysis is that the expert witness properly plays a prominent role in protecting not just him- or herself, but both retaining and opposing counsel, as well as the adversarial system of justice itself.

Part one examines five important principles that pervade our discussion of the myriad conflicts of interest the expert witness must be vigilant to avoid. The second part analyzes the standard of review by which courts exercise their inherent power to disqualify expert witnesses. A fundamental understanding of this concept is essential, before appreciating the myriad types of conflicts that may result in disqualification itself. The third part discusses the myriad practices and pitfalls that fall under the broad category of conflicts of interest. In particular, we examine, first, conflicts of interest in their traditional setting—unrelated engagements and the phenomenon known as *side switching*, then we discuss several related areas of potential concern for experts, namely, permissible and impermissible forms of compensation and the expert's equally important involvement during the discovery process and, ulti-mately, trial. Finally, we conclude by recapping the expert's concomitant burden of self-preservation, to ensure that their unique role in the American legal system, as well as their own participation in the process itself, is preserved.

FIVE PRINCIPLES

There are five overarching principles that bear mentioning at the outset: First, courts are rightfully hesitant to disqualify expert witnesses, once they have been retained by counsel at the behest of the client counsel represents. Second, unlike retained counsel, who must advance a partic-ular cause, experts enjoy a unique independence and objectivity in the American legal system. Third, the treating physician stands on even greater independent footing than the "civilian" expert, because treat-ment of the client transforms the expert into a veritable eyewitness, of sorts. Fourth, the expert is nevertheless part of the team, for which they are engaged to assist in the presentation of retained counsel's theory of the case. And fifth and finally, because of the nature of the professional engagement, otherwise privileged communications and confidences, secured in the expert–client relationship, are necessarily vitiated in anticipation of the expert's participation in litigation.

Disqualification Is a Last Resort

First, courts are, and should be, reticent to disqualify expert witnesses. This reticence has one foot in policy, recognizing a public interest, and another in practice, encouraging that reasonable steps should be taken to protect confidences and confidential relationships (Richmond, 1997). To be sure, courts must take care to "preserve parties' confi-dences and to prevent a party from profiting by exploiting its adversary's work product" (Richmond, 2000, p. 298). Nevertheless, "disqualification motions have great potential for abuse as a litigation strategy," and judges must be vigilant in "preventing parties from wielding conflict of interest and confidentiality rules as procedural weapons" (Richmond, 2000, p. 928). Thus,

> as a matter of policy, courts must balance (1) the need to protect opinion
> work product and client confidences and maintain the integrity of the judicial

process with (2) the need to ensure that parties have access to qualified expert witnesses who possess useful specialized knowledge. In conjunction with both elements, courts must be mindful that if experts are too easily disqualified, attorney and parties 'will be encouraged to engage in a race for expert witnesses holding adverse opinions and . . . to create some type of inexpensive relationship with those experts' in order to conflict them out of cases. Such behavior threatens the integrity of the judicial process by depriving courts of the benefit of experts' knowledge and insight, and it deprives parties of the assistance of qualified expert witnesses. (Richmond, 2000, pp. 926–927)

Therefore,

from a practical standpoint, courts should disqualify experts cautiously "because lawyers seeking to invoke the confidential relationship have the knowledge, experience, and the ability to avoid the conflict[s]"; thus, they rightfully bear the consequence for failing to take appropriate precautions. (Richmond, 2000, p. 927)

Focusing thus on the attorney's burden, one seeking to retain the services of an expert, and establish a confidential relationship, should make this intention unmistakably clear and confirm the same in writing:

The lawyer should include in the engagement letter an explanation of the expert's duty of confidentiality. The lawyer may instruct the expert not to discuss the case with other lawyers or colleagues, although such specificity is not required. Broad confidentiality obligations are the best for all concerned. If the lawyer provides the expert with any materials or communicates with him in writing, work product should be clearly identified. Attorneys should also inquire into the expert's previous employment in order to ferret out potential problems. Before sharing confidential information, counsel should ask potential experts to run formal conflict checks or to make the best inquiry they can in their particular situation. (Richmond, 2000, pp. 927–928)

Independence and Objectivity

The second important general principle is that, party alliance or affiliation aside, an expert witness enjoys a unique independence in an otherwise adversarial legal system. In short, expert witnesses owe no shade of allegiance or undivided loyalty to their employer, as does the employer (the lawyer) to the client (Richmond, 2000; Lubet, 1999). "While a lawyer is an advocate for his client, an expert witness is supposed to be a source of knowledge and opinions that will aid the trier of fact"

(Richmond, 2000, p. 910). As such, expert witnesses are viewed as "independent servants of the court" (Richmond, 2000, p. 910).

For this reason, as a general rule, experts may accept concurrent engagements for and against the same party, lawyer, or law firm, and may even testify against former clients in "successive engagements" (Richmond, 2000; Lubet, 1999). An expert's professional freedom is not absolute, however, because agency principles come into play to require that the witness "reasonably safeguard client confidences and refrain from trading on confidential information for personal gain or any other improper purpose" (Lubet, 1999, p. 472; Richmond, 2000, p. 911).

The Doubly Unique Role of the Treating Physician as an "Eye" Expert Witness

Distinct from other types of expert witnesses, treating physicians who double as experts present an even more independent front (Richmond, 2000). Unlike a treating physician, a "civilian" expert, retained solely for litigation purposes, may still be considered "part of the litigation team since the expert is oftentimes responsible for developing a party's theory of the case" (*Donovan v. Bowling*, 1998, p. 941). Conversely, "The doctor's opinions are based on facts actually observed, not on the theory of the case developed by people involved in the litigation phase" (Richmond, 2000, p. 923). As spoken in *Donovan*:

> First-hand and on-scene observations by a witness, expert or not, should be always and equally accessible to both parties. To allow one party to contact a treating physician and then claim that the treating physician has been retained as a possible expert witness, thereby effectively barring the other party from access to that physician's unique first-hand perspective, would be highly unfair to litigants, regardless of whether the party sits at the plaintiff's or the defendant's counsel table. (*Donovan*, p. 941)

In this fashion, the distinction between counsel and expert, particularly the expert engaged in a client-treatment role, becomes crystallized. The attorney is expected to behave in a biased manner, although not improperly so. The expert, on the other hand, is to "remain objective and independent, both in fact and in appearance" (Parker, 1991, pp. 1371–1372).

"The single most important obligation of an expert witness is to approach every question with independence and objectivity" (Lubet, 1999, p. 467). The admissibility of expert testimony is predicated upon the ability of the expert's specialized knowledge to "assist the trier of fact to understand the evidence" (Federal Rules of Evidence 702, 1997). The necessary corollary to this principle is, of course, that the expert's opinion must be "candidly and frankly based upon the witness's own investigation, research and understanding" (Lubet, 1999, p. 467). As an objective observer, the expert is called upon to view facts and data "dispassionately, without regard to the consequences for the client" (Lubet, 1999, p. 467). Indeed, the truly independent expert "is not affected by the goals of the party for which she was retained, and is not reticent to arrive at an opinion that fails to support the client's legal position" (Lubet, 1999, p. 467).

Still, temptation or fantasy aside, no expert witness is an island. Rather, experts must cope with, and work with, lawyers, in order to fulfill their function in an adversarial legal system (Lubet, 1999). Remember that it is the lawyer's job to be the advocate, to make the best possible argument on behalf of the client, in order to win the case (Lubet, 1999). The lawyer, unlike an expert, does not testify under oath, and may often find themselves believing that the advance of a particular position will lead to a victory of sorts, "without necessarily believing that the view is correct," and without even having to "convince yourself" (Lubet, 1999, p. 468). At times, then, a lawyer may indeed be duty-bound to make arguments which, although they do not convince themselves, might very well convince the factfinder to whom they urge it (Lubet, 1999). This is the "classic formulation of the advocate's duty . . . not know[ing] it to be good or bad till the judge determines it" (Boswell, p. 47; Lubet, 1999, p. 468).

And therein lies the inherent clash between the attorney as advocate and the expert witness, who, to the contrary, has no such latitude in their distinct role, apart from, not as part of, membership on the litigation team:

> As a witness testifying under oath, an expert is not entitled to state a position "which does not convince yourself" in the hope that it may convince the judge or jury. The entire system of expert testimony rests upon the assumption that expert witnesses are independent of retaining counsel, and that they testify sincerely. Most lawyers understand and accept this on an intellectual level. Still, in the heat of adversary battle, it is not unknown for lawyers to seek to "extend" or "expand" an expert's opinion in just the right direction.

This is wrong. It is no more acceptable for a lawyer to attempt to persuade an expert to alter her opinion than it would be to convince an eyewitness to change his account of the facts. (Lubet, 1999, p. 468)

Still an Integral Part of the Team

Recognizing that litigation is often a complex endeavor, and almost always an interactive one, the need for independence and objectivity certainly cannot, and does not, prevent experts from working closely with the lawyers who retain them (Lubet, 1999). As long as their respective professional roles are not blurred, "it is entirely legitimate for expert witnesses to cooperate closely with retaining counsel" (Lubet, 1999, p. 469). To this end, experts properly may depend on their employers to provide information, explanations, or descriptions about the case, or disregard the same, if legally irrelevant or inadmissible; advise of the legal standard to be addressed in the formation of the expert's opinion; even convey facts not otherwise readily accessible, in the form of reasonable and clearly identified hypothetical questions (Lubet, 1999).

It is likewise proper for retaining counsel to make suggestions to, or ask questions of, the expert; to seek that the expert reconsider a previous conclusion in light of additional information; to inject pointed questions to ensure the validity of the expert's position; to suggest ways in which the expert's opinion could be solidified; even to assist the expert's preparation for deposition and trial (Lubet, 1999). What is improper is for retaining counsel to pressure the expert to change their opinion, or to instruct the expert how to testify (Lubet, 1999). Neither may an attorney, as the expert must beware, "try to stretch a witness's expertise, either as a cost saving measure or in an effort to broaden the impact of the testimony" (Lubet, 1999, p. 471), as is sometimes their natural impulse to put the expert through such double duty. So too must the expert guard against the slightly more insidious tack of counsel's effort to "induce or inveigle an expert to offer opinions that are truly beyond the scope of her expertise," which, if given, "puts the witness out on a limb that may be sawed off during cross-examination" (Lubet, 1999, p. 471).

In the end, "tactics aside, experts must be both qualified and independent" (Lubet, 1999, p. 471). "A lawyer must ultimately be willing to take the bad news with the good, and to realize that an expert's opinion may be unfavorable to, or not fully supportive of, the client's position" (Lubet, 1999, p. 470). From this, a silver lining emerges: "A lawyer with integrity will normally accept a negative opinion, or even appreciate it, since that may help counsel and client formulate a settlement strategy rather than take a losing case to trial" (Lubet, 1999, p. 470). It is imperative, therefore, that the expert resolve any such issues by this appropriate inquiry: "Either the witness is legitimately able to opine on subject, in which case the engagement proceeds on that basis, or the witness lacks the necessary skills or qualification, in which case the subject is dropped" (Lubet, 1999, p. 471).

Diminished Confidentiality

Professional obligations of confidentiality and secrecy are well recognized in both federal and state courts. The employment of an expert witness, however, necessitates a different result. Notwithstanding the privilege normally accorded privileged communications, the expert witness must be prepared to heed, even expect to be compelled, to reveal client confidences (Lubet, 1999). Such is the very nature of the engagement:

> Forensic evaluation and testimony do not fall within the ordinary practice of most professions. Communications made to a retained witness, for the purpose of facilitating testimony in court, do not fall within the "zone of privacy" necessary for the invocation of an evidentiary privilege. (see, e.g., Federal Rules of Civil Procedure 26(a)(2)(B); Lubet, p. 472)

For the expert witness, then, the watchword is caution:

> Expert witnesses should assume that all of their communications, with either the client or retaining counsel, may be subject to disclosure through the process of discovery. Additionally, the witness' research files, work papers, notes, drafts, correspondence, and similar materials may have to be revealed to the attorneys for opposing parties. (Lubet, 1999, p. 472)

Hence, although, in some jurisdictions, discovery rules may mitigate against discovery disclosure, "prudence dictates that the witness presume that her entire file will be an open book" (Lubet, 1999, p. 472).

> Because of the complex interplay among professional ethics standards, rules of evidence, discovery, and other law, it is best to clarify expectations of confidentiality at the outset of every engagement. According to the ABA Standing Committee on Professional Conduct, a retention letter "should

define the relationship, including its scope and limitations, and should outline the responsibilities of the testifying expert, especially regarding the disclosure of client confidence." (Lubet, 1999, p. 473)

THE STANDARD OF REVIEW

"Life is oftentimes better understood backwards," it has been said. Thus, a discussion of the legal standard upon which courts exercise their discretion to disqualify expert witnesses is apropos before speaking to the issues of the conflicts of interest warranting disqualification. Although instances of disqualification are rare, its happenstance has significant ramifications, beyond that of terminating the services of a particular expert witness. Indeed, both the expert and lawyer or law firm retaining them are subject to disqualification, as well as fee forfeiture or, worse, professional discipline.

Federal and state courts alike possess the inherent power to disqualify experts and attorneys. To determine whether the expert witness or attorney/employer is ripe for disqualification, a two-part test is generally applied, which focuses on the mere appearance of impropriety (Richmond, 1997). Thus, the inquiry asks, "First, was it objectively reasonable for the first party who retained the expert to believe that a confidential relationship existed, [and s]econd, did that party disclose any confidential information to the expert?" (see *Cordy v. Sherwin-Williams, Co.*, 1994, p. 580; *Shadow Traffic Network v. Superior Court*, 1994, pp. 699–700). "Many lower courts have considered a third element: the public interest in allowing or not allowing an expert to testify" (*Koch*, p. 1181; Lubet, p. 488, n. 39).

The answers to both questions must be affirmative, and the public interest not compelling, in order to disqualify the witness (Richmond, 2000). After all, "if the party crying foul should not have reasonably believed that it shared a confidential relationship with the expert, the expert should not be disqualified" (Richmond, 2000, p. 914). By the same token, "if neither the complaining party nor its counsel disclosed confidences, . . . something akin to attorney–client communications or opinion work product, . . . the expert should not be disqualified" (Richmond, 2000, p. 914).

Courts that do not apply the "appearance of impropriety" test have opted for a more "careful, precise and reality based standard" (*Proctor & Gamble, Co. v. Haugen (Haugen I)*, 1998, p. 573). To the court in *Haugen I*, only "real interference" with work product or similar interests, not the mere appearance of impropriety, should require disqualification of counsel (*Haugen I*) or the enlisted expert witness who was only informally consulted (see *Proctor & Gamble, Co. v. Haugen (Haugen II)*, 1999, pp. 412–413). *Haugen II* thus considered four factors in balancing the relative interests: (1) of paramount import, whether the communication originated in confidence or other privilege that it would not be disclosed; (2) to a lesser degree, whether confidentiality is essential to the full and satisfactory relations between the parties; (3) whether the confidentiality at issue breeds a community sense that the relation ought to be sedulously fostered, to the exclusion of production of the evidence; and (4) whether the injury that would occur to the relation by disclosure is greater than the benefit gained for the appropriate resolution of the litigation (*Haugen II*; Richmond, 2000).

Accordingly, in *Haugen II*, the court was not compelled to disqualify an expert witness with whom counsel had only informally consulted. The informal consultation was that the expert was paid a consultation fee and discussed at length material relevant to the case with counsel. Counsel did not, however, reveal its litigation strategy. Thereafter, counsel did not consult further with the expert or exchange any additional information. No further effort was made to contact the expert nor was any indication made to prevent the expert from discussing the case with others. As a matter of fact, the expert never considered himself to have been employed by the party; he did not conduct any research or calculate any data, either. In sum, there was no evidence to suggest he had been retained as an expert in any capacity. Some 2 years later, opposing counsel contacted and retained the expert, but took care not to ask him anything about his prior consultation, which was fully revealed.

In *Haugen I* and *II*, neither present counsel nor the expert was disqualified. Counsel had done nothing to protect its work product, mental impressions, or any of its communications with the expert. Nor did any privilege or basis for disqualification arise as a consequence of the informal consultation with the expert. After all, the expert was not retained, nor had he been privy to any strategic thoughts or impressions. Prior counsel could show no prejudice nor could it demonstrate that the expert owed any duty of confidentiality. In essence, all disqualification would have served to accomplish was exclude relevant evidence— something that the court was surely not willing to do for the sake of formality, favoring instead, in balancing competing interests, the expert's continued participation in the case (*Haugen II*; Richmond, 2000).

PRACTICES AND PITFALLS

From this vantage point, and upon engaging the gentle balance of the expert witness as both independent servant of the law and party-agent, our analysis of the potential problem areas begins.

Traditional Conflicts of Interest

Conflicts of interest involving expert witnesses threaten, equally, litigants on both sides of a dispute (Richmond, 2000).

> Parties may consult with *numerous* [italics added] experts before settling on one who will testify at trial. Those communications are sometimes sensitive and significant, as counsel may have to share their opinion work product or divulge confidential information in order to judge an expert's suitability. (Richmond, 1997, p. 557)

And, of course, circumstances sometimes arise in which "a party may also hire consulting experts unbeknownst to its adversary" (Richmond, 1997, p. 557).

Although the independence of the expert witness is an accepted axiom, it is arguable that the axiom exists only in a cerebral context. For the public at large, probably most of the clients, and certainly some of the bench and bar, believe—or urge themselves to believe, in advancing their particular agenda—that

> in addition to the bias that naturally results from the selection process, the expert witness is influenced by another form of unconscious bias resulting from partisan associations during trial preparation. It is widely acknowledged that witnesses often participate extensively in trial preparation and are carefully prepared to present only favorable testimony on the stand. . . . Attorneys intent on recovering compensation for their clients often try to instill a favorable bias in the expert and sell them the proposed theory of liability. As a result of this partisan bias, witnesses sometimes resort to special purpose studies, the omission of certain factors, and other manipulations in order to support their positions. (Parker, 1991, p. 1386)

Thus, issues of client loyalty and conflicts of interest predominantly arise in two different contexts: *Unrelated engagements,* which asks in which an expert may accept concurrent engagements for and against the same party; and the phenomenon in which an expert switches sides in litigation, otherwise known as *side-switching* (Lubet, 1999, p. 474).

Unrelated Engagements

As noted previously, the legal and ethical obligations of retained counsel and experts unto their clients coexist in a distinct tandem. As a matter of legal ethics, it is well-established that lawyers may not represent any interest directly averse to a current client, as in suing and defending the same party (Lubet, 1999).

> Expert witnesses, on the other hand, do not owe that sort of loyalty to their clients: An expert is not the client's "champion," pledged faithfully to seek the client's goals. Indeed, in many ways the expert's role is precisely the opposite. She must remain independent of the client and detached, if not wholly aloof, from the client's goals. There is no reason that an objective expert could not conclude—and explain—that a party is correct in one case and wrong in another. (Lubet, 1999, p. 474)

"Consequently, there is no general ethical principle that prevents an expert from accepting concurrent engagements both for and adverse to the same party," or even testifying adversely to a former client or law firm that had previously retained the expert (Lubet, 1999, p. 474).

Again, it is agency principles that curtail an expert's exercise of absolute freedom in engagement and "imposes an obligation to refrain from exploiting a client's confidences for the benefit of another" (Lubet, 1999, p. 474). An example of this might be an expert's accepting conflicting engagements, "either concurrently or successively, that are factually related, since this could risk exploitation or betrayal of a client's confidences" (Lubet, 1999, pp. 474–475).

Apart from an actual, or case-specific, conflict of interest, there exists a more amorphous specter of conflict that might also act to constrain an expert's acceptance of an engagement of services. Even when no threat of revelation of client confidences exists, or even when the matters requiring the expert's testimony are utterly unrelated, a law firm or client would surely find "discomfort to see their expert turn up on the opposite side of another lawsuit" (Lubet, 1999, p. 475). Indeed, the expert's dual position may necessarily place the employer in the "troublesome position of having to extol the expert's opinion in one case while attacking it in another" (Lubet, 1999, p. 475). The mere existence of this scenario, rather than a conflict-of-interest-in-fact, may inure to the expert's professional detriment:

> Needless to say, most lawyers would find this situation damaging to the expert's credibility in case one, damaging to the client's position in case two, or both.

No doubt, the retaining lawyer would prefer to avoid this dilemma if possible, even if there is no ethical bar to the expert's actions. (Lubet, 1999, p. 475)

Again, the better part of valor, as a matter of courtesy and professionalism, is to resolve such issues at the very outset of the engagement. Consequently

[a] lawyer may reasonably request that the expert refrain from accepting potentially adverse engagements, least for the duration of the retention. The expert may accept or decline the proposed restriction, or may suggest other terms. The absence of an ethics rule does not prevent the attorney and expert from negotiating a mutually agreeable resolution to what could perhaps become a sticky problem. In any event, a forthright discussion of terms and conditions can prevent the development of an awkward situation down the road. (Lubet, 1999, p. 475)

It is common, of course,

for opposing experts to know one another, to be familiar with each other's work, and perhaps to have worked together. Many experts do not hesitate to call a colleague to inquire about a theory, question data reported in an article, or discuss new methodologies or studies. This is especially true when the experts have forged a personal relationship through service or involvement in professional associations. (Richmond, 2000, p. 924)

Side-switching

This phenomenon is well presented in the following query:

Imagine that an expert has been retained by the plaintiff in a lawsuit. The expert conducts her research and arrives at an opinion that is quite unfavorable to the plaintiff, who then discharges the witness. May the expert subsequently testify for the defendant, whose position is supported by the expert's work? (Lubet, 1999, p. 475)

As stated earlier, because of their uniquely independent role, there is no per se rule prohibiting an expert from switching sides in a lawsuit (Lubet, 1999). Stated another way, because it is the province of the expert not to join irrevocably with a party, but to "arrive at an independent opinion, it cannot be disloyal for the witness to begin working for one party and end up working for the other" (Lubet, 1999, p. 475).

Whether an expert may stray from one camp to another depends ultimately upon the nature and extent of the relationship between the expert and the original client. In brief, an expert may not switch sides, even following discharge or release, if that would violate the original client's reasonable expectation of confidentiality. This in turn will depend on a number of factors. . . . How extensive was the communication between the expert and the client or the client's counsel? Was the expert provided with non-public or privileged information? Did the expert participate in strategy discussions with counsel, or otherwise learn of the client's decision-making strategy? (Lubet, 1999, pp. 475–476)

And, although courts are likely to apply one of the two analyses previously addressed to weigh these factors, the question called turns more often than not on the expert's access to otherwise confidential information (Lubet, 1999). Such was the case in *English Feedlot, Inc. v. Norden Lab., Inc.* (1993), which demonstrates both that an expert who only participates for a brief while in preliminary discussions with counsel, is "free to accept retention from the other side" (Lubet, 1999, p. 476) and that litigants' silence or inconsistent conduct may waive any confidentiality their professional relationship otherwise might bring (Lubet, 1999).

In *English Feedlot*, the defendant tried to disqualify plaintiff's expert and counsel alike. The defense had retained the expert as a veterinary consultant in one matter, then, some years later, the expert served on behalf of several of defendant's customers, agreeing about their complaints about the defective nature of its vaccines. Between the expert's engagements, he made public his opinions about plaintiff's products, and plaintiff, surprisingly, did not protest or object to "dissemination of this information on 'confidentiality' grounds" (*English Feedlot*, 1993, p. 1504; Richmond, 2000, p. 925), essentially acquiescing to the expert's criticisms of their products.

Although the court did find that the two shared a confidential relationship, plaintiff never revealed any confidential information to the expert. And even assuming the plaintiff did, "the company waived any claims of confidentiality" (Richmond, 2000, p. 925).

Waiver is the intentional relinquishment of a known right or privilege. "A waiver may be explicit . . . or it may be implied, as, for example, when a party engages in conduct which manifests an intent to relinquish the right . . . or acts inconsistently with its assertion." Here, SmithKline repeatedly acquiesced to Brown's public criticism of its products. It is thus inconsistent, after impliedly relinquishing this right, for SmithKline to now assert that [the] information is confidential. There, assuming arguendo SmithKline disclose[d] confidential information to Brown, SmithKline waived its right to assert confidentiality at this late date. (*English Feedlot*, p. 1504; Richmond, 2000, pp. 925–926)

And, since the expert had not received any confidential information from plaintiff, the expert could not taint defense counsel (his new employer), thus warranting its disqualification, either (Richmond, 2000).

Waivers may be more subtly imputed, too, however:

For example, a party might allow its consulting expert to share information with its testifying expert in order to help the testifying expert shape his opinions. Assuming that confidential information passes from the consulting expert to the testifying expert and the testifying expert considers that information in forming his opinions, the party has likely waived any confidentiality claims otherwise attending its relationship with the consultant. If a consulting expert's work is part of the foundation for another expert's testimony and the sponsoring party does not object to related deposition questions posed to the testifying expert, the party has probably waived any confidentiality arguments. (Richmond, 2000, p. 926)

"Conversely, an expert who had performed an extensive fact investigation, working closely with counsel, would more likely be barred from switching sides," as in *Wang Laboratories, Inc. v. Toshiba Corp* (Lubet, 1999, p. 476). And concededly, although precedential authority is sparse, an expert who, in a rare instance, defects, that is, either deliberately setting out to switch sides or having been lured away by opposing counsel— compared to one who is discharged or initially declines an engagement—is surely subject to disqualification, because, "not only is such a witness likely to have compromised confidences, but a defecting witness also creates the appearance of chicanery," and thus an affront to the fair administrating of justice (Lubet, 1999, p. 476).

As before,

most difficulties can be avoided if there is a frank discussion at the outset of the engagement. A well-drafted retention letter will spell out the expert's duties and the client's expectations concerning confidential information, as well as the expert's options in the event of discharge or release. (Lubet, 1999, pp. 476–477)

In *Cordy*, for example, the plaintiff was injured while riding his bicycle over railroad tracks. In communicating with an engineer as a prospective expert witness, plaintiff's counsel spoke with him over the telephone about 10 times, ultimately entering into a retainer agreement. After receiving a host of plaintiff's investigative materials, the expert rendered an oral opinion, although he did not provide a written report. After the expert subsequently resigned, returning the retainer as well, he was contacted by defense counsel, and, although he revealed that he had indeed been consulted by plaintiff, the expert was hired by the defense and, as a precaution, instructed not to disclose anything to the defense the expert had learned from his association with plaintiff. The expert ultimately concluded, in a written report, that defendant was not responsible for the accident.

The court easily found that plaintiff's counsel rightly concluded that the expert must have shared confidential information with the defense. All in all, the court found that it was "simply not possible" for the expert to "ignore what he learned" from plaintiff's counsel (*Cordy*, p. 582; Richmond, 2000, p. 915). The court not only disqualified the expert, but defense counsel as well, because, "at the very least, the defense counsel should have contacted Plaintiff's counsel" (*Cordy*, p. 584) to investigate or discover the nature of the relationship between the parties. Whether the defense "chose to ignore the warning signs or actually encouraged" the expert's misconduct was of no interest to the court (*Cordy*, p. 584; Richmond, 2000, p. 915).

There are other instances in which the conflict of interest is between the expert witnesses themselves. The key to whether disqualification is warranted is the degree to which confidential information is shared. Consider, for example, the unique case of *Hansen v. Umtech Industrieservice Und Spedition, GmbH*, a products liability action in which opposing experts were engaged by the same client. The first expert employed by Umtech assured the corporation that there were no conflicts of interests of concern. This expert then shared client confidences, discussed the case at length, and assessed with counsel the relative strengths and weaknesses of the defendant's position. A letter was then sent to the expert confirming his retention, including a request for confidentiality. In return, the expert faxed a letter identifying documents typically necessary for him to review. However, no one took any action with respect to the fax or the case in general (*Hansen v. Umtech*, 1996, p. *2; Richmond, 2000, p. 919).

A short time later, plaintiff engaged its own expert—from the same firm as previously employed by the defendant. Plaintiff's expert ran a computerized conflict-of-interest check, which failed to reveal the prior representation, because defendant's expert "had not entered his representation of Umtech on the system" (Richmond, 2000, p. 920). To make matters worse, the defense expert was on vacation at the time plaintiff sought assistance and therefore was unavailable to properly advise the new expert as to the conflict.

The court disagreed with Umtech that plaintiff's expert, and his firm, should be disqualified, based on its prior relationship with its own expert. The uniqueness of the facts of this case—namely, the fleeting memory of the initial expert engaged—made the court's task less complicated than it otherwise might have been:

> While [defense counsel] stated that she discussed her analysis of the case, including its strengths and weaknesses, with [its expert], [the expert] has no recollection of the details of that conversation. Additionally, [counsel's] disclosures in connection with the liability phase of the case are not germane to either [the expert's] expertise or expert opinion. Further, [the expert] forgot about the case entirely until the conflict was made known to him by [plaintiff's expert and defense counsel]. It is clear, then, that to the extent that counsel disclosed confidential information, [its expert] did not in any way use that information. Furthermore, and more importantly, [he] never discussed the case with anyone, including [plaintiff's expert]. Suffice it to say that if the expert himself can't remember any of the information, he certainly could not have passed it along to the other expert. (*Hansen v. Umtech*, p. *8; Richmond, 2000, p. 920)

In *Palmer v. Ozbek*, the defendant's expert consulted directly with two of plaintiff's experts for a matter of a few hours. This was their sole contact. Plaintiff's counsel never communicated directly with the expert nor did they form a confidential or fiduciary relationship with him. Plaintiff's experts also did not disclose any trial strategies or confidences. Indeed, the only information disclosed was subject to discovery, anyway. Based thereupon, the court declined to disqualify the expert (*Palmer*, 1992; Richmond, 2000). *Palmer* has been cited as a well-reasoned decision, because "experts' communications with one another should not be punished unless a party's confidences or counsel's work product are revealed. If trial lawyers are concerned about such communications, they must instruct their experts not to discuss their engagement with colleagues" (Richmond, 2000, pp. 924–925).

As stated, state courts, too, must resolve conflicts of interests involving experts and whether to disqualify them, along with counsel. In *Shadow Traffic Network v. Superior Court*, a California court disqualified the defendant's entire law firm for engaging experts who had been consulted, although not retained, by the plaintiff (Richmond, 2000). The defense argued, perhaps understandably so, that it should not be prevented from hiring experts whom plaintiff chose not to retain, that is, plaintiff's communications could not be deemed confidential as a matter of law (Richmond, 2000). Applying the standard two-step disqualification analysis, the court disagreed:

> Communications made to a potential expert in a retention interview can be considered confidential and therefore subject to protection from subsequent disclosure . . . as long as there was a reasonable expectation of such confidentiality. (*Shadow Traffic*, 1994, p. 700; Richmond, 2000, p. 921)

Even when opposing counsel is unaware, whether through inadvertence of innocent oversight, of the dual retention of consulting experts, courts may easily conclude that the whole lot of experts should be disqualified (Richmond, 2000). Such was the case in *Mitchell v. Wilmore*, in which neither plaintiff nor defendant realized that they had engaged the same experts—first, the defense to prepare for deposition, then plaintiff, for trial. Applying the same standard test, the court agreed with defendant that disqualification was appropriate, given its "objectively reasonable belief that their relationship with [the experts] was a confidential one and that the matters discussed would remain inviolate" (*Mitchell v. Wilmore*, 1999, pp. 176–177; Richmond, 2000, p. 922).

A final consideration examined by courts, to determine whether a party should be allowed to compel the testimony of opposing counsel's former expert, is the availability of other experts on the topic at hand:

> Courts are unlikely to compel an adversary's former expert to testify where the party seeking to compel the expert's testimony has other available options. The party seeking to compel testimony in that situation cannot claim unfair prejudice if the court precludes the expert's testimony. (Richmond, 2000, pp. 932–933)

However, it stands to reason that, "if a court compels the testimony of a party's former expert, it would not allow the jury to hear that the expert was once employed by the party he is testifying against" (Richmond, 2000, p. 933).

Hence, under a traditional evidentiary balancing test, courts are likely to conclude that

> evidence of the prior retention is substantially more prejudicial than probative. Jurors might assume that counsel for the party who first employed the

expert is trying to suppress unfavorable evidence by not calling the expert, thus destroying the attorney's credibility. If it appears that jurors may be able to infer how the expert became involved in the case without mention of his prior engagement or if his prior engagement places the party that originally retained him at too great a disadvantage on cross-examination, it may be necessary to exclude the expert's testimony altogether. (Richmond, 2000, p. 933)

Compensation

The expert witness is once again considered in a unique context when it comes to the financial aspect of the practice. For, unlike other witnesses who, though testifying, are traditionally reimbursed only for expenses, an expert is paid a fee for preparing and testifying in court. It is here that much of the criticism of the use of expert witness testimony arises, and the darker side the business of the practice rears its ugly head (Lubet, 1999).

> Litigators regularly shop around for experts to support a partisan theory rather than accepting a neutral expert who speaks with objectivity. Attorney skepticism of the "so-called impartial educator" is so high, in fact, that many attorneys refuse to employ "an objective, uncommitted, independent expert." (Parker, 1991, pp. 1385–1386)

Some have even said that, "because lawyers act as zealous advocates in pursuit of a client's allegedly rightful compensation, 'the object is to win' and 'in striving to win, lawyers resort to biased interpretations of facts, partial truths, manipulation, and distortion' " (Parker, 1991, p. 1386). And often, the

> fees to employ necessary expert witnesses constitute substantial litigation expenses and thus potentially act as a bar to effective litigation by litigants who are not wealthy or whose counsel are unable to advance witness fees and absorb them if the case is unsuccessful. (Parker, 1991, p. 1368)

It has thus been argued that "a major hurdle in obtaining adequate compensation for losses is the prevalence of prohibitively high access fees" (Parker, 1991, p. 1368). The gravamen of the problem is the perception, let alone the fact, of denying a claimant the realistic opportunity to pursue a claim—not so much an issue of physical access to courts, but that prohibitively high fees work as an effective bar to recovery, just as if a physical one had been erected (Parker, 1991).

As recognized, "the realities of modern medical malpractice may necessitate resort to technical assistance for the education of counsel inexperienced in such litigation, endeavoring to obtain expert witnesses, and marshalling evidence to support the claim" (Parker, 1991, p. 1385). Thus, despite the evidently pervasive fear that "witness shopping" may occur, for the most part, the more rational conclusion is that "the need for competent experts outweigh[s] the possibility of biased testimony" (Parker, 1991, p. 1385).

An Exorbitant or a Reasonable Fee?

How times have changed. Not so long ago, a court would not sheepishly extol the ethics of an expert witness, as well as our perceptions of good will, in upholding a contingent fee:

> It would be a serious and unwarranted reflection upon the integrity of a physician to say as a matter of law that his testimony was warped or influenced by the fact that, unless a recovery was had, he would not be paid for his services, in examining or treating the patient. (*Lack Malleable Iron Co. v. Graham*, 1912, p. 1018)

The modern experience is altogether differently expressed.

Experts often demand minimum fees, for preparation, deposition, and trial testimony,

> far exceeding that which they would earn were they to charge their regular hourly rate for the actual . . . time. . . . . Experts may charge the party deposing them an hourly rate exceeding that which they charge the party employing them. Treating physicians may charge expert witness fees far above their regular chargers to their patients, a practice roundly criticized by reviewing courts. (Richmond, 1997, p. 566)

Both federal and state courts have long recognized the problems posed by these supposed abusive fee demands (Richmond, 1997, p. 566). "Apparently the litigious nature of society has caused litigation participants to forget the adage 'an honest day's work for an honest day's pay' " (Richmond, 1997, p. 566). Critics, then, are thankful for the extensive judicial regulation that has come to the fore (Richmond, 1997, p. 566). Federal Rule of Civil Procedure 26(b)(4)(C)(i) provides that courts "shall require that the party seeking discovery pay the expert a reasonable fee for time spent responding to discovery."

But what is reasonable? A seven-factor test has been applied by both federal and state courts, to evaluate reasonableness, in light of: (1) the expert's area of expertise; (2) the education and training required to provide the expert the insight that is sought; (3) the prevailing rates of comparable experts; (4) the nature, quality, and complexity of the discovery responses provided; (5) the fee actually being charged to retaining counsel; (6) the fee the expert traditionally charges on related matters; and (7) any other factor likely to be of assistance to the court in balancing the interests implied by Rule 26 (*Jochims v. Isuzu Motors, Ltd.*, 1992, p. 496; Richmond, 1997, pp. 567–568). Assessing whether a fee is reasonable, under such a balancing of interests, is rather straight-forward.

Still, the oft-cited decision by the court in *Anthony Abbott Laboratories* perhaps best illustrates the legal system's frustrations with exorbitant expert witness fees. When the defendant balked at paying one of the plaintiff's key expert's hourly deposition fee, the court, in reducing the fee, waxed so prophetic that we take considerable time here to relate the court's thoughts on the matter:

> For a person with little or no discernible overhead, a rate of $420 hourly strikes this court as unconscionable. Based on a standard (40 hour) work week, annualization would produce an income to [the expert] of $840,000 yearly. He may well be a genius in his field, but this court cannot find that even so important and prestigious a profession as medicine has a right to command such exorbitant rewards. . . . There must be some reasonable relationship between the services rendered and the remuneration [*sic*] to which an expert is entitled; and [the expert's] all-that-the-traffic-will-bear approach falls well outside the outer limits of the universe of rationally-supportable awards.
>
> To be sure, we live in an age where a grown man may be paid a seven figure annual salary to dribble a small round ball. But, the forces of the marketplace are at work in such a situation: not only supply and demand, but the variegated effects of the superstar's presence on attendance, television revenues, and the all-hallowed won/lost record. And, most important, the employer and the employee square off and bargain at arm's length in order to determine an equitable stipend, each with something to lose and something to gain. In the Rule 26(b)(4)(c) context, however, such factors are noticeably absent; the plaintiffs have handpicked the expert, and the defense has neither options nor bargaining power if it desires to obtain the pretrial discovery which the rule permits. Unless the courts patrol the battlefield to ensure fairness, the circumstances invite extortionate fee-setting. (*Anthony Abbott Laboratories*, 1998, pp. 464–465; Richmond, 1997, p. 570)

But the court was not done, harkening back to the mainstay of the American legal system:

> Our citizens' access to justice, which is at the core of our constitutional system of government, is under serious siege. Obtaining justice in this modern era costs too much. The courts are among our most treasured institutions. And, if they are to remain strong and viable, they cannot sit idly by in the face of attempts to loot the system. To be sure, expert witness fees are both the tip of an immense iceberg. But, the skyrocketing costs of litigation have not sprung full-blown from nowhere. Those costs are made up of bits and pieces, and relaxation of standards of fairness threatens further escalation across the board. The effective administration of justice depends, in significant part, on the maintenance and enforcement of a reasoned cost/benefit vigil by the judiciary. (*Abbott Laboratories*, p. 465; Richmond, 1997, p. 570)

Contingent Fee Contracts

The American legal system has sought to alleviate the economic barrier preventing access to courts by purportedly prohibitive attorney fees, "by allowing claimants to employ counsel on a contingent basis" (Parker, 1991, p. 1363). Although an expert is properly paid for their testimony, it is utterly impermissible to pay them—let alone foster a legal system predicated upon the use of testimony—bought and paid for on a sliding scale, that is, dependent upon the outcome of the case. As stated previously, it is the independence of the expert witness that we cherish and hold sacrosanct. Hence, it is a near-universal principle that contingent expert witness fees are unethical, and the rationale for the rule is obvious:

> Such fees are prohibited because they create an unacceptable incentive for the expert to tailor her opinion to the needs or interests of the retaining party. In other words, the expert's independence and objectivity become impaired when payment hinges on the success of the litigation. (Lubet, 1999, p. 477)

Value Billing

Value billing travels a parallel course, because the fee is determined not by the amount of work actually performed, but by the "value or benefit conferred by the work," rather than the "number of hours devoted to the task" (Lubet, 1999, p. 477). For the expert witness, "value billing can come uncomfortably close to charging on the basis of the content of the testimony" (Lubet, 1999, p. 477). It is not only the fact of, but the appearance of, impropriety that is to be avoided, as well. Thus, for example, an expert's policy of returning fees, when their opinion cannot be used by retaining counsel, may, at first blush, appear munificent as a cost-cutting grace. The flip side of that coin, however, is a clear result, whether inadvertent, that the expert receives additional monies when their opinion is favorable to the client (Lubet, 1999). A similar fate might befall an expert who adjusts their hourly rate—up or down—following their initial research or evaluation of a subject, pursuant to an engagement of services (Lubet, 1999).

Steering clear of such contingencies is rather simple. In order to avoid any undue suggestion, experts should bill "at a constant hourly rate" (Lubet, 1999, p. 478). Then, even when an initial consultation or evaluation leads to a further engagement preparing for deposition or trial, this additional work, although obviously resulting in greater total compensation, is not considered a contingent fee (Lubet, 1999).

Flat Fees, Minimums, and Retainers

Thankfully, there are several other ethical means by which to arrange fee structures, namely flat fees, minimums, and retainers (Lubet, 1999). A *flat fee* is, as it suggests, a set amount of remuneration for all, or a limited portion of, the engagement.

> For example, a flat fee could cover the entire engagement all the way through testimony at trial, or it could be determined in stages—perhaps one amount for the initial research and work-up, another if a written report becomes necessary, and a final amount for deposition and trial time. (Lubet, 1999, p. 478)

In a similar vein, by charging a *minimum fee*—usually alongside an hourly assessment—the expert is assured that they will be paid a certain amount, irrespective of the amount of work performed (Lubet, 1999). Finally, a *retainer*, also known as an *advance*, traditionally "provides the witness with some or all of her payment at the outset of the engagement, rather than billing exclusively as work is performed" (Lubet, 1999, p. 478).

What is critical about each of these fee structures is that in none of them is payment guaranteed, based upon the content of the expert's testimony. For this reason, such financial arrangements are considered by courts to be the flip side of the contingent fee and provide security for experts that they will indeed be compensated for their services (Lubet, 1999).

Lock-Up Fees (aka the Signing Bonus)

A final consideration is the *lock-up fee*, which essentially represents a nonrefundable payment to the expert at the outset of the engagement of services, the purpose of which is "to compensate the witness for agreeing to forego retention by the other parties in the litigation" (Lubet, 1999, p. 478). Here, the expert's uniquely independent role in the legal system rises anew.

There is certainly an element of financial risk in an expert's agreeing to work for one party and receiving client confidences in return. In this instance, as discussed above, the expert may not be permitted to switch sides of the litigation. Imagine the expert's dismay at learning only a short while into the case that their opinion is indeed adverse to the client, rendering their testimony impotent for the duration of the case for either party. The lock-up fee is an effort to resolve this dilemma "by, in essence, providing the expert with a 'signing bonus' in exchange for agreeing to work exclusively with one client in the matter" (Lubet, 1999, p. 479).

When it comes to retaining counsel, such nonrefundable fee arrangements have been roundly criticized as oppressive and exploitative, particularly as they impact on a client's absolute right to disengage their services (Lubet, 1999). The chief objection to the attorney's nonrefundable retainer is that the forfeiture of the retainer creates "a *de facto* impediment to firing the lawyer" (Lubet, 1999, p. 479). Such procedural or substantive constructs, which chill the free exercise of client rights—constitutional, statutory, or otherwise—are frowned upon. Indeed, these types of signing bonuses have been either banned outright, or severely limited, as used by attorneys across the country, resulting not only in return of monies, but in professional discipline as well (Lubet, 1999).

But the expert witness does not operate under these same constraints. Here, too, there is an inherent interest in protecting the client from financial loss resulting from an entrapped marriage of sorts. Yet, although an expert, too, may be fired at will by retaining counsel, "no comparable public policy is served" in similarly shielding the client, whose relationship with counsel has been solidified prior to the engagement (Lubay, 1999, p. 480). The expert is the independent, authoritative source they have solicited to employ (Lubet, 1999). Retaining parties should therefore be prepared to accept some risk of cost or penalty in disengaging the services of an expert, whether they have performed some or all of the services contracted for. "Consequently, lock-up fees should not be considered unethical when used by expert witnesses" (Lubet, 1999, p. 479).

During Discovery

An expert's utility to the retaining party is certainly not limited to their performance at trial. Indeed, while many cases involve the engagement of expert witnesses, but only a small percentage of them actually proceed to trial. Most legal disputes, whether as a sheer consequence of volume or for other more practical reasons, achieve a settlement before the jury reaches a verdict. Therefore, the role the expert plays in discovery, particularly helping to develop the theory of the case, then advance the cause toward resolution, cannot be underemphasized. The expert's broad spectrum of involvement is touched upon below.

In addition to the areas addressed herein, an expert's familiarity with procedures embodied in rules such as Federal Rules of Civil Procedure 26 and 37, discussing, generally, disclosure requirements, rebuttal, and impeachment testimony, for testifying and consulting experts alike, are highly recommended (Richmond, 1997, pp. 533–543).

Communicating with Adverse Counsel

An expert must always remain alert to the potential pitfalls incurred by communicating with lawyers from the opposing party. In order to maintain at least a modest vigilance, the expert too must know of the distinction between *testifying experts* and those referred to merely as *consulting* or *nontestifying experts* (Lubet, 1999, p. 480). The Federal Rules of Civil Procedures, and corresponding provisions in most states, limit the right to, and scope of, such contact (Lubet, 1999). "Although there are limited exceptions, only testifying experts are broadly subject to discovery. Purely consulting experts, other than in extreme circumstances, are exempt from discovery" (Lubet, 1999, p. 480; Fed. R. Civ. P. 26[b][4]).

Still, an expert, even a consulting one, cannot turn a blind eye to an impermissible contact. Predictably, most of the discovery rules promulgated to date proscribe conduct by counsel. Most rules thus probably do not constrain experts themselves, but, once again, it is agency principles that require the expert to take reasonable steps to maintain client confidences (Lubet, 1999). The burden is a rather facile one: "A responsible expert, therefore, should notify retaining counsel in the event that she is approached for substantive information by the attorney for an adverse party" (Lubet, 1999, p. 480).

Document Production

As discussed herein, the prudent expert, particularly the testifying expert, while keeping client confidences inviolate, knows full well that their file may, at some juncture, be subject to full disclosure to the adverse party (Lubet, 1999). Whether a testifying or nontestifying expert, however, the decision whether to turn over materials in discovery is eminently a legal one. Fortunately, this makes it for the lawyers to hash out. "Experts are neither expected nor allowed to decided on their own which materials should and should not be disclosed" (Lubet, 1999, p. 480).

For the time being, then, for the expert's purposes, the critical obligation—to client, counsel and court alike—is most obvious:

> It is unethical, and perhaps even criminal, to conceal or destroy material that has been subpoenaed or requested in discovery. Of course, disclosure may be resisted. There can be objections to discovery and subpoenas may be quashed. But that process nonetheless requires good faith compliance, or at least acknowledgment of the existence of the requested items. (Lubet, 1999, pp. 480–481)

This limitation is not applicable merely to documents previously requested by the adverse party. As the expert thus abides cautiously by obeying counsel's directives whether to, and, if so, the scope of, the revelation of otherwise privileged documents or confidences, the experts themselves must take care to "never destroy any item, document, object, photograph, or record for the purpose of concealing it from discovery or obstructing another party's access to evidence" (Lubet, 1999, p. 481). This is not to say that, in the course of normal housekeeping, certain papers and objects may be discarded (Lubet, 1999). Understandably, this transgression is easiest to discern once the discovery has been requested, and preservation thereof, until the request has been complied with by the expert, or disallowed by the court, is manifest (Lubet, 1999). It is the matter of concealing materials potentially subject to discovery that is a similarly nefarious undertaking and should give the expert pause before taking any hasty route that may lead to sanction.

For example, in *House v. Combined Insurance Co.*, a sexual harassment suit, defendant/insurance company retained a psychiatrist to conduct an independent examination of plaintiff, to discern whether she indeed suffered from emotional distress, and subsequently designated that the expert would testify at trial. In preparing for the expert's deposition, plaintiff sought production of his report in discovery. Probably harboring knowledge that the expert's opinions were adverse to the defense, defendant then moved for a protective order regarding the report, and, although it did not recede from having designated him as an expert witness, it did drop him from its final witness list and apprise the court it did not intend to call him at trial (Richmond, 2000).

The court noted that there were "three possible standards to apply when determining whether a party should have access to an adversary's former expert" (Richmond, 2000, p. 930):

> The first option is the "exceptional circumstances" standard in Federal Rule of Civil Procedure 26(b)(4)(B), which deals with the consulting experts. The second is a " 'discretionary' or 'balancing' standard," which weighs the "interests of the [discovering] party and the court against the potential for prejudice to the party who hired the expert." The third and most lenient standard is an "entitlement" standard, drawn from a few cases holding that a party is entitled to call an adversary's expert notwithstanding the adversary's opposition. (*House*, 1996, p. 240)

Because the case dealt, not with testifying experts, but with the "very significant difference from the situation in which an expert has merely been consulted by a party, but never designated as likely to testify at trial," the court rejected the "exceptional circumstances" standard (*House*, p. 245).

> Parties should be encouraged to consult experts to formulate their own cases, to discard those experts for any reason, and to place them beyond the reach of an opposing party, if they have never indicated an intention to use the expert at trial. Such a consulted-but-never-designated expert might properly be considered to fall under the work product doctrine that protects matters prepared in anticipation of litigation. . . . For this reason also, the ability of an opposing party to call a never-designated expert at trial should depend upon a showing of "extraordinary circumstances." (*House*, p. 245)

The court continued:

> However, once an expert is designated, the expert is recognized as presenting part of the common body of discoverable, and generally admissible, informa-

tion and testimony available to all parties. A party's designation of an expert as a witness to be called at trial, even if later revoked, removes the expert from the category of consulting experts whom are protected from compelled testimony absent a showing of exceptional circumstances. (*House,* p. 245)

When it came to the case at hand, however, the court ultimately applied the intermediate level, discretionary or balancing standard, which best balanced " 'the court's [objective] interest in the proper resolution of the issues' with the parties' interests in presenting their claims and preserving their defenses" (*House,* p. 246; Richmond, 2000, p. 931). This case demonstrates that the role the public interest plays in shaping such decision is significant. Thus, *House* held that the expert's testimony should, in fact, be presented to the jury, to "aid in the proper resolution of the issues" (Richmond, 2000, p. 931).

Still, the court placed a logical restriction upon plaintiff's presentation of evidence, in order to, as always, keep the playing field as even as possible in the pursuit of the fair administration of justice:

> The court was concerned, however, that [the expert's] testimony would unfairly prejudice [the defendant] if the plaintiff was allowed to elicit testimony that [defendant] originally hired the doctor and then dropped him as a witness once his opinions became known. (Richmond, 2000, p. 931)

Therefore, in equity, the court held that the plaintiff could indeed call the expert as her expert at trial, "provided that evidence of *how* he became involved in the case was excluded" (*House,* p. 248; Richmond, 2000, p. 931).

> *House* teaches what should be obvious: a party who hires an expert should do so carefully. The case also illustrates that health care providers who testify as experts based on independent medical examinations performed under Federal Rules of Civil Procedure or state court equivalents may be treated differently from other experts. (Richmond, 2000, p. 931)

Note, however, that

> [a] party's designation of an expert to testify at trial does not always entitle an opponent to depose that expert or to call him as a witness at trial if he switches sides. A party should not be allowed to call an adversary's former expert in an attempt to cure the mistake of not designating its own expert. Nor should a party be allowed to call its adversary's former expert where the expert's testimony is not relevant or is only "indirectly pertinent." (Richmond, 2000, p. 931)

Depositions

Simply stated, a "deposition is pretrial testimony, taken under oath for the purpose of discovering what the witness has to say" (Lubet, 1999, p. 481). There are few ethical pitfalls for the expert to beware of here, "though all of the standard issues such as confidentiality, coaching, and candor certainly can and do arise" (Lubet, 1999, p. 481). That no judge is present, however, does present a question worthy of note: whether to act upon the advice of counsel, received on or off the record, in the face of a contrary directive by opposing counsel. Since local procedures play a large role in directing the expert's response, the more cautious approach will be recommended here (Lubet, 1999). Of course, when the witness is apprised of more definitive authority, a more precise course of action may be justified.

Conferences between expert witness and retained counsel are commonplace during deposition. In days past, it was

> considered routine almost everywhere for lawyers to pull aside their witnesses so long as there was no question pending at that particular moment. While most such conferences were no doubt conducted in good faith to clarify a point, to preserve a confidence, or to calm down a nervous witness, they were also the occasion of much abuse. Too many lawyers used off-record conferences to obstruct the deposition, coach the witness, or worse. (Lubet, 1999, pp. 481–482)

Rules governing counsel's right to confer with a witness now vary greatly among jurisdictions. For our purposes, the import of this development was to free the expert from the quandary of facing "a great variety of environments" and not always being able "to count on the lawyers for clear or knowledgeable directions" (Lubet, 1999, p. 482), although it is to them, ironically, that procedural rules are particularly aimed. The soundest advice is for the expert to take matters into their own, educated hands, thusly:

Remember that retained counsel is not the expert's counsel (Lubet, 1999). "The expert is there to provide an independent analysis and opinion. Since the expert is not a party to the case, the expert is not represented by either of the attorneys" (Lubet, 1999, p. 485). Indeed, expert witnesses are rarely, if ever, accompanied by their own attorney at deposition (Lubet, 1999).

Hence, if adverse counsel does not object to the expert's conferring with retained counsel, there is obviously little reason for concern (Lubet,

1999). When a squabble does arise, however, especially those requiring undue revelation of client confidences or responses beyond the scope of expertise, seldom is it "the witness's job to resolve" (Lubet, 1999, p. 482). The lawyers are there for something. Unless the expert has "reliable independent knowledge of the jurisdiction's rule, the best approach to this problem is probably to follow the directions of the retaining lawyer" (Lubet, 1999, p. 483). Stated more succinctly:

> Recall that an expert has specific professional obligations to the client, including a duty to take reasonable steps to protect certain confidences. It is the retaining lawyer who speaks for the client, and it is the retaining lawyer who is most knowledgeable about the effect of the deposition upon the client's confidences. Hence, the prudent path is usually to accept the retaining lawyer's understanding of the rules. (Lubet, 1999, p. 483)

This is not to say, of course, that lawyers are not infallible (Lubet, 1999). In other words, if something sounds too good to be true, even from your counsel, it probably is. Consequently,

> [a]n expert should never violate or disregard a court order, no matter how many assurances are forthcoming from retaining counsel. . . . More importantly, even where conferencing is freely allowed, an expert should likewise never permit retaining counsel to dictate or alter the content of her testimony. (Lubet, 1999, p. 483)

And only "in extreme or extraordinary circumstances, the expert should consider whether she needs to consult her own attorney" (Lubet, 1999, p. 483).

But what of conflicting directives, when the deposing and retaining lawyers dispute the authority of the expert to reveal a confidence or opinion? Ostensibly, the expert may now be in a bind: "Retaining counsel has instructed her not to answer but the deposing lawyer insists threatening court action is she refuses. Which lawyer is right? Which one should the witness believe? Most important, how should the witness respond?" (Lubet, 1999, p. 484).

It does not take an expert to answer this one. Once the cat is out of the bag, so to speak, the damage is already done. Consequently, the expert "must always be sensitive to the need to shield privilege information. Once information has been revealed, it may lose its protected nature even if the deposing lawyer was never entitled to it in the first place" (Lubet, 1999, p. 484). The better course, then, is for the expert to decline to answer when an impediment arises or an apparent abyss presents itself. After all, there is little downside to a temporary halt in the proceedings:

> Here is the solution. If the witness improperly declines to answer, the informa-tion can always be provided later. Thus, there is relatively little harm in refusing to answer a particular question, pending resolution by the lawyers or a ruling by the court. On the other hand, information can never be retrieved once it has been disclosed. Great damage can be done by ignoring an objection and by proceeding to reply. . . . Thus, in the absence of other factors, the best approach for a witness is to decline to answer questions once retaining counsel has objected on the basis of privilege or confidentiality. A polite refusal to answer will preserve the objection so that it may, if necessary, be brought before the court. (Lubet, 1999, p. 484)

For example, a suitable response to a deposing lawyer's admonition, whether the expert is going to follow their lawyer's instructions and refuse to answer the question, may thus be: "I am not following *anyone's* [italics added] instructions, but I decline to answer that question. It is not my job to resolve disputes between counsel about privilege or discoverability" (Lubet, 1999, p. 485).

At Trial

As the litigation enters the trial phase, the basic principles of profes-sional ethics continue to govern the expert's conduct (Lubet, 1999). There are, however, a few trial-specific issues worthy of mention.

Ex Parte Communications

An ex parte communication is one that involves less than the total number of parties legally entitled to share it or to be present during its discussion. Thus, as a general rule, "all communication with the court must take place in the presence of all attorneys" (Lubet, 1999, p. 485). Like any other witness or party-agent, the expert witness should take care to avoid any formal or informal private conversation with a judge on any pending matter, even at the appellate level, particularly discussions of "the substance of the case or the content of the witness's testimony" (Lubet, 1999, p. 485). This admonition is indeed rather straightforward.

Do not think for a moment, however, that the only culprit might be you. "Unfortunately, it also occurs that judges seek out witnesses even without legal justification. Perhaps the judge is curious, incautious, or simply unaware of the extent of the rule against ex parte communication" (Lubet, 1999, p. 486). Frankly, the "why" does not matter very much at all. "Whatever the reason, such contact can obviously cause much discomfort for the witness" (Lubet, 1999, p. 486). To be sure, "most witnesses would never presume to question the judge's knowledge of law or ethics" (Lubet, 1999, p. 486). Might the communication therefore be appropriate? After all, "the judge is the judge" (Lubet, 1999, p. 486).

Alongside the regal stature of the expert's independent status in the sphere of litigation comes some responsibility considered perhaps above and beyond the ken. Foremost, outside of testimony on the witness stand, experts should remain vigilant to remain away from such communications, whether with the court or, for that matter, with jurors (Lubet, 1999). The expert witness, as any witness, should make an effort to limit contact with the court or the jury—in the hallway, elevator, or cafeteria—to a polite smile or greeting, if that. And, surely, "under no circumstances should a witness *ever* discuss a case with a sitting juror" or judge (Lubet, 1999, p. 486).

Third-Party Communications

The rules proscribing the expert witness's communications with others during trial, including other witnesses, are rather straightforward, as well. More commonly known as the Rule of Sequestration (or "The Rule"), once invoked by one or both of the parties, or by the court on its own motion, witnesses are normally excluded from the courtroom while others are testifying (Lubet, 1999). The purpose is to engender as pristine a result as possible, in which one witness's testimony is not unduly influenced, tainted, or tilted by another. Obviously, knowledge of other witnesses' testimonies can be gleaned not merely from sitting in the courtroom, but from discussing prior testimony with them before the expert takes the stage (Lubet, 1999). Don't. "An expert should not debrief another witness who has already testified and should not read the transcript of earlier testimony, other than at the direction of trial counsel" (Lubet, 1999, p. 487). And remember, should trial counsel direct you to do so, an insistent bell should go off in your head that you and you alone are ultimately responsible for the candor and tenor of your conduct.

Experts, however, are different. Because of their uniquely independent character in the litigation process, expert witnesses are sometimes excepted from this proscription (Lubet, 1999). Therefore, the expert should "always check with retaining counsel before attending the trial as an observer" (Lubet, 1999, p. 486).

When it comes to contact between the expert and retained counsel, particularly contact during trial, and communications during recesses in the witness's testimony, rules vary from courthouse to courthouse. In some jurisdictions, broad dialogue is permitted; in others, there may be limited, if any, contact at all, once the expert is placed under oath (Lubet, 1999). And, in still others, access to speak with the expert is dependent upon when during the expert's testimony the recess is taken, that is, during, or upon the conclusion of, the witness's direct examination (Lubet, 1999). The best rule, then? "Needless to say, expert witnesses should determine the applicable rule for the court in question. Whatever the rule, the witness should comply" (Lubet, 1999, p. 487).

Speaking to the Media

In most litigation, it does not suite the press's fancy to seek public commentary by the parties or witnesses. Most cases are, after all, routine. For this reason, trial courts are rarely called upon to enter this fray. There are times, however, when this is not the case. "In the absence of a gag order or secrecy statute, witnesses are free to speak with the press about the trials in which they have participated" (Lubet, 1999, p. 487). Still, an expert's sense of professionalism may, and usually should, cause them to think twice before doing so (Lubet, 1999).

> Ordinarily, a party to litigation does not retain an expert for the purpose of speaking to the press. The party may not want the case publicized and may not want to risk the exposure of confidences. In this regard, experts should take their cue from retaining counsel. (Lubet, 1999, p. 487)

The cue from most prudent counsel is, in general, to decline comment, especially in pending litigation. In only the rarest instances will trying the case in the press assist the trier of fact—unless, of course, that is your particular style. And when it will assist in advancing the course of a case, rest assured that retaining counsel will likely let the expert know.

Excluded Evidence

As discussed, it is predominantly retained counsel's responsibility to apprise the expert of what information is available to them, the legal standard to be addressed, and, ultimately, where their opinion fits in the party's theory of the case. However, "with or without the expert's knowledge, certain evidence may have been ruled inadmissible by the court," either in limine, that is, pretrial, or even during the trial itself (Lubet, 1999, p. 487). Trial, after all, is a dynamic, not a static, process. It is incumbent upon counsel, then, to inform the expert of any limitations on their testimony to come. And, of course, "once evidence has been ruled inadmissible, either during or before the witness's testimony, it is unethical to sneak it in 'through the back door' " (Lubet, 1999, p. 487).

The expert, playing it safe and ethical, as always, once instructed to refrain from eliciting certain matters, "should not attempt to blurt out the proscribed information on the pretext of answering an unrelated question" (Lubet, 1999, pp. 487–488).

CONCLUSION

"It is widely recognized that expert testimony is 'virtually indispensable' in cases where the facts are outside the realm of understanding of lay jurors or judges" (*Natural Soda Prods. v. City of Los Angeles*, 1952, p. 994). Expert witnesses indeed play a prominent role in the American litigation process, but, as discussed, the legal system is ultrasensitive to the potential for abuse—as it bombards triers of fact with potent, scientific testimony, as well as its affect, real or perceived, upon access to courts.

In light of all of the foregoing, and in accord with the adage "Ignorance is not bliss" (Richmond, 2000, p. 928), it is recommended that experts take it upon themselves to ensure both the propriety of the engagement of services and the sanctity of the ensuing agent relationship. From the outset, experts ought to take care "to avoid conduct that contributes to a lack of clarity about the relationship" (*Wang Laboratories*, p. 1250; Richmond, 2000, p. 928) either with counsel or the opposing party. Should an expert wish to decline employment, the prudent course is to "express their doubts clearly" (*Wang Laboratories*, p. 1250; Richmond, 2000, p. 928). Obviously, "if an expert does not want to share a confidential relationship with a prospective employer, she should decline the engagement" (*English Feedlot*, p. 1505; Richmond, 2000, p. 928). And, if an expert does not wish to be employed, is unsure about their desire for the employment, or, perhaps most importantly, does not want to be obligated to maintain client confidences, they must take care not to accept information or materials relating to the case (Richmond, 2000; *Wang Laboratories*). Moreover, in such cases, experts should also "decline a retainer or any other fee advance" (Richmond, 2000, p. 929). And finally, when an expert has consulted with a party in a case and is subsequently contacted by another party to the litigation, it stands to reason that it is incumbent upon them to "inform the second party of the prior consultation" (*Haugen II*, p. 414; Richmond, 2000, p. 929).

A conscious effort to take care to observe these simple and straightforward guidelines should serve the expert to avoid conflicts of interest that may lead to rather unanticipated and unpleasant results.

REFERENCES

Anthony Abbott Laboratories, 106 F.R.D. 461 (D. R.I. 1985).

Black's Law Dictionary (5th ed.). (1979).

Boswell, J. (1887). *The Life of Samuel Johnson.*

Cordy v. Sherwin-Williams, Co., 156 F.R.D. 575 (D. N.J. 1994).

Daubert v. Merrell Dow Pharmaceuticals, Inc., 509 U.S. 579 (1993).

Donovan v. Bowling, 706 A.2d 937 (R.I. 1998).

English Feedlot, Inc. v. Norden Labs, Inc., 833 F.Supp. 1498 (D. Colo. 1993).

Federal Rule of Civil Procedure 26(a)(2)(B).

Federal Rule of Civil Procedure 26(b)(4).

Federal Rule of Evidence 702.

Hansen v. Umtech Industrieservice Und Spedition, GmbH, No. 95-516 MMS, 1996 WL 622557, at *1 (D. Del. July 3, 1996).

House v. Combined Insurance Co., 168 F.R.D. 236 (N.D. Iowa 1996).

Jochims v. Isuzu Motors, Ltd., 141 F.R.D. 493 (S.D. Iowa 1992).

Joiner v. General Electric Co., 78 F.3d 524 (11th Cir. 1996), *cert. granted*, 117 S.Ct. 1243 (1997).

Koch Ref. Co. v. Jennifer L. Boudreaux MV, 85 F.3d 1178 (5th Cir. 1996).

Kumho Tire Co. v. Carmichael, 526 U.S. 137 (1999).

Lack Malleable Iron Co. v. Graham, 143 S.W. 1016, 1018 (1912).

Lubet, S. (1998, Spring). Expert witnesses: Ethics and professionalism. *Georgetown Journal of Legal Ethics, 12,* 465.

Mitchell v. Wilmore, 981 P.2d 172 (Colo. 1999).

Murphy v. A.A. Mathews, 841 S.W.2d 671 (Mo. 1992).

Natural Soda Prods. Co. v. City of Los Angeles, 240 P.2d 993 (Cal. App. 1952).

Palmer v. Ozbek, 144 F.R.D. 66 (D. Md. 1992).

Parker, J. J. (1991, July). Contingent expert witness fees: Access and legitimacy. *Southern California Law Review, 64,* 1363.

Proctor & Gamble, Co. v. Haugen (Haugen I), 183 F.R.D. 571 (D. Utah 1998).

Proctor & Gamble, Co. v. Haugen (Haugen II), 184 F.R.D. 410 (D. Utah 1999).

Random House Webster's college dictionary (edition). (1991). New York: Random House.

Richmond, D. R. (2000, Summer). Expert witness conflicts and compensation. *Tennessee Law Review, 67,* 909.

Richmond, D. R. (1997, Summer). Regulating expert testimony. *Mo. Law Review, 62,* 485.

Selvidge v. United States, 160 F.R.D. 153 (D. Kan. 1995).

Shadow Traffic Network v. Superior Court, 29 Cal. Rptr.2d 693 (Cal. Ct. App. 1994).

Wang Laboratories, Inc. v. Toshiba Corp., 762 F.Supp. 1246 (E.D. Va. 1991).

Weisgram v. Marley Co., 120 S.Ct. 1011 (2000).

Special Areas

Chapter 16

Forensic Neuropsychology with Children

Jeffrey B. Titus and Raymond S. Dean

The practice of forensic neuropsychology involves the assessment of a litigant in a criminal or civil proceeding, using neuropsychological techniques. The original interest of using neuropsychology for this purpose developed out of personal injury claims of brain injury, over the past few decades, requiring testimony about the neurological integrity of litigants. Neuropsychologists became experts of preference in this regard, because of their specialized knowledge of brain functioning and behavioral sequelae of damage (Giuliano, Barth, Hawk, & Ryan, 1997). In addition, neuropsychologists are trained to utilize techniques that provide quantitative and more objective data than that produced by medical experts. The use of such data can make neuropsychological testimony more credible in the courtroom (Glass, 1991). However, because the credibility of neuropsychologists weighs so heavily upon the quality and interpretation of the test results, it is important for neuropsychologists to have a strong justification for the measures they use, as well as the reasoning behind the manner in which the results were interpreted. This point can be emphasized even more, when considering the challenges that children pose in neuropsychological assessment. Assessment of children, especially in a legal context, requires a high degree of complexity, and it is important to consider this population in isolation from adults.

In general, personal injury, competency, and custody are the most common reasons children are considered for neuropsychological assessment in forensic cases. *Personal injury* refers to the determination of whether a child has experienced a significant brain injury as the result of insult (e.g., motor vehicle accident, physical abuse, perinatal complications). Assessment for the purposes of establishing *competency* is a determination of whether a child possesses a certain level of awareness about the proceedings and can offer valid testimony. Last, *custody* considerations in legal proceedings are common, when parents are feuding about the best interests of the child. In this situation, assessment focuses upon the emotional state of the child and the ability of each parent to successfully rear the child.

Being qualified to make these determinations requires a solid foundation of knowledge in development and childhood pathology. Moreover, the clinician must be trained in clinical neuropsychology, with understanding of common childhood neurological conditions and issues related to their assessment. A qualified clinician should be licensed in psychology, preferably with a degree or postdoctoral training in pediatric neuropsychology, school psychology, or child clinical psychology. High standards of proficiency would be evidenced through board certification by the American Board of Professional Psychology, the American Board of Professional Neuropsychology, or the American Board of Pediatric Neuropsychology. The American Board of Forensic Examiners also provides certification, but membership does not require formal graduate training or supervision.

ASSESSMENT

This chapter includes specific considerations that need to be made regarding personal injury, competency, and custody, when assessing children. However, certain elements should be present in all neuropsychological evaluations of children. These include the following:

1. A comprehensive review of developmental history, including perinatal events.
2. Examination of medical history, including past mental health treatment and medications.
3. Determination of any exposure to toxins or head injuries.
4. Examination of educational history, with special attention regarding special education.
5. Psychosocial functioning, including peer relationships and interactions with authority.
6. Comprehensive mental status examination.
7. Comprehensive neuropsychological testing.

The goal of neuropsychological testing should be to develop a thorough understanding of the child's neuropsychological functioning, through multiple measures that tap a variety of constructs. Oftentimes, in forensic cases, multiple measures of the same construct are desired, to assure the validity of the findings. However, of particular interest in forensic cases is the assessment of constructs that can provide an indication of level of functioning, brain damage, the presence of emotional disturbance, or a probability of malingering. These constructs include the following:

1. Cognitive ability (including memory, fluid reasoning, crystallized knowledge, and visual and auditory processing).
2. Achievement (particularly in reading, mathematics, and language).
3. Sensory performance (simple and complex).
4. Motor performance (including subcortical).
5. Emotional status (personality assessment).

Each of these constructs can offer unique contributions to the assessment of an individual. Primarily, a cognitive measure can provide an understanding of the child's overall level of functioning. However, it also provides examination of individual aspects of higher cortical functioning, which can contribute to the determination of head injury or even preexisting pathology. For example, although memory and fluid reasoning are typical deficits following head injury, crystallized knowledge (such as linguistic information) has been shown to remain relatively stable following injury, providing clues to premorbid functioning (Wechsler, 1958). Moreover, assessment of academic achievement can also provide clues in this regard; however, in children, this becomes more difficult, because of the necessity of an adequate exposure to learning. That is, the younger the child, the less reliable achievement scores are, because they are based upon a smaller amount of learned information.

Assessment of sensory performance should always include both simple and complex stimuli, as presented on both hands and simultaneously to the hand and face. Such assessment provides adequate information on the integrity of the sensory pathways and sensory processing systems in the brain. In addition, careful examination of differences between left and right performance can provide further evidence of underlying neurological dysfunction. This is a similar consideration when assessing motor performance. Individuals with brain impairment can show significant differences between performance on their left or right, depending upon the nature and location of the injury. Examination of motor skills should cover competencies in manual dexterity, strength of grip, fine and gross coordination, speech expression, and balance. Investigation of subcortical functioning is also important and can be of particular interest in younger children, who are still experiencing significant cortical development.

Finally, neuropsychological assessment of children in forensic cases should always include a comprehensive assessment of the child's emotional status. Combining results from the mental status examination with results from objective personality measures can offer information about the existence of difficulties with depression, anxiety, inattention, oppositional behavior, obsessive–compulsive features, withdrawal, hyperactivity, and poor social skills. This can shed light upon the presence of disorders that may affect the results of the neuropsychological examination or suggest the presence of preexisting conditions that are not related to the injury.

In working with all of this information, neuropsychologists must be aware of the challenges that are faced when assessing children. No two children can be considered to be the same, developmentally. Stage theorists have proposed a relatively uniform pattern of development in children (Piaget, 1952), but a more accurate view, based upon the many biological and environmental influences on children, emphasizes the uniqueness of each individual. Moreover, especially in assessment of personal injury, factors such as delayed effects and plasticity in the recovery of function must be considered, before a true understanding of a child's level of functioning can be developed.

PERSONAL INJURY

In the case of personal injury, the most important issue is the recovery of function. However, this concept becomes more complicated in children, because a lost function may not have been developed prior to the injury-inducing event. Therefore, consideration must be made about whether the injury prevented the function from developing normally. Courchesne, Townsend, and Chase (1995) offer an explanation of how an insult to a developing brain can result in future pathology. They describe neural network development in terms of a *self-organizing phenomenon*.

That is, each emerging structure and process leads to the formation of more structures and processes, to progress from a state of relatively simple interactions to one of more complex interactions. Once the process of development is set in motion, the development and survival of neurons, synapses, and structures is shaped by the functional use of preceding neurons, synapses, and structures. In this way, the network self-organizes itself to work most effectively and efficiently. The more complex and stable neural network that results is dramatically different from its predecessor. Many structures or operations that are needed for development of function are not necessarily needed at the end of development. For this reason, the end product of neural development may not resemble the process of development. For example, it may have taken A-B-C-D-E-F to create the function of G, but the final network may only contain A-D-G, since B, C, E, and F are not needed for use, maintenance, or elaboration of the function.

Abnormal organization in this system can occur in a similar self-organizing way, to create a neural network that is not organized, but rather misorganized. In the same way that organization breeds more organization, misorganization can breed more misorganization. Misorganization at any stage in development can lead to the omission of intended operations or the inclusion of unintended operations (Courchesne et al., 1995). One such misorganization can occur from abnormal functional activity. In this case, the inactivity or overactivity of a certain function can create organization of the neural network that is not intended. For example, lack of, or abnormal, visual stimulation early in brain development can cause a lack of development in the primary visual cortex (e.g., Dehay, Horsbaugh, Berland, Killackey, & Kennedy, 1989) or a reorganization of the cortex, which can lead to vision being located somewhere other than in the occipital lobes (e.g., Sur, Garraghty, & Roe, 1988).

A second misorganization during neural network development can occur in remote areas, as a result of abnormal development in primary areas. This effect on remote areas occurs in correlation to the loss in the primary area and tends to become more pronounced as development progresses (Courchesne et al., 1995). For example, magnetic resonance imaging studies with autistic children have suggested a loss of cortical tissue in the parietal lobe and somatosensory and motor cortices, secondary to primary damage in the cerebellum (e.g., Courchesne, Press, & Yeung-Courchesne, 1993). This phenomenon emphasizes the importance of healthy brain functioning in the process of normal development. If one part of the brain becomes misorganized, it can lead to misorganization in multiple areas of the brain and potential abnormal brain functioning.

Delayed Effects

When assessing a child, the examiner must keep in mind that the effects of a brain injury may not be observable until sometime later (Goldman, 1974). For example, a child who has a head injury at the age of 3 years may not demonstrate the lost ability to decode symbols in reading until the typical maturational exhibition of that skill, at around 5 or 6 years. Although the child may appear to be performing at a normal level at the time of assessment, there may be an unmeasurable loss of a functional precursor to reading.

Another version of this effect is explained by the *crowding hypothesis* (Levin, Ewing-Cobbs, & Benton, 1984). This occurs when a child experiences a brain injury and the young brain rewires to compensate for the lost function. There is recovery of function following the injury, but the actual loss does not become apparent until the child needs to develop more advanced cognitive skills that would normally be reserved for the portion of the neural network used to compensate for the loss of function. In this situation, the child's brain is said to be overcrowded, because it does not have room to add the new skills. Therefore, the loss is not observed until the child reaches a developmental milestone that cannot be adequately achieved.

Plasticity

The *Kennard principle* is the concept that recovery of function is inversely related to age at the time of injury. This suggests that the younger a brain injury is experienced, the better chance there is for the child to regain those functions that were associated with the damaged area, because of the high degree of plasticity in the immature brain (Kennard, 1942). This phenomenon, however, has not held true with all functions. For instance, replications of Kennard's research have not been successful, to this point, with the recovery of motor functions (Passingham, Perry, & Wilkinson, 1983). Moreover, recovery of cognitive skills is not universal (e.g., Woods, 1980) and may be more a function of the sensitivity of the psychometric instruments being used (Miner, Fletcher, & Ewing-Cobbs, 1986).

This inconsistency in recovery of function across tasks could result from a number of factors. Some research has suggested that the type, location, and severity of an injury, rather than age, has more to do with whether function is recovered (e.g., Banich, Levine, Kim, & Huttenlocher, 1990). Fletcher, Miner, and Ewing-Cobbs (1987) emphasize the importance of the developmental sequence in looking at plasticity. Injury to the young brain is dependent upon what developmental processes have been disturbed. If the injury occurs at a particularly crucial time, recovery of function may be less likely.

Because brain injury in children involves disruption to a highly complex system that is under constant change, it is important to use an assessment system that provides thorough and reliable examination of the child's neuropsychological functioning. To do this, one can choose to utilize either a flexible battery or a fixed battery. A flexible battery consists of a set of tests handpicked by the examiner to address what is seen as the presenting problem. For instance, if the child is seen to have significant memory impairment prior to testing, the examiner will select and administer tests designed to assess memory. Such an approach can give detailed information about the presenting problem, but the exclusion of other measures creates weaknesses that can be a problem in forensic cases (Williams, 1997). These include the lack of objective evidence about the functioning of other cognitive abilities, the overreliance on the clinician's initial perceptions of the presenting problem, and the vulnerability of a flexible battery to manipulation by the neuropsychologist. Especially if the clinician is hired by the defense, a flexible battery can offer temptation to select tests that will provide a desired outcome.

Fixed batteries refer to a collection of tests that have been assembled and standardized for use with a variety of different presenting problems (Williams, 1997). All examinees are given the same set of tests, in the same manner, allowing for comparisons between profiles and more objective interpretation. The ability to conduct research with fixed batteries has led to confidence of psychometric properties and diagnostic results. A number of fixed batteries have been used, such as the Halstead–Reitan Neuropsychological Test Battery, the Luria–Nebraska Neuropsychological Test Battery, and a recent battery, which provides a more functional approach to neuropsychological assessment—the Dean–Woodcock Neuropsychological Assessment System (D-WNAS) (Dean & Woodcock, in preparation).

The D-WNAS provides a comprehensive evaluation of cognitive, sensorimotor, and emotional status. It can be interpreted on at least two levels. One level includes consideration of the neurological implications of a subject's performance. A second level involves interpretation at an information-processing or functional level. This second level moves beyond previous fixed batteries, which focused upon the ability of the battery to predict brain damage and localize dysfunction. However, because of advances in brain imaging techniques, this purpose is outdated, especially for the forensic setting. To pick up on the subtle functional deficits that are commonly associated with milder head injuries, the D-WNAS offers a comprehensive assessment of functional abilities in terms of Gf–Gc theory (Horn, 1988, 1991). This is especially important when assessing children who present at varying levels of development and require thorough examination of all areas of brain functioning, to determine where impairment may exist. Moreover, because brain development in children is not limited to cortical maturation, the D-WNAS provides assessment of subcortical functioning, with emphasis on the importance of multiple layers of functioning (Dean & Woodcock, 1999; Luria, 1973).

PREEXISTING DISORDERS

Another consideration in the assessment of children for personal injury is the presence of preexisting pathology. As mentioned, early insult to the developing neural network can result in abnormal functioning that may not surface until later in a child's development. Because of this, it is important to look at perinatal factors and history, when assessing the functional integrity of a child's neural network. Perinatal variables, such as low birth weight, hypoxia, substance abuse, and distress during delivery, have been found to be associated with impaired (or diminished) intellectual functioning (e.g., Goldstein, Caputo, & Taub, 1976) and later educational placement (i.e., regular education versus special education) (Fitzhardinage & Steven, 1972; Minick-Vanhorn, Titus, & Dean, in press). Indeed, preterm infants have been shown to have a higher prevalence of neurological dysfunction and neuropsychological impairment, when they reach school age (e.g., Ross, Lipper, & Auld, 1996).

Although clinicians have understood the need to assess for perinatal complications for some time, the ability to do so has been hindered by an inability to keep up with the rapid expansion of research in the area and the lack of psychometrically sound perinatal assessment measures. However, the *Maternal Perinatal Scale* (MPS), developed by Dean and Gray (1985), provides a systematic and highly structured self-report format that can provide valuable information about perinatal events. It consists of a pool of items developed from known and suspected perinatal factors (e.g., Commey & Fithardinge, 1979) that may place a child at risk for perinatal complications and further abnormal development. The MPS is completed by the mother, to create an overall impression of the child's functioning level at birth. Mothers' responses have been shown to correlate with medical records at levels of .90 and above (Gray, Dean, Rattan, & Bechtel, 1988). Even past the age of 9 years, mothers' responses have been found to be a reliable source of perinatal information (Gray & Dean, 1991).

A child's history is also important when considering the influence of preexisting disorders. A structured interview with a parent is helpful in identifying medical conditions (seizures, etc). and previous head injury, which might be impacting functioning. In addition, although it is often difficult to examine the effect of factors such as education and socioeconomic status, both have been shown to be related to performance on psychological measures, in general, and on measures of neuropsychological functioning, specifically (Dean, 1989). The degree to which these factors affect performance varies for individual patients, but is, nonetheless, important to assess, as well. Combining information obtained about the patient's developmental, medical, and social history can generate an understanding about the neurological integrity of the child prior to injury. This is particularly important because of the effect of early closed-head injury on neuropsychological performance. Injury early in life can create behavioral and emotional sequelae that persist many years later (e.g., Hoofien, Gilboa, Vakil, & Donovick, 2001). Therefore, a comprehensive history must be gathered, even about seemingly unrelated factors, to help explain inconsistencies in a child's performance that may arise.

COMPETENCY

With the increasing use of children's testimony in court cases that deal with issues such as child abuse, the need for assessing children concerning their ability to provide accurate testimony is great. Judges are left to make the final decision about competency, but the information provided by the psychologist is of utmost importance to the decision.

Myers (1993) identifies three major elements judges consider when deciding the competency of a child. First, the child must possess adequate capabilities to observe the proceedings of the court. These capabilities include adequate memory to recall information after a delayed period. Complete understanding of the material is not necessary, but the child must demonstrate retention of facts presented. In addition, the ability to make a moral distinction between right and wrong is necessary. Such a determination can be made by conducting a clinical interview with the child that includes scenarios of moral judgment (e.g., the difference between telling the truth and lying). For example, this determination could be established objectively through item analysis of the Comprehension subtest on the Wechsler Intelligence Scale for Children—Third Edition (WISC-III). Moreover, the child must possess the capability to appropriately participate in the court proceedings. That is, the child should be able to attend adequately, concentrate on the questions, and demonstrate appropriate behavior control. Determination of these behaviors would be delineated best through an objective measure of personality completed by a parent or teacher (e.g., Personality Inventory for Children [PIC]; Behavior Assessment Scale for Children [BASC]).

Another element identified by Myers (1993) as a determining factor with judges is whether or not the child has personal knowledge of the facts in the case. This issue comes under the federal guidelines for the submission of evidence (Federal Rules of Evidence Rule 602), but can be facilitated by the psychologist's assessment. Most children are not prone to offering information in a novel situation. This is especially true when the situation involves legal proceedings with significant personal consequences. Therefore, the use of projective measures, in assessing children who are resistant to offering details about the knowledge they have, can be beneficial. Projective measures (e.g., Thematic Apperception Test) allow children to talk about sensitive information in an indirect manner, which can later help the child in discussing details with more ease. In addition, they also provide an indication of whether or not a child possesses any information that may be of value to the case.

Last, Myers (1993) identifies the prerequisite that children understand the oath that is required upon taking the stand. Not all states require this, but most judges prefer an indication of comprehension, before a child is deemed competent to testify. This requirement is related to the child's ability to distinguish right from wrong and truth from lie. Assessment of this ability can be done through interviewing the child or, if objective analysis is preferred, with the Vocabulary subtest of the WISC-III or other measure of semantic knowledge (e.g., Shipley Institute of Living Scale). Also, reading comprehension scales could be used for this purpose (e.g., *Woodcock–Johnson Tests of Achievement—Third Edition*). However, to determine adequate vocabulary knowledge for the comprehension of an oath, one must first establish at what grade level the oath is presented. Once this is agreed upon, comparison can be made between the oath and an objective score of grade equivalency.

Another factor that is important to consider, when assessing the competency of a child, is the tendency for the child to exaggerate or offer fictional testimony. Although oftentimes, younger children are more apt to generate false stories that are based in fantasy rather than reality, false testimony from older children, and adolescents, would be better explained as a volitional attempt to manipulate an outcome for secondary gain (Cullum, Heaton, & Grant, 1991). It is unlikely an adolescent would have difficulty separating fantasy and reality, unless extremely low intellectual functioning is present. In assessing younger children in this regard, one must investigate for the presence of bizarre mentation or delusional ideation. The presence of such thought patterns would be indicative of a tendency to overlap fantasy with reality. Measures for evaluating this would include the Psychosis scale of the PIC or the Atypicality scale of the BASC. In adolescents, assessment of the tendency to confuse imagination with reality is also important. The PIC can be used with this population until the age of 16 years. However, the Minnesota Multiphasic Personality Inventory for Adolescents (MMPI-A) offers thorough evaluation of this, on the Schizophrenia scale. An adolescent's tendency to manipulate testimony for secondary gain, in cases of personal injury or abuse (malingering), can also be assessed with the MMPI-A, through examination of the L and F validity scales. The K scale can offer information about whether the individual is attempting to portray themselves in a more positive light than is accurate. In addition, self-report measures of neuropsychological symptomology have proven to detect the presence of malingering among patients involved in litigation (e.g., Neuropsychological Symptom Inventory) (Rattan, Dean, & Rattan, 1989; Ridenour, McCoy, & Dean, 1996).

Finally, the subject of competency with children should consider the appropriateness of placing a child on the stand, in relation to their emotional and overall psychological health. The environment that surrounds legal proceedings can be highly charged with confusing emotions and anxiety-provoking situations. The child who enters such an environment, with already established emotional disturbance, will be unlikely to adequately deal with the legal proceedings and may suffer negative psychological consequences as a result (Arrigo, 2000). Therefore, it is important for the psychologist to consider the emotional and behavioral status of a child, before deeming the child competent from a mental health perspective. Moreover, from a legal point of view, children are much more likely to offer inaccurate testimony when experiencing a high degree of anxiety (Pina, Silverman, Saavedra, & Weems, 2001). Not only can this affect their ability to recall events, but it can lead to fabrication of details, especially when being faced in the courtroom with the presence of someone who may have perpetrated an illegal action against them.

CUSTODY

Unfortunately, the issue of custody in civil cases does not lend itself solely to the concern of the child. Originally, children were viewed as property of the parents, and custody was awarded to the parent who had a legal right to the property within the marriage. Not until the late nineteenth century did courts begin to implement the *tender years doctrine*, which gave custody precedence to the mother when the child was below a certain age (Gudjonsson & Haward, 1998). This assumed that young children would be served best by being reared by the mother. However, by the 1970s, courts began to decide child placement decisions according to the *best interests of the child doctrine*. To date, this standard prevails in judges' decisions, because it allows for a consideration of the capability of each parent to care for the child (Arrigo, 2000). However, this same subjectivity has brought a great deal of criticism of this standard.

Best Interest

The premise of the best interests criterion is one that is preferable to psychologists (Arrigo, 2000). The concept that the environment and well-being of the child will be considered, before placement decisions are made, is ideal. However, two overarching problems exist. First, the concept of best interest is vague, because there is no generally accepted criterion for what determines when a child's best interests are being met. *Best interest* is a general term with a very subjective definition. What may be an ideal situation for one, may not be ideal for someone else. Second, the lack of an operational definition of best interest makes its assessment essentially impossible. Therefore, the task of determining the best placement for a child, based upon this criterion, is a subjective endeavor, at best (Arrigo, 2000).

If a psychologist is able to make a professional judgment regarding the best placement for a child, through assessment, the issue of whether or not that information will be recognized by the court is still debatable. At this point in time, the determination of what psychological information is admissible in custody decisions is up to the judge. Nothing requires the judge to consider the opinion of the psychologist or the psychological well-being of the child. In the same manner, the psychological state of the parents does not have to be considered. To downplay the impact of psychological assessment in custody decisions even more, the judge will likely side with legal precedence over psychological evidence. Even though the opinion of the psychologist may be to place the child in the custody of one parent over the other, the judge is more likely to make the determination according to legal precedent. In essence, the opinion of the psychologist is either used to validate the decision of the court or may not be used at all.

Recent trends in dealing with children's issues in the courts are beginning to turn toward the rights of the child. Family law, to this point, has essentially ignored the emotional needs and well-being of children, but interest groups, such as the National Task Force for Children's Constitutional Rights, have begun to advocate consideration of children at the same legal level as adults (Wynne, 1997). That is, just as adults have the right to their family, children have the right to a safe and loving home that will help them mature and develop into fully functioning adults. With this children's rights movement, there is hope that courts will begin to give more consideration to the emotional state of children and the family dynamics involved, before making custody decisions.

Assessment

Determination of a child's well-being through assessment should be made primarily from a cognitive, emotional, and relational point of view. A parent could possess adequate, even exemplary, skills to be a competent parent, but, if a child's emotional needs are not met in the situation, appropriate development is less likely to occur. Emotional status of a child is best determined through somewhat subjective means. An initial clinical interview with the child aids in elucidating the child's emotional needs. Objective assessment can offer aberrations in emotional functioning, but it does not offer much in the area of the emotional needs of the child. Moreover, most objective measures for young children utilize parental report, which is likely to be biased in a court proceeding. Offering more evidence about a child's emotional well-being can be gleaned through the use of projective measures (e.g., Thematic Apperception Test). Such measures can provide indications of possible problems in the emotional development of the child and open up avenues for further investigation. Incomplete sentence instruments are particularly good for this task, allowing the examiner to guide the child in discussing emotional concerns. Direct observation of the interactions between the child and each parent is also of great value in determining the emotional well-being of a child, concerning parental placement. Following custody decisions, the child will begin life in a single-parent home, rather than the dual-parent home experienced prior to the separation. Observations of interactions must take into account which parent is best prepared to deal with the child's emotional distress from the new situation and which is prepared to shoulder the majority of the responsibility in helping the child develop, not only from a biological point of view, but from a social, emotional, and moral perspective, as well.

BRAIN DEVELOPMENT

Of primary importance when assessing any individual, but especially children, is the foundational assumption that all individuals possess a level of uniqueness. The neuropsychologist must have a good understanding of the complex development of the human nervous system and how deviations to that development can lead to misorganization of brain function and potential long-term impairment. Therefore, this section provides a general description of the development of the nervous system and what can be expected, structurally and functionally, at different ages.

The structural antecedents of the human nervous system are evident within the first month following conception (Minkowski, 1967). Although the embryo is less than 5 cm in length (rump to crown), the embryonic neural plate, which gives rise to all future divisions of the adult nervous system, may be seen. Following this meager beginning, development of the nervous system proceeds at a phenomenal rate. During some 40 weeks of gestation, the fetal brain grows to an average of 350 g. This rate of growth continues postnatally, with the infant's brain weight increasing by a factor of two during the first year of life, representing approximately 70% the size of a normal adult brain (1,500 mg [male brain]) (Himwich, 1970). The remaining gain in brain weight is accomplished over the next 10–12 years. Following the first year of life, the maturation of functional capacities is far more remarkable than changes in structure or size of the brain (Folch, 1955).

The enlargement of the postnatal brain is more the function of continued nerve cell development than an increase in the number of cells (Davison, Dobbing, Morgan, & Wright, 1959). In fact, the complement of neurons in the cerebral cortex has been shown to be nearly complete prior to birth (Folch, 1955; Schulte, 1969). Although multiplication and migration of cells (glial, cerebellar granule cells) continue during infancy and childhood, just as important in the growth of postnatal brain is the myelination of axons and arborization of dendrites (Schulte, 1969).

Myelination

Myelination has long been seen as the growth of a fatty sheath around the axons, which may be seen to facilitate synaptic activity (Davison et al., 1959; Flechsig, 1901; Peiper, 1963; Shulte, 1969). The increase in the thickness of the myelin sheath seems to be a necessary condition for the development of complex behavior and early intellectual functions. Myelination may be viewed as a measure of the maturity of the individual cell and the ability to transmit messages efficiently (Himwich, 1970). At birth, axons resemble long, thin strands capable of the transmission of impulses at a relatively slow rate. The slow, awkward responses of the infant may in part be attributed to the lack of myelination in higher-order control areas (Dodge, 1964). After myelination, their efficiency is dramatically improved. Although the rate of myelination slows with age, the process has been followed into the fifth and sixth decade of life (Folch, 1955; Schulte, 1969).

The patterns of myelin development of the nervous system are uneven, but they follow a consistent course across individuals (Minkowski,

1967). Primary projection areas (large pathways of neurons), such as those required in vision and audition, as well as the thalamocortical pathway and the corticospinal tract, are myelinated soon after birth (e.g., Peiper, 1963). However, axonal myelination of pathways between association areas of the cerebral cortex follows a much slower course, which corresponds to the development of functional behavior in the child (Dodge, 1964). Thus, whereas the complement of the cerebral cortex seems nearly complete before birth, the lack of myelination reduces the functional efficiency of these cells. From this point of view, deviations from normal myelination may be reflected in behavior reminiscent of primitive subcortical functions.

Arborization

The process of myelination, in general, is a necessary, but not sufficient, condition for the functional development of the brain. Dendritic arborization, or the formation of axodendritic synapses, is often viewed as important as myelination in the early development of the nervous system (Sperry, 1968). The growth of neuronal dendrites involves the formation of efficient axodendritic synapses, which form the basis of impulse transmission between neurons (Gazzaniga, 1975). Arborization is complete in the spinal cord and some subcortical structures in the full-term newborn, but continues at a high rate in early postnatal development, for the upper subcortical and cortical structures (Sarsikov, 1964). During these periods of rapid perinatal growth, the brain is particularly susceptible to injury by a variety of toxic and metabolic substances (Langman, 1975).

The anatomical and functional development of the brain proceeds in an orderly and predictable fashion (Gazzaniga, 1975; Sperry, 1968). Although it is necessary to rely in part on research with lower forms of life, the movement from undifferentiated to specialized functions seems to be an invariant trend in both cortical and subcortical human development. The formation of higher-order abilities (e.g., language, thought) is determined by the degree of maturation in the cerebral cortex, which, in turn, is dependent upon development of lower levels of the nervous system during development (Luria, 1973). Development favors increased localization of functions, but the interdependence of all components of the nervous system cannot be minimized (Gazzaniga, 1975; Luria, 1973). Hence, in evaluating sophisticated aspects of neuropsychological functioning, subcortical aspects must be considered (Dean, 1983). Because components of the brain develop at contrasting rates, and systems are interdependent, when evaluating children, greater care needs to be taken not to attribute localized dysfunction from behavioral inadequacies established with adult subjects (e.g., Dean, 1989).

The Influence of Evolution

From conception, the anatomical and functional development of the nervous system follows a sequence that has been argued to reflect the evolutionary past of the species (e.g., Green, 1958; MacLean, 1970; Penfield, 1958). Theoretically, the present configuration of the human brain evolved by the addition of increasingly complex structures, which in turn allowed the species to function in the environment more effectively. With the addition of each component came increased capacity for reasoning and the potential for more sophisticated motor functions. Support for this notion comes both from the hierarchical organization of the human nervous system and sequential development of successively more complex adaptive mechanisms (Luria, 1973).

MacLean (1970) has portrayed these evolutionary changes by subdividing of the human nervous system. In this scheme, MacLean characterized the upper spinal areas, the midbrain, basal ganglia, and diencephalon as the *protoreptilian brain*. The second evolutionary stage, or the *paleomammalian brain*, includes components of the limbic system, together with those of the protoreptilian brain. The propensity for analytic thought, corresponding to upper cortical structures, was distinguished as the *neomammalian brain*.

This theoretical conceptualization has neuroanatomical and neuropsychological support, when the neurological development of the child is examined (Goldman, 1972). A good deal of evidence suggests that nonfunctioning of the cerebral hemispheres of the brain of the neonate, such as that found with hydranencephalic and anencepehalic infants, causes few aberrations in the postnatal neurological examination (Dodge, 1964). Moreover, these gross abnormalities in structure are not exhibited behaviorally until later in development and are congruent with the developmental sequence associated with neocortical functioning (Goldman, 1972). This phenomenon is also portrayed by Ford (1976), in a study that showed normal neurological evaluations of newborns who later exhibited spastic cerebral palsies associated with defects present at birth. Thus, when assessing children, it is important to obtain a comprehensive history of medical conditions, with special emphasis upon perinatal events. Moreover, in correlation with cortical maturation, reexamination of children well into middle adolescents (14–16 years) is necessary to ensure normal functioning of the brain, particularly the frontal and prefrontal cortices (Caviness, Kennedy, Bates, & Makris, 1996).

DEVELOPMENTAL CONSIDERATIONS

Perinatal–Infant Development

The differentiation of cells into the neural plate is evident during the third week after conception. Areas that mark the limits of developing structures can be observed on the surface of this plate (Minkowski, 1967). Cell division in the embryo is such that early hemispheric pairing may be observed by the end of the second month of gestation. Into the third month, the early beginnings of the hemispheres of the brain are clearly present, and the thalamus and cerebellar structures are distinguishable (Himwich, 1970).

The lateral ventricles of the brain are seen as separate structures by the beginning of the fourth gestational month. The major divisions of the cerebral and cerebellar hemispheres are recognizable by the end of this fourth month of development. Unlike the valleys (sulci) and plateaus (gyri) of the adult brain, the surface of the embryonic nervous tissue is rather smooth. Into the fourth month of postconceptional development, fissurization begins. This is first observable with the early indications of what will become the sylvian fissure (which serves to separate the temporal lobe from the cerebrum). Fissurization in the posterolateral fissure of the cerebellum also becomes clearly demarcated during this period. Small fissures (sulci), which give the brain a convoluted appearance, do not develop until the last trimester of gestation and are completed during the first 2 years of postnatal life (Sperry, 1968). This process of fissurization increases greatly the surface area of the cerebral cortex, while allowing containment within a reasonable-sized skull vault.

Corresponding to MacLean's (1970) notions of the protoreptilian brain and the median brain (Yakovlev & Lecours, 1967), the structures of the basal ganglia, brain stem, and other subcortical motor nuclei develop at a faster rate than higher-order areas (Yakovlev & Lecours, 1967). In fact, within the 12 months following conception, these areas are more nearly functionally matured than any other area of the brain (Gazzaniga, 1975). Overall, these structures are concerned with large behavioral patterning of overt responses of the entire body. These areas seem to serve simple integration of functions and those necessary for life maintenance (Himwich, 1970). Early lesions of basal ganglia produce gross behavioral defects in posture, posture control, equilibrium, and locomotion (see Freeman & Brann, 1977). The brain stem reticular system and accompanying motor nuclei seem responsible for the level of activation and gross movements of the head, eyes, and trunk (Freeman & Brann, 1977). Thus, if early insult occurs in this system, deficits may be noted in attention, concentration, and arousal (Young & Pigott, 1999).

Specific functional capacities remain unclear in the fetus, because of its inaccessibility. Prior to the age of viability (that point at which life-support systems are developed to the extent that the fetus can function independently of the mother), much of our knowledge is based on anatomical research and is localized for more mature organisms. The age of viability is usually considered to occur some 30 weeks after conception. Information concerning early functional development is gleaned from premature births in which gestational age may be followed (e.g., Watson & Lowrey, 1954). Therefore, information concerning functional capacities would seem to be lower bound, because the effects of a premature birth on the child's development are not clear.

Many of the early-appearing reflexes have little adaptive value for the infant, but rather provide evidence of the child's basic neurological development. The absence of these reflexes at an early age provides evidence of aberrations in normal neurological development (Dodge, 1964). Clearly, behavioral development reflects movement toward functional organization of subcortical structures and developing myelination of primary projection areas involved in vision, audition, and those in the thalamocortical area. For example, the visual pathway is developed to the extent that, after 1 month of postnatal life (40 weeks gestational age), the normal infant is briefly able to follow an object. Therefore, if an infant cannot visually attend to this extent, he may be seen as impaired in that area. Such a conclusion is limited, however, because injury to the cerebral cortex may not be evident in behavior. This is because of the general lack of integration of these areas in the early developmental period (Penfield, 1958). Without unequivocal evidence of damage, a prognosis from the absence of the behavioral signs is a hazardous pursuit. At this point in development, constellations of behavioral abnormalities (e.g., spasticity, hyperreflexia) increase the probability of neurological abnormality over a single sign, but such deductions still remain inconclusive (Dodge, 1964; Freeman & Brann, 1977).

Neurological development during the perinatal period can be characterized as progression of areas of the brain involved with functions necessary for survival and arousal of the organism. Piaget (1952) characterized development here as sensorimotor in nature. The emergence of cooing (prior to 3 postnatal months) and babbling (above 4 postnatal months) are seen as more motoric exercises than early emergence of language development (Molfese, Freeman, & Palermo, 1975). In fact, there is some neuropsychological and developmental evidence that only after some 48 months of postnatal life is the child neurologically able to move from the simple stimulus–response elements of language toward verbal thought (Vygotsky, 1962). Aspects of learning within this early stage of development amount to little more than simple response patterns and some early indications of discrimination learning (Sarsikov, 1964).

Early Childhood Development

Aspects of development, characterized by MacLean (1970) as paleomammalian and rudiments of the neomammalian brain, are of primary interest during the early childhood years (12–50 postnatal months). During this phase of development, the undifferentiated reflexive behavior seen in the infant begins to be inhibited. This period is characterized by the increasing acquisition of skills requiring cerebellar and cortical control. The primitive reflexes (e.g., Moro, tonic neck responses), indicative of control at lower levels, are repressed, with control moving to higher structures (Van der Vlugt, 1979; Yakovlev & Lecours, 1967). This fact is evident in the neurological examination of the child's reflexive responses. Here, the child's level of neurological development is inferred from the presence of these reflexes, in light of the chronological age since conception (Dodge, 1964; Freeman & Brann, 1977).

When evaluating an infant, the rapid pace of development in the early months of life dictate the use of age since conception, rather than the time since birth, as a measure of age. This fact is of considerable importance in evaluating the premature child's development. Therefore, a 3-month-old infant, born at the 28th week of gestation, should be more similar developmentally to an average full-term newborn than to a 3-month-old child. Consequently, lesions to the paleomammalian structures may be observed, behaviorally, in a general lack of inhibition of more primitive responses indicative of lower levels (Peiper, 1963).

Although some of these behaviors may continue to be elicited during infancy, most are not present during early childhood. These behaviors hold significance as developmental markers, both from their time of appearance and the degree to which they are repressed during early childhood. The neurological development of the infant is characterized by the loss of reflexes (e.g., Moro and tonic neck response) and the disappearance of flexor tone (Dodge, 1964; Prechtl, 1965). The lack of these behaviors in early childhood is seen as movement of functional organization from the diencephalon, or midbrain level, to those skills that are more indicative of cerebellar and lower cortical control. Deviance from this developmental pattern is viewed as significant.

The paramedian zone, or, if you will, the paleomammalian brain, is the developmental focus in the full-term infant. This, a most active developmental period, involves myelination and cell migration (Robinson, 1969). In tandem with development of the paramedian zone, maturation of cortical structures increases (Prechtl, 1965), although functional expression and general level of maturity of these areas lag behind lower structures (Schulte, 1969). In what may be seen as the first move toward self-awareness, control begins to move to the limbic zone (Isaacson, 1974). Still, visceral components structures involved here compose what is known, in the adult brain, as the limbic system. With direct projections to the hypothalamus, these areas are often seen to suppress more primitive behavioral sequences. In general, the development of the limbic system opens the way for the learning of new temporary associations. This conclusion is evident in children who have experienced a lesion in this area (Pribram & Isaacson, 1975). It seems that, with a lack of appropriate functioning in this area, the limbic system may serve to intensify behavior patterns arising at a more primitive level. For example, a child who has damage in this area is likely to exhibit significant aggressive behavior (Siegel & Edinger, 1983).

At the central position in the limbic system, the hippocampus is involved in the integration of information from the septal areas and external information from sensory systems. Thus, the structure serves to filter continuous sensory input of the auditory and tactile/kinesthetic systems. In this way, the overall level of attention, concentration, and arousal is involved (Pribram & Isaacson, 1975). In lower forms of life, lesions inflicted to the hippocampal formations result in hyperactive behaviors (Kimble, 1968). Although concluding that there is correspondence between hyperactive behaviors in children and developmental aberrations in this area is tempting, such behavioral excesses are not observed in adults with lesions to the hippocampus (Douglas, 1975). Specific stimulation of the hippocampus, which is central in the limbic system, has been reported to cause a suppression in ongoing behaviors (Isaacson, 1974; Kimble, 1968). Damage to the hippocampus can be related to specific deficits in memory, which would, in turn, affect overall cognitive performance (Akhondzadeh, 1999).

Research that has involved the behavioral effects of lesions to the hippocampus suggests its importance in learning. Bilateral lesions to this structure are seen, behaviorally, in gross impairments in new learning to all but simple stimulus responses (Ford, 1960). Although unilateral lesions to the hippocampus produce few lasting effects in adults, a catastrophic effect on subsequent adult behavioral control (e.g., memory) is observed when the lesion occurs prior to maturation of the limbic system (Isaacson, 1974). Pate and Bell (1971), using a spontaneous alternation paradigm, present some inferential evidence that elements of these structures reach a developmental plateau after some 48 months of postnatal life. Jones (1970) argues in favor of the development of response flexibility and the reduction of perseveration associated with development in the hippocampal area. Thus, the role of this structure in learning may well relate to attentional control and, at best, retrieval of functions.

The precursors of higher-level cognitive functions associated with the neomammalian brain may be seen to develop during the early years of childhood (Peiper, 1963; Robinson, 1969). Geschwind (1968) points out that the primordial zones of the neomammalian brain, which begin to mature during this time in development, have the more efferent and afferent connections with subcortical structures. He portrays the gradual invariant evolution of cortical control, from lower, more primitive areas to those responsible for higher-order cognitive functions, which characterize human behavior. For example, the exhibition of emotion, which has been associated with subcortical structures (i.e., the limbic system), has been shown to be regulated by higher cortical areas, such as the prefrontal cortex (Davidson, 2000).

Thus, as would be expected, myelination of terminal zones (e.g., left angular gyrus) and corticocortical (within cerebral cortex) connections occur at a slower rate than myelination of subcortical and subcorticocortical areas mentioned above (Schulte, 1969). It would appear that corticocortical pathways, which serve in the mediation of complex language and thought processes, are not functionally efficient during early years of childhood. Myelination of axonal pathways between some association areas of the cerebral cortex continues for some four to five decades of life (Todd, Swarzenski, Rossi, & Visconti, 1995). However, although postnatal specialization exists, functions in early childhood are diffusely represented within hemispheres (Peiper, 1963).

The fine-grained analysis of the external environment, seen in later years, is not present during early childhood. Neurologically, this seems true because control of functions is served by lower neurological regions (Robinson, 1969). However, this conclusion is not meant to discount the role of subcortical function in the total behavior of the mature organism. One needs to appreciate that higher-level functioning is determined by the maturity of both the cerebral cortex and subcortical formations (Sarsikov, 1964). This view stresses the critical importance of subcortical development as a prerequisite to more refined functions of the neocortex. Although obvious within the present context, perhaps, clinical applications of neuropsychology often focus on cerebral functions in isolation and fail to appreciate the interdependence of cortical areas on more caudal structures (Luria, 1973).

Increasing development of neocortical structures and successively more refined adaptive mechanisms in early childhood are integrated in a complex fashion later in development (Hartlage & Telzrow, 1983). This process is exhibited in the child's development of fine-grained movement of the extremities, corresponding to increasing control over subcortical brain stem regions (Isaacson, 1974). Thus, as motor control passes from more caudal areas of the brain, the child reaches for objects, first with the entire hand, then with increasing pincer movements of the fingers and thumb. Haaxma and Kuypers (1975) offer evidence that, with damage to primary motor areas of the neocortex, the development of the fine-grained movements is lost, resulting in motor behavior that is indicative of subcortical control. Integration of these motor functions also is displayed with the child's crossing of midline to transfer objects from hand to hand, and with sitting, standing, and beginning to walk (Todd et al., 1995). Such skills also depend, to increasing degrees, on the relatively early myelination that has occurred in the primary projection areas (e.g., vision, auditory), the corticospinal tract, and the thalamocortical sensory pathways. However, skills that require increased integration of functioning areas are still lacking and continue to develop through late adolescence (Robinson, 1969).

As one would gather, learning at this state is more efficacious when sensory integration or cross-modality responses to stimuli are minimized (Dean & Rothlisberg, 1983). This observation would seem to hold for the motor control necessary for speech development. Although some 24 months of postnatal development are required for rudimentary speech, the integration with other higher-order areas is necessary for human language. In sum, the neurological development during early childhood corresponds closely to Piaget's (1952) notion of a preoperational stage of behavioral development and Bruner's (1968) conception of the enactive representational base. Assessing the child for the functions seen by Piaget and Bruner at this stage can help one assume the progress of the neurodevelopmental process of the child.

Later-Childhood–Adolescent Development

Later childhood is marked more by functional development in the brain than observable structural changes (Robinson, 1966). In fact, by gross anatomical, biochemical, and physiological measurements, the human brain has reached adult parameters at 15 years of life (e.g., Freeman & Brann, 1977). The commissural (connective pathways between hemispheres) and associative systems (outermost or supralimbic cerebral cortex) have the longest maturational cycle (Sperry, 1968). Evidence suggests that a relatively slow maturation of these areas may well be responsible for the selective consolidation of functions by the hemispheres of the brain and the late onset of symbolic thought. Hence, maturation of these formations, which continues beyond the first two decades of life, may be responsible in part for the progressive asymmetrical lateralization of visual perception, thought, and language. This slow consolidation may vary in relation to the myelination of the corpus callosum and the projectional and association axons of the cerebral hemispheres. Thus, the commitment to the consistently reported left hemisphere specialization for language may be viewed in a progression congruent with development in these secondary areas.

About 5–7 years of life mark a shift in processing that has been clearly documented in the developmental psychology literature. Referred to by various terms, this shift represents a neuropsychological potential for concrete thought (Bruner, 1968; Ingram, 1970; Piaget, 1952; White,

1965). Vygotsky (1962) portrays this period as that point at which speech, and hence language, become distinct from early motor dependence and may become integrated into verbal thought. Moreover, the child gains facility with the use of language as a tool in learning and understanding the environment. This shift may well relate to maturation of tertiary areas of sensory integration and terminal zones (parietal lobe), in conjunction with continuing myelination of corticocortical connections (Geschwind, 1968). In normal children, neuropsychological evidence suggests this shift corresponds to increased visuospatial, symbolic integration (Ingram, 1970; Peiper, 1963). This conclusion seems related to Van der Vlugt's (1979) findings of a sharp decrease in perceptual rotation and position reversals of letters between the ages of 6 and 8 years. These changes are attributed to both brain development associated with visual–verbal integration and natural language mediation, which is present during this period.

Gibson (1968) has outlined cognitive stages in reading development that coincide closely with the evolving maturation of the child's brain. The first cognitive stage necessary in the early reading process is seen to involve the child's ability to discriminate orthographic symbols. This skill would seem to develop in the early childhood phase of neurological maturation, but not until the age of 5 to 8 years would this ability be firmly established (e.g., Vygotsky, 1962). The second stage, according to Gibson, concerns the decoding process, in which visual stimuli are transformed to their speech-sound component. This process requires increased maturation of the associative areas of the cerebral cortex. The utilization of complex linguistic units, which approach the adult reading process, characterizes Gibson's third cognitive phase of the reading process. The maturation of the prefrontal lobes of the brain and intercortical connections, which are functional at the period from 12 to 15 years (Doty & Overman, 1977; Peiper, 1963), would seem to facilitate this process. The functional progression associated with this final cognitive stage translates behaviorally to what Piaget (1952) has portrayed as formal operations and is characterized by cognitive-abstract thought. As Piaget points out, and what is clear from the research in this area, both the maturation of the brain and the quality of environmental stimulation are important to the development of such cognitive skills (Sparrow & Satz, 1970). Thus, at this stage, one should expect the child to perform abstract tasks and complex problem solving. In the classroom, this would lend itself to such learning as algebra.

In examination of the developmental sequence of the human nervous system, it becomes clear that the developing brain is not simply a smaller version of the adult brain. On the contrary, the human brain, at different ages, possesses unique structural and functional qualities that may or may not be present in the final product. Because of this, neuropsychologists must take special care in the assessment of children.

CONCLUSION

The purpose of this chapter is to provide an understanding of the relevant issues that surround forensic neuropsychological assessment with children. At the heart of working with children in the legal setting is the understanding that children are not simply smaller versions of adults. Biologically, it is understood that children possess brains that are in constant development. The complexity of this development is encompassed in the different developmental processes that occur, both structurally and functionally, at varying ages in a child's life. Not only does brain development not occur in a linear fashion, but neuronal processes and structures that may be present during development may not be present in the final adult version of the brain.

These complicated aspects of brain development offer a picture of how the effects of personal injury in children can have devastating consequences later in life. If precursors for more complex processes are damaged in childhood, the expression of skills, such as reading and writing, may be forever impaired. Therefore, the neuropsychologist who considers the true degree of injury suffered by a child must take into account the complexity of the developmental process. Specific considerations that should be made are issues such as delayed effects and plasticity. *Delayed effects* refers to the tendency for children to not express true deficits until later in development. Therefore, accurate assessment of the consequences of injury cannot be determined immediately after the injury. In addition, although children possess a better probability of recovery of function than adults, the true benefits of plasticity are inconsistent. As it stands, there is little understanding or consensus about how recovery of function can be expected and what abilities should be expected to return.

In issues of competency and custody, the final determination is always up to the judge hearing the case. To establish competency, the child must possess certain capabilities, such as the ability to observe and participate in the legal proceedings. Moreover, the child must possess the mental capabilities to recall facts of the case, respond appropriately to questions, and understand the meaning of the oath to testify. Custody determinations require adequate assessment of the emotional well-being and needs of the child. Making this assessment is a subjective matter, which can be aided by the use of examination techniques that will give insight into the ability of each parent to adequately provide for the child.

In working with children in legal matters, it is most important to consider the unique qualities that children bring into the situation. The courtroom is an adult environment that can cause significant stress for the young child. Consideration of the issues presented in this chapter can help the neuropsychologist provide the best services, not only to the court, but, more importantly, to the well-being of the child.

REFERENCES

Akhondzadeh, S. (1999). Hippocampal synaptic plasticity and cognition. *Journal of Clinical Pharmacy and Therapeutics, 24*(4), 241–248.

Arrigo, B. A. (2000). *Introduction to forensic psychology: Issues and controversies in crime and justice.* San Diego, CA: Academic Press.

Banich, M. T., Levine, S. C., Kim, H., & Huttenlocher, P. (1990). The effects of developmental factors on IQ in hemiplegic children. *Neuropsychologia, 28,* 35–47.

Bruner, J. S. (1968). The course of cognitive growth. In N. S. Endler, L. R. Boulter, & H. Osser (Eds.), *Contemporary issues in developmental psychology* (pp. 329–362). New York: Holt, Rinehart, & Winston.

Caviness, V. S., Kennedy, D. N., Bates, J. F., & Makris, N. (1996). The developing human brain: A morphometric profile. In R. W. Thatcher, J. Rumsey, & R. W. Thatcher (Eds.), *Developmental neuroimaging: Mapping the development of brain and behavior* (pp. 3–14). San Diego, CA: Academic Press.

Commey, J. O., & Fitzhardinge, P. M. (1979). Handicap in the preterm small-for-gestational age infant. *The Journal of Pediatrics, 94,* 779–786.

Courchesne, E., Press, G. A., & Yeung-Courchesne, R. (1993). Parietal lobe abnormalities detected on magnetic resonance images of patients with infantile autism. *American Journal of Roentgenology, 160,* 387–393.

Courchesne, E., Townsend, J., & Chase, C. (1995). Neurodevelopmental principles guide research on developmental psychopathologies. In D. Cicchetti & D. J. Cohen (Eds.), *Developmental psychopathology: Vol. 1. Theory and methods* (pp. 195–226). New York: John Wiley & Sons.

Cullum, C. M., Heaton, R. K., & Grant, I. (1991). Psychogenic factors influencing neuropsychological performance: Somatoform disorders, factitious disorders, and malingering. In H. O. Doerr & A. S. Carlin (Eds.), *Forensic neuropsychology: Legal and scientific bases* (pp. 141–171). New York: Guilford Press.

Davidson, R. J., Putnam, K. M., & Larson, C. L. (2000). Dysfunction in the neural circuitry of emotion regulation: A possible prelude to violence. *Science, 289,* 591–594.

Davison, A. N., Dobbing, J., Morgan, R. S., & Wright, G. (1959). Metabolism of myelin: The persistence of (4-^{14}C) cholesterol in the mammalian central nervous system. *Lancet, 1,* 658–660.

Dean, R. S. (1983). Neuropsychological assessment. In Staff College (Ed.), *Handbook of diagnostic and epidemiological instruments.* Washington, DC: National Institutes of Mental Health.

Dean, R. S. (1989). Perspectives on the future of neuropsychological assessment. In B. S. Plake & J. C. Witt (Eds.), *Buros-Nebraska series on measurement and testing.* New York: Lawrence Erlbaum.

Dean, R. S., & Gray, J. (1985). *Maternal Perinatal Scale.* Muncie, IN: Ball State University.

Dean, R. S., & Rothlisberg, B. A. (1983). Lateral preference patterns and cross-modal sensory integration. *Journal of Pediatric Psychology, 8,* 285–292.

Dean, R. S., & Woodcock, R. W. (1999). *The WJ-R and Bateria-R in Neuropsychological Assessment* (Research Report Number 3). Itasca, IL: Riverside.

Dean, R. S., & Woodcock, R. W. (in preparation). *Dean-Woodcock Neuropsychological Assessment System.* Itasca, IL: Riverside.

Dehay, C., Horsburgh, G., Berland, M., Killacky, H., & Kennedy, H. (1989). Maturation and connectivity of the visual cortex in monkey is altered by prenatal removal of retinal input. *Nature, 337,* 265–267.

Dodge, P. R. (1964). Neurologic history and examination. In T. W. Farmer (Ed.), *Pediatric neurology.* New York: Harper & Row.

Doty, R. W., & Overman, W. H. (1977). Mnemonic role of forebrain commissures in macaques. In S. Harmad, R. W. Doty, L. Goldstein, J. Jaynes, & G. Krauthamer (Eds.), *Lateralization in the nervous system.* New York: Academic Press.

Douglas, R. J. (1975). The development of hippocampal function: Implications for theory and for therapy. In R. L. Isaacson & K. H. Pribram (Eds.), *The hippocampus: Vol. 11, Neurophysiology and behavior.* New York: Plenum Press.

Fitzhardinge, P. M., & Steven, E. M. (1972). The small for dates infant: Later growth patterns. *Pediatrics, 49,* 671–681.

Flechsig, P. (1901). Developmental (myelogenetic) localization of the cortex in human subjects. *Lancet,* 1027–1029.

Fletcher, J. M., Miner, M. E., & Ewing-Cobbs, L. (1987). Age and recovery from head injury in children: Developmental issues. In H. S. Levin, J. Grafman, & H. M. Eisenberg (Eds.), *Neurobehavioral recovery from head injury.* New York: Oxford University Press.

Folch, J. (1955). Composition of the brain in relation to maturation. In H. Waelsch (Ed.), *Biochemistry of the developing nervous system.* New York: Academic Press.

Ford, B. (1976). Head injuries: What happens to survivors. *Medical Journal of Australia, 1,* 603–605.

Ford, F. R. (1960). *Diseases of the nervous system in infancy, childhood and adolescence.* Springfield, IL: Charles C Thomas.

Freeman, J. M., & Brann, A. W. (1977). Central nervous system disturbances. In R. E. Behrman (Ed.), *Neonatal-perinatal medicine* (pp. 129–146). St. Louis: C. V. Mosby.

Gazzaniga, M. S. (1975). Brain mechanisms and behavior. In M. S. Gazzaniga & C. Blakemore (Eds.), *Handbook of psychobiology*. New York: Academic Press.

Geschwind, N. (1968). Neurological foundations of language. In H. R. Myklebust (Ed.), *Progress in learning disabilities: Vol. 1* (pp. 232–257). New York: Grune & Stratton.

Gibson, E. J. (1968). Learning to read. In N. S. Endler, L. R. Boulter, & H. Osser (Eds.), *Contemporary issues in developmental psychology*. New York: Holt, Rinehart & Winston.

Giuliano, A. J., Barth, J. T., Hawk, G. L., & Ryan, T. V. (1997). The forensic neuropsychologist: Precedents, roles, and problems. In R. J. McCaffrey, A. D. Williams, J. M. Fisher, & L. C. Laing (Eds.), *The practice of forensic neuropsychology: Meeting challenges in the courtroom* (pp. 1–36). New York: Plenum Press.

Glass, L. S. (1991). The legal base in forensic neuropsychology. In H. O. Doerr & A. S. Carlin (Eds.), *Forensic neuropsychology: Legal and scientific bases* (pp. 3–16). New York: Guilford Press.

Goldman, P. S. (1972). Development determinants of cortical plasticity. *Acte Neurobiologiae Experimentalis, 32*, 495–511.

Goldman, P. (1974). An alternative to developmental plasticity: Heterology of CNS structures in infants and adults. In D. G. Stein, J. J. Rosen, & N. Butters (Eds.), *Plasticity and recovery from brain damage* (pp. 149–174). New York: Academic Press.

Goldstein, K. M., Caputo, D. V., & Taub, H. B. (1976). The effects of prenatal and perinatal complications on development at one year of age. *Child Development, 47*, 613–621.

Gray, J. W., & Dean, R. S. (1991). *Neuropsychology of perinatal complications*. New York: Springer.

Gray, J. W., Dean, R. S., Rattan, G., & Bechtel, B. A. (1988). Mothers' self-reports of perinatal complications. *Journal of Clinical Child Psychology, 17*(3), 243–247.

Green, J. D. (1958). The rhinencephalon and behavior. In G. E. W. Wolstenholme & C. M. O'Connor (Eds.), *CIBA foundation symposium on the neurological basis of behavior*. London: J. & A. Churchill.

Gudjonsson, G. H., & Haward, L. R. C. (1998). *Forensic psychology: A guide to practice*. London: Routledge.

Haaxma, R., & Kuypers, H. G. J. M. (1975). Intrahemispheric cortical connections and visual guidance of hand and finger movements in the rhesus monkey. *Brain, 98*, 239–260.

Hartlage, L. C., & Telzrow, C. F. (1983). Neuropsychological assessment. In K. D. Paget & B. A. Bracken (Eds.), *The psychoeducational assessment of preschool children*. New York: Grune & Stratton.

Himwich, W. A. (1970). *Developmental neurobiology*. Springfield, IL: Charles C Thomas.

Hoofien, D., Gilboa, A., Vakil, E., & Donovick, P. J. (2001). Traumatic brain injury (TBI) 10–20 years later: A comprehensive outcome study of psychiatric symptomology, cognitive abilities and psychosocial functioning. *Brain Injury, 15*(3), 189–209.

Horn, J. L. (1988). Thinking about human abilities. In J. R. Nesselroade & R. B. Cattell (Eds.), *Handbook of multivariate psychology—Revised* (pp. 645–685). New York: Academic Press.

Horn. J. L. (1991). Measurement of intellectual capabilities: A review of theory. In K. S. McGrew, J. K. Werder, & R. W. Woodcock, *WJ-R technical manual* (pp. 197–232). Itasca, IL: Riverside.

Ingram, T. T. S. (1970). The nature of dyslexia. In F. A. Young & D. B. Lindsley (Eds.), *Early experience and visual information processing in perceptual and reading disorders.* Washington, DC: National Academy of Sciences.

Isaacson, R. L. (1974). *The limbic system.* New York: Plenum Press.

Jones, S. J. (1970). Children's two-choice learning of predominantly alternating and predominantly non-alternating sequences. *Journal of Experimental Child Psychology, 10,* 344–362.

Kennard, M. A. (1942). Cortical reorganization of motor function. *Archives of Neurological Psychiatry, 48,* 227–240.

Kimble, D. P. (1968). Hippocampus and internal inhibition. *Psychological Bulletin, 70,* 285–295.

Langman, J. (1975). *Medical embryology: Human development: Normal and abnormal* (3rd ed.). Baltimore: Williams & Wilkins.

Levin, H. S., Ewing-Cobbs, L., & Benton, A. L. (1984). Age and recovery from brain damage: A review of clinical studies. In S. W. Scheff (Ed.), *Aging and recovery of function in the central nervous system.* New York: Plenum Press.

Luria, A. R. (1973). *The working brain: An introduction to neuropsychology.* New York: Basic Books.

MacLean, P. D. (1970). The triune brain, emotional and scientific bias. In F. O. Schmitt (Ed.), *The neurosciences: Second study program.* New York: Rockefeller University Press.

Miner, M. E., Fletcher, J. M., & Ewing-Cobbs, L. (1986). Recovery versus outcome after head injury in children. In M. E. Miner & K. A. Wagner (Eds.), *Neural trauma: Treatment, monitoring and rehabilitation issues* (pp. 233–254). Stoneham, MA: Butterworth.

Minick-Vanhorn, R. E., Titus, J. B., & Dean, R. S. (in press). Maternal perinatal events as predictors of educational placement: Computation of relative risk ratios. *International Journal of Neuroscience.*

Minkowski, A. (1967). *Regional development of the brain in early life.* Philadelphia: F. A. Davis.

Molfese, D. L., Freeman, R. B., & Palermo, D. (1975). The ontogeny of brain lateralization for speech and nonspeech stimuli. *Brain and Language, 2,* 356–368.

Myers, J. E. B. (1993). The competency of young children to testify in legal proceedings. *Behavioral Sciences and the Law, 11,* 121–133.

Passingham, R. E., Perry, V. H., & Wilkinson, F. (1983). The long-term effects of removal of sensorimotor cortex in infant and adult rhesus monkeys. *Brain, 106,* 675–705.

Pate, J. L., & Bell, G. L. (1971). Alternation behavior in children in a cross-maze. *Psychonomic Science, 23,* 431–432.

Peiper, A. (1963). *Cerebral function in infancy and childhood.* (B. & M. Nagler, Trans.). New York: Consultants Bureau.

Penfield, W. (1958). *The excitable cortex in conscious man.* Liverpool, England: Liverpool University Press.

Piaget, J. (1952). *The origins of intelligence in children.* New York: International Universities Press.

Pina, A. A., Silverman, W. K., Saavedra, L. M., & Weems, C. F. (2001). An analysis of the RCMAS lie scale in a clinic sample of anxious children. *Journal of Anxiety Disorders, 15*(5), 443–457.

Prechtl, H. F. R. (1965). Prognostic value of neurological signs in the newborn infant. *Proceedings of the Royal Society of Medicine, 58,* 3–4.

Pribram, K. H., & Isaacson, R. L. (1975). Summary. In R. L. Isaacson & K. H. Pribram (Eds.), *The hippocampus.* New York: Plenum Press.

Rattan, G., Dean, R. S., & Rattan, A. I. (1989). *Neuropsychological Symptom Inventory.* Muncie, IN: Author.

Ridenour, T. A., McCoy, K. D., & Dean, R. S. (1996). An exploratory stepwise discriminant function analysis of malingered and nondistorted responses to the Neuropsychological Symptoms Inventory. *International Journal of Neuroscience, 87,* 91–95.

Robinson, R. J. (1966). Cerebral function in the newborn. *Developmental Medicine and Child Neurology, 8,* 561–567.

Robinson, R. J. (1969). Cerebral hemisphere function in the newborn. In R. J. Robinson (Ed.), *Brain and early behavior.* New York: Academic Press.

Ross, G., Lipper, E., & Auld, P. (1996). Cognitive abilities and early precursors of learning disabilities in very-low-birthweight children with normal intelligence and normal neurological status. *International Journal of Behavioral Development, 19*(3), 563–580.

Sarsikov, S. (1964). The evolutionary aspects of the integrative function of the cortex and subcortex of the brain. In D. P. Purpura & J. P. Schade (Eds.), *Growth and maturation of the brain: Vol. 4. Progress in brain research* (pp. 27–42). Amsterdam: Elsevier.

Schulte, F. J. (1969). Structure–function relationships in the spinal cord. In R. J. Robinson (Ed.), *Brain and early behavior.* New York: Academic Press.

Siegel, A., & Edinger, H. M. (1983). Role of the limbic system in hypothalamically elicited attack behavior. *Neuroscience and Biobehavioral Review, 7*(3), 395–407.

Sparrow, S., & Satz, P. (1970). Dyslexia, laterality, and neuropsychological development. In D. J. Bakker & P. Satz (Eds.), *Specific reading disability: Advances in theory and method.* Rotterdam: Rotterdam University Press.

Sperry, R. W. (1968). Plasticity of neural maturation. In *Developmental Biology,* Supplement 2, (27th Symposium). New York: Academic Press.

Sur, M., Garraghty, P. E., & Roe, A. W. (1988). Experimentally induced visual projections into auditory thalamus and cortex. *Science, 242,* 1437–1441.

Todd, R. D., Swarzenski, B., Rossi, P. G., & Visconti, P. (1995). Structural and functional development of the human brain. In D. Cicchetti & D. J. Cohen (Eds.), *Developmental psychopathology: Vol. 1. Theory and methods* (pp. 161–194). New York: John Wiley & Sons.

Van der Vlugt, H. (1979). Aspects of normal and abnormal neuropsychological development. In M. S. Gazzaniga (Ed.), *Handbook of behavioral neurobiology: Vol. 2, Neuropsychology* (pp. 111–132). New York: Plenum Press.

Vygotsky, L. S. (1962). *Thought and language* (E. Haufmann & G. Vakar, Trans). Cambridge, England: MIT Press and Wiley. (Original work published 1932).

Watson, E. H., & Lowrey, G. H. (1954). *Growth and development of children.* Chicago: Year Book.

Wechsler, D. (1958). *The measurement and appraisal of adult intelligence* (4th ed.). Baltimore: Williams & Wilkins.

White, S. H. (1965). *Evidence for a hierarchical arrangement of learning processes: Advances in child development and behavior: Vol. 2.* New York: Academic Press.

Williams, A. D. (1997). Fixed versus flexible batteries. In R. J. McCaffrey, A. D. Williams, J. M. Fisher, & L. C. Laing (Eds.), *The practice of forensic neuropsychology: Meeting challenges in the courtroom* (pp. 57–70). New York: Plenum Press.

Woods, B. T. (1980). The restricted effects of right-hemisphere lesions after age one: Wechsler test data. *Neuropsychologia, 18,* 65–70.

Wynne, E. E. (1997). Children's rights and the biological bias in biological parent versus third party custody disputes. *Child Psychiatry and Human Development, 27,* 179–191.

Yakovlev, P. I., & Lecours, A. R. (1967). The myelogenetic cycles of regional maturation of the brain. In A. Minkowski (Ed.), *Regional development of the brain in early life* (pp. 25–48). Oxford: Blackwell.

Young, G. B., & Pigott, S. E. (1999). Neurobiological basis of consciousness. *Archives of Neurology, 56*(2), 153–157.

Chapter 17

Forensic Neurotoxicology

Raymond Singer

INTRODUCTION

Neurotoxicity describes the harmful effects of toxic substances on the nervous system. All parts and aspects of the nervous system are susceptible to neurotoxicity, including the central and peripheral nerves, the brain, sensory organs, autonomic function, motor function, neurochemical processes, cognition, emotion, conation, perception, personality, and so on.

Many substances are known to be neurotoxic, either from clinical experience or animal testing. Few commercial products have been adequately tested for their potential to cause neurotoxic injuries (Kilburn, 1998; Singer, 1990a). The substances for which we have some agreement regarding neurotoxicity include many pesticides, some herbicides (Singer, Moses, Valciukas, Lilis, & Selikoff, 1982), fumigants, solvents, and some metals.

The number of people with significant neurotoxic chemical exposures and potential chemical brain injuries remains very high and uncharted. To determine that number, we need an accurate assessment of, and agreement for, which substances are neurotoxic. We also would benefit from knowing the conditions necessary for a substance to produce neurotoxicity, quantifying factors such as potency, duration of exposure compared to levels of exposure, and host factors such as gender, age, race, prior function of the immune, hepatic and renal systems, prior neurotoxic chemical exposures, concomitant exposures, possible additive or synergistic effects of all of these factors, and so on.

Every person touched by modern civilization is at risk of significant chemical exposure and neurotoxicity. Significant neurotoxic injury may result from occupational exposures in such diverse occupations as insurance office personnel (Singer, 1997a), automobile sales managers (Singer, 1997a), dentists (Singer, 1995), electrical products (transformer) salvage (Singer, 1994), herbicide workers (Singer et al., 1982), and postal workers (Singer, 1985). Even if a person does not work, they may suffer neurotoxicity from use of consumer products (Singer, 1996a), prescription drugs (Singer, 1997b), medical devices (Singer, 1996b), drinking water at home (Singer, 1990b), or drinking beverages at a restaurant (Singer, 2000).

Simply going to school can be hazardous for both students and teachers (Singer, 1999a), if your school district is repairing the roof of your school while school is in session. Or, when trying to get away from the pressures of modern life, and building a life in a beautiful rural county, one can be exposed to a witches brew of human and industrial waste, called sewage sludge. Municipalities can pay your neighbor to spread sewage sludge, creating a hazardous dump for the neighborhood (Singer, 1999b).

Pesticides are especially promiscuous in their targets. Even if a person does not work or consume, they may live in or enter a structure with pesticide over application, or be drizzled by pesticide drift when walking down a country lane, or sitting in their rocking chair on their front porch, or sleeping in their bed in an agricultural area (Singer, 1999c).

A product as seemingly innocuous as carbonless copy paper can cause relentless neurotoxicity, when it is amassed in large quantities in an office, under poor ventilation conditions, and with lengthy exposure time periods (Singer, 1998).

Living far from industrialization may not always provide protection from hazardous chemical products: The highest levels of polychlorinated biphenyl (PCB) have been found among the Inuit (Eskimo) people of Baffin Island, near the Arctic circle, thousands of miles from where PCB is used. As the result of various atmospheric processes, industrial effluent discharged into the air in the tropics can collect in polar regions (Lean, 1996).

Once neurotoxic chemicals have been used in manufacture and production of consumer goods, and the product is stabilized, this does not mean that we are forever safe from its reach. For example, neurotoxic substances can be released by fire, as found in the wake of the World Trade Center attack, with high levels of benzene, dioxin, metals, and other substances being discharged into the air and water at ground zero (Gonzales, 2001).

When people are hurt by neurotoxic products, they have the right to demand compensation for their injuries. These matters are often brought to court for adjudication. The forensic neurotoxicologist and neuropsychologist will be called upon to help the judge and jury understand the nature and extent of possible nervous system injury. With that in mind, let us now examine the common symptoms of neurotoxicity.

SYMPTOMS OF NEUROTOXICITY

The residual neurobehavioral symptoms of neurotoxicity from various substances are similar (Singer, 1990a). They include:

1. Cognitive changes
   a. Attentional dysfunction, concentration difficulties: The affected person reports difficulty with keeping his mind in focus. His thoughts may drift and seem fuzzy. There will be increased susceptibility to distraction.
   b. Learning dysfunction, caused by disruption of memory processes: Often with sparing of memory prior to exposure and onset of illness
   c. Cognitive and psychomotor slowing, which may be described by the subject as confusion or "brain fog."
2. Personality changes
   a. Irritability: Reduction of cognitive and emotional capacities from neurotoxicity can be frustrating and perplexing. The subject may report frequent strife with family members, friends, and coworkers, or difficulty with conformity.
   b. Increased sadness, depression, crying. Helplessness and hopelessness can develop from neurotoxic injuries.
   c. Social withdrawal occurs as the person becomes increasingly frustrated with his disabilities. He may feel that people are staring at or scrutinizing him. Word dysfluency often is present. Upon personality testing, the examiner might find avoidant personality disorder.
3. Disturbance of executive function: Difficulty with planning, multitasking, organizing, assessing outcomes, and changing plans accordingly.
4. Sleep disturbance: Choppy sleep patterns, frequent awakening. Disruption of endocrine and hormonal systems are suspected

with neurotoxicity. Sleep disturbance contributes to learning dysfunction and chronic fatigue.

5. Chronic fatigue: Subjects may report that they are always tired, with reduced ability to lift, carry, climb stairs, walk distances, or stay awake.
6. Headache, which may be diagnosed as migraine, tension, or of other type.
7. Sexual dysfunction: Males may have difficulty maintaining an erection. In both genders, there is usually reduced desire for sexual activities, perhaps secondary to fatigue, emotional dysfunction (i.e., irritability) or self-concept issues.
8. Numbness in the hands or feet (depends upon the substance)
   a. Some neurotoxic agents damage peripheral nerves. Nerves with very long axons, such as nerves that serve the feet (and the hands to a lesser extent) are more susceptible to damage from neurotoxic agents.
   b. Disruption of the peripheral nervous system may be described by the patient as numbness, tingling, "pin and needles" sensation, or a feeling that the limb "falls asleep."
9. Multiple chemical sensitivity

Other frequent symptoms include:

1. Motor dysfunction (tremor, reduced dexterity, etc.): This symptom may be expressed as difficulty in walking or handling tools, and can progress to severe motor loss. Neurotoxicity may be misdiagnosed as multiple sclerosis (Singer, 1996a), "MS-like" disease (Singer, 1990b), amyotrophic lateral sclerosis, opsoclonus–myoclonus, seizures, and other diseases affecting the neuromotor system.
2. Sensory-perceptual disturbances: Blindness, hearing loss, pain, burning sensations, and kinesthetic dysfunction are examples of sensory disturbance that can occur with neurotoxicity. If the peripheral and central nervous system degenerate, the nerves have reduced ability to transmit accurate information to the central nervous system (CNS). Any sensory system can be affected, to the point of system failure.

SCOPE OF NEUROTOXICITY

The main classes of neurotoxic substances include pesticides, solvents, some metals, and gases such as carbon monoxide. Pesticides are perhaps the most egregious neurotoxic offender.

Exposure of Agricultural Workers to Pesticides

Approximately 1 billion pounds of pesticides are used annually in agriculture in the United States, costing $5 billion. Agricultural workers exposed to pesticides include field workers, pesticide applicators, food transporters, and storage personnel (Office of Technology Assessment [OTA], 1990). An estimated 5 million Americans farm as a primary source of income. Children under the age of 16 years are often involved in agriculture. About 3 million workers in the United States are migrant and seasonal agricultural workers, and there are an estimated 1 million pesticide handlers that are certified (OTA, 1990).

The estimated prevalence of pesticide poisoning in the United States is 300,000 cases, only 1–2% of which are reported (OTA, 1990). Estimated prevalence rates need to account for the low rate of identification of pesticide neurotoxicity, because few clinicians are trained to diagnose neurotoxicity. Cases of neurotoxicity (1) may not come to the attention of health care workers, (2) may be dismissed without a diagnosis, or (3) may be diagnosed as psychiatric or neurologic disorders, without awareness of cause of the illness.

Examples of Neurotoxic Pesticides

Organophosphate and carbamate pesticides are widely used. Because of their rapid toxicity, they are the most common cause of acute pesticide poisoning. These pesticides affect insects and humans by interfering with the biochemistry of nerve transmission. Acute symptoms can include hyperactivity, breathing difficulties, sweating, tearing, urinary frequency, abnormal heartbeat, anxiety, gastrointestinal disturbance, weakness, dizziness, convulsions, coma, and death. Typical organophosphorus pesticides include Parathion, Thimet, EPN (ethyl p-nitrophenl thionobenzene phosphate, chlorpyrifos, Dursban, DDVP, dichlorous), and Vapona. Carbamate pesticides include aldicarb, Temik, carbaryl, and Sevin (OTA, 1990).

Organochlorine pesticides are less acutely toxic than organophosphate and carbamate pesticides, but they have a greater potential for chronic toxicity, because of their persistence in the environment and in the affected person's body. From 1940 through the 1970s, several organochlorine pesticides were widely used, including DDT, aldrin, mirex, lindane, chlordane, and heptachlor. Chlordane, introduced in 1947, was banned in 1978 for most uses, except in termite control (OTA, 1990). Chlordane is highly persistent, and has an estimated half-life of 20 years.

Pyrethroids are a group of insecticides that are highly toxic to insects, but less toxic to humans than the organophosphate and organochlorine pesticides. They are replacing the more toxic pesticides.

Fumigants are gases used to kill insects (including termites) and their eggs, and are the most acutely toxic pesticides used in agriculture. Methyl bromide is a particularly problematic pesticide, because it is colorless, almost odorless, and relatively inexpensive. It has caused death and severe neurotoxic effects in fumigators, applicators, and structural pest control workers (exterminators) (OTA, 1990).

Neurotoxic herbicides include 2,4-D (2-4-dichlorophenoxyacetic acid); 2,4,5-T (Trichlorophenoxyacetic acid); MCPA (d-methyl-4-chlorophenoxyacetic acid); and Silvex. Although the Environmental Protection Agency suspended some of their uses, they continue to be used widely in forest management, and for weed control in agricultural and urban settings, including children's soccer fields. These herbicides may be contaminated with dioxins (TCDD) (2,3,7,8-tetrachloro dibenzo-p-dioxin) (OTA, 1990).

Nonagricultural Exposure to Pesticides

Two billion dollars are spent annually on nonagricultural pesticide products (OTA, 1990). Neurotoxic pesticides are used to control termites, cockroaches, and other household insects. The elderly, adults, and children are exposed to these substances in environments including the home, school, public and private offices, restaurants and other public stores, and public parks. Usually, the person being exposed is not aware that an exposure is occurring, nor is there awareness of the potential for neurotoxicity. Additional exposures to pesticides and herbicides can occur during chemical treatment of lawns, golf courses, and playing fields.

Pesticide Residue in Foods

An estimated 17% of the preschool population in the United States are exposed to neurotoxic pesticides above levels the federal government has declared as safe (Natural Resources Defense Council [NRDC], 1989; OTA, 1990). This analysis was based upon raw fruits and vegetables alone, and does not consider other sources of pesticide exposure. Children are considered to be more at risk of neurotoxicity than adults, because they absorb more pesticides per pound of body weight, their immature development makes them less able to detoxify substances, and their nervous system is developing and may be more vulnerable to permanent disruption (OTA, 1990).

Pesticides banned for use in the United States can return to the food supply via produce from other countries with fewer regulations. For example, DDT, which was banned in the United States years prior, was still found in the U.S. food supply (General Accounting Office [GAO], 1989a; NRDC, 1984). This phenomena has been termed *banned pesticide rebound*. Pesticides may be overapplied by applicators who have difficulty reading the manufacturer's instructions, which may only be available in English. The U.S. Food and Drug Administration is too short-staffed to adequately monitor the pesticide status of imported food (GAO, 1989b).

Pesticides can also contaminate water supplies. Highly persistent pesticides, such as aldicarb, have been found in groundwater supplies (Barrette, 1988).

Effects of Chronic Exposure to Pesticides and Other Neurotoxic Substances

The effects of chronic exposure to pesticides may be difficult to detect, for a number of reasons.

1. Difficulties for detection of neurotoxicity by the untrained observer: Mental deterioration from exposure to low levels of

neurotoxic chemicals may not be noticed by a person, because (1) the brain lacks the ability to detect pain resulting from brain cell death or injury, and therefore lacks sensitivity to destruction of brain tissue itself, and (2) mental deterioration often occurs in small increments, so that gradual and subtle change is difficult to notice. Over time, such gradual decrements can cause significant decline in mental function. As the person's mental processes deteriorate, he is less able to use logic, perception, memory, and other mental processes to determine the extent or cause of mental deterioration.

2. Lack of knowledge: Doctors may be aware of the acute effects of pesticides, but they often are unaware of chronic or residual effects of pesticides or neurotoxic substances, in general. Acute exposure to neurotoxic agents also may have a delayed effect, which further confounds the ability of the physician to determine the cause of subsequent neurobehavioral deterioration.

3. Accumulation of neurotoxicity: Dead brain cells are not replaced, so many of the functional deficits caused by damage to the brain and spinal cord are permanent (Aguayo, 1987).

   a. Some scientists have theorized that Alzheimer's disease and other neurological and neuropsychological conditions may be caused by exposure to environmental toxic substances occurring years before the onset of the disease. Spencer et al. (1987) have linked an environmental (food) chemical exposure, occurring many years earlier with no apparent effects, with neural disease occurring later, specifically, amyotrophic lateral sclerosis, Parkinsonism, dementia. Spencer thought that other environmental chemicals may also act as triggers for neuronal death. Calnes, McGeer, Eisen, and Spencer (1986) speculated that Alzheimer's disease may be caused by environmental damage to the CNS. Although damage may remain subclinical for several decades, it may make those affected especially prone to the consequences of age-related neuronal attrition (Lewin, 1987). Arezzo and Schaumburg (1989) also suggested that neurotoxic damage early in life can enhance CNS dysfunction that occurs late in life, such as Parkinson's disease.

   b. The relationship between dementia and neurotoxicity was discussed by Butler (1987), former head of the National

Institute of Aging. Function of the CNS provides a primary marker of aging. Neurotoxic damage to the CNS tends to be irreversible and cumulative. Neurotoxic damage is not all-or-nothing; neurotoxic nervous system deterioration is produced on a continuum.

c. Chemically induced neurological disorders are often virtually indistinguishable from other causes of disease, suggesting the possibility that environmental chemicals mimic the action of metabolically generated chemical substances circulating in the blood. The decline of neurologic integrity associated with the aging process might be linked with the cumulative effects of endogenous or exogenous poisons (Williams et al., 1987).

d. Determination of the possible relationship between neurotoxic chemical exposure and such neural diseases as senile dementia is hampered by the delayed or cumulative effects of neurotoxicants. We are now aware that some diseases, such as cancer from asbestos exposure, may take 20 years to develop. Without careful study, the causal connection of asbestos and cancer could have been overlooked. Degenerative brain disease could have a long latency period after exposure has occurred.

ELEMENTS OF THE FORENSIC EVALUATION FOR NEUROTOXICITY

Symptoms

Perhaps the most important element of this evaluation is the detection and assessment of symptoms. The examiner should assess for the presence of a constellation of symptoms characteristic of neurotoxicity. An instrument that I have found helpful is the *Neurotoxicity Screening Survey* (Singer, 1990a; Singer, 1990c), which helps quantify the frequency and severity of neurotoxicity symptoms in 10 factors. This instrument also aids in record keeping, because it assesses the extent to which the subject may have had similar symptoms prior to exposure. It also has a measure of distortion, so that the examiner can determine if the subject is overreporting symptoms.

Interview

The subject's overall condition can be assessed during the interview, and useful information regarding the degree of the subject's veracity can emerge. To help keep a record of the interview, behavioral observations can be recorded on an extended checklist, such as that provided by Zuckerman (1991). A head and shoulder photograph for the case records can help refresh the expert's memory, if testimony is needed. It is often helpful to interview members of the family or household, to obtain their perspective on any disabilities the subject may have, and to help determine the impact of the illness on family members. Collateral interviews can help an examiner determine the consistency of his and other's observations of the case, in relation to the subject's self-report. Statements or interviews of employers, clergy, and long-time friends of the case can be helpful.

Past Mental and Emotional Function

To develop a preexposure criteria of cognitive function, preexposure record examination may include records of all educational and scholastic activities, any standardized tests, military service, and evidence of intellectual achievement, such as papers, patents, and so on. These materials can be used to quantify overall prior mental function, and determine specific levels of cognitive function in various cognitive, perceptual, and emotional domains.

In addition, demographic equations, to predict premorbid intellectual function, are available. Because crystallized cognitive function is more resistant to recent insults than more fluid cognitive functions, this differential can be helpful in estimating overall premorbid intellectual function and in determining possible declines. Collateral and family interviews, as described above, may also be helpful.

Psychometric Tests

Cognitive function can be assessed, using the numerous commercially available tests for intellectual, memory, and other cognitive functions. The overall intelligence quotient may be a misleading indicator of a person's actual ability, because of disabling deficits in specific domains forming the quotient.

For the analysis of the onset of neurotoxicity, it is important to analyze the results regarding the possible discrepancy between crystalized and fluid cognitive functions. Crystalized functions are more resistant to neurotoxic effects. Perceptual distortions are common with neurotoxicity.

Interpretation of test results must account for prior cognitive ability. The person should not be compared with the hypothetical average.

Emotional Function

It is often helpful to quantify emotional function. Tests, such as the Beck Depression and Anxiety Scales, can help assess the extent of emotional factors in the case's pathology. Disruption of emotional function may result from the actual neurotoxic injury or may be secondary to loss of cognitive and physical function. In addition, these measures may help in differential diagnosis. Yet, even if depression is found, the responses should be checked, to determine if the depression shows the classic stigmata of feelings of guilt and low self-worth, or whether responses are more weighted toward psychomotor slowing and hopelessness, which often accompanies neurotoxicity.

Personality Function

Many neuropsychologists routinely use the MMPI-2 to identify personality pathology. However, the MMPI-2 has not been normed on patients with neurotoxicity or other neurological disorders, so it is not valid for differentiating between neurotoxicity and personality disorders. The MMPI-2 test results are often difficult to explain to a jury, in part because of the antiquated names that have been applied to the scales. More modern tests, such as the NEO Personality Inventory, offer clearer evidence to help juries adjudicate cases.

General Well-Being

Instruments such as the Human Activity Profile or the General Well Being Schedule help quantify the impact of the sickness on general functioning.

Malingering and Distortion

These issues are covered in separate chapters.

Neurophysiological Tests

Many neurotoxic substances also affect the peripheral nervous system. Nerve conduction velocity tests offer a reliable and inexpensive way to evaluate peripheral nerve function (Kimura, 1989; Singer, 1990a). Choose to measure nerves that are most susceptible to neurotoxicity, such as the median sensory and sural nerves, and measure both sides of the body.

Other techniques that may provide helpful information include the various brain potential tests (somatosensory, etc.) and evoked potential measures of attentional processes. Because sleep is so often disrupted, laboratory sleep studies might provide helpful information to the examiner.

CNS Imaging

Typically, routine computerized axial tomography (CAT) and magnetic resonance imaging (MRI) brain imaging are only helpful to rule out other causes of pathology. Positron emission tomography (PET) and single proton emission computed tomography (SPECT) scans are sensitive and more controversial methods. They might be useful to the diagnostician, but also might not be accepted as probative in court.

Testing for Traces, Metabolites, or Other Indications of Exposure in Blood

These measures might be valuable when assessing acute exposures, but, in general, these tests are of little value for assessing the effects of a substance months or years after exposure.

Antimyelin Antibody

These measures are often elevated in neurotoxic conditions.

NEW FRONTIERS OF FORENSIC NEUROTOXICOLOGY

Neurotoxicity can be a factor in an accused criminal's mental state when he or she committed a crime. It can affect executive function, ability to plan, decide, judge, comprehend, control impulses, and so on. In cases in which an accused faces the death penalty, the jury may find that neurotoxic injury can be a factor mitigating against death. Also, the horrors of war in the modern age may contain new neurotoxic attacks (Sloyan, 1996a, 1996b).

REFERENCES

Aguayo, A. J. (1987). Regeneration of axons from the injured central nervous system of adult mammals. In G. Adelman (Ed.), *Encyclopedia of the brain* (Vol. 1). Boston: Birkhauser.

Arezzo, J. C., & Schaumburg, H. H. (1989). Screening for neurotoxic disease in humans. *Journal of American College of Toxicology, 8,* 147–155.

Barrette, B. (1988). The Rhode Island Department of Health (DOH) Private Well Surveillance Program. *Northeast Regional Environmental Public Health Center Newsletter, 2,* 1–2.

Butler, R. (1985). Keynote address, Workshop on Environmental toxicity and the aging process. In S. R. Baker & M. Rogul (Eds.), *Environmental toxicity and the aging process, Vol. 1* (1st ed.) (pp. 11–18). New York: Alan R. Liss.

Calnes, D. B., McGeer, E., Eisen, A., & Spencer, P. (1986). Alzheimer's disease, Parkinson's disease, and motoneurone disease: Abiotropic interaction between ageing and environment? *Lancet,* 1067–1070.

Ecobichon, D., & Joy, R. (1982). *Pesticides and neurological disease* (1st ed.). Boca Raton, FL: CRC Press.

General Accounting Office (GAO). (1989a). *Pesticides: Export of Unregistered Pesticides is not Adequately Monitored by EPA* (GRD/HRD89128). Washington, DC: Author.

GAO. (1989b). *Imported Foods: Opportunities to Improve FDA's Inspection Program* (GAO/HRD89128). Washington, DC: Author.

Gonzales, J. (2001, October 26). A toxic nightmare at disaster site: Air, water, soil contaminated. News and Views | City Beat.

Kilburn, K. (1998). *Chemical brain injury.* New York: Van Nostrand Reinhold.

Kimura, J. (1989). *Electrodiagnosis in diseases of nerve and muscle: Principles and practice* (2nd ed.). Philadelphia: F. A. Davis.

Lean, G. (1996, December 15). World industry poisons Arctic purity. *Independent* (London, England), p. 15.

Lewin, R. (1987). Environmental hypothesis for brain diseases strengthened by new data. *Science, 284,* 583–584.

National Resources Defense Council (NRDC). (1984). *Pesticides in food: What the public needs to know.* San Francisco: Author.

NRDC (1989). *Intolerable risk: Pesticides in our children's food.* Washington, DC: Author.

Office of Technology Assessment. (1990). *Neurotoxicity. Identifying and controlling poisons of the nervous system* (OTABA436). Washington, DC: Office of Technology Assessment, Congress of the United States.

Singer, R. (1985, August). Neuropsychological evaluation of neurotoxicity. In *Neurobehavioural Methods in Occupational and Environmental Health: Document 3. Environ-*

mental Health (pp. 86–90). Second International Symposium, Copenhagen, Denmark: World Health Organization.

Singer, R. (1990a). *Neurotoxicity guidebook.* New York: Van Nostrand Reinhold.

Singer, R. (1990b). Neurotoxicity can produce "MS-like" symptoms. *Journal of Clinical and Experimental Neuropsychology, 12*(1), 68.

Singer, R. (1990c). *The Neurotoxicity Screening Survey.* Santa Fe, New Mexico.

Singer, R. (1994, March). Chronic polychlorinated biphenyl exposure and neurobehavioral effects. *The Toxicologist, 14*(1).

Singer, R. (1995, March). Neuropsychological assessment of a practicing dentist with elevated urinary mercury. *The Toxicologist, 15*(1).

Singer, R. (1996a). Neurotoxicity from outdoor, consumer exposure to a methylene chloride product. *The Toxicologist, 30*(1), 3–4, Part 2.

Singer, R. (1996b). Neurobehavioral screening of breast implant women. *Archives of Clinical Neuropsychology, 11,* 5.

Singer, R. (1997a). Wood-preserving chemicals, multiple sclerosis, and neuropsychological function. *Archives of Clinical Neuropsychology, 12*(4), 404.

Singer, R. (1997b, March). Sick building syndrome: Neuropsychological study. Fundamental and Applied Toxicology, Supplement: *The Toxicologist, 36*(1), 59, Part 2.

Singer, R. (1998, January). Evaluating a carbonless copy paper neurotoxicity case. *Archives of Clinical Neuropsychology, 13*(1), 127.

Singer, R. (1999a, Winter). Neuropsychological evaluation of bystander exposure to pesticides. *Journal of Neuropsychiatry and Clinical Neurosciences, 11*(1), 161–162.

Singer, R. (1999b, March). Neurobehavioral screening of child and adult bystander exposure to toluene diisocyanate application. Fundamental and Applied Toxicology, Supplement: *The Toxicologist, 48,* 1-S, 359.(a)

Singer, R. (1999c). Neurotoxicity from municipal sewage sludge. *Archives of Clinical Neuropsychology, 14,* 160.

Singer, R. (2000, March). Neurobehavioral evaluation of residual effects of acute chlorine ingestion. Fundamental and Applied Toxicology, Supplement: *The Toxicologist, 54*(1), 181.

Singer, R., Moses, M., Valciukas, J., Lilis, R., & Selikoff, I. J. (1982). Nerve conduction velocity studies of workers employed in the manufacture of phenoxy herbicides. *Environmental Research, 29,* 297–311.

Sloyan, P. J. (1996a, October 11). Release of gulf war study postponed. *Newsday.*

Sloyan, P. J. (1996b, September 27). CIA reports 120,000 exposed to nerve gas. *Newsday.*

Spencer, P. S., Nunn, P. B., Hugon, J., et al. (1987). Guam amyotrophic lateral sclerosis–Parkinsonism–dementia linked to a plant excitant neurotoxin. *Science,* 517–522.

Williams, J. R., Spencer, P. S., Stahl, S. M., et al. (1987). Interactions of aging and environmental agents: The toxicological perspective. In *Environmental toxicity and the aging process* (pp. 81–135). New York: Alan L. Liss.

Zuckerman, E. (1991). *The clinician's thesaurus.* Pittsburgh: Three Wishes Press.

Chapter 18

Forensic Neuropsychological Assessment in Criminal Law Cases

Robert J. Sbordone, Martha L. Rogers, Veronica A. Thomas, and Armando de Armas

INTRODUCTION

Neuropsychologists typically evaluate individuals who complain or present with alterations in their cognitive, behavioral, and emotional functioning, following a known or suspected cerebral insult. They utilize specialized tests and methods to identify these alterations and determine their severity. Forensic neuropsychologists involved in personal injury cases, however, must determine whether these alterations were caused by a specific cerebral injury that occurred during an accident, or reflect preexisting conditions (e.g., attention deficit disorder, prior brain insults) or nonneurological factors (e.g., motivation, psychiatric illness) that are unrelated to the accident (Purisch & Sbordone, 1997). The forensic neuropsychologist is also asked to express their opinions about the plaintiff's progress for recovery, what treatments are needed to alleviate the plaintiff's cognitive and behavioral deficits, and whether the plaintiff is able to work (or will ever be able to work). Forensic neuropsychologists involved in criminal cases, however, must utilize their test data to determine the criminal defendant's competence to stand trial, sanity, and suitability for probation. They are also asked for their opinions on sentencing/mitigation issues, if the defendant has been found guilty of committing a crime.

Although personal injury and criminal forensic psychological examinations both assess a person's cognitive, behavioral, and emotional functioning, the plaintiff's current subjective complaints following a specific event (e.g., automobile accident, exposure to toxic substances, slip-and-fall accident), in personal injury cases, mostly determine which neuropsychology tests will be administered to the plaintiff (Sbordone & Saul, 2000). In criminal cases, however, the defendant's cognitive functioning and intentions at the time the crime was committed (instant offense), usually determine which tests and methods are likely to be employed and are usually the focus of the examination.

NEUROPSYCHOLOGICAL ASSESSMENT: CIVIL AND PERSONAL INJURY VERSUS CRIMINAL CASES

Civil and Personal Injury Cases

Neuropsychological assessment in personal injury or civil cases is typically conducted in comfortable settings, such as the neuropsychologist's office, a quiet conference room at a law firm or hotel, or in a court reporter's office (e.g., if the examiner has to travel to the examination), which are free of distracting stimuli, to optimize test performance. This type of environment has been a standard in the field, to reduce the extraneous negative influences that can occur during a psychological or neuropsychological examination (Cronbach, 1984). In personal injury cases, the examiner typically can control the lighting, room temperature, and ambient noise level, and is usually able to minimize the likelihood of any potential distractions that might occur in these settings.

An examiner can usually administer a wide variety of neuropsychological tests to assess the plaintiff's cognitive, emotional, and behavioral functioning. The examiner can also provide the plaintiff with rest and lunch breaks whenever they are needed. The examiner's ability to control these factors tends to facilitate the plaintiff's motivation to perform to the best of their ability during testing. In addition, the attorney requesting the examination will typically furnish the neuropsychologist with the plaintiff's educational, vocational, and medical records prior to the scheduled examination. The examination will typically start at a prearranged time and will frequently last until it is completed, unless prior arrangements have been made to continue the examination at a later date.

Criminal Cases

Neuropsychological assessments in criminal cases are rarely, if ever, conducted in the neuropsychologist's office or in comfortable or quiet settings. Instead, they are usually conducted in the jail or prison where the criminal defendant is held. The examination usually cannot take place unless the examiner has a valid court order that grants permission to enter the attorney/bonds section of the jail or prison where the inmate resides. These areas may only permit direct contact with the defendant over a plexiglass divider; other facilities have a thick wire-meshed screen between the examiner and examinee, with a small space below the wire-meshed screen for passing very thin materials back and forth. Some facilities allow the examination to occur in the infirmary, which can result in the examination of a rapist in a gynecological examination room or a schizophrenic in the employees' lunch area.

After the examiner has filled out all of the necessary paperwork, after arriving at the jail or prison, it is not uncommon for the examiner to wait for hours until the defendant is made available. When the inmate arrives in the examination area, the examiner and examinee are often electronically locked in opposing booths. The lighting is generally dim. There are typically no windows in the room. The examiner has no control over the lighting (which may occasionally go out) or ambient noise level. It is not uncommon to have the examination interrupted by guards yelling at the prisoners, prisoners talking loudly nearby, or announcements occurring over the PA system.

Other inmates, attorneys, or examiners often work in adjacent booths, which affords little privacy as to what can be said or who hears what is being said. This is particularly troublesome when examining alleged child molesters, since the examiner must discuss emotionally charged events with a defendant, often within earshot of other inmates, potentially subjecting them to negative treatment by other inmates when the examination concludes (as a consequence, many defendants are instructed by their attorneys not to discuss the alleged crime with anyone).

If the defendant has reading glasses or a hearing aid, he will often arrive for the examination without such corrective devices, since they are usually left in his or her cell. As a consequence, the defendant must return to his or her cell to retrieve them, usually accompanied by a guard, which requires yet more delay. If, during the examination, which is usually timed around the inmates feeding and counting schedules, the defendant must use the restroom, a deputy must escort the inmate back to his or her cell block. When a sufficient number of personnel are unavailable to accommodate this need, the examiner is often forced to terminate the session and return another day.

Depending on the seriousness of the crimes with which the defendant has been charged, one or more deputies may be in attendance during the examination, usually standing directly behind the defendant. Furthermore, some criminal defendants with histories of violence may not even be permitted to use their hands during the examination, which markedly restricts the choice of psychological and neuropsychological assessment measures that can be administered to them. For example, an examination of the defendant's motor skills is virtually impossible, if the inmate's arms are shackled at their waist.

In criminal cases, the neuropsychologist must take their test materials to the jail or prison where the defendant is being held. Everything from writing instruments, tape recorders, laptop computers, test stimuli booklets, and response forms, and all of the test instruments utilized, must be mobile and portable. In some examination areas, there may not be any electrical outlets available. Although some electrical outlets may be found in the attorney/bonds area, the forensic examiner must bring a long extension cord, a flashlight, and batteries to the examination. In addition, some neuropsychological tests (e.g., hand dynamometer) may not be brought into the examination area without a specific court order and must pass security clearance, because of the risk of being misused as a lethal weapon.

The criminal forensic neuropsychologist frequently has little or no background information about the defendant, other than the pending criminal charges and a police report, at the time of the examination. Thus, the examination is usually conducted without the neuropsychologist having access to the defendant's educational, medical, or psychiatric records. During the examination, the defendant and examiner are often forced to sit on narrow metal stools that are attached to the floor and are quite uncomfortable. These conditions frequently cause the examiner to feel physically uncomfortable and may also cause the defendant to feel uncomfortable and less motivated to perform to the best of their ability. Not only is this environment dramatically different from the standard clinical environment, but there are no normative comparison data available for individuals being tested under such conditions (Sbordone, Strickland, & Purisch, 2000).

CULTURAL, ETHNIC, EDUCATIONAL, LINGUISTIC, AND SOCIOECONOMIC FACTORS IN CRIMINAL CASES

Although neuropsychological tests are frequently utilized to detect subtle organic brain pathology and cognitive deficits, many neuropsychologists have naïvely assumed that a criminal defendant's performance on these tests can simply be compared to standardized test norms, to determine whether the defendant is mentally retarded, cognitively impaired, or "brain damaged." Setting aside for a moment the issue of whether it is practical or even ethical to apply the normative data available for a neuropsychological test to individuals who are being tested under these conditions, strict reliance on standardized test norms is clearly inappropriate, if the defendant's cultural, ethnic, educational, and/or linguistic background differ significantly from the subjects upon which the test were normed. Such invidious comparisons are likely to result in inaccurate diagnoses (e.g., mental retardation, brain damage) and/or inappropriate treatment recommendations (e.g., continued incarceration, denial of probation). There has been a growing recognition of the importance of obtaining a detailed history in forensic criminal cases, but relatively little attention has been paid to cultural, educational, linguistic, socioeconomic, and acculturation factors (Fletcher-Janzen, Strickland, & Reynolds, 2000). This practice becomes more problematic when the criminal defendant is not perceived as being part of mainstream society. Some of these factors are discussed below.

Cultural Factors

In clinical and forensic personal injury neuropsychological evaluations, the examiner and examinee frequently share the same general cultural background. However, in criminal forensic cases, the neuropsychologist is likely to encounter a high percentage of culturally/racially diverse individuals. As a consequence, the cultural mismatch between the neuropsychologist and the examinee is usually the rule rather than the exception. When such a cultural mismatch occurs, it is crucial to consider how cultural differences may influence the interaction between these individuals and, ultimately, the examiner's opinion. Wong, Strickland, Fletcher-Janzen, Ardila, and Reynolds (2000) have pointed out that, when this occurs, overestimation or underestimation of psychopathology is likely to occur, even if the neuropsychologist relies on valid and reasonably reliable neuropsychological tests and measures. For example, the neuropsychologist may inappropriately attribute the criminal defendant's poor performance on a particular test or measure either to impaired neurological functioning or to motivational factors.

Educational Factors

There appears to be mounting evidence in the neuropsychological literature that the level of education may significantly affect an individual's performance on neuropsychological tests and measures (Perez-Arce & Puente, 1996). For example, less-educated individuals tend to do poorly on neuropsychological tests and are at high risk for being erroneously identified as cognitively impaired (Karken, 1997; Sbordone & Purisch, 1996). Some investigators have advocated the use of educationally adjusted norms (Kittner et al., 1985; Magaziner, Bassett, & Hebel, 1987; O'Connor, Pollitt, Treasure, Brook, & Reiss, 1989), other investigators (e.g., Berkman, 1986) have argued against the use of educationally adjusted norms in screening criminal defendant's and determining risk calculations.

Although many neuropsychological tests and batteries employ educational corrections, the level of education only accounts for between 30% and 50% of the variance in intelligence (Matarrazo, 1972; Neisser et al., 1996). Thus, an individual's educational background may not necessarily be a critical component in determining their premorbid level of intellectual functioning. Furthermore, Perez-Arc and Puente (1996) have argued that individuals who have low levels of education are most likely to be recent immigrants from other countries and may not be motivated to perform to the best of their abilities on neuropsychological tests and measures.

Linguistic Factors

A number of investigators (e.g., Wong et al., 2000) have strongly argued that neuropsychological assessment of the non-English speaker, by an examiner who is unfamiliar with the language, is "not only risky but could potentially be unethical" (p. 8). They point out that an examiner unfamiliar with the examinee's language is unlikely to detect abnormal prosody or unusual syntax or other symptoms suggesting a neurologically based language disorder. Similarly, it would also be difficult to assess the examinee's mood, affect, or thought processes, if the examiner lacks familiarity with the examinee's language. They also argue that employing professional translators does not eliminate this linguistic dilemma. For example, they point out that the issue of establishing client rapport through an interpreter has not been adequately researched and that the translators themselves may be influenced by cultural variables at the time of the examination, which may result in distortions of the examinee's responses.

There are many potential ways in which accuracy can be lost with use of interpreters. On occasion, an interpreter may overidentify with his or her countryman and fail to interpret accurately, in the mistaken belief she or he is assisting the defendant. Some defendants may be less willing to disclose certain kinds of information to an interpreter of the opposite sex, or may not want to "lose face" by admitting crimes in front of a fellow countryman.

Ethnicity/Socioeconomic Factors

The Halstead–Reitan Neuropsychological Test Battery (HRNTB) has been validated on numerous occasions for its efficacy in detecting brain damage (Russell, 1995) and is perhaps the most widely used neuropsychological battery in clinical settings, but Steinmeyer (1986) has pointed out that the majority of the data in support of its validity was based on middle-aged, well-educated, and primarily Caucasian subjects. Although Heaton, Grant, and Matthews (1991) have developed normative corrections for the HRNTB, based on the patient's age, education, background, and gender, no attempt was made to provide norms for racially diverse individuals or for individuals with low socioeconomic status (Evans, Miller, Byrd, & Heaton, 2000).

RECOGNIZING THE IMPORTANCE OF TEMPORAL FACTORS WHEN ASSESSING CRIMINAL DEFENDANTS

Unlike personal injury cases, in which the psychologist is asked to evaluate a plaintiff's current intellectual, cognitive, and psychological functioning, neuropsychologists in criminal cases are frequently asked to reconstruct the criminal defendant's behavioral, cognitive, and emotional functioning at the time the alleged crime was committed. This is usually quite difficult, since many changes may have occurred in the patient's behavioral, cognitive, and psychological functioning since the alleged crime. For example, the cognitive abnormalities present at the time when the alleged crime was committed may not be present when the defendant is later evaluated, particularly if the defendant has been in custody for several months or even years. Often, the defendant's cognitive functioning has markedly improved, as a result of institutionally imposed cessation of alcohol and substance abuse, reinstituting neuroleptic medications (which the defendant may have stopped taking prior to the commission of the alleged crime), more consistent nutrition, and being removed from the environmental stressors that were in effect at the time of the alleged crime.

The Realities of the Criminal Forensic Examination

Attorneys handling criminal cases are usually overburdened and have limited investigative or secretarial staff. Thus, the likelihood of obtaining the defendant's prior academic, medical, military, prison, or psychiatric records, in a timely fashion, is often poor. Even when significant others (e.g., mother, wife, sibling) may be available to interview, the criminal defendant may not permit the neuropsychologist to contact them or sign an authorization form. Although prior criminal reports, custody, or probation records may exist, there may not be any civilian medical or psychiatric records. Juvenile records may exist, but they are often sealed, which requires that the neuropsychologist request them from the court, without any guarantee that the court, will grant this request.

Interview with the Criminal Defendant

Since neuropsychologists involved in criminal cases are primarily interested in the defendant's thoughts and cognitive and emotional functioning at the time that the crime was allegedly committed, they must reconstruct the defendant's thought processes at the time of the instant offense and determine which factors may have contributed to the defendant's actions at that time. In doing this, the neuropsychologist often must rely heavily on the criminal defendant's recollection (autobiographical memory) of the alleged crime.

A review of the literature on the accuracy and validity of a criminal defendant's autobiographical memory (Ross, 1991; Rubin, 1986; Schwarz & Sudman, 1994; Thompson, Skowronski, Larsen, & Betz, 1996) reveals that the major problems in utilizing a defendant's recollection of what occurred during the alleged crime is that their memory of this event is likely to change over time, particularly if they have consulted with an attorney, or have become aware of witness statements and the evidence against them. Thus, the defendant is likely to recall the alleged crime in a manner that decreases their culpability, to avoid going to prison. To complicate matters even further, other inmates will often coach the defendant to fake memory problems or to assert that they have been having hallucinations. Finally, the presence of guards standing nearby, the ability of other inmates to listen to what the defendant is saying at the time of the examination, and, at times, the instructions of the defendant's attorney to avoid discussing the alleged crime, serve to make the neuropsychologist's job very difficult, at best.

Determining the Validity of the Criminal Defendant's Memory of the Alleged Crime

The neuropsychologist must try to determine whether the defendant's memory for events is what really occurred at the time of the alleged crime, or was constructed through conversations with their attorney, investigator, or other inmates. The defendant's recollection may also be influenced by low intellectual functioning, motivational factors, cultural and linguistic factors, or memory deficits caused by brain damage as a result of frequent fights, motor vehicle accidents, or chronic substance abuse. Thus, the neuropsychologist must rule out these possible explanations through a process of elimination. This process usually begins by ruling out low intellectual functioning, to determine whether the defendant understands the criminal charges that have been brought against them and can talk about them.

The neuropsychologist must determine the extent to which the defendant has adequate receptive language skills, and is able to comprehend and respond to the questions they are being asked during the interview. The neuropsychologist should rule out the likelihood that the defendant has a well-recognized memory disorder, which could contaminate their ability to recall past events. The neuropsychologist should also assess whether the defendant's thinking is logical, coherent, and relevant.

The manner in which the defendant organizes their thoughts, and initiates and discusses information, particularly during a lengthy interview and over multiple sessions, permits the examiner the opportunity to assess the defendant's executive functions. The neuropsychologist should also try to assess the degree to which the defendant can be influenced by others or is suggestible. For example, low-intellectual-functioning defendants with dependent personality disorders are at higher risk for being unduly influenced by others. For example, their recollection of the alleged crime may reflect the suggestions of others, and is unlikely to accurately reflect what actually occurred. To rule out this possibility, neuropsychologists should become familiar with the methodology developed by Gudjonsson (1992), when assessing defendants who are at risk of being unduly influenced by others or making false confessions.

Neuropsychologists should try to rule out changes in the defendant's memory of the crime by the use of clinical interview techniques, by tests of autobiographical memory, and by comparing the defendant's current recollection of the crime with their recollection of the crime taken shortly after the instant offense was committed (e.g., statements given to the police). It is often helpful to ask the defendant to recall concurrent events in the same time frame in which the crime was committed, which are not threatening to their case and can be validated by others. The defendant's ability to accurately recall these events can be utilized to assess their remote memory. Some defendants may claim that they are unable to recall the crime or that they have a poor memory, but the use of neuropsychological validity measures designed to assess feigning of memory deficits (e.g., Test of Memory Malingering, Victoria Symptom Validity Test) may be helpful in determining whether the defendant's claim of having a poor memory reflects motivational issues.

The defendant may have psychogenic amnesia of the alleged crime as a result of blocking out certain aspects of what took place, because of an acute or posttraumatic stress disorder (particularly if it involved violence). These defendants, however, may be able to later recall these events, after their stress disorder dissipates and they have established a good rapport with the examiner. Defendants who are anxious or depressed may also exhibit a selective or overgeneralized recall (Eysenck, 1992; Mazzoni & Nelson, 1998; Teasdale & Barnard, 1993), which may also produce an inaccurate recollection of the crime. Schizophrenics may exhibit memory retrieval problems and a general paucity of thought, when they are asked to provide a narrative recall of the crime (Green, 1998).

The use of personality measures, such as the Minnesota Multiphasic Personality Inventory 2 (MMPI-2) or Personality Assessment Inventory (PAI) may be helpful in ferreting out an underlying psychiatric disorder that may account for the defendant's unreliable recollection of the alleged crime. The defendant's clinical profile should, however, be consistent with the examiner's observation of the defendant's behavior and be corroborated by prior medical and psychiatric records, as well as collateral interviews with significant others.

If the defendant has genuine memory deficits or their recollection of the crime has been colored by their suggestibility, through contacts with others, neuropsychologists should inform the court that the defendant's recollection of the alleged crime is unreliable. If, on the other hand, a neuropsychologist is asked by the court, "How do you know the information you obtained from the defendant is accurate?" it is often helpful to point out to the court the various steps that were taken to rule out the sources of invalidity and memory contamination and the various methods that were utilized to determine whether the defendant's recollection of the alleged crime is consistent with other information.

Neuropsychologists should utilize sources of information in addition to the defendant's or witnesses' accounts of how the alleged crime occurred. For example, physical evidence at the scene of the crime (e.g., location, sources of blood, or other biological materials) can be compelling and tells its own story. Neuropsychologists should also consult with investigators and criminologists and carefully review crime scene photographs, videotapes, autopsy reports, or victim photographs and laboratory findings. Reviewing these materials may provide additional information as to how the alleged crime was committed, particularly whether it corroborates what the defendant stated actually occurred. Neuropsychologists should also review ambulance and emergency room records, and witness statements, to help reconstruct what happened to the victim.

The Validity of the Criminal Defendant's Symptoms

The validity of the criminal defendant's symptoms is an important concern in any forensic context, and they are particularly important in criminal cases (Hall & Pritchard, 1996; Rogers, 1997). Although many psychologists utilize the MMPI-2 or the PAI to determine whether a defendant's symptoms are valid, many psychologists involved in criminal cases utilize the Structured Interview of Reported Symptoms (SIRS) (Rogers, Bagby, & Dickens, 1992), to assess the validity of a defendant's symptoms. This 172-item structured interview consists of detailed and repeated inquiries to assess response consistency, and general inquiries to assess the validity of specific symptoms, general psychological problems and symptom patterns.

Research has shown that the SIRS can identify individuals with psychiatric disorders from those who are feigning a psychiatric disorder. For example, Rogers et al. (1992) compared 25 suspected malingerers with 26 psychiatric inpatients. They found that 9 of the 13 SIRS scales discriminated between the two groups with excellent interrater reliability. The SIRS scores of the suspected malingerers were highly correlated with MMPI indicators of simulation. For example, 78% of the SIRS scales were significantly correlated with the MMPI fake bad scales. Based on these findings, Rogers (1997) has argued that the SIRS may supplement, but not replace, the MMPI, to determine whether a criminal defendant is malingering psychiatric illness.

Hall and Pritchard (1996) have developed a Forensic Distortion Analysis, which forces the examiner to focus on the symptoms of individuals who are feigning or malingering psychiatric illness. Their model has been designed to provide testable hypotheses for further inquiry and can be specifically tailored to the specific questions of the examiner.

Understanding Important Legal Issues

Two of the most common legal issues raised in the criminal justice system are the defendant's competency to stand trial, and sanity at the time of the alleged criminal offense. Neuropsychologists who are relatively inexperienced in this area, or who do not possess a good understanding of these issues, are encouraged to review an excellent text on these issues by Melton, Petrila, Poythress, and Slobogin (1997).

Competency to Stand Trial

Approximately 60,000 criminal defendants are evaluated for competency to stand trial each year in the United States (Melton et al., 1997). The legal standard for competency to stand trial in each state is usually some variant of *Dusky v. United States* (1960): The defendant must have a factual understanding of the proceedings against them and must have the present ability to consult with their attorney with a reasonable degree of rational understanding. This definition requires that the criminal defendant understands the charges that have been brought against them and has the cognitive and behavioral skills to assist their counsel and function appropriately in court. Understanding the criminal charges brought against the defendant includes the knowledge that they have been arrested and what specific charges (e.g., murder, sexual assault) have been brought against them. The defendant must also be able to communicate with their counsel in a meaningful fashion in preparing for trial and making informed decisions.

The assessment of competency must address the defendant's current mental state and the prognosis for maintaining their mental state throughout the trial (which may last several weeks or months). In some cases, the stability of the defendant's mental state may depend on their willingness to continue to take psychotropic medications during trial. However, should the criminal defendant's ability to behave appropriately or ability to communicate with their attorney markedly deteriorate during trial (e.g., the defendant believes that their attorney is the son of Satan, or begins barking like a dog in the courtroom), then psychological and/or psychiatric examinations may be ordered by the court. In some cases, the judge may postpone trial until the defendant regains competency.

It is often assumed that, if the criminal defendant is competent to stand trial, they must be competent to enter a plea (guilty, innocent, or no contest). Entering a plea requires that the defendant waive some of their rights and assumes that they understand the consequences of entering such a plea. This assumption, however, is not always valid. For example, although defendants waive their constitutional rights when entering a plea of guilty or no contest, they may not understand the implications of their decision, as a result of their limited educational background, low level of intellectual functioning, cultural or linguistic background, psychiatric illness, or cognitive deficits.

Psychologists typically do not become involved in competency issues, until the defense raises the issue of the defendant's competency to stand trial. When this occurs, all legal proceedings immediately cease, until the issue of the defendant's competency is resolved. Neuropsychologists, in particular, need to consider the following factors when determining whether a particular criminal defendant is competent to stand trial: a psychiatric illness, low intellectual functioning, cognitive impairment, and the defendant's cultural and linguistic background (which may prohibit an understanding of the U.S. legal system).

If the defendant has a psychiatric illness, the neuropsychologist must determine whether the defendant's psychiatric disorder impairs their ability to cooperate with counsel (keeping in mind that the presence of a psychiatric disorder may not render the defendant incompetent to stand trial). For example, if the defendant has a severe delusional disorder that incorporates the defense counsel, the judge, or the prosecutor, they will most likely be found incompetent to stand trial. If, on the other hand, the defendant's delusional disorder is more circumscribed and does not significantly affect their ability to deal with the facts of the case and communicate with and assist counsel, then the defendant is likely to be found competent.

Impaired intellectual and cognitive functioning may not meet the criteria for incompetency. For example, if special procedures can be utilized to compensate for the defendant's limited intellectual resources (e.g., by providing the defendant with extra support to follow court testimony and point out errors to their counsel), they may be found competent to stand trial. When this occurs, the neuropsychologist can also request the court to slow the pace of trial, and simplify the vocabulary and grammar of witnesses. The court will also permit the defendant to signal their attorney when they do not understand what is being said during trial. Frequent breaks may also be granted to allow the defendant to discuss the testimony of witnesses with their attorney.

In some cases, however, the defendant may be found incompetent to stand trial as a result of severe cognitive impairment, which obviates any realistic possibility of compensating for the defendant's cognitive deficits or the defendant regaining competency in the foreseeable future. For example, a male defendant attempted suicide after he was arrested for killing his wife, by locking himself in a garage with his car engine running. After this episode, he exhibited such poor anterograde memory that he was judged incompetent to stand trial, since he was unable to follow court proceedings, point out any errors in the testimony of witnesses, and was unable to meaningfully assist his counsel. His cognitive deficits were documented by neuropsychological testing and led to a dismissal of the charges that were brought against him.

A criminal defendant's inability to recall having committed a crime is not a deterrent to being found competent to stand trial. However, if the defendant has significant amnestic problems that interfere with their ability to cooperate and assist counsel (as in the above example), they may be found incompetent. If the defendant is unable to remember the charges brought against them or recall discussions with their counsel, the defendant may also be found to be incompetent to stand trial. If the defendant's cognitive deficits improve, they may be later found to be competent to stand trial. For example, in *Wilson v. United States* (1968), a defendant who had been charged with assault and robbery suffered a skull fracture and concussion while being apprehended by the police. Although the defendant was unable to recall the crime, he was found competent to stand trial when the cognitive deficits, stemming from his postconcussion syndrome, resolved.

Criminal defendants may also be motivated to be found incompetent to stand trial, so that they can be transferred to a state psychiatric hospital, where less restrictions are placed on their freedom. Some criminal defendants, on the other hand, who are incompetent to stand trial as a result of their severe cognitive impairments, may not wish to be labeled or perceived as mentally ill and may actually feign normalcy, even though they do not adequately understand the charges that have been brought against them and are unable to meaningfully assist their attorney.

Incompetency to stand trial does not include the defendant's unwillingness to cooperate with legal proceedings, as long as the lack of cooperation is not the product of mental deficiency or psychiatric illness. For example, many individuals with chronic personality disorders exhibit considerable resistance in cooperating with their attorneys and are often dishonest with them. However, the line between "can't" and "won't" is often difficult to determine and may require the gathering of additional information.

Psycholegal Assessment of Competency

The MacArthur Competence Assessment Tool—Criminal Adjudication (MacCAT-CA) (Hoge, Bonnie, Poythress, & Monahan, 1996, 1999; Poythress et al., 1999) is a structured interview and rating system that can assist the forensic examiner to determine whether a criminal defendant is likely to be found competent to stand trial. It assesses the defendant's ability to discriminate which information would be most relevant to disclose to their attorney on the basis of various criminal scenarios (e.g., accidental, self-defense) in a hypothetical assault case. This instrument assesses reasoning, problem solving, and executive function skills, which are essential for a defendant to meaningfully assist their counsel.

This instrument can also be used to assess the ability of low-intellectual-functioning defendants to apply basic reasoning skills and demonstrate a sufficient level of knowledge of the legal process to function effectively as a criminal defendant. The test items explore the defendant's understanding of their situation and ability to assess the implications of various legal outcomes. It can be verbally administered in approximately 45 minutes. Neuropsychologists using the MacCAT-CA should be aware that this instrument has not been validated on mentally retarded defendants or juveniles.

Hoge et al. (1997) and Otto et al. (1998) have evaluated the psychometric properties of this instrument, utilizing an eight-state sample of 722 criminal defendants. They found that it measures three factors (the defendant's understanding, reasoning skills, and ability to understand their legal situation) with an average internal consistency of 0.85, as measured by Cronbach's alpha. They also reported that the classification accuracy of this instrument could be significantly improved with the addition of demographic, historical, and clinical factors. They found that defendants' reasoning skills and appreciation of their particular legal situations were strong predictors of competency.

Although this instrument provides norms that can serve as guidelines to assist a neuropsychologist in determining the competence of a particular defendant, it does not utilize strict cutoff scores. It also assumes that other factors must be taken into account before any criminal defendant can be determined to be competent. For example, the neuropsychologist should consider the following factors: the defendant's propensity to exaggerate or minimize cognitive or psychiatric impairment, the complexity of the defendant's pending legal case (e.g., the defendant might be competent for purposes of adjudicating a petty theft, drunk driving, or trespassing charge, yet may be incompetent to participate in their defense in a murder charge), the defendant's psychiatric history, current mental status, ability to communicate relevant information in a fairly coherent manner, and ability to function effectively in court. The assessment of competency should not be based simply on the results of the MacArthur instrument, since mental health, education, and investigatory (e.g., police, criminal, probation) records are also needed to assess a criminal defendant's competence to stand trial (Roesch, Hart, & Sapf, 1996; Skeem & Golding, 1998).

Use of Neuropsychological Tests to Determine Competency

Since assessment of the criminal defendant's competency to stand trial involves assessment of their current cognitive functioning, neuropsychological tests may be particularly helpful in determining a defendant's competency to stand trial. For example, the usefulness of neuropsychological tests to determine a defendant's competency to stand trial has been carefully examined by Nestor, Daggett, Haycock, and Price (1999). They examined a total of 181 criminal defendants on a neuropsychological inpatient service, who had undergone competency evaluations. They carefully analyzed the cognitive demands required for competency and utilized a battery of neuropsychological tests to assess the defendants' cognitive functioning. They found that defendants who were competent to stand trial possessed relatively intact attention, memory, verbal reasoning, and social awareness skills. Their findings suggest that neuropsychological tests may be helpful in identifying the underlying cognitive skills, which are necessary for competence to stand trial.

Neuropsychological studies on juvenile and adult prisoners who had committed violent crimes (e.g., assault, homicide, rape) have shown that a high percentage of these individuals tested in the impaired range, when they were administered the HRNTB (Lewis et al., 1988; Lewis, Pincus, Feldman, Jackson, & Bard, 1986; Yeudall, 1977; Yeudall & Fromm-Auch, 1979). These studies suggest that a significant number of prisoners who commit violent crimes have brain dysfunction or damage, but these investigators appear to have utilized standardized HRNTB test norms and essentially ignored cultural, ethnic, educational, linguistic, and socioeconomic factors, not to mention any normative data on incarcerated prisoners for control purposes.

Neuropsychologists should not rely solely on the defendants' poor test scores to determine whether they are competent to stand trial. They should seek out convergent and consistent sources of information to increase their understanding of the defendant's mental capacity and/or competence in their particular ecological niche. For example, no one specific neuropsychological test or measure can accurately determine a criminal defendant's mental capacity or competency to stand trial, if their cultural, ethnic, linguistic, educational, and socioeconomic background is dramatically different from the published test norms and the examiner's background or experience. Thus, impaired performances on neuropsychological measures may not necessarily be indicative of impaired functional skills or even remotely predictive of the defendant's competence to stand trial. Neuropsychological tests, however, are likely to have more predictive value if the measures used during testing more closely match or simulate the demands on the defendant's functioning in everyday or real-world settings. Unfortunately, few assessment measures have demonstrated adequate ecological validity (Sbordone & Guilmette, 1999; Sbordone et al., 2000).

Determining Criminal Responsibility:
Not Guilty by Reason of Insanity

The forensic neuropsychologist must determine if the criminal defendant understood that their behavior was right or wrong, acceptable or unacceptable (based on societal norms) or was legal or illegal (based on legal statutes), at the time the alleged criminal offense was committed. Since the statutes controlling criminal responsibility determination vary across different legal jurisdictions, the neuropsychologist should become familiar with the definitions of criminal responsibility within the legal jurisdictions in which they offer testimony.

Modern definitions of legal insanity are attributed to the aftermath of *M'Naghten* (1843) in Great Britain. For example, M'Naghten tried to kill the British prime minister, but instead killed his secretary, as a result of his persecutory and delusional thinking. Since Queen Victoria did not approve of the finding of insanity, she selected a group of judges to develop more rigorous legal standards. In many ways, this is similar to the controversies and legal revisions that were seen in the United States after President Reagan was shot in 1981.

The M'Naughten standard states

> to establish a defense on the ground of insanity, it must be clearly proved that at the time of committing the act, the party accused was laboring under such a disease of the mind, as not to know the nature and quality of the act he was doing; or he did not know it, that he did not know what he was doing was wrong. (p. 718)

The American Law Institute (Model Penal Code, 1962) has broadened the M'Naughten standard to include cognitive and emotional factors. For example, they state,

> a person is not responsible for criminal conduct if at the time of such conduct as a result of mental disease or defect, he lacks substantial capacity either to appreciate the criminality (wrongfulness) of his conduct or to conform his conduct to the requirements of the law. (p. 325)

Their interpretation of the M'Naughten standard implies that, from a neuropsychological perspective, a criminal defendant's cognitive and intellectual deficits could render them incompetent to stand trial (Martell, 1992).

Most legal insanity definitions in use today are variations of the M'Naughten standard, and usually include criteria such as whether the defendant suffers from a mental disease or defect that results in cognitive impairments severe enough that they were unable to understand the nature and quality of their act, or recognize that the act was wrong or illegal at the time it was committed. Depending on the particular legal jurisdiction in which the case is tried, there may be legal standards that focus more on the defendant's ability to control their behavior versus the defendant's cognitive awareness of whether their actions were right or wrong at the time when the alleged crime was committed. The reader is encouraged to review Slovenko (1995) to gain a better understanding of these issues.

One of the most difficult issues to evaluate is the criminal defendant's state of mind at the time the crime was committed, since, as pointed out earlier, the defendant's state of mind at the time of assessment is likely to be different than when the alleged crime was committed. This may reflect a variety of factors, such as guilt, incarceration, being charged with the crime, the passage of time, being confined to a jail or prison, as well as the defendant's present psychiatric state and cognitive functioning. One simply cannot assume that a defendant's mental state at the time of examination is an extension of their state of mind at the time of the instant offense. For example, if a criminal defendant killed his wife, after developing a paranoid delusion that his wife was going to kill him, as the result of taking amphetamines for several days, his mental status at the time of the examination (6 months later) would most likely be considerably different as a result of being drug free. In some cases, defendants were not substantially impaired at the time of the offense, but later became significantly impaired, to the point that they were determined to be incompetent to stand trial. For example, a defendant, who killed his girlfriend after he discovered that she was cheating on him, became so guilt-ridden that he shot himself in the head. Although he would have not been found to be insane or incompetent to stand trial at the time the crime was committed, he was found to be incompetent to stand trial as a result of his severe cognitive deficits stemming from his head injury.

Since psychologists are rarely afforded the opportunity to evaluate a criminal defendant immediately after a criminal offense, they must try to reconstruct how the alleged crime occurred and the defendant's mental state at the time the alleged crime was committed. Since the information from the criminal defendant may be biased, self-serving, and inaccurate, neuropsychologists are typically compelled to seek a more objective basis for determining the defendant's mental state at the time of the instant offense.

Hall and Pritchard (1996) developed a comprehensive framework to assess a defendant's mental state at the time of the instant offense. Their approach systematizes the collection of a forensic database and its analysis. It also links a defendant's executive functions with the criminal offense and other ongoing activities. This methodology helps determine how a criminal defendant planned or committed the crime. It also examines a defendant's history of self-regulation and violent behavior. Hall and Pritchard's approach allows neuropsychologists to integrate discrepant information into a unified timeline and focus on key areas that need to be more closely examined. It permits the examiner to develop a decision path, to weigh the importance of various pieces of information, and an objective method of assessing a defendant's mental state, based on the available data. This approach is based on the assumption that

> even primarily cognitive impairments must always be expressed through overt behavior, because it is the only manner by which those impairments can be observed or deduced. Cognitive impairments are second-order inferences derived from possible behavioral aberrations. All cognitive impairments, therefore, presuppose volitional impairments in the sense that problems in thinking must be reflected through behavioral responses. (Hall & Pritchard, 1996, p. 72)

Determination of Insanity

Although neuropsychologists must establish that the criminal defendant met the criteria for insanity when the alleged crime was committed, they must also present evidence that the defendant met these criteria prior to the commission of the alleged crime. Neuropsychologists should determine whether any neurological, medical, metabolic, or toxic factors may have affected the defendant's cognitive functioning at the time of the alleged crime or may have possibly contributed to the alleged crime. Neuropsychologists should also determine whether the criminal defendant's actions at the time of the instant offense were the result of impaired cognitive functioning caused by delusional or psychotic thinking that resulted in a loss of reality testing. If the defendant, however, did not show evidence of psychotic behavior and poor reality testing prior to the criminal offense, it is very difficult to argue that such behavior initially occurred at the time of the instant offense.

Case Study

A mother killed her two young children, based on her delusional belief that a stalker was following them with the intent of raping her children. The neuropsychologist assigned to the case determined, after careful questioning of the defendant, family members, and acquaintances, that the defendant had publicly accused three different men of stalking her within 10 days prior to the instant offense. Police investigations had not uncovered this crucial information. The neuropsychologist determined that the defendant had a well-documented preexisting psychiatric history of major depression with psychotic features, which included unrealistic fears that her children were going to be raped.

Recent studies, which have examined the number of insanity acquittals, have shown that many more persons are evaluated for sanity than are actually acquitted (Cirincione & Jacobs, 1999). In fact, insanity defenses are typically unsuccessful (Pasewark et al., 1979; Steadman, 1980). For example, the average number of acquittals per state is only 33 per year, with Florida and California having the highest annual number of (110 and 134, respectively) (Cirincione, 1996). In fact, Steadman, Pantle, and Pasewark (1983) have estimated that the sanity issue might only be raised 2–3% of the time and is only successful in one of four times it is raised. Similarly, Rogers and Sewell (1999) found that 23% of a total of 413 criminal defendants in their database, who were evaluated for sanity, were found to be insane at the time of the instant offense. Although developmental or acquired neurocognitive deficits are common among criminal defendants, a plea of not guilty by reason of insanity (NGRI), based solely on the defendant's neuropsychological deficits, appears to be relatively uncommon. When such pleas are successful, the level of impairment is typically obvious, rather than subtle.

Most successful NGRI defendants are found to be psychotic at the time of the offense, with their cognitive functioning seriously impaired as a result of a lengthy history of alcohol and substance abuse. Although a few defendants (without a history of psychosis) may report dissociating during the commission of the crime, this rarely makes for a successful

NGRI. Perhaps, since such claims of being unable to recall the crime are so common, it frequently raises the issue of malingering.

Many defendants will claim to be unable to remember all or part of the alleged crime. After the psychosis defense, a claim of amnesia is perhaps the single most common defense utilized in sanity cases. However, one cannot make a finding of NGRI simply because the defendant does not remember what they were thinking at the time of the crime. In such cases, one must carefully evaluate the circumstances, the physical and behavioral evidence, and the role of chronic or recent substance abuse, as well as rule out whether any psychiatric or neurological disorder present at the time of the alleged crime could have produced an amnestic disorder.

Defendants frequently do not understand that their failure to later remember what they did during an alleged crime is not a defense for what occurred at that time. In fact, most claims of memory loss typically consist of a circumscribed dense memory loss, often with sharp demarcating boundaries around the incident, with no evidence of an alteration of consciousness prior to and following the alleged crime. In the majority of cases, there is typically no evidence of retrograde or anterograde amnesia or memory complaints consistent with a well-recognized amnestic disorder (Kapur, 1999).

Case Study

A defendant who robbed a building supply store and shot the manager was able to describe in detail all of his thoughts and actions up to the moment he walked into the store, and from the moment he ran out of the store while fleeing the scene, but denied any recollection as to what occurred during the 45 minutes he spent in the store. Witness accounts indicated, however, that he appeared to be fully aware of his actions, which included making threats and specific instructions given to store personnel, while holding a loaded weapon. His performance on neuropsychological tests was generally within normal limits, but he performed poorly on tests that were designed to detect malingering of memory.

A related but separate grounds for acquittal, which is often raised in neuropsychologically impaired defendants, is the defense of unconsciousness or automatism, in which the defendant claims to lack awareness of the crime that was being committed. Of the neurologically based defenses, the most common is the defendant's claim of becoming violent as a result of having a seizure at the time of the instant offense. Neuropsychologists evaluating such claims should review Delgato-Escueta et al. (1981). Their study correlated the patient's clinical history, EEG recordings, and videotaped observations of ictal violence. They found that any aggressive behavior occurring during a seizure usually consists of random, flailing, and nonpurposeful movements, particularly when someone tried to physically restrict the patient during a seizure. They argued that more specific and goal-directed violence is extremely rare during seizures and that most violence reflects conscious intent and is carried out by individuals who are neurologically intact with no history of seizures.

Case Study

A young man, who was a neighbor of a woman, gained entrance into her home by asking her if he could use her telephone. Once inside of her home, he physically and sexually assaulted her. During this time, reciprocal verbal and physical exchanges between the assailant and victim occurred. As he was leaving her home, he asked her not to tell his parents what had transpired. He then returned home and went to bed. When he was later apprehended by the police, he claimed that he could not remember anything from the time he left his home until he woke up in bed. Although he had an abnormal EEG, he had never had a seizure. Thus, his claim of unconsciousness made little sense in light of his obvious goal-directed behavior, including his verbalizations during and after the assault.

Psycholegal Measurement of Sanity

The Rogers Criminal Responsibility Assessment Scales (R-CRAS) (Rogers, 1984) was designed to review and evaluate factors that are believed to be particularly relevant to determine a criminal defendant's sanity at the time of the instant offense. This instrument consists of a set of rating scales, which ensure that the examiner systematically reviews all of the factors that may contribute to a finding of insanity. This instrument was validated on 260 criminal defendants, who were being held in custody in five different states. Two independent evaluations of each defendant were performed, in which each examiner rated each case in different time frames (an average of 3 weeks apart). These investigators found that R-CRAS had moderately high reliability for individual variables, and even higher kappa ratings for decision variables, with an average coefficient Kappa of 0.81 and a 97% concordance rate with the ultimate clinical judgment (Rogers & Schuman, 2000).

Although the R-CRAS has many strengths, including its high interrater reliability and high rate of concordance between opinions based on its ratings and court verdicts, Melton et al. (1997) have stressed that examiners should not rely solely on the R-CRAS ultimate issue items in determining a criminal defendant's sanity. On the other hand, Rogers and Schuman (2000) have argued that the strength of the R-CRAS lies in its ability to carefully systematize areas, which should be explored to improve the reliability and validity of any professional judgments, even if it is not used to arrive at the ultimate issue.

From a neuropsychological perspective, the R-CRAS includes several items that can be utilized to assess the influence of cognitive impairment or brain dysfunction on criminal behavior. For example, the examiner is asked to rate the relationship between a defendant's cognitive dysfunction from brain damage and the commission of the alleged crime. Rogers (1997) has stressed that, although brain dysfunction may affect a defendant's predilection to commit a crime, the effect is often subtle, rather than dramatic.

Use of Neuropsychological Tests to Determine Sanity

The prevailing standard in most jurisdictions is that neuropsychological assessment should be performed in death penalty cases. The primary argument for its use, however, is that, although a defendant's cognitive deficits at the time of the instant offense are often an inadequate defense for the crime, they may be helpful in mitigating the culpability of the defendant for sentencing purposes. For example, the neuropsychological test data may be used to demonstrate that the defendant's cognitive deficits diminished their capacity to organize and plan their behavior to form the legal intent to commit murder, to cause the trier of fact to find the defendant guilty of committing a lesser crime (e.g., manslaughter).

The relationship between neuropsychological testing and the determination of NGRI has been carefully examined by Nestor and Haycock (1997), who archivally examined the clinical status, neuropsychological functioning, and perpetrator–victim relationships of 28 adult patients who had committed homicide and had been involuntarily committed to a forensic psychiatric facility. They divided the patients into two groups: defendants who had been found not guilty by reason of insanity, and convicted murderers. In comparison to convicted murderers, the NGRI subjects were more likely to be psychotic at the time of the crime and to have killed blood relatives, particularly a parent. By contrast, convicted murderers were more likely to have killed a significant other, usually a spouse or lover. A history of substance abuse was more likely to have been present at the time of the crime in convicted murderers than in the NGRI acquittals.

The NGRI acquittal group and the convicted murderers, however, did not differ in their performance on neuropsychological measures. In fact, both groups generally performed within normal limits. Their results suggest that NGRI murderers may be triggered by an acute psychosis directed toward blood relatives, against a backdrop of well-preserved neuropsychological functioning. Psychotic NGRI murderers generally performed better on neuropsychological tests than patients with chronic schizophrenia. Their data suggest that NGRI murderers most likely represent a distinct group of psychotic patients who are characterized by malignant paranoid delusions with well-preserved cognitive functioning. These findings suggest that the intact cognitive abilities of convicted murderers may provide them with the ability to organize and act upon their psychotic perceptions and delusional beliefs.

These findings may not generalize to younger groups of murderers. For example, Nestor (1992) found that males between the ages of 17 and 25 years (mean age of 20.2 years) were more likely to have a history of prior arrests (suggestive of long-standing antisocial/conduct disorder), as well as a developmental reading disability, as determined by neuropsychological testing. An older group, consisting of 18 men with the mean age of 46.4 years (range 30–67 years), was more likely to be diagnosed with a psychotic disorder at the time of the psychiatric evaluation, but were less likely than the younger group to have a record of prior arrest or history of learning disabilities. Both groups, however, had a high incidence of prior substance abuse. These findings suggest that a neurodevelopmental disorder, in conjunction with a childhood conduct disorder, is often associated with the onset of violence in late adolescence and early adulthood (Lewis et al., 1988; Mannuzza et al., 1989; Nestor 1992). Others (e.g., Swanson et al., 1990) have also suggested that substance abuse may interact with specific neuropsychological impairments, to substantially increase the likelihood of violence.

ADMISSABILITY OF EXPERT NEUROPSYCHOLOGICAL TESTIMONY

Legal rulings during the past 20 years have served to establish the admissibility of neuropsychological testimony in the courtroom. For example, in *People v. Wright* (1982), the Colorado Supreme Court determined that a neuropsychologist's testimony regarding minimal brain dysfunction was properly admitted into evidence to support a criminal defendant's successful insanity defense. In the *Horne v. Goodson Logging Co.* (1985) case, the American Psychological Association, together with the North Carolina Psychological Association, submitted an amicus brief that resulted in the North Carolina Court of Appeals upholding the admissibility of neuropsychological evidence, although it left the issue of the credibility of the expert to the trial court judge (Bersoff & Majestic, 1986).

Although the rules governing the admissibility of neuropsychological evidence vary by jurisdiction, and often by the judge who is hearing the case, the Federal Rules of Evidence (1975) permit judges the discretion to admit neuropsychological testimony, as long as it assists the trier of fact and its probative value does not outweigh its prejudicial impact (Monahan & Walker, 1990). Since neuropsychological testimony can have a powerful impact on the trier of fact, the forensic neuropsychologist should carefully discuss and rule out alternative interpretation of their test data, as well as recognize the limitations of the available norms that are utilized (Martel, 1992; Matarrazo, 1990; Purisch & Sbordone, 1997; Sbordone & Purisch, 1996).

Every forensic neuropsychologist should also be well acquainted with two particular legal cases, as well as the subsequent analyses of their implications: *Daubert v. Merrell Dow Pharmaceuticals* (1993) and *Kumho Tire Co. v. Carmichael* (1999). The U.S. Supreme Court, in both cases, found that expert testimony, based on scientific, technical, or clinical evidence, or other specialized forms of knowledge, was subject to review for its admissibility. The Court suggested that several criteria should be used to assess its admissibility: whether a specific theory or technique has been tested and assessed for its ability to be falsified, and for its known or potential error rates, or whether the methods used have ever been subject to peer review, or published, and have been accepted as reliable within the relevant scientific community.

Neuropsychologists entering the criminal forensic arena should review some of the past history and debate on the relationship between psychology and the law, in general (Roesch, Hart, & Sapf, 1996), social science evidence (Monahan & Walker, 1994), and the admissibility of neurological data, and, in particular, neuropsychological testing (*Chapple v. Ganger*, 1994). In *Chapple*, the experts' reasoning processes, validation of testing as applicable to a particular population being tested, and past experience with similar cases were major factors in having experts' opinions admitted into evidence under the *Daubert* standard. Ultimately, a neuropsychologist's opinions should be based on a combination of methods, such as a structured interview, prior educational, employment, medical, and psychiatric records; psychological and neuropsychological testing, interviews with significant others, and observations of the defendant's behavior over time (Meyer et al., 2001; Sbordone & Saul, 2000). Neuropsychologists should also be mindful that the results of the neuropsychological tests should not be analyzed blindly (Sbordone & Purisch, 1996) and should be corroborated by real-world observations (Sbordone & Long, 1996). Finally, neuropsychologists should remain cautious, given the limitations of human judgment, which frequently influences a neuropsychologist's decision making skills (Garb, 1998; Stone et al., 2000).

RECOMMENDED BASIC WORKING LIBRARY

The following volumes are those which the authors believe will be most helpful in integrating neuropsychology and criminal forensic psychological practice.

Ayd, F. J., Jr. (2000). *Lexicon of psychiatry, neurology and the neurosciences* (2nd ed.). Philadelphia: Lippincott Williams & Wilkins.

Baddeley, A. D., Wilson, B. A., & Watts, F. N. (1995). *Handbook of memory disorders*. New York: John Wiley & Sons.

Douglas, J. E., Burgess, A. W., Burgess, A. G., & Ressler, R. K. (1992). *Crime classification manual: A standard system for investigating and classifying violent crimes*. New York: Lexington Books.

Fletcher-Janzen, E., Strickland, T. L., & Reynolds, C. R. (2000). *Handbook of cross-cultural neuropsychology.* New York: Kluwer Academic/Plenum.

Gacono, C. B. (Ed.). (2000). *The clinical and forensic assessment of psychopathy: A practitioner's guide.* Mahwah, NJ: Lawrence Erlbaum.

Garb, H. N. (1998). *Studying the clinician: Judgment research and psychological assessment.* Washington, DC: American Psychological Association.

Hall, H. V., & Sbordone, R. J. (1993). *Disorders of executive functions: Civil and criminal law applications.* Winter Park, FL: PMD Publishers.

Hess, A. K., & Weiner, I. B. (1999). *The handbook of forensic psychology.* New York: John Wiley.

Horton, A. M., Jr., Wedding, O., & Webster, J. (Eds.). (1997). *The neuropsychology handbook* (Vol. 1 and 2). New York: Springer.

Laws, D. R., & O'Donohue, W. (1997). *Sexual deviance: Theory, assessment, and treatment.* New York: Guilford.

Melton, G. B., Petrila, J., Poythress, N. G., & Slobogin, C. (1997). *Psychological evaluations for the courts: A handbook for mental health professionals and lawyers* (2nd ed.). New York: The Guilford Press.

Miller, B. L., & Cummings, J. L. (Eds.). (1999). *The human frontal lobes: Functions and disorders.* New York: Guilford Press.

Quinsey, V. L., Harris, G. T., Rice, M. E., & Cormier, C. A. (1998). *Violent offenders: Appraising and managing risk.* Washington, DC: American Psychological Association.

Roesch, R., Hart, S. D., & Ogloff, J. R. P. (1999). *Psychology and law: The state of the discipline.* New York: Kluwer Academic/Plenum.

Rogers, R. (1995). *Diagnostic and structured interviewing: A handbook for psychologists.* Odessa, FL: Psychological Assessment Resources.

Rogers, R. (1997). *Clinical assessment of malingering and deception* (2nd ed.). New York: Guilford Press.

Rogers, R., & Schuman, D. (2000). *Conducting insanity evaluations* (2nd ed.). New York: Guilford Press.

Sbordone, R. J., & Long, C. (1996). *Ecological validity of neuropsychological testing.* Delray Beach, FL: GR Press/St. Lucie Press.

Sbordone, R. J., & Saul, R. E. (2000). *Neuropsychology for health care professionals and attorneys* (2nd ed.). Boca Raton, FL: CRC Press.

Stringer, A. Y. (1996). *A guide to adult neuropsychological diagnosis.* Philadelphia: F. A. Davis.

Tulving, E., & Craik, F. I. M. (Eds.). (2000). *The Oxford handbook of memory.* New York: Oxford University Press.

Zamble, E., & Quinsey, V. L. (1997). *The criminal recidivism process.* New York: Cambridge University Press.

REFERENCES

Berkman, L. F. (1986). The association between educational attainment and mental status examination: Of etiologic significance for senile dementia or not? *Journal of Chronic Diseases, 39,* 171–174.

Bersoff, D. N., & Majestic, A. L. (1986, August). Motion for leave to file brief of *Amici Curiae* and brief of the American Psychological Association as *Amici Curiae* in support of appellant. North Carolina Court of Appeals Docket #1-1606. *Horne v. Goodson Logging and Self Insured.*

Chapple v. Ganger, 851 F. Supp. 1481 (1994).

Cirincione, C. (1996). Revisiting the insanity defense: Contested or consensus? *Behavioral Science and the Law, 14,* 61.

Cirincione, C., & Jacobs, C. (1999). Identifying insanity acquittals: Is it any easier? *Law and Human Behavior, 23*(4), 487–497.

Cronbach, L. J. (1984). *Essentials of psychological testing* (4th ed.). New York: Harper and Row.

Daubert v. Merrell Dow Pharmaceuticals, Inc., U.S. 113 S. Ct. 2786 (1993).

Delgado-Escueta, A. V., Mattson, R. H., King, L., Goldensohn, E. S., Spiegel, H., Madsen, J., et al. (1981). Special report. The nature of aggression during epileptic seizures. *New England Journal of Medicine, 305,* 711–716.

Dusky v. United States, 362 U.S. 402 (1960).

Evans, J. D., Miller, S. W., Byrd, D. A., & Heaton, R. K. (2000). Cross-cultural applications of the Halstead-Reitan Batteries. In E. Fletcher-Janzen, T. L. Strickland, & C. R. Reynolds (Eds.), *Handbook of cross-cultural neuropsychology* (pp. 287–304). New York: Kluwer/Plenum.

Eysenck, M. W. (1992). *Anxiety: The cognitive perspective.* London, UK: Lawrence Erlbaum.

Fletcher-Janzen, E., Strickland, T. L., & Reynolds, C. R. (2000). *Handbook of cross-cultural neuropsychology.* New York: Kluwer Academic/Plenum.

Garb, H. N. (1998). *Studying the clinician: Judgment research and psychological assessment.* Washington, DC: American Psychological Association.

Green, M. F. (1998). *Schizophrenia from a neurocognitive perspective: Probing the impenetrable darkness.* Boston: Allyn and Bacon.

Gudjonnson, G. (1992). *The psychology of interrogations, confessions, and testimony.* New York: John Wiley.

Hall, H. V., & Pritchard, D. A. (1996). *Detecting malingering and deception: Forensic Distortion Analysis (FDA).* Delray, FL: St. Lucie Press.

Hall, H. V., & Sbordone, R. J. (1993). *Disorders of executive functions: Civil and criminal law applications.* Winter Park, FL: PMD Publishers Group.

Heaton, R. K., Grant, I., & Matthews, C. G. (1991). *Comprehensive norms for an expanded Halstead-Reitan Battery: Demographic corrections, research findings, and clinical applications.* Odessa, FL: Psychological Assessment Resources.

Hoge, S. K., Bonnie, R. J., Poythress, N., & Monahan, J. (1996, 1999). *The MacArthur Competence Assessment Tool—Criminal Adjudication.* Odessa, FL: Psychological Assessment Resources.

Hoge, S. K., Bonnie, R. J., Poytthress, N., Monahan, J., Eisenberg, M., & Feucht-Haviar, T. (1997). The MacArthur adjudicative competence study: Development and validation of a research instrument. *Law and Human Behavior, 21*(2), 141–177.

Kapur, N. (1999). Syndromes of retrograde amnesia: A conceptual and empirical analysis. *Psychological Bulletin, 125*(6), 800–825.

Karken, D. A. (1997). Judgement pitfalls in estimating premorbid intellectual functioning. *Archives of Clinical Neuropsychology, 12*(8), 701–710.

Kittner, S. J., White, L. R., Farmer, M. L. S., Woltz, M., Kaplan, E., Moes, E., et al. (1985). Methodological issues in screening for dementia: The problem of education adjustment. *Journal of Chronic Disease, 39*(3), 163–170.

Kumho Tire Co. v. Carmichael, 119 S. Ct. 1167 (1999).

Lewis, D. O., Pincus, J. H., Feldman, M., Jackson, L., & Bard, B. (1986). Psychiatric, neurologic and psychoeducational characteristics of 15 death row inmates in the U.S. *American Journal of Psychiatry, 143,* 838–845.

Lewis, D. O., Pincus, J. H., Bard, B., Richardson, E., Prichep, L. S., Feldman, M., et al. (1988). Neuropsychiatric, psychoeducational, and family characteristics of 14 juveniles condemned to death in the United States. *American Journal of Psychiatry, 1435,* 581–588.

Magaziner, J., Bassett, S. S., & Hebel, J. R (1987). Predicting performance on the Mini-Mental State Examination. *Journal of the American Geriatric Society, 35,* 996–1000.

Mannuzza, S., Gittleman, K. R., Horowitz, K. P., & Giampino, T. L. (1989). Hyperactive boys almost grown up: IV Criminality and its relationship to psychiatric status. *Archives of General Psychiatry, 46,* 1073–1079.

Martel, D. A. (1992). Forensic neuropsychology and the criminal law. *Law and Human Behavior, 16*(3), 313–336.

Matarazzo, J. D. (1972). *Wechsler's measurement and appraisal of adult intelligence.* Baltimore: Williams and Wilkins.

Matarrazo, J. D. (1990). Psychological assessment v. psychological testing: valid from the Binet to the school, clinic, and courtroom. *American Psychologist, 45*(9), 999–1017.

Mazzoni, G., & Nelson, T. O. (Eds.). (1998). *Metacognition and cognitive neuropsychology: Monitoring and control processes.* Mahwah, NJ: Lawrence Erlbaum.

McNaghtan Case (1843). 10 Cl., & Fin.20., 8 Eng. Rep 718.

Melton, G. B., Petrila, J., Poythress, N. G., & Slobogin, C. (1997). Competency to stand trial. *Psychological Evaluations for the Courts: A Handbook for Mental Health Professionals and Lawyers* (2nd ed., pp. 119–155). New York: Guilford.

Meyer, G. J., Finn, S. E., Eyde, L. D., Kay, G. G., Moreland, K. L., Dies, R. R., et al. (2001). Psychological testing and psychological assessment: A review of evidence and issues. *American Psychologist, 56*(2), 128–165.

Model Penal Code (1962). Section 4.01: American Law Institute formulation of the insanity defense.

Monahan, J., & Walker, L. (1990). *Social science in law: Cases and materials* (2nd ed.). Mineola, NY: The Foundation Press.

Monahan, J., & Walker, L. (1994). *Social science in law: Cases and materials* (3rd ed.). Westbury, NY: The Foundation Press.

Neisser, U., Boodoo, G., Bouchard, T. J., Boykin, A. W., Ceci, S. J., Halpern, D. F., et al. (1996). Intelligence: Knowns and unknowns. *American Psychologist, 51*(2), 77–101.

Nestor, P. G. (1992). Neuropsychological and clinical correlates of murder and other forms of violence in a forensic psychiatric population. *Journal of Nervous and Mental Disease, 180,* 418–423.

Nestor, P. G., Daggett, D., Haycock, J., & Price, M. (1999). Competence to stand trial: A neuropsychological inquiry. *Law and Human Behavior, 23*(4), 397–412.

Nestor, P. G., & Haycock, J. (1997). Not guilty by reason of insanity of murder: Clinical and neuropsychological characteristics. *Journal of American Academy of Psychiatry and Law, 25,* 161–171.

Nestor, P. G., Haycock, J., Doiron, S., Kelly, J., & Kelly, D. (1995). Lethal violence and psychosis: A clinical profile. *Bulletin of American Academy of Psychiatry and the Law, 23,* 331–345.

O'Connor, D W., Pollitt, P. A., Treasure, F. P., Brook, C. P. B., & Reiss, B. B. (1989). The influence of education, social class, and sex on Mini-Mental State scores. *Psychological Medicine, 19,* 771–776.

Otto, R. K., Poythress, N. G., Nicholson, R. A., Edens, J. F., Monahan, J., Bonnie, R. J., et al. (1998). Psychometric properties of the MacArthur Competence Assessment Tool—Criminal Adjudication. *Psychological Assessment, 10*(4), 435–443.

Pasewark, R. A., Pantle, M. L., & Stedman, A. J. (1979). Characteristics and disposition of persons found not guilty by reason of insanity in New York State, 1971–1976. *American Journal of Psychiatry, 136,* 655.

People v. Wright. 648 P.2d 665 (1982).

Perez-Arce, P., & Puente, A. E. (1996). Neuropsychological assessment of ethnic minorities: The case of assessing Hispanics living in North American. In R. J. Sbordone & C. J. Long (Eds.), *Ecological validity of neuropsychological testing* (pp. 283–300). Delray Beach, FL: GR Press/St. Lucie Press.

Poythress, N. G., Nicholson, R., Otto, R. K., Edens, J. F., Bonnie, R. J., Monahan, J., et al. (1999). *MacCAT-CA: The Macarthur Competence Assessment Tool—Criminal Adjudication professional manual.* Odessa, FL: Psychological Assessment Resources.

Purisch, A., & Sbordone, R. (1997). Forensic neuropsychology: Clinical issues and practice. In A. M. Horton, Jr., D. Wedding, & J. Webster (Eds.), *The neuropsychology handbook, Vol. 2* (pp. 309–356). New York: Springer.

Roesch, R., Hart, S. D., & Sapf, P. A. (1996). Conceptualizing and assessing competency to stand trial: Implications and applications of the MacArthur treatment competence model. *Psychology, Public Policy, and Law, 2*(1), 96–113.

Rogers, R. (1984). *Rogers Criminal Responsibility Assessment Scales (R-CRAS) and test manual.* Odessa, FL: Psychological Assessment Resources.

Rogers, R. (1997). *Clinical assessment of malingering and deception* (2nd ed.). New York: Guilford Press.

Rogers, R., & Schuman, D. (2000). *Conducting insanity evaluations* (2nd ed.). New York: Guilford Press.

Rogers, R., & Sewell, K. W. (1999). The R-CRAS and insanity evaluations: A reexamination of construct validity. *Behavioral Sciences and the Law, 17,* 181–194.

Rogers, R., Bagby, R. M., & Dickens, S. E. (1992). *SIRS: Structured Interview of Reported Symptoms: Professional manual.* Odessa, FL: Psychological Assessment Resources.

Ross, B. M. (1991). *Remembering the personal past: Descriptions of autobiographical memory.* New York: Oxford University Press.

Rubin, D. C. (Ed.). (1986). *Autobiographical memory across the lifespan.* Cambridge, England: Cambridge University Press.

Russell, E. W. (1995). The accuracy of automated and clinical detection of brain damage and lateralization in neuropsychology. *Neuropsychology Review, 5,* 1–68.

Sbordone, R. J., & Guilmette, T. J. (1999). Ecological validity: Prediction of everyday and vocational functioning from neuropsychological test data. In J. Sweet (Ed.), *Forensic neuropsychology: Fundamentals in practice* (pp. 227–254). Lisse, Netherlands: Swets & Zeitlinger.

Sbordone, R. J., & Purisch, A. D. (1996). Hazards of blind analysis of neuropsychological test data in assessing cognitive disability: The role of confounding factors. *Neurorehabilitation, 7,* 15–26.

Sbordone, R. J., & Long, C. (1996). *Ecological validity of neuropsychological testing.* Delray Beach, FL: GR Press/St. Lucie Press.

Sbordone, R., & Saul, R. (2000). *Neuropsychology for health care professionals and attorneys* (2nd ed.). Boca Raton, FL: CRC Press.

Sbordone, R. J., Strickland, T. L., & Purisch, A. D. (2000). Neuropsychological assessment of the criminal defendant: The significance of cultural factors. In E. Fletcher-Jansen, T. L. Strickland, & C. R. Reynolds (Eds.), *Handbook of cross-cultural neuropsychology* (pp. 335–344). New York: Klewer/Plenum.

Schwarz, N., & Sudman, S. (1994). *Autobiographical memory and the validity of retrospective reports.* New York: Springer-Verlag.

Skeem, J. L., & Golding, S. L. (1998). Community examiners' evaluations of competence to stand trial: Common problems and suggestions for improvement. *Professional Psychology: Research and Practice, 29*(4), 357–367.

Slovenko, R. (1995). *Psychiatry and criminal culpability.* New York: John Wiley.

Steadman, H. (1980). Insanity acquittals in New York Sate, 1965–1978. *American Journal of Psychiatry, 137,* 321.

Steadman, H., Pantle, M., & Pasewark, R. (1983). Factors associated with a successful insanity plea. *American Journal of Psychiatry, 140,* 401.

Steinmeyer, C. H. (1986). A meta-analysis of Halstead-Reitan test performances of non-brain damaged subject. *Archives of Clinical Neuropsychology, 1,* 301–307.

Stone, A. A., Turkkan, J. S., Bachrach, C. A., Jobe, J. B., Kurtzman, H. S., & Cain, V. S. (Eds.). (2000). *The science of self-report: Implications for research and practice.* Mahwah, NJ: Lawrence Erlbaum.

Swanson, J. W., Holzer, C. E., Ganjo, V. R., & Jono, R. T. (1990). Violence and psychiatric disorder in the community: Evidence from epidemiologic catchment area surveys. *Hospital and Community Psychiatry, 41,* 761–770.

Teasdale, J. D., & Barnard, P. J. (1993). *Affect, cognition, and change: Remodeling depressive thought.* London, UK: Lawrence Erlbaum.

Thompson, C. P., Skowronski, J. J., Larsen, S. F., & Betz, A. L. (1996). *Autobiographical memory: Remembering what and remembering when.* Mahwah, NJ: Lawrence Erlbaum.

Wilson v. United States, 391 F.2d 460 (1968)

Wong, T. M., Strickland, T. L., Fletcher-Janzen, E., Ardila, A., & Reynolds, C. R. (2000). Theoretical and practical issues in the neuropsychological assessment and treatment of culturally dissimilar patients. In E. Fletcher-Jansen, T. L. Strickland, & C. R. Reynolds (Eds.), *Handbook of cross-cultural neuropsychology* (pp. 3–48). New York: Kluwer/Plenum.

Yeudall, L. T. (1977). Neuropsychological assessment of forensic disorders. *Canada's Mental Health,* 25(2), 7–15.

Yeudall, L. T., & Fromm-Auch, D. (1979). Neuropsychological impairment in various psychopathological populations. In J. Gruzielier & P. Flor-Henry (Eds.), *Hemisphere asymmetries of function in psychopathology.* Amsterdam: Elsevier/North Holland.

Chapter 19

Neuropsychological Evaluations in the Context of Competency Decisions

Michael D. Franzen

Clinical neuropsychology has developed mostly in a medical context, but it possesses utility in other contexts, including the legal arena. An important facet of legal–neuropsychological assessments is the evaluation of competency. Competency is a legal, not a clinical, concept. It includes fiduciary competency (the ability to make decisions regarding the deployment of financial resources), testamentary competency (the ability to sign one's name to legal documents, thereby committing oneself to certain responsibilities), competency to consent to treatment (the ability to make decisions regarding medical disposition), and competency to live independently (the ability to maintain hygiene, safety, and health). Other forms of competency, which are less formally defined in our legal and social system, include driving and responsibility for others, such as the competency required to be a caregiver or teacher. There is an area related to competency to consent to treatment, in the form of competency to consent to research procedures, whether for reasons of cognitive impairment (Bonnie, 1997) or for reasons of depression (Elliott, 1997). Although this issue has received increasing attention in the literature related to institutional review boards (Hirschfield, Winslade, & Krause, 1997), as yet, clinical evaluations have not been involved.

There are multiple issues implicated when the question of competency is raised. Zaubler, Viederman, and Fins (1996) provide an overview of some of the issues related to psychiatry and the legal realm. This chapter provides a brief description of the issues to which a clinical neuropsychologist should attend, and a review of selected instruments is provided, to give some idea of the tools available to the neuropsychologist. Although competency and commitment are frequently related (Bloom & Faulkner, 1987), this chapter deals narrowly with the issues specific to competency only.

The requests for clinical neuropsychologists to conduct competency evaluations reflects at least two distinct sets of concepts and variables. The first set of variables is legal in nature and is comprised of a consideration of the power of the state to curtail aspects of personal freedom and autonomy under certain circumstances. Included in this realm of variables is the role of the clinical neuropsychologist as an agent of social control. The second realm of variables is related to the clinical neuropsychologist as an emissary of the scientific world to the practical legal world. The clinical neuropsychologist should be aware of the legal standards and regulations involved in the venue in which the competency decision is being made.

The curtailment of personal freedom is based on a decision that the greater good, whether for the subject, or for the individuals in the subject's social environment, would be served by this curtailment. This curtailment of the sphere of personal power can be invoked to prevent the harmful consequences of behaviors: For example, to prevent an individual from squandering his financial resources, that person might be relieved of the capacity to spend those resources at will. As Schopp (2001) points out, the issue of determination of competency contains a basic conflict between protecting individual liberty and promoting well-being. In fact, there is a presumption of competency, that is, adults are presumed to be competent until there is convincing evidence to the contrary. Furthermore, although a legal proceeding may result in that presumption being revoked, there is a reversible character to the decision: Someone, once adjudicated to be incompetent, can be later found to be competent.

Competency to Consent to Treatment

Competency to consent to treatment is the name by which this set of concepts is known, but, in practicality, the question is, actually, competency to refuse treatment (Farnsworth, 1990). As long as the patient agrees to treatment, there is no question raised about the competency of the patient, even though, at least for psychiatric patients consenting to voluntary hospitalization, this assumption may not be tenable for the majority of patients (Appelbaum, Mirkin, & Bateman, 1981). Yet another study found that, for residents of a nursing home, nearly one half were incompetent to give consent for treatment, even though their oral consent had been relied upon in treatment decision implementation (Barton, Mallik, Orr, & Janofsky, 1996). This form of competency evaluation is a familiar activity among neuropsychologists who work in a psychiatric context. Appelbaum and Roth (1981) discuss the issues related to a psychiatric evaluation of competency to consent to treatment, but the same issues are relevant to an evaluation in which the issue of cognitive capacity is in question. As those authors point out, the accuracy and completeness of the information conveyed by the patient should be considered by the clinician, and the stability of the patient's mental status should be evaluated and commented upon.

The issues to be addressed include whether the patient understands the need for treatment, whether the patient can explain the possible outcomes of treatment, including side effects, and whether the patient can predict the likely consequences of not getting treatment. Roth, Meisel, and Lidz (1977) describe the relevant content areas being able to evidence a choice, having an understanding of the outcome, having the choice based on rational reasons, and having the ability to understand, as well as having actual understanding.

Both the cognitive condition and the emotional state of the patient are relevant here. Severe depression may interfere with the capacity to make rational decisions about treatment. A related area is the advance directive, in which a patient states preferences regarding treatment that may be contemplated in a situation in which the patient is unable to provide consent, or even to communicate. In the healthy adult who records advance directives, there is usually no question about the mental status. In progressive dementing conditions, it may be necessary to document the competency of the patient to make decisions about treatment options and to record those decisions, as guidance for surrogate decision makers later in time (Grossberg, 1998).

Fiduciary Competency

Fiduciary and testamentary competency are multifaceted. These are legal decisions, not clinical ones. However, the trier of fact (judge) makes these decisions, utilizing information from different sources, including clinical sources. The extent to which a given judge relies on clinical information depends upon the experience and knowledge of the judge, combined with the opinion regarding the clinician held by the judge. It is incumbent upon the neuropsychologist to represent accurately and dispassionately the status of clinical science in answering the relevant legal questions.

Fiduciary competence requires basic arithmetic skills (or the ability to use a calculator), as well as judgment and problem solving skills. The upper boundary of fiduciary skill, involving the disposition of large sums of money and complicated financial plans, is not an issue in these evaluations. Even the most astute manager of his own funds would utilize some form of financial advisor, in order to optimize the return on his resources. The relevant issue in determining fiduciary competence is whether the patient is allowed to choose or turn down such advisement and whether they possess adequate cognitive skills to understand the likely consequences of certain financial decisions. For example, although the patient may not be able to determine whether the best (most productive) form of investment would be a limited partnership real estate operation or a stake in a hedge market, the patient would be required to understand that some risk was involved in each undertaking and that writing a check to cover either investment would decrease liquid assets by the same amount. That is, some degree of reasonable knowledge is expected, but not an above-average ability.

Objectives

The objectives for conducting a fiduciary competency evaluations are (1) to gain an understanding of the financial tasks required of the patient, (2) to obtain a history of recent financial decision made by the patient, and the outcomes, (3) to determine the cognitive skills of the patient required to make the necessary financial decision, (4) to draw reasonable conclusion about the ability of the patient to make reasonable financial decisions in the near future, and (5) to make accurate predictions about the effect of changes in the person's situation or neuropsychological condition (is the condition static or progressive, is it reversible?) There are several different domains relevant to the evaluation of financial competence, including basic money skills, conceptual knowledge related to financial operations, the ability to conduct cash transactions, management of a personal checkbook, ability to read and understand a common bank statement, and ability to make rational decisions related to financial options and plans.

Testamentary Competency

Testamentary competency can be intertwined with fiduciary competency, although it is also possible to separate the two. The complication arises because signing one's name can encumber financial resources. However, there is at least one area in which testamentary competency is separate from financial competency, namely, in the capacity to sign a will. A will is signed in the presence of a witness who could theoretically testify later as to the mental state of the patient. But challenges after the fact, especially after the death of the individual involved, are not uncommon. Of course, the clinical neuropsychologist can most confidently provide information regarding testamentary competence when an evaluation is requested a priori. Requests for clinical input after the death of the individual require the collection of information from collateral observations and from an examination of the activities and decisions made contemporaneous to the act of signing the document (Spar & Garb, 1992). In order for a person to be found competent to sign a will (testamentary competence), it is necessary that cognitive skills be reasonably intact, that the person understand the identity of the recipients of the benefits of the will, understand that signing one's name to that document will require the survivors to implement the desires expressed in the will, and understand that dying while the will is in effect will set in motion a series of events that is irrevocable.

Objectives

The objectives in this case include (1) to obtain information regarding the cognitive skills of the patient, (2) to obtain a description of the patient's ability to understand the responsibilities and consequences attendant upon signing the document, and (3) to provide a reasonable conclusion regarding the capacity of the individual to commit oneself to the exigencies of the contract or document.

Criminal Competency

Criminal competency can be related to more than one concept. There is the question of whether the individual understood and appreciated the criminal act, whether the criminal can participate in the preparation of his own defense, and whether the criminal is cognitively aware enough to experience the punishment.

Objectives

Grisso (1988) has listed five objectives to be achieved in conducting competency to stand trial: (1) functional description of specific abilities, (2) causal explanations for deficits in competency abilities, especially whether these can be considered to be irreversible or treatable, and reversible diagnosis of relevant mental disorders, (3) interactive significance of deficits in competency abilities, (4) conclusory statements (may be the purview of the presiding legal authority, and (5) prescriptive, that is, whether treatment can remediate the deficits.

GENERAL CLINICAL MODEL FOR THE ASSESSMENT OF COMPETENCE

Competency evaluations are, in the final measure, clinical evaluations. The purpose is to obtain an accurate depiction of the person's level of cognitive skill and emotional and behavioral functioning, to make reasonable inferences about the likely etiologies, and to make valid predictions about extra-test behaviors. There are some differences from the typical evaluation, however. As an initial difference, with the exception of questions of competency to refuse treatment, which are initiated by physicians, most competency evaluations are initiated either by family members or by the court. As another important difference, the competency evaluation, more so than any other type of neuropsychological evaluation, is going to have implications for the civil rights of the patient. Although the neuropsychologist does not make the final competency decision, they contribute to a process that is essentially moral in nature, rather than strictly legal or clinical.

In any form of competency hearing, competency itself is situational. A person may be competent in one realm and not another, competent in one situation and not another, competent at one time and not another. Therefore, the evaluation should be designed with a consideration of which variables would influence the competency of the patient for a given task in a given setting.

The first step would be to clarify which type of competency is at question. Determining the type of competency will help delineate which neuropsychological content areas are of importance. For example, arithmetic skill would be more pertinent to an evaluation of financial competency than for competency to consent to treatment, and memory skill would be especially pertinent in competency to stand trial and assist in defense. Executive functions would play a role in various types of competency, but would be essential in decisions related to independent living.

It would be important to determine what types of physical limitations are present and how these would interact with the cognitive profile and demands of the task situation. For example, language-based deficits, especially deficits in receptive language skills, would curtail one's ability to make reasonable decisions in one's own best interest, because of limitations in the accuracy of information received by the patient. Physical impairment would compound the effects of any cognitive deficits related to competency to live independently.

The next step would be to choose instruments with adequate and appropriate normative information. In many, but not all, of these situations, geriatric norms would be necessary. Additionally, it would be preferable to use norms that more closely approximate the descriptive characteristics of the patient. For example, for some neuropsychological instruments, norms are available for comparison to subjects living in a nursing home versus subjects living independently. Age and level of education are also important variables to consider. Gender and race may be important in some neuropsychological content areas, especially language-based skills. The most likely relevant content areas for assessment in competency are orientation, attention, memory, communication, perception, and executive functions.

The clinical neuropsychologist should clarify the audience/client recipient of the information. For most competency questions, the recipient is a legal authority, such as a magistrate or judge. These legal officials have varying degrees of knowledge and familiarity with neuropsychological constructs and diction. It is important to keep professional lingo to a minimum and to describe the everyday consequences of the assessment results. For example, in reporting a memory impairment related to recalling only 12% of the Wechsler Memory Scale—Third Edition Logical Memory content over the standard delay, the neuropsychologist should be careful to include a statement that the subject will not remember textual or narrative material, even if it is repeated once, and multiple repetitions may be necessary to ensure that important material is actually encoded.

As well as knowing the question to be asked and the patient to be assessed, the neuropsychologist should know how the information is to be used. The clinical neuropsychologist needs to be conversant with the state laws and regulations regarding competency. In some states, only a physician can sign the necessary paperwork to petition for a competency hearing. However, even in those situations, many physicians will not sign the forms without first reviewing the results of cognitive testing.

A second important set of information is to examine the ecological validity of the test instruments chosen. In instances from either end of the continuum of skill level, ecological validity may be less relevant. A person who scores well into the range of severe dementia is unlikely to possess fiduciary competency. In contrast, a person who scores in the above-average range on cognitive measures is unlikely to be found incompetent. It is in the middle ranges, where a person scores in the moderate range of memory impairment and the moderately severe range of executive dysfunction, that it would important to examine what types of limitations would be empirically supported.

Test data alone is insufficient to determine competency. The clinician must supplement this data with individualized questions directed at the subject, as well as interview information. For example, in conducting an evaluation related to competency to stand trial, it would be necessary to obtain information related to the subject's understanding of the charges pending, particulars of the legal process, and the roles of the opposing attorneys and the presiding judge.

Another facet of the clinical evaluation of competency is obtaining informed consent, which is somewhat different from the concept of consent in treatment or other assessment contexts. The most obvious facet is that the level of cooperation may differ drastically from that in a typical clinical situation. The evaluation may be court ordered, and the outcome may have untoward effects, from the perspective of the subject. In court-ordered situations, the subject does not have the right to refuse assessment, although, certainly, the subject retains control over behavioral aspects of cooperation. Depending upon the results, the person may lose aspects of personal freedom and autonomy. Poythress et al. (1999) discusses some of the concepts related to this type of consent in a criminal proceeding.

Yet another complicating difference from usual treatment is that obtaining informed consent depends upon an assumption that the person is competent to provide consent, when the outcome of the evaluation is a determination that the person does not possess competence to make those decisions and grant that consent. The clinician in those cases needs to document what information is provided to the subject and make every effort to provide the information at a level of complexity that can be reasonably understood.

An important element in some clinical evaluations for competency purposes is the issue of detecting an exaggeration of impairment. The issue of exaggeration does not usually occur when the patient can be reasonably assumed to be motivated to give the best effort. However, just as in any clinical neuropsychological evaluation, the motivation to give best effort may be less than complete. Not all of these instances may involve an individual who is trying to escape responsibility for an action by feigning cognitive impairment. Incomplete effort may also be the result when an individual, who is somewhat impaired, is being evaluated in a context in which they fear the consequences of the evaluation and do no trust the health care professional involved. In either case, that of deliberate exaggeration or that of incomplete effort, it is necessary to make some objective evaluation of the level of effort expended by the patient. Wynkoop and Denney (1999) present a case of an attempt to magnify deficits during a pretrial competency evaluation. They suggest the use of techniques that have also been used in general and forensic neuropsychological evaluations.

Review of Relevant Instruments

There are many clinical instruments available to the clinical neuropsychologist conducting a competency evaluation. These include the standardized and familiar tests of memory, attention, abstract problem solving, perception, and emotional functioning. There are also specialized instruments designed to evaluate content areas that would be important in the competency assessments.

The MacArthur Competence Assessment Tool—Criminal Adjudication (MacCAT-CA) is a tool that can be useful in the determination of competency to stand trial or, as the authors term it, "competence to proceed" (Poythress et al., 1999). The instrument evaluates three abilities, namely, the ability to understand general information related to the legal process, the ability to reason specific choices related to mounting a defense, and appreciation or awareness of the meaning and consequences of the legal process, as related to the individual. An early evaluation of the psychometric properties indicated adequate face validity. Furthermore, the instrument was able to reliably separate individuals who were incompetent via independent team determinations, individuals who demonstrated significant psychopathology, but who were competent, and individuals who were competent. Interrater reliability was above 0.75 for the three subscales, and internal consistency was above 0.81. The three subscales demonstrated adequate correlations with clinical instruments that evaluated similar or related constructs (Otto et al., 1998).

One way of examining the characteristics of competency to stand trial would be to compare subjects who were adjudicated incompetent and those who were evaluated and subsequently adjudicated to be competent. Nicholson and Kugler (1991) reviewed 27 studies, which compared those two sets of subjects on differing variables. Those studies involved more than 8,000 subjects, of which approximately 31% were found to be incompetent. Examining effect sizes, those researchers determined that the variables most highly related to a decision of "incompetent" were poor performance on psychological tests specifically designed to evaluate competence, a diagnosis of psychosis, and symptoms of severe psychopathology. Other variables, such as the demographic variables of marital status, minority racial identity, and previous legal involvement, also predicted the outcome of the competency decision.

Yet another form of competency is related to independent living and the capacity to manage one's finances and personal decisions. Frequently, these decisions are made within the context of cognitive testing results and observations regarding the person's performance in the open environment. Because of concerns about the limitations of formal cognitive testing in predicting everyday behavior, new instruments have been developed to evaluate practical skills in a more ecologically valid manner. The Independent Living Scales (Loeb, 1996) is an example of such an instrument. The subscales include Memory/Orientation, Managing Money, Managing Home and Transportation, Health and Safety, and Social Adjustment. Because there is no external criterion for competence, there are not strict cutoff scores. But there are standard scores available, computed from a sample of 400 independent-living adults over the age of 65 years. Additionally, optimal cut scores, to separate these individuals from dependent-living adults, were calculated. It remains to be seen whether these scores and classifications will be accepted in court.

Instruments to Evaluate Competency to Consent to Treatment

The area of competency to consent to treatment has received the most attention from test developers. Most of these assessment procedures are simple and can be completed at bedside, which is an important practical consideration. However, most of these instruments have been developed on a certain population and their generalizability to other populations is unknown. Edelstein, Nygren, Northrop, Staats, and Pool (1993) devised an instrument to evaluate competency to consent to treatment for subjects in a long-term residential care facility. This particular instrument combines direct questions with analog assessment of behavioral skills in areas related to competency decisions.

Janofsky, McCarthy, and Folstein (1992) developed the Hopkins Competency Assessment Test, which can also be used at bedside. In this instrument, patients are given brief essays to read, then are asked to answer questions derived from the information contained in the essays and related to the issue of consent. Interrater reliability was adequate ($r = 0.95$). Validity was assessed by comparison to competency evaluation conducted by a board-certified psychiatrist. Using the psychiatrist's ratings as the external criterion and an optimal cut-point, 100% sensitivity and specificity was achieved in a limited sample of inpatients. The Hopkins test was more accurate than the Folstein Mini Mental State Exam in determining competency.

Another approach to the assessment of competency is to combine measures of cognitive function and measures of competency-related operations. Pruchno, Smyer, Rose, Hartman-Stein, and Henderson-Laribee (1995) report the development of a short assessment instrument that combined the Folstein exam with questions regarding two vignettes that are read to the patient. The initial empirical investigation of the instrument indicated 86% accurate classification in a sample of residents of a long-term care facility.

Marson, Ingram, Cody, and Harrell (1995) have developed an analog assessment instrument, which presents the patient with hypothetical situations, then asks questions related to evidence for treatment choice, appreciating the consequences of the choice, providing rational reasons for the choice, and understanding treatment situation and choices. The answers are scored according to standardized criterion, which demonstrated adequate interrater reliability in a sample of patients with Alzheimer's disease. The greatest single predictor of scores on the instrument developed by Marson et al. was verbal fluency (Marson, Cody, Ingram, & Harrell, 1995). Subsequent research indicated that the four areas and scores could be interpreted as factors of verbal conceptualization/reasoning and verbal memory (Dymek, Marson, & Harrell, 1999). Further research is needed to determine whether the scores can identify competent and incompetent individuals with a diagnosis of other than Alzheimer's disease.

The Competency Interview Schedule (Bean, Nishisato, Rector, & Glancy, 1994) is a brief bedside instrument designed to evaluate the competency of an individual to consent to medical treatment. It evaluates the patient's capacity in four areas; awareness of a choice, ability to understand the issues related to treatment, evidence of a rational reason for the choice, and appreciation of the nature of the situation. It has been reported to have reasonable internal consistency reliability (Cronbach's alpha = 0.96) and interrater reliability (intraclass $r = 0.79$). Initial research indicated that it could separate between competent and incompetent patients with low specificity (8%) and high sensitivity (98%).

Future Research

Existing assessment instruments are fragmented and frequently pertain only to a narrow population. Future research needs to focus on the development of broadly applicable, reliable, and valid assessment instruments. In particular, the external validity of the test instruments needs to be addressed. In this context, external validity would refer both to the decisions made regarding competency, independent of the assessment instrument, e.g., by the trier of fact, and to accurate prediction of the patient's ability to perform the relevant tasks accurately. Ecological validity is more a concern here than perhaps in most other areas of clinical neuropsychological assessment.

The other major area is to develop models for the assessment of different types of competency, using existing assessment instruments of cognitive function. As a first step in the conceptualization of competency assessments, it would be important to have an agreed upon taxonomy of the skills necessary for the various forms of competency and the types of instruments that would be necessary to evaluate that area. Next, research would need to be performed concerning the degree of impairment necessary to declare that a task is unlikely to be adequately performed. Finally, those cutoff points for the impairment ratings would need to be validated against empirical observations of the patients in the open environment, performing the relevant behaviors.

CONCLUSIONS

Competency evaluations carry with them their own set of values, challenges, and issues. However, this is an area in which clinical neuropsychologists have much to offer. The objective evaluation and quantification of behavioral skills is a significant contribution to the legal process of deciding whether to assign culpability or whether to restrict personal freedoms. The neuropsychologist working in this area needs to be aware of the clinical science supporting the procedures, as well as the legal definitions, regulations, and relevant rulings in the venue being served. Finally, the neuropsychologist needs to be aware of the moral implications of serving as an agent of social control. It is a rewarding area, because of these requirements.

REFERENCES

Appelbaum, P. S., & Roth, L. H. (1981). Clinical issues in the assessment of competency. *American Journal of Psychiatry, 138,* 1462–1467.

Appelbaum, P. S., Mirkin, S. A., & Bateman, A. L. (1981). Empirical assessment of competency to consent to psychiatric treatment. *American Journal of Psychiatry, 138,* 1170–1176.

Barton, C. D., Malli, H. S., Orr, W. B., & Janofsky, J. S. (1996). Clinician's judgment of capacity of nursing home patients to give informed consent. *Psychiatric Services, 47,* 956–960.

Bean, G., Nishisato, S., Rector, N. A, & Glancy, G. (1994). The psychometric properties of the Competency Interview Schedule. *Canadian Journal of Psychiatry, 39,* 368–376.

Bloom, J. D., & Faulkner, L. R. (1987). Competency determinations in civil commitment. *American Journal of Psychiatry, 144,* 193–196.

Bonnie, R. J. (1997). Research with cognitively impaired subjects: Unfinished business in the regulation of human research. *Archives of General Psychiatry, 54,* 105–111.

Dymek, M. P., Marson, D. C., & Harrell, L. (1999). Factor structure of capacity to consent to medical treatment in patients with Alzheimer's disease: An exploratory study. *Journal of Forensic Neuropsychology, 1,* 27–48.

Edelstein, B., Nygren, M., Northop, L., Staats, N., & Pool, D. (1993, August). *Assessment of capacity to make financial and medical decisions.* Paper presented at the 101st Meeting of the American Psychological Association. Toronto, CA.

Elliott, C. (1997). Caring about risks: Are severely depressed patients competent to consent to research? *Archives of General Psychiatry, 54,* 113–120.

Farnsworth, M. G. (1990). Competency evaluations in a general hospital. *Psychosomatics, 31,* 60–66.

Grisso, T. (1988). *Competency to Stand Trial Evaluations: A Manual for Practice.* Sarasota, FL: Professional Resource Exchange.

Grossberg, G. T. (1998). Advance directives, competency evaluation, and surrogate management in elderly patients. *American Journal of Geriatric Psychiatry, 6,* S79–S84.

Hirschfield, R. M. A., Winslade, W., & Krause, T. L. (1997). Protecting subjects and fostering research. *Archives of General Psychiatry, 54,* 121–123.

Janofsky, J., McCarthy, R. J., & Folstein, M. R. (1992). The Hopkins Competency Assessment: A brief method for evaluating patient's capacity to give informal consent. *Hospital and Community Psychiatry, 43,* 132–136.

Loeb, P. A. (1996). *Independent Living Scales: Manual.* San Antonio, TX: The Psychological Corporation.

Marson, D. C., Cody, H. A., Ingram, K. K., & Harrell, L. E. (1995). Neuropsychological predictors of competency in Alzheimer's disease using a rational reasons standard. *Archives of Neurology, 52,* 955–959.

Marson, D. C., Ingram, K. K., Cody, H. A., & Harrell, L. E. (1995). Assessing the competency of patients with Alzheimer's disease under different legal standards. *Archives of Neurology, 52,* 949–954.

Nicholson, R. A., & Kugler, K. E. (1991). Competent and incompetent criminal defendants: A quantitative review of comparative research. *Psychological Bulletin, 109,* 355–370.

Otto, R. K., Poythress, N. G., Nicholson, R. A., Edens, J. F., Monahan, J., Bonnie, R. J., et al. (1998). Psychometric properties of the MacArthur Competence Assessment Tool—Criminal Adjudication. *Psychological Assessment, 10,* 435–443.

Poythress, N. G., Nicholson, R., Otto, R. K., Edens, J. F., Bonnie, R. J., Monahan, J., et al. (1999). *The MacArthur Competence Assessment Tool—Criminal Adjudication: Professional Manual.* Odessa, FL: Psychological Assessment Resources.

Pruchno, R. A., Smyer, M. A., Rose, M. S., Hartman-Stein, P. E., & Henderson-Laribee, D. L. (1995). Competence of long-term care residents to participate in decision about their medical care: A brief, objective assessment. *The Gerontologist, 35,* 622–629.

Roth, L. H., Meisel, A., & Lidz, C. W. (1977). Tests of competency to consent to treatment. *American Journal of Psychiatry, 134,* 279–284.

Schopp, R. F. (2001). *Competence, condemnation, and commitment.* Washington, DC: American Psychological Association.

Spar, J. E., & Garb, A. S. (1997). Assessing competency to make a will. *American Journal of Psychiatry, 149,* 169–174.

Wynkoop, T. F., & Denney, R. L. (1999). Exaggeration of neuropsychological deficit in competency to stand trial. *Journal of Forensic Neuropsychology, 12,* 29–53.

Zaubler, T. S., Viederman, M., & Fins, J. J. (1996). Ethical, legal, and psychiatric issues in capacity, competency, and informed consent: An annotated bibliography. *General Hospital Psychiatry, 18,* 155–172.

Chapter 20

The Future of Forensic Neuropsychology

Arthur MacNeill Horton, Jr.

In the preceding chapters, efforts were made to describe the current status of forensic neuropsychology. Chapters dealt with foundations of forensic neuropsychology, ethical issues, issues unique to brain injury, practice issues, and special area in forensic neuropsychology. In this chapter, however, the intent is to speculate about possible future directions and likely developments in forensic neuropsychology. At the same time, these speculations are based on the judgments of the chapter author, and no guarantees are provided, nor should any be expected. In terms of organizing this chapter, future developments are listed in terms of new concepts, new techniques, and new populations.

NEW CONCEPTS

In this section, the new concepts of managed care, the Internet, and credentialing are addressed.

Managed Care and Forensic Neuropsychology

It is fairly clear that future forensic neuropsychology directions will involve activities that will be strongly influenced by the changing U.S. health care system (Sbordone & Saul, 2000). There is ample warrant to expect significant health care changes in the near future. The history of health care in the last two decades has been one of drastic change

(Cummings, 1986). Although, in the 1970s, and perhaps in the early 1980s, there was great attention to the quality of health care services, this has changed. In the late 1980s and 1990s, the watchword in health care became *cost containment*. Essentially, national health care costs have been increasing over the years at a rate greater than the inflation rate and at a far greater rate than the production of other goods and services for the United States (Strosahi, 1994). Simply put, while the productivity of the American worker had been increasing up until perhaps the early 1970s, year by year that productivity appeared to level off in the 1970s.

This has created a difficult situation, because inflation has continued to rise and there is continued pressure from employees to have annual wage increases. Unfortunately, the amount of surplus capital or new productivity to pay for wage increases has not been available in the American economic system. Therefore, one has greater demands for wages and health care, with fewer resources to pay for wages and health care.

Health care has perhaps taken an even more disturbing trend, in that, as earlier noted, the rate of increase has gone up expeditiously over the past few decades. To a great extent, this is, or should be, caused by greater use of expensive technological procedures and the use of heroic efforts to keep terminally ill patients alive through artificial means. In addition, however, there is increasing concern regarding runaway physician fees and inefficient health care systems. In health care, the public perception has been that there is basically no accountability with respect to cost of procedures (Armenti, 1993).

In recent years, the specter of managed care has arisen in such a way as to make every day Halloween for U.S. health care providers. To put it in simplest perspective, managed care applies a cost metric to health care. That is to say, there is review of the allocation of health care dollars and questioning as to whether money should have been spent. In recent years, this has become at times a maddening array of paperwork and health care treatment plans in managed care organizations, which have bedeviled doctors, nurses, physicians' assistants, psychologists, and other health care professionals, almost to the point of major mental disturbance (Strosahi, 1994). As managed care reduces the incomes of clinical psychologists, many will probably move into the forensic psychology area, in order to gain income (Otto & Heilbrun, 2002). Forensic neuropsychology is an attractive area of practice, because of the ability of psychologists to charge high fees.

What is most unfortunate is the perception that managed care organizations, which review the utilization of care, may disavow services that have, in many cases, been delivered without an accurate research base to make these decisions. As noted by Peterson and Harbeck (1988), regarding pediatric psychology, the development of a research base is critical to the maturing of any field, and their comments are relevant to managed care. Little is known about the impact of management care, and less research has gone on in terms of evaluating the effects of managed care on forensic neuropsychology services (Armenti, 1993). As far as clinical neuropsychologists are concerned, however, the extant research findings concerning managed care influences on forensic neuropsychology are gloomy at best and disastrous at worst (Sweet, Westergaard, & Moberg, 1995).

Nonetheless, because of federal budget deficits and the need to reduce health care costs, there have been efforts to apply rigid cost-containment strategies, in the form of managed care. That is to say, the plans imposed are based on the fact that health care costs need to be cut, and there is little thoughtful planning as to how to best do this (Cummings, 1986).

How will the forensic neuropsychologist's role change in order to deal with managed care settings and the pressures of the evolving health care system? It would appear clear that there are going to be greater pressures on cost accountability and specification of problem and outcome. In addition, forensic neuropsychology will have to include explicit methods to promote generalization of effects to other settings, demonstrating ecological validity of findings (Purish & Sbordone, 1997), and to evaluate the degree to which the person treated approximates, after treatment, the untreated members of their peer groups, who at least initially were without the identified problem.

It would be expected that forensic neuropsychologists would be encouraged to be precise in terms of the problems they are addressing and to collect specific outcome data demonstrating that their interventions were effective (Hall & Cope, 1995). Although that is all and good, it would appear likely that there would be pressures to treat even complex clinical cases in a limited number of sessions.

As a result, it may be difficult to treat cases with appropriate amounts of resources, unless proper attention is given to the issue of making determinations of the degree of complexity of specific cases. In medicine, there are descriptors of whether the services provided may be relatively uninvolved or brief, or whether it is complex or difficult. There would need to be some sort of consideration producing a similar system for forensic neuropsychology.

It may be, in some cases, that the forensic neuropsychology activity would require quite some time, whereas, in some other cases, the activity might be relatively brief. Nonetheless, forensic neuropsychologists will have to take great care to document what they do and also demonstrate that they are efficient. The time component will be very important in terms of delivery of services, as long as services are calculated on an hour-for-hour basis.

The focus of outcome care, at least in the foreseeable decade, will be on containment cost. Health care providers will be pressured, and in some cases severely pressured, to contain costs to provide adequate clinical services economically. In time, the hope is that there would be some efforts to move toward a greater emphasis on quality of care.

The great danger in managed care is that an excessive focus on cost containment will cause a diminution of quality service, to the point at which clinical care may be given, but may be so watered down as to be inefficient. Therefore, although some treatment services are provided, the treatment provided could be so inadequate as to argue for the abolishment of the service. In some cases, the effect of managed care appears to have been to reduce the quality of health care. This could be a very serious development, because the denial of adequate care can have horrible consequences to ill and impaired individuals.

Many health care providers have their horror stories of managed care errors. There is the case of one young woman who complained of severe headaches and went to her HMO and was not even examined, because they had felt that she was somewhat hysterical. The woman was made to sit down on a bed in the clinic, was never examined by a physician, physician's assistant, nurse, or nurse practitioner, then was sent home. The woman, unfortunately, was having transient ischemic attacks and later had a stroke. The fact that she was young (about 29 years old) was apparently no barrier to stroke, and a lawsuit ensued. The woman's clinical history was noteworthy for the fact that she had a clear family history of relatives having strokes in their thirties. This unfortunate situation at least appears to be an example of when efforts to curtail the use of health care services may cause significant harm to patients and destroy the confidence of consumers in the U.S. health care system.

The Internet and Forensic Neuropsychology

The practice of real estate can be summed up in the phrase "location, location, location, and location." The issue of technological influences on forensic neuropsychology might be summed up as "computers, computers, computers, and computers." The explosive development of the Internet and World Wide Web has changed the way that human beings in the United States, and indeed the whole world, approach information processing, information transfer, and information storage, and will continue to do so for centuries to come. The information superhighway is a reality for citizens of the world. The computer revolution is such that individuals can trade information with others halfway around the world in moments. Internet news groups regularly have international contributions from individuals in South American, Australia, England, and Canada, as well as the United States.

One of the most fascinating aspects of the news groups, with respect to forensic neuropsychology, is that, very often, a member of a news group will present a forensic neuropsychological case and ask for comments, and, within that 24 hours, the person posting the message in the news group can receive specific advice and suggestions from individuals who they have never previously heard from, half a world away.

It is also remarkable how the comments on the news group can provide a wide range of suggestions, so that it almost seems like a very good case conference in forensic neuropsychology. The value for forensic neuropsychology might be that, in the future, there could be electronic chat rooms devoted to forensic neuropsychology problems. A master consultant could moderate interactions among individuals seeking advice and those who can provide advice in such a way that suggestions can be given and participants can be helped in a positive manner.

The speed with which information can be transferred is amazing and potentially of fantastic value, in terms of forensic neuropsychology, for the treatment of patients. In addition to information transfer, the computer can facilitate the development of expert systems. That is to say, various problems in forensic neuropsychology could be reduced to a number of key considerations and essential factors. Computer programs in a computer network could be developed to provide forensic neuropsychology guidance in elementary cases. Software could be developed so that suggestions can be made to persons seeking forensic neuropsychology. There are already a number of computer programs, for instance, for making neuropsychological interpretations related to patients' neuropsychological test data. These appear best for making a simple diagnosis of brain damage, but are less capable when one deals with the questions of etiology, localization, or process of cerebral injury. Nonetheless, the potential for further development is available. Additional work could possibly develop systems of training individuals in forensic neuropsychology and, specifically, in behavioral procedures that could be useful in behavioral forensic neuropsychology.

It could be that a person could put in various parameters of a problem, then come back with possible suggestions, based on research literature and expert judgment of what would be seen as state-of-the-art methods of approaching various neurobehavioral problems. Although such an undertaking would require a great deal of time and effort, it nonetheless could yield particularly powerful and positive results.

One need only consider the ubiquitous computer interpretations of psychological tests, to realize the potential value. While Minnesota Multiphasic Personality Inventory-2 and Millon Clinical Multiaxial Inventory—III interpretations may or may not fit individual clients, in all cases, nonetheless, their use over a number of years has established them as significant aids to clinicians. The production of computerized psychological test interpretations is now a significant economic activity for psychologically oriented business persons.

It might be expected that forensic neuropsychology services could be operated in the same way over the Internet, whereby anyone in any setting could request some initial suggestions regarding forensic neuropsychology services. In addition, when various problems come up, the computer can provide additional suggestions as to what would be possible viable strategies for overcoming various difficulties. The potential to improve forensic neuropsychology practice is great.

On a more personal level, there is always a possibility of case conferences done through video services, in which people at various locations can be visually linked through transmission of pictures of persons in other settings. Even movies are transmitted through the Internet. For example, this could include observations of a child in a free-play situation going through a behavioral treatment session. Experts, hundreds and even thousands of miles away, could consult on the case and make suggestions regarding the appropriate strategies for dealing with the child.

Such technological avenues of information could allow world-famous experts to consult widely and significantly enhance the standardization of high-quality forensic neuropsychology services on a national, even international, basis.

Credentialing and Forensic Neuropsychology

As noted by Otto and Heilbrun (2002), forensic psychology as a specialty is at a crossroads, and efforts need to be made to respond to current challenges. It might be averred that forensic neuropsychology is at a similar crossroads. Perhaps the most serious challenge lies in the area of credentialing. Indeed, there is a long and controversial history of credentialing efforts in clinical neuropsychology. Because this history has been treated elsewhere (Horton, 1997a) only brief comments are offered here.

In clinical neuropsychology, there are two major diplomate boards offering board certification credentials. These are the American Board of Clinical Neuropsychology (ABCN), which is affiliated with the American Board of Professional Psychology (ABPP), and the American Board of Professional Neuropsychology (ABPN). In the interests of appropriate disclosure, the author is a past president of ABPN. Both ABCN and ABPN utilize an application process, work sample review, and oral examination procedures. ABCN uses a multiple-choice test and ABPN uses an essay exam.

Recently, ABPN has begun to offer an advance qualification in a number of specialty areas, one of which is forensic neuropsychology. The expectation is that professional practice standards in forensic neuropsychology will show continual development. The establishment of a free standing American Board of Forensic Neuropsychology (ABFN) is a likely development of increasing professionalism in this specialty area.

NEW TECHNIQUES

In this section, the new techniques of neuropsychological measures, neurodiagnostic measures, and malingering measures are covered. At the same time, however, it must be noted that the *Daubert* decision (*Daubert v. Merrell Dow Pharmaceuticals,* 1993) has imposed new standards for technique assessment. Although it is not possible to adequately deal with the complex issues posed by the *Daubert* decision in the limited space of this chapter, nonetheless, some brief and oversimplified remarks will be offered. The *Daubert* decision has promulgated standards for helping trial judges to assess the value of scientific evidence offered in the context of litigation. The intent is to weed out "junk science" from the courtroom. The intent, of course, is praiseworthy, but many forensic neuropsychologists are concerned about the actual application of scientific standards in the hands of individuals such as trial judges, who, although highly intelligent and interpersonally astute persons, are not usually formally trained in science. Future clarification of the *Daubert* decision in actual court decisions is expected, and the degree to which

Daubert achieves its purpose will determine if a lasting contribution is made.

Neuropsychology Assessment Measures and Forensic Neuropsychology

The hallmark of neuropsychological assessment measures has been their careful validation in relation to neurological criteria (Reitan & Davison, 1974; Reitan, 1974; Reitan & Wolfson, 1993). There is clear agreement among scientists and researchers as to the impressive empirical validity of neuropsychological tests to determine the presence of brain damage and lateralization of the brain damage (Horton, 1997b). On the other hand, there has been a paucity of specific research with the ability of neuropsychological tests to address completely forensic/legal questions, and the argument has been made that empirical evidence for the ecological validity of neuropsychological tests needs to be much better developed (Sbordone & Saul, 2000). It is to be expected that a future trend will be to address this important area.

Neurodiagnostic Assessment Measures and Forensic Neuropsychology

Neurodiagnostic measures, such as magnetic resonance imaging (MRI) and positron emission topography (PET) scanning, have provided new windows through which to visualize the human brain (Bigler, Lowry, & Porter, 1997). The expectation is that increased use of these exciting brain-imaging techniques will be the norm in forensic neuropsychology. The interactive use of neuropsychological testing and neurodiagnostic measures, such as MRI and PET scans, might be expected to yield dramatic new insights into the workings of the human brain and further develop the empirical basis for forensic neuropsychology.

Malingering Measures and Forensic Neuropsychology

In the last decade, the most dramatic development in forensic neuropsychology has been the explosive growth of test measures designed to detect biased responding on neuropsychological tests (Franzen & Iverson, 1997). Both the development of new measures and the use of specific profiles, item-response patterns, and cutoff scores on standard neuropsychological tests have been investigated. Future research in this area is expected.

NEW POPULATIONS

In this section, possible new populations that forensic neuropsychology may address are mentioned. Such populations might include medical/ health care patients and minority groups.

Medical/Health Care Patients and Forensic Neuropsychology

In medical neuropsychology (Horton, 1997a), there are many opportunities for forensic neuropsychologists to make important contributions. Patients who have had systemic illnesses that have secondary brain effects (such as lung disease, cardiovascular disorders, liver disease, and selected ontological disorders), as well as cases in which the effects of pharmaceuticals are at question, are clear candidates for forensic neuropsychological assessment, to determine if brain damage has occurred. In addition, cases in which medical complications or treatment may have a direct or indirect impact on neural integrity, and in which neurotoxic effects of chemicals/substances are suspected, are considered within the possible scope of forensic neuropsychology (Hartman, 1995).

Minority Groups and Forensic Neuropsychology

As the population of the United States grows increasingly more diverse, greater attention to the neuropsychological assessment of minority groups is an inevitable development. The expectation is that appropriate neuropsychological assessment may have to be tailored to fit the cultural context of new immigrants to the United States and those who maintain a different cultural perspective than the majority culture. The extant research on neuropsychological assessment in a multicultural context, however, is actually quite rudimentary (Horton, Carrington, & Lewis-

Jack, 2001). When minority group members are neuropsychologically assessed and forensic/legal questions are at issue, a firm empirical basis for decision making is needed. At present, much additional work is needed to address the area of forensic neuropsychological assessment within a multicultural context.

SUMMARY

This chapter discusses the possible impact of the future on forensic neuropsychology practices in the United States. It is postulated that the advent of managed care will drive clinical psychologists into forensic practice, as traditional psychological practices prove to be less profitable under managed care. Health care practices will be more influential than legal developments in shaping the focus of forensic neuropsychology. In addition, the potential value of computers and the Internet, for improving forensic neuropsychology practices and facilitating access to experts in forensic neuropsychology, is briefly outlined. Issues related to credentialing are also briefly mentioned, in an oversimplified manner.

Also, the need for ecological validity for legal questions for neuropsychological tests, the future uses of MRI and PET scans, and need for measures to assess biased responding are mentioned. The populations of medical/health care patients and minority group members are proposed as areas in need of future forensic neuropsychological assessments. The hope and expectation is that this book can serve to expedite the future progress of forensic neuropsychology in the United States and, thereby, in some small way, facilitate the search for truth and justice in the forensic neuropsychology area.

REFERENCES

Armenti, N. (1993). Managed health care and the behaviorally trained professional. *The Behavior Therapist, 14,* 13–15.

Bigler, E. D., Lowry, C. M., & Porter, S. S. (1997). Neuroimaging in clinical neuropsychology. In A. M. Horton, Jr., D. Wedding, & J. S. Webster (Eds.), *The Neuropsychology Handbook, Vol. 1* (2nd ed.) (pp. 171–220). New York: Springer.

Cummings, N. (1986). The dismantling of our health care systems: Strategies for the survival of psychological practice. *American Psychologist, 41,* 426–431.

Daubert v. Merrell Dow Pharmaceuticals, 113 S. Ct. 2786 (1993).

Franzen, M. D., & Iverson, G. L. (1997). Detection of biased responding in neuropsychological assessment. In A. M. Horton, Jr., D. Wedding, & J. S. Webster (Eds.), Vol. 2, *The neuropsychology handbook* (2nd ed.) (pp. 393–423). New York: Springer.

Hall, K. M., & Cope, D. N. (1995). The benefits of rehabilitation in traumatic brain injury: A literature review. *Journal of Head Trauma Rehabilitation, 10*(1), 1–13.

Hartman, D. (1995). *Neuropsychological toxicology* (2nd ed.). New York: Plenum Press.

Horton, A. M., Jr. (1997a). Human neuropsychology: Current status. In A. M. Horton, Jr., D. Wedding, & J. S. Webster (Eds.), *The Neuropsychology Handbook, Vol. 1* (2nd ed.) (pp. 3–29). New York: Springer.

Horton, A. M., Jr. (1997b). Halstead-Reitan neuropsychological test battery: Problems and prospects. In A. M. Horton, Jr., D. Wedding, & J. S. Webster (Eds.), *The Neuropsychology Handbook, Vol. 1* (2nd ed.) (pp. 221–254). New York: Springer.

Horton, A. M., Jr., Carrington, C. H., & Lewis-Jack, O. (2001) Neuropsychological assessment in a multicultural context. In L. A. Suzuki, J. G. Ponterotto, & P. J. Meller (Eds.), *Handbook of Multicultural Assessment* (2nd ed.) (pp. 233–260). San Francisco: Jossey-Bass.

Otto, R. K., & Heinbrun, K. (2002). The practice of forensic psychology. *American Psychologist, 57*(1), 5–18.

Peterson, L., & Harbeck, C. (1988). *The Pediatric Psychologist.* Champaign, IL: Research Press.

Purish, A.D., & Sbordone, R. J. (1997). Forensic neuropsychology: Clinical issues and practice. In A. M. Horton, Jr., D. Wedding, & J. S. Webster (Eds.), *The Neuropsychology Handbook, Vol. 2* (2nd ed.) (pp. 309–373). New York: Springer.

Reitan, R. M., & Davison, L. A. (Eds.). (1974). *Clinical neuropsychology: Current status and applications.* New York: John Wiley.

Reitan, R. M. (1974). Psychological effects of cerebral lesions in children of early school age. In R. M. Reitan & L. A. Davison (Eds.), *Clinical neuropsychology: Current status and applications* (pp. 53–90). New York: John Wiley.

Reitan R. M., & Wolfson, D. (1993). *Halstead-Reitan Neuropsychological Test Battery.* Tucson, AZ: Neuropsychology Press.

Sbordone, R. J., & Saul, R. E. (2000). *Neuropsychology for health care professionals and attorneys* (2nd ed.). Boca Raton, FL: CRC Press.

Strosahi, K. (1994). Entering the new frontier of managed mental health care: Gold mines and land mines. *Cognitive and Behavioral Practice, 1,* 5–23.

Sweet, J. J., Westergaard, C. K., & Moberg, P. J. (1995). Managed care experiences of clinical neuropsychologists. *The Clinical Neuropsychologist, 9*(3), 214–218.

Index